A GLOSSARY OF
TERMS USED IN
HERALDRY

APPRENDRE ET TENIR.

1. Richard Willoughby, Esq.
quartering arms of

2. Frevile	5. Mountforte	8. Buttetourt
3. Marmion	6. De la Plaunche	9. Dudley
4. Kilpeck	7. Haversham	10. De la Zouch

see p. 396

A GLOSSARY OF
TERMS USED IN
HERALDRY

BY

JAMES PARKER

A NEW EDITION

With One Thousand Illustrations

CHARLES E. TUTTLE CO.: PUBLISHERS

RUTLAND, VERMONT

Representatives
Continental Europe: BOXERBOOKS, INC., *Zurich*

Published by the Charles E. Tuttle Company, Inc.
of Rutland, Vermont & Tokyo, Japan
with editorial offices at
Suido 1-chome, 2–6, Bunkyo-ku, Tokyo, Japan

Copyright in Japan, 1970 by Charles E. Tuttle Co., Inc.

Library of Congress Catalog Card No. 77–94021

International Standard Book No. 0-8048-0715-9

First Tuttle edition, 1970
Second printing, 1982

PRINTED IN JAPAN

PUBLISHER'S FOREWORD

———•———

THE use of heraldry is far more extensive today than it was in medieval times. Decorative and symbolic today, heraldry seems to have increased in popularity with the centuries, so that there is a distinct and even urgent need for a quick and authentic reference work for this science of recording genealogies and blazoning arms or ensigns armorial.

Here are the ancient and established terms, as distinguished from later, fanciful terms which may have little foundation in fact, and thus little more justification than an exercise of ingenuity on the part of later writers.

Many of the illustrations in this appealing volume are based upon material found in early manuscripts, brasses, stained glass and sepulchral monuments, but they are all presented in their illustrative rather than in their archaeological and historical aspects.

Painstaking research among the Rolls and Visitations in the British Museum have paid off in authenticity and consequent admiration for this work. And the beauty of this compelling compilation lies in its simplicity of presentation and convenience for quick reference.

A complete synoptical table presents the chief terms under logical headings and in systematic order. This is followed by the completely alphabetized terms which are set off and embellished by 1,000 illustrations. Words such as charge, bearing, ordinary, tincture field, fess, and many others then take on new meaning and luster for the student as well as those wise in the ways of heraldry and old world lore. And heraldry gains new adherents; it is destined never to die. This work was originally published by James Parker and Company in 1894.

PREFATORY NOTE.

IT is now nearly fifty years since my father published a work entitled, "A Glossary of Terms used in British Heraldry."

The book had been out of print for several years, and finding that it was still enquired for, and that it had not been actually superseded by more recent works, I determined some little time back to reprint it. As no author's name appeared to the book, and as my father had left me no details as to the circumstances attending the original publication, I thought I would myself be responsible for such revision as would be necessary for a new edition, since in years gone by I had paid some attention to Heraldry as a branch of Archæology.

At the first glance at the work I thought this could be done very readily and in a very short time, but after revising the first few sheets I was troubled with the large number of general statements respecting various charges without examples given of their occurrence in any coat of arms. The result was that I came to the conclusion that several fanciful terms, for which I found no authority further than the exercises of ingenuity on the part of writers of the seventeenth century, might be omitted, or at any rate should be distinguished from ancient and established terms which had been actually adopted in recognised coats of arms. Also, as regarded the more ancient charges, it seemed to me that examples ought to have been given from the early Rolls of arms which have been preserved. I further found that it was necessary to follow some more systematic ar-

rangement with regard to synonyms and the grouping of
terms more or less allied to one another, and whose separate
treatment left ·the description somewhat obscure.   To assist
in this I decided to place a large number of the Terms at
the foot of the page with cross references to the words under
which the charge would be found described, either under
another name or in its relation to similar charges; and with
these cross references I thought it well to place such words
as only required a very brief explanation.

In adopting this new system, the frequent omissions, trans-
positions, and very considerable additions left practically
hardly anything of the original printed copy standing.

I was tempted at times to go into historical questions, but
this would have added much to the extent of the work, and
would not have been consistent with its purpose.   I feel,
however, the history of the rise and progress of Heraldry
remains to be written—not culled from the fanciful treatment by the sixteenth and seventeenth century writers on
the subject, but based upon the material supplied by the
illustrations which early Manuscripts, Brasses, Sepulchral
Monuments, Stained Glass and the like afford.   It is true that
many of the illustrations in the present volume are derived
from these sources, but they are presented in their illustrative
rather than in their archæological and historical aspect.

I should mention that after I had gone some little way
with my task an interleaved copy of the Glossary, with several
notes by the late Mr. Wyatt Papworth, came into my hands.
As the author of that laborious and useful work, " An Ordinary
of English Arms," his references to it, and additional notes
were of much help.   And I should acknowledge that the
ordinary itself was also of great assistance to me.

I should further add that the copy of the whole had been
prepared, and actually about half of it had been printed, when
I received a letter from Mr. HENRY GOUGH, who I learnt
had projected and assisted very largely in the original com-

pilation, and indeed had been mainly responsible for the first edition. He in the kindest way possible offered to look over the proofs. As at times I had begun to be very much disheartened at the difficulties which seemed rather to increase as I went on, I gladly accepted his generous offer of help, and availed myself of many notes and suggestions which he sent to me.

With respect to the long delay which has intervened since the first announcement that the book was in the press, I should state that I found the work was growing to such an extent under my hands and required so considerable an amount of uninterrupted attention, that I transferred all my MS. notes and my books of reference to my residence at Fyfield, looking upon the work rather as a recreation than as a matter of business. Further, I had there also the great advantage of my eldest daughter's assistance, who made herself thoroughly acquainted with the principles which I adopted in compiling the work, as well as with the original material, by researches amongst the Rolls and Visitations preserved in the British Museum, and who, besides, rendered me considerable aid in supplying some 250 illustrations which it seemed to me were required above and beyond those which appeared in the first edition. The main part of the work had been practically finished while I was residing at Fyfield. Having, however, been obliged from a sudden and terrible domestic affliction to leave that place, with all its happy memories, the proofs and incidental papers were packed up. For a long while they remained so, as I had not the heart to set again to the work (connected as it was with so many sad associations), and draw up the tables and indices and complete all that was necessary for issuing the book to the public. Feeling, however, that I had allowed it to remain too long unfinished, and with an effort I have now completed the indices and introductory remarks, so that the last sheets might be printed off and the book sent to the binders.

I am well aware that the editorial work involving such an amount of research and technical knowledge should have been entrusted to a more competent hand, and had I foreseen when first I began how different the labour would prove from that of simple revision, I should not have attempted it.

JAMES PARKER.

Oxford, October, 1894.

INTRODUCTORY.

THIS work, following the title of the older book, is called a Glossary, the object being primarily to describe and explain the several terms connected with the study of Heraldry which a reader is at all likely to meet with.

The terms are put in one complete alphabetical order; a few of less importance, or where only a line is required to explain them, or where they are best explained under some other term, are, for the sake of saving of space, printed at the foot of the page in somewhat smaller type.

Most of the recognised Heraldic terms are derived from the old Norman French of the thirteenth and fourteenth century; but have acquired different interpretations in process of time, together with different modes of spelling. The use of these words has been illustrated as far as possible by quoting examples from the early Rolls, a list of which will be found given at p. 325 of the Glossary. There exist some few others, but these are the more important.

A great deal of additional Heraldic nomenclature, however, is derived from writers of the sixteenth and seventeenth century. To search out the name of the writer who first used each term, and in what sense he used it, and how far succeeding writers have adopted or misapplied the terms, would be laborious work to a compiler, tedious to the reader, and wholly useless in result. All that has been done is to give a sufficient description to enable the reader to interpret the terms when he meets with them in any Heraldic, Genealogical, or Topographical works, which he may consult. A list of the chief Heraldic writers, often termed 'Authorities,' will be found given under the word *Heraldry* in the Glossary, p. 323.

But besides these there are a large number of ordinary and every-day terms, including names of plants and animals, as well as of inanimate objects, which have been adopted as charges by families, sometimes possibly from some historic event, but more often because of the play upon the name. It has been thought necessary to take note of these, not so much with a view of description as with that of shewing what families use them; how they are generally represented; and what tinctures are applied to them.

In a few cases Crests, Supporters, Badges, &c., have been noted, and especially where the animal or object does not occur amongst charges.

It will be seen at once that these various classes of Terms have to be treated in a variety of manner. In nearly all cases, however, examples are given of the use of the older terms from the earliest instances in which they are found employed. In the case of modern terms, either characteristic examples of the words are selected, or else cases where the charges, &c., are borne by well-known families. As a rule the French equivalent is given, as in many instances there is much similarity, and in others it may be useful where French works on Heraldry have to be consulted. Occasionally also examples of modern French coats of arms are introduced by way of illustration. In describing the terms it has not been thought well to enter to any extent into the various discussions arising from opinions of writers; the object has been to explain the actual use of the terms. Neither has it been thought necessary, as regards the more modern Coats of Arms, to go behind such substantial works as Burke's "General Armory," Papworth's "Ordinary," and similar compilations. It has been considered that, as a rule, the compilers of those books made use of the best information.

While primarily the object of the work, as has been said, is to describe and explain terms used in Heraldry, and more especially in the blazon of Coats of Arms, the practical side of Heraldry has not been overlooked. Under such articles as *Marshalling*, *Arms*, *Achievements*, and the like, several of the rules of Heraldry are introduced. Also the various Titles of Nobility, &c.; Orders of *Knights; Heralds*, &c., will all be found in the Glossary, with such information given in a condensed form as it is thought will be of use to those students of Heraldry who pursue the subject otherwise than as an adjunct to Genealogical and Archæological enquiry.

It has been attempted, as far as possible, for the sake of condensation, to bring similar terms together, and it is thought that the cross references at the foot of the page will afford every facility for finding any word: for the sake, however, of assisting those who use the book to grasp the principle of the arrangement, a very full SYNOPTICAL TABLE is given after this Introduction, in which the terms are arranged under several headings in systematic order; and such terms as are found in the Alphabetical Glossary being given in italic, those following the chief term will be found described beneath the same. Apart from the use which it has been to the compiler, and apart from that which it may be to those who use the book, it is thought that such a synoptical view will not be otherwise than interesting, as shewing the vast range of subjects over which those who have had duly assigned to them (or unduly taken to themselves) coats of arms have extended their choice. Objection may perhaps be taken to the classification of the Ordinaries and Conventional Charges as not being one generally recognized. There is so much disagreement, however, amongst writers, that it has been thought better to adopt an independent system, guided rather by convenience than by any so-called authority.

The Synoptical Table, it will be observed, is not confined to Ordinaries and Charges themselves, but is extended to the several modifications of form or position to which the charges are subject, as well as the various general Heraldic Terms, Titles, &c., which belong to the application of the study of Heraldry. In fact it has been attempted to classify and arrange under it, in systematic order, all the words which occur in the Glossary.

But few abbreviations have been used. The very slight space saved by such, rarely compensates for the trouble which they sometimes give in interpreting them.

The INDEX OF NAMES at the end of the volume will give easy reference to the families whose arms are blazoned as illustrations of the terms described in the book. The spelling followed is that adopted in the source from which the blazon has been taken. As it comprises nearly four thousand references to the coats of arms blazoned, it cannot be without some use to the student of Heraldry, though perhaps but of little to the Genealogist. As far as possible repetition has been avoided, but in so large a series of examples this has not been always possible.

A SYNOPTICAL TABLE

OF THE CHIEF TERMS USED IN BRITISH HERALDRY.

N.B. The terms in Italic type will be found in their alphabetical order in the Glossary. Those in ordinary type will, in nearly all cases, be found described under the preceding *Italic word*. Where there is any difficulty, the cross reference must be turned to in the double column at the foot of the page throughout the Glossary.

I. TINCTURES.

1. *Or* (Gold).
2. *Argent* (Silver).
3. *Gules* (Red).
4. *Azure* (Blue).
5. *Sable* (Black).
6. *Vert* (Green).
7. *Purpure* (Purple).
8. *Tenné* (Orange or Tawny ?).
9. *Sanguine* (Bloodcolour).

FURS.

| *Ermine.* | Ermines. | Pean. | *Vair.* |
| Erminois. | Erminites. | *Potent* or Meirré. | Counter vair. |

IRREGULAR TINCTURES (used chiefly in crests and supporters).

Colours, ash, bay, brown, carnation, earth, grey, russet, white, &c.

II. ORDINARIES.

1. *Chief.*

2. *Fess.*
3. *Bar* [a].
4. *Bend* dexter.
5. *Bend sinister.*
6. *Pale.*
7. *Chevron.*
8. *Cross* [b].
9. *Saltire.*

III. LINES.

A. LINES OF PARTITION APPLIED CHIEFLY TO THE FIELD.

Per *fess.* Per *bend* [dexter]. Per *pile.* *Quarterly*, (i.e. per cross)
Per *pale.* Per *bend sinister.* Per *chevron.* Per *saltire.*
Gyronny (i.e. per cross and saltire, &c.).

B. LINES OF DIVERSITY APPLIED CHIEFLY TO THE FIELD.

Barry.	*Pily.*	*Lozengy.*	*Fretty.*
Paly.	*Chevronny.*	*Fusilly.*	Latticed.
Bendy [dexter].	*Chevronelly.*	*Masculy.*	*Gobony.*
Bendy sinister.	*Chequy.*	*Tortilly.*	Masoned.

C. LINES OF DIVERSITY APPLIED CHIEFLY TO ORDINARIES.

Embattled.	*Raguly.*	*Dovetailed.*	*Champaine.*
Bretessed.	*Dancetty.*	*Engrailed.*	*Undy* or *Wavy.*
Counter embattled.	*Indented.*	*Invected.*	*Nebuly.*

N.B. The lines of Diversity under C may be combined with most under A in partitioning the field, and with some beneath B in diversifying the field.

---

[a] By only a few Heralds considered as a diminutive of the fesse.
[b] And of this there are a large number of varieties to which different names are applied. See the alphabetical list given on page 179.

LINES (*continued*).

D. LINES OF TRUNCATION OF THE SHIELD (considered as abatements).

Plain *Point.*	*Point* dexter.	*Point* dexter base.
Point pointed.	*Gore* dexter.	*Gore* sinister.
Point champaine.	*Gusset* dexter.	*Gusset* sinister.

IV. POINTS OF THE ESCUTCHEON.

dexter chief *point.*	middle chief point.	sinister chief point.
dexter base point.	honour or collar point.	sinister base point.
	fess point.	
	nombril point.	
	middle base point.	

V. CONVENTIONAL CHARGES (INCLUDING SUB-ORDINARIES).

A. DIMINUTIVES OF THE ORDINARIES [c] AND THE LIKE.

Fillets.	*Bendlets.*	*Chevronels.*
Viure (?).	*Scarpes.*	*Crosslets.*
Barrulets.	*Closets.*	*Saltorels.*
Pallets.	*Cotises.*	

B. SUBORDINARIES WHICH APPARENTLY ENCROACH UPON THE FIELD.

Canton.	*Bordure.*	*Pile* [d].
Quarter.	*Orle.*	*Gyron.*
Inescutcheon.	*Tressure.*	*Flaunches.*

C. SUBORDINARIES [e] AND OTHER CONVENTIONAL RECTILINEAR CHARGES.

Fret.	*Mullet* and *Rowel.*	*Lozenge.*
Pall.	*Billet.*	*Mascle.*
Skakefork.	*Cube.*	*Fusil.*
Baton.	*Delf.*	*Rustre.*
Label.	*Esquire.*	*Triangle.*

D. CONVENTIONAL CURVILINEAR CHARGES.

Annulet.	*Roundles.*	*Pomey* (vert).
Gurges.	*Bezant* (or).	*Golpe* (purpure).
Gouttes.	*Plate* (argent).	*Guze* (sanguine).
Crescent [f]	*Hurt* (azure)	*Orange* (tenne).
Estoile [f].	*Torteau* (gules).	*Fountain* (argent and
Fer de moline [f].	*Pellet* (sable).	[azure).

---

[e] By some Heralds the diminutives of the Ordinaries are reckoned as SUBORDINARIES.

[d] By many Heralds reckoned as an Ordinary.

[e] Besides the nine SUBORDINARIES in list B, the Fret, the Pall, and the Label, are usually considered subordinaries; but there is much disagreement amongst authors.

[f] These three are rather charges of which the drawing is conventional.

X. CHARGES TAKEN FROM BIRDS.

NATATORES.

Duck.
Drake.
Sheldrake.
Wildduck.
Mallard.
Teal.
Shoveller.
Cannet.
Muscovy Duck.
Smew, or
White Nun.
Goose.
Magellan Goose.
Wildgoose.
Barnacle Goose.
Swan.
Cygnet.
Cormorant.
Sea Aylet.
Gannapie.
Sea Gull.
Sea Mew.
Tern.
Sea Pewit.
Sea Fowl.
Auk.
Murr.
Razorbill.
Pelican.

GRALLATORES.

Coot.
Baldcoot.
Moorhen.
Crane.
Heron.
Heronshaw.
Bittern.
Fencock.
Spoonbill.
Plover.

Stork.
Snipe.
Curlew.
Avocetta.
Lapwing.
Pewit.
Tirwhitt.
Sea pie.
Bustard.

CURSORES.

Ostrich.
„ feathers.

RASORES.

Heathcock or
Blackcock.
Moorcock or
Grouse.
Cock, i.e.
Barn-door Cock.
Hen.
Gamecock.
Cockerells.
Capon.
Pheasant.
Mitus.
Partridge.
Peacock.
Peahen.
Turkey.
Dove.
Ring Dove.
Turtle Dove.
Stock Dove.
Pigeon.
Wood Pigeon.

SCANSORES.

Parrot.
Parroquet.
Popinjay.

INSESSORES.

Raven.
Rook.
Crow.
Daw.
Cornish Chough.
Beckit.
Magpie.
Jay.
Starling.
Stern.
Finches.
Goldfinch.
Bullfinch.
Chaffinch.
Brambling.
Canary.
Linnet.
Pinzon.
Lark.
Bunting.
Sparrow.
Blackbird.
Wren.
Robin Redbreast.
Martlet.
Swallow.
Martin.
Kingfisher.

RAPTORES.

Eagle.
Eaglet.
Alerion.
Falcon.
Hawk.
Sparrowhawk.
Goshawk.
Kite.
Sacre.
Merlion.
Vulture.
Owl
Horned Owl.

XI. CHARGES TAKEN FROM REPTILES.

CHELONIA.	OPHIDIA.	AMPHIBIA.
Tortoise.	*Serpent.*	*Frogs.*
	Snake.	Tadpoles.
LACERTILIA.	Bisse.	Powets.
Lizard.		Toads.
Cameleon.	*Adder.*	
CROCODILIA.	Asp.	*Effets.*
Alligators.	Viper.	Askers.
Crocodile.		Newts

XII. CHARGES TAKEN FROM FISH.

OSSEOUS FISHES.	*Bream.*	*Turbot.*
Perch.	*Lucy*, or Pike.	Sole.
Chabot.	Ged.	Flook.
Gurnet.	*Flyingfish.*	Flounder.
Mullet.	*Salmon.*	
Mackerel.	Trout.	———
Swordfish.	Smelts.	*Eels.*
Gudgeon.	*Herring.*	Congereels.
Loach.	Cobfish.	Grigs.
	Sprats.	
———	Pilchard.	CARTILAGENOUS FISHES.
Barbel.	Garvin.	*Sturgeon.*
Tench.	*Cod.*	*Shark.*
Mogul, fish of.	Hake.	Dogfish.
Carp.	Ling.	*Lampreys.*
Chub.	Whiting.	
Minnow.		

XIII. CHARGES TAKEN FROM INVERTEBATE CREATURES.

INSECTA.	*Bees.*	ANNULOIDA.
Grasshoppers.	Hornets.	*Sea Urchins.*
Crickets.	Beehives.	CRUSTACEA
———	*Ants.*	*Crab.*
Fly.	Emmets.	*Lobster.*
House-fly.	*Beetles.*	Crevices.
Gad-fly.	Stag Beetles.	*Shrimps.*
Gadbee.		Prawns.
Brimsey.	ANNULOSA.	MOLLUSCA.
Butterfly.	*Horseleech.*	*Escalop.*
Harvest-fly.	*Spider.*	*Whelks.*
Silkworm-fly.	*Scorpion.*	*Snails.*

XIV. CHARGES taken from PARTS OF MEN and ANIMALS.

A. Of Men, Women, Children, &c.

Head, Man's.	*Head*, Woman's.	*Bones*.
,, Saracen's.	,, Lady's.	Human skull
,, Turk's.	,, Maiden's.	Jaw-bone.
,, Negro's.	,, Nun's.	*Heart*.
,, Moor's.	,, Children's.	*Arm*.
,, Savage's.	,, Infant's.	*Hand*.
,, Chieftain's.	*Eye*.	*Leg*.
,, Saxon's.	*Hair*.	*Foot*.
,, Egyptian's.	*Limbs*.	

B. Of Animals.

Heads of Beasts.	*Gambes* of Beasts.	*Ears* of Beasts.
,, of Birds.	Paws.	*Attires* of Deer.
,, of Fish.	*Legs* of Beasts.	Tynes ,,
,, of Monsters.	*Horns* of Beasts.	*Lambs*' Kidneys.
Wings of Birds.	*Tails* of Beasts.	Cows' *Horns*.

XV. CHARGES taken from MONSTERS.

Monsters with Wings.	Beasts with Fishes' Tails.	Man Monsters.
Griffin.		*Satyrs*
Dragon.	*Sea Horse*.	Satyral.
Alce.	Sea Lion.	Centaur.
Opinicus.	Sea Dragon.	Sagittarius.
Cockatrice, with	Sea Dog.	Triton.
Wyvern.	Sea Wolf.	Lampago.
Basilisk.		Man Tiger.
Amphistere.		
Hydra.	Combined beasts.	Women Monsters.
	Unicorn.	*Sphinx*.
Beasts with Wings.	[*Allocamelus*.]	Harpy.
Pegasus, with	[*Apre*.]	[Chimera.]
Winged Stag.	[*Bagwyn*.]	*Mermaid*.
Winged Bull.	[*Musimon*.]	Siren.
Python.	[*Yale*.]	
Winged Ox.	Deer-*goat* (heads).	Creatures in Fire.
Winged Lion.	Lion-*goat* (heads).	*Phœnix*.
		Salamander.

XVI. CHARGES taken from the VEGETABLE KINGDOM.

A. Forest Trees, &c.

Alder berry.
Ash tree.
rowan branches.
ashen Keys.
Beech branch.
Birch branches.
,, leaves.
Elder leaves.
Elm tree.
,, leaves.
Hawthorn tree.
,, leaves.
Whitethorn.
Mayflowers.

Holly tree.
,, branches.
,, leaves.
Ivy branches.
Laurel tree.
,, branches.
,, leaves.
,, bay leaves.
Linden leaves.
Maple tree.
Oak tree.
,, leaf.
Acorn.
Acorn cup.

Palm tree.
Cocoa nut tree.
China Cokar.
Pine tree.
,, cone.
Fir tree.
Cedar.
Cypress.
Poplar tree.
Aspen leaf.
Staff tree leaves.
Willow tree.
Salix.
Osier.
Yew tree.

B. Fruits and Fruit-trees.

Almond slip.
,, leaves.
Apple tree.
,, fruit.
Barbary branch.
Cherry tree.
,, fruit.
Fig tree.
Hazel leaves.
Nuts.
Filberts.
Mulberry.

Olive tree.
,, branch.
Orange tree.
,, fruit.
Pear.
Warden pear.
Pine apple.
Ananas.
Plum.
Pomegranate tree.
,, fruit.
Apple of Granada.

Quince fruit.
Strawberry sprigs.
,, leaf.
Frasier.
Vine.
,, branch.
,, leaves.
Grapes.
Walnut leaves.
,, [tree].

C. Flowers and Flowering Plants.

Balm.
Betony leaf.
Carnation.
Pink.
Broom.
Planta genista.
Bluebottle.
heydodde ?
Columbine.
Daisy.
Gilly flower.
Heliotrope.

Honeysuckle.
Lily.
Iris.
Marigold.
Narcissus.
Nettle.
Pansy
Poppy.
Primrose.
Rose.
,, damask.
,, heraldic.

Sengreen.
Silphium.
Sunflower.
Heliotrope.
Thistle.
Teazel.
Trefoil leaf.
Shamrock.
Tulip.
Violets.
Gletver *Leaf.*

CHARGES TAKEN FROM THE VEGETABLE KINGDOM (*continued*).

D. MISCELLANEOUS PLANTS, GRAIN, &c.

Beans.
  Beancods.
  Ornamental leaves.
Cloves.
Cotton tree.
Cummin.
Dock leaf.
  Bur leaf.
Fern leaves.
  Adder's tongue.
Garlic.
Gourds.
[*Graintree.*]
Grass, tufts.
  ,, spires.

Hopbines.
  Hop poles
Mandrake.
Parsley leaves.
Peascods.
Pepper pods.
Reeds, bundles of.
  ,, sheaves of.
  ,, tufts.
  Rushes.
  Bulrushes.
Seaweed.
  Laver.
Sugar canes.

Tobacco.
Turnip.
Watercress leaves.
Wheat ears.
  ,, sheaves.
  Big wheat.
  Guinea wheat.
  Barley ears.
  Corn ears.
  Oat sheaves.
  Rye ears.
  ,, stalks.
Garbe.

E. PARTS OF TREES, CHAPLETS, CONVENTIONAL FORMS, &c.

Tree.
  branch.
  limb of tree.
  scrogs.
  twigs.
  sprigs.
  slips.
  graft.
  stock.
  stump.
  trunk.

Chaplet of roses.
  ,,   of flowers.
  ,,   of laurel.
  ,,   of holly.
  ,,   of hazel.
  ,,   of rue.
  ,,   of oak (or
    Civic) wreath.
  Bramble wreath.
Bush.
Faggot.

Flower.
Fruit.
Leaf.
Root.
Staff raguly.
  Wand.
Foil.
Trefoil.
Quatrefoil.
Cinquefoil.
Sexfoil.
Fleur de lis.

XVII. CHARGES TAKEN FROM ARMOUR, ACCOUTREMENTS, &c.

Helmet, Sovereign's.
  ,,   Duke's.
  ,,   Baronet's.
  ,,   Esquire's.
  visor.
  beaver.
  gorget.
Cap of Steel.
  Basnet.
  Burgonette.
  Morion.

Hauberk.
  Habergeon.
Cuirass.
  Breastplate.
Shield.
  Target.
Escutcheon.
Belt.
  Baldrich.
Arm.
  Brassarts.

Gauntlet.
Buckle.
  Fermail.
  Arming buckle.
Escarboucle.
Straps.
  Wriststraps.
Fetterlock.
  Shackle bolts.
  Manacles.

XVIII. CHARGES TAKEN FROM WEAPONS, WAR MATERIAL, &c.

A. GUNS, BOWS, AND ARROWS, &c.

Guns.
- Cannon.
- Field piece.
- Chamber piece.
- Chamber.
- Culverin.

Mortar.

Matchlock.

Matches, Roll of.

Musket.
- Potgun.
- Pistol.

Bow.
- Long-bow.
- Hand-bow.
- Cross-bow.
- Bowstring.

Arrow.
- Bundle of arrows.
- Broadarrow.
- Quarrels.
- Bolts.
- Bird bolts.

Pheon.

Shot.
- Chain shot.
- Star stone.

Fireball.
- Bombs.
- Bombshells.
- Grenados.
- Hand grenades.

Sling.
- Sweep.
- Balista.

Quiver.

B. SWORDS, SPEARS, AXES, &c.

Sword.
- Arming sword.
- Irish sword.
- Claymore.
- Brand.
- Hilt.
- Pomel.
- Scabbard.
- Bouterol.
- Chape.
- Crampet.

Sabre.
- Falchion
- Scimitar.
- Seax.
- Badelaire.
- Hanger.
- Cutlas.

Dagger.
- Dirk.
- Rapier.
- Poignard.
- Skean.

Spear.
- Lance.
- Javelin.
- Dart.

Cronel.

Rest.
- Clarion.

Axe.
- Battle axe.
- Danish axe.
- Tomahawk.
- Lochabar axe.
- Pole axe.

Staff.
- Pikestaff.
- Club.
- Truncheon.

C. WAR MATERIAL, TENTS, FLAGS, &c.

Beacons.
- Cressets.

Torch.
- Firebrand.

Fire.
- Fascines.

Battering ram.

Grappling irons.

Caltrap.

Ladder (Scaling).

Target.

Quiver.

Shield.

Tent.
- Tent staff.
- Pavilion.

Scroll.
- Ribbon.

Flag.
- Standard.
- Union Jack.
- [Gonfanon.]
- Guidon.
- Pennon.
- Pennoncel.
- Streamer.

Banner.
- Beauseant.

D. HORSE-GEAR, &c.

Horse trappings.

[*Hame*].

Bit.
- Boss.

Bridle.

Saddle.

Stirrup.

Spur.
- Rowel.

Whip.

Horse shoe.

Horse picker.

Barnacles.

Breys.

Curry comb.

XIX. CHARGES taken from Articles of ATTIRE and ORNAMENT.

A. Articles of Attire.

Crown.
  imperial.
  royal.
  mural.
  celestial.
  eastern.
  naval.
  civic.
  prince's coronet.
  ducal.   ,,
  earl's   ,,

Mitre.
Tiara.
Wreath.
Cap.
  Chapeau.
  Infula.
  Ducipers.
Bonnet.
Hat.
  Hatband.
Robe.

[*Mantle.*]
Maunch.
  Sleeve.
Boot.
  Dutch boots.
  Irish brogues.
  Shoes.
Hose.
Garter.
Glove.

B. Personal Ornaments, Decorations, Jewels, &c.

Sceptre.
Orb.
  Mound royal.
Regalia.
Mace.
  Civic mace.
Collar.

Plumes.
  Feathers.
Ring (gem).
  jewelled.
Diamonds.
  Crystals.
  Brilliants.
Ruby.

Medal.
  medallion.
  clasp.
  pagoda.
  penny yard penny.
[*George.*]
Riband.
Angles.

XX. CHARGES from Articles of DOMESTIC USE.

Mirror.
Tapestry.
Cushions.
  Pillow.
  Tassel.
Child's Cradle.
Chair.
Trestle.
Basket.
  ,, of wastel cakes.
  Dorcer.
  Vane.
  Shruttle.
Mortars.
  Pestle.
Brush.
  Besom.
Lamp.
Candlestick.
  Pricket.
Ferris.
Comb.

Purse.
  Pouch.
Bellows.
Pattens.
Stilts.
Clock.
Hourglass.
  Sandglass.
Balances.
Key.
  Wards.
Spoon.
Scoop.
Hook.
  Fleshhook.
  Hangers.
Gridiron.
Cauldron.
Trivet.
[*Firechest.*]
Cup.
  Drinking Pots.
  College Pots.

Pot.
  Possenet.
  Fleshpot.
  Waterpot.
Ewer.
  Laver-pot.
  Jug.
  Pitcher.
  Flagon.
Buckets.
  Pails.
Waterbouget.
Urn.
  Vase.
Tun.
  Barrel.
  Tub.
Bottle.
Bowl.
Salt.
Dishes.
  Platter.

XXI. CHARGES TAKEN FROM HOME STUDIES, RECREATION, &c.

LITERATURE.

Book.
　Bible.
　Song Book.
　Music Book.
　Musical Lines.
　Clasps.
　Seals.
Chart.
Letters.
　Greek letters.
　Numerals.
　Astronomical
　　　　　Signs.
Roll of Parchment.
Penner.
　Pens.
　Ink horn.
　Sandboxes.

SCIENCE.

Armillary *Sphere.*
　Globe.
Astrolabe.
　Quadrant.
Magnetic Needle.
　Compass Dial.
Level staff.
Compasses.
Spectacles.
Telescope.

GAMES.

Cards.
　Ace.
Dice.
Backgammon Table.
Chessrook.
　Zules.
Top.
　Peg-top.
　Playing top.

MUSIC.

Harp.
　Irish Harp.
　Jew's Harp.
　Cloyshacke.
Violin.
　Fiddle.
Lyre.
Rest.
　Clarion.
Trumpet.
　Sackbut.
　Hautboy.
Bugle Horn.
　Hunting Horn.
Pipes.
　Flutes.
　Shepherd's pipe.
　Organ pipes.
Bagpipes.

XXII. CHARGES TAKEN FROM IMPLEMENTS AND MANUFACTURES.

A. IMPLEMENTS USED IN HUSBANDRY.

Spade.
　Half Spades.
　Spade-irons.
　Shovels.
Fork.
　Pitchforks.
　Dungforks.
　Hayfork.
Deebles.

Rake.
　Thatcher's rake.
　Thatcher's *Hook.*
Plough.
　Ploughshares.
　Coulters.
　Laver cutters.
Harrow.
　Pruning *Knife.*

Sickle.
　Scythe.
　Reaping Hook.
　Pruning Hook.
Bill.
Churn.
Waggon.
　Cart *Wheel.*
Barrow.

B. TOOLS, AND ARTICLES USED IN CARPENTRY AND BUILDING.

Hammer.
　Clawed Hammers.
　Broken Hammers.
　Mallet.
Axe.
　chipping-.
　adze.
　hatchet.
Saw.
　handsaw.
　framed Saw.
　crooked Saw.
Chisel.

Awl.
　Gimlet.
Augur.
　Wimble.
Pincers.
Carpenter's *Square.*
　　,,　　*Reel.*
Mason's *Square.*
Yard measure.
Trowel.
Hone-stone.
Level.
　Plummet.

Nail.
　Spikes.
Cramp.
Hook.
　Tenterhooks.
Staples.
Swivels.
Locks.
　Padlock.
Hinges.
Wedges.
Laths.

CHARGES taken from IMPLEMENTS and MANUFACTURES (*continued*).

C. Implements and Articles connected with Manufacture and Trade.

Baker's *Peel*.
,, *Manchet*.
Bale of silk.
Bag of madder.
*Basket*maker's iron.
,, prime.
,, cutting knife.
,, outsticker.
Blacksmith's *Anvil*.
Bowyer's *Float*.
,, *Hank*.
Bricklayer's *Axe*.
Butcher's Block *Brush*
,, Slaughter *Axe*.
Cloth, piece of.
Clothier's preen.
,, habbick.
Coaches.
Cords.
Knots.
Cooper's *Grose*.
Cotton *Hank*.
Currier's shave.
Distillatory.
Eel-spear.
Harpoon.
Embroiderers—
broaches.
trundles.
quils of yarn, &c.
Fan-maker's shaving iron.
Farrier's *Buttrices*.
Fish *Weel*.
Fish basket.
Eel-pots.
Fish *Hook*.

Founder's fining.
,, tongs.
,, melting pot.
Glazier's nippers.
,, grossing iron.
,, cripping iron.
Hatmaker's *Merillion*.
Hemp brake.
Ironmonger's *Gad*.
Knitting frame.
Marbler's *Axe*.
Metal.
Blocks of metal.
Ingot of gold.
Cake of Copper.
Pig of Lead.
Mill-wheels.
-clacks.
-rinds.
-hoppers.
-stones.
-picks.
Needles.
Bodkins.
Net.
Pattenmaker's pattens.
,, Cutting knife.
Pewterer's *Limbeck*.
Pick-*axe*.
Coal pick.
Paviour's pick.
Plasterer's *Brush*.
Plumber's cutting knife
,, Shavehook.
,, Soldering iron.
,, Cross-staff.

Rope hook
Shoemaker's *Knife*.
Silk hank.
,, bundle.
Silkthrower's mill.
Sugar-loaves.
Surgeon's *Fleam*.
,, Lancet.
,, Spatula.
Tailor's *Scissors*.
Weaver's spindles.
,, slea.
,, shears.
,, shuttle.
,, slippers.
,, *Burling iron*.
Wine press.
,, piercer.
,, broach.
Wire, bundle of.
Wire drawer's iron.
,, copper.
,, point.
,, ring.
,, [engrossing block.]
Woodmonger's *Faggots*.
Wool card.
Working card.
Stock card.
Wool comb.
Flax comb.
Jersey comb.
Wool-pack.
,, sack.

[N.B. Many of the charges on this page are from Insignia of London Companies.]

XXIII. CHARGES TAKEN FROM SHIPS AND SHIPPING.

Ship.	*Lymphad.*	*Rudder.*
Spanish brig.	Galley.	*Anchor.*
[Shambrogue].		Stock.
Hulk.	*Boat.*	Beam.
Stern.	Lighter boat.	Fluke.
Mast.	Open boat.	Cable.
Topmast.	Bark.	Ship's *Lantern.*
Rigging.	Skiff.	Boatswain's *Whistle.*
Sail.	Raft.	*Mariner's* Cross-
	Oars.	staff.
	Boat-hook.	

XXIV. CHARGES TAKEN FROM OBJECTS SEEN IN THE HEAVENS.

Sun.	*Moon.*	*Planet.*
Eclipse.	Decrescent.	Polar *Star* [h].
Ray.	Increscent.	*Clouds.*
Rainbow.	*Crescent* [g].	*Comet.*

XXV. CHARGES TAKEN FROM LANDSCAPES, BUILDINGS, AND PARTS OF BUILDINGS.

A. OBJECTS IN A LANDSCAPE.

Mount.	*Ocean.*	*Park.*
Mountain.	Waves.	Park-pales.
Hill.	*Well.*	*Wood.*
Mound.	Fountain of water.	forest.
Water.	*Weir.*	grove.
River.	*Bridge.*	hurst.
Bubble.	*Gate.*	*Rock.*
Loch.	*Turnstile.*	*Cave.*
Pond.		*Mine.*

B. BUILDINGS AND PARTS OF BUILDINGS.

Town.	*Royal Exchange.*	*Pillar.*
City.	*Lighthouse.*	Column.
College.	*Windmill.*	Capital.
Castle.	Watermill.	Base.
,, Fortress.	*Dovecote.*	Pedestal.
,, Barbican.	*Gateway.*	*Degrees.*
,, Bartizans.	Door arches.	Steps.
,, Trench.	*Tower.*	*Window.*
,, Parapet.	Turret.	*Bracket.*
Portcullis	Steeple.	*Brick-kiln.*
Church, &c.	Cupola.	Bricks.
See under Series	*Spire.*	*Stones.*
No. VII.	*Vane.*	*Flagstones.*
Temple.	Weathercock.	*Wall.*
,, antique.	*Arches.*	Dyke.

[h] See also *Crescent* and *Estoile,* ₹ V. (D), under Conventional Curvilinear charges.

XXVI. DESCRIPTIVE TERMS APPLIED TO ORDINARIES AND CHARGES ABOVE NAMED.

A. RELATING TO THE POSITION OF ORDINARIES OR CHARGES AS REGARDS THE FIELD OR AS REGARDS ONE ANOTHER.

sinister.	*the quadrilateral or*	*ambidextral.*
dexter.	*ensigned by.*	*interlaced.*
in chief.	*enfiled by.*	*embraced.*
in base.	*pierced with.*	*concentric.*
in pale.	*surmounted by.*	*cottised.*
in fesse.	*supporting.*	*gemel.*
barwise.	*sustaining.*	*fimbriated.*
bendwise.	*surtout.*	*cousu.*
saltirewise.	*over all.*	*accosted.*
enhanced.	*brochant sur le tout.*	*accompanied.*
embelief.	*depressed.*	*confronting.*
sovereign.	*debruised.*	*affrontant.*
abased.	*throughout.*	*contourné.*
transposed.	*transverse.*	*reversed.*
two and one.	*issant.*	*addorsed.*
two and two.	*jessant.*	*conjoined.*
three, two, one.	*naissant.*	*appointé.*

B. AFFECTING THE OUTLINES OF ORDINARIES AND SOME FEW CHARGES.

humetty.	*inarched* (of a chevron).	*barby* (of a cross).
alèsé.	*couched* ,,	*flory* ,,
dimidiated.	*fracted* ,,	*avellane* ,,
demi.	*debruised* (of a bend).	*recercellé* ,,
rebated.	*embowed.*	*ancetty* ,,
pery.	*biparted.*	*bourdonné* ,,
enty.	*fitchy.*	*cramponné* ,,
bevilly.	*aiguisé.*	*annuletty* ,,
parted.		*nowy* ,,
voided.		See also p. 179.

See also under III. A. Lines of Partition, and C. of Diversity.

C. APPLIED MORE ESPECIALLY TO THE HUMAN FIGURE.

armed (of men).	*bowed, embowed* (of arms, &c.).	*apaumy* (of hands).
environed (of heads).	*reflexed.*	*avenant* ,,
envelloped ,,	*vambraced.*	*clenched* ,,
wreathed ,,		
crined ,,		

DESCRIPTIVE TERMS APPLIED TO ORDINARIES AND CHARGES (*continued*).

D. APPLIED MORE ESPECIALLY TO BEASTS [i].

passant.
guardant.
regardant.
respectant.
in trian aspect.
sejant.
affronty.
statant.
at gaze.
rampant (of a lion).
couchant   ,,
clymant (of a goat).
segreant (of a griffin).
salient (of a deer).
at bay   ,,
browsing ,,
trippant ,,

rearing (of a horse).
cabré   ,,
careering ,,
in full career ,,
at random (of dogs).
combatant (of 2 lions).
fettered (of a horse).
caparisoned ,,
spancelled ,,
barded   ,,
maned   ,,
belled (of a cow, &c.)
attired (of a deer).
chevillé   ,,
defamed (of a lion).
winged (of a bull).
courant (of a dog).

armed.
membered.
dismembered.
unguled.
incensed.
vulned.
chained.
baillonné.
accolé.
erased (of heads).
couped   ,,
caboshed   ,,
massacre   ,,
erect   ,,
upright   ,,
dejected   ,,
nowed (of tails).
queued   ,,
coward   ,,

E. APPLIED ESPECIALLY TO BIRDS, REPTILES, FISH, AND INVERTEBRATE CREATURES, &c.

beaked (of birds).
membered.
crested.
jellopped (of a cock).
wattled   ,,
preying (of birds).
lolling   ,,
rising   ,,
volant   ,,
surgerant   ,,
soaring   ,,
pecking   ,,
perched   ,,
pruning its wings
collying   ,,
in his majesty (of an eagle).

in her piety (of a pelican).
grilleté (of a falcon).
jessed   ,,
chaperonné   ,,
belled   ,,
Lure   ,,
Hood   ,,
close (of wings).
disclosed   ,,
overt   ,,
endorsed   ,,
espanture   ,,
expanded   ,,
conjoined   ,,
in lure   ,,

naiant (of fishes).
haurient   ,,
urinant   ,,
vorant   ,,
ingulphant   ,,
pamé   ,,
finned   ,,
ecaillé   ,,
moucheté (of lampreys).
gradient (of tortoises).
involved (of serpents).
nowed   ,,
tergiant (of lobsters).
volant en arrière (of insects).

---

[i] A few of these terms as regards position are also applied to Birds.

DESCRIPTIVE TERMS APPLIED TO ORDINARIES AND CHARGES (continued).

F. APPLIED ESPECIALLY TO CHARGES BELONGING TO THE VEGETABLE KINGDOM.

fructed (of trees).	*acorned* (of oaks).	*husked* (of an acorn).
lopped ,,	*slipped* (of stalks).	*graminy* (of chaplets).
snagged ,,	*barbed* (of leaves).	*stalked* (of flowers).
trunked ,,	*bearded* (of wheat).	*seeded* ,,
eradicated ,,	*aulned* ,,	*leaved* ,,
blasted ,,	*bladed* ,,	*banded* (of garbs).

G. APPLIED TO SPECIAL OBJECTS.

barbed (of arrows, &c.)	*purfled* (of armour, &c.)	*inflamed* (of a beacon).
pheoned ,,	*close* (of helmets).	*flamant* ,,
in *sheaves* ,,	*corded* (of bales, &c.)	*fumant* (of a kiln).
in *bundles* ,,	*stoned* (of rings).	*antique* (of vessels, &c.
shafted (of weapons,&c.)	*adorned* (of dress).	in *splendour* (of the sun).
hafted ,,	*fringed* (of a pall).	*radiate* ,,
emmaunched ,,	*chained* (of anchors,&c.)	*rayonnant* ,,
embowed ,,	*cabled* ,,	*increscent* (of the moon).
stringed (of bows).	*masoned* (of buildings).	*decrescent* ,,
buckled (of straps).	*ajouré* ,,	in her *complēment* ,,
bataillé (of a bell).	*quadrangular* (of castles)	*pendent* (of a crescent).
clawed (of hammers).	*Degrees* (of a cross).	
Doubling (of a mantle).	*fired* (of a cannon).	

XXVII. GENERAL HERALDIC TERMS.

A. TERMS CONNECTED ESPECIALLY WITH BLAZON.

Field.	*Bearings.*	*impaling.*
Tinctures.	*Trick.*	*quartered.*
[See ante I.]	*Sides.*	*counter.*
Ordinaries.	*Panes.*	*counterchanged.*
[See ante II.]	*Traits.*	*semé.*
Points.	*Interstices.*	*crusilly.*
[See ante IV.]	*Verge.*	*diapered.*
Charges.	*proper.*	*accolé* (of shields).
[See ante V.—XXV.]	*plain.*	

GENERAL HERALDIC TERMS (*continued*).

B. TERMS CONNECTED WITH THE THEORY AND PRACTICE OF HERALDRY.

Heraldry.	*Crest.*	*Arms* of Dominion.
Armorie.	*Lambrequin.*	—— of Pretension.
Rolls of Arms.	*Mantle.*	—— of Succession.
Visitations.	*Motto.*	—— Family.
Shield.	*Escroll.*	—— of Assumption.
Arms.	*Cordon.*	—— of Alliance.
Insignia.	*Supporters.*	—— of Adoption.
Achievements.	*Surcoat.*	—— of Concession.
Escutcheon.	*Tabard.*	—— of Patronage.
Chaperonnes.	*Badge.*	—— of Office.
Emerasses.	*Device.*	—— of Communities.
Marshalling.	*Rebus.*	Insignia of *England.*
Baron et Femme.	*Merchant's Mark.*	—— of *Scotland.*
Composed arms.	*Abatements.*	—— of *Ireland.*
Cadency.	*Stainand colours.*	—— of *Wales.*
Difference.	*Augmentations.*	
Ulster Badge.	*Armes pour enquerir.*	

XXVIII.   TITLES,   ORDERS,   KNIGHTS,   HERALDIC   OFFI-
CERS, &c., &c.

King.	Orders (*continued*).	*Heralds.*
Duke.	Hanoverian or Guelphic	Garter King of Arms.
Marquess.	Of Knights Hospital-	Clarenceux ,,
Earl.	lers.	Norroy ,,
Viscount.	Of SS. Michael and	Bath ,,
Baron.	George.	Lord Lyon ,,
Baronet.	Of the Passion.	Ulster ,,
Marshal.	Of S. Patrick.	Chester Herald.
Knights.	Of the Round Table.	Lancaster ,,
—— Grand Cross.	Of the Royal Oak.	Richmond ,,
—— Commanders.	Templars.	Somerset ,,
—— Companions.	Of the Thistle, or of	Windsor ,,
—— Bachelor.	S. Andrew.	York ,,
—— Banneret.	Of the Star of India.	Pursuivants.
Esquire.	Of S. Lazarus.	Rouge croix.
Orders of Knights	Of Victoria and Albert.	Blue mantle.
Of the Bath.		Rouge Dragon.
Of the Garter.		Portcullis.

DESCRIPTIVE TERMS APPLIED TO ORDINARIES AND CHARGES (*continued*).

D. APPLIED MORE ESPECIALLY TO BEASTS [i].

passant.	*rearing* (of a horse).	*armed.*
guardant.	*cabré* ,,	*membered.*
regardant.	*careering* ,,	*dismembered.*
respectant.	*in full career* ,,	*unguled.*
in trian aspect.	*at random* (of dogs).	*incensed.*
sejant.	*combatant* (of 2 lions).	*vulned.*
affronty.	*fettered* (of a horse).	*chained.*
statant.	*caparisoned* ,,	*baillonné.*
at gaze.	*spancelled* ,,	*accolé.*
rampant (of a lion).	*barded* ,,	*erased* (of heads).
couchant ,,	*maned* ,,	*couped* ,,
clymant (of a goat).	*belled* (of a cow, &c.)	*caboshed* ,,
segreant (of a griffin).	*attired* (of a deer).	*massacre* ,,
salient (of a deer).	*chevillé* ,,	*erect* ,,
at bay ,,	*defamed* (of a lion).	*upright* ,,
browsing ,,	*winged* (of a bull).	*dejected* ,,
trippant ,,	*courant* (of a dog).	*nowed* (of tails).
		queued ,,
		coward ,,

E. APPLIED ESPECIALLY TO BIRDS, REPTILES, FISH, AND INVERTEBRATE CREATURES, &c.

beaked (of birds).	*in her piety* (of a pelican).	*naiant* (of fishes).
membered.		*haurient* ,,
crested.	*grilleté* (of a falcon).	*urinant* ,,
jellopped (of a cock).	*jessed* ,,	*vorant* ,,
wattled ,,	*chaperonné* ,,	*ingulphant* ,,
preying (of birds).	*belled* ,,	*pamé* ,,
lolling ,,	*Lure* ,,	*finned* ,,
rising ,,	*Hood* ,,	*ecaillé* ,,
volant ,,	*close* (of wings).	*moucheté* (of lampreys).
surgerant ,,	*disclosed* ,,	
soaring ,,	*overt* ,,	*gradient* (of tortoises).
pecking ,,	*endorsed* ,,	*involved* (of serpents).
perched ,,	*sepurture* ,,	*nowed* ,,
pruning its wings	*expanded* ,,	*tergiant* (of lobsters).
collying ,,	*conjoined* ,,	*volant en arrière* (of insects).
in his majesty (of an eagle).	*in lure* ,,	

---

[i] A few of these terms as regards position are also applied to Birds.

XXVI. DESCRIPTIVE TERMS APPLIED TO ORDINARIES AND CHARGES ABOVE NAMED.

A. RELATING TO THE POSITION OF ORDINARIES OR CHARGES AS REGARDS THE FIELD OR AS REGARDS ONE ANOTHER.

sinister.	in quadrature.	cantoned.
dexter.	ensigned by.	interlaced.
in chief.	enfiled by.	embraced.
in base.	pierced with.	concentric.
in pale.	surmounted by.	cottised.
in fesse.	supporting.	gemel.
barwise.	sustaining.	fimbriated.
bendwise.	surtout.	cousu.
saltirewise.	over all.	accosted.
enhanced.	brochant sur le tout.	accompanied.
embelief.	depressed.	confronting.
sovereign.	debruised.	affrontant.
abased.	throughout.	contourné.
transposed.	transverse.	reversed.
two and one.	issant.	addorsed.
two and two.	jessant.	conjoined.
three, two, one.	naissant.	appointé.

B. AFFECTING THE OUTLINES OF ORDINARIES AND SOME FEW CHARGES.

humetty.	inarched (of a chev-	barby (of a cross).
alèsé.	ron).	flory ,,
dimidiated.	couched ,,	avellane ,,
demi.	fracted ,,	recercellé ,,
rebated.	debruised (of a bend).	ancetty ,,
pery.	embowed.	bourdonné ,,
enty.	biparted.	cramponné ,,
bevilly.	fitchy.	annuletty ,,
parted.	aiguisé.	nowy ,,
voided.		See also p. 179.

See also under III. A. Lines of Partition, and C. of Diversity.

C. APPLIED MORE ESPECIALLY TO THE HUMAN FIGURE.

armed (of men).	bowed, embowed (of	apaumy (of hands).
environed (of heads).	arms, &c.).	avenant ,,
envelloped ,,	reflexed.	clenched ,,
wreathed ,,	vambraced.	
crined ,,		

XXIII. CHARGES TAKEN FROM SHIPS AND SHIPPING.

Ship.	*Lymphad.*	*Rudder.*
Spanish brig.	Galley.	*Anchor.*
[Shambrogue].		Stock.
Hulk.	*Boat.*	Beam.
Stern.	Lighter boat.	Fluke.
Mast.	Open boat.	Cable.
Topmast.	Bark.	Ship's *Lantern.*
Rigging.	Skiff.	Boatswain's *Whistle.*
Sail.	Raft.	*Mariner's* Cross-
	Oars.	staff.
	Boat-hook.	

XXIV. CHARGES TAKEN FROM OBJECTS SEEN IN THE HEAVENS.

Sun.	*Moon.*	*Planet.*
Eclipse.	Decrescent.	Polar *Star* [h].
Ray.	Increscent.	*Clouds.*
Rainbow.	*Crescent* [g].	*Comet.*

XXV. CHARGES TAKEN FROM LANDSCAPES, BUILDINGS, AND PARTS OF BUILDINGS.

A. OBJECTS IN A LANDSCAPE.

Mount.	*Ocean.*	*Park.*
Mountain.	Waves.	Park-pales.
Hill.	*Well.*	*Wood.*
Mound.	Fountain of water.	forest.
Water.	*Weir.*	grove.
River.		hurst.
Bubble.	*Bridge.*	*Rock.*
Loch.	*Gate.*	*Cave.*
Pond.	*Turnstile.*	*Mine.*

B. BUILDINGS AND PARTS OF BUILDINGS.

Town.	*Royal Exchange.*	*Pillar.*
City.	*Lighthouse.*	Column.
College.	*Windmill.*	Capital.
Castle.	Watermill.	Base.
,, Fortress.	*Dovecote.*	Pedestal.
,, Barbican.	*Gateway.*	*Degrees.*
,, Bartizans.	Door arches.	Steps.
,, Trench.	*Tower.*	*Window.*
,, Parapet.	Turret.	*Bracket.*
Portcullis.	Steeple.	*Brick-kiln.*
Church, &c.	Cupola.	Bricks.
See under Series	*Spire.*	*Stones.*
No. VII.	*Vane.*	*Flagstones.*
Temple.	Weathercock.	*Wall.*
,, antique.	*Arches.*	Dyke.

[h] See also *Crescent* and *Estoile,* ⸹ V. (D), under Conventional Curvilinear charges.

CHARGES TAKEN FROM IMPLEMENTS AND MANUFACTURES (*continued*).

C. IMPLEMENTS AND ARTICLES CONNECTED WITH MANUFACTURE AND TRADE.

Baker's *Peel*.
  ,,   *Manchet*.
Bale of silk.
  Bag of madder.
*Basket*maker's iron.
  ,,   prime.
  ,,   cutting knife.
  ,,   outsticker.
Blacksmith's *Anvil*.
Bowyer's *Float*.
  ,,   *Hank*.
Bricklayer's *Axe*.
Butcher's Block*Brush*
  ,,   Slaughter *Axe*.
Cloth, piece of.
Clothier's preen.
  ,,   habbick.
Coaches.
Cords.
  Knots.
Cooper's *Grose*.
Cotton *Hank*.
Currier's shave.
Distillatory.
Eel-spear.
  Harpoon.
Embroiderers—
  broaches.
  trundles.
  quils of yarn, &c.
Fan-maker's shaving
  iron.
Farrier's *Buttrices*.
Fish *Weel*.
  Fish basket.
  Eel-pots.
Fish *Hook*.

Founder's furnace.
  ,,   tongs.
  ,,   melting pot.
Glazier's nippers.
  ,,   grossing iron.
  ,,   cripping iron.
Hatmaker's *Merillion*.
Hemp brake.
Ironmonger's *Gad*.
Knitting frame.
Marbler's *Axe*.
Metal.
  Blocks of metal.
  Ingot of gold.
  Cake of Copper.
  Pig of Lead.
Mill-wheels.
  -clacks.
  -rinds.
  -hoppers.
  -stones.
  -picks.
Needles.
  Bodkins.
Net.
Pattenmaker's pattens.
  ,,   Cutting knife.
Pewterer's *Limbeck*.
Pick-*axe*.
  Coal pick.
  Paviour's pick.
Plasterer's *Brush*.
Plumber's cutting knife
  ,,   Shavehook.
  ,,   Soldering iron.
  ,,   Cross-staff.

Rope hook.
Shoemaker's *Knife*.
Silk hank.
  ,,   bundle.
Silkthrower's mill.
Sugar-loaves.
Surgeon's *Fleam*.
  ,,   Lancet.
  ,,   Spatula.
Tailor's *Scissors*.
Weaver's spindles.
  ,,   slea.
  ,,   shears.
  ,,   shuttle.
  ,,   slippers.
  ,,   *Burling iron*.
Wine press.
  ,,   piercer.
  ,,   broach.
Wire, bundle of.
Wire drawer's iron.
  ,,   copper.
  ,,   point.
  ,,   ring.
  ,,   [engross-
    ing block.]
Woodmonger's *Fag-gots*.
Wool card.
  Working card.
  Stock card.
Wool comb.
  Flax comb.
  Jersey comb.
Wool-pack.
  ,,   sack.

[N.B. Many of the charges on this page are from Insignia of London Companies.]

XXI. CHARGES taken from HOME STUDIES, RECREATION, &c.

LITERATURE.	SCIENCE.	MUSIC.
Book.	Armillary *Sphere.*	*Harp.*
Bible.	Globe.	Irish Harp.
Song Book.	*Astrolabe.*	Jew's Harp.
Music Book.	Quadrant.	Cloyshacke.
Musical Lines.	*Magnetic Needle.*	*Viollm.*
Clasps.	Compass Dial.	Fiddle.
Seals.	*Level* staff.	*Lyre.*
Chart.	*Compasses.*	*Rest.*
Letters.	*Spectacles.*	Clarion.
Greek letters.	*Telescope.*	*Trumpet.*
Numerals.		Sackbut.
Astronomical	GAMES.	Hautboy.
Signs.	*Cards.*	*Bugle Horn.*
Roll of Parchment.	Ace.	Hunting Horn.
Penner.	*Dice.*	*Pipes.*
Pens.	*Backgammon Table.*	Flutes.
Ink horn.	*Chessrook.*	Shepherd's pipe.
Sandboxes.	Zules.	Organ pipes.
	Top.	*Bagpipes.*
	Peg-top.	
	Playing top.	

XXII. CHARGES taken from IMPLEMENTS AND MANUFACTURES.

A. IMPLEMENTS USED IN HUSBANDRY.

Spade.	*Rake.*	*Sickle.*
Half Spades.	Thatcher's rake.	Scythe.
Spade-irons.	Thatcher's *Hook.*	Reaping Hook.
Shovels.	*Plough.*	Pruning Hook.
Fork.	Ploughshares.	*Bill.*
Pitchforks.	Coulters.	*Churn.*
Dungforks.	Laver cutters.	*Waggon.*
Hayfork.	*Harrow.*	Cart *Wheel.*
Deebles.	*Pruning Knife.*	*Barrow.*

B. TOOLS, AND ARTICLES USED IN CARPENTRY AND BUILDING.

Hammer.	*Awl.*	*Nail.*
Clawed Hammers.	Gimlet.	Spikes.
Broken Hammers.	*Augur.*	*Cramp.*
Mallet.	Wimble.	*Hook.*
Axe.	*Pincers.*	Tenterhooks.
chipping-.	Carpenter's *Square.*	*Staples.*
adze.	,, *Reel.*	*Swivels.*
hatchet.	Mason's *Square.*	*Locks.*
Saw.	*Yard measure.*	Padlock.
handsaw.	*Trowel.*	*Hinges.*
framed Saw.	*Hone-stone.*	*Wedges.*
crooked Saw.	*Level.*	*Laths.*
Chisel.	Plummet.	

XIX. CHARGES TAKEN FROM ARTICLES OF ATTIRE AND ORNAMENT.

A. ARTICLES OF ATTIRE.

Crown.	*Mitre.*	[*Mantle.*]
imperial.	*Tiara.*	*Maunch.*
royal.	*Wreath.*	Sleeve.
mural.	*Cap.*	
celestial.	Chapeau.	*Boot.*
eastern.	Infula.	Dutch boots.
naval.	Ducipers.	Irish brogues.
civic.	*Bonnet.*	Shoes.
prince's coronet.	*Hat.*	*Hose.*
ducal. ,,	Hatband.	*Garter.*
earl's ,,	*Robe.*	*Glove.*

B. PERSONAL ORNAMENTS, DECORATIONS, JEWELS, &c.

Sceptre.	*Plumes.*	*Medal.*
Orb.	Feathers.	medallion.
Mound royal.	*Ring* (gem).	clasp.
Regalia.	jewelled.	pagoda.
Mace.	*Diamonds.*	penny yard penny.
Civic mace.	Crystals.	[*George.*]
Collar.	Brilliants.	*Riband.*
	Ruby.	*Angles.*

XX. CHARGES FROM ARTICLES OF DOMESTIC USE.

Mirror.	*Purse.*	*Pot.*
Tapestry.	Pouch.	Possenet.
Cushions.	*Bellows.*	Fleshpot.
Pillow.	*Pattens.*	Waterpot.
Tassel.	*Stilts.*	*Ewer.*
Child's Cradle.	*Clock.*	Laver-pot.
Chair.	*Hourglass.*	Jug.
Trestle.	Sandglass.	Pitcher.
Basket.	*Balances.*	Flagon.
,, of wastel cakes.	*Key.*	*Buckets.*
Dorcer.	Wards.	Pails.
Vane.	*Spoon.*	*Waterbouget.*
Shruttle.	*Scoop.*	*Urn.*
Mortars.	*Hook.*	Vase.
Pestle.	Fleshhook.	*Tun.*
Brush.	Hangers.	Barrel.
Besom.	*Gridiron.*	Tub.
Lamp.	*Cauldron.*	*Bottle.*
Candlestick.	*Trivet.*	*Bowl.*
Pricket.	[*Firechest.*]	*Salt.*
Ferris.	*Cup.*	*Dishes.*
Comb.	Drinking Pots.	Platter.
	College Pots.	

XVIII. CHARGES TAKEN FROM WEAPONS, WAR MATERIAL, &c.

A. GUNS, BOWS, AND ARROWS, &c.

Guns.
- Cannon.
- Field piece.
- Chamber piece.
- Chamber.
- Culverin.

Mortar.

Matchlock.

Matches, Roll of.

Musket.
- Potgun.
- Pistol.

Bow.
- Long-bow.
- Hand-bow.
- Cross-bow.
- Bowstring.

Arrow.
- Bundle of arrows.
- Broadarrow.
- Quarrels.
- Bolts.
- Bird bolts.

Pheon.

Shot.
- Chain shot.
- Star stone.

Fireball.
- Bombs.
- Bombshells.
- Grenados.
- Hand grenades.

Sling.
- Sweep.
- Balista.

Quiver.

B. SWORDS, SPEARS, AXES, &c.

Sword.
- Arming sword.
- Irish sword.
- Claymore.
- Brand.
- Hilt.
- Pomel.
- Scabbard.
- Bouterol.
- Chape.
- Crampet.

Sabre.
- Falchion
- Scimitar.
- Seax.
- Badelaire.
- Hanger.
- Cutlas.

Dagger.
- Dirk.
- Rapier.
- Poignard.
- Skean.

Spear.
- Lance.
- Javelin.
- Dart.

Cronel.

Rest.
- Clarion.

Axe.
- Battle axe.
- Danish axe.
- Tomahawk.
- Lochabar axe.
- Pole axe.

Staff.
- Pikestaff.
- Club.
- Truncheon.

C. WAR MATERIAL, TENTS, FLAGS, &c.

Beacons.
- Cressets.

Torch.
- Firebrand.

Fire.
- Fascines.

Battering ram.

Grappling irons.

Caltrap.

Ladder (Scaling).

Target.

Quiver.

Shield.

Tent.
- Tent staff.
- Pavilion.

Scroll.
- Ribbon.

Flag.
- Standard.
- Union Jack.
- [Gonfanon.]
- Guidon.
- Pennon.
- Pennoncel.
- Streamer.

Banner.
- Beauseant.

D. HORSE-GEAR, &c.

Horse trappings.

[*Hame*].

Bit.
- Boss.

Bridle.

Saddle.

Stirrup.

Spur.
- Rowel.

Whip.

Horse shoe.

Horse picker.

Barnacles.

Breys.

Curry comb.

CHARGES TAKEN FROM THE VEGETABLE KINGDOM (*continued*).

D. MISCELLANEOUS PLANTS, GRAIN, &c.

Beans.
  Beancods.
Cinnamon leaves.
Cloves.
Cotton tree.
Cummin.
Dock leaf.
  Bur leaf.
Fern leaves.
  Adder's tongue.
Garlic.
Gourds.
[*Graintree.*]
Grass, tufts.
  ,,   spires.

Hopbines.
  Hop poles
Mandrake.
Parsley leaves.
Peascods.
Pepper pods.
Reeds, bundles of.
  ,,   sheaves of.
  ,,   tufts.
  Rushes.
  Bulrushes.
Seaweed.
  Laver.
Sugar canes.

Tobacco.
Turnip.
Watercress leaves.
Wheat ears.
  ,,   sheaves.
  Big wheat.
  Guinea wheat.
  Barley ears.
  Corn ears.
  Oat sheaves.
  Rye ears.
  ,,   stalks.
Garbe.

E. PARTS OF TREES, CHAPLETS, CONVENTIONAL FORMS, &c.

Tree.
  branch.
  limb of tree.
  scrogs.
  twigs.
  sprigs.
  slips.
  graft.
  stock.
  stump.
  trunk.

Chaplet of roses.
  ,,   of flowers.
  ,,   of laurel.
  ,,   of holly.
  ,,   of hazel.
  ,,   of rue.
  ,,   of oak (or
        Civic) wreath.
  Bramble wreath.
Bush.
Faggot.

Flower.
Fruit.
Leaf.
Root.
Staff raguly.
  Wand.
Foil.
Trefoil.
Quatrefoil.
Cinquefoil.
Sexfoil.
Fleur de lis.

XVII. CHARGES TAKEN FROM ARMOUR, ACCOUTREMENTS, &c.

Helmet, Sovereign's.
  ,,   Duke's.
  ,,   Baronet's.
  ,,   Esquire's.
  visor.
  beaver.
  gorget.
Cap of Steel.
  Basnet.
  Burgonette.
  Morion.

Hauberk.
  Habergeon.
Cuirass.
  Breastplate.
Shield.
  Target.
Escutcheon.
Belt.
  Baldrich.
Arm.
  Brassarts.

Gauntlet.
Buckle.
  Fermail.
  Arming buckle.
Escarboucle.
Straps.
  Wriststraps.
Fetterlock.
  Shackle bolts.
  Manacles.

XVI. CHARGES TAKEN FROM THE VEGETABLE KINGDOM.

A. FOREST TREES, &c.

Alder berry.
Ash tree.
   ашеп branches
   ashen Keys.
Beech branch.
Birch branches.
   ,, leaves.
Elder leaves.
Elm tree.
   ,, leaves.
Hawthorn tree.
     ,,   leaves.
   Whitethorn.
   Mayflowers.

Holly tree.
   ,,   branches.
   ,,   leaves.
Ivy branches.
Laurel tree.
   ,,   branches.
   ,,   leaves.
   ,,   bay leaves.
Linden leaves.
Maple tree.
Oak tree.
   ,, leaf.
Acorn.
   Acorn cup.

Palm tree.
   Cocoa nut tree.
   China Cokar.
Pine tree.
   ,, cone.
   Fir tree.
   Cedar.
   Cypress.
Poplar tree.
   Aspen leaf.
Staff tree leaves.
Willow tree.
   Salix.
   Osier.
Yew tree.

B. FRUITS AND FRUIT-TREES.

Almond slip.
   ,, leaves.
Apple tree.
   ,, fruit.
Barbary branch.
Cherry tree.
   ,, fruit.
Fig tree.
Hazel leaves.
   Nuts.
   Filberts.
Mulberry.

Olive tree.
   ,, branch.
Orange tree.
   ,, fruit.
Pear.
   Warden pear.
Pine apple.
   Ananas.
Plum.
Pomegranate tree.
   ,, fruit.
   Apple of Granada.

Quince fruit.
Strawberry sprigs.
   ,, leaf.
   Frasier.
Vine.
   ,, branch.
   ,, leaves.
   Grapes.
Walnut leaves.
   ,, [tree].

C. FLOWERS AND FLOWERING PLANTS.

Balm.
Betony leaf.
Carnation.
   Pink.
Broom.
   Planta genista.
Bluebottle.
   heydodde ?
Columbine.
Daisy.
Gilly flower.
Heliotrope.

Honeysuckle.
Lily.
   Iris.
Marigold.
Narcissus.
Nettle.
Pansy
Poppy.
Primrose.
Rose.
   ,, damask.
   ,, heraldic.

Sengreen.
Silphium.
Sunflower.
   Heliotrope.
Thistle.
   Teazel.
Trefoil leaf.
   Shamrock.
Tulip.
Violets.
   Gletver *Leaf.*

XIV. CHARGES TAKEN FROM PARTS OF MEN AND ANIMALS.

A. OF MEN, WOMEN, CHILDREN, &c.

Head, Man's.	*Head,* Woman's.	*Bones.*
,, Saracen's.	,, Lady's.	Human skull.
,, Turk's.	,, Maiden's.	Jaw-bone.
,, Negro's.	,, Nun's.	*Heart.*
,, Moor's.	,, Children's.	*Arm.*
,, Savage's.	,, Infant's.	*Hand.*
,, Chieftain's.	*Eye.*	*Leg.*
,, Saxon's.	*Hair.*	*Foot.*
,, Egyptian's.	*Limbs.*	

B. OF ANIMALS.

Heads of Beasts.	*Gambes* of Beasts.	*Ears* of Beasts.
,, of Birds.	Paws.	*Attires* of Deer.
,, of Fish.	*Legs* of Beasts.	Tynes ,,
,, of Monsters.	*Horns* of Beasts.	*Lambs'* Kidneys.
Wings of Birds.	*Tails* of Beasts.	Cows' *Horns.*

XV. CHARGES TAKEN FROM MONSTERS.

MONSTERS WITH WINGS.	BEASTS WITH FISHES' TAILS.	MAN MONSTERS.
Griffin.		*Satyrs*
Dragon.	*Sea Horse.*	Satyral.
Alce.	Sea Lion.	Centaur.
Opinicus.	Sea Dragon.	Sagittarius.
Cockatrice, with	Sea Dog.	Triton.
Wyvern.	Sea Wolf.	Lampago.
Basilisk.		Man Tiger.
Amphistere.		
Hydra.	COMBINED BEASTS.	WOMEN MONSTERS.
	Unicorn.	*Sphinx.*
BEASTS WITH WINGS.	[*Allocamelus.*]	Harpy.
Pegasus, with	[*Apre.*]	[*Chimæra.*]
Winged Stag.	[*Bagwyn.*]	*Mermaid.*
Winged Bull.	[*Musimon.*]	Siren.
Python.	[*Yale.*]	
Winged Ox.	Deer-*goat* (heads).	CREATURES IN FIRE.
Winged Lion.	Lion-*goat* (heads).	*Phœnix.*
		Salamander.

XI. CHARGES TAKEN FROM REPTILES.

CHELONIA.	OPHIDIA.	AMPHIBIA.
Tortoise.	*Serpent.*	*Frogs.*
	Snake.	Tadpoles.
LACERTILIA.	Blind.	Powots.
Lizard.		Toads.
Cameleon.	*Adder.*	
CROCODILIA.	Asp.	*Effets.*
Alligators.	Viper.	Askers.
Crocodile.		Newts

XII. CHARGES TAKEN FROM FISH.

OSSEOUS FISHES.	*Bream.*	*Turbot.*
Perch.	*Lucy*, or Pike.	Sole.
Chabot.	Ged.	Flook.
Gurnet.	*Flyingfish.*	Flounder.
Mullet.	*Salmon.*	
Mackerel.	Trout.	_____
Swordfish.	Smelts.	*Eels.*
Gudgeon.	*Herring.*	Congereels.
Loach.	Cobfish.	Grigs.
	Sprats.	
_____	Pilchard.	CARTILAGENOUS FISHES.
Barbel.	Garvin.	*Sturgeon.*
Tench.	*Cod.*	*Shark.*
Mogul, fish of.	Hake.	Dogfish.
Carp.	Ling.	*Lampreys.*
Chub.	Whiting.	
Minnow.		

XIII. CHARGES TAKEN FROM INVERTEBATE CREATURES.

INSECTA.	*Bees.*	ANNULOIDA.
Grasshoppers.	Hornets.	*Sea Urchins.*
Crickets.	Beehives.	CRUSTACEA
	Ants.	*Crab.*
_____	Emmets.	*Lobster.*
Fly.	*Beetles.*	Crevices.
House-fly.	Stag Beetles.	*Shrimps.*
Gad-fly.		Prawns.
Gadbee.	ANNULOSA.	MOLLUSCA.
Brimsey.	*Horseleech.*	*Escalop.*
Butterfly.	*Spider.*	*Whelks.*
Harvest-fly.	*Scorpion.*	*Snails.*
Silkworm-fly.		

X. CHARGES TAKEN FROM BIRDS.

NATATORES.

Duck.
  Drake.
  Sheldrake.
  Wildduck.
  Mallard.
  Teal.
  Shoveller.
  Cannet.
  Muscovy Duck.
  Smew, or
  White Nun.
Goose.
  Magellan Goose.
  Wildgoose.
Barnacle Goose.
Swan.
  Cygnet.
Cormorant.
  Sea Aylet.
  Gannapie.
Sea Gull.
  Sea Mew.
  Tern.
  Sea Pewit.
  Sea Fowl.
Auk.
  Murr.
  Razorbill.
Pelican.

GRALLATORES.

Coot.
  Baldcoot.
  Moorhen.
Crane.
Heron.
  Heronshaw.
  Bittern.
  Fencock.
  Spoonbill.
Plover.

Stork.
Snipe.
  Curlew.
  Avocetta.
Lapwing.
  Pewit.
  Tirwhitt.
  Sea pie.
Bustard.

CURSORES.

Ostrich.
  ,, feathers.

RASORES.

Heathcock or
  Blackcock.
Moorcock or
  Grouse.
Cock, i.e.
  Barn-door Cock.
  Hen.
  Gamecock.
  Cockerells.
  Capon.
Pheasant.
  Mitus.
Partridge.
Peacock.
  Peahen.
Turkey.
Dove.
  Ring Dove.
  Turtle Dove.
  Stock Dove.
  Pigeon.
  Wood Pigeon.

SCANSORES.

Parrot.
  Parroquet.
  Popinjay.

INSESSORES.

Raven.
  Rook.
  Crow.
  Daw.
Cornish Chough.
  Beckit.
Magpie.
  Jay.
Starling.
  Stern.
Finches.
  Goldfinch.
  Bullfinch.
  Chaffinch.
  Brambling.
  Canary.
  Linnet.
  Pinzon.
Lark.
Bunting.
Sparrow.
Blackbird.
Wren.
  Robin Redbreast.
Martlet.
Swallow.
  Martin.
Kingfisher.
    RAPTORES.
Eagle.
  Eaglet.
  Alerion.
Falcon.
  Hawk.
  Sparrowhawk.
  Goshawk.
  Kite.
  Sacre.
  Merlion.
Vulture.
Owl
  Horned Owl.

VIII. CLASSICAL AND MYTHOLOGICAL CHARGES.

Apollo.	*Hercules* (?).	*Neptune.*
Bacchus' *Faces.*	Jupiter's *Thunderbolt.*	Neptune's *Trident.*
Britannia.	Mercury's *Caduceus.*	Pallas' *Shield.*
Golden *Fleece.*	Midas' *Head.*	Roman *Fasces.*
Æsculapius' Rod.		

IX. CHARGES TAKEN FROM BEASTS.

QUADRUMANA.

Ape.
  [Monkey].

PROBOSCIDEA.
Elephant.

CETACEA.
Whale.
Dolphin.

CHEIROPTERA.
Bat.
  Reremouse.

INSECTIVORA.
Hedgehog.
Mole.

RODENTIA.
Hare.
  Rabbit.
  Coney.
  Levrets.
Porcupine.
Beaver.
Rat
Squirrel.

CARNIVORA.
Lion.
  Leopard.
  Lioncel.
Tiger.

Panther.
  Ounce.
  Lynx.
Cat.
  Mountain Cat.
  Wild Cat.
  Musion.
  Lezard.
Dog.
  Alant.
  Bloodhound.
  Greyhound.
  Hound.
  Levrier.
  Mastiff.
  Spaniel.
  Talbot.
Wolf.
Fox.
  Tod.
  Genet.
Otter.
Weasel.
  Ermine.
  Foine.
  Marten.
Civet Cat.
Badger.
  Gray.
  Brock.
Bear.
  Sea Bear.
Seal.
  Sea Calf.
  Morse.

UNGULATA.

Rhinoceros.
Horse.
  Nag.
  Colt.
Ass.
  Mule.
Camel.
Deer.
  Stag.
  Buck.
  Doe.
  Fawn.
  Hart.
  Hind.
  Roebuck.
  Reindeer.
  Brocket.
Antelope.
  Ibex.
Goat.
  Assyrian Goat.
Sheep.
Ram.
Lamb.
Bull.
  Ox.
  Cow.
  Calf.
  Buffalo.
Boar.
  Hog.
  Sanglier.
  Grice.
  Marcassin
  [Camelopard].

VI. CHARGES TAKEN FROM THE HUMAN FIGURE.

Archer.	*Man,* wild.	*Man,* Soldiers
Armour, man in.	,, savage.	,, Danish Warrior.
Chevalier.	,, Negro.	,, Watchman.
King.	,, Moor.	,, [Russian].
Bishop.	,, Blackamoor.	,, [Highlander].
Child.	,, African.	,, Woodman.
Boy.	,, Indian.	,, Gardener.
Infant.	,, [Mandarin.] [g]	,, Miner.

VII. RELIGIOUS AND ECCLESIASTICAL CHARGES.

Trinity (Symbol of the).	*Saint* Michael.	*Crosier.*
	,, Giles.	Episcopal Staff.
Crucifix.	,, Boniface.	Bishop's Crook.
Crown of *Thorns.*	,, Columb.	Pastoral Staff.
Passion Nails.	,, Andrew.	*Pilgrim's* Staff.
Lamb (Paschal).	,, Bryce.	,, Crutch.
Virgin Mary, The.	,, Columba.	,, Scrip.
The Infant Saviour.	,, Giles.	*Staffs,* various.
Evangelistic symbols	,, Magnus.	*Escallop* Shell.
Letter ℳ.	and others.	*Rosary.*
Letters A and Ω.	S. John's *Head* in	Beads.
Angel.	a charger.	*Church.*
Charity.	S. George's *Cross.*	Cathedral.
Justice.	S. Andrew's *Cross.*	Chapel.
Cherub.	S. Patrick's *Cross.*	Porch.
Paradise, Tree of.	S. Antony's *Fire.*	Shrine.
,, Adam and Eve in	S. Bartholomew's	Altar tomb.
Noah's Ark.	*Knife.*	*Tombstone.*
Moses' *Head.*	S. Peter's *Keys.*	*Altar.*
Burning *Bush.*	S. Catherine's *Wheel.*	*Monastery.*
Mount *Ararat* with	S. Guthlac's *Scourges*	*Ruins* of old Abbey.
Raphael and To-	*Cross* of Calvary.	Church *Bell.*
bias in base.	,, Jerusalem.	*Censer.*
Nimbus.	,, S. Antony.	*Fanon.*
Pall, Archiepiscopal.	,, S. Julian.	*Chalice.*
Prester John.	,, S. Chad.	*Mortcour.*
Kings of Cologne.		

[g] N.B. Those printed within brackets have not been met with by the Editor as Charges, but most of them occur as Supporters, Crests, or Badges.

A GLOSSARY

OF TERMS USED IN

HERALDRY.

A or *a* in heraldic memoranda and sketches of arms in *trick*, is employed to signify *Argent* [and is better than *ar.*, which might be mistaken for *az*, or for *or*].

Abased, (fr. *abaissé*): this term is used when a *chevron*, *fesse*, or other ordinary, is borne lower than its usual situation. Charges, however, when placed low down in the shield are said to be *in base*.

Abatements, sometimes called *Rebatements*, are marks of disgrace attached to arms on account of some dishonourable act of the bearer. They are shewn by pieces of different shapes being to all appearance cut out of, or off from, the shield; their shapes and positions are represented by the following varieties, which are nine in number, and must be either *sanguine* or *tenné*, which the old writers call "staynande colours," otherwise they are no abatements but honourable charges, viz.—

1. *Delf.*	4. *Point dexter.*	7. *Gore sinister.*
2. *Inescutcheon* reversed.	5. *Point pointed.*	8. *Gusset dexter.*
3. *Plain Point.*	6. *Point champaine.*	9. *Gusset sinister.*

As the use of arms is not compulsory, a bearer would of course rather relinquish them than publish his own disgrace by bearing them abated. Abatements such as the above exist only in systems of heraldry, and no instance of their actual use is on record: but under the several headings diagrams will be found explaining the meaning of the terms which are used by heraldic writers.

Broken chevrons, and beasts turned towards the sinister, are supposed by some heraldic writers to have been given as abatements.

"And Edward the Third of England ordained two of six stars which a gentleman had in his arms to be effaced, because he had sold a seaport of which he was made governor." [According to Sir George Mackenzie, in allusion to AYMERY OF PAVIA, a Lombard, governor of Calais in 1349, who bore azure, four mullets or.]

There is another mark of disgrace which is due only to the traitor: it consists in *debasing* or reversing the entire coat.

Accolé: 1. (from fr. *col*, the neck,) having a collar is synonymous with *gorged* (and occasionally with *wreathed* or *entwined*).   2. Is used still with French heralds when two shields are joined side by side; a practice sometimes adopted in England previously to the introduction of *impaling*.

Accosted, (fr. *accosté*): 1. a term used when charges are placed on each side of another charge, as, a pale accosted by six mullets; though English heralds would generally say, between six mullets pallet-wise. 2. Applied to two beasts walking or running side by side. Unless they are *accosted passant counter-passant* the more distant should be a little in advance of the other.

Azure, a chevron between six rams accosted, counter trippant, 2, 2 and 2 argent, attired or—HARMAN, Suffolk.

Abacot. See *Cap*.

Abbey. See *Monastery*, also *Ruins*.

Abisme en, (fr.); in the middle fesse *point*.

Aboutés, (fr.): with the ends united in the centre, e.g. of four ermines. See *Cross* of four ermines, § 8.

Absconded: entirely hidden by a superimposed ordinary, or charge.

Accidents, (fr. *accidents*): a comprehensive term applying to marks of *difference* and the like.

Accompanied, (fr. *accompagné*), used only by old heralds, is practically the same as 'between;' e.g., a cross accompanied by four crescents, or a chevron accompanied by three roses.

Accorné, (fr.): *horned*, but used only when the horns are of a different tincture.

Accroupi, (fr.): said of a lion or wild beast in a resting posture.

Accrued: full-grown; applied to trees.

Ace: See *Cards*.

Achievements, spelt sometimes *atchievements*, and more frequently *hatchments :* coats of arms in general, and particularly those funeral escutcheons, which being placed upon the fronts of houses or in churches, or elsewhere, set forth the rank and circumstances of the deceased. The arms upon the latter may in all cases be either single or quartered.

When the deceased is the last of his line a *death's head* may be placed over his arms instead of, or besides, the crest.

A. OFFICIAL PERSONAGES. 1, 2. *A king or reigning queen, whether married or not.*— The royal arms complete, upon a ground entirely black.

3. *A queen consort.*—The achievement of a queen consort should be arranged in a manner similar to that of the lady of a peer.

4. *Archbishops and bishops.*—An archbishop or bishop has his paternal arms impaled after the insignia of his see, both being surmounted by a mitre. The ground must be per pale, white on the dexter side, signifying that the see never dies, and black on the sinister, denoting the decease of the bishop. Whether the bishop be married or unmarried will make no difference in the arrangement of his achievement.

The arms of the bishops of Winchester and Oxford (the one, prelate, and the other, chancellor of the order of the garter) should be encircled by the garter, and have their badges pendent. The archbishops of Armagh and Dublin bear the badge of the order of S. Patrick in the same manner. Prelates having temporal jurisdiction, (as the bishops of Durham had,) may bear a crosier and sword saltirewise behind their arms ; the hilt of the sword should be uppermost.

5, 6. *The dean of a cathedral or collegiate church, or the head of a college, whether married or not.*—The insignia of the deanery or college impaled with the paternal coat must be placed upon a ground parted per pale white and black, as in No. 4. A dean or other clerk should by no means bear a helmet, mantle, or crest.

The deans of Windsor, Westminster, and S. Patrick's, Dublin, should bear the badges of their respective orders.

7 *Kings of Arms.*—The achievement of a king of arms should

contain the insignia of his office and his paternal coat impaled together, and surmounted by his helmet, crest, mantling, and crown. Some kings of arms have encircled their shields with the collar of SS belonging to their office. The ground of this achievement must be, like the above, per pale white and black.

B. BACHELORS. All bachelors (official personages already mentioned being excepted), must have their arms complete, that is to say, with all the external ornaments belonging to their condition, upon a black ground, namely, if an esquire, with his wreath, helmet, and crest, and perhaps it may be with a mark of cadency on the arms. The arms being without any impalement, or any escutcheon of pretence, shews that the bearer was an unmarried man.

Achievement in case of a Bachelor.

C. HUSBANDS. 1. *In general.*—All husbands (except those whose wives are peeresses in their own right) should have a shield with the external ornaments proper to their rank, containing their own arms on the dexter side, impaled with their wives' on the sinister side, or if the latter be heiresses theirs must be upon an escutcheon of pretence. In all cases the ground will be per pale black and white, the dexter being black to denote the husband's decease.

Achievement in case of a Husband.

According to some modern heralds it is not proper for a knight to include the arms of his wife within the collar, ribbon, or other insignia of his order. In compliance with this opinion it is customary for the achievement of a knight (whether a peer or not) to be arranged thus :—Two shields are placed side by side, the first, which is encircled by the garter or other distinction

Achievement in case of a Knight.

of the order, contains the husband's arms alone, and the second those of the husband and wife. Both these shields are included within the external ornaments pertaining to the husband's rank. The ground is perpendicularly divided at the middle of the second shield, the dexter side black, the sinister white.

Marriages previous to the last one should not be noticed upon achievements.

2. *A husband of any rank, whose lady is a peeress in her own right.* — Two escutcheons; the dexter containing the arms of the husband with the lady's upon an escutcheon of pretence ensigned with her coronet: the sinister lozenge-shaped, with the lady's alone. Each must be accompanied by all its proper external ornaments. The ground should be perpendicularly divided at the middle of the dexter escutcheon, and painted black and white.

D. WIDOWERS. Their funeral achievements only differ from those of husbands, under similar circumstances, in the ground being totally black.

Women (sovereign princesses excepted) may not bear helmets, crests, or mantlings, but a peeress is entitled to her robe of estate.

E. UNMARRIED LADIES OF ANY RANK. The arms of an unmarried lady must be placed in a lozenge, but no external ornaments of an heraldic nature should be used, unless she were a peeress. In that case her supporters, robe of estate and coronet, should be added: the ground entirely black. Shells, cherubims' heads, and knots or bows of ribbon, are often placed above the arms of women, whether spinsters, wives, or widows.

F. WIVES. 1. *In general.*—Their achievements are arranged precisely as their husbands' would be, except that the helmet, crest, mantle, and motto, are omitted, and the ground painted per pale, white and black, or, to speak more accurately, black under the arms of the wife, and white under those of the husband.

2. *The wife of an archbishop or bishop.*—It is customary to arrange the achievement of the wife of a prelate thus:—Two shields, the first containing the impaled arms of the see and the

bishop, surmounted by a mitre, and the second, the family arms of the bishop with those of his wife, and over them a knot of ribbons or a cherub's head : the ground all white except that part under the arms of the wife (i.e. about one third per pale on the sinister side), which must be black.

G. WIDOWS. The achievements of widows differ from those of wives in two respects ; the escutcheon or escutcheons are lozenge-
shaped (escutcheons of pretence excepted), and the ground is entirely
black. The arms should be encircled
by a silver *Cordon*, which is the special symbol of widowhood.

As the episcopal dignity is one in
which a wife cannot participate, the
achievement of a prelate's widow

Achievement in case of a Widow.

should not differ from that of the widow of a private gentleman. The same may be said of the widow of a knight.

The place for affixing the arms above described is against the residence of the deceased; but some years ago in many churches, but now in very few, helmets and banners of some deceased knight were frequently found remaining hung up in some aisle or chapel, and these also went by the name of *hatchments*. The banners in St. George's, Windsor, afford the most complete example of the survival of an old custom, and here also the achievement is engraved on a plate in the stall held by each successive knight of the Order of the Garter.

In France the *litre*, or *lisiere*, hung around the churches, answers, perhaps, to the *hatchment*.

Acorn, (fr. *gland*, old fr. *cheyne*) : this is usually repre-
sented *vert*, but they may be of other colours. They may also be *slipped* or leaved. An *acorn-sprig* is not unfrequently used in the arms, and is often used also as a *crest*. Sometimes, too, the *acorn-cups* are represented alone.

Sire Rauf de Cheyndut, de azure, a un cheyne de or, e un label de goules—Roll of Arms, temp. EDW. II.

Argent, three martlets azure, on a chief gules an acorn between two mullets or—CAIRNS.

An acorn slipped and leaved—Seal of town of WOKINGHAM.

Argent, three acorns slipped vert—AIKENHEAD and TATTON.

Vert, three acorns or—HARDING and SMITH, Middlesex.

Quarterly, per fess indented first and fourth gules in chief a maunch argent, in base an acorn sprig—AKERMAN, Surrey.

Argent, three cups of acorns, azuré—ATHOL.

Acorns are also borne by the families of ASHTON, Marketfield; ATASTER (or AKASTER); BRETTELL, Worcester; BOYS; CROMIE, Kildare; CUDDERLEY, Derby; DALLING; DUNCAN, Essex; FYFIELD; IFIELD; JOHNSON, Warrington; PALMER, Middlesex; SEVENOKE, and others.

Adders, (old fr. *givre* or *vivre*, from lat. *vipera*) or *asps :* appear not to be distinguishable from *serpents* and snakes, except as regards size. They are represented as *nowed, embowed,* or *erect.* When not otherwise described they would be represented fesswise, but curling. *Vipers' heads* also occur.

Gules, an adder nowed or—NATHERLY.

Sable, three chevrons ermine between as many adders argent—WISE, Warwick. The same between three adders erect or—WISE, Brompton. Also embowed vert—WISE.

Vert, three adders erect argent—HASSELL, Wraysbury.

Azure, on a bend argent, three adders embowed of the first—CASTLETON, Surrey.

Argent, three viper's heads erased proper—HATSELL, 1708.

Vert, three asps in pale or—ASPENDALL.

Addorsed, or *endorsed* (fr. *adossé*) : said of two animals turned back to back. These terms (generally the latter) are also used with reference to axes (*bills*), to keys, when the keybits or wards are turned outwards, and to other similar objects, and more especially to wings and heads of birds, &c.

Argent, two lions rampant addorsed, the 1st azure, 2nd gules—LUCAS.

Sable, two greyhounds endorsed argent—BARNARD, Hants.

Sable, two bills addorsed in saltire argent—BILLINGFORD, Norfolk.

Azure, an eagle's wings endorsed or—EDMUNDS, Lyndhurst.

Gules, two keys addorsed in bend or, interlaced with a sword in bend sinister argent, hilt and pomel of the second—PLIMPTON Monastery.

Acorned, (of an oak)= fructed with acorns (fr. *englanté*).

Adam and Eve. See *Paradise.*

Adextre par, (fr.): having a charge on the right or *dexter* side.

Adder's tongue. See *Fern.*

Adorned, (fr. *adorné*): a chapeau or other article of dress, charged, is sometimes said to be adorned with such a charge.

Adumbration, or *Transparency :* the shadow of a charge, apart from the charge itself, painted the same colour as the field upon which it is placed, but of a darker tint, or, perhaps, in outline only.   The term belongs rather to the romance of heraldry than to its practice, and is imagined by the writers to have been adopted by families who, having lost their possessions, and consequently being unable to maintain their dignity, chose rather to bear their hereditary arms adumbrated than to relinquish them altogether.   When figured by a black line the bearing is said to be *entrailed.*

Affrontant, (fr. *affronté*) : used when two animals face each other, e.g. of *goats,* stags, greyhounds ; but the terms *Confronting* and *Respecting each other,* are more properly employed.

Sable, on a mount vert, two stags salient affrontant argent, attired or—JOHN FISHER, Bp. of Exeter, 1803 ; Bp. of Salisbury, 1807—25.

Gules, two greyhounds salient affrontant or—DOGGETS, Norfolk.

Affronty, (fr. *de front*) : facing the spectator (as the lion in the crest of Scotland), or *in full aspect,* which is the more correct term when applied to a bird.   It is applied to a *helmet, savage's head,* &c.   [See a remarkable example given under *Monastery.*]

Per saltire, or and argent . . . in the chief centre section an open helmet affronty unbarred proper . . .—POWER.

Gules, three savage's heads affronty erased argent—VIGNE.

Azure, a bull's head affronty couped at the neck argent, between two wings or . . . . HOSTE.

Alder : there is one species of alder bearing berries, and to this probably the arms following refer.

Argent, three bunches of alderberries proper—ALDERBERRY.

Adz, or *Addice.*   See *Axe.*

African.   See *Man.*

Agnus Dei.   See *Lamb (Holy).*

Aigrette, (old fr.) : an Egret or tufted *heron.*

Aiguiere, (fr.)   See *Ewer.*

Aiguise, (fr.) or *Equisé :* sharply pointed, e.g. of a *cross* pointed.

Aislé, (fr.) : *winged ;* but used only in respect of animals naturally without wings.

Ajouré, (fr.) : 1. of a chief when the upper part is *crenellé,* and the field shewn through ; 2. of a building with the openings shewing the field at the back.

Alant.   See *Dog.*

A la quise.   See *erased.*

Albanian Bonnet.   See *Cap.*

Alberia : a shield without ornament or armorial bearings, so called from being white.

Allerions, (fr. *alérions*): resembling *eaglets* displayed, but without beak or feet, and the points of the wings downward.

Gules, three allerions displayed or—LIMESEY.

Or, on a bend gules, three allerions argent—Duchy of LORRAINE.

[These arms are supposed to have originated from the circumstance of Godfrey of Boulogne, duke of Lorraine, shooting three allerions with an arrow from a tower at Jerusalem " upon the direction of a prophetick person." A far more probable supposition is, that the arms were intended as a play upon the name of the duchy.]

Alesé, or *Alaisé* (fr.), when an ordinary does not extend to the edge of the shield: but the English term *couped* is more usual, and of a cross *humetty*, § 7.

Alligator, and *Crocodile*. The only case of either of these borne in English arms is,

Gules, a chevron argent between three alligators. . . .—HITCHCOCK.

Per chief gules and or, in base an olive-tree eradicated and fructed proper, in chief the head and fore-legs of a crocodile issuant proper—DALBIAC, Bedford.

Allocamelus, called by Holmes an *Ass-camel*, is a fictitious beast borne as a crest by the EAST LAND COMPANY, and so far as has been observed by this Company alone.

[The Company was incorporated 1579, and Charter confirmed by Charles II.]

Allocamelus.

Almond: parts of the Almond-tree are sometimes found, e.g.

Argent, an almond slip fructed proper—ALMOND.

Sable, an eagle displayed between two bendlets argent; on a chief or three almond leaves vert—JORDAN, Surrey.

Altar: a tall circular pedestal, generally borne *inflamed*.

Sable, on a fesse dancetty of four, between three lions rampant gardant argent, each supporting an altar or, flaming proper, nine billets of the field. —SMIJTH, of Hill Hall, Essex.

Altar.

Alcyon, (fr.): an aquatic bird represented in its nest amidst the waves of the sea—MASSILLON, Ile de France.

Alce. See *Griffin*.

Alembick. See *Limbeck*.

Alerons, *Ailettes* or *Alettes*. See *Emerasses*.

Allumé: applied by French heralds to the eye of a beast or bird when touched with red.

Altar tomb. See *Church*.

Anchor, (fr. *ancre*): this is frequently used as a charge, or *crest*, emblematical of hope, or of naval service. In old examples it is not unfrequently *ringed* at the point as well as at the head The parts are thus named: the shank or *beam* (fr. *stangue*): the *stock, timber,* or cross-piece (fr. *trabe*): the *cable* (fr. *gumène*): and the *fluke* (fr. *patte*). In some coats the anchor has a *chain* attached instead of a cable.

Argent, an anchor sable—SKIPTON.

Gules, an anchor argent, the ring or—ZACHERT.

Gules, an anchor argent, the stock or—GOADEFROY.

Azure, a lion rampant supporting a cabled anchor or; on a chief wavy . . . . —RICHARDSON.

SKIPTON.

Argent, an anchor erect (without a stock) proper, environed on the centre with the letter C or—CLEMENTS INN.

An anchor between two smaller ones, within the beam and fluke—Seal of NAVY OFFICE. [See also MARINERS' Company, Newcastle-on-Tyne, under *Whistle.*]

Angel, (fr. *Ange*): The figure is always represented *in full aspect*, the wings extended with points upwards. Angels' wings also occur; and in the singular arms of the family of RAPHAEL, Surrey, the angel Raphael is named in connection with *Ararat*, q.v. Angels are found as supporters, and a single angel frequently as a *crest*.

Argent, on a chevron sable three angels kneeling, habited in long robes close girt, their hands conjoined elevated upon their breasts, wings displayed or—MAELOR CRWM, Caernarvon.

Azure, a pillar erect between two angel's wings, elevated or—AWBORN.

Alternate, or alternated, is sometimes applied to the tinctures; e.g. of a plume of feathers, where every other one is of a different tincture. In the use of the terms *barry, chequy*, and the like, ' alternately ' is understood.

Ambulant: walking; *passant* generally used.

Amethyst. See *Purpure.*

Amphistere. See *Cockatrice.*

Ampty, or *Anty.* See *Enty.*

Ananas. See *Pine-apple.*

Ancettée. See *Cross* humetty, § 7.

Anché, (fr.): curved; used of a scimetar, &c.

Anchored (fr. *ancré*), or ancred. See under *Cross moline,* § 24.

Ancient, or *anshent*: 1. a kind of *flag;* 2. used in the sense of *Antique.*

Andrew, S., *Cross of,* and *Banner of.* See *Saltire.*

Andrew, S., *Order of.* See *Knighthood.*

Gules, an Angel standing erect with hands conjoined and elevated on the breast, habited in a long robe, girt argent, wings displayed or—BRANGOR (or Berenger) of Cervisia, 1413.

Angles: this bearing seems intended to represent the hook or fastening of a waistband (the arms of Wastley being allusive), and for this purpose the rings are attached; possibly for the same purpose, namely, that it might serve as a dress fastening, rings were attached to the *Cross annuletty.* This charge might be described also as two chevrons interlaced and couped.

Angles.

Argent, three pairs of Angles interlaced fesswise; at each end an annulet azure—WASTLEY.

Annulet, (fr. *Anneau* and *Anelet,* written sometimes in plural *Anelettz* or *Anels:*) a small ring, possibly derived from the links composing chain armour. It is of frequent occurrence as a charge, and generally more than one appear: the two annulets are often linked in fess, or *embraced;* or they may be *conjunct.* Three may in like manner be *interlaced* in triangle. When three rings are interlaced the expression *gimbal rings* is sometimes used, and when more, they form a *chain,* q.v.

The single annulet is likewise the *difference,* or mark of *cadency,* assigned to the fifth son.

Azure, three annulets argent, (of another branch or)—ANLETT.

Sir Nicholas de VEPOUND de or a vj aneus de gules—Roll, temp. ED. II.

Sire Johan de CROMWELLE de goules a vj aneus de or—Ibid.

Monsire de BARTON de Fryton port d'ermin, sur fes gules trois anneletts d'or—Roll, temp. ED. III.

Argent, two annulets linked together gules, between three crosses formy sable — THORNHAGH, Nottingham.

ANLETT.

Angemnes, (lat. *ingemmæ*): a series of round ornaments. See *Sexfoils.*

Anille. See *Fer de Moline.*

Animé, (fr.). See *Incensed.*

Annodated : bowed embowed, or bent in the form of the letter S.

Argent, two annulets conjunct sable, within an orle of trefoils slipped vert—John Eton.

Ermine, three annulets interlaced in triangle gules—Mandere.

conjunct.

Gules, six annulets embraced or, two, two and two—Bracer.

Gules, six annulets interlaced palewise in pairs, and a chief or—Clench.

embraced.

Argent, nine annulets in saltire interlaced [chain], five gules and four azure—Hatchet.

Ermine, three annulets, one within another, gules—Fytton.

(See also under roundles 'faux rondelets'.)

interlaced.
Annulets.

Annuletty, *Annulated,* or *Ringed :* crosses and saltires are occasionally *couped* and ringed at the ends. See *angles* and *Cross annuletty,* the couping being implied.

Ant, (fr. *fourmi*). Of the insecta of the animal kingdom there are but few representatives. The *ants,* and with them the *emmets,* may be mentioned: the former are generally represented on their *ant-hill* (fr. *fourmiliére*).

Vert, an ant argent—Kendiffe.

Sable, on a chevron between three ant-hills or, each charged with four ants proper, as many holly leaves azure—Benedictine Abbey of Pershore.

Argent, a bend azure between three emmets sable—Massy.

Antelope : it is now customary with herald-painters to draw animals as they appear naturally, which is, generally speaking, directly contrary to the practice of ancient artists, who drew them conventionally. Hence arises the distinction between the *heraldic antelope* and the *natural.* The form of the antelope, as drawn by the old heralds, has a mane and long tail, and differs considerably from the fawn-like appearance of the animal in nature. Antelopes' heads

Harris.

are also frequently named, and both the animal and the head appear among the *crests.* The antelope gorged with a crown occurs amongst the badges of Henry V., and with an ordinary collar with chain attached amongst those of Henry VI.

Argent, an heraldic antelope gules, tusked, horned, maned and hoofed or—ANTILUPE.

Sable, an antelope salient argent, attired, unguled, tufted, and maned or—HARRIS, Monm. and Devon.

Argent, on a bend gules, three antelopes passant of the first, attired or —HALLIWELL, Taunmster.

Azure, a fess nebuly ermine between three antelope's heads erased argent—SNOW, London.

Sable, three antelope's heads couped argent armed or—BRUSARD.

With the heraldic Antelope must be grouped the *Ibex,* which resembles it, although belonging to the goat-tribe.

Argent, a fess engrailed between three ibexes passant sable—SEDBOROUGH, York.

Lozengy argent and vert, on a bend azure an annulet in chief of two heraldic ibex's heads or—Sir John YOUNG, Lord Mayor of London, 1466.

Antique, (fr.): a word not infrequent in the blazoning of coats of arms, signifying that the charge, &c., is to be drawn after the antique or ancient manner; e.g. an antique *crown, boot, bow, escutcheon, ship, temple, plough, hulk,* &c. The *antique crown,* for instance, is encircled by a series of plain triangular rays.

Argent, a lion rampant gules, crowned with an antique crown or—ROCHE, Ireland.

Azure, an antique bow in fess, and arrow in pale argent.—MULLER.

Or, on a lion rampant sable, an antique escutcheon or, charged with a cross patty gules—POWNALL.

Anvil : this charge appears to be borne but rarely, and annexed is the form it takes.

Per chevron argent and sable, three anvils counterchanged—SMITH of Abingdon, Berks.

Azure, an anvil or—ARNULF.

Gules, a smith's anvil argent—ANVAILE or ANVIL.

Anvil.

Apaumy, or *Appalmed,* (fr. *appaumé*) : said of a *hand* open, shewing the palm. The term is, however, scarcely necessary, as every hand not blazoned as aversant, or *dorsed,* is supposed to be appalmed.

Vert, an arrow fesswise in chief and a dexter hand apaumy couped in base argent—LOUGHMAN, Ireland.

Ape : this is the only representative of the Quadrumana used as a charge ; a monkey occurs sometimes as a crest.

Sable, a chevron or between three apes argent, chained of the second —LOBLEY.

Vert, an ape sejant holding up the paw braced round the middle, and chained to the sinister side of the escutcheon argent—APPLEGH.

Apollo : a figure of Apollo, as the inventor of Physic, occurs in the insignia of one Company.

Azure, Apollo proper with the head radiant, holding in the left hand a bow, and in the right hand an arrow or, supplanting [or bestriding] a serpent argent—APOTHECARIES' Company [inc. 1617].

Apple, (fr. *pomme*) : the apple-tree is rarely borne ; the fruit is more frequently so.

Argent, an apple tree vert fructed proper—ESTWIRE.

Gules, a bird argent standing upon an apple or—CONHAM, Wilts.

Argent, a fesse sable, between three apples gules stalked vert—APPELTON.

Argent, on a bend sable, three apples slipped or—APULBY.

Azure, a bar argent ; in base three apples erect proper—HARLETON.

Azure, a bar argent ; in base three apples transposed or—HARLEWYN.

Apre : a fictitious animal, resembling a bull with the tail of a bear.

Apre.

The sinister supporter of the arms of the Company of MUSCOVY Merchants.

Ararat : this mount is mentioned in a very curious manner, namely, in the arms of the family of RAPHAEL.

Quarterly azure and argent a cross moline or, in the first quarter the sun in splendour ; in the second the ark on the summit of Mount Ararat, and a city at the base, with this inscription in the Armenian language, NAKSIVAN ; in the third quarter the angel Raphael and Tobias standing on a mount, thereon a fish proper ; in the fourth an anchor with the cable entwined in bend or—RAPHAEL, Ditton Lodge, Surrey.

Apple of Granada. See *Pomegranate*.

Appointé, (fr.) : of two charges whose points meet, e.g. cf. chevrons, swords, arrows, &c.

Aquilon, (fr.) : the north wind is represented by an infant's features with the cheeks puffed out (perhaps used only in French coats of arms).

Arbalette, (fr.) · a steel cross-*bow*.

Arch : this may be single or double, i.e. springing from two or three *pillars*, which may be of a different tincture from the ꞇꞷꞷᵗ, ꬰꞩ ꬰꞁꞩꞷ may the imposts, or caps, and bases. See also *Bridge*.

Gules, three arches, two single in chief, and one double in base argent, the imposts or—ARCHES.

Gules, three arches conjoined in fess argent; caps and bases or—ARCHES [Harl. MS. 613].

ARCHES.

Archer: this figure is used as a charge only on one coat of arms, but it occurs at times as a supporter.

Gules, three archers azure—ABRENCIS or AVERING, Kent.

Argent, (fr.): the tincture *Silver*. By those who emblazon according to the Planetary system it is represented by the *Moon*, just as the tincture of gold is represented by the Sun. Hence it is sometimes fancifully called *Luna* in the arms of princes, as also *Pearl* in those of peers. As silver soon becomes tarnished, it is generally represented in painting by white. In engraving it is known by the natural colour of the paper; and in *tricking* by the letter *a*. In the doubling of mantles it may be called *white*, because (as the old heralds say) it is not in that case to be taken for a metal, but the skin of a little beast called a Litvite. Sometimes, too, in old rolls of arms the term *blanc* is used.

Argent, simple—BOGUET, Normandy.

Blank ung rey de soleil de goules—RAUF DE LA HAY, Roll, temp. 1240.

Argent.

Arm, (fr. *bras*, but usually *dextrochere* or *senestrochere*, q.v.) : the human arm is often found as part of a crest, although it is not very frequent as a charge. It should be carefully described as being *dexter* or *sinister ; erect, embowed*, or

---

Arched, or *Archy :* said of an ordinary which is *embowed*.

Ardent, (fr.): inflamed and burning.

Ark: see *Noah's Ark*.

Armes parlantes : canting-arms.

Armoiries, (fr.) : Coats of *Arms; Achievements*.

Armoyé, (fr.) : charged with a shield of arms.

Arms accollés. See *Marshalling*.

Arms composed. See *Marshalling*.

counter-embowed ; vested, vambraced, armed, or *naked,* as the case may be: sometimes it is *cuffed.* If *couped,* care should be taken to describe where. When couped at the elbow, it is called a *cubit-arm.* When armed the metal-plates for the elbow are termed *brassarts.*

Gules, three dexter arms conjoined at the shoulders, and flexed in triangle [like the legs in the ensign of the Isle of Man], vested or, with fists clenched, proper—TREMAYNE, Cornwall.

Sable, three dexter arms conjoined at the shoulders, and flexed in triangle, vested or, cuffed argent, the fists clenched, proper—ARMSTRONG.

Gules, three dexter arms braced [i.e. vambraced] argent, hands proper—ARMSTRONG, Ballycumber.

TREMAYNE.

Gules, a naked arm embowed, issuing from the sinister holding a battle-axe erect proper—HINGENSON, Bucks.

Gules, an arm in armour proper, holding a Danish battle-axe argent —HINGSTON, Holbeton, Devon.

Gules, issuing from the sinister side a cubit dexter arm unvested, fesswise grasping a sword proper—CORNOCK, co. Wexford.

The arm is also borne by the families of ARMORBERY—DE LA FOY—PUREFOY—BORLASE—ARMORER—RONNCEVALE—HANCOKE—CHAMBERLAYNE, and many others.

An *Arm,* when used as a *Crest,* more frequently holds a dagger, arrow, &c.; also two arms sometimes occur.

Armed, (fr. *armé*): when any beast of prey has teeth and claws, or any beast of chase (except stags, &c.) horns and hoofs, or any bird of prey beak and talons, of a tincture different from its body, it is said to be armed of such a tincture, though, as regards hoofs, *hoofed,* or *unguled* (fr. *onglé*), is the more accurate term. The lion is usually *langued* of the same tincture. The application to beasts and birds of prey is because their talons are to them weapons of defence.

Argent, three bars azure, over all an eagle with two heads gules, armed or—SPEKE, Cornwall.

Armes pour enquerir, (fr.): Applied to Arms where there is irregularity, e.g. metal on metal, as in the Arms of Jerusalem, or colour on colour. See *Cross Potent,* § 31.

When the term is applied to arrows it refers to their iron points : and when a Man is said to be *armed at all points* it signifies that he is entirely covered with armour except his face.

Armour: the grants of coats of arms having been of old frequently for services rendered in the battle-field it is but natural that portions of the armour should at times form devices emblazoned on the shields, and be used for *Crests*. The *Helmet*, for instance, besides being an appendage to the shield, became a charge, and was represented differently, besides which there were several varieties of metal head-coverings, such as the *Cap of Steel*, the *Bassinet*, the *Burgonet*, and the *Morion*, all different from the esquire's helmet, which was that usually represented. The *hauberk* and the *habergeon*, as well as the *cuirass*, or breastplate, are found as bearings. So also armour and *brassarts* for the *arm*, *gauntlets* for the hand, and *greaves* for the leg occur. We find a "*Man in Armour*," or, as he may be termed, a *Chevalier*, and this last is often employed as a ' *supporter*.' To describe all the various portions of armour, and their several names at different periods, would be beyond the limits of this work, though in its origin Heraldry, as the " Science of Armoury," is intimately associated with the subject.

Vert, a horse thereon a man in complete armour, in the dexter hand a sword proper—MAGUIRE.

Sable, a chevalier in full armour with halbert proper—ARGANOR.

Sable, a demi-chevalier in plate armour, couped at the thighs proper, holding in his dexter hand a battle-axe—HALFHEAD.

A man on horseback in full speed, armed cap-a-pie, and bearing on his left arm his shield charged with the arms of France and England quarterly; on his helmet a cap of maintenance; thereon a lion statant guardant ducally crowned; his dexter arm extended and holding a sword erect, the pomel whereof is fastened to a chain which passes from the gorget; the horse fully caparisoned—Seal of the Town of WALLINGFORD.

A man in armour also borne by families of MONCURRE, ANSTROTHER, ARMSDRESSER, O'LOGHLEN, GRIMSDITCH, NEVOY, &c.

Arms in heraldry signify the *Armorial bearings* (fr. *Armoiries*), and strictly speaking the term is applied only to those borne upon the *shield*. Crests, badges, and the like are not

Armined, i.q. *Ermined*.

properly so described. The origin, or even date, of the earliest
examples of armorial bearings has occasioned much dispute,
so that the subject requires a treatise to itself.

The various modes of acquiring, and reasons for bearing arms
are differently described by different writers, but the following
varieties will be found to represent the more usual classification.

Arms of Dominion are those borne by sovereign princes;
being those of the states over which they reign: while *Arms
of Pretension* are those borne by sovereigns who have no actual
authority over the states to which such arms belong, but who
quarter them to express their prescriptive right thereunto.

Arms of Succession, otherwise called *feudal arms*, are those
borne by the possessors of certain lordships or estates: while
Arms of Family are hereditary, being borne (with proper differences) by all the descendants of the first bearer.

Arms of Assumption are such as might rightfully be taken,
according to certain laws, from the original bearer otherwise
than by grant or descent: and *Arms of Alliance* are those
of a wife, which a man impales with his own, or those which
he quarters, being the arms of heiresses who have married into
his family. *Arms of Adoption* are those borne by a stranger,
when the last of a family grants him the right to bear his
name and arms, as well as to possess his estates: and *Arms
of Concession* are granted when an important service has been
rendered to the Sovereign. The grant almost always consists
of an *Augmentation*, q.v. *Arms of Patronage:* those of the
lesser nobility or gentry derived from the arms of the greater.

Arms of Office, such as those borne by *Bishops, Deans, Kings
of Arms*, &c.; and lastly,

Arms of Community, those borne by cities, towns, abbeys,
universities, colleges, guilds, mercantile companies, &c. The
arms of abbeys and colleges are generally those of their founders,
to which the abbeys usually added some charge of an ecclesiastical character, as a crosier, mitre, or key. Such arms, as
well as those borne by Sovereigns, are more properly termed
Insignia.

The Royal Arms. Arms have been assigned in subsequent times to all the early kings of England from Alfred the Great onwards, but the earliest English sovereign for whose insignia wo have any contemporary authority is Richard Cœur-de-Lion. From that time onwards the series is complete; and in most cases the great seal of each successive reign affords a good illustration. The following notes will be found to represent a brief summary of the more important changes.

Though we have no *authority* for the arms of WILLIAM I., WILLIAM RUFUS, or HENRY I., writers agree in ascribing to them the following.

Gules, two lions [or leopards] passant gardant in pale or.

Some ingenious writer, knowing that the *Sagittarius* was ascribed as the badge of King STEPHEN, substituted it for the lions in the Royal arms, but following

WILLIAM I , &c. STEPHEN.

late examples, placed three instead of two upon the shield.

According to a theory of comparatively late date, HENRY II., upon his marriage with Eleanor, daughter and heiress of the

Duke of Aquitaine and Guyenne, added another lion, and hence the *Insignia* of *England* (q.v.)

Gules, three lions passant gardant in pale [called the lions of England] or.

These arms appear very distinctly upon the great seal of his successor, RICHARD I., but there is a second

HENRY II.   RICHARD I. (?)

great seal of this king (perhaps even earlier), in which a portion of the shield is shewn, and (possibly by carelessness of the die-cutter) this contains a *lion counter-rampant.*

The great seals of JOHN, HENRY III., and EDWARD I. exhibit the arms of England very clearly. The seal of EDWARD II. is without a coat of arms, but there is abundance of other evidence for ascribing the same to him.

Le Roy de ENGLETERRE, porte de goules a iij lupars passauns de or— Roll, temp. ED. II.

EDWARD III., for some years after his accession, bore the same arms, but after 1340 he bore—

Quarterly 1 and 4 ; azure semy of fleurs-de-lis or [for France] 2 and 3, arms of ENGLAND.

On the seal is represented, for the first time, a distinct *crest* (a lion passant on a chapeau).

There are several authorities for the same arms being borne by RICHARD II. ; but towards the end of his reign he impaled the

EDWARD III.

imaginary arms of EDWARD THE CONFESSOR, his patron Saint.

Azure, a cross patonce between five martlets or.

HENRY IV. bears on his great seal the same arms, and apparently a similar crest. The *badges* of HENRY V. are sometimes given as the *supporters* of the arms of HENRY IV., but on no good authority.

HENRY V. bears the same arms, but CHARLES VI. of France having reduced the number of *fleurs-de-lys* in the arms of that kingdom to three, the arms of HENRY V. were then altered, and appear so in the great seal.

HENRY VI. the same ; and the arms appear with two antelopes argent, attired, unguled, and spotted or, gorged with crowns as *supporters*, and the *motto, Dieu et mon droit.*

EDWARD IV., EDWARD V., and RICHARD III., the same arms, with *supporters* ' a lion rampant argent, and a bull sable armed and unguled or ;' and in one case ' two white boars armed, unguled, and bristled or.'

HENRY VII. and HENRY VIII., EDWARD VI., MARY and ELIZABETH the same arms, excepting that after Mary's marriage with King Philip, she bore the arms of the two sovereigns impaled, viz. with that of PHILIP on the dexter.

Throughout the *supporters* appear varied. A dragon gules and a greyhound argent appear with the arms of HENRY VII. A dragon and greyhound, also a lion and greyhound, with those of HENRY VIII. A lion and dragon with those of EDWARD VI. A lion and greyhound with those of MARY, and a lion and dragon with those of ELIZABETH. But the authorities, chiefly in sculpture and painting, are not much to be depended on.

JAMES I. On his great seal we find the following:—

Quarterly, I. and IV. counter quartered: 1 and 4 FRANCE; 2 and 3 ENGLAND. II. Or, a lion rampant within a double tressure flory counter flory gules—SCOTLAND. III. Azure, a harp or stringed argent—IRELAND.

These arms were continued to be used by CHARLES I., CHARLES II., and JAMES II., and are usually represented in carving, painting, &c., with the same *supporters,*

JAMES I.

namely, the lion and the unicorn. It may be noted, however, that CROMWELL, as Protector, bore:—

Quarterly 1 and 4; argent a cross gules [i.e. of St. George, for ENGLAND]. 2, Azure, a saltire argent [i.e. of St. Andrew, for Scotland]. 3, Azure, a harp or, stringed argent [for IRELAND], and on an escutcheon surtout sable a lion rampant gardant argent [for CROMWELL].

WILLIAM and MARY bore the same arms, but the former with an escutcheon *surtout* bearing the arms of NASSAU (Azure, semé of billets and a lion rampant or).

Queen ANNE bore the arms of JAMES II., but on the union with Scotland in 1707 the Royal Arms were marshalled:—

Quarterly 1 and 4, ENGLAND impaled with SCOTLAND; 2 FRANCE; 3 IRELAND.

GEORGE I. and GEORGE II. the same, except that in the fourth quartering the arms of HANOVER were substituted for ENGLAND.

GEORGE III. After the Treaty of Amiens in 1801 the Arms of France were abandoned and the Royal Arms were:—

Quarterly 1 and 4 ENGLAND; 2 SCOTLAND; 3 IRELAND; an escutcheon with the arms of HANOVER surtout ensigned with the electoral bonnet [afterwards with a crown].

GEORGE IV. and WILLIAM IV. the same. VICTORIA as follows:—

Quarterly 1 and 4 ENGLAND; 2 SCOTLAND; 3 IRELAND.

From JAMES I. onwards the Lion and Unicorn remained the *supporters,* generally with the same motto, *Dieu et mon droit.*

Arraché, (fr.), or *arrasht:* (1) of trees, pulled up by the roots = *eradicated;* (2) of heads of animals, &c., torn off=*erased.*

Arrière, (fr.): *Volant en arrière* of a bird or insect flying with the back to the spectator.

Arrondi, (fr.): rounded off.

Arrow, (fr. *fléche*): the ordinary position of an arrow is in pale, with the point downward, that is, falling (fr. *tombante*), but to prevent the possibility of a mistake, it would be better always to mention it, because in French coats they are more frequently the other way. When represented as rising, it should be stated "with point upwards," &c. Arrows appear blazoned as *barbed* (fr. *ferré*) or *armed* (fr. *armé*) of the tincture of their points, and *flighted* or *feathered* (fr. *empenné*) of that of their feathers; also *notched* (or *nooked*) (fr. *encoché*) of the

STANDARD.

tincture of the end which rests on the bowstring. The tincture given is that of the shaft, but with French heralds it is sometimes named as shafted (fr. *futé*) of such a tincture.

Vert, an arrow in pale, point downwards, or, barbed and feathered argent—STANDARD, Oxfordsh. [A particular arrow was called a standard, and hence this is a *canting* coat.]

Gules, two arrows in saltire argent, over all a fess chequy of the second and first—MACAULAY.

Argent, two arrows in saltire, points upward azure between four 5-foils of the last—JAMESON.

Per pale embattled gules and azure an arrow in bend or, barbed and feathered argent, point upward—CUGLER, Hertfordshire.

Gules, three arrows double pointed or—HALES.

When arrows are in *bundles* such bundles are called *sheaves of arrows* (the number and position being in some cases mentioned).

Gules, three bundles of as many arrows argent—BYEST, Salop.

Gules, three sheaves of arrows points upwards argent—JOSKYN.

Gules, three bundles of as many arrows, two in saltire and one in pale or, feathered headed, and tied in the middle with a string argent—BESTE.

A *bird-bolt* again differs, not being barbed as an ordinary arrow: it may be described as a blunt-headed arrow used to shoot birds, and shot from a cross-bow. An old French word, '*boson*,' also occurs, which appears to mean the same.

Argent, three cross-bows bent, each loaded with a three-headed bird-bolt sable; a chief vert—SEARCHFIELD, Bp. of Bristol, 1619.

Argent, three bird-bolts gules, headed and feathered or—BUSSHAM, Lincolnshire.

Argent, three bird-bolts in fess gules—BOLTON.

Argent, three bird-bolts in pile gules—BOUZUN.

Argent, three bird-bolts gules, headed or, and feathered of the first—BOWMAN, Norfolk.

Or, three bird-bolts gules, nooked and pointed of the first; a label gules—BEARUM.

Sire Peres BOSOUN de argent a iij bosons de gules —Roll, temp. Hen. III.

Bird-bolts.

A broad arrow differs somewhat, perhaps, from the above in the head, and resembles a *pheon* (q.v.), except in the omission of the jagged edge on the inside of the barbs. By the term *broad arrow*, the head alone is meant. The *bolt* and the *quarrel* were shorter arrows, used with the *cross-bow*.

Argent, three broad arrows azure—HALES, Stafford.

Gules, a broad arrow between two wings argent—ZINGELL.

Argent, three bolts in pale gules—BOLTSHAM, Devon.

Gules, three quarrels argent—BAGGSHAM.

Arrows are also borne by the families of ARCHARD, HYAM, ZINGEL, TINGEWICK, FLOYER, FORSTER, and many others.

Broad arrow.

Ash : this tree occurs in more than one coat, rather, perhaps, in consequence of the frequency of the syllable ash in proper names. It probably refers to the common ash (i.e. *fraxinus*), unless otherwise expressed. But examples occur of *mountain ash*, properly called the *rowan*-tree (and in one case *rodey*).

Argent, an ash-tree proper issuing from the bung of a tun—ASHTON, Cornwall.

Argent, an ash-tree vert—ESTWREY. [By one branch of the family a chevron vert between three bunches of ashen keys proper.]

Argent, on a chevron gules between three branches of rowan [or rodey] tree proper, as many crescents or. [Also by another blazoning between three trees proper, fructed of the second]—RODEY, Liverpool.

Argent, on a chevron azure, between three branches of mountain-ash vert, as many crescents of the first—ROWNTREE.

The seed-vessels of the common ash-tree are called *Ashen keys.*

Argent, three ashen keys vert between two couple-closes sable—ASHFORD, Devon.

Argent, a chevron between three branches of ashen keys vert—ASHFORD, Cornwall.

Ashen keys.

Arrow-head. See also *Pheon.*

Ascents, or *Degrees* : steps.

Ascendant: said of rays, flames, or smoke issuing upwards.

Aspect: a term expressive of the position of an animal, as *in full aspect* means full-faced, or *affronty* (fr. *de front*). *In trian aspect* means between *passant* and *affronty*.

Or, an eagle in full aspect gules, standing on a perch issuing out of the sinister side argent—Body.

Gules, on a mount vert a stork in trian aspect to the sinister argent—Arnalt.

Ass, (fr. *âne*): this animal in theoretical heraldry is emblematical of patience, but appears mainly to be used in arms as punning upon the name. The *Mule* is sometimes named, (but erroneously in arms of Moyle. See under *Bull*).

Sable, an ass argent—Assil.

Argent, a fesse between three asses passant sable—Askewe.

Sable, a fesse between three asses passant argent—Ayscough, Bp. of Salisbury, 1438—50.

Argent, an ass's head erased sable—Holknell.

Gules, an ass (or mule) passant within a border argent—Moyle, Kent.

Sable, a fesse ermine between three mules passant argent—Stompe, Berks.

Astrolabe: the old astronomical instrument described by Ptolemy, used for taking altitudes.

Az, an astrolabe or—Astroll.

Per fess or and gules, an astrolabe proper held in the dexter paw of a lion rampant counterchanged armed and langued az.—Middleton, Frazerburgh.

Attire, (fr. *ramure*): may be used for a single horn of a stag. Both the horns are commonly called *a stag's attires* (sometimes written *tires*), and are generally borne *affixed to the scalp* (fr. *massacré*). The word *attired* (fr. *chevillé* and *ramé*) is used when stags and some other beasts, e.g. goats, are spoken of, because it

---

Ash. See *Colour.*

Asker. See *Effet.*

Asp. See *Adder.*

Aspectant: used improperly for *respectant.*

Aspen leaf. See *Poplar.*

Aspersed: the same as (fr.) *semé, strewed,* or *powdered.*

Assaultant, or *Assailant*: i.q. *Salient.*

Assis, (fr.) sitting; of domestic animals: of wild animals *sejant.*

Assumption. See *Arms of.*

Assurgent: rising out of.

Astroid: another name for an ordinary *mullet.*

Astronomical signs. See *Letters.*

Asure, and *Assure:* written sometimes for *Azure.*

At bay. See *Deer.*

At gaze: a term applicable to beasts of the stag kind, as *statant gardant* is to beasts of prey.

is supposed that their horns are given them as ornaments, and not as weapons. The main stem of the antler is termed the *beam*.

Sable, a chevron or, between three stag's attires fixed to the scalps argent—COCKS (Viscount Eastnor and Earl Somers).

Sable, a stag lodged regardant, and between the attires a bird or—NORTOST, Norfolk.

Argent, a chevron between three stag's attires fixed to the scalps azure—COCKS.

Argent, a hart statant azure, attired or—HARTINGTON.

COCKS.

Auger, or *wimble :* a tool for boring.

Gules, three augers argent, handles or—BUNGALL.

Ermine, a pile gules, charged with a lion passant gardant in chief or, and a wimble in base proper ; a fesse chequy azure and of the third ; thereon two escalops sable—WIMBLE, Lewes.

Augmentations: additional charges to the family arms granted to persons by their sovereign as a special mark of honour. Such marks frequently consist of portions of the royal arms, as lions, or roses, that flower being one of the royal badges.

Richard II. is the first English sovereign who is recorded to have granted augmentations of arms to his subjects. Having added the legendary arms of S. Edward the Confessor (i.e. azure, a cross patonce between five martlets or) to his own, he granted the same in 1394 to Thomas Mowbray, Duke of Norfolk, to be impaled by him in the same manner. One of the charges brought against this nobleman's descendant, Henry Howard, Earl of Surrey, in the reign of Henry VIII., was the bearing of this augmentation, which, it was alleged, implied a claim to the crown. King Richard also gave the same arms, with a bordure ermine, to Thomas Holland, Duke of Surrey, and Earl of Kent.

The augmentation of arms granted by K. Henry VIII. to Thomas Howard, Duke of Norfolk, for his victory over the Scots at Bramston, or Flodden-Field, where James IV., king of Scotland, fell (Sep. 9, 1513), is an escutcheon or, charged with a demi lion rampant, pierced through the mouth with an arrow, within a double tressure flory counter-flory gules. It will be observed that this augmentation bears a considerable resemblance to the arms of the vanquished king.

K. Henry granted an augmentation to the family of SEYMOUR, upon his marriage with his third queen, Jane, in 1536. It is ' or, upon a pile gules, between six fleurs-de-lis azure, three lions passant gardant in pale or,' and is generally borne quarterly with their paternal coat, in the first and fourth quarters.

Another of Henry's grants was to Richard Gresham, mayor and alderman of London, whose arms were argent, a chevron ermine between three mullets sable pierced of the first. To these were added, on a chief gules a pelican close between two lion's gambs, erased or, armed argent.

Sir Stephen Fox, who faithfully served K. Charles II. during his exile in France, was very appropriately rewarded with a canton azure, charged with a fleur-de-lis or, being a portion of the insignia of that kingdom.

Anciently the chief, the quarter, the canton, the gyron, the pile, flasques, and the inescutcheon, were chosen to receive the augmentations of honour. In modern times the chief and canton have been generally used.

Many of the augmentations granted for naval and military services about the commencement of the present century are so absurdly confused, that all the terms of heraldry cannot intelligibly describe them. Indeed they sometimes rather resemble sea views and landscapes than armorial bearings.

Foreign sovereigns have occasionally granted augmentations to British subjects.

In 1627 Gustavus Adolphus, King of Sweden, knighted Sir Henry Saint George (who was sent to him with the Garter), and gave him the arms of SWEDEN (azure, three crowns or) to be borne in an inescutcheon; and the king of Prussia, and the Prince of Orange, conferred certain augmentations of arms upon the Earl of Malmesbury, which K. George III. gave him permission to assume in 1789.

From the nature of the usual method of exhibiting the augmentation on the coat of arms, the original charge is frequently *debruised* (as it is also by the marks of *cadency*); hence with the French heralds both are included under the term *brisures*. The example of the arms of the family of PAYLER, possibly arising from an augmentation, exhibits this in a remarkable manner, as the central lion is nearly *absconded*. But the debruising must not be supposed in any way to be a mark of *abatement*, as it is quite the reverse.

PAYLER.

Gules, three lions passant gardant in pale argent, over all a bend or charged with three mullets—PAYLER.

Auk, (lat. *alca*) : this bird occurs in the following arms, and as in another blazoning of the same arms the term *murr* occurs instead of *auk*, we may presume that it is synonymous. The name *Razor-bill* (*alca torda*) also occurs on one coat of arms.

Or, a chevron sable between three auks (or murra) proper—CARTHEU, Cornwall.

Or, the head of an auk proper—AUKES.

Argent, three razor-bill's heads, couped sable—BRUNSTAUGH.

Awl : the ordinary brad-awl used by carpenters, and with this may be named the *gimlet*.

Azure, a chevron between three awls, points reversed argent, hafts or—AULES.

Argent, a chevron gules between three [nine] gimlets sable—CLAPHAM.

Common hatchet.

Axe, (fr. *hache*) : there are various kinds of axes and hatchets. It is impossible to classify them, or give the whole of the varieties ; but the following will be found the chief forms which appear. The handle of the axe is sometimes called the *stave*, or an axe may be *hafted* (fr. *manché*), and the *blade* is often referred to.

1. The common *axe* or *hatchet*, is usually represented as shewn in the margin.

In the arms of the TURNERS' Company it is represented somewhat differently.

Gules, three axes argent—AXALL.

Azure, three axes argent, handles or—AXTELL, Devon.

Turner's axe.

2. *Adz* or *Addice :* this has the blade set transversely to the flattened handle, and is sometimes called the *carpenter's axe.*

Argent, three addices azure, handles or—ADDICE.

Azure, three carpenter's axes argent—WRIGHT, Scotland.

Gules, a chevron between three carpenter's axes or, hafted argent—PENFOLD.

Aulned, *Awned,* or *Bearded :* words used when ears of corn are spoken of. See *Wheat.*

Auré, (fr.). See *Gutté d'or.*

Auriflamme. See *Banner.*

Avellane. See *Cross*, § 12.

Averdant: covered with green herbage : applied chiefly to a mount.

Averlye, (old fr.), i.q. *Semé.*

Aversant, or *Dorsed :* of a hand of which the back only is seen.

Avocetta. See *Snipe.*

3. Brick, or *Bricklayer's-axe :* a charge in the armorial insignia of the Company of BRICKLAYERS and TILERS, of London. The metal portion only of the axe is exhibited, and this is made broad with the sides hollowed, as shewn in the margin.

Azure, a chevron or; in chief a fleur-de-lys argent enters [i.e. between] two brick axes palewise of the second; in base a bundle of laths of the last—BRICKLAYERS' Company, incorp. 1508.

Bricklayer's axe.

4. Chipping-axe : this occurs in the arms of the London Company of MARBLERS (afterwards united to the MASONS), and is the axe which is still used by quarrymen in chipping the stones before they leave the quarry.

Gules, a chevron argent between in chief two chipping-axes of the last and in base a mallet or—Company of MARBLERS.

Chipping-axe.

5. The *Slaughter-axe.* The axe used by butchers for killing animals. Such an axe occurs in the arms of the BUTCHERS' Company.

Azure, two slaughter-axes addorsed in saltire argent, handled or between three bull's heads couped as the second armed of the third, viz. two in fess and one in base, on a chief silver a boar's head couped gules, between two block brushes (i.e. bunches of knee holly or butcher's broom) vert—COMPANY OF BUTCHERS, London and Exeter.

Slaughter-axe.

6. The *Pick-axe* seems to be the miner's pick-axe, also called the *hew ;* somewhat similar to it is the double *Coal-pick,* and the tool called a *Paviour's pick.*

Sable, three pick-axes argent—PIGOTT, Cambridge.

Argent, three hews or miner's pick-axes sable—William CHARE, in Trinity College Chapel, Cambridge.

Pick-axe.

Azure, three pick-axes or—PACKWOOD, Warwick.

Argent, three pick-axes gules—PICKWORTH.

Argent, on a cross engrailed sable a compass dial in the centre between four pheons or; a chief gules charged with a level staff enclosed by two double coal-picks or—FLETCHER, co. Derby, granted 1731.

See also *Mill-pick.*

Paviour's Pick.

7. *Battle-axe* (fr. *hache d'armes*), is variously represented. The common form is given in the margin, and it is found very frequently employed as a *crest*.

Azure, a battle-axe or, headed argent, the edge to the sinister—~~Iloxxaxwxxn~~.

Argent, a battle-axe, head downwards, held by a lion rampant guardant proper, within a border azure—CRACKNELL, Devon.

Azure, three battle-axes or, staves argent—BAIN-BRIDGE.

Azure, a battle-axe in pale or, headed argent—OLDMIXON, Somerset.

Battle-axe.

8. The *Broad-axe* seems to be so called only from the breadth of the blade differing in no other respect from other axes.

Sable, three broad axes argent—Sir John PORTER.

Gules, three broad axes argent, a demi fleur-de-lis joined to each handle with inside or, between as many pierced mullets of the last—Thomas TREGOLD.

Broad-axe.

9. The *Danish axe* was probably so called because it occurred in the royal arms of that kingdom, in which it is drawn like a Lochabar axe, but some apply the name to an axe whose blade is notched at the back. There is a form without the notch borne by HAKELUT, and called a *Danish hatchet*. The Indian *tomahawk* occurs in the arms of HOPKINS, granted 1764.

Sire Walter HAKELUT, de goules, a iij haches daneys de or, e une daunce de argent—Roll, temp. EDW. II.

Danish axe.

Sable, three Danish axes argent—DAYNES, Devon.

Gules, five Danish axes palewise in saltire argent—ROGER MACHADO, [Clarenceux King of Arms, temp. Henry VIII.]

Gules, a Danish battle-axe argent, held by an arm in armour proper—HINGSTON, Devon.

10. The *Lochabar axe* has a curved handle and a very broad blade, and represents perhaps a Scotch axe.

Gules, a Lochabar axe between three boar's heads erased argent—RANKEN, Scotland.

Argent, two Lochabar axes in saltire heads upward, between a cock in chief and a rose in base—MATHESON, Benetsfield.

Lochabar axe

11. *Pole-axe*, or *Halbert*, (fr. *haillebarde*) : the axe with a long pole, often called the *halbert* or *halberd*. It was used by the men at arms in processions and on great occasions for keeping back the crowd.

Argent, two halberts in saltire azure—Eccles, Scotland.

Gules, two pole-axes in saltire or, headed argent, between four mullets of the last—Pitman, Suffolk.

Gules, three pole-axes or—Sir Walter Hakelett, temp. Edward I.

Azure, a halbert or, the edge to the sinister, its lance-head argent—Heyngeston.

Ermine, two halberts in saltire sable—Magdeston, Lincoln.

Pole-axe.

Azure, bright blue, i.e. the colour of an eastern sky, probably derives the name from the Arabic *lazura* (conf. *lapis lazuli*, Gr. λαζωριον, Span. *azul*, Italian, *azurro*, Fr. *azur*), the name being introduced from the East at the time of the Crusades. It is sometimes called *Inde* from the sapphire, which is found in the East: (see example under *cadency*.) Heralds who blazon by planets call it *Jupiter*, perhaps from his supposed rule over the skies; and when the names of jewels are employed it is called *Sapphire*. Engravers represent it by an indefinite number of horizontal lines.

Azure.

Backgammon Table : this singular device is borne by the following family.

Azure, three pair of backgammon tables open of the first, pointed argent, edged or—John Pegrez.

Badge, or *Cognizance :* a mark of distinction somewhat similar to a crest, though not placed on a wreath, nor worn upon the helmet. They were rather supplemental bearings quite independent of the charge of the original arms, and were borne on the banners, ensigns, caparisons, and even on the breasts, and more frequently on the sleeves of servants and followers.

Aylet. See *Cormorant.*
Ayrant. See *Eyrant.*

Az : in *tricking* may be used for *azure*, but *bl.* is more usual.

The badges borne by the Kings of England are very numerous, and are to be found on tombs, carvings, embroidery, stained glass, and paintings. The earliest which can be any way reckoned as a badge, is the *Planta genista*, or *Broom;* and of the others, of which a list is given, it must be admitted that several rest upon solitary instances, or on the authority of the writers whose names are appended.

STEPHEN. A *Sagittary ?*
Ostrich *feathers* (Guillim).
HEN. II. *Escarbuncle* (Mackenzie).
Sword and olive-branch (Cotton).
RIC. I. *Star* within crescent (Great Seal).
Star and crescent separate (Great Seal).
Armed *arm* holding lance (Cotton).
Sun on two anchors (Guillim).
JOHN. *Star* within crescent (Silver penny).
HEN. III. *Star* within crescent (Great Seal).
ED. I. *Rose*, stalked (MS. Harl.)
ED. II. Hexagonal *castle* (Great Seal).
ED. III. *Rays* from clouds (Camden).
Stump of *tree* (MS. Harl.)
Ostrich *feathers* (MS. Harl.)
Falcon.
Griffin (Private Seal).
Sword and three crowns (MS. Harl.)
RIC. II. *Sun* in splendour (MS. Harl.)
Sun behind cloud (effigy).
A branch of *broom* (?) (effigy).
White *hart* couchant.
Stump of tree.
White falcon (Hollingshed).

LANCASTER.
Red *rose*.
Red *rose en soleil*.
Collar of SS.
HEN. IV. A *genet* (on his tomb).
Eagle displayed (ibid.)
Tail of a *fox* pendent (Camden).
Crescents (Hollingshed).
Panthers and *eagles* crowned (MS. Harl.)
HEN. V. A *beacon* inflamed.
Antelope gorged with a crown.
Swan gorged with a crown.

HEN. VI. *Antelope* collared and chained.
Two *feathers* in saltire (MS. Bib. Reg.)
Spotted *panther* passant guard. (MS. Harl.)

YORK.
A white *rose*.
White *rose en soleil* (MS. Bib. Reg.).
ED. IV. *Falcon* within *fetterlock* (ironwork).
Bull sable [for Clare].
Dragon sable [for Ulster].
Sun in splendour (Baker).
White *hart*.
White *wolf* (MS. Lansd.)
ED. V. *Falcon* within *fetterlock* (painting).
RIC. III. Rose and sun separate (Great Seal).
Falcon with maiden's head (Sculpture).

TUDOR.
Red and white *roses* united.
Roses separate and crowned.
Portcullis.
Fleur de lis.
HEN. VII. A red *dragon* (Baker).
Hawthorn bush crowned (glass).
Dun *cow* (Baker).
Greyhound courant (for Beaufort).
HEN. VIII. *Greyhound* courant.
ED. VI. *Sun* in splendour (Cotton).
MARY. Double *rose* impaled with a sheaf of arrows within a semicircle (MS. in Coll. of Arms).
Rose and pomegranate.
ELIZABETH. Harp crowned [for Ireland].
A *Rose*.

STUART.
Roses united [for England].
Fleur de lis [for France].
Thistle, leaved [for Scotland].
Harp [for Ireland].

The above representative badges for the four kingdoms were continued by the House of BRUNSWICK and in George the Third's reign (i.e. 1801) they were settled by sign manual, the old badge for ENGLAND, namely, the *Cross of S. George*, being retained in the national banner of the *Union Jack* (q.v. under *Flag*).

A white rose within a red one, barbed, seeded, slipped and leaved proper, and ensigned with the imperial crown, for ENGLAND.

A thistle, slipped and leaved proper, and ensigned with the imperial crown, for SCOTLAND.

A harp or, stringed argent, and a trefoil vert [i.e. shamrock] both ensigned as before, for IRELAND.

Upon a mount vert, a dragon passant, wings expanded and endorsed, gules, for WALES.

Certain OFFICERS also wore badges; thus: Crown-keepers, or yoemen of the crown, bore on their left shoulders a crown, which, under the Tudor sovereigns, surmounted a rose. Four examples have been noticed on brasses: one of them is in the possession of the Society of Antiquaries, from which this illustration is taken.

Crown Keeper's Badge.

From about the time of Richard II. badges have been occasionally borne by SUBJECTS. This practice is alluded to by Shakspere, who mentions both the cognizance and the crest.

Old Clifford.—Might I but know thee by thy *household badge.*
    Warwick.—Now by my father's *badge*, old Nevil's *crest*,
        The rampant bear chained to the ragged staff, etc.

The PERCIES have a *crescent* for their badge, and the VERES used a *mullet*.

Badges are frequently represented on brasses, and often beneath the feet. Occasionally a badge was engraved on the dress; thus a *swan* (or as some say a pelican) is embroidered on the collar of Lady Peryent, 1415, as represented on the brass in Digswell church, Herts.

Brass of LADY PERYENT.

The *Hame* of Saint-John will be found in its alphabetical order, and the cognizances of several other families under *Knots*.

Another class of distinguishing *marks* may also be included under the head of *badges*, though not heraldic badges, namely, those connected with TRADE. The theory of the grant of armorial bearings was such that engagement in commerce was incompatible with the bearing of arms, which was permitted only to gentlemen; and this was strictly the case throughout the middle ages. Still the merchants had their badges; the Guilds and Companies, of which the great London Companies are the survivors, had their distinctive marks or *devices*, and no doubt it is these which in later years, when the dignity of successful commerce came to be recognized, were incorporated into the arms of their companies. Similar also were the *Merchants' Marks*, and these will be noted in their place. Lastly, there were the signs, i.q. *ensigns*, of the chief houses of trade, by which the house was known, e.g., at the "Bible and Crown in Fleet-street." With scarcely an exception (and those mostly cases of revival) these signs have been only retained by inns and hostelries.

Badger, (fr. *blaireau*): in blazon this is often called a *Brock*, and occasionally a *Gray*.

Or, a badger passant sable—BADGER.

Or, on a fesse sable between three brocks passant proper two cinquefoils pierced argent, on each foil an ermine spot — James BROKS, Bp. of Gloucester, 1554-8.

Argent, three brocks proper—BROCK.

Argent, a chevron between three badger's legs erased sable—YARMOUTH.

Bagpipes are only named in connection with the *hare* playing on them.

Argent, three hares sejant playing upon bagpipes gules—HOPWELL, Devon.

Argent, three hares sejant gules, playing upon bagpipes or—FITZ-ERCALD, Derby.

[The illustration of a hare playing upon the bagpipes is from MS. Harl. 6563, written in the fourteenth century.]

Hare playing on bagpipes.

Bacchus faces. See *Faces*.

Badelaire, (fr.): a broad-bladed sword, or *scimetar*, slightly curved. The *sabre* comes nearest to it.

Bagwyn : an imaginary beast like the heraldic antelope, but having the tail of a horse, and long horns curved over the ears, was the dexter supporter of the arms of CAREY, Lord Hunsdon.

Balances, a pair of, (fr. *balance*) : besides appearing in the arms of the Company of BAKERS both of London, Newcastle-on-Tyne, and Exeter (in which they are sometimes blazoned as a pair of *scales*), the following may be noted.

Azure, a pair of balances within an orle of eight estoiles or—STARR.

Azure, a pair of balances supported by a sword in pale argent, hilt of pomel or, within a balance of the last—JUSTICE, Scotland.

Bale, or *bag :* a package of merchandise corded : one containing silk occurs in the arms of the Company of SILKMEN, while a *bag of madder* occurs in that of the DYERS. Madder was a plant much used in dyeing, and is named but in this one instance. It is to be noted especially that the *cords* are of a different tincture from the rest. The *bale*, or *bag*, is to be distinguished from the *bundle*, or *hank* (e.g. of *cotton*, silk, &c.)

Bale corded.

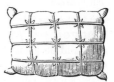

Bag of madder.

Argent, a ship of three masts in full sail on the sea in base, all proper ; on a chief or, a bale of silk corded proper, between two bundles of silk pendant of the last—Company of SILKMEN, London [Inc. and arms granted, 1631].

Sable, a chevron engrailed argent, between three bags of madder of the last, corded or—Company of DYERS [Inc. 1471].

Balm : this plant, the common balm (*melissa*) of our fields, seems to be used only in a canting coat.

Argent, three sprigs of balm flowered proper—BALM.

Bague, (fr.) : a *gem*, or finger-*ring*.

Baillonné, (fr. *baillon :* a gag). Of animals when they have a *baton* in their mouth.

Balcanifer, or *Baldakinifer :* the standard-bearer of the Knights Templars.

Baldcoot. See *Coot*.

Baldrick. See *Belt* and *Bend*.

Balista. See *Sling*.

Ball. See *Fire-ball*.

Bandé, (fr.) : for *bendy*.

Bande, (fr.) : for a bend dexter.

Banded, (*empoigné*) : is used when two or more objects (e.g. a garb or branches of a tree) are bound together with a band of a different tincture.

Banner, (old fr. *ban*, also *baniere*) : a kind of *flag* painted
or embroidered with arms, and of a size pro-
portioned to the rank of the bearer. The banner of an emperor is prescribed to be six feet
square, that of a king five feet, that of a prince
or duke four feet, and that of a nobleman of
any rank from marquess to baron three feet,
that of a Knight banneret was still smaller.
Whether these rules were at any time strictly
observed is very doubtful. Banners were often

Banner.

(but not, it would seem, until a rather late period) fringed with
the principal metal and colour of the arms.

The chief distinction between the term *banner* and other flags
such as *standards*, *pennons*, &c., is that it is square (or nearly so),
while the others are, as a rule, elongated. See under *Flag*.

The *Funeral banner*, or *Banneroll*, was a square flag whereon
the arms of the deceased, and those of his ancestors, were
painted, with crest or coronet, but without helmet, mantle,
or supporters. The colour of the banner itself follows the same
rules as that of the grounds of *achievements*. It was usually
fringed with the principal metal and colour of the arms. The
great banner, used at funerals, contained all the quarterings of
the deceased, occupying the entire field, the edge being fringed.
Funeral banners are not restricted to Knights banneret and
persons of higher rank, but may be carried at the interment
of gentlemen bearing arms, and even at funerals of women.

The *Beauseant*, or *Ancient*, was the name of the banner of
the Knights Templars in the thirteenth century, though it might
be described as an oblong *flag*, per fess, sable and argent, one
of the longer sides being affixed to the staff.

Le baucent del HOSPITALE, de goules a un croyz d'argent fourme.—
Le baucent [another MS. Le Auncient] del TEMPLE, dargent, al chef
de sable a un croyz de goules passant—Roll, temp. HEN. III.

The *Military Banners* most frequently borne in the English
army during the middle ages (besides those of Knights bannerets and other noblemen) were those embroidered with the

---

Banderolle, (fr.). See *Flag*.   Banneroll (?). See *Banner*.

arms of the sovereign, or with the legendary arms of SS. George, Edmund, and Edward the Confessor, patrons of England. The military banner might contain quarterings, but not impaled arms.

A red banner, charged with the symbol of the Holy Trinity, was borne at the battle of Agincourt, A.D. 1415.

The banner of S. John of Beverley was borne in the English army 24 Edw. I. (1295) by one of the vicars of Beverley college.

S. Cuthbert's banner was carried in the English army by a monk of Durham in the wars with Scotland, about 1300 ; and again in 1513.

The *Oriflamme* was the *military banner* of the French army, being derived from a banner anciently belonging to the Abbey of S. Denis, near Paris. It was charged with a *saltire* wavy, with rays issuing from the centre crossways, and from these rays the name *auriflamme* was no doubt derived.

The oriflamme borne at Agincourt was (according to Sir N. H. Nicolas) an oblong red flag, split into five points.

The *banner* was used also as a charge, occurring generally hung from the walls of a castle, and the *Paschal Lamb* is usually represented carrying a banner.

Gules, on a banner or, an imperial eagle charged with an escutcheon argent, the staff held by a griffin segreant of the last—GARBETT.

Quarterly, first and fourth gules, a banner displayed argent ; thereon a canton azure charged with a S. Andrew's cross of the second ; second and third or, a cross moline azure within a bordure engrailed argent— BANNERMANN, Elsick.

Azure, three banners bendwise in pale flowing to the sinister or—KINGDOM.

Argent, on a cross gules a Paschal Lamb or, carrying a banner argent charged with a cross of the second—Hon. Society of the MIDDLE TEMPLE.

Bar, (fr. *fasce en divise;* lat. *fasciola*): resembles the *fess* in form, but occupies about one-fifth of the field. Although practically a diminutive of the fess, it is not reckoned as such, but a distinct ordinary. It is seldom (and in such few cases there is a chief) borne singly, and consequently is not confined, like the fess, to the middle of the shield. It has two diminutives, the *closet,* which is half the bar, and the *barrulet* (fr. *burèle*), which is a quarter. As the bar occupies one-fifth of the field a greater number than four cannot be borne together. When three or four bars are borne in the same arms, they are, for the sake of

proportion, drawn considerably narrower than one-fifth of the
height of the shield.

William Maudyt,—d'argent a deus barres de
goulz—Roll, temp. Henry III.

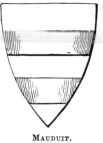

MAUDUIT.

Richard de Hammestede, d'or a deux barres de
goules—*Ibid.*

Sire Andreu le Grimstede, de goules a iij
barres de veer—Roll, temp. Ed. II.

Sire Wary Martin, de argent a ij barres de
goules besantes de or—*Ibid.*

Monsire Hugh Seinttle, port d'asur a deux
barres d'argent; au chief de gules—Roll, temp.
Ed. III.

In ham, or *harwise,* signifies the horizontal arrangement of
charges in two or more rows; the term *in fesse* being proper
only when there is but one row, i.e. placed across the fess-point.

Bar-gemel, or *gemelle :* bars-gemels are bars voided, or *closets*
placed in couples (they derive their name from the Latin *ge-
mellus,* double, or fr. *jumelles*), and with the old writers the word
gemelle was used for *bar*-gemel. But two bars-gemels are not
always distinguishable from four bars, nor three bars-gemels
from six barrulets, nor four bars-gemels from eight. For the
odd number the term *barrulet* must be used. Palliot fancifully
describes bars generally as *immolés,* and the expression ' *bar and
a-half*' is found in one roll of arms.

Tremon de Menyll,—d'azur a trois gemelles, et ung cheif d'or—Roll,
temp. Hen. III.

Roand le Connestable de Richemund, de goules a ung cheif d'or, a deus
gemeus de l'un en l'autre d'or—*Ibid.*

Sire Wauter de Hontercombe, de ermyne, a ij
barres gymeles de goules—Roll, temp. Edw. II.

Azure, a bar and a-half argent, in the sinister
quarter a garb or—Scheffeld (Glovers ordinary).

ERCALL.

And sometimes it appears that each bar
of a bar-gemel was counted as a *gemelle.*

Argent, three bars-gemels sable—Ercall.

Sr Thom's de Richmond port de gules le chef
d'or ov quatre gemeus d'or—Harl. MS. 6589.

Argent, three bars-gemels gules—Barry, Earl of Barrymore, Ireland.
Gules, three bars-gemels and a canton ermine—Bardwell.

Bars like the fesse may be *embattled, dancetty, nebuly, wavy,* &c., and a shield may be divided *per bar* and per *base bar,* q.v.

Ermine, three bars wavy gules—LACY.

[In Roll, temp. Edw. II. Sir Johan de LACY, oundee de gules et de ermine].

Argent, two bars embattled ermine—BURNBY, co. Devon.

Argent, two bars counter embattled gules—JAMES, co. Essex.

Gules, two bars dancetty or—SAMLER.

Argent, two bars nebuly sable, a bend or—POWER, co. Surrey, 1601.

Azure, two bars wavy or—Sir Walter de la POOLE.

LACY.

N.B. In French heraldic works the word *barre* is used as equivalent to a *bend sinister,* and this is supposed in many cases to be a mark of bastardy. Hence the expression is often found of a *bar sinister,* meaning a *bend sinister.* The modern French equivalent for the bar, *fasce en divise,* means that it is a fesse of half its ordinary width. See also under *Barbel.*

Barry, (in old fr. *barré,* sometimes *burelé,* in modern fr. *fascé*): denotes that the field is horizontally divided into a certain even number of equal parts. If the number of divisions were odd the same tincture would appear in chief and in base, and the pieces of the other tincture would be so many *bars,* or *barrulets.*

Richard de GREY, barry d'argent et d'azure—Roll, temp. HEN. III.

Alayn de Fitz Brian, barree d'or et de gules—*Ibid.*

Patrick de CHAURCY, burele d'argent et de goules—Roll, temp. HEN. III.

Barry of six, ermine and gules—HUSSEY, Wilts.

Barry of ten, argent and gules—BARRY, Lord Barry.

Barry of ten, argent and sable—BARRALL.

Barry of twelve, or and sable—BOTFIELD, Salop.

DE GREY.

Barry of twenty, argent and azure—BRUN.

Per pale or and argent barruly wavy gules—Sire Richard de AUNTES-HEYE.

Barry dancetty azure and argent—TURBERVILLE.

The division of the shield into party-coloured pieces by means of lines is not unfrequent, and the *barry* is combined for the sake of variety with other line-divisions. The following will give some idea of the varieties.

Barry bendy or *Barry bendy lozengy* may be employed when a field is divided bar-wise, each piece being subdivided bendwise also, the tinctures being counterchanged. *Barry bendy sinister* also occurs.

Barry bendy of six argent and gules—AMERY.

Barry bendy lozengy argent and gules—QUARM, DUTON.

Bendy sinister and barry, gules and argent—WYER.

Barry-bendy. Barry-bendy sinister.

Barry indented and *Barry dancetty* have the lines drawn so that apex falls beneath apex.

Barry of four indented or sable or azure—Richard MITFORD, Bp. of Chichester, 1389, of Salisbury, 1396—1347.

Barry indented, argent and gules—John BALUN.

Barry dancetty of six azure and argent—TODENHAM.

Barry indented, the one in the other, may be blazoned *Lozengy . . . . couped per fesse,* or better still *Lozengy . . . . parted barwise and counterchanged.*

Barry indented.

Barry of six argent and sable, indented, the one in the other—GUISE, or GYSE, Glouc.

Barry indented, the one in the other, or and azure, on a chief gules, three cross crosslets of the first--MOUNTAINE, Westminster, 1613.

Barry nebuly, when the lines instead of being drawn straight across the shield are drawn as in the margin; and *barry wavy,* with the bars as shewn in previous page.

Barry nebuly.

Barry nebuly of six argent and azure, on a bend gules a lion passant gardant or—HABERDASHERS' Company. Arms granted in 1571.

Barry nebuly of six, or and gules—DOLSEBY, London.
Barry nebuly of six, or and sable—BLOUNT, Bart. 1642.
Barry wavy of six, ermines and argent—MORRIS.

Barry pily: divided into an even number of pieces by piles placed horizontally across the shield. If the number of pieces were uneven, it would rather be called so many piles barwise, proceeding from the dexter or sinister side. It is difficult to find examples, as the proper position of the ordinary is upright.

Barry pily of eight, or and gules—HOYLAND, Linc.

Barry pily.

Barry pily of eight, gules and or—VANCE, Ireland.

Barry per pale counterchanged is when the field is divided into several pieces barwise, and by a party-line palewise the tinctures on each side of that line are counterchanged. For *barry paly* see *billetty*.

Barry of six, sable and or, per pale counterchanged—SCURFIELD.

Barry of twelve, per pale azure and argent counterchanged—MOORE, Salop.

N.B. In modern French heraldic works *barré* seems to be used generally as the equivalent of *bendy sinister*, just as the bar is used for the bend sinister, as has already been noted.

Barberry: one example only appears of this shrub (*berberis*), with its bright red berries, in allusion evidently to the name.

Argent, a barberry branch fructed proper—BERRY.

Barbed, (fr. *barbé*); bearded: an expression chiefly applied to the metal point of an *arrow*, sometimes also to the green leaves of a *rose*, when any of these are of a different tincture. By the French also to the gills of *cocks*, &c. A cross when 'barbed' is called a *Cross barby*.

Gules, three arrows argent, barbed or—Nicholas HALES.

Argent, on two bars gules, three roses of the field, barbed vert, seeded or, two and one—ORLEBAR, Bedford.

De gueules, a trois coqs d'argent, becqués, crêtes, barbés, et membrés d'or—SANDELIN, Artois.

Barbel, (fr. *barbeau*, lat. *cyprinus*): the fresh-water fish, so named from the barbs attached to the mouth ; and with this may be classed the *Tench* (*tinca vulgaris*) as similar in character.

Sr John de BARE porte d'azure ov ij barbes d'or croisele d'or, ov la bordure endente de gules—Falkirk, roll, Harl. MSS.

Azure, semé of cross crosslets fitchy at foot or, and two barbels embowed and endorsed of the same, eyes argent—Arms of the duchy of BARRE, which are quartered by QUEENS' COLLEGE, Cambridge.

Argent, two barbels haurient, respecting each other sable—COLSTON.

Borne also by families of BARWAIS, BARDIN, BARE, BERNARD, BURES, &c.

Azure, a fesse or, between three tenches argent—WAYTE, Norfolk.

Borne by families of VON TANQUES and of Marshall TENCHE, Flanders.

The *bar* in French heraldry sometimes means the barbel, but generally the sea fish so named (lat. *sciæna*).

Le Counte de BAR, d'azur, pudre a croisile dor a deux bars de mer—Roll, temp. HEN. III.

Gueules, a un bar contourné d'argent, la tête surmountée d'une fleur-de-lis d'or—Ville dê BARFLEUR, Normandy.

Barnacle, or *Barnacle goose*, (old name *Bernak*): it is known now as the Cleg or Clark goose, perhaps the same as the Solan or Orkney goose; *Anser bernicla* is recognized by all naturalists.

Sire William BERNAK de argent a une fesse e iij bernaks de sable—Roll, temp. EDW. II.

Sable, a barnacle goose argent; Azure, three barnacles argent—BARNACLE.

Gules, a barnacle goose argent—BARNER.

Argent (?), a chevron ermines between three barnacle birds close proper —WYKE.

Barnacle or *Horse-barnacle :* generally spoken of as a *Pair of barnacles*, and in a roll of Henry III. called *Breys*, is supposed to represent an instrument used by farriers (fr. *morailles*) to curb unruly horses. It is occasionally borne extended, that is, horizontally.

With the French heralds this charge has caused much discussion. Three *broyes* are borne by the family of BROYES (as well as by that of JOINVILLE and GOY), and have been supposed

Barbican. See *Castle.*

Barby, (fr. *barbée*). See *Cross*, § 13.

Barded, (fr. *bardé*): of a horse *caparisoned.* The *barde* was ori-ginally the armour-plating covering the chest of a horse in battle, but came in time to signify ornamental covering of any kind.

to be respectively architectural festoons, instruments for torture of criminals, hemp crushers, as well as the meaning given above.

WYATT.

Gules, a barnacle argent—WYATT, Kent.

Argent, three pair of barnacles, expanded in pale sable—BRAY, Cornwall.

Argent, four bars wavy azure on a chief gules, three pair of barnacles or—SMITH, Suffolk.

The most celebrated instance of the barnacle expanded is the coat of the illustrious French family of Joinville, or as the English called it, Geneville.

Geoffrey de GENEVILE d'azure, a trois *breys* d'or au cheif d'ermyne ung demy lion de goules—Roll temp. HEN. III.

Simon de GENEVILL a trois breys d'or, au chief d'argent ung demi-lion de goules—Ibid.

JOINVILLE.

Baron: the fifth and lowest rank of the British peerage. The title, introduced into England immediately after the Norman conquest, was originally applied to all the Thanes (or feudal lords under the rank of earl) who held great fiefs of several Knights' fees, but was subsequently restricted to those summoned by writ to parliament, a practice which dates from the reign of John. The first baron by patent was John Beauchamp of Holt, who was raised to the peerage by K. Richard II. in the eleventh year of his reign (Oct. 10, 1387) by the title of baron of Kidderminster. No other instance occurs until 10 Hen. VI.

Barons are not recognised as part of the English nobility quâ Baron, i.e. Lord of the manor, unless they are duly summoned to be a Peer of Parliament; and before the reign of Charles II. barons, even though peers of the realm, were not allowed to wear *coronets* q.v., but only the crimson cap, with a plain gold band.

Baron and Femme are words employed in describing impalements of the arms of husband and wife; that on the *dexter* being the paternal achievement of the man, that on the *sinister* the family arms of the woman. See *Marshalling*.

Baronets may be distinguished as follows.

I. *Baronets of Great Britain:* An order founded by King James I., May 22, 1611, ranking below that of a peer and above that of a knight. The dignity is bestowed by patent and is hereditary, but generally limited to the heirs male of the grantee. It was in the first instance bestowed upon knights and esquires (being duly qualified), each of whom stipulated to maintain thirty foot soldiers in Ireland at 8d. per diem for the term of two years. Upon the establishment of the order it was arranged that the number of baronets should never exceed two hundred, and that upon the extinction of a baronetcy no other should be created to fill the vacancy; but these regulations were soon dispensed with, and the number became unlimited.

The qualifications required of those who were admitted into the number of baronets are thus described in the instructions of the royal founder to the commissioners, for the admission of proper persons into the order:—

"Provided always that you proceed with none, except it shall appear unto you upon good proof that they are men for quality, state of living, and good reputation, worthy of the same: and that they are at least descended of a grandfather by the father's side that bore arms: and have also a certain yearly revenue in lands of inheritance of possession, one thousand pounds per annum de claro, or lands of the old rent, as good (in account) as one thousand pounds per annum of improved rents, or at the least two parts in three to be divided of lands to the said values in possession, and the other third part in reversion, expectant upon one only life, holding by dower or in joynture."

The first baronet created was Sir Nicholas Bacon.

The precedence assigned to baronets is before all knights bannerets, except those made by the king himself, or the prince of Wales under the royal banner in actual war, and next after the younger sons of viscounts and barons.

The badge of baronetage, namely a sinister *hand* (*q. v.*) erect, open, and couped at the wrist gules (being the arms assigned to the ancient Kings of Ulster), was granted in 1612. It may be borne upon a canton, or upon an inescutcheon, which may be placed either upon the middle chief point or the fesse point, so as least to interfere with the charges composing the family arms. It should never be placed upon the intersection of two or more coats quartered, unless the baronet has two surnames, and bears the arms belonging to them quarterly.

In the same year in which this badge was granted, King James knighted the heirs of all existing baronets, and ordained that their eldest sons might for the future claim knighthood upon attaining their majority. This privilege was abolished by George IV., but has since been restored, though never claimed.

II. *Baronets of Ireland :* An order established by James I. in 1619. Their qualifications, privileges, and badge, are the same as those of the baronets of Great Britain. It is believed that this dignity has not been conferred since the union of 1801.

III. *Baronets of Scotland and Nova Scotia.* An order similar to those before mentioned, projected by the same monarch, but founded by Charles I. in 1625, immediately after his accession. The object of this order was to encourage the plantation of Nova Scotia, in which colony each baronet had granted to him by his patent eighteen square miles of land, having a sea-coast, or at least the bank of some navigable river, three miles in length, and an extent of six miles inland.

The arms of baronets of this order are not now distinguished by any badge, although one appears to have been in use until the year 1629, viz. a small shield argent charged with a saltire azure, in the centre of which upon an escutcheon or is the lion of Scotland within a tressure gules. No creations have taken place since 1707.

Barrow : borne on the seal of DROITWICH (see *Sword*) : also, Sable, a hand-barrow between nine roses or—BEARWELL.

Barrulet, *Barrelet,* or *Bracelet,* and *Barruly.* The *Barrulet* is a diminutive of the Bar, of which it is one-fourth, that is to say, a twentieth part of the field; the *closet* being one half of the bar. It is never borne singly.

Bark. See *Boat.*
Barley. See *Wheat.*
Barre (fr.) = a *bend sinister* [not
    bar].

Barrel, (fr. *Barillet*). See *Tun.*
Barry. See under *Bar.*
Bartizan. See *Castle.*
Basilisk. See *Cockatrice.*

Argent, four barrulets gules; on a canton of the second a mullet of six points of the first—WACE.

Azure, six barrulets gemel [=12 barrulets] and a chief or—MENELL, York.

Argent, seven barrulets gemel azure [=14 barru-lets] ᵀᴴᴱᴼᴮᴬᴸᴰ ????

Sable, eight barrulets gemel [=16 barrulets] and a canton or on two bars azure, as many barrulets dancetty argent. A chief indented of the second —SAWBRID, [Indented argent—BUCKTIN, York.]

WACE.

Beyond this the term *barruly* [or *barruletty*, fr. *burellé*, old fr. *burlé*] is used by some writers in describing a field horizontally divided into ten or any higher even number of equal parts; practically, however, the term *barry* might be used in most cases.

Patrik de CHAURCY, burele d'argent et de goules—Roll, temp. HEN. III.

Le Counte DE LA MARCHE, burule de une menue burlure dargent et de azur—Another Roll, temp. HEN. III.

Sire Robert de ESTOTEVILE, burlee de argent e de goules a un lion rampand de sable—Roll, temp. ED. II.

Base: 1. (fr. *bas de l'ecu*.) The lower part of the shield, hence *in base* means that the charge is so to be placed. 2. *Base-bar*, or *Baste:* a portion of the base of a shield, equal in width to a bar, parted off by a horizontal line. It is identical with the *plain point*, q. v. under *Point*. 3. For *base* in architecture see *Pillar*.

Argent, a lion rampant and a base indented purpure—John de SKIPTON, Harl. MSS. 1386.

Basket, (fr. *corbeille*): there are several varieties of baskets found figured in coats of arms.

1. Ordinary or *hand-baskets*, sometimes termed *wicker* baskets.

Azure, three baskets or—GARDEN.

Sable, three baskets [like fig. 1] argent—LITTLEBURY.

1. Basket.   2. Wicker Basket.

Sable, three wicker baskets [otherwise dossers] with handles argent—Sir John LITTLEBORNE.

Sable, a bend or, between three hand baskets argent—WOOLSTON, co. Devon, 1716.

Gules, three covered baskets or—PENTNEY Priory, Norfolk.

2. In one or two cases Religious houses seem to have borne a kind of *bread* basket filled with loaves or *wastel cakes*.

Sable, three baskets full of bread argent—MIDDLETON Abbey, Dorset.

Azure, three baskets or.—GARDEN.

Argent, two bars sable . . . . . a basket of bread (i.e. wastel-cakes) or on the sinister side—London, BETHLEHEM Hospital.

Azure, a basket of fruit proper between three mitres or—JANE, Bp. of Norwich, 1499—1501.

Bread-basket.

3. *Winnowing-baskets.* These have various names, that of *Vane* or *Vannet* being the commonest. But the same kind of basket, which has, when badly drawn, been mistaken for an *escallop-shell*, is also termed *Fan, Fruttle,* and *Shruttle.*

Sire Robert de SEVENS de azure, a iij vans de or—Roll, temp. ED. II.

[N.B. The brass of Sir H. de Septvans in Chartham Church, Kent (ob. A.D. 1306), has the three vanes only, and not seven, as might have been expected from the name.]

Winnowing-basket.

The four implements, viz. *prime, iron, cutting-knife,* and *outsticker,* used in basket-making are represented on the insignia of the Basket-makers' Company :—

Azure, three cross-baskets in pale argent between a prime and an iron on the dexter, and a cutting knife and an outsticker on the sinister of the second—BASKET-MAKERS' Company.

4. *Fish-baskets.* See *Weel.*

Bat : This mammal, not infrequent in English arms, is usually represented displayed ; its *proper* tincture is sable. Blazoned sometimes by the older name of *rere-mouse.*

"Some war with rere-mice for their leathern wings"—SHAKESPERE, Mids. Night's Dream.

Bats' wings are also borne.

Argent, a bat displayed proper—STAININGS.

Or, a bat volant gules ; a rere-mouse vert—ATTON.

Or, a bat's wing gules, surmounted of another azure—ALDEN.

STAININGS.

Basnet, *Bassinet.* See *Cap* of *Steel.*

Bataillé, (fr.) : of a bell when the clapper (*batail*, old fr. for battant) is of a different tincture.

Bath, Order of the. See *Knights.*

Baton-cross. See *Cross,* §§ 8, 31.

Battelly, (fr. *bastille*) or *battled.* See *embattled.*

Battle-axe. See *Axe.*

Battled. See *Embattled.*

Baton, (fr. *bâton*), (though the old fr. *Baston, Battoon,* or *Batune,* is used almost entirely for the *bendlet*). It resembles the diminutive of the *Bend sinister* (and hence often called a *sinister baton*) in general form, but usually *couped* at both extremities. The *sinister baton* was in later times made to be a mark of the illegitimacy of the first bearer, and to be of metal when assigned to the illegitimate descendants

Baton.

of royalty, but in every other case to be of colour, even though placed upon another colour. Accordingly, the following arms were assigned by modern heralds:—

Gules, two lions passant guardant [HENRY I.] with a batoon sinister azure—REGINALD, base son of Henry I., created Earl of Cornwall.

It was said that the baton should not be laid aside until three generations had borne it, and not then, unless succeeded by some other mark assigned by the king of arms, or unless the coat was changed. *Dexter batons* are but rarely met with. Sometimes a small *baton* ap-

REGINALD, Earl of Cornwall.

pears in the mouths (fr. *baillonné*) or between the paws of animals, such as lions, dogs, bears, &c., but this almost entirely in crests.

Quarterly vert and or a couped baston of the second—DE HISPANIA.

Gules, on a bend engrailed or, a baston azure—ELLIOT (1666).

Gules, a chevron raguly of two bastons couped at the top argent—Christopher DRAIESFIELD, Harl. MS. 1386.

Argent, a lion rampant azure, a dexter baton compony or and gules—Sir Richard de DOCKESSEYE.

Argent, a lion rampant gules, over all a dexter baston compony or and azure—Piers LUCIEN.

Argent, a lion rampant sable holding a baton in pale azure—WILLISBY.

In the sense of an ordinary *bendlet*, (q.v.)

Monsire JEFFREY DE CORNEWALE, d'argent, une lyon de gules couronne d'or: une baston de sable charge de trois mullets d'or—Roll, temp. ED. III.

Baudrick, (fr. *Baudrier*): a sword *belt*, possibly the prototype of the *Bend*.

Bay, *At Bay*. See *Deer*.

Bay. See *Colour*.

Bay leaf. See *Laurel*.

Battering-ram, (fr. *bélier*): this military charge seems to occur only in the arms of one single family, but occurs also as a *crest.*

Battering-ram.

Argent, three battering-rams barwise proper, headed azure, armed and garnished or—BERTIE.

Beacon, (A.-Sax. *becn*, fr. *phare*): an iron cage or trivet, containing blazing material, placed upon a lofty pole served to guide travellers; or to alarm the neighbourhood in case of an invasion or rebellion. The *cressets,* or lights anciently used in the streets of London were similar in form.

Beacon.

A beacon or, inflamed proper—Badge of HENRY V.

Sable, three beacons with ladders or, fired proper—DAUNT.

Azure, three beacons, with ladders or, fired proper—GERVAYS.

Beans, (bean-*cods*, bean-*pods*, and *sheaves* of beans), represent the common bean (*faba vulgaris*), and their exact position is usually given.

Azure, three beans or—MERTON.

Argent, three bean-cods transverse the escutcheon proper—HARDBEANE.

Gules, three bean-cods pendent or—BEANE.

Argent, a chevron gules, between three bean-pods vert—RISE, Cornwall.

Argent, a chevron between three sheaves of beans sable—BLAKE, Northumberland.

Bear, (fr. *ours*): frequent in German arms, and in some instances in Scottish arms, but comparatively rare in English arms, though not unfrequent as a crest, and sometimes the head or jambs are chosen for the latter apart from the body. In one coat of arms *Sea-bears* are named: it is not clear what is meant,

---

Beads. See *Rosary.*

Beaked, (fr. *becqué*): of an *eagle,* or other birds, griffins, and the like, when the beak is of a different tincture.

Beaker. See *Ewer.*

Beam. 1. See *Attire;* 2. See *Anchor;* 3. See *Sun.*

Bearded, or *aulned.* See *Wheat.*

Bearing: an expression very frequently used to signify a *charge,* or anything included within the escutcheon. The old French formula of speaking of the charges upon arms was 'il porte.'

possibly Seals, but more probably *Polar-bears*. The Canton of Berne in Switzerland, as well as the Abbey of S. Gall, exhibit the bear in their insignia. Bears appear also as supporters.

Argent, a bear rampant sable, muzzled or—BER-NARD.

Sire Richard de BARLINGHAM de goules a iij ours de argent—Roll, temp. ED. II.

Gules, on a bend or a bear passant sable—Canton of BERNE.

Argent, a bear erect sable—Abbey of ST. GALL.

Azure, a fesse or; in chief a bear's head proper muzzled and ringed of the second—BARING [Bp. of Gloucester and B., 1856; of Durham, 1861–79].

BERNARD.

Per chevron sable and argent three sea-bears counterchanged—FLOWERDEW, NORFOLK.

Beasts, (fr. *animaux*): the ordinary beasts of the field, with others included under Mammalia, add considerably to the charges of Coats of Arms, as will be seen by the printed Synopsis. A general classification is given there, as a minute and accurate classification would be out of place. It will be found that there are between eighty and ninety varieties to be more or less distinguished both in the drawing and in the blazoning amongst modern coats of arms, but in the earlier arms there were few varieties. If, for instance, we take the well-known roll of arms, temp. Henry III., containing over 200 arms, we find forty instances of the *lion* (including the *leopard*), and some few *lioncels* (as the lions are termed when there are several, or when they have to be drawn on a small scale); but beyond this, if we except an instance of *boars' heads* (borne by Adam de SWYNEBOURNE), no other beast is represented. And when we take the roll of the siege of Carlaverock, temp. Edw. I., containing over 100 coats of arms, and a fine roll, temp. Edw. II., containing over 1,000 coats, and a third roll, temp. Edw. III., containing over 600, the sum total of the mammals to be added to the above list amounts only to six, namely, the *bear*, the *greyhound*, and the *dolphin*, and the heads of *goats*, *stags*, and *wolves*. In time, however, the *tiger* and the *panther* (with the lynx and ounce) were added to the lion tribe, as also the *cat*. Besides the greyhound, other *dogs* were chosen, viz. the bloodhound,

mastiff, spaniel, and the 'alant' and 'talbot.' The *stag*, too, was
no longer represented by only one variety, and only one name,
for we find the buck, the doe, the roebuck, the hart, the hind,
and the reindeer; while the *boar* is known as sanglier, grice,
and marcassin. On account of the fur the *weasel* was prized,
and this, with the ermine, the foine, and the marten, as well as
the *civet* (or civet-cat), appear on the arms. For the skin, too,
the *otter* and the *beaver*, and for its quills the *porcupine*, seem
to have been sought after, and to have been selected for charges
on arms. From the north, the polar *bear* and the *seal*, the
whale and the *dolphin;* while from other parts, the *elephant*,
the *rhinoceros*, the *buffalo*, the *camel*, the *antelope*, and the ibex,
provided subjects for the arms. At home, the *goat* and the
sheep (the latter with the varieties of the lamb, the ram, and
the toison, or fleece), the *bull* (with the varieties of ox, cow,
and calf), the *horse*, the *badger*, and the *fox* were also added
to the list. Nor were lesser animals overlooked, e.g. the *hare*
and the rabbit, the *squirrel*, the *hedgehog*, the *mole*, and the
rat, and lastly, the reremouse, or *bat*.

Beaver, (fr. and lat. *castor*), occurs in the insignia of BEVER-
LEY, Yorkshire, and in other arms where the name suggests it;
but it is used more frequently as a *crest*.

Vert, on a base barry of five argent and azure two beavers, rampant
combatant or—Thomas BEVERIDG, co. Chester, 1595.

Or, a fesse azure between lions rampant in chief gules, and a beaver
passant in base proper—BEAVER.

Argent, three beaver's tails [erect] gules—BEAVER.

Argent, a cross gules between four beavers passant proper—HUDSON
BAY Company [Inc. 1670].

Bee, (fr. *abeille*) : is always represented flying, with wings
extended, and generally upwards, and this is sometimes expressed by *erect*, but more correctly *en arriere*, i.e. flying away
from the spectator. The *Hornet* also occurs on one coat.

Beauseant.   See *Banner*.

Beaver, or *Beauvoir :* the part of
the *Helmet* which opens to shew
the face.

Bebally : a word, now disused, for
party per pale.

Beckit : a bird resembling a *Cornish chough*, q.v.

Azure, three bees volant erect or—BYE.

Azure, three bees volant en arriere argent—BYE.

Sable, a chevron between three bees volant erect argent—SEWELL.

Azure, on a fesse argent a bee volant arriere sable—DE VERTHON.

Or, on a bend azure, three bees volant argent—BUTTERFIELD.

Gironny of eight ermine and gules, on each of the last a bee volant argent—CAMPBELL, Gargamock.

Sable, a hornet argent—BOLLARD.

BYE.

Bee-hive, (fr. *ruche*): this device was granted to a Cheshire family named ROWE during the Commonwealth, but was afterwards also granted to several other families. Both the bee and the bee-hive appear as crests.

Argent, a bee-hive, beset with bees diversely volant sable—ROWE.

Argent, a bee-hive, beset with bees volant proper—TREWEEK, Cornwall.

Ermine, a fesse sable between three bee-hives or—FRAYE.

Argent, on a bee-hive sable a hart lodged argent, attired or—SANDELLAYER, Stafford.

ROWE.

Beech. Only one reference to this tree has been noticed.

Azure, an eagle displayed argent, in his beak a branch of beech or; on a chief of the last a rose between two crosses bottonny gules—BULLINGHAM, Bp. of Gloucester, 1581–89.

Beetle: possibly this is but an error of some writer, who has mistaken the *flies* for beetles (as the name of the bearer suggests); however, the *stag beetles* (*lucanidæ* of naturalists) occur.

Argent, a chevron vert between three beetles proper—MUSCHAMP.

Per pale gules and azure, three stag beetle's wings extended or—DOORE, Cornwall.

Beffroy, or *Beffroy de vair*: an old French term for *vair.*

Belfry. See *Bell.*

Belic: an old word, now disused, for *gules.*

Belled: is applied to a hawk, or falcon, having bells affixed to its legs (fr. *grilletté*); or to other animals, e.g. cows, sheep, &c. (fr. *clariné*).

Bell, (fr. *cloche*), or as it is sometimes called a *Church bell*, is a large bell of the usual form. Smaller bells of a different shape are attached to the legs of hawks and *falcons*, q.v., when they are said to be *belled;* also to necks of *bulls*, &c. (fr. *clariné*).

When the *clapper* is of a different tincture it is to be so described (fr. *bataillé*). The *cannon* or ear may be also of a different tincture from the body or *barrel* of the bell.

Sable, three church bells argent—PORTER.

Sable, a fesse ermine between three bells argent—BELL.

Argent, three war bells gules—KEDMARSTON, co. Suffolk.

Church Bell.

Azure, a lion rampant guardant within an orle of bells argent, cannoned or—OSNEY, co. Lincoln.

Sable, a doe passant between three bells argent—DOOBEL, Sussex, 1695.

Argent, on a cross gules five bells of the first—SEDGEWICKE, Cambridge.

Or, four bars sable ; on three escutcheons argent as many church bells of the second, clappers of the first—HALL, Essex.

A *belfry* occurs as a crest to the family of PORTER, and in this a bell argent is represented as supported between two pillars roofed and spired or, and on the spire a vane of the last.

Bellows: these are of the usual form, and are borne with the pipes downwards.

Argent, three pair of bellows sable—SCIPTON.

Belt: this charge is but rarely borne, and usually only a small portion of the leather is shewn (as in the margin); hence it is often blazoned *half a belt*, and the buckles (fr. *boucle*) should be named as to position, tincture, &c. The belt worn over the shoulder, and crossing the chest and back, was termed anciently a *baldrich* or *baudrick*, and to the lower part was attached the sword. It is not borne by this name, but has been said, amongst other suppositions, to have been the origin of the *bend*.

Belt.

Argent, a demy belt fixed in fesse azure buckled edged and garnished or —BELTMAINE.

Argent, three belts, the under parts couped in fesse azure, buckled and garnished or—NARBON.

Gules, two pieces of belts [otherwise half-belts] palewise, in fesse, argent, the buckles erect in chief or—PELHAM.

Bend, (fr. *bande*): the *bend dexter* is perhaps one of the most frequently used of *Ordinaries*, q.v., being a straight piece extending from the dexter corner to the opposite edge of the shield. It is said to derive its origin from the *belt, baudrick* ~~or baldrick (Balthous, Cingulum militare),~~ which was once a mark of knighthood; other heralds, however, have seen in it the idea of a scaling-ladder. According to Legh and other heraldic writers, the bend should occupy one-third of the field when charged, and one-fifth when plain. In English arms the bend is always placed straight athwart the shield, and never bowed as in foreign ~~arms: at the same time,~~ in some late MSS. it is fancifully drawn with a curve, in order to represent the convexity of the shield.

FOLIOT.

Gules, a bend argent—FOLIOT [or as it is written in a Roll of arms, temp. Henry III. 'Richard Fo-LIOTT, de goulz ung bend d'argent'].

William de GAUNT, barreé d'argent et d'azure, ung bend de goules—Roll, temp. HEN. III.

John de VAUX, ung bend escheque d'argent et de goules—*Ibid.*

Gules, a bend ermine between six bezants— [? Sir Armoyne COUGHTE, from arms in Dorchester Church, Oxon.]

COUGHTE?

A bend is very frequently subjected to a modification of its margin, and is *engrailed, invected, indented, embattled, counter-embattled, bretessed, raguly, champaine* (or *warriated*), *nebuly, wavy ;* also *bevilled, cotticed* and *fimbriated,* all of which terms will be found explained.

Robert WALROND, d'argent ung bend engrele de goules—Roll, temp. HEN. III.

Sire Aleyn PLOKENOT, de ermyn a une bende engrele de goules—Roll, temp. EDW. II.

Sir Johan de PENZRET, de goulys, a une bende batille [embattled] de argent—*Ibid.*

Beloochee soldier. See *Man.*

Bend per. See *Party.*

Bendwise, or *bendways:* when the charge is placed lengthways in the middle of the shield, like a bend. Cf. *barwise.*

A *bend* is also frequently charged with various devices, and
when *charged upon the upper part* this should be noticed, because when a bend is simply described as *charged*, it signifies it
is so on the centre or fesse-point. All charges placed upon a
bend, in bend, or between cottices, must stand bendwise, not perpendicularly. Even the *furs* follow this rule, although generally
upright on all other ordinaries. Illustrations of bends besides
those given in the present article will be found under *compony,
cottised, embowed, engrailed, fleury, pierced, raguly, wavy,* and
also bearing such charges as *magnet, mullet, spear, wyvern,* &c.

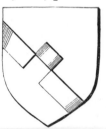

Gules, on the upper part of a bend between six
crosses crosslet fitchy argent, an escutcheon or
charged with a demi lion rampant, pierced through
the mouth with an arrow, within a tressure flory
counter flory gules—HOWARD, Baron Howard, Earl
of Surrey.

Gules, on a bend between crosses botonny argent,
a mullet in the point of the bend sable—Monsire de
ORMESBY, Harl. MS. 6589.

HOWARD.

Bend archy, bowed or *embowed* (q.v.), not found in English
arms, only on the Continent, and more frequently in German
arms; an example may be seen in the *Crown of Rue*, q.v.

Bend debruised, or *fracted,* otherwise
dauncet, or *downset :* various forms are
inserted in English heraldic books, but
it may be questioned whether the old
' dancetty' was not quite distinct from
the idea of the barbarous term *downset.*

De argent a une bende daunce de vert a ij
coties daunce de goules Sir Edmund de KEN-
DALE—Roll, A.D. 1308–14 (Lansd. MS. 855).

Bend double downset?

Azure, a bend double dancetty argent—LORKS.

Per bend fracted [in another MS. double dancetty] or and gules, two
birds in bend sinister counterchanged—RAUFF.

Per bend sinister fracted [in another MS. double dancetty, and a third
MS. rompu] argent and sable six martlets counterchanged—John AL-
LEYNE, Suffolk.

A *bend* may be composed of charges placed bendwise, e.g.

A bend of five lozenges combined or—Jon le MARESCAL, Harl. MS. 6137.

In bend is a term used when bearings are placed *bendwise*.

Per bend: see *Party.*

The diminutives of the bend are the *bendlet, garter,* or *gartier,* which is half its width, the *cost* or *cottice* which is one-fourth, and the *riband* which is one-eighth.

Bend sinister, (fr. *barre*): an ordinary resembling the Bend in form, but extending from the *sinister* chief to the *dexter* base.

It is, however, borne in English arms but rarely. Its diminutives are the *scarpe,* which is half its width, and the *baton* (q.v.), which is half as wide as the *scarpe* and *couped.*

Argent, a bend sinister gules—BIZZET, Scotland.

Or, a bend sinister azure—TRYE [originally from France].

Argent, three bendlets engrailed sable; over all a scarpe gules—BLAGE, Kent.

BIZZET.

According to Nisbet, bends sinister were formerly much borne in Scotland, but have generally been changed to dexter bends of late, from a mistaken notion that they always betokened illegitimacy. It is the sinister *baton* (or diminutive *bend* couped), which alone conveys this disgrace. In Germany the bend is borne almost as frequently sinister as dexter.

Bendlet: a diminutive of the bend, nominally half the width of that ordinary, though often much narrower. In old French rolls there does not seem to be any distinction, as frequently two and three '*bends*' are blazoned as on the shield. According to Guillim, a single bendlet should be placed as in the sketch in the margin, which position, however, is not observed in practice. A bendlet azure over a coat was of old frequently used as a mark of cadency. It ap-

BOTRINGHAM.

pears sometimes to be called a *garter,* and by Planché a '*cotice single,*' (which cannot be).

Argent, a bendlet gules—BOTRINGHAM. Another branch bears three bendlets.

Or, two bendlets azure—DOYLEY, Oxfordshire.

Argent, a bendlet gules; over all a cross or—GALLWAY, Ireland.

Bendlets are occasionally *enhanced* or placed *in chief sinister*. They are also subject to the same variations as the bend, both as to margin and
as to charges.

Argent, three bendlets enhanced gules—BYRON,
co. York.

Argent, two bendlets, one enhanced, the other
in base azure; over all a saltire gules—DORIEN.

Or, three bendlets enhanced gules—GRYLLS,
Cornwall.

Gules, three bendlets enhanced or—GREILEY
[or Gresley], Lord of Manchester. [Also City
of MANCHESTER.]

BYRON.

Argent, three bendlets crenellé sable—H. DE COSTELLO, Bp. of Hereford,
1504.

Gules, on two bendlets or, six fleurs-de-lis vert—DRAPER.

Sir Walter de FRENES, de goules a ij bendes endentes de or et de
azure, le un en le autre—Roll, temp. EDW. II.

There are cases where the word '*baston*' is used for '*bendlet*,'
e.g. in the arms of SEGRAVE. The glass existing in Dorchester
Abbey Church, Oxon, exhibits the ancient
drawing of the 'baston' of the roll, which
may well be contemporary with the glass.

Sire Henri de SEGRAVE, de sable, a un lion rampand de argent [corone de or] e un baston de
goules—Roll, temp. ED. II.

Argent, Robert de WELLE, d'argent ov deux bastons (= bendlets) de goules besante d'or. Roll,
temp. HEN. III.

SEGRAVE.

Bendy, (fr. *bandé*): said of a field or charge divided bendwise into an even number of equal parts; or, as it may be
otherwise described, as a field bearing a series of diagonal
stripes of alternate tinctures (and liable to the same variations
of the edges as the *bend*), but so that there is an equal number of each. It stands to reason that if the same tincture appears in chief as in base, the shield must be blazoned as a field
bearing so many bendlets. As a rule, the first tincture is

named; but in the case of a metal and colour, though the latter is first in order, the metal is to be first named.

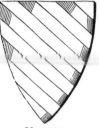

Monsire de MONTFORT port bende de X. peces d'or et d'azure—Roll, temp. ED. III.

Monsire de St. PHILIBERT port bende de VI. peces d'argent et d'asur—Roll, temp. EDW. III.

Bendy of six, champaine purple and argent —BOWBRIDGE.

Bendy wavy of six, argent and azure—PLATER, Suffolk.

MONTFORT.

Bendy sinister (fr. *barré*), with the lines drawn from the left-hand upper or *sinister* corner of the shield, is rarely found.

Bendy sinister of eight, gules and argent—SCHBEBSDOBF, Bavaria.
Bendy sinister of ten, azure and or—Piers de MOUNTFORTH.

Bendy barry: this practically amounts to *Barry bendy*, before described, and of which illustrations have been given.

Bendy barry of eight, gules and or—HOLLAND.
Bendy barry argent and gules—CRISPIN, co. Lincoln.

Bendy paly, or *Paly bendy*. According to the late Mr. Wyatt Papworth (from whose MS. note-book these illustrations are taken) *Paly* bendy is the better term, since, although it is not known to occur, the same might have to be drawn *Paly bendy sinister*.

Paly bendy.

Paly bendy sinister.

As will be seen, it is a combination of bendy and paly, less accurately called sometimes *Lozengy bendy*.

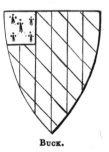

Bendy paly of eight? or and azure, a canton ermine—BUCK (Bart.), Linc.

Bendy paly or and azure—BUCK, Agecroft Hall, Manchester.

Bendy paly argent and gules—SYDENHAM.

Paly bendy gules and azure, martlets in orle or—HENDLEY.

BUCK.

Bendy lozengy, and *Bendy lozengy sinister :* lozengy, each lozenge being placed in bend, or in bend sinister.

Bendy lozengy or and gules —Isabel, daughter of Aylmer, Earl of ANGOULEME, and wife of King John.

Bendy lozengy, argent and sable—CROFTS, co. Lancaster.

Bendy lozengy (? paly) of eight, or and azure—BUCK, co. Lincoln.

Bendy lozengy barry, sable and or—IPRE.

Bendy lozengy barry or and sable—CANCELLOR.

Bendy lozengy.   Bendy lozengy sinister.

Bendy lozengy (? paly), argent and azure—BAVARIA [Sandford's Genealogical History].

Bendy dexter and sinister would appear as in the margin, that is, the lines would produce squares, which would be similar to those of a field *chequy*, only placed diamond wise. They would differ from *lozengy*, q.v., which is more of a diamond shape, and fusilly, which is still narrower.   An illustration is here given, but it is, we believe, a theoretical coat, and not one actually borne.

Bendy dexter and sinister.

Bendy pily or *pily bendy :* divided into an even number of pieces by piles placed bendwise across the escutcheon. Although

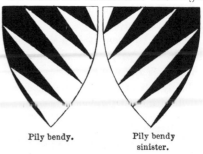

this seems to be referred to in several books on heraldry, no example has been found by way of illustration.   The engravings here given, like the others illustrating the varieties of the fesse and bend in conjunction with other lines of partition,

Pily bendy.   Pily bendy sinister.

are from sketches by the late Mr. Wyatt Papworth.

Betony leaf, (*Betonica officinalis* of Linnæus): a common wood-plant of the nettle tribe, appears in a solitary instance, unless the *bethune* leaf is the same.

Or, a betony leaf proper—BETTY.

Azure, on a fesse between three lozenges or, a bethune leaf slipped vert —BETHUNE, Nethertarvit.

Bevilly (fr. *bevillé*), or *bevilled:* a term of doubtful origin, and omitted by most writers on heraldry. It signifies a kind of break forming a bevel, or acute angle. It is applied to the chief, bend, &c.

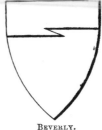

BEVERLY.

Or, a chief bevily vert—BEVERLY.
Gules, a bend bevilled or—BOVILE.
Per pale beviled azure and or—ALTHAM.

Bezant, *Besant* (fr.), or *Besaunte* = a *Roundlet or.* It represents the gold coin of Byzantium (Constantinople), and should therefore be drawn flat. It is said that this money, once current, had no device whatever stamped on it. This and the other *roundles* were no doubt introduced into English heraldry by the crusaders. The French term it *Besant d'or,* while they call the *plate, Besant d'argent;* they also write *Besant de gueules* when the *Roundle* (q.v.) is red.

DYNGHAM.

Gules, three bezants—DYNGHAM.

Monsire de WORSELEY port [d'argent, une bend entre vi merletts gules] a trois besands en la bend—Roll, temp. ED. III.

Bezanty, (fr. *besanté*): signifies *semé of bezants,* and is usually applied to bordures, but it may be applied to other ordinaries, as well as to the field itself.

Le Conte de CORNEWAIL argent, ung Lion de goulz coronne or, ung borde de sable besante d'or —Roll, temp. HEN. III. [i.e. Richard PLANTAGENET, king of the Romans, and earl of CORNWALL, son of King John].

RICHARD, KING OF
THE ROMANS.

Béqué, or *becqué* (fr.): beaked.
Berly: disused term for *Barruly.*

Bernak: old name for *Barnacle.*
Besom. See *Brush.*

Monsire Alen de ZOUCH port gules besante—Roll, temp. ED. III.

Argent, a fret of six pieces bezanty—WYKE.

Azure, bezanty—BESLET, BYSSETT, BYSET, &c.

Bill, or *Wood-bill*, (A.-Saxon *Bil*): an instrument used by woodmen for the purpose of lopping trees. The head alone is more frequent as a charge than the entire instrument. The wood-bill, as represented in fig. 2, occurs in the arms of FUST, and is more probably intended for an implement of war. For *Stone-bill*, see *Wedge*.

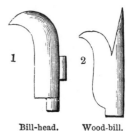

Bill-head.   Wood-bill.

Ermine, two wood-bills sable with long handles proper in saltire a chief azure . . . . . . &c.—William BILL, D.D. ob. 1561.

Ermine, three bills sable—DENNYS, Devon.

Argent, three wood-bills in sable—GIBBES.

Sable, three bill-heads (like fig. 1) argent—LEVERSEGE.

Billet, (fr. *billette*): a small oblong figure. In architecture blocks of a similar shape bear this name, and are frequent in Ionic and Corinthian, and are continued in Norman, mouldings; but while they are in architecture either exact squares or else cylindrical, in heraldry they are brick-shaped, and should be drawn twice as long as wide. The theory that it was meant to represent a written letter (i.e. modern French ' *billet* ') will scarcely bear examination. The term rarely appears in ancient rolls as a separate charge, but often under the term *billette*.

Or, three billets gules— MERLING.

Gules, ten billets, 4, 3, 2, and 1 or, within a bordure engrailed argent, charged with ten torteaux—SALTER.

Monsire Bartholomew GABRIEL, or, a vi billetta sable —Roll, temp. ED. III.

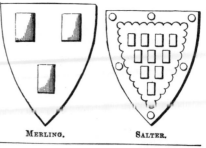

MERLING.   SALTER.

Bible. See *Book*.

Bicorporated: having two bodies, e.g. of a lion.

Bicapitated: having two heads.

Bigarré, (fr.): of variegated colours, e.g. of a butterfly.

They are not always straight-sided, being sometimes *raguled*, and this possibly illustrates the original meaning, namely, that they were blocks of wood cut with the *bill*, or woodman's *axe*. An example of a *carved stone* billet also occurs.

Argent, a billet, raguled and trunked sable, inflamed in three places proper—BILLETTES.

Argent, three stone billets carved gules—BILLERBERG.

Billetty, (fr. *Billetté*), i.e. *semé of billets:* this occurs frequently in ancient rolls of arms. It is agreed that the term 'billetty' involves that there should be at least ten in the field, and they should be placed in rows barwise, not one beneath the other, but alternately, and leaving the corners sufficiently distant so as not to be mistaken for *chequy*.

Azure, semé of billets, and a lion rampant or—Earl of ROCHFORD. [These are the NASSAU arms.]

Mahewe de LOVAYNE, goules billete d'or, une fece d'argent—Roll, temp. HEN. III.

Geffrey GACELYN, d'or billety de sable, ung label de goules—*Ibid.*

William de ST. OMER D'azure, billety d'or a ung fece d'or—*Ibid.*

Earl of ROCHFORD.

Billetty counter billetty is a mode of blazoning *barry* and *paly*, when the divisions of the former are as wide again as those of the latter, so as to be distinguished from *chequy*.

Billetty counter billetty gules and argent—BILLINGER.

Birch, (lat. *betula*): Birch branches and leaves occur in one or two canting arms.

Gules . . . . &c., a chief embattled argent, with three nine-leaved birch branches vert—BYRCH, Essex.

Sable, a fesse between three birch-leaves argent—BURCHE, Devon.

Or, three birch-twigs sable—BIRCHES.

Birds. The Birds, as will be seen by the Table in the Appendix, are as varied in their names as the Beasts, though it is doubtful if the same variety could be detected in the actual emblazonment of the arms. As in the case of the Beasts, in the ancient rolls of arms comparatively few varieties of Birds

---

Biparted. See *Cross*, § 8.

Birdbolt. See *Arrow.*

occur, and further the arms in which birds appear are not to be compared in number with those in which the beasts occur, amongst which the *lion* and *leopard* are so general. The little *martlet* is the most frequent, which in the Roll of Henry III., referred to under *Beasts*, occurs in eight coats of arms, the *eagle* in two, the *popinjay* in two, the *raven, heron,* and *cock* respectively in one coat. And if we go further through the same rolls before referred to, viz. Edw. I., II., and III., though the number of arms bearing the above is considerably increased, we add only two additional names to the list, the *falcon,* and *pinzon.*

But in the fifteenth and sixteenth centuries, and more especially in the seventeenth and eighteenth centuries, the list becomes swollen to over one hundred varieties at least in name. For it will be observed that in very many cases the name is adopted for the sake of the pun, and often a mere local name is given, such as the *beckit* for A'BECKET, and the like. All will be found mentioned under the forty articles or so represented by the names printed in the Synopsis in the italic type.

There are some few cases in which a *bird* is named, but no designation of what the bird is, and when so referred to it should be drawn in the form of the blackbird. Thus:—

Gules, a bird standing upon an apple or—CONHAM, Wilts.

Gules, a bird on a rock proper—ROCK.

According to heralds, birds, unless the contrary is specified, are to be emblazoned with their wings *close,* as it is termed, except in the case of the eagle, when it would be drawn with wings *displayed.* But there is much variety of terminology applied to the mode of representing birds, and, according to theoretical heraldry, by a combination of the following terms the variety may be increased almost *ad infinitum.* For instance, a bird might be represented as: 1. *Close;* and beneath this the following varieties,—cl. *embowed,* cl. *preying,* cl. *in full aspect,* cl. *aspectant,* or *at gaze,* cl. *in brian aspect,* and cl. *in brian aspect at gaze.* 2. *Displayed;* and under this, displ. *erect,* displ. *inverted,* displ. *with double head,* displ. *without wings,* displ. *in majesty,* displ. *surgeant.* 3. *Expansed;* and under this exp. *elevated,* exp. *sepurture,* exp. *disclosed.* Examples of one or two

of the above will be found under *Eagle, Falcon,* &c., but practically the terms more frequently met with are less technical;
e.g. a bird is *regardant,* or *recursant, perched, standing, sitting,
feeding, pecking, preying* or *trussing, pruning* its wings, *rising,
volant, singing, croaking* (of ravens), and *pendent* when dead and
hanging. Again, a bird may be *membered, collared, armed,
crested, beaked, legged, jelloped,* and *combed* (of cocks) of a different tincture; birds may also be *jessed, hooded,* and *belled* (of
falcons), and *vulned,* or *in piety* (of pelicans). References are
also frequently made to the *wings, head,* &c., which still
further add to the variety of description.

Bishop: In ancient times the bishops and other ecclesiastics frequently took a vigorous part in military affairs, and
hence in the insignia borne by sees and by religious houses
the ordinary military charges appear. In modern times the
Mitre (q.v.) has taken the place of the helmet and crest upon
all episcopal arms. The bishop *impales* the arms of the see
with his paternal coat, the former on the dexter, the latter on
the sinister side. (See *Achievements* and *Marshalling.*)

A *figure of a bishop,* also in his pontifical vestments, occurs in
the arms of the see of CLOGHER, as well as in those of some of
the Scotch sees.

Azure, a bishop [some say S. Michael] mitred and vested standing in
the porch of a church, the dexter hand elevated praying over a cauldron
on a fire, and containing three children all proper; in his sinister hand
a crozier or—See of ABERDEEN.

Bit, *Manage :* a charge in the armorial
ensigns of the LORINERS or bit-makers.

Azure, on a chevron argent, between three
manage-bits or, as many bosses sable—Company of LORINERS. [Founded temp. HEN. VII.,
but incorporated 1712.]

Snaffle-bit. This appears to be distinguished from the manage-bit, and is
thus represented.

Sable, three snaffle-bits or— MILNER, Pudsey,
Yorksh., [also of London, 1633-4].

Manage-bit.

Snaffle-bit.

Birt-fish. See *Turbot.*
Bittern. See *Heron.*

Bisse, (fr., Ital., *biscia*) : a kind of
snake. See *Serpent.*

Boss of a bit : this is another charge in the same arms of the Company of Bit-makers, as will be seen above, and it is represented as shewn in the margin.

Boss.

Bl. An abbreviation of the word blue, often found in sketches or *tricking* of arms for azure. B. alone is preferable.

Blackbird, (fr. *merle*) : this is the *merula vulgaris* of naturalists. It is borne by several families. By the first named below it was probably chosen from the sound of the Latin name.

Azure, three blackbirds proper [and in other arms of same family with a chief dancetty sable]—Mellor, co. Derby.

Argent, a blackbird singing perched upon a vine vert, thereon a bat or —Ronayne, co. Waterford.

Vert, a cross raguly humetty or, on a chief of the last three blackbirds proper—Beck, Surrey : granted 1864.

Argent, on a chevron azure between three blackbirds proper, a crescent enclosed by two cinquefoils or—Sleigh, Scotland.

Blazon, (fr. *Blason*) : a word which, whatever may be the derivation and original meaning, now signifies to describe a coat of arms in such a manner that an accurate drawing may be made from the description. In order to do so, a knowledge of the *tinctures, ordinaries, charges*, and *points* of the shield is particularly necessary.

1. In blazoning a coat of arms the first thing to be mentioned is the *FIELD*, whether it be of one tincture, as *Gules ;* or parted, as *Per fesse; Per pale;* or *Quarterly* (and then add ' first,' or ' first and fourth '), &c.; or if it be of any of the patterns frequently used, as *Checquy, Bendy, Fretty, &c. ;* or if the field be *semé*, or strewed with any small charges without regard to number (and they are to be named next after the field itself), always naming the *tincture* or *tinctures*.

Azure, semé of trefoils argent, a lion rampant of the last—Holland.

Black: always blazoned *sable*.

Blackamoor's head. See *Head*.

Bladed, (fr. *tigé*): an expression used when the blade or sprout of any grain is of a different tincture.

Black-cock. See *Heath-cock*.

Blanc, white : see *argent*, but used sometimes perhaps for *ermine*.

Blasted : leafless, applied to *trees*.

2. The principal *ORDINARY* is next to be mentioned, with its peculiarities of form (if any) and *tincture*, as

NEVILL.

Gules, a saltire argent—NEVILL, Earl of Warwick.

Azure, a chevron or—D'AUBERNOUN, Surrey.

Argent, a bend engrailed sable — RADCLIFFE, Sussex.

Per saltire argent and azure, a saltire gules—GAGE, Hengrave, Suffolk.

3. The *CHARGES*, if any there be, between which the ordinary is placed, are next to be mentioned, as,

Gules, a chevron between three mullets of six points, pierced, or—DANVERS, Northamp.

Or, a fesse between three lions rampant gules—DANNERTON, Salop.

Of the charges placed above, below, or beside the principal bearing, whether on *sinister* or *dexter* side; those in *chief* are named before those in *base*, and those on the *dexter* take precedence of those on the *sinister*.

WAKE.

Argent, two bars gules, in chief three torteaux—WAKE, Linc.

Gules, three hands holding respectively a crown a key and a purse or—Arms ascribed to NIGELLUS, Bp. of Ely, 1133—69.

If there be no ordinary, the principal charge, or the charge or charges which cover the fesse-point, or are in the midst of the field, should first be named, and any charge whose position is not specially mentioned, or at least implied to be otherwise, is understood to be in the middle of the shield.

WILLIAMS OF THAME.

Azure, two organ-pipes between four crosses patée or—Lord WILLIAMS of Thame.

Sable, a lion passant guardant or, between three esquire's helmets argent—COMPTON, Northamp.

Azure, two trumpets pileways between eight crossed crosslets 3, 3, 2, or—TRUMPINGTON.

If there be no charges of the kinds already mentioned, whatever charges there may be must be named after the field, notice being taken of their position with regard to one another, as

Sable, three ducal coronets in pale or—The see of BRISTOL.

Azure, ten estoiles, four, three, two, one, or—ALSTON, Beds.

Sable, fifteen bezants, five, four, three, two, and one—County of CORN-WALL.

When three charges are borne *two and one* it is superfluous to say so, as they are always to be drawn in that position if no other be mentioned.   Example:—

Or, three torteaux— COURTENAY.

Consequently the arms of England, when the three lions are one beneath the other, are not rightly blazoned, unless they are said to be *in pale.*

It is also highly necessary to describe the position of each charge individually, whenever there is the possibility of a mistake.   It would of course be quite superfluous to describe a crescent or a billet as *erect,* because that is their natural position, but there are many charges which may be placed several ways with equal propriety: keys, for instance, may be *in pale* (*palewise in pale* is implied), *barwise in pale, bendwise in pale, palewise in fesse,* and in many other positions which it would be useless to enumerate here.   The wards need not be described as turned to the dexter, because that is their ordinary position, though they are often *endorsed.*

4. Next come charges upon the ordinary or central charge, as

Argent, on a fesse sable, between three hawks rising proper, a leopard's face between two mullets or—STONEHOUSE, Radley, Berks.

5. The BORDURE and the charges thereon are next to be mentioned.

6. The CANTON or CHIEF with all charges upon them are to be emblazoned next.

Sable, on a cross engrailed argent, a lion passant gules, between four leopard's faces azure; on a chief or, a rose of the third, seeded of the fifth, barbed vert, between two Cornish choughs proper—The arms of Cardinal WOLSEY, now borne by CHRIST CHURCH, Oxford.

Cardinal WOLSEY.

It often happens that one ordinary or charge is superimposed over some other or others, and this, if so, should be named last, and expressed by the term *over all.*

7. Lastly come the DIFFERENCES or marks of cadency, and the baronet's badge.

In *blazon* repetition should be avoided: the name of a tincture should never be used twice in describing the same coat. To avoid this it is customary to say *of the third, of the field, &c.,* as in the arms of WOLSEY above. If the field be all of one tincture, a charge of the same may be said to be *of the field*, but otherwise *of the first* or *second*. Some heralds of the seventeenth century used the word *gold* to avoid the repetition of *or*. The word *silver* was, though less frequently, used for *argent*.

If two charges consecutively named are of the same tincture, the tincture mentioned after the latter serves for both, as in the arms of DANVERS and STONEHOUSE given above; but except in very simple cases it is better to name the tincture after the former, describing the latter as *of the last*.

The way to avoid the repetition of numbers may be shewn by the following example—

Sable, on a chevron or, between three estoiles of the second (or last), as many crosses pattée fitchée gules—Archbishop LAUD.

While conciseness in blazoning is sought after, it should never be forgotten that the best blazon is that which is the most perspicuous. Tautology and diffuseness in describing a coat of arms are undoubtedly faults, but ambiguity is a much greater one. In the choice of technical terms, English ones are in general to be preferred to French, and those whose signification is undisputed to those which have different meanings.

It may, perhaps, be mentioned with greater propriety here than elsewhere, that every charge in which there is the distinction of front and back is ordinarily to be turned towards the *dexter* side of the escutcheon, unless directed to be placed otherwise (see *Counter - couchant,* &c.); but in banners the charges should be turned towards the staff, and upon the caparison of a horse towards his head. In the oldest plates remaining in the stalls of the knights of the garter, at S. George's Chapel, Windsor, all the shields and charges are inclined towards the altar, so that those on the north side are turned contrary to the usual practice.

Blue-bottle : the flower of the *cyanus*, and the bright blue occupant of the corn-field has been chosen in one or two instances for armorial bearings.

Argent, a chevron gules, between three blue-bottles slipped and leaved proper—BOTHELL.

Argent, a chevron between three blue-bottles azure cupped vert—CHORLEY.

Blue-bottle.

In one coat of arms (Harl. MS. 2151, fol. 110) *heydoddes* are named. As they appear to be a kind of flower, and are blazoned azure, possibly blue-bottles are meant.

Argent, a chevron gules between three heydoddes azure slipped vert— DODD.

Boar: this word implies the wild-boar, and occurs perhaps more frequently in Scottish than in English coats of arms. It was called with the old heralds *sanglier*. A young wild-boar is termed a *Grice*, and is borne by families of that name. The term *Marcassin* is also used for a young wild-boar, and this should be represented with tail hanging down, instead of twisted. The terms *Hog* and *Porc* are also employed.

The boar, besides being represented in the various ways common to other animals, e.g. *passant, rampant, statant*, &c., may be represented *enraged*. It may also be represented *crined, tusked, cleyed, membered, unguled, armed, bristled*, &c.

More frequently the heads (fr. *hure*) were borne than the whole animal, and are represented as lying lengthways, unless expressed otherwise. The snout (fr. *boutoi*) is in some French arms of a different tincture. It should be stated whether the heads are *couped* or *erased*.

Blemished: having an abatement. A sword having the point broken off may be said to be blemished or *rebated*.

Block. See *Metal*, *Cube*, and *Delf*.

Block-brush. See *Brush*.

Blood-colour: the term *Bloody*, which occurs at times in the works of some old heraldic writers (as a bloody hand, heart, &c.) does not seem to signify *sanguine* but gules. The Latin *blodius* also is probably to be interpreted the same, though there are instances in which *blodius* is presumed to be used for 'blue,' i.e. azure.

Blind : without an eye ; applied to the *quatrefoil* and *cinquefoil*, when not pierced.

Bloodhound. See *Dog*.

Blue: always blazoned *Azure*, though in *tricking* the *b* is used.

Argent, a boar passant gules armed or—TREWARTHEN.

Vert, a boar or—BOAR.

Argent, on a bend sable three grices passant of the first—GRICE.

Argent, on a mount vert a boar passant sable crined or—KELLET, co. Cork.

Argent, a fesse between two boars passant sable tusked, cleyed, and membered or; on the fesse a rose between two eaglets displayed of the fourth—BUSHE, Bp. of Bristol, 1542-54.

Argent, a boar passant sable enraged and unguled gules—PERROT.

Or, a hog lying fesswise, a raven feeding on his back sable—DANSKINE, Scotland.

Argent, a chevron between three porcs sable—SWYNETHWAYTE.

Argent, three boar's heads couped sable armed or—CRADOCK.

Argent, a chevron between three boar's heads erased azure—COCHRANE.

Argent, a chevron between three boars sable—BERHAM, also SWYNEY.

Adam de SWYNEBOURNE, de goules a trois testes de senglier argent—Roll, temp. HEN. III.

CRADOCK.　　COCHRANE.

Sire Johan de SWYNEFORD d'argent a iij testes de cenglers de goulys—Roll, temp. ED. II.

Sire Johan de WYNSINGTONE, de sable a iij testes de senglier de argent—Roll, temp. EDW. II.

Boars are sometimes found as supporters, e.g. as dexter supporter in the arms of Garden CAMPBELL, Perth, and in one MS. they are seen as supporters to the royal arms of Richard III. This same king had, when Duke of Gloucester, adopted the boar as his badge, and it is supposed from this that he called one of his heralds *Blanch Senglier*. The wild-boar is also occasionally used as a *crest*, as well as the *Boar's head*.

Boat: besides the larger *ships* q.v., which are somewhat frequent, there are smaller vessels of various kinds used as charges, which may better be classed with the *boat*. *Lighter-boat, open boat, bark, skiff*, and *raft*. *Boat-hooks*, also the *boat-oars* are borne separately. A common boat is the crest of the family of AMES.

Sable, in base an open boat with oars in a sea proper, on a chief argent three crescents vert—MACNAB.

Barry, wavy of six argent and azure, on the middle bar a boat or ; on a chief of the second two oars in saltire of the third between two cushions of the first tasselled or—Company of WATERMEN [Inc. 1556].

Or, a lighter-boat in fesse gules, [in one blazoning, a lighter vessel without masts]—DE WOLFO, Swevland.   Azure, three barks or—AYER.

Argent, a boar . . . . a skiff with oars sable between the two in base —O'MALLEY, co. Mayo.

Gules, a raft or float removed or—BRETVILL.

Per pale gules and or, two boat-oars in saltire azure—TORRANCE.

Bones: it is singular that human bones should be so frequently chosen as devices for coats of arms, and it will be found that they are separated into varieties in the blazoning, though probably the *shank* bone, *thigh* bone, and *leg* bone are generally intended for the same, viz. the *femur*.   By the *shin* bone is probably meant the *tibia*.

Sable, two shin-bones in saltire, proper, the sinister surmounted by the dexter—NEWTON.

[Another branch of the family appears to bear the sinister uppermost.]

Sable, a shin-bone in pale, proper, surmounted of another in fesse—BAYNES, Cumb. [The family seem to have borne originally a saltire.]

Sable, two shank-bones in cross, that in pale surmounting the one in fesse argent—BAINES, York.

NEWTON.

Or three broken shank-bones fesswise in pale gules—DE COSTA.

So far as has been observed in all cases the bones are intended for human bones.

The human *skull*, or *death's head*, also is borne, but not frequently.   The *jaw-bone* also occurs occasionally

Argent, on a chevron gules, three human skulls of the first—BOLTER.

Sable, a chevron between three human skulls argent—BOULTER.

BOLTER.

Paly of six, or and gules, a jaw-bone in pale azure—DAMBOYS.

Bodkin. See *Needle*.

Boltant, or *Bolting* : said of a hare or rabbit springing forward.

Bolt. See *Arrow* and *Fetterlock*.

Bomb-shell. See *Fire-ball*.

Bonnet, Albanian.   See *Cap*.

In *Achievements* a *skull* is sometimes placed over the shield instead of the crest, to signify that the deceased is the last of his line.

Bonnet: the ordinary bonnet appears to be borne only in the insignia of a Company.

Argent, a fesse between three bonnets azure, impaled with or a chevron gules between three woolpacks proper — Company of BONNETMAKERS, Edinburgh.

The velvet cap of crimson, within a *coronet*, q.v., is also called a bonnet.

Bonnet, Electoral: a cap of crimson velvet turned up with ermine. This was borne over the arms of Hanover until some time after the erection of that state into a kingdom in 1814, when a crown was substituted in its stead.

Electoral Bonnet.

Book: books are borne in arms, either open, as in those of the University of OXFORD, or closed, as in those of the University of CAMBRIDGE and the Company of STATIONERS. Their position, and *clasps* or *seals*, if they have any, should be mentioned.

Azure, on an open book proper, having on the dexter side seven seals or [Rev. v. 1], between three ducal coronets of the last the words DOMINVS ILLVMINATIO MEA. (Ps. xxvii. 1.)—UNIVERSITY OF OXFORD.

[Previous to King James' reign SAPIENTIA ET FELICITATE occurs (e.g. in glass in Bodleian Library, and in a typographical device, 1585). Still earlier, in a typographical device, the motto on the books runs VERITAS LIBERABIT BONITAS REGNABIT.]

OXFORD UNIVERSITY.

Argent, three books closed gules, leaved, clasped, and garnished or— PAYNTER, Norfolk.

Gules, a clasped book open between three buck's heads erased or—Seal of John BUCKNER [Bp. of Chichester, 1798—1824].

Amongst Books the *Bible* is the one most frequently mentioned by name.

Vert, in chief, the holy Bible expanded proper, in base a sand-glass running argent—JOASS, Scotland.

Argent, on a fesse gules, three Bibles of the second garnished or, a falcon volant between two suns of the last—SLAMBERG.

Argent, an eagle displayed double-headed sable, armed gules, on a chief azure a book of the Holy Scriptures, open proper, stringed or—W. MOR-GAN, Bp. of Llandaff, 1549.

Bible,
STATIONERS' COMPANY.

Azure, on a chevron or between three Bibles fesse-wise, clasps downwards gules, garnished and leaved of the second, an eagle rising proper enclosed by two red roses seeded or barbed vert; from the chief a demi-circle of glory edged with clouds proper, therein a dove displayed and nimbed argent—Company of STATIONERS, London [Incorporated 1556].

Argent, a chevron azure between three pheons gules; on a chief of the second an open Holy Bible proper edged and sealed or, inscribed, Proverbs, cap. xxii. ver. 6, enclosed by two crosses flory of the last—JOHNSON.

The *Music,* or *Song-book,* borne by the parish clerks of London, is of oblong form, and similar to that in the margin. *Musical lines* also occur, consisting of five parallel lines of music extending across the shield horizontally.

Song-book,
PARISH CLERKS.

Azure, a fleur-de-lis or; on a chief gules a leopard's head between two song-books (shut) of the second, stringed vert—Company of PARISH CLERKS, [Inc. 1233, arms granted, 1582].

Azure, on a fesse argent 5 musical lines sable charged with a rose gules, and two escallops of the third in chief . . . . &c.—TETLOW, Lancaster. [Arms granted, 1760.]

Argent, two bars wavy azure, on a chief of the second an open music-book or between two swords in saltire of the first hilted and pommelled of the third—THE ACADEMY OF THE MUSES, London.

Books also occur in the arms of Dean and Chapter of RAPHOE.—College of S. Mary at Manchester in LANCASTER.—Company of SCRIVENERS, London; and in those of the families of CONROY, co. Montgomery.—JOASS, Scotland.—GRANT.—SMITH, Edinburgh.—EVANS, Norwich.—B. PORTEOUS, Bp. of Chester, 1777.—FARDELL, co. Lincoln, and many others.

Boot: the boot is referred to under different designations, e.g. the *Irish brogue,* the *Dutch boot, Antique boot,* &c.: with these should be named the *shoe.*

Argent, a boot sable, top turned down or, soled gules—BOOT.
Or, three boots sable—HUSSEY.
Argent, three antique boots sable, spurs or—MANN.

Argent, two Dutch boots, the soles erect, embowed at the knee and endorsed sable, issuant out of a pile in base vert, spurred or—BOOTE.

Argent, a shoe proper, on a canton per chevron gules and ermine, three covered cups or, two and one—O'HAGAN.

Argent, three men's boots sable—COKER, co. Dorset.

Gules, a chevron between three brogues or—ARTHURE, Ireland.

Irish brogue.

Bordure, (fr.) or *Border :* this bearing, which is reckoned among the *sub-ordinaries,* occupies one-fifth of the field. It is generally used as the mark of a younger branch of a family. Charged bordures in ancient armoury are supposed to allude to maternal descent. In some cases they are possibly *augmentations.* It is, however, evident from the bordure being sometimes the only charge in a coat, that it is a distinct and original bearing.

Ermine, a bordure gules—HUNDESCOTE.

Or, a bordure vair—GWINE, or GYNES.

Ermine, a bordure compony or and sable— RENDELL, Harl. MS., 1441.

HUNDESCOTE.

The bordure is placed over all ordinaries, except the chief, the quarter, and the canton, which invariably surmount it, with perhaps some few exceptions, which are in such cases to be specially described.

Azure, a chief paly of six gules and or within a bordure engrailed sable—KEITH, Scotland.

Quarterly gules and or a bordure counterchanged; over all a chevron vair—FENWYKE.

When a coat having a bordure is *impaled* with another coat the bordure may be omitted where they join. [See *Impaling.*] If it be charged with eight bezants (for example) only three whole ones will be seen, and two halves. *Quartered* coats, on the other hand, should retain their bordures entire.

Quarterly, first and fourth France and England quartered within a bordure argent; second and third or, a chevron gules—STAFFORD, Duke of Buckingham.

STAFFORD.

When a bordure is *bezanté, billetté,* or the like, the number of bezants or billets is generally eight, unless some other number is particularized. The arms of Richard, King of the Romans, are represented sometimes with eight, sometimes with more, *bezants,* q. v.

Bordures charged with *bends* (blazoned *bendy*), *bars chevrons,* or other ordinaries, shew only those portions of the charges which would have fallen upon the bordure if it had composed a part of a field so charged.

The line of the *bordure* may be *indented* (e.g. DE VERE), *wavy, embattled, engrailed, recerselé,* &c.

It may also be *chequy lozengy, vair,* and the like.

HUGH DE VERE.

Sire Hue de VEER quartile de or e de goules a un molet de argent od la bordure endente de sable—Roll, temp. ED. II.

John le FITZ GEFFREY, esquartele d'or et de goules, a la bordur de verree [i.e. *vair*]—Roll, HEN. III.

William de SAY, autiel [i.e. the same] sans le bordure—*Ibid.*

A *bordure compony* should consist of sixteen pieces. It was supposed to have been a mark of illegitimacy, in cases where a natural son has succeeded by bequest to the estates of his father.

Bordure enaluron : a name given to one charged with eight birds of any kind, and it may be blazoned an *enaluron* of (say) eagles, which would imply that it was a border, and that it was charged with eight eagles. The word is probably only a corruption of the French *en orle.*

Analogous to the above is the *Bordure entoyer* or *entier :* charged with eight figures of any kind, except animals or plants, and *Bordure verdoy,* charged with eight leaves or flowers.

Gules, three garbs, within a bordure engrailed or, entoyré of pomeis—KEMP.

Or, a lion rampant azure armed and langued argent, within a bordure of the second entowry of mitres-gold—William of S. Mary-Church, Bp. of LONDON, 1199—1221.

Boson. See *Arrow.*
Boss. See *Bit.*

Boteroll, (fr. *bouterolle*). See *Scabbard,* under *Sword.*

Bordure enurney, charged with eight beasts, and so *bordure of England* is a bordure gules, *enurney* of lions, i.e. charged with eight lions of England.

Le Comte de RUGEMOND les armes de GARENE a un quarter de ermine, od la bordure de Engleterre—Roll, temp, ED, II.

The *Bordure of France* is azure, charged with eight fleurs-de-lis or: and the *Bordure of Scotland* is the double tressure flory counter flory gules, or more properly, a bordure or, charged with such a tressure.

The bordure has no diminutive, but it is said that one may be surmounted by another of half its width. It is not the same as the *Orle,* though so used by some writers.

Bottle, *Leather :* borne only by the Company.

Argent, on a chevron between three leather-bottles sable, as many bugle-horns stringed of the first—Company of BOTTLE-MAKERS and HORNERS [Incorporated 1638].

Bottle.

Bow, (fr. *Arc*) : the *long-bow, hand-bow,* or *string-bow,* and the *cross-bow* (fr. *arbalette*), as well as *arrows,* are of frequent occurrence in coat-armour. In one case the term *stone-bow* occurs, in allusion to the name ; in another, an *antique-bow.* Their position should be mentioned, and also whether they are *strung* of a different tincture. The *bowstring* also occurs alone.

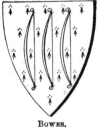

Ermine three long bows, in fesse gules—BOWES.

Argent, a chevron between three stone-bows sable—HURLESTONE.

Azure, an antique bow in fesse and arrow in pale argent—MULLER.

Azure, a bowstring in fesse fretted with eight arrows interlaced in bend dexter and sinister, argent and feathered or—Town of SHEFFIELD.

Gules, two long bows bent and interlaced in saltire or stringed argent, between four bezants each charged with a fleur-de-lis azure—REBOW, Essex, 1685.

BOWES.

Botonné. See *Cross,* § 14.

Bouclé, (fr.) : buckled, i.e. having a buckle ; e.g. of a collar.

Bourchier's-knot. See *Cords.*

Bourdon. See *Pilgrim's Staff.*

Bourdonné : terminating in a round knob, or pomel. See *Cross* pomellée, § 29.

Bout, or *Bouse,* and *bouz :* contracted forms of *water-bouget.*

Boutonné, (fr.) : of flowers, having the centre, or bouton, of a different tincture.

Bowed. See *Embowed.*

Bower. See *Wood.*

Sable, a hand-bow in bend between two pheons argent—CARWARDING, Hertford.

Sable, two string-bows endorsed in pale or, garnished gules, between two bundles of arrows in fesse, three in each, gold, barbed and headed argent, tied as the third—BENBOW, Scotland.

Argent, two bows one within the other in saltire gules, strung or—BOWMAN.

Ermine, a cross-bow bent in pale gules—ALBASTER, Stafford.

Ermine, a cross-bow bent point downwards, between three moorcocks sable—HIGHMORE, Cumberland, temp. HEN. IV.

Bowl: called *open* or *standing-bowls*, and in one case *wassail-bowls*. They are represented as ordinary bowls.

Or, two bars gules, on a chief argent three open bowls of the second, the insides of the third—HALGHTON.

Azure, three standing-bowls argent, out of each a boar's head or—BOWLES, co. Lincoln.

Gules, on a bend sable, three wassail bowls or—CHRISTMAS, Kent.

Braced, written *brased, embraced, brazed:* i.e. interlaced, as the *chevronels* in the arms here figured, or as the *annulets*, q.v.

FITZ-HUGH.

Azure, three chevronels braced (or interlaced) in the base of the escutcheon or, a chief of the last —Robert FITZ-HUGH, Bp. of London, 1431-36.

Sable, six annulets braced palewise in pairs argent two and one—ANDERTON, Lancaster.

Bracket: one instance occurs of this device only.

Argent, three double brackets sable—BIDDLE.

Bream, and *sea-bream*: these appear to be two different kinds of fish; the former, or *carp-bream*, as it is called (*cyprinus* of Linnæus, and *abramis* of later naturalists), is a fish which inhabits rivers and lakes, and in some districts is plentiful. The latter is the marine fish of that name (*sparus* of Linnæus, *pagrus vulgaris* of later writers), and is said to be taken frequently in the Mediterranean by anglers. The arms of Doxey are often, however, blazoned as "three halves."

Azure, three breams bendwise, 2 and 1, or—DE LA MARE, Abbot of Peterborough.

Gules, three breams haurient argent—DE LA MARE, Fisherton, Wilts.

Vert, three sea-breams haurient or—DOXEY.

Azure, three breams or—BREAME, Essex.

Brick: a charge resembling a *billet*, but shewing its thickness in perspective. Only one instance occurs.

DE LA MARE.

Argent, a rose between three bricks sable—BRICKS.

Brick-kiln: this occurs but in one coat of arms.

Argent, on a mount in base vert, a brick-kiln of four stories gules flamant and fumant on the second and top stories—BRICKILL.

Bridle: this occurs but seldom by itself, though a horse with bridle, or *bridled,* is not unfrequent.

Argent, a bridle or—BRIDLED, Devon.

Argent, a horse's head gules bridled of the first—GRONO GOCH.

Argent, a horse's head erased sable bridled or—FLINN.

Bridge, (fr. *pont*): when this charge occurs, the number of its arches, and all its other peculiarities, should be carefully noticed in the blazon. The charge occurs in the insignia of several towns, e.g. BIDEFORD, BRIDGWATER, GRAMPOUND, &c.

Gules, a bridge of one arch argent, masoned sable, with a stream transfluent proper—BRIDGE, Scotland.

Gules, three bridges of as many arches . . CRAIG, Ireland.

Azure, a bridge of two arches argent—POUNT.

Or, on a bridge of three arches gules, masoned sable, the streams transfluent proper, a fane argent—TROWBRIDGE, Wilts. [Another, the field argent, the flag or. Another, as above, a tower gules, thereon a fane argent.]

TROWBRIDGE.

Breast-plate. See *Cuirass.*

Breathing: applied to the stag, has the same meaning as *at gaze.*

Bretesse. See *Embattled.*

Breys, *brize,* or *broyes :* old fr. word for the horse *barnacle.*

Brilliants. See *Diamond.*

Brimsey. See *Gad-fly.*

Brisé, (fr.) : 1. broken, as of *chevrons,* &c.; 2. *debruised.*

Brisures, (fr.). See *Cadency;* also *Augmentation;* also note '*debruised.*'

Britannia: this figure occurs on the seal of the BANK OF ENG-
LAND, and of the Commissioners of "TRADE AND PLANTATIONS."

The figure is represented on an island, seated and holding in the right
hand an olive-branch, in the left a spear erect, surmounted with the cap
of liberty, her arm resting on a shield charged with the union cross,
and near it several bales of goods lying on the ground: over all is the
legend, 'TRADE AND PLANTATIONS.'

Broom: the common wild shrub of this name is the *Cytisus*
scoparius of botanists, the *Planta-genista* (fr.
genêt) of old writers. A sprig of this shrub was
chosen as the badge of the royal house of Plantagenet, who are said to have derived their surname from the circumstance of one of their
ancestors having worn a branch of broom in his
helmet, either by way of penance, or in token
of humility, of which the broom is a symbol. It
appears on the Great Seals of Ric. I.

Planta-genista.

Louis IX., of France, also instituted an order of knighthood
under the name of this flower, with the motto EXALTAT HUMILES.

Azure, a hand erect between three broomslips proper—BROOME, Salop
Vert, semy of broomslips, and over all a lion rampant or—Sandde
HARDE, Denbigh.

Argent, three broom-branches vert—BROME, Somerset.

Brush, (fr. *brosse*): the *block-brush* is perhaps the most important; it represents a bunch of the herb called
knee-holm, or sometimes *knee-holly* (the knee-holy of
monastic, and *ruscus* of modern botanists), used by
butchers to clean their blocks, hence called *butcher's*
broom. It is borne in the insignia of the BUTCHERS'
Company, q.v. under Slaughter-*axe*, but has often
been drawn as a *garbe* or wheatsheaf.

Block-brush.

Broohant, or *Bronchant*: an old
French term signifying placed
over a field semé of any small
charges, but used by modern
French writers for overlying generally.

Broaches. See 1. *Embroiderers;*
2. *Winepress.*
Brock. See *Badger.*
Brocket: a young stag. See *Deer.*
Brogue, Irish. See *Boot.*
Brown. See *Colour.*
Browsing. See *Deer.*

The *Besom* is also found mentioned, and a *flat-brush* (such as is used by whitewashers) is borne in the arms of the PLASTERERS' Company. See *Hammer*.

Argent, on a chevron azure three brushes of the first —PENWALLIS.

Azure, two besoms in saltire or —DURSTON.

Argent, a chevron between three besoms gules—BROME.

Flat-brush.

Bucket: of buckets there are several varieties. That most usually borne in arms is the common *well-bucket*, but they are sometimes hooped and have feet; they are sometimes blazoned *dossers*. See under *Water-bouget*.

Argent, three well-buckets with feet sable, hoops and handles or—PEMBERTON, Yorkshire.

Bucket.

Argent, an annulet suspending two buckets saltire-wise sable between three fleurs-de-lys gules—BANNISTER.

Argent, a fess between three pails sable hooped and handled or—FITZ HOW.

Buckle (fr. *boucle*), or *fermail* (old fr. *fermaille*): from an early period buckles were used as charges.

Sire William ROSSELYN de azure a iij fermaus de or—Roll, temp. ED. II.

Sire Peres ROSSELYN de goules a iij fermauls de argent—*Ibid*.

ROSSELYN.

Sire Robert MALET de sable a un cheveron e iij fe:mals de argent—Ibid.

As buckles of various forms occurred in heraldry it became necessary to mention the shape. An *arming-buckle* is in the form of a lozenge.

Azure, an arming-buckle argent, between three boar's heads or—FERGUSON, Kilkerran.

Argent, three lozenge- (or mascle-, or arming-) buckles gules—JERNINGHAM or JERNEGAN, Suff.

Arming-buckle.   Square buckle.

Argent, a fesse sable in the dexter chief a square buckle gules—GILBY.

Brusk. See *Tenné*.
Bubble. See *Water*.

Buck. See *Deer*.
Buckler. See *Shield*.

We find besides, square buckles, circular buckles, and even oval buckles figured. In some examples the tongues are turned to the dexter, in others to the sinister; and to the variety of buckles may be added the *gar* buckle (possibly contraction for *garter* buckles), and the *belt-buckle*.

Sable, three round buckles argent, tongues pendent—JODDREL, Cheshire.

Azure, three gar-buckles argent (possibly garter-buckles)—STUKELEY.

Argent, a chevron between three circular buckles sable—TRECOTHIK.

Round buckle.   Round buckle.

Or, a lion rampant gules; over all on a bend wavy sable an oval buckle tongue upwards, between two mascles argent—SPENCE, Edinburgh.

Argent, three belt-buckles sable—SAPCOTT.

Argent, a fesse azure between three belt-buckles gules —BRADLEY.

With cross-bar.

A strap or garter with a buckle may be termed *buckled*, and generally the buckle is of another tincture.

Gules, three men's garters nowed and buckled argent—SYDEMERS.

Bugle-horn, or *hanchet* (fr. *huchet*): this may be *garnished* with encircling rings or *virols*, and with French heralds the end opening may be *enguiché* of another tincture. It is usually *stringed*, i.e. suspended by strings.

Argent, a torteau between three bugle-horns gules stringed or—VARNECK, Baron Huntingfield.

Argent, a bugle-horn sable, stringed gules—DOWNES.

Argent, a bugle-horn sable garnished gules, within the baldrick a mullet, in chief three holly-leaves proper—BURNET, Bp. of Salisbury, 1689.

Argent, an arrow or, feathered gules, between three bugle-horns stringed sable, and interlacing the lower one—HAULE, Devon.

Vert, three greyhounds courant argent, on a chief of the last as many bugle-horns sable, stringed gules—HUNTER.

VARNECK.

DOWNES.

The *Hunting-horn* (fr. *cor de chasse*) is often represented as the *bugle-horn ;* another form is shewn in
the margin; there is also the *trumpet*, q.v.

Azure, a hare salient argent, round the neck a hunting-
horn sable, stringed gules—KINEILAND, Scotland.

Hunting-horn.

Gules, two huntsman's horns in saltire between four
crosses crosslet or—NEVILL.

The *Cornet* is named in some works (but probably erroneously) as borne by HULME Abbey. See under *Crosier*.

Sable, a crozier in pale or with two ribbons (or tassels) entwined about
it argent, between four golden cornets (should be coronets)—Benedictine
Abbey of HULME.

Bull, (fr. *taureau*): is rare in ancient rolls of arms, but in
later times tolerably frequent; and we find also the *ox* (fr.
bœuf), the *cow* (fr. *vache*), and the *calf* (fr. *veau*), all duly blazoned; the latter is distinguished in heraldry by the absence of
the horns: the term *buffalo* (fr. *buffle*) is rarely used in English
blazon for bull. The charge is often used associated with the
name, as in the case of OXFORD, OXENDON, &c. A bull may be
horned, hoofed, unguled, and *armed* of a different tincture; and
it may be *collared*, and even *belled* (fr. *clariné*). *Moile* (drawn
erroneously as a mule) is really an ox without horns.

Bendy wavy argent and azure, an ox gules
passing over a ford proper—City of OXFORD [ac-
cording to some ; according to others, Argent, an
ox gules, armed and unguled or, passing a ford
of water in base proper].

Ermine, a bull passant gules armed and unguled or—BEVILLE.

Argent, a chevron between three bulls passant
sable—OXENDON.

Or, a bull passant sable collared and belled
gold—HULL, Dorset (? temp. Hen. III.).

City of OXFORD.

Argent, an ox passant gules through reeds proper—RIDLEY.

Argent, a fess gules between three oxen sable—OXLEY, Yorkshire.

Ermine, a cow statant gules within a bordure sable, bezanty, a crescent for difference—CORVELL.

Buffalo. See *Bull*.
Bullet : the *ogress* or *pellet*.

Bulfinch. See *Finch*.
Bulrushes. See *Reeds*.

Argent, three cows passant sable, eyes gules, collared or—Benedictine Alien Priory at COWICK, Devon.

Ermine, a calf passant gules—CAVELL, Cornwall.

Argent, a fess gules between three calves passant sable—CALVERLEY.

Argent, on a bend sable three calves passant or—VEAL.

Gules, a moile passant argent—MOILE, Cornwall.

Bulls' heads are perhaps more commonly found than the animal itself, generally *erased*, sometimes *couped*, rarely *caboshed*. Generally the *horns* are blazoned of a different tincture. It is not certain what is meant by the *sea*-bull's *head* blazoned below.

Argent, a bull's head erased sable—TURNBULL, Scotland.

Argent, a chevron gules between three bull's heads couped sable—BULLEINE [the same family as Anne BOLEYN, one of Henry the Eighth's Queens].

TURNBULL.

Argent, three bull's heads caboshed sable, armed or—WALROND.

Argent, three bull's heads erased sable, breathing fire proper—TRUMBULL, Berks.

Argent, three cow's heads erased sable—VACH or VEITCH.

A bull armed or is one of the supporters to the arms of DARCY, Westmeath.

Argent, a sea-bull's head couped sable—BULLOCK.

WALROND.

Bunting, or *bunten :* this refers to the English species of the *Emberiza* (called sometimes the Corn-bunting). It has only been adopted for the sake of the name, as will be seen.

Argent, a bend gules between three bunten-birds proper—BUNTEN, Ardoch, Scotland.

Argent, three bunten birds azure; on a chief of the last a sword fess-wise as the first, hilt and pomel or—BUNTEN, Kilbride, Scotland.

Argent, a bend engrailed gules between three bunting-birds proper—BONTEINE, Mildovan.

Argent, a chevron sable between three bunten-birds proper—BUNTEN, Buntenhall, Scotland.

Quarterly or and gules three birds (probably buntings) counterchanged—BUNTING.

Bundle. See *Arrow, laths, cotton, reeds, silk, wire, wheat,* &c.

Burling-iron: an instrument used by WEAVERS. It is a sort of large pointed tweezers, held in the right hand to pick out knots and other defects left in the weaving. It occurs in the arms of their company at Exeter.

Burling-iron.

Sable, a chevron between three burling-irons argent—BURLAND.

Gules, three burling-irons argent—BURLINGER.

Bush: the simple term '*bushes*' occurs, but the *flaming* or *burning bush* is the most striking form. The latter is borne differently, as will be seen, by different branches of the BRANDER family.

Gules, from behind bushes vert, a stag courant argent, on a chief azure three castles of the field one and two—JAMES, Brecknock.

Gules, a flaming bush on the top of a mount proper, between three lions rampant argent, in the flanks two roses of the last—BRANDER, Elgin.

Gules, a burning bush proper between two roses argent in fesse, in chief two lions rampant, and a third in base of the last—BRANDER, Surrey.

Bustard: this bird, belonging to the genus *Otis,* is almost quite extinct in England, but is found generally distributed in Europe. One or two instances of its use occur.

Argent, a fesse between three bustards, gules--BUSTARD.

Azure, three bustards, rising argent—NEVILL.

Or, a chevron sable between three bustards vert—LANDON.

Argent, a chevron between three bustards gules—KITCHING, Hereford.

Argent, a cross engrailed azure, between four bustards respecting each other sable—SMALRIDGE, Bp. of Bristol, 1714–19.

Butterfly, (fr. *papillon*): this insect is generally borne *volant en arriere*, its four wings being expanded. When borne so, it is not necessary to add any intimation of its position.

The *harvest-fly* is nearly similar, but shews two wings only, and the legs prominently shewn. What it is intended to represent it is impossible to say.

Butterfly.

Burèles, and *burèlé*, (fr.) = *barrulets* and *barruly :* vide sub-*Bar.*

Burdock. See *Dock.*

Burgonette. See *Cap* of *Steel.*

Bur leaf. See *Dock.*

Burre, (old fr.): *cronel* of a lance.

Bust, (fr. *buste*). See *Heads.*

Butt-fish. See *Turbot.*

Argent, two bars between three butterflies volant sable—FLEMINGS.

Gules, a griffin passant, wings elevated argent; on a canton indented or, a butterfly volant azure—BUTTERFIELD, Surrey.

Argent, on a bend azure, three butterflies or—BUTTERWIKE.

Argent, on a bend sable, three butterflies of the first—BOTERFORD, Devon.

Harvest-fly.

Azure, a harvest-fly volant argent—BUTTERFLY.

Sable, a harvest-fly, volant en arriere—BOLOUR or BOLOWRE.

Buttrices: an old name for the knives used for paring horses' hoofs. They seem to be used solely for the punning on the name, but sometimes blazoned as *Farriers' Implements.*

Argent, three buttrices in fesse sable—BUTTRISS.

Azure, three buttrices, handles erect in fesse argent—BUTTRISCH.

Caboshed, *Cabossed,* or *Caboched,* otherwise *Trunked* (old fr. *caboche*) : terms applied to the heads of beasts, when borne full-faced and with no part of the neck being visible, so that it appears like the mark of a head. An example will be seen above, under *bull,* also under *leopard :* in the case of *leopards' heads,* however, as the word is not found used, it does not appear to be necessary. The term *rencontre* supplies the nearest equivalent in French heraldry ; thus arms here figured would be blazoned in French *rencontre de cerf.*

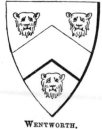

TRYE.

WENTWORTH.

Argent, a buck's head caboshed gules, attired or—TRYE, Glouc.

Sable, a chevron between three leopard's heads or—WENTWORTH.

Argent, in chief, sable three leopard's heads or—NORMAN.

Cabled, (fr. *câblé*) : 1. of a cross with a cable pattern, i.e. of twisted rope ; 2. of an anchor, &c., having a rope cable.

Cabré (fr.) is applied by French heralds to a horse which, brought to a check, is rearing (but not so much as *acculé*).

Cadency, *marks of,* otherwise called *Distinctions,* or *Differences* (fr. *brisures*): variations of the original arms of a family, or marks attached to them for the purpose of pointing out the several branches, and the relation in which they stand to each other and to their common ancestor.

In ancient heraldry "a plain *Label*" (as Sir N. H. Nicolas remarks), "most frequently azure, appears to have been the distinction of the eldest son and heir apparent;" as, for instance, at the Siege of Caerlaverock, Maurice de BERKELEY, who joined in the expedition, is described as having over his arms (gules, crusilly with a white chevron) a label azure, because his father was still alive:

"E. Morices de Berkelée,   Croissillie o un chievron blanc,
  Ki compaigns fu de cele alée,   Ou un label de asur avoit,
  Banier ot vermeille cum sanc,   Por ce que ses peres vivoit."

And again, one bore his arms in no manner different from his father [the Earl of Lennox] except the *azure* label:

"Cele au Conte de Laonois . . . .   Ne la portoit par nul aconte
  Patrik de Dunbar, fiz le Conte   Fors de une label de *inde* diverse."

It also appears "that younger sons bore the label variously charged, sometimes with the whole or part of their mother's arms, or the arms of a distinguished family from which they were descended; that more distant branches changed the colours, or charges, of the coat; placed a bend over it; surrounded it with a bordure, or assumed a canton, plain or charged."

Although the charge of tinctures, and the addition, removal, or alteration of charges are very frequently marks of *cadency*, it must not be supposed that all families of the same name, and between whose arms there is some resemblance, are descended from the same ancestors, for the arms of ancient families have often been very unjustly granted with slight alterations to persons whose relation to such families consisted only in similarity of name.

The differences now in use may be divided into two classes; those used by the royal family, and those which should be borne by all others. The sons and daughters of the sovereign all bear labels of three points argent. That of the Prince of Wales is plain, but those of the other princes and princesses are charged with crosses, fleurs-de-lis, hearts, or other figures for the sake of distinction. Princes and princesses, being the sons and daughters of the above, are distinguished by *labels of five points* charged in the same manner. All such differences should be borne on the arms, crest, and supporters.

The *differences* now in use for all families except that of the sovereign may be partially traced to the time of Edward III. They are as follows :—

I.　　　　II.　　　　III.　　　　IV.　　　　V.　　　　VI.

FIRST HOUSE.

First son. A *label* of 3 points.　　Fourth son. A *martlet*.

Second son. A *crescent*.　　　　Fifth son. An *annulet*.

Third son. A *mullet*.　　　　　Sixth son. A *fleur-de-lis*.

Some heralds pretend that the seventh son was marked by a *rose*, the eighth by a *cross moline*, and the ninth by *eightfoil;* but this theory does not seem to be borne out in practice.

The first son of the first son of the first house bears a label upon a label (or more agreeably to ancient custom a label of five points). The second a label charged with a crescent, and so on for all other sons of this branch.

SECOND HOUSE. First son. A crescent charged with label of three points.

Second son. A crescent charged with a crescent.

And so on for the rest, but it is not usual to bear more than double differences. There are no differences for sisters (except in the royal family), as they are all equal, but they should bear the differences which pertain to their fathers.

Crescents, mullets, &c., used as differences, should be drawn smaller than usual, to distinguish them from ordinary charges. They may be placed upon any part of the arms which is most convenient. There does not appear to be any rule respecting their tinctures.

Sire Johan FILOL, de veer a un quarter de goules. Sire Johan sun filz meisme les armes en le quarter un molet de or—Roll, temp. ED. II.

Caduceus, (fr. *caducée*): the rod of Mercury, with wings attached, and two snakes round it. Used chiefly as a crest.

Per saltire or and erminois, on a saltire azure between a caduceus in chief and a pine-apple in base proper, two swords in saltire argent, pomels and hilts gold—BARROW, Bath.

Caltrap, written also *Calthrop,* and *Galtrap,* and by French heralds *Chausse-trap,* is an abbreviated form of *Cheval-trap:* an instrument thrown upon the ground to injure feet of horses, consisting of four iron spikes, one of which is ever uppermost.

Caltrap.

Argent, three cheval-traps sable—TRAP, Glouc.

Azure, a cross between four caltraps or—WESTFALING, Bp. of Hereford, 1586—1603.

Vert, on a lion rampant or caltraps sable—LIGHTORLES.

Camel : the camel is borne but on few arms. Several branches of the CAMMEL family bear it.

Argent, a chevron between three camels sable—CAMMEL.

Azure, a camel statant argent—CAMELL.

Argent, a camel passing through a ford of water proper—CAMELFORD.

Also borne by the following :—FALLOWES, Cheshire ; FALWITZ, Alderley; CLOVES, Wilts.; WHEELER, Surrey ; WILKIE of St. Vincent [a Camel's head] ; STUTOILE [Ibid].

Cameleon, or *Chameleon :* the proper tincture is green, and it is drawn as in the margin.

Argent, a chevron sable between three cameleons vert—LANDON.

Azure, in chief a sun or, in base a chameleon on sandy ground proper—ORY.

Cameleon.

Sable, three chameleons erect or, within a bordure argent charged with eight martlets sable—WORTHAM.

Camelopardel : the camelopard, or giraffe, with two long horns slightly curved backward, used only as a *crest.*

Candlestick, (fr. *chandelier*). The *taper-candlestick,* borne in the arms of the FOUNDERS' Company, and usually drawn as represented in the annexed engraving, has a spike, or, as it is technically termed, a *pricket,* upon which the taper is placed. Vide also *Mortcour,* which is used at funerals.

Candle-stick.

Calamine stone. See *Metal.*

Calf. See *Bull.*

Campaned: having bells attached.

Cannelé, (fr.) *invected.*

Or, three candlesticks sable—KYLE, Scotland.

Azure, two candlesticks [? chalices] in fesse or—EMERLE.

Ermine, three candlesticks, each enfiled with a wreath of laurel, and in chief . . .—TORRENS.

. . . . A book expanded having a candlestick with a lighted candle in it above the book, on the leaves the words 'Lucerna pedibus,' &c.—College of S. Mary, MANCHESTER.

Canting Arms (sometimes called *allusive* or *punning arms,* and by French heralds, *armes parlantes*) are very generally distributed. They are arms containing charges which are allusive to the name of the bearer. A few examples are annexed.

Gules, a castle triple towered or, and argent, a lion rampant gules (sometimes purpure, and often crowned or), quarterly—The kingdom of CASTILE and LEON.

Sable, six swallows (fr. *hirondelles*), 3, 2, 1, argent—ARUNDEL, Wardour, Wilts.

Barry of six, argent and gules—BARRY, Ireland.

Gules, three covered cups or—BUTLER. [This family was originally named FITZWALTER, and bore Or, a chief indented azure, but one of them being appointed to the

CASTILE.

office of lord Butler of Ireland, they took the surname of BUTLER at the same time as their arms.]

Argent, three eagles displayed gules—EGLESFIELD, Cumb. (Founder of Queen's College, Oxford, 1340).

Argent, three eels naiant in pale sable—ELLIS, Norf.

Crest, a holy lamb—EVANS, Wales. [This is an allusion to S. John the Baptist; Evan being the Welsh form of the Christian name John.]

Gules, on a chevron between three ostrich feathers argent, a pellet (or gun-stone)—FETHERSTON, Herts.

Argent, on a mount in base vert, a hart lodged gules—HARTHILL.

Crest, a talbot's head couped argent, collared sable, to the collar a ring of the first—HAYWARD, Surrey. [This is a specimen of heraldic allusions of a more recondite character, the reference being to the Saxon haᵹan-peaþð, a house-dog.]

Or, three boots (hosen) sable—HUSSEY.

Azure, a cross moline or—MOLINEUX, Hawkley, Lanc.

Gules, a fesse between four dexter hands couped argent—QUATRE-MAYNE, Oxfordsh.

Azure, seven acorns, 2, 3, 2, or—SEVENOKE (Lord Mayor of London, 1418).

Argent, a stork sable, beaked and membered gules—STARKEY, Chesh.

Azure, two trumpets pileways, between eight cross crosslets, 3, 3, 2, or—TRUMPINGTON, Cambr. (Sir Roger de Trumpington, ob. 1289).

Many even of early coats of arms allude, in some way or other, to the names of their bearers, and perhaps more than is commonly suspected would be found to be so, if we could always recover the early chance names given to the charges of which they are composed.

Geoffrey de LUCY, de goules a trois lucies d'or—Roll, temp. HEN. III.

Nicholas de MOELES, d'argent a deux barres de goules, a trois molets en le cheif de goules—*Ibid.*

Thomas CORBETT, d'or, deux carbeaux noir—*Ibid.*

Roger de MERLEY, barree d'argent et de goulz, a la bordur d'azure, et merlots d'or en le bordur—*Ibid.*

Odinel HERON d'azur a trois herons d'argent—*Ibid.*

Armes parlantes do not often occur of later date than King James I., about which time they began to grow into disrepute from ignorance and misapplication, and were nick-named canting or punning arms. They were numerous at all preceding periods, not only in England, but throughout Christendom.

Canton, (fr. *canton,* but also *franc quartier* appears to be often used in this sense): resembles a first *quarter* of the shield in form, but of smaller dimensions; its size does not appear to be fixed, but is generally about one-third of the chief. In old French *cauntel,* (i.e.) *canton,* is used for *Quarter,* q.v.

When the word is used alone, a *dexter* canton is intended; it may, however, be placed upon the *sinister* side, if so blazoned, and when with a bend. Cantons *in base* occur upon foreign arms, but it is believed are never used in English armory.

The canton is sometimes the only charge in a coat; but generally it is supposed to be an *augmentation* of the original arms, or a *difference.*

Argent, a canton sable—Oliver SUTTON, Bp. of Lincoln, 1280–99; Charles SUTTON, Bp. of Norwich, 1792, and Abp. of Canterbury, 1805–28; [also SUTTON, Baron Lexington, 1645, and other families of that name].

SUTTON.

Argent, fretty gules, a canton azure—IREBY, Cumberland.

Gul. LONGESPE, dazur, a sis liuncels dor—Soun frer au tel a une cauntel dermine—Roll, temp. HEN. III.

Where there is a bordure the canton always surmounts it, and when borne upon a coat consisting of three charges (2 and 1) it generally covers the whole or greater part of the first. If more than three it generally covers the whole of one, if not of more. In very exceptional cases, however (and then the arrangement must be duly described), the canton itself is partially covered by some ordinary (e.g. a bend).

It is often charged with another bearing, though generally plain, and the most frequent tincture is ermine, which rather tends to bear out a theory that its origin was suggested by some badge of honour placed upon the shoulder of the warrior.

Sable, a lion rampant argent, on a canton of the last a cross gules (i.e. a canton of S. George) —CHURCHILL, Duke of Marlborough. [Arms of Earl of Marlborough, 1689.]

Gules, on a bordure sable eight estoiles or; on a canton ermine a lion rampant of the second; in fesse point an annulet of the third for difference—S. JOHN BAPTIST's College, Oxford [founded by Sir Thomas WHITE, 1557].

MARLBOROUGH.

Or, three lioncels passant sable langued gules; on a canton of the second three bezants—GODWIN, Bp. of Bath and Wells, 1584-90.

Monsire Philip le DESPENCER, port barre d'or et d'asur de vj peeces, a une quarter d'ermin— Roll, temp. ED. III.

Azure, six lions rampant argent; on a canton or a mullet gules—KIRBY, Kent. [The arms engraved are from Haseley Church, and perhaps are those of LONGESPEE, Earl of Salisbury, with the canton for a difference.]

KIRBY [?].

Sire Walter TOUK de sable, billeté de or e un quarter de ermyn—Roll, temp. ED. II.

Sire Rauf de ZEFOUL, d'argent, a une croys patee de verd; e en le cauntel un oysel de goulys —Roll, temp. ED. II.

Calvary.   See *Cross of.*

Canary.   See *Finch.*

Cannet.   See *Duck.*

Cannon.   See *Bell*, also *Gun.*

Cantoned.   A cross or saltire be-tween four charges is sometimes said to be *cantonnée*, or *cantoned* with such charges. A fesse joined to a canton is also sometimes called a fesse cantoned.

A *canton* and *fesse* of the same tincture, as in the arms of WOODVILLE, should join, without even a line to part them. The same remark will apply to the uppermost of two or more bars, when occurring with a canton; but this is not so with a bend. When a canton and chief occur on the same coat the canton overlies it.

WOODVILLE.

Argent, a fesse and canton gules—WOODVILLE.

Argent, two bars azure on a canton of the second a cinquefoil or—PYPARD. [From glass formerly at Haseley.]

Ernaud de BOYS, argent deux barres et ung canton goulez—Roll of Arms, temp. HEN. III.

Barry of six argent and azure, a chief ermine and a canton of the first—HOTHAM. [In some branches of the family a canton or.]

Barry wavy of six argent and sable, a chief gules and a canton ermine—BARLOW, Derby.

PYPARD.

Barry of six argent and sable; a canton quarterly or and argent—BELSTED, Norfolk.

Barry of five argent and gules, a canton as the last; over all a bend sable—Sire Johan du BOYS, Roll of Arms, 1308-14; M. Roger le BOYS, Roll of Arms, 1392-97.

Cap: the principal caps in use as charges, parts of crests, or accessories to coats of arms, are the following:

The *Lord Mayor's* cap usually placed over the insignia of the city of London, or arms of a lord mayor, is thus represented. It is worn by the sword-bearer, and is of brown fur.

Lord Mayor's Cap.

The caps borne by MAUNDEFELD are of a peculiar form, similar to that of the 'Doge's' cap. Those borne by DROKENSFORD, and called *pilia pastoralia* (if caps at all), were possibly similar.

Quarterly, azure and or four caps counterchanged—DROKENSFORD.

MAUNDEFELD.

The family of CAPPER bear caps, like the figure annexed.

Argent, three caps sable banded or—CAPPER, Cheshire.

CAPPER.

A *Cardinal's cap* or *hat* is always red, and has tassels pendent from its labels in five rows, instituted by Innocent IV., at the Council of Lyons, 1245. The continental archbishops and bishops (especially those of France) bear green hats of the same form over their mitres, the former with five rows of tassels, and the latter with four. A black cap of the same shape, with three rows of tassels, belongs to abbats. Prothonotaries use a similar hat with two rows of tassels. A black hat or cap, with one tassel on each side, belongs to all other clergymen.

Cardinal's Cap.

Cap of dignity or *maintenance*, called also *Chapeau*, is a cap generally of red velvet turned up with ermine, formerly peculiar to dukes (whence it is sometimes called a *duciper*), but now often used to place crests upon instead of a wreath.

Argent, three chapeaus sable (or caps of maintenance)—HALWORTH.

The cap of maintenance occurs as a charge in the insignia of the city of GLOU-CESTER, and on the seals of Towns of WALLINGFORD and STAINES.

Cap of Maintenance.

The term *chapeau*, however, is variously used for a cap or hat of any kind. In the arms of COPE it is probably a cap of maintenance; in that of KINGESTON it is probably a hat of some kind.

Quarterly ermine and azure, a chapeau gules turned up of the first between two greyhounds courant in pale or—COPE, Osbaston, Leicester.

Argent, a chapeau azure [elsewhere a steel cap proper], with a plume of ostrich feathers in front gules—John KINGESTON, 1390.

The *doctor's cap* in the arms of SUGAR refers probably to the University degree.

Sable, three sugar-loaves argent, in chief a doctor's cap proper—SUGAR, Somerset.

The *long Cap*, of a peculiar shape, which occurs in the crests of WALPOLE and BRYDGES, is shewn in the margin, and a cap somewhat similar is termed an *Albanian bonnet*, probably that worn by the peasantry.

Azure, a trois bonnets Albanois d'or—VAUX, France.

Long Cap.

The *Abacot*, a mere corruption of *bycocket*, is said in Spelman's Glossary to have been given to a cap worn by ancient kings of England, and is so copied into heraldic books.

The *Infula* is used in one case in the sense of a cap.

Argent, an infula embowed at the end gules, turned up in form of a hat, and engrailed with a button and tassel at the top or—BRUNT.

Caps of Steel: of these there are various kinds, and they cannot properly be included under the term helmet. The first is the *Basinet* (fr.), or *Basnet*, properly a plain circular helmet resembling a basin, though sometimes they are drawn (improperly) like squires' helmets. The *Burgonet* is a steel cap, worn chiefly by foot-soldiers, and of the shape shewn in the margin.

Burgonet.

There is also the *Morion* (fr. *chapeau de fer*), which was worn by foot-soldiers, and is usually of the plain shape annexed, but it may be ornamented. In many ancient examples the points of these morions are turned to the dexter.

A somewhat different morion is given on the crest of CECIL, Marquis of Salisbury.

Morion.

Argent, a chevron gules between three basnets proper—BASNET.

Argent, a fesse azure between three burgonettes [elsewhere morions] of the second garnished and nailed or—EVINGTON, Enfield, 1614.

Morion.

Argent, a chevron gules between three morions proper—BRUDENEL, Earl of Cardigan.

Caps (fr. *chaperons*) are also used for *Falcons*, q.v.

Caparison, or *housing* (old fr. *barde*): the embroidered covering of a horse, which was often charged with the arms of the knight to whom the horse belonged, as on the seal of Edward CROUCHBACK, Earl of Lancaster. The horses represented upon his monument, and that of AYMER DE VALENCE, both in Westminster Abbey, are examples of the practice. The horses upon the great seals of King Edward I. and many of his successors are caparisoned with the royal arms.

All animals embroidered upon the housing of a horse should face his head. The same may be said of all charges which are different on each side; thus a bend upon the right side of the caparison of a horse would appear as a bend sinister.

Cards: playing cards are used in the arms of the company.

Gules, on a cross argent between in chief the aces of hearts and diamonds, but in base the aces of clubs and spades proper, a lion passant guardant—Company of CARDMAKERS.

Carnation: (1) improperly used for flesh-colour, as no such tincture is recognised in heraldry (but frequent with French heralds); (2) a flower. The *pink* is also found.

Argent, three carnations gules, stalked and leaved vert—NOYCE.

Azure, on a bend or within a bordure argent two pinks, slipped proper—WADE.

Pinks are also borne by families of EDSIR (Surrey), of MARLOW, and of LEVINGSTON, and by SKEVINGTON, Bp. of Bangor, 1510–33.

Castle, (fr. *chateau*): the word castle used alone generally signifies either a single *Tower*, q.v. or two towers with a gate between them. A *castle triple-towered* is represented in the ensign of the kingdom of CASTILE, and is frequently found quartered in the arms of Queen Eleanor. The illustration is from glass still existing in Dorchester Church, Oxon.

Argent, a lion rampant sable, quartering gules, a castle triple-towered or—CASTILE and LEON.

Gules, three castles triple-towered within the royal tressure argent—Burgh of ABERDEEN.

CASTILE.

Sable, a castle triple-towered or — TOWERS, Bp. of Peterborough, 1639–49.

Amongst other varieties which occur, are *triangular* and *quadrangular* castles; castles seen *in perspective,* and castles extending quite across the field. Castles are also described as *domed, turreted* (fr. *donjonné*), *embattled, breached, &c.,* and it is not uncommon to describe in detail *towers, gates, loopholes, windows, vanes, portcullises,* and the like. Where the masonry is shewn by the addition of lines the term *masoned* is used. The windows and doors are sometimes represented as of a different tincture, and then are supposed to be closed; and the same if they are of that of the castle itself; but if of the tincture of the field they are supposed to be open, and the term *ajouré* might be used. *Coulissé* signifies that the *portcullis* is down.

Sable, two bars between three castles masoned or—CLEAVER, Bp. of Chester, 1788; of Bangor, 1800; and of S. Asaph, 1806-15.

Gules, a castle towered and domed argent, masoned sable; on the dome a flag—Town of BARNSTAPLE, Devon.

Sable, a castle with towers turreted in perspective argent standing in water wavy azure and argent—CASTLEFORD.

Per fesse azure and argent; in base on a rock a castle breached, the Indian colours struck and flag-staff proper; in chief two eagles rising or —STIBBERT, London (1768).

Argent, a castle (or tower) triple-towered sable, chained transverse the port or—OLDCASTLE, Kent.

Per fesse vert and gules, in base a lion passant guardant or; in chief a quadrangle of castles walled argent—Town of LANCASTER.

Argent, on a rock proper a castle triple-towered and embattled sable, masoned of the first, and topped with three vanes gules, windows and portcullis shut of the last—City of EDINBURGH.

Sometimes the terms *Fort, Fortress, Citadel,* &c., are used. The Castle, too, may be surrounded with a *fortification.*

Argent, on a fesse azure, between two Cornish Choughs proper in chief, and in base a lion passant gules crowned or, a fort of the field—GARSTON.

Vert, on a chevron embattled . . . &c.; a chief charged with the gates and fortress of Seringapatam proper—HARRIS, Baron Harris, 1815.

Per chevron azure and argent . . . . and on a chief silver the fortress of Khelat; a canton charged with the Dooranee badge—WILTSHIRE, 1840.

Per chevron vert and argent; on a chevron or between, in chief two castles of the second, in base another surrounded by a fortification proper, three torteaux—GREEN, Kent, Baronetcy, 1786.

In connection with the Castle the *Barbican* (that is to say the advanced work) is described in some insignia, and the projecting turrets overhanging the embattled wall, called *Bartizans*, in others. Other additions are occasionally named, e.g. a *trench*, or the castle, may be standing in *water* or surrounded by a *wall*.

Gules, the barbican of a castle having loopholes, gate, and portcullis, with two pointed side towers; on each of the latter a pennon waving argent, and ensigned on the centre of the battlement by a royal coronet or—Town of DONCASTER.

Gules, out of water in base, an embattled wall enclosing a castle with three gables from the embattled parapet, a piece of tapestry hung along the front between the bartizans and displaying three *shields* [shields described] . . . Town of NEWCASTLE-UNDER-LYNE.

JANE SEYMOUR.

The *badge* of Jane Seymour, third queen of Henry VIII., blazoned upon a grant of lands made to her in 1536, presents a good example of a castle. The tinctures are as follows:—

The walls argent, the ground vert, the tree of the same fructed gules, the Phœnix or, in flames proper, and the roses alternately white and red.

Castles occur rarely in the old rolls of arms.

Monsire de GRANSON pale d'argent et d'azure de vi. piéces, a chastelez d'or en une bend gules—Roll, temp. ED. III.

The Castle is borne very frequently in the insignia of cities and towns, with other charges; of these insignia, however, the evidence is often only derived from the seal. The following may be named, but the list might probably be extended.

ABERDEEN; BARNSTAPLE; BEDFORD; BERKHAMSTEAD, (Hertford); BISHOPS CASTLE, (Salop); BOSNEY, (Cornwall); BRIDPORT; BRIDGEWATER, (Somerset); BRIDGENORTH, (Salop); BRISTOL; CARDIGAN; CARLISLE; CARMARTHEN; CLITHERO, (Lancashire); CORFE, (Dorset); DENBIGH; DEVIZES; DONCASTER; DORCHESTER, (Dorset); DUBLIN; DUNBAR; EDINBURGH; EXETER; FORFAR, (Scotland); GUILDFORD, (Surrey); HAVERFORDWEST; KINGHORN, (Scotland); KNARESBOROUGH; LANCASTER; LAUNCESTON, (Cornwall); LINCOLN; LUDGERSHALL, MALMESBURY; NEWBURY; NEWCASTLE under Lyne; NEWCASTLE upon Tyne, (three); NORTHAMPTON; NORWICH; ORFORD; PEMBROKE; PLYMOUTH; PONTEFRACT; QUEENBORO'; SAFFRON WALDEN; STAFFORD; TAUNTON; TEWKESBURY; THETFORD; TIVERTON; WARWICK; WINCHESTER (five); WORCESTER; YARMOUTH, (Hants).

Cat, (fr. *chat*): occurs not infrequently. Probably the wild-cat is generally intended, though the special reference to the *Cat-a-mountain* in several arms seems to imply a distinction. A *spotted cat* is also referred to.

Cats are found blazoned most frequently *passant*, but also *rampant, salient, statant,* and *couchant*. With French heralds the term *effarouché* is used to signify the cat when rampant (as if scared), and *herissonée* with 'the back up.' The *wild-cat* is supposed always to be represented *guardant*, although it be not stated in the blazoning. *Musion*, a fanciful name for a cat, is used by Bossewell.

A *cat's head* is also found on one coat.

KEATE.

Argent, two cats passant gules—Catt.

Gules, two cats passant guardant argent—Catton.

Per fesse azure and vert, in chief a cat argent couchant, coward; in base a pierced cinquefoil of the last—Catharne, Pembroke.

Vert, a cat statant, tail erect argent, within an orle of eight trefoils slipped or—Vaghan.

Argent, three mountain-cats passant in pale sable—Keate, Herts.

Per pale sable and gules, a mountain-cat between three roses argent—Limpenie.

Sable, on a fesse argent, between three mountain-cats or, a cross formy of the field—Hill, Berks.

Sable, a chevron ermine, between three spotted cats passant argent—Harthorp, London.

Cats are also borne by the families of Chivas, Aberdeen; Duane, London; Adams, Northampton; Tibbett; Lippingcote, Devon, Gibbs, Dorset; and Keats, Dover.

Azure, a cat's head erased argent, between eight crosses crosslet of the second, 3, 2, 2, and 1—Tolderrey, Kent.

The *crest* of the Duke of Sutherland is a cat-a-mountain sejant guardant proper: and two wild-cats are the *supporters* to the arms of Farquharson of Invercauld; while the *lezard*, a beast somewhat resembling the wild-cat, is the dexter supporter of the Skinners' and Muscovy Merchants' Companies, as well as the crest of the former.

Cat-a-mountain.

Cauldron : is found only in connection with the children in the cauldron. See example under *Bishop*.

Cave : this singular charge occurs in one coat of arms.

Gules, a cave proper, therefrom issuant a wolf at full speed regardant argent—WILLIAMS.

Censer, (fr. *encensoir*) : no example having been found in English arms the following French example is given.

D'or, à l'encensoir d'azur—LAMBERT, Limousin.

Chain, (fr. *chaine*) : (1) a series of *annulets* (q.v.) when interlaced are commonly called a chain, and are borne as distinct charges, as in the insignia of the kingdom of NAVARRE.

Gules, a cross and saltire of chains, affixed to an annulet in the fesse-point, and to a double orle of the same, all or—NAVARRE, taken after the battle of Tolosa, 1212.

Argent, three circles of chains sable—Hoo.

Argent, a chain of nine links in saltire, five gules and four azure—HATCHET.

Azure, a chain couped in chevron between three mitres all argent; at the dexter end of the chain a padlock of the last—EVESHAM Benedictine Abbey.

Gules, a chain of seven links in pale argent—KENDALL.

Sable, three chains each of four links palewise argent—ANDERTON, co. Lancaster.

(2) *Chains* are also often fixed to the *collars* of animals and to other charges, e.g. to a *portcullis*, an *anchor*, &c., and are frequently of a different tincture from the charge, and the term *chained* is used either when two animals are chained together, or when a chain is attached to the collar of a single animal.

Argent, two barbels haurient, respecting each other, sable, collared and chained together or; the chain pendent and ringed at the end—COLSTON, Essex.

Gules, a stag statant argent collared and chained or—BOIS, co. Brecknock.

Oaterfoil — *quatrefoil*.

Cathedral. See *Church*.

Catherine Wheel. See *Wheel*.

Caudé, (fr.) : of tails of *comets* when of a different tincture.

Cautel, or *Cauntel* (old fr.), found also spelt *cantel* and *chuntel* : appears to be generally a corner at the *Sinister chief point* of the shield, but superseded in modern heraldry by the *canton*. See *Quarter*.

Chair: this is used in one case in a singular manner.

Or, out of a chair resembling a mural coronet reversed argent a demi-lion rampant sable—TALSTOCK.

Chalice: generally drawn in old examples as in the margin, though often with an octangular foot.

Chalice.

Azure, a sun in splendour, in base a chalice or; [otherwise a chalice or and in chief a sun]—VASSALL.

Azure, two chalices in fesse or [elsewhere blazoned candlesticks]—EMERLE.

Champaine, (1) *Champaine* (corrupted by some writers to *Champion*), otherwise *urdé* and *warriated :* is an embattled line, but with the top and bottom of each division pointed instead of square, and so resembling somewhat the line usually drawn in *vair*. It occurs, though rarely, as a line of partition.

Purpure, a bend champaine argent—ARCHBY.

Argent, a pale champaine vert—BOWMAN.

Bendy of six champaine purple and argent—BOWBRIDGE.

Champaine.

Gyronny of four champaine or, enarched argent and gules—BRAUNECK.

(2.) The term *Point Champaine*, or *Champion* (q.v.) also is used. It is included in the forms of *Abatement*.

Chaperonne, *Chapourn,* or *Shafferoon :* (1) a name given to the small shields containing crests, initials, deaths' heads, &c., placed upon the heads of horses, either with or without a hood, at pompous funerals; (2) *Chaperonné*, or *chapourné*, appears also to be used to signify *hooded*, being applied to *falcons*, &c.

Cedar. See *Pine-tree.*

Centaur. See *Satyr.*

Centre-point: the fesse-point. See *Points* of the escutcheon.

Cercelé. See *recercelé* and *Cross cercelée.*

Cerclé, (fr.): encircled, e.g. of a *Tun* or barrel.

Cercle, (fr.): a large voided circle, only used in French arms.

Chafant, (fr.): enraged, and is applied to the wild *boar.*

Chabot. See *Perch.*

Chaffinch. See *Finch.*

Chain-shot. See *Shot.*

Chamber-piece. See *Gun.*

Chameleon. See *Cameleon.*

Chamfrain, (old fr.): signifying the armour-plates which cover the head of a horse.

Champagne : rarely and irregularly used for the lower part of the shield generally, i.e. the 'ground.' See *Point.*

Chapé: a partition of the shield used by French heralds,
and formed by two lines drawn from the centre of the upper
edge of the shield, diverging towards the flanks, and leaving
the field resembling somewhat a wide *pile* reversed; the tincture is applied to the two portions thus parted off.

Chaussé is similar to *Chapé*, but with the lines diverging

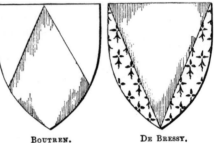

from the base towards
the two corners, and
leaving the field re-
sembling an expanded
pile. The line may be
curved, and the parti-
tion is then blazoned
chaussé arrondi, &c.

BOUTREN.   DE BRESSY.

De gueules, chapé d'ar-
gent—BOUTREN de Franqueville, Normandie.

Ecartelé d'argent, et de gueules, chapé de l'un en l'autre—DE MONTBAR,
Bourgogne.

De gueules, chaussé d'hermines—DE BRESSY de Sablous, Normandie.

Chaplet, (old fr. *chapelet*, pl. *chapeus*): is, when not otherwise described, a garland of leaves with four
flowers amongst them, at equal distances. It
is to be distinguished from the *wreath* (q.v.),
and though usually composed of *leaves* will be
found blazoned of various tinctures.

Chaplet.

Sire Rauf LE FITZ WILLIAM, burele de argent e de
azure, a iij chapels [in Falkirk roll ' chapeus '] de goules—Roll, temp.
ED. II.

Party per fesse, argent and azure, three chaplets counterchanged—DUKE.
Sable, three chaplets argent—JODRELL, Stafford.
Sable, three chaplets gyronny argent and gules—DYRWARD.

It is more usual, however, to designate the
material of which the chaplet is composed. It
may be of *roses* (and this, perhaps, is the most
frequent) or of *flowers* generally, or it may be of
leaves, and often of *laurel leaves*. In the latter
case it is termed a *crown triumphal*.

Crown Triumphal.

Monsire William PLAICE, port d'asur, au cheif d'argent deux chapeaux des roses vermals—Roll, temp. ED. III.

Monsire de HILTON de Haderness, port d'argent, a trois chepeletts de roses vermaux—*Ibid.*

[Chaplets of roses are also borne by the families of SAXTON; DEAN; FAULDER; GREYSTOCK; FITZRALPH; LASCELLES, and others.]

Argent, on a chevron sable, between three chaplets of flowers gules, another chevron ermine—BOROUGH.

Argent, a lion rampant azure, holding in his dexter paw a chaplet of laurel vert, in chief a scroll sable, thereon the word "Emmanuel" or—EMMANUEL COLL., Cambridge.

Or, two bars azure, on a canton argent a chaplet of laurel proper—HOLME.

Argent, a garland of laurel vert, between three pheons gules—CONQUEROR, Frierton.

[Chaplets of laurels are also borne by the families of PELLEW; KEATS, Dover; NIGHTINGALL, Norfolk.]

Rarer instances occur of chaplets of *holly*, or of *hazel*, or of *brambles*, while the single instance of the *chaplet of rue* is a name sometimes given to the *crown of rue* (q. v.) which occurs in the arms given by Frederick of Barbarossa to the Duke of SAXONY.

Argent, a fesse engrailed humetty sable, between three chaplets of holly leaves proper—Nicholas BUBBEWYTH, Bp. of Salisbury, Bath and Wells, 1408—24.

Gules, on a chevron argent, between, in chief three chaplets of hazel or, and in base a plough proper, three shakeforks sable—PEER, Hazelwood, Devon.

Argent, a lion rampant gules encircled by a wreath of brambles proper—DUSILVA, Portugal.

When the material is *oak* the device is often blazoned as a *wreath*, and there is especially a 'wreath of oak acorned' which bears the name of the '*Civic wreath*,' or the *Civic Crown*. It is supposed to represent the Roman crown conferred upon public benefactors, especially upon those who had saved the life of a citizen. The leaves should be represented tied together by a ribbon. The *Ducal Coronet* (q. v. under *Crown*) had originally oak leaves, but strawberry-leaves have been substituted.

Civic Crown.

Argent, a chevron gules; in base an oak wreath vert, tied azure; on a chief of the second, three mascles of the first—PELLEW, Cornwall, [1796].

Azure, on a fesse, between three garbs or, a wreath of oak vert between two estoiles gules—SANDBACH, Lancaster.

[Chaplets of oak also borne by the families of STUDD, Ipswich; DICKSON, Norfolk; LLOYD, Sussex; MURRAY, Mexico, and others.]

Gules, a lion passant guardant, and in chief two civic wreaths or, a chief wavy, charged with a ship of war before Algiers proper—PELLEW.

Argent, a civic crown or wreath of oak acorned proper, on a chief azure a serpent nowed or, and a dove of the field respecting each other—SUTTON, Norfolk.

The *Crown obsidional* is also mentioned in old works on heraldry, which is a *chaplet graminy,* i.e. composed of twisted grass, and is fancifully said to have been bestowed upon any general who had held a city against a besieging force.

Gules, an eagle displayed argent armed or; on a canton of the second a chaplet graminy vert—GOODALL, Suffolk [granted Mar. 1, 1612].

The term *garland* as well as *wreath,* it will be observed, is used sometimes instead of chaplet.

Charge, (fr. *meuble,* but more accurately *meuble d'armoirie,* or *meuble de l'ecu*): anything borne on a coat of arms, whether upon the field, as was more usually the case in ancient arms, or upon an ordinary, or indeed upon another charge. The position of a charge, unless occupying the centre of the field, i.e. the fesse-point, has to be stated. (See under the article *blazon.*) The great variety of the charges which have been adopted in Coats of arms, will be seen by the Synoptical view given in the Appendix, and this by no means contains all the minor varieties, nor all the extraordinary objects chosen in more recent times. The contrast between recent arms and the more simple bearings of the thirteenth, fourteenth, and fifteenth centuries is very marked.

Charged with, (fr. *chargé*), signifies having a charge thereon.

Champion. See *Champaine.*

Chape. See *Sword.*

Chapeau. See *Cap.* See also *Chapeaux* under *Chaplet.*

Chapel. See *Church.*

Chapourne. See *Chaperonne.*

Charboucle. See *Escarboucle.*

Chased. See under *Thunderbolt.*

Charity: the representation of charity is thus blazoned from a seal.

A figure of Charity with one child in her arms, and three others standing near her naked; on the dexter side a shield hung on a tree, with the cross of S. Andrew on it, to which the figure is pointing; on the sinister side of the escutcheon a thistle issuing from the ground in base, stalked and leaved; over it a regal crown—The Scots Corporation [Incorporated 1665].

Chart: This device seems to be used in a solitary instance.

Per chevron wavy, azure and erminois, a chart of Chesterfield's Inlet, between in chief two estoiles argent and in base on a mount vert a beaver passant proper—Christopher, London.

Chequy, *Checky, Checquer-bearing,* (fr. *échiqueté,* old fr. *eschequeré):* terms applied to a field or charge divided by perpendicular and horizontal lines, into small squares of metal and colour alternately. There should be at least twenty squares in the shield. If less, the number is named (as in the shield of Toledo, where there are 15). When only 9, with the French heralds the term *equipollé* is applied.

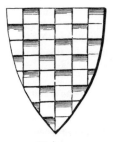

WARREN.

This pattern is said by some to be derived from the game of chess, which if not originally introduced into Europe by the Crusaders was certainly revived by them. Others, however, with greater probability derive it from the Steward's or 'chequer' board. In the Exchequer of the kingdom, and the Chancellor of that department, the word is still retained; and the 'Checkers,' a frequent sign of small inns, with the board

---

Chastel: written sometimes for *Castle.*

Chataignier, (fr.): the Chestnut-tree, but not noted in any English arms.

Châtelé, (fr.): by French heralds signifies charged with castles (e.g.

the bordure of the royal arms of Portugal is so blazoned.

Chausé. See *Chapé.*

Chausse-trap. See *Caltrap.*

Chaudière, or *Chaudron,* (fr.): a cauldron, in French arms, but rarely.

painted in squares on the outside, still hands down the tradition of the account board. It is not, however, impossible that this board gave the name to the game of chess played upon it.

While the number of pieces in the field must be, as already said, at least twenty, a *fesse* or other *ordinary* when blazoned *chequy* must contain three rows of squares, for if there be but one, the ordinary will be *compony*, and if but two, *counter-compony*. At the same time the field may have but two rows in chief of a fesse, for so the arms of Lord Clifford are represented in the glass windows at Dorchester, Hasely, &c.

When a *bend*, *chevron*, or *saltire* is *checquy*, the squares are not placed perpendicularly, but slanting in the direction of the ordinary.

CLIFFORD.

Roger de CLIFFORD escheque d'or et d'azur ove ung fesse de goulz—Roll, temp. HEN. III.

Le Conte de GARENNE [i.e. Warren] escheque d'or et d'azur—Ibid.

Rauf le BOTELLIER de goules a ung fesse escheque d'argent et de sable et croiseletts d'or —Ibid.

Or, a fesse chequy argent and azure—STEWARD, Scotland.

Chequy of nine pieces or and azure—GENEVA.

Chequy of twelve, sable and argent—ST. BARBE, Somerset.

At the same time there are some peculiar forms which may be noted.

Chequy in perspective argent and sable—PROSPECT.

Chequy of lines palewise and chevronwise gules and or—SPOTWORTH.

Cherry: both the tree and the fruit of the tree are found in armorial bearings. The fr. *crequier* (q.v.) also is sometimes referred to as the wild cherry-tree. The *griotte* also occurs.

Argent, a cherry-tree fructed proper—ESTOWER.

Argent, three cherry-trees, 2 and 1 vert fructed gules, each on a mount of the second—SHRUBSOLE, Canterbury.

Argent, a saltire sable between four cherries gules slipped vert SERGEAUX.

... on a chevron between three martlets ... as many cherries stalked; in chief three annulets ... .—CHERITON, Bp. of Bangor, 1436-47.

The charge is also borne by the families of MESSARNEY and THORNTON.

Cherub, or *Cherub's head* (fr. *cherubin*): this is drawn as the head of an infant between a pair of wings.

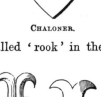

Argent, a chevron dancetty, between three cherubs gules—ADYER, Kent.

Azure, a fesse dancetty between three cherub's heads argent—ADNEY.

Sable, a chevron between three cherubim or—CHALONER, Yorksh.

Azure, a fesse dancetty between three cherubim's heads or, faces argent—ADY, Kent.

CHALONER.

Chess-rook, (old fr. *rok*): the figure called ' rook ' in the game of chess, from the Italian *rocca*, a tower or castle. The chess-rook is an ancient bearing, and of frequent occurrence. It is also in the arms of ZULEI-STEIN termed a *zule*, and this is borne on an escutcheon surtout by the Earls of ROCHFORD.

Chess-rooks.

Sire Richard de WALSINGHAM,—de goules a iij roks de argent—Roll, temp. ED. II.

Gules, three chess-rooks ermine—Simon le FITZ SYMON, Roll, temp. ED. I., Harl. MS. 6137.

Or, three chess-rooks gules—COLVILL.

Azure, a fesse between three chess-rooks or—BODENHAM, Hereford.

Gules, three zules argent ; a label of three points of the last—ZULEISTEIN.

The charge is also borne by the families of MARSHALL, AOLUITE, OGILVIE, and ORROCK.

Chevron, (fr. *chevron*, old fr. *cheveron*): an ordinary occupying one-fifth of the field. The origin and meaning of this term has afforded ground for many guesses, but in diversifying the forms which bars across the shield may take, that of the *chevron* is a very natural one. The name itself is derived directly from the fr. *chevron*, i.e. a rafter of a roof.

It is found in the earliest of the Rolls of Arms, and is one of the most frequently employed of the Ordinaries. At

---

Chevalier, (fr.): a man in complete *Armour*, q.v.

Cheval-trap. See *Caltrap*.

Chever. See *Goat*.

Cheverons: old term for ' *party per chevron*.'

the siege of Caerlaverock, for instance (A.D. 1300), Henry le
TYES had a banner argent, or, as the poet writes, 'whiter
than a brightened lily,' with a chevron gules in the midst.
And at the same siege, Robert FITZWALTER, "who well knew
of arms the business," on a yellow banner
had a fesse between two red chevrons. Both
of these arms are to be seen in stained
glass in Dorchester Church, Oxon, in a
window which was probably nearly contemporary with the siege, and perhaps recording the benefactors to the Church.

> Baniere ot Henris li TYOIS
> Plus blanche de un poli lyois
> O un chievron vermeil en mi.

TYES.

> O lui Robert le FIZ WATER
> Ke ben sout des armes le mester . . .
> En la baner jaune avoit
> Fesse entre deus cheverons vermaus.

It has two diminutives, the *chevronel*,
which is half its width (more or less),
and the *couple-close*, which is half the *chevronel*.

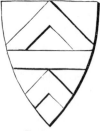

FITZWALTER.

Moris de BARKELE,—goules ung cheveron d'argent—Roll, temp. HEN. III.
Le Conte de WARREWIK,—chequy d'or et d'azur, a ung cheveron d'ermyn—*Ibid*.

A chevron is subjected to the same kind of variation in respect of outline as the *bend*, that is, it may be *engrailed*, *indented*, *embattled*, *counter-embattled*, *dauncetty*, *wavy*, *raguly*,
fimbriated, &c.

Azure, a chevron embattled ermine—REYNOLDS, co. Leicester.
Azure, a chevron dauncetty or—HAMELL, co. Buckingham, and HAMIL-
TON, co. Gloucester.
Argent, a chevron ermine fimbriated sable, between three annulets
gules—CLUTTON.

Chevillé, (fr.) = *attired*, is used
of the stags' horns, when they
have five or any greater number
of branches. The word *ramé* (fr.)

is also used, and appears to be
synonymous.
Chevronelly, i.q. *Chevronny*. See
at end of *Chevron*.

In one early roll two chevrons appear to be blazoned as a chevron *gemel*.

Sire William de HOTOT,—de azure, a iij cressanz de argent e un cheveron de or—Roll, temp. ED. II.

Sire Johan de HOTOT,—meisme les armes, le cheveron gymile—*Ibid.*

It may be *party* as to tincture, *compony* or even *quarterly*, and, on the other hand, it may be *voided*, that is, the field may be made visible through it, leaving merely a narrow outline.

Argent, a chevron per pale or and gules—WESTON.

Argent, a chevron quarterly sable and gules—HONYWOOD, Kent.

Ermine, a chevron compony gules and argent—HILL.

Further, the *chevron* may be *charged* with other devices of various kinds, and amongst these is especially to be noted the surmounting of one chevron by another. In the arms of STEER it will be observed that we have two different blazonings for the same arms, one describing the chevron as *voided*, the other as one chevron on another. And in the case of the arms of STALEY we have a further complication, since this chevron may be blazoned in two different ways, either as a chevron *engrailed* surmounted by a chevron *plain*, or as a *plain* chevron *fimbriated*. Precisely similar arms, as re-gards outline, are those of DUDLEY, which are blazoned as *voided*. It seems to be a case where authority can be found for either system of blazon, and it is difficult to say which is best.

DUDLEY.

Argent, a chevron voided gules—STEER, Ire-land.

Argent, on a chevron gules another of the first—STEER.

Azure, a chevron engrailed, voided or—DUD-LEY, Berks and Bucks.

Argent, on a chevron engrailed azure an-other plain sable—STALEY.

[Or as it is elsewhere blazoned—Argent, a plain chevron sable, fimbriated and engrailed azure—STALEY.]

STALEY.

Gules, on a chevron argent three bars gemells sable — THROCK-
MORTON.

Gules, on a chevron argent .... bars nebuly
sable—HANKFORD.

Or, on a chevron engrailed azure bars wavy
argent—BROWNE.

Or, on a chevron gules bars sable—Lewis
PROUDE, Charterhouse, 1619.

THROCKMORTON.

A chevron may be *enhanced*, that is,
borne higher up on the escutcheon (no
instance has been observed in which it is *abased*), and it may
be *reversed*, that is, it may have its point downwards, like a
pile, or it may be combined with a *pile*, but such variations are
of rare occurrence.   It is also sometimes found *couped*, that
is, not extending to the edge of the escutcheon, or with the
apex terminated by some other charge, when it may be said to
be *ensigned* of such a charge.

Gules, a chevron enhanced argent—CARLYON.

Argent, a chevron reversed gules—GRENDON.

Ermine, a chevron couped sable—HUNTLEY; also JONES, 1730.

Ermine, a chevron couped gules—AMOCK.

Argent, a chevron embattled and ensigned on the top with a banner
between, in chief two estoiles, and in base a sun gules—EUENE.

Argent, a chevron supporting on its point a cross patty sable—TRE-
NEREEK.

Sable, a chevron ending in the middle point with a plain de lis
argent—KEY.

Argent, a chevron, the top ending with a cross patty sable—FINDON;
Harl. MS. 1386.

Argent, a chevron sable and a pile counterchanged—ATWELL, co. York;
Harl. MS. 1465.

Chevron couched: one which springs
from one of the sides of the escutcheon.
It should be mentioned whether it is
dexter or sinister.

Or, a chevron couched dexter gules—TOURNEY.

Or, a chevron couched dexter azure—DOUBLET.

Argent, two chevrons, couched (and counter-
pointed?) vert—COUCHMASTER.

Purpure, a chevron couched sinister or—
BIGHTINE.

Chevron couched.

Chevron inarched. Of this form there are two varieties, as shewn in the margin, found in modern heraldic designs, but probably no ancient authority for the form exists.

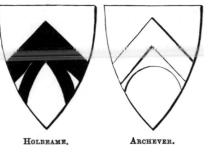

Argent, a chevron inarched sable — HOLBEAME, Lincoln.

Purpure, a chevron inarched argent—ARCHEVER, Scotland.

HOLBEAME.   ARCHEVER.

A *Chevron arched* (fr. *courbé*), resembles a semi-circular arch across the field. It only occurs in foreign arms, and is to be distinguished from the arched fesse by the curve being somewhat more decided.

For *Chevrons interlaced,* see *Angles.*

Besides the above there are various forms of *broken chevrons.* But the terms do not appear very distinctly defined by heralds, and the actual examples are but few. We find the terms *fracted, disjoint, bruised,* or *debruised* (fr. *brisé*), and *rompu* or *downset,* the last term, to all appearance, being a barbarism derived from the French *dauncet,* which would be equivalent to dancetty.

Argent, a chevron debruised between three crosses botonny fitchy sable—BARDOLPH, Stafford.

Argent, a chevron debruised sable, between three cross-crosslets fitchée of the last—GREENWAY [Glover's Ordinary].

Per pale argent and sable, a chevron bruised at the top, and in base a crescent counterchanged—ALEXANDER, Kinlassie.

. . . . a chevron debruised by a fesse charged with a crescent, all between three annulets . . . . HEDLEY, Newcastle-on-Tyne.

Azure, a chevron disjoint or broken in the head or—BROKMALE.

Per fesse gules and sable, a chevron rompu counterchanged—ALLEN, Sheriff of London, 18° Jac. I.

Or, a chevron rompu between three mullets sable—SALT, Yorks.

Broken chevron, fig. 1.

In the margin are given illustrations of one or two forms found in books, but no ancient examples have been observed. With the French engravers the *chevron brisé* is generally drawn in a similar manner to fig. 1, though the two portions are often still further apart, so as

Broken chevron, fig. 2.   Broken chevron, fig. 3.

not to touch at all. *Rompu* and *failli* seem to be used by them when the sides of the chevron are broken into one or more pieces.

In chevron would be applied to charges arranged chevronwise.
Per chevron. See *Party.*

Chevronny, (fr. *chevronné*): is used when the field is divided into an even number of equal portions chevronwise. *Chevronelly* appears to be used more correctly.

Chevronelly of four, argent and gules—WHITHORSE.

Chevronelly of five, argent and gules, over all a lion rampant sable—WINTHORP, Suffolk.

Chevronelly of six, gules and argent—CHALKHILL, Middlesex.

Chevronelly of seven, or and gules, over all a lion rampant of the last—HASARD, Essex.

Chevronel: a diminutive of the chevron, of which it is nominally one half the width; the term being used properly when there is more than one chevron. With the older writers, however, the term chevron is used, and so may still be used when there are two or even three chevrons.

Or, three chevronels gules.—CLARE.

Or, three chevronels per pale, the first azure and gules, the second gules and azure, the third as the first.—WALTER DE MERTON, Bp. of Rochester, 1274-77, and founder of Merton College.

Argent, two chevronels sable, between three roses gules, barbed and seeded proper.—William of WYKEHAM, Bp. of Winchester, 1367—1404. [Founder of the Colleges of S. Mary at Winchester and at Oxford.]

CLARE.

Other ordinaries may be charged with the *chevronel,* while it
in its turn is subjected to the same vari-
eties as the chevron; though, of course,
but rarely such varieties occur.

Argent, on a fesse sable, three chevronels
couched sinister of the field.—TRENOWITH, *Corn.*

Chevronels are sometimes interlaced, **or**
braced, and under the latter term an illustration will be found. See also *Couple-close.*

TRENOWITH.

Chief, (fr. *chef*) : the first of the *Ordinaries,* and occupying about one-third of the shield from
the top downward.

The *fillet* is by some considered its diminutive, while others hold that it can
have none. Some English heraldic books,
and most foreign, speak of instances of
two *chiefs,* one *abased* below the other
in the same coat, but no English examples are ever adduced.

A chief is frequently charged with other

LUMLEY.

bearings, and it may be *nebuly, wavy, indented, dancetty, engrailed, embattled, bevilly, &c.,* but it is only the lower side
which is subjected to these variations.

Robert de MORTEYN BRETON, d'ermyn a la cheif de goules. Roll, temp.
HEN. III.

Raulf le FITZ RANDOLF d'or ung cheif endente d'azur.—Ibid.

Sire William DABETOOT, de ermyne od le chef bende de or e de sable.
Roll, temp. ED. II.

Or, a chief gules—LUMLEY, Essex.

Paly of six, argent and sable ; a chief wavy azure—BURMAN.

Argent, gouty de poix ; a chief nebuly gules—ROYDENHALL.

Argent, a chief dancetty azure—GLANVILE, Earl of Suffolk.

A chief may also be party *per pale, per bend, &c.,* or even
quarterly. When divided by a horizontal line the expression
per chief is more accurate than *per fesse.*

Cheyne: old fr. for *Acorn.*   Chieftain.   See *Head.*

Ermine, a chief quarterly gules and or—Peckham, [Abp. Cant. 1219–92].

Quarterly; first and fourth argent, a cross bot-
tonnee gules; second and third gules, three suns
in splendour or; over all on a chief party per
pale gules and argent, three cinquefoils counterchanged—John Christopherson, Bp. of Chichester, 1557-58.

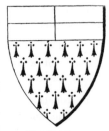

Barry wavy of six, argent and azure; a chief
per pale ermine and gules—Barlowe, Derbyshire.

Barry of six, gules and or per pale counterchanged; a chief, the dexter side per bend as the
first and second, the sinister, per bend sinister

Abp. Peckham.

like the second and first; over all an escutcheon argent—Hageley.

Chequy gules and azure; a chief per chevron wavy of the first and or
—Sir Nicholas Hauberkes. [From Glover's Ordinary.]

Chequy azure and or; a chief per chief nebuly of the first and second
—Tavestoke. [Ibid.]

The chief does not, as a rule, surmount other charges, and
consequently such have often to be abased.
The bend, for instance, starts from the dexter
corner just beneath the chief. When associated with a bordure (unless there is direct
statement to the contrary) the bordure would
be turned and continued beneath the base
line of the chief.

Gules, a chief dancetty argent within a bordure
azure—Baret [or Barratt, Sheriff of London, 1379.]

Carey.

Argent, on a bend sable, three roses of the first; on chief gules three
crosses patty or—Carey, Bp. of Exeter, 1820, afterwards Bp. of S. Asaph,
1830-46.

It is contended by some writers that the *chief* has a diminutive, and to a figure as shewn in the
margin is given the name of *fillet*. French
heralds, however, blazon this as *chef retrait*,
the word *filet* being used for a diminutive of
the *cotice*. The word *cumbel* is also given by
some English heraldic writers as meaning the
same thing. It is said that the fillet does
not occur at all in English arms, but perhaps
the following example may be cited—

Fillet.

Argent, two bars and a canton gules; over all a fillet sable—BOIS or DEBOYS, 1315, Ingham Church, Norfolk.

In Chief is a term frequently used when the charges are to be placed upon the upper part of the escutcheon, and differently from their ordinary position. There are also three *points* (q. v.) in the escutcheon connected with the chief, viz. the *dexter chief point, middle chief point,* and *sinister chief point.*

Child : *Children, boys,* and *infants* are represented on armorial bearings as early as the sixteenth century, and in a great variety of ways. Perhaps some of the oldest are those where the eagle snatches away the child from its cradle, which occurs in different families, and is variously depicted in the arms of the branches of the same family. Of course such arms are readily associated with tradition, but it is scarcely within the scope of a 'glossary' to discuss them. More frequently, however, the children's *heads* (q.v.) alone occur.

Argent, an eagle sable, crined gules, standing on a child proper, swathed or lying in a cradle vert—COULCHIEFE.

Azure, an eagle preyant sable upon a child swaddled gules—CULCHETH, Lancaster.

Argent, a tree eradicated sable; on it a nest of the first, in which is a child proper, swaddled gules, seized on by an eagle volant of the second.—RISLEY.

The three children in a tub or vessel are generally referred to the miracle of S. Nicolas, who restored them after they had been murdered and salted down for food : and in the insignia of the SEE OF ABERDEEN the Bishop is represented as praying over them. (See under *Bishop.*) Some curious legend must account for the origin of the following.

Sable, a goat argent, attired or, standing on a child proper, swaddled gules, and feeding on a tree vert—DAVIES, Hope, Co. Montgomery.

To another, (probably that of W. de ALBINI) is due the arms of Richard BARNES, Bishop of Carlisle, in which a naked child, front faced, is represented as holding in both hands the tongue of a bear. The following is one blazon.

Azure, on a bend argent, between two estoiles or, a bear passant sable, semie des estoiles of the third, ready to devour a naked child of the fourth; on a chief of the second, three roses gules radiated with rays of the sun proper—Richard BARNES, Bp. of Carlisle, 1570 ; Bp. of Durham, 1577-87.

Other blazoning of these arms is found.

Azure, a bend argent between two estoiles or, a bear passant sable estoiled or, seizing a man proper; on a chief azure three roses gules radiated or—BARNES.

BARNES.

Azure, on a bend argent, between two estoiles or, a naked boy, front faced, holding in both hands proper sable the tongue of a bear statant of the last estoiled gold, a chief as the second charged with three roses gules radiated like the third.—BARNES [the arms confirmed 1571, Harl. MS. 5847].

The FOUNDLING HOSPITAL in London has for its insignia :

Per fesse azure and vert; in chief a crescent argent between two mullets of six points or ; in base an infant exposed and stretching out its arms for help proper.　*Motto*, ' Help.'

Chisel : this occurs variously in different branches of the family of CHESSELDEN.　It also occurs in the crest of the Company of MARBLERS drawn as in the margin.

Argent, a chevron sable between three chisels or handled of the second—CHESELDON, Harl. MS. 1386.

Chisel.

An arm embowed vested azure cuffed argent, holding in the hand proper an engraving chisel of the last—Crest of the MARBLERS' Company.

Chub, (*leuciscus cephalus*) : this fish, common to England and belonging to the order *cyprinidæ*, seems only to have been chosen for the sake of the punning name, since it is only borne by the family of CHOBBE.

Vert, three chub fish haurient sable—CHOBB.

Gules, on a chevron between three chub fish argent three shovellers sable ; on a chief dancetty of the second three escallops of the first— CHOBBE [and one of the quarterings borne by Lord DORMER, of Wing, Bucks].

Chimera.　See *Sphinx*.　　　China Cokar.　See *Palm*.

Together with the above must be classed the *roach* (*leuciscus rutilus.* fr. *rosse*). The most authentic instance of a delineation of this charge is perhaps found on Lord de la Roche's seal.

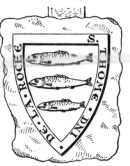

Gules, three roach naiant in pale argent —Seal of Thomas Lord DE LA ROCHE affixed to the Barons' letter to Pope Boniface VIII., 1301.

Again it is represented on the seal of Thomas Arundel, Abp. of Canter-bury, 1397—1414, where the shield bearing the fish (which are supposed

Seal of Lord DE LA ROCHE.

to be roach) is represented as borne by one of the four mur-
derers of Thomas à Becket, though what connection they had with the Roche family is not known.

It may perhaps be noted that the application of this charge to the name of the family is a singular instance of the punning adopted in heraldic devices, for the remains of Roche Castle, founded by Adam de la Roche, still exist on an insulated rock (fr. *roche*) of great height, and it has been suggested that the proverb 'sound as a roach' has its origin in the same confusion of the French and English language.

The roach is found borne differently by different descendants of the family, e.g.

Gules, three roach naiant or within a bordure engrailed argent—Sir David ROCHE of Carass, Limerick.

Sable, three roach naiant in pale argent—De la ROCHE, Herefordshire.

Azure, three roach naiant argent within a bordure or—Walter ROCHE of Bromham, Wilts.

Gules, three roach naiant in pale argent—Peter de RUPIBUS [or Sir Pierre des ROCHES], Bp. of Winchester, 1206-38.

Or, a bull passant gules between three roach haurient proper, a chief chequy or and azure—Sir William ROCHE, Lord Mayor of London, 1540.

Argent, on a bend sable three roach of the field—HUYSHE, Devon-shire.

Gules, a chevron engrailed between three roach naiant argent; on a chief of the second three herons sable, billed and membered gules—HOBBS, Middlesex.

Church: this is not unfrequently represented in coats of arms of recent date, but there seem to be no special characteristics to be noted in the several examples, and the method of representing the church seems somewhat arbitrary. This is so in a very marked way on the insignia of the Burgh of CULROSS.

Azure, a fesse or, in base a church argent—TEMPLETON.

A church with a spire; on the dexter chief the sun in splendour, on the sinister a crescent; at the dexter end of the church three ears of corn on one stalk, at the sinister end of the church a saltire—Seal of town of ASHBURTON, Devon.

Azure, a perspective view of the church of S. Servanus, shewing the south side, in which there is a gate, with a window on each side; the top of the west end [!] of the church ensigned with a passion cross: in the west end another gate, and two windows over it and one window over the two last; a square steeple terminating the building towards the east [!], above the battlements of which is a cupola ensigned with a ball on the top of a rod, all argent masoned sable—Burgh of CULROSS, Scotland.

Together with the church will be conveniently grouped the *cathedral* and the *chapel* (fr. *chapelle*). These, like the church, are found only in one or two modern coats of arms.

Azure, on a cross argent, between four suns or, a Cathedral church gules—NICHOLSON, Virginia [granted 1693-4].

Per fesse argent and vert, a chapel of the first, roofed gules between four escallop shells counterchanged—CHAPPELL, Cambridgeshire.

Beneath the same heading will be conveniently noted the *Porch*, the *Shrine*, and the *Altar-tomb*.

Gules, three porches of churches with double doors expanded argent—LESINGTON.

. . . . A shrine of Gothic work; over it an angel holding an escutcheon gules; three lions passant guardant in pale or—Seal of borough of WILTON, Wiltshire.

Gules, on an altar-tomb a lamb passant guardant argent carrying a banner of the last charged with a cross of the first, resting the dexter forefoot on a mound or—Augustinian College of ASHRIDGE, co. Buckingham.

Churn: this device seems to be borne only by one family, but the origin of the selection has not been ascertained.

Azure, three butter churns or—READE, Wales.

Chough. See *Cornish* Chough.   Church-bell. See *Bell*.

Cinquefoil, (fr. *quintefeuille*) or *quinte-foil*: a bearing of conventional form, having five leaves, as the name implies, and, as a rule, with the centre pierced.

Gules, a cinquefoil pierced ermine. Town of LEICESTER.

Robert QUENCY de goules ung quintefueile de hermyne—Roll, temp. HEN. III.

William BARDOLF d'azur a trois quinte feuiles d'or—*Ibid.*

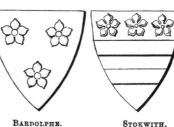

Town of LEICESTER.

Sire Johan PAYNEL de goules a un quintefoil de argent—Roll, temp. ED. II.

Or, a cinquefoil gules—VERNON.

Or, three cinquefoils gules—DYKE.

Gules, a cinquefoil or—ALLIN.

Azure, a cinquefoil ermine pierced of the field—ASHLEY.

Argent, a cinquefoil azure—MOTON or MUTTON.

BARDOLPHE.   STOKWITH.

Argent, three cinquefoils gules—DARELL.

Argent, two bars gules, in chief three cinquefoils of the second—STOKWITH.

Cinnamon: a solitary instance of the leaves of this tree, which is a native of Ceylon, occurs as follows.

Or, on a chevron gules, between in chief two cinnamon leaves erased vert, and in base a negro girt with white linen striped blue, carrying on a bamboo yoke two bundles of cinnamon proper, three cinnamon leaves as the first—PYBUS, Hertford (granted 1768).

Civet, (fr. *civette*), or, as it is commonly called, the *Civet Cat* (*viverra civetta* of Linnæus): appears at least upon one coat of arms.

Sable, three civet cats passant in pale argent—SEEVES, Scotland.

Cimier. See *Crest.*
Cinabar, or *Cinabre.* See *Gules.*
Circle of Glory. See *Nimbus.*
Citadel. See *Castle.*

City. See *Town.*
Civic Crown, and *Civic wreath.* See *Chaplet.*
Civic Mace. See *Mace.*

Clock: this charge is believed to be confined to the bearings of the company which have been thus blazoned.

Sable, a clock, each of the four corner pillars of the case erected on a lion couchant, and on each capital a mound ensigned with a cross pattée, and on the dome of the case an imperial crown supported by circular arches springing from the pillars, under which arches the bell appears, and on the centre of the dial-plate a double rose, all or—CLOCK-MAKERS' Company, London.

The credit of this minute example of blazon (presenting a great contrast to the simple insignia of more ancient companies) is due to Sir Edw. Walker, Garter, who granted it in 1677.

Closet: this may be considered as the diminutive of the *Bar*, of which it is half the width, i.e. a tenth of the shield, so that only nine closets can be borne in one shield; the term *closetty* is sometimes used signifying *barry* of many pieces, though the term *barry* may be used of any even number of pieces.

Argent, a chevron between two closets gules—MALBISE.
Argent, three bars closetted gules [= 9 barrulets]—BERNSTEAD.
Argent, three closets sable—ANCHILECK, Scotland.

Cloth, *Piece of:* this is a charge borne by the Company of TAILORS OF CHESTER. A somewhat similar bearing in the insignia of the MERCHANT TAILORS OF LONDON is called a *Parliament-robe*.

Argent, a tent between two pieces of scarlet cloth; on a chief azure . . . .—Company of Merchant TAILORS, Chester.

Piece of Cloth.

Clacks. See *Mill-wheels*.
Clam: a local term for the cockle, or *escallop*, by Scottish heralds.
Clapper. See *Bell*.
Clarenceux. See *Heralds*.
Clariné, (fr.): belled; applied to cows, sheep, &c., having bells.
Clarion, or *Claricord*. See *Rest*.
Clasp. See *Book* and *Medal*.
Claws of, and *Clawed*. See *Hammer*.
Claymore, or *Clymore*. See *Sword*.

Cleché. See *Cross* clechée, § 16.
Clenched: of a *hand* when closed.
Cleyed: i.q. clawed, applied to *boars*, 'tusked and cleyed or.'
Close: a term applied to *wings* of birds; and to *helmets*.
Closing-tongs. See *Founder's tongs*.
Cloué, (fr.): nailed; said of horseshoes, dog-collars, &c., when the nails are of a different tincture.

Clothiers' implements. The *habick* was a tool used for holding the cloth firm whilst it was operated on by the *teazel* or other instrument. The word is probably a corruption of the 'habiting hook,' and it is represented on the arms of the Company, as shewn in the margin.

The *teazel* is referred to elsewhere, under *thistle*. The *shears* for cropping the pile or nap for rendering the surface smooth will be found under the implements of *Weavers*.

Habick.

The *preen* appears to be an instrument which was used for much the same purpose as the teazel. It does not, however, occur in the insignia of any of the companies, but it is found in the arms of a private person, where it seems to have been chosen for the sake of the name.

Azure, a preen or—PREENER.

Sable, a chevron ermine between two habicks in chief argent and a teazel in base slipped or—CLOTHWORKERS' Company, London [originally incorporated 1482, by the style of the Fraternity of the Assumption of the Blessed Virgin

PREENER.

of the Sheermen of London; confirmed in 1528, but incorporated as Clothworkers' Company by Queen Elizabeth: arms granted 1530].

Clouds (fr. *nuée*) sometimes occur as bearings, as in the cases of the MERCERS' and DRAPERS' Companies, and a few families. Very frequently arms, &c., are represented issuing from the clouds; and in French arms still more so, since the *dextrochere* as it issues from the side of the shield is generally surrounded by clouds. The partition-line called *nebuly* (fr. *nuagé*), which may be considered as a conventional representation of clouds, is common in heraldry. See also examples under *Ray* and *Tiara*.

Azure, three clouds proper radiated in base or; each surmounted with a triple crown of the second, the cap gules—DRAPERS' Company [arms granted 1439].

Sable, a hand proper vested argent issuing out of the clouds in chief of the second rayonnée or, feeling the pulse of an arm also proper issuing from the sinister side of the shield, vested argent: in base ... &c.—College of PHYSICIANS, incorporated 1523.

Gules, a cloud as a chief nebuly azure and argent, with thirteen rays alternately plain and wavy descending palewise or—LESUNE, Harl. MS. 4199.

Gules, a battle-axe held by a dexter arm in fesse issuing from clouds on the sinister; in chief two mullets argent—PETTET.

Clove: the spice so called. It is usually drawn not exactly in its natural form, but as in the margin, resembling the arms of the *Cross Avellane*, to which the filbert has been supposed to supply the design.

Argent, a chevron gules between nine cloves sable, three three and three [or better, perhaps, in 'three groups of three'] —GROCERS' Company, Lond. [Inc. 1346, arms granted 1531].

Or, a camel passant between three cloves sable—CLOVE, Wilts.

Sable, a chevron between three cloves or—DUFFIELD.

Vair, on a fesse gules, five cloves argent—BUSHBY, Cumberland.

Cloves.

Coach: such a charge will be found only in the arms of the Company.

Azure, a chevron between three coaches or—Company of COACHMAKERS and COACH HARNESS-MAKERS [Incorporated and arms granted 1677].

Cock (fr. *coq*), sometimes called *barn-door cock* or *dunghill-cock*, but as other species are always mentioned with some additional epithet, no such distinction is necessary. The *game-cock* is sometimes specially named, and so is the *hen*.

The *Cock* is found, though rarely, in ancient rolls of arms. And with the Cock should be grouped the *Capon* and the *Cockerell* (fr. *coquerelle*). It will be observed that in very many instances the charge is borne for the sake of the play upon the name of the bearer.

Clover-leaf. See *Trefoil*.

Cloyshacke. See *Harp*.

Club. See *Staff*.

Cluster of Grapes. See *Vine*.

Clymant, or *Climant*. saliant, applied to the goat.

Coal-pick. See *Axe*.

Coambulant: rarely used for walking side by side.

Coat of Arms, or *Coat-armour*: the general term for the *escutcheon* or shield of arms, but properly applicable to the *Surcoat*, and especially to that of a pursuivant.

Cob-fish. See *Herring*.

Cockerel. See *Cock*.

Cockle-shell. See *Escallop*.

A cock with the *comb* of a different tincture may be blazoned *crested* or *combed* (fr. *crêté*) of such tincture; so also with the *gills*, or *uncelles*, when the term *jellopped* (written frequently *jowlopped*) or *wattled* (fr. *barbé* or *barbelé*) is used. Other terms are also found; *armed* (fr. *armé* or *onglé*); legged or *membered* (fr. *membré*); spurred (fr. *éperonné*); beaked (fr. *becqué*). With the French the term *hardi* is used when the right leg is raised; and in both English and French arms *crowing* (fr. *chantant*), when the beak is represented as open.

William de Estotevile de la Marche, burelé d'argent et de goulz a trois cockes noirs—Roll, temp. Hen. III.

Sire Richard de Cokfeld, de azure a une crois e iiij coks de or—Roll, temp. Ed. II.

Argent, three barn-door cocks crested and jowllopped sable—Cockayne [also borne by Cockburne, Scotland].

Gules, three barn-door cocks argent, armed, crested, and jowllopped or—Cock.

Azure, a dunghill-cock perched upon an escallop or—Otterbury.

Argent, a cock gules—Cheke.

Azure, three cocks argent—Chanticleer, Cornwall.

COCKAYNE.

Sable, three cocks or, membered gules—Ovington, Kent.

Argent, three cocks sable, armed, crested, and wattled or—Pomfret, 1730.

Argent, three game-cocks gules, crested and wattled sable—Cockman.

Argent, a fesse between three hens sable—Ayloft.

Argent, three capons sable armed, crested, and jowllopped or—Caponhurst.

Argent, on a chevron vert three cockerells of the first membered gules—Chickerin, Norwich.

Gules, a chevron between three cocks crowing argent—Crow, Suffolk.

D'argent, au coq hardi de sable, crêté becqué, barbé et membré de gueules—Le Cocq, Artois.

D'or, au coq chantant de gueules—Le Coq, de Bièville, Normandie.

The *Cock's head* is also frequently borne as a charge.

Argent, on a fesse between three cock's heads erased sable crested and jellopped gules a mitre or, all within a bordure of the third, charged with eight ducal coronets of the fourth—Jesus College, Cambridge.

Argent, on a fesse between three cock's heads erased sable, crested and

jowllopped gules, a mitre or—John ALCOCK, Bp. of Rochester, 1472; Bp.
of Worcester, 1476; Bp. of Ely, 1486—1500.

Cockatrice: amongst the monsters with wings the *Cockatrice* and the *Wyvern* (Sax. *wivere*, a serpent) are frequently represented in heraldry.   They differ from the groups of *Griffins* and
Dragons, inasmuch as they have only two legs, and the hinder
part of the body ends in a large and long tail. The Cockatrice is
represented as having the head of a *cock*, but the tongue extended and barbed. Otherwise it is very similar to the *wyvern*,
the essential difference being that the *wyvern* has the head of
a *serpent*, but with the tongue extended and barbed.   The frequency of such devices was due, no doubt, to the tales of travellers brought from the East, which had a special charm for
many a designer of arms.

The *Cockatrice*, perhaps, when correctly drawn, should have
the legs and feet of a cock—the *Wyvern* those of an eagle, but
these details are seldom observed in representation.

Argent, a cockatrice azure, combed, beaked, wattled, and membered
gules—DANCYE, Lancaster.

Argent, a cockatrice volant sable, crested,
membered, and beaked—LANGLEY, Lancaster.

Or, a cockatrice, the tail nowed with a serpent's head sable, comb, wattles, and head
gules; in the beak a trefoil vert—ASHEN-
HURST, Derby.

Argent, a wyvern, wings endorsed, gules—
DRAKE, of Ashe, Devon. (Bart., 1660.)

Argent, on a bend sable, between two lions
rampant of the last, a wyvern volant, in bend
of the field, langued gules—RUDINGS.

DRAKE.

Argent, a wyvern passant azure—DAVET.

Argent, a wyvern with wings endorsed sable
—TILLEY, Devon.

Gules, a wyvern volant or—SOUTHWELL.

Gules, a wyvern or, on a chief azure three
mullets or—Priory of S. Peter, HEREFORD, and
also of HAVERFORDWEST.

Vert, a wyvern-dragon passant volant argent
swallowing a child proper — WARRINGEHAM
[from Harl. MS. 1404].

RUDINGS.

Sire Johan de FOLEBOURNE de or, a un cheveron de sable e ij wyvres de sable—Roll, temp. ED. II.

Sir Edmon de MAULEE, de or, a une bende de sable: en la bende iij wyvres de argent—*Ibid.*

Or, a wivern between three fleur-de-lys vert—HINCHLIFFE, Bp. of Peterborough, 1769-94.

Gules, a wivern or, on a chief azure, three mullets pierced of the second—HEREFORD Priory, Pembrokeshire.

[The figure of the Wyvern here given in the margin is from one of the supporters of the arms of KENNEDY, co. Ayr.]

KENNEDY.

Cockatrices also occur in the arms of the families of DRAKE; BRENT, Co. Kent; BOOTH; BOGAN, Devon; BROWN, Norfolk; JONES; Henry SEYNES, Newark.

Wyverns are borne by TAME, Oxford; DRAPER, Oxford, 1613; BRENT, Oxford, 1613; MACBEATH, Scotland; DE WINTON, Gloucester.

Similar to the Cockatrice is the *Basilisk*, and it is usually held to be synonymous with it, but it is said in books of heraldry to have an additional head, like that of a dragon, at the end of the tail, and hence the *Basilisk* is sometimes termed an *Amphisian Cockatrice*. Similar also is the *Amphistere*, which is found frequently in French coats of arms, and is described as a winged serpent with dragons' feet, of which the tail ends in another serpent, or in more than one serpent; in the latter case it is said to be *gringolé* of so many serpents. The *Hydra* (fr. *hydre*) also occurs in heraldic designs, but though compared with the dragon it is more like the wyvern, having only two legs, even if it has those. The peculiarity is that it partakes somewhat of its mythological prototype, inasmuch as it has seven heads—though in one case the blazoning especially reduces the number to five.

Argent, a cockatrice with wings endorsed and tail nowed; at the end thereof a dragon's head all sable—LANGLEY, Dalton, Yorkshire.

Argent, a basilisk, wings endorsed, tail nowed sable—LANGLEY, Hathorpe Hall, Yorkshire.

D'azure, a l'amphistere d'or—DU BOURG SAINTE-CROIX, Bresse.

Paly of six or and azure, on a chief gules, three five-headed hydras as the first—GRANDPRÉ.

A hydra, wings endorsed, vert, scaled or—Crest of BARRET of Avely.

Cod. The representations of different varieties of fish are not always to be distinguished, though the names are so in the blazon. The *Cod*, the *Hake*, the *Ling*, and the *Whiting* (all belonging to the family of *Gadidæ*), are found on various coats of arms. The *Hake* is rather more slender, and comparatively larger about the head, than the cod, but otherwise the drawing does not distinguish the several kinds. Indeed the drawing of fish in heraldry is very arbitrary, and it will be observed it is mostly in punning arms that fish occur.

Sable, a chevron between three codfishes naiant argent—Codd.

Azure, three codfishes naiant in pale argent—Beck.

Azure, three hake fishes hauriant argent—Hake.

Argent, on a bend sable, three whitings proper—Whiting.

Azure, three whitings hauriant argent—Whittington.

Argent, on a fesse dancetty azure, three ling's heads erased or—Caldwell, Staffordshire.

On a fesse wavy between three dolphins embowed, three hakes naiant with a coronet over each—Mayor's Seal, town of Wexford.

Gules, three hakes hauriant argent—Hakehed, Ireland.

Azure, three hakes hauriant argent—Hacket.

Vert, three hakes hauriant argent—Doney. [Blazoned sometimes as *breams*.]

CALDWELL.

The *haddock* (which is grouped by naturalists under the same division) does not occur in any coat of arms, but the crest of the family of Haddock, Lancashire, is—

A dexter hand holding a haddock.

A species of *ling* is called sometimes the *burbot*, but it lives in fresh water; and this

HADDOCK.

is also called the *coney fish*, and supposed to be allusive in the following arms.

Argent, on a chevron azure, a coney courant between two burbot or coney fish hauriant of the field. On a chief chequy argent and azure a rose gules—Richard Cheyney, Bp. of Gloucester, 1562-79.

Cœur. See *Heart*. With French heralds ' en cœur' means in the fesse-*point*.

Cocoa-nut. See *Palm*.

Cog. See *Mill-wheel*.

Cognizance. See *Badge*.

Collar. A plain collar is not unfrequently found surrounding the necks of *Dogs, Lions,* &c. It is generally of gold, sometimes of silver, rarely of another tincture. The plain collar does not appear to be employed separately as a charge, but when an animal is said to be 'collared' or *gorged* (fr. *accolé* or *colleté*) a plain collar is implied; still animals are often gorged with ducal and other *coronets.*

When a beast is *gorged and chained,* the chain must be affixed to the collar and reflected over the back, as in the annexed example. Sometimes a double collar is named.

Argent, a lion rampant, gules, ducally gorged and chained or—PHILIPPS, Pembroke.

PHILIPPS.

Sire Johan de HAVERINGE, de argent a un lion rampaund de goules od la couwe forchie e un coler de azur—Roll, temp. ED. II.

Argent, three annulets or, on a chief argent a greyhound courant gules collared of the second—RHODES.

Sable, a lion rampant ermine with a collar gemel azure ; therefrom pendent an escutcheon of the last charged with a mullet argent—POWNALL, Lancaster.

Collar of SS. Collars studded with the letter S, or consisting of many of that letter linked together, either alone or alternately with other figures, have been at times much worn by persons holding great offices in the State, as well as by the gentry of various ranks from esquires upwards. They were worn by the Lords Chief Justices, the Lord Chief Baron of the Exchequer, the Lord Mayor of London, the Kings of Arms, and Heralds, and the Serjeants at Arms, though frequently they are little more than ordinary chain collars with the links twisted so as to resemble the letter S.

Cointise: a *surcoat;* old fr. term used for the *lambrequin* or *mantle,* q.v.

Cokar, *China.* See *Palm.*

Coler (old fr.), *collar.*

Collar-point. See *Point.*

Collared, i.q. *gorged* (fr. *colleté*): having a *collar,* q.v.

The signification of the letter S in connection with the collar has been variously explained. Perhaps the best conjectures are, either that the device was invented to represent the word 𝔖𝔬𝔲𝔢𝔯𝔞𝔤𝔫𝔢, the favourite motto of Henry IV., which he bore when Earl of Derby, and retained when he succeeded to the throne; or else that that word was suggested by an after-thought of some courtier, or perhaps of the royal jeweller himself, as explanatory of the form which the workman had adopted, and which was so suitable to chain-work.

There is ample evidence that the collar of SS was originally a badge of the house of Lancaster, and that Henry IV. was the first sovereign who granted to the nobility as a mark of royal favour a licence to wear it; and, according to an old chronicle, Henry V., on the 25th day of October, 1415, gave to such of his followers as were not already noble permission to wear "un collier semé de lettres S de son ordre."

The right of knights to wear such a collar of gold was recognised by Act of Parliament, 24 Hen. VIII., but restricted to persons who were not below that grade.

The collar of SS begins to appear upon monuments at the beginning of the fifteenth century, and upon distinguished persons of both sexes. It is represented as if worn by Sir Thomas Burton, in 1381, on the brass at Little Casterton Church (though the brass was not executed till *circa* 1410). It is also represented as worn by Sir Robert de Hattfield, who is attired as a civilian, and by his wife, on the brass in Oulton Church, Yorkshire, which is dated 1409. On a brass in Hereford Cathedral it is represented as worn by Lady Delamere (1435), but not by her husband. The monumental effigy in Little Dunmow Church, Essex, to Matilda, Countess of Huntingdon, who lived *temp.* King John, is of no value as evidence, as the effigy is of the fifteenth century. The example here given is from the brass of Sir John DRAYTON, 1411, which exists in Dorchester Church, Oxon.

Sir John DRAYTON.

The *Collar* of *Suns* and *Roses* also should be mentioned here, being one of the badges of Henry IV. It occurs on several brasses, and the right to bear this mark of favour was no doubt acquired direct from the sovereign. This collar was not so common as that of the SS. According to Haines, it occurs on brasses at Rougham, Norfolk, *c.* 1470; at Lilling-

Collar of Suns and Roses.

ston Lovell, Oxon, 1471; at Broxbourne, Herts, 1473; at Sardley, Derbyshire, 1478; at St. Albans, 1480; and at Little Easton, Essex, 1483.

Some *kings of arms* and *heralds* have also encircled their arms with the collars pertaining to their degrees.

College. In one case only as yet a representation of a College occurs in a coat of arms, and it can scarcely be said to be an English example.

Vert, a college argent masoned proper; in chief the rising sun or, the hemisphere of the third—VIRGINIA College.

Colours. Although, properly speaking, there are but the nine *tinctures* in Heraldry (q.v.), of which two are metals, yet in some coats of arms certain *colours* are incidentally and perhaps irregularly named. Such, for instance, as a *lion* partly of an *ash* colour; a horse, of a *bay* colour; a horse's head and wild-ducks, *brown;* the *mine,* in the arms of the Miners' Company (q.v.), of *earth* colour, with the chief *brown* colour. The *carnation* is frequently used with the French heralds for pink or flesh colour, applied to human subjects, and especially the face; *grey* is applied to hair, *russet* is said of a parrot, and *yellow* of a pheasant's breast. With respect to *white,* it may be used instead of argent for the lining of mantles, which are not generally taken for cloth of silver, but a pure white fur,

---

College of Arms. See *Herald.*

College-pots. See *Cups.*

Collying: a term applied by writers on falconry to the bird with head erect when preparing to take flight, and may be found applied by some heralds to the *eagle* also.

Cold-wells. See *Wells.*

which some call the litvit's skin. It often happens, too, that certain charges are blazoned ' proper,' and these when rightly represented frequently require the use of other colours than the recognised tinctures of heraldry. *Gold* and *silver*, with heralds of the seventeenth century, are terms used for *or* and *argent* in complicated arms, where these tinctures have been already named, but solely for the purpose of avoiding repetition of the same word.

Argent, a lion rampant sable, the head, paws, and half of the tail ash colour—GWILT, South Wales.

Argent, a horse passant, bay colour, between two tilting-spears in fesse sable—SHEKEL, Pebworth.

Argent, a horse passant, bay colour, holding in his mouth a tulip slipped proper—ATHERTON. [Noted by Glover as a quartering.]

. . . . . A chief or charged with three horse's heads erased brown— WRENNE.

Gules, a chevron argent between three wild ducks brown—WOLRICH.

D'argent, aux deux jumeaux accouplés de carnation posé sur une terrasse de sinople—Martin de BOUDARD.

Gules, three men's heads couped at the shoulders argent, crined grey— EDYE.

Per pale, argent and gules, in the dexter fesse point a parrot russe, beaked and legged or—Richard SENHOUSE, Bp. of Carlisle, 1624-26.

Argent, a chevron azure between three pheasant cocks vert, beaked and legged gules, breast yellow—Richard CHOPIN, Alderman of London.

In poetical blazon, however, with old writers, other than technical terms are used. For instance, at the Siege of Caerlaverock, which took place A.D. 1300, we learn from a contemporary poem of the siege that Robert FITZ-ROGER had his banner

" De or e de *rouge* esquartelée, O un bende tainte en *noir*,"

which we should now blazon

Quarterly or and gules, a bend sable.

And the Earl of Hereford had

" Baniere out de *Inde* cendal fort   De or fin, dont au dehors asis
O une *blanche* bandelée   Qt en rampant lyonceaus sis,"
De deus costices entrealée

which would be blazoned now as

Azure, a bend argent cotised or, between six lioncels rampant of the second.

Other examples will be found, e.g. in an example given under *cadency*, where it will be seen that ' gules' is described as 'red as blood,' *vermeille cum sanc;* and under *chaplet*, 'deux chapeaux des roses *vermals*.'

Columbine, or Columbian *flower*, (*aquilegia vulgaris*), seems to be used more frequently than many other flowers. Possibly this may be owing to the fact that it was the *badge* of the House of LANCASTER. It occurs in one of the London insignia. The ancient and heraldic method of drawing is shewn in the margin, but in modern times it has been drawn as shewn below, in the arms of HALL, Bishop of Oxford. The fr. *ancolie* is borne by the family of BACONEL, Picardie, while the allied *campanule* is borne by that of HESPEL, Artois.

Columbine.

Argent, a chevron sable between three columbines azure slipped proper—COVENTRY, Lord Mayor of London, 1425.

Argent, a chevron between three columbines pendent azure, barbed gules, slipped vert—TIMOTHY HALL, Bishop of Oxford, 1688–90.

Argent, a chevron engrailed gules between three columbines proper, stalked and leaved vert—COOKS' Company, incorporated 1472.

Sable, a bend argent between three columbines of the second—WALSHE, Norfolk.

Argent, a saltire chequey or and azure between four columbines proper—COLLINGBORNE, Devon.

HALL, Bishop of Oxford.

Or, on a bend azure three buckles of the first, in chief a Columbian flower slipped proper—STIRLING, Dundee.

Or, three columbine buds vert—CADMAN.

Argent, two columbine slips crossed and drooping proper, flowered purple—BESSELL.

Or, a chevron sable between three columbines azure—CHEPMERDEN.

Colt. See *Horse.*

Comb. (1) See *Flax - comb* and *Wool-comb* under *Woolcard;* (2) See *Curry-comb;* (3) See *Cock's comb.*

Column. See *Pillar.*

Combed : used of a *cock* when the comb is of a different tincture.

Combel. See *Chief.*

Comb, (fr. *peigne*) : the comb when blazoned without any prefix is to be represented as in the margin. It is not uncommon, as will be seen. More frequently the kind of comb is named : e.g. the *Jersey-comb* or *wool-comb, flax-comb, curry-comb*, &c.

Comb.

Gules, a chevron between three combs argent—PONSONBY.

Azure, a lion passant guardant between three combs or—Company of COMBMAKERS, incorporated 1636.

Sable, three combs argent—TUNSTALL, Bp. of London, 1522 ; of Durham, 1530–59.

Ermine, on two bars sable three combs argent—LUCAS.

Argent, a fesse wavy between three combs gules—TERNOM, Essex.

Argent, on a bend gules three combs or—COMBE.

Comet, (fr. *comète*), or *Blazing-star :* an estoile of six points, with a tail extending from it in bend. The term *bearded* (fr. *caudé*) is applied to the tail when the tincture is different.

Azure, a comet or—CARTWRIGHT, Scotland. [Otherwise, Azure, a comet in the dexter chief point with rays streaming in bend or.]

Azure, a four-pointed comet star . . .—HURS-TON.

Per fesse or and azure, a pile counterchanged; in the chief a lion rampant; in base on each side of bottom of pile a blazing comet counterchanged—COLDWELL, Prebendary of Ely, 1702.

CARTWRIGHT.

Combatant: a word expressive of the position of two lions rampant face to face, or of two goats. The word rampant, though sometimes used as well, is superfluous.

Or, two lions (rampant) combatant gules, armed and langued azure—WYCOMBE.

Argent, two goats salient, combatant argent—KIDD.

Commisse. See *Tau Cross*, § 34.

Complement: fulness ; the *moon* in her complement = 'full moon.'

Compony. See *Goboné.*

Conché, (fr.) : applied to a Dolphin much curved, the head nearly touching the tail (i.e. like a spiral shell).

Compartment: a term peculiar to the heraldry of Scotland. An ordinary compartment is a kind of carved panel placed below the shield bearing the motto, and the supporters standing upon it. It has no fixed form, but may be varied at pleasure.

Compartments of special forms, however, have been attributed to certain Scottish families.

Compasses, (fr. *compas*): in the insignia of the Company of Carpenters, as well as in others named, this instrument is borne expanded chevronwise, as shewn in the margin. For the *Compass Dial,* see under *Magnetic Needle.*

Compasses.

Argent, a chevron engrailed between three pairs of compasses expanded at the points sable—Company of CARPENTERS.

Argent, an annulet between the legs of a pair of compasses sable—HADLEIGH.

Azure, three pairs of compasses extended or, pointed sable—BONNY.

Per chevron crenelly or and sable, three pairs of compasses extended counterchanged—CARTWRIGHT.

Gules, a chevron argent between two pairs of compasses in chief extended at the points and a sphere in base or; on a chief of the last a pale azure between two roses of the first seeded of the third barbed vert; on the pale an escallop of the second—JOINERS' Company [Inc. 1569].

Sable, on a chevron engrailed between three towers argent a pair of compasses of the first—MASONS' Company [Inc. 1411; arms granted 1473].

Sable, on a chevron between three towers argent a pair of compasses open chevronways of the first—The FREEMASONS' Society [as given by Edmondson].

Composed arms: a name given by heraldic writers in cases where a man has, or is supposed to have, added a portion of the arms of his wife or ancestors to his own, to shew his alliance or descent. The introduction of *marshalling,* q.v., is considered to have superseded it.

Cone: of a *pine,* q.v.

Coney. See *Hare.*

Confronting: said of two animals facing, or respecting each other. Conf. *Affrontant.*

Congers, or *Conger-eels.* See *Eels.*

Conjoined, or *Conjunct,* or *Joinant:* joined together, so as to touch each other; e.g. of *annulets* (not to be represented as interlaced): applied also sometimes to *Mascles.*

Coot, or *Baldcoot:* amongst the family of the·Rails (*rallidæ*) the *Coot* (*fulica atra*) and the *Moor-hen* (*gallinula chloropus*) alone are found on coats of arms.

Argent, three coots proper—COOTE, Lincoln.

Argent, a chevron between three coots sable—SOUTHCOTE, Devon.

Sable, a bend between six baldcoots or—BOULCOTT, Hereford.

Gules, on a bend argent three baldcoots sable, beaked and legged of the first, in the sinister chief a unicorn's head erased as the second—MARSDEN, Manchester.

Argent, a chevron between three moor-hens . . . LUXMOORE, Devon.

Borne also by families of COOLIN, KILBURNE, &c.

Cord : cords by themselves are but seldom borne, but are very frequently attached to other charges, which are there described as *corded* (fr. *cordé*), and this is used of almost any charge bound with or having cords, when those cords are of a different tincture, e.g. a *bale*, *woolpack*, *bag*, *bow*, *harp*, &c., though some of these are described also as *stringed*. In one or two exceptional cases an ordinary is corded, e.g. a *bar*, *Cross*, &c., meaning that it is wreathed round with a cord, and not to be confused with *cabled*.

Or, a chevron ermine between three cords erased at each end and tied in knots vert—CLEAVER.

Azure, four hawk's bells or conjoined in saltire by a double and wreathed cord alternately argent and sable—Sir Ralph JOSSELYN, Alderman of London.

Sable, two bars argent, corded or wreathed gules—WAYE, Devonshire, confirmed 1574].

Although not borne by name, cords are frequently so in fact, under the name of *knots*, of which there are the following varieties, though they are chiefly employed as badges, and not as charges. It may be noted that theoretically the cords are of silk.

Contourné, (fr.) : of animals, turned (contrary to the general rule) towards the sinister side of the shield.

Contre hermine: the fr. term for *ermines*.

Contrary-conyd: used by Upton for *gyronny* ; perhaps only meaning *counter-posed*.

Contre, (fr.) i.q. *Counter*.

Contre trevis : old fr. term for party per fesse.

Bourchier's Knot. This device is many times repeated
upon the tomb of Abp. Bourchier (1486) at
Canterbury, hence the name. It appears also
in the east window of the Dean's chapel in
that cathedral, where it is tinctured *or*.

Bourchier's Knot.

The *Bowen's Knot* is a name which is given to a knot known
as the *Tristram* or *true-lovers'* knot, and which is
figured as in the margin; but with the French the
lacs d'amour, which sometimes occurs, is figured
rather differently.

Bowen's Knot.

Gules, a chevron between three tristram or true-love knots
argent—BOWEN. [Sir James ABOWEN,—also Abp.OWEN and BOWEN.]

Gules, a chevron between in chief two true-love knots, in base a lion
rampant or—Sir Jamys ap OWAIN.

Or, on a chevron gules a true-lovers' knot of the first—Town of STAF-
FORD.

Azure, a lion rampant or, in a true-love knot argent between four
fleurs de lys, their stalks bending towards the centre of the second—
HOGHE.

D'azur, à un lacs-d'amour de sable, accompagné de trois molettes
d'éperon du même—GUILBERT, Normandie.

The DACRE family are recorded to have a peculiar and distinctive knot on their badge or
cognizance. The Arms of the family who were
established in Westmoreland and Cumberland
are as follows :—

Dacre's Knot.

Gules, three escallops or—DACRE. And it will be observed that the scallop shell is repeated in the badge.

The Lincolnshire branch of the HENEAGE family
have, according to the visitation of the county, a peculiar badge
or cognizance in the shape of a knot which is suggested by the motto "Fast though united." This
knot does not appear to have been used as the crest,
which is a *greyhound courant*.

Heneage's
Knot.

The three following knots in a similar manner are
respectively the badges of the three families of LACY,

Copper. (1) See *Wiredrawers;*   Coquilles. See *Escallops.*
(2) *Cake of.* See *Metal.*   Corbie, and *Corbeau.* See *Raven.*

S<small>TAFFORD</small>, and W<small>AKE</small>.   The last is borne by the family as a crest.

Lacy's Knot.   Stafford's Knot.   Wake's Knot.

The *Harington Knot* is simply an ordinary *fret* q.v., while the *Gordian Knot* is a term applied to the insignia of the kingdom of N<small>AVARRE</small>.

The *Hatband* (q.v.) of the F<small>ELTMAKERS</small>' Company might be considered a kind of knot, and the *hanks* of silk or cotton are also frequently termed knots.

Cordon (fr. *Cordelière*), is the silver cord which encircles the arms of widows. Its institution has been attributed to Anne of Bretagne, widow of Charles VIII. King of France, "who," says Ashmole (Order of G., p. 126), "instead of the military belt or collar, bestowed a cordon or lace on several ladies, admonishing them to live chastly and devoutly, always mindful of the cords and bonds of our Saviour Jesus Christ; and to engage them to a greater esteem thereof, she surrounded her escocheon of arms with the like cordon."   The special use is to distinguish the arms of widows from those of wives; but in England it is but rarely painted upon funeral achievements. The precise form and number of the knots is arbitrary. The arms given in the illustration are thus blazoned.

Cordon.

Argent, a bend engrailed sable—R<small>ADCLIFFE</small>; and sable a saltire argent —A<small>STON</small>.—The arms within a cordon.

Cordals : the tasselled cords sometimes attached to mantles and robes of estate.

Cormorant (lat. *Phalacrocorax*, fr. *Cormoran*), written by some naturalists, *Corvorant*, occurs at times in arms. The bird in the arms of WARBURTON, and forming a portion of the insignia of LIVERPOOL, is a cormorant, but it is known and blazoned there by name of the *lever*. Perhaps the *Sea Aylet* also may be considered similar to the Cormorant. *Cormorants' heads* sometimes are borne, as also *Sea Aylet heads*.

Sable, a cormorant argent—POPELLER.

Azure, three cormorants or—SEVENS, or SEVANS, Kent.

Gules, on a bend wavy argent three cormorants sable, beaked and membered or—Sir Robert READE [Puisne Justice of the King's Bench, 1496].

Argent, a cormorant sable, beaked and legged gules, holding in the beak a branch of sea-weed called laver inverted vert—City of LIVERPOOL

Or, on a chevron azure between three cormorant's heads erased sable as many acorns slipped of the first—CHIDDERLEGH, Cornwall.

Argent, a cross sable between four sea aylets of the second, beaked and membered gules—John AYLMER [Bp. of London, 1577].

Quarterly; first and fourth, argent, a chevron between three cormorants sable; second and third, a fret—WARBURTON [Bp. of Gloucester, 1760-79].

AYLMER, Bp. of London.

Probably allied in shape to the Cormorant, but not determinable to what species it belongs, is the *Gannapie*, which is found in some arms and referred to in heraldic works.

Argent, a chevron counter compony vert and azure between three gannapies of the last membered gules—WYKES [Glover's ordinary].

Argent, a chevron chequy azure and vert between three gannapies proper—WIKES, Devon.

Argent, a chevron sable between three gannapies [elsewhere drakes] azure—YEO, Colliton, Devon.

Cornish Chough: a bird of the crow kind, very common in Cornwall. It is bluish black, with red or orange-coloured beak and legs. This bearing was confined to Cornish families until Barker, who was Garter King of Arms, temp. Hen. VIII. granted it indiscriminately to any applicants for arms, and Cornish Chough.

amongst others to Cardinal WOLSEY, who was born in Suffolk; and so now borne by CHRIST CHURCH College, Oxford. [See an illustration of these arms under *blazon*.]

Argent, three Cornish choughs proper—PENESTON, Cornwall [and PENISTON, Oxfordshire].

Argent, a Cornish chough proper—TREVETHIN, Cornwall.

Argent, a fesse gules between six Cornish choughs —ONSLOW, Shropshire.

Azure, a bend or, and on a chief argent two Cornish choughs proper—VYNER.

Azure, three Cornish choughs proper; on a chief gules a lion passant guardant or—Town of CANTERBURY.

PENESTON.

Sable, guttee d'eau, on a fesse argent, three Cornish choughs—CORNWALLIS, Bp. of Lichfield, 1750; Abp. of Cant., 1768-83.

Or, a cross engrailed gules, in the dexter chief a Cornish chough proper—MASSENDEN, co. Lincoln.

Argent, three arrows gules one and two between as many Cornish choughs proper two and one—CHASTEIN.

Azure, a lion passant or; on a chief argent three Cornish choughs proper—ROFFEY.

The *Beckit* is supposed to resemble the Cornish chough, though the name does not appear in works by modern naturalists. But it is interesting as the canting arms ascribed (at what date is not clear) to S. Thomas A BECKET.

Argent, three Cornish choughs [beckits] proper two and one—BECKET, Abp. of Canterbury, 1162-70. [These, with the addition of a lion of England on a chief gules, were taken as the insignia of the city of CANTERBURY].

[Cornish Choughs are also borne by S. Thomas' Priory, Canterbury, S. Gregory's Priory, Canterbury, and by NICHOLS, Bp. of Bangor, 1408-17.]

Corner, (old fr. *corniere*). See *Point* and *Esquire*.

Cornet, used erroneously for *Bugle-horn*. Example cited from S. Benet's, HULME, instead of *coronets*. Vide *Crown*.

Corn. See *Wheat*.

Coronel. See *Cronel*.

Coronet. A small crown, or a crown borne by those who are not sovereigns; but generally synonymous with *Crown*, q.v.

Cottices or *Cottises*, (fr. *cotice;* old fr. *custere; liste* is also used) are mostly, if not invariably, borne in pairs, with a bend, or a charge or charges bendwise between them. More frequently the term *cotticed* is used, and as long as the bend is *plain* (i.e. with straight sides) and the *cottices* the same, to say a bend *cotticed* is more convenient than to say a bend between two *cottices*. But as it happens sometimes that the bend is plain and the cottice not so, then the latter blazoning is found to be the most convenient.

BOHUN.

Le counte CHAUMPAINE, dazur a une bende dargent a custeres dor diasprez—Roll, temp. HEN. III.

Humphry de BOUN, d'azur ung bend d'argent entre six leonceux d'or cotisee d'or [ove ung labell de goules]—*Ibid.*

Le counte de HERFORD, dazur a sis Liuncels dor a un bende dargent lyte [i.e. with listes] dor—Another Roll, temp. HEN. III.

When a single 'cottice' is shewn, it is called a *cost* (lat. *costa*, a rib). The cottice may be considered as the diminution of a bend containing one fourth part of the breadth of the ordinary.

Although the term *cotticed* is strictly applicable to the bend only, it is sometimes applied also to fesses, pales, chevrons, &c., and ordinaries are occasionally to be met with which are *double* and even *treble cotticed*. An instance of cottising with demi *fleurs-de-lis* may be seen under *fleur-de-lis*. *Cottisé* with French heralds is sometimes used for describing a field covered with ten or more bendlets of alternate colours, and for a diminution of the *cotice* they use the term *filet*.

COVE.

Gules, a bend argent, cotticed or—COVE.

Argent, a bend between two cotices engrailed sable—WHITFIELD.

Argent, on a bend engrailed, cotised plain sable three mullets or—Lancelot ANDREWES, Bp. of Chichester, 1605 ; of Ely, 1609; afterwards of Winchester, 1619—1626.

Argent, a lion passant between two cotices gules—GAWLER.

Sable, a bend between two cottices dancetty or—CLOP-TON.

Ermine, a fesse gules, cotised wavy sable—DODD.

Argent, a fesse double cotised sable—GULFORD, Staffordshire.

Gules, a fesse double coticed argent—PRAYERS, Essex.

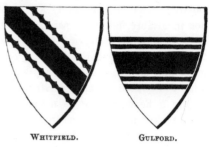

WHITFIELD.   GULFORD.

Argent, a fesse ermine, double cotised sable—HARLESTON.

Cotton : we have cotton incidentally mentioned in one or two arms. We have the *cotton tree* (Gossypium) or *cotton plant* notably in the arms of the great founder of the firm of ARKWRIGHTS, and cotton-*hanks* (q.v.) as well as *bundles of cotton* are found borne by families bearing the name of COTTON.

ARKWRIGHT.
(Cotton-tree.)

Argent, on a mount vert, a cotton-tree fructed proper, on a chief azure between two bezants an inescutcheon of the field charged with a bee volant proper—ARKWRIGHT, Derby.

Barry of six argent and azure, three bundles of cotton or.—COTTON.

Couchant, (fr. *couché*), i.e. lying down, is a term not often used, but it may be applied both to beasts of prey as well as to beasts of chase, that is to the lion as well as to the deer. Beasts thus described should be drawn with their heads upright, to distinguish their position from dormant. With beasts of chase the more usual term to represent this position is *lodged*.

Cotoyé, (fr.) : a term used by French heralds with similar signification to *accompagné*, only that the charges are placed along the sides of, or in the same direction as the sides of, the ordinary to which the term is applied.

Couched. See *Chevron*.

Coué, (old fr.), or *cowé* : i.q. *coward*. See *Tail*.

Coulissé, (fr.): a castle is so described when the *herse* or *portcullis* is down, and fills up the gateway.

Coulter of a *Plough*, q.v.

Argent, a chevron gules between three lions couchant of the second—NEWMAN, co. Cork.

Argent, on a mount, a buck couchant under a tree all proper—HISLOP, Devon.

Argent, a chevron between three talbots couchant sinister argent—TRASAHER, Cornwall.

Counter, (fr. *contre*), simply means opposite; but with this general sense it is variously employed.

When applied to the position of two animals, it signifies that they are turned in contrary directions, i.e. back to back, as two foxes *counter-salient* in saltire. If but one animal is spoken of, it means that it faces the sinister, as a lion *counter-rampant*, that is in an opposite direction to that which is usual. Two lions accosted *counter-couchant* means that they lie side by side, with their heads in contrary directions. Again, two lions *counter-couchant in pale* denotes that one occupies the upper part of the shield, and the other the lower, one facing the dexter, the other the sinister. One lion counter-couchant always faces the sinister. The term *counter-passant* (fr. *contre passant*) is used in the same way. A good example of *counter-trippant* will be found under *Deer*.

When applied to the *tinctures* the term *counterchanged* is of frequent occurrence, and signifies that the field consists of metal and colour separated by one of the lines of partition named from the ordinaries (per pale, per bend, &c.), and that the charges, or parts of charges, placed upon the metal are of the colour, and vice versa. *Counter-coloured* is sometimes, but erroneously, used. The annexed illustration affords a simple instance.

Per pale argent and sable, a chevron counter-changed— S. BARTHOLOMEW's Hospital, London. [Identical with those of LAWSON, Cumberland, (Bart., 1688.)]

S. BARTHOLOMEW'sHospital.

Counter-compony See *Gobony*.
Counter-vair. See *Vair*.

Counter-embattled, i.e. *embattled*, q.v., on both sides.

Sometimes the counterchange is more complicated, as in the following.

Barry of six, argent and gules, per pale indented, counterchanged — PETOE, Chesterton, Warwick.

Party per chevron or and azure, three mullets counterchanged—George DAY, Bp. of Chichester, 1543-51 and 1554-56.

Party per pale azure and purpure, three bars counterchanged—Adam HOUGHTON, Bp. of S. David's, 1361-89.

PETOE.

Or, a chevron paly of eight gules and argent, per chevron counterchanged—SUBRIDGE.

When *roundles* occur in counterchanged arms (whether cut through by the line of partition or not) they are not called bezants, torteaux, &c., as in other cases, but retain the appellation of roundles.

In old French rolls the term *de l'un en l'autre* occurs, and is still used by French heralds: it is in most cases practically equivalent to the more recent term *counterchanged*. The following are examples, and another will be found previously given under *bar gemel*. See also under *Party*.

Sire Robert de FARNHAM quartile de argent e de azure, a iiij cressauz de lun en lautre—Roll, temp. ED. II.

Monsieur de METSED, quarterly, d'or et gules, a quatre escallops de l'une et l'autre—Roll, temp. Ed. III.

Applied to various ordinaries and other charges, expressions like *counter-embattled* (fr. *contre-bretesse*), *counter-fleury* (fr. *contre-fleuré*), imply that both sides have alternate projections, while amongst the furs, *counter-vair* (fr. *contre-vaire*), *counter-potent* (fr. *contre-potencé*), &c., mean that the pieces are turned round contrary to their usual position. Examples are given under the several headings. *Counter-camp* is only a corruption of *counter-compony*. *Counter-ermine* is a term used by Nisbet for *Ermines*.

Applied to two chevrons the term *counter-pointed* would mean that the two chevrons are drawn in opposite directions, their points meeting in the centre of the shield.

Couped, or *Coupy*, (fr. *alaisé*), cut off in a straight line, as is often the case with the heads and limbs of animals, and so distinguished from *erased* [see example under *Boar*]. It is important to say where a head or limb is couped ; for instance, if *couped close* it would signify cut off close to the head. A *hand* is often said to be *couped at the wrist*.

The word *couped* is sometimes applied to the extremities of ordinaries, but they are more often said to be *humetté* or *alesé*.

Per fesse sable and or, a tree couped and eradicated counterchanged —BUCHER.

Azure, a dexter hand couped at the wrist argent—BROME, co. Salop.

Couped-fitchy is an expression used to signify that the cutting is not by a clean straight stroke, but that a point is left projecting.

Heraldic writers say that an ordinary when blazoned *couped* and *voided* would differ essentially from the same ordinary blazoned *voided* and *couped ;* but as no examples are given shewing that the difference exists in fact, it is hardly necessary to lay it down as a rule.

The French *coupé* has a distinct meaning, and is frequently employed to signify the partition of the shield horizontally into two equal parts. English heralds would describe the same as *party per fesse.*

Couple-close : this is one of the diminutives of the *chevron*, of which it should be one-fourth the width. Couple-closes are always borne in pairs, from which circumstance they derive their name. They are often borne with the chevron, which is then said to be between *couple-closes*, a more exact expression perhaps than *coticed.*

Argent, on a chevron between two couple-closes indented sable three escallops or—GONVILL. [The arms of Gonville and Caius College, Cambridge, founded 1348.]

Coupé, (fr.): used by French heralds for *party per fesse.*

Coupe, (fr.): *Cup.*

Couple-close. See *Chevronel.*

Courant, *Current*, or *Cursant:* running at full speed as a *Horse.* See also *Deer*, and Greyhound under *Dog.*

Cousu, (fr.), meaning 'sewed to,' and the term is practically a device used by French heralds in blazoning arms, when a chief and the field are both of a metal or both of a colour, in order to avoid the breach of the rule which forbids metal to be placed upon metal, or colour on colour. The same would apply to a canton or any other charge where the rule is broken. But while German and Spanish arms are frequently regardless of the rule, and the French sometimes, breaches are exceedingly rare in English armory.

Purpure, a cross moline or; on a chief cousu gules a lion passant of the second charged on the body with the letter L—Professorship of Law at CAMBRIDGE.

Crab: the common crab (lat. *cancer*, fr. *ecrevisse*) occurs on the coats of arms of several families.

Argent, on a bend sable between two crabs of the second a cross crosslet of the first—CROSSE.

Argent, a crab sable—SHRODER.

Argent, a chevron engrailed azure between three crabs gules—BRIDGER, co. Gloucester.

Argent, three crabs erect sable—ALLYM.

Argent, three crabs erect, gules—ALVANSTON.

Cramp, or *Crampoon*, and sometimes *cramp-iron* (fr. *Crampon*), are similar to the pieces of iron bent at each extremity, used for the purpose of strengthening a building. In their origin the irons are supposed to represent the hooked attachments to the scaling-ladders. Hence a *cross* may be *cramponny* (fr. *cramponné*) when the ends are thus terminated. Cramps are generally borne in pairs, and are sometimes (though erroneously) called *Fleams* or *Grapples*.

TIDERLEIGH.

Ermine, two cramps in saltire, sable—TIDERLEIGH, Dorset.

Argent, a chevron gules between three crampoons erect, sable—CHETHAM, Suffolk.

Or, a fesse between three cramp irons sable—HAGEN.

Covered pots. See *Cups*.

Cow. See *Bull*.

Coward: with the tail between the hind legs. See *Tail*.

Crane: this bird (*grus cineria*, fr. *grue*) is in heraldry often confounded with the *heron* and *stork*, it being in ordinary drawing precisely similar. It is borne by the following, and in two cases it will be observed that the crane holds in the dexter foot a *stone*, a somewhat singular device.

Argent, a crane sable standing on a staff raguly in base vert—CRANE, Cornwall.

Azure, a crane thrust through with a sword argent—FITHIE, Scotland.

Gules, a saltire ermine, between two cranes in pale argent and two garbs in fesse or—KIRSOPP, Northumberland.

Gules, a crane without the head argent—FINNIE, Scotland.

Argent, a crane holding a stone in the dexter foot gules; on a chief vert three crescents of the first—SIMPSON, Scotland.

Per chevron or and gules, in chief two cinquefoils of the second stalked and leaved vert, and in base a crane argent, in the dexter foot a stone sable—DEARMAN.

Crequer plant, (fr. *créquier*): is described as a wild plumtree, or cherry-tree, the fruit of which bears the name of '*creques*' in the patois of Picardy, and from the peculiar representation in the following arms the word *crequier* will be found sometimes given in dictionaries as meaning a sevenbranched candlestick.

Or, a crequer plant of seven branches eradicated sable—GIRFLET.

Crescent, (fr. *croissant*, old fr. *cresaunt*, pl. *cressanz*): a half-moon with the horns uppermost. The other positions of the half-*moon*, viz. *increscent* and *decrescent*, will be found mentioned under *moon*.

A crescent is the ancient ensign of the Turks, and was without doubt introduced into heraldry (properly so called) by the crusaders, and hence in arms dating from Henry III.'s reign onwards it is very frequently employed. It is also the mark of *cadency* assigned to the second house.

LUCY.

Cradle, a child. See under *Child*.

Crampet. See *Sword*.

Crampiron, *Crampoon*, and *Crampouné*. See *Cramp*.

Crancelin. See *Crown of Rue*.

Crenelly, *Crenellé*, and *Crenellated*. See *Embattled*.

Cresset. See *Beacon*.

Azure, a crescent argent—LUCY, London.

Frank de BOUN, de goules ung croissant de hermyn, ung urle dez merlotts d'ermyn—Roll, temp. HEN. III.

Sire William de RYTHE de azure a iij cressans de or—Roll, temp. ED. II.

Sire Johan de HANLON de goules a iij cressanz de argent—*Ibid.*

Monsire de RITHERE port d'asur a trois cressants d'argent—Roll, temp, ED. III.

Monsire de WAUTLAND d'argent un fes gules a deux cressents gules en le chief—*Ibid.*

Sable, a fesse dancetty or, between three crescents argent—ROUS, Earl of Stradbroke.

Gules, five crescents or—William de KILKENNY, Bp. of Ely, 1254-56.

Argent, a lion rampant gules between five pierced mullets, the two in chief enclosing a pair of crescents sable, the others as the second—DYSON.

ROUS.

In some coats it is noted that the *crescents* are to be reversed, i.e. with the horns downwards, and they are then blazoned as *pendent.*

Gules, a bend argent between six crescents 'pendent' or—Esmond FOLLYOT.

Crest, (fr. *cimier*): a figure anciently affixed to the *helmet* (fr. *casque*) of every commander, for his distinction in the confusion of battle, and in use before the hereditary bearing of coat armour: it is not unfrequently confounded with the *badge* or *cognizance*, which is a different thing. The word *timbre* includes the crest, helmet, wreath, &c., in short everything which is above the shield.

Crests do not appear to have been considered as in any way connected with the family arms until the fourteenth century, when Edward III. conferred upon William of Montacute, Earl of Salisbury, the right to bear an *eagle.*

The earliest representations of a crest in mediæval times in this country upon any authentic record is perhaps that on the

---

Crested, (fr. *crêté*) : of a bird when of another tincture. See under *Cock.* (2) Of a *helmet*, q.v.

Crevice, (corrupted from *écrevisse*), but used for the crayfish. See *Lobster.*

great seal of Richard the First, on which a lion appears figured on the helmet. It does not, however, seem to be a separate attachment, but to be a part of the helmet, and also appears in old illustrations to have been attached to the head of the horse as well as to that of the rider.

The royal crest of England—a lion upon a cap of estate—appears for the first time during the reign of King Edward III., upon one of his great seals. It continues the same to the present day, but is now generally placed upon the royal crown. The following are early instances of family crests:—

Quarterly; first and fourth barry of six or and azure, on a chief of the first, two pallets between as many esquires based of the second, over all an inescutcheon argent—MORTIMER. Second and third or, a cross gules—DE BURGH. *Crest*, out of a ducal coronet proper, a plume of feathers azure. Supporters, two lions guardant argent, their tails coward and reflected over their backs—Seal of Edmund MORTIMER, Earl of March [who died in 1424].

MORTIMER.

A plume of seven feathers in one height, ermine, placed upon a ducal coronet gules, is the *Crest* of Sir Simon de FELBRIGGE, K.G. [upon his stall-plate at Windsor].

Le timbre sur le heaulme ung teste morien, &c.—Grant of Arms to Alan TROWTE, 1376.

Ancient crests were, for the most part, the heads of men, or of birds, or of animals, or plumes of feathers. Such inappropriate figures as rocks, clouds, and rainbows, were never used for crests while heraldry was in its purity. The list of the varieties of crests found on arms at the present time would fill several pages, but it may be observed that heads and portions of men and animals are still found to be the most frequent.

Unless the contrary be expressly mentioned, a *crest* is always to be placed upon a *wreath*, and such was, in general, the most ancient practice, nor was it until the time of COOKE, Clarenceux, in Queen Elizabeth's reign, that the *ducal coronet* and the *chapeau* (which is also proper to a duke) were indiscriminately granted. Mural and other crowns are occasionally used in the same way.

Though corporate bodies may bear the arms of their founders just as the founders themselves bore them, it is scarcely in accordance with principle for them to bear helmets and crests (as many of the mercantile companies of London do). The oldest mercantile crest, perhaps, is that of the TALLOW-CHANDLERS, with the *Head* of S. John the Baptist in the charger, q. v.

Crickets: the *gryllus domesticus* of the naturalists has been chosen for the bearings in at least one coat of arms.

Argent, three blackbirds proper between two bars dancetty gules ; in chief a griffin segreant between two crickets of the second—GRIFFITHS, Hereford.

Cronel, or *Coronel,* (old fr. *burre :* see Harl. MS. 1392): the head of a jousting-lance, somewhat resembling a crown, whence its name.

Cronel.

Argent, a bend between three cronels sable.—CORNALL, or CROWNALL.

Argent, a chevron engrailed between three coronels sable—BYKELEY. [But in the arms of another branch of the family blazoned ducal coronets.]

Ermine, on a fesse gules, three cronels or—CROMWELL.

Azure, a chevron between three coronels or—SCOPLEY, Middlesex.

Crosier, or *Crozier,* (lat. *Crocia,* a crook, fr. *Croc,* not from *crux* or *cross*): this word is properly restricted to the crook of an Archbishop, a Bishop, or an Abbot.

Crible, (fr.): a sieve; used only in foreign arms.

Cri di guerre. See *Motto.*

Crined, (fr. *chevelé*): used with respect to the hair of a man's head, or the mane of a horse when of another tincture. See *Hair.*

Cripping iron. See *Glazier's* nippers.

Critched : old form of crutched, applied to a staff.

Croaking of a *raven,* q.v.

Crocodile. See *Alligator.*

Croisé, (fr.): used by French heralds, of a banner bearing a cross.

Croissant, fr. for *Crescent.*

Croix, *Rouge.* See Poursuivants under *Heralds.*

Croix, (fr.) : a *cross.*

The *Archbishop*, besides his *Crosier*, made use also of a *Staff* surmounted by a *cross;* that of the Pope having a triple cross. That of the see of Canterbury is represented as surmounted by a *cross formy*. In actual examples, some few of which remain, the Archbishop's Staff is found to be of various patterns and highly ornamented. The annexed cut represents the *Staff* of Archbishop Warham (who died 1520), from his tomb at Canterbury. It is borne of this form, but not so highly ornamented, in the ensigns of the archiepiscopal sees of Canterbury, Armagh, and Dublin.

The *Crosier* of a bishop ends in a curve resembling that of a shepherd's crook, from which there is every reason to believe it was derived, notwithstanding the opinion of some, that its origin is to be traced to the lituus of the priesthood of pagan Rome. There are many existing specimens of episcopal staves, which, while they all retain the general form of a crook, differ very much in their enrichments. In heraldry the Crosier. simple form shewn in the margin is generally adopted.

Staff of Abp. Warham.

The *Crosier* and *Staff* surmounted by a cross are, however, often confounded under the general term *Pastoral Staff*, and the French term *Crosse* is used equally for the crosier as for the staff with the cross.

Azure, a crosier in pale or, ensigned with a cross formée argent, surmounted of a pall of the last, edged and fringed of the second, charged with four crosses formée fitchée sable— See of CANTERBURY.

Azure, on a chevron gules between three Cornish choughs as many pastoral staves erect or—Henry DEANE, Bp. of Bangor, 1496; Bp. of Salisbury 1500; afterwards Abp. Cant. 1501-30.

Azure, a bend or; over all a crosier in bend sinister, the staff argent, the crook or—Abbey of S. Agatha, RICHMOND, Yorkshire.

Argent, three bars gules, over all a crosier in bend, staff argent, head or—Gilbertine Priory at ALVINGHAM, co. Lincoln.

Azure, two crosiers endorsed in saltire or; in chief a mitre of the last —See of ARGYLL, Scotland.

Azure, two pastoral staves in saltire, and a mitre in chief or—SPOFFORD, Bp. of Hereford, 1522-48.

Gules, three lions passant guardant, over all a crosier, the staff gules, crook sable, all within a bordure of the last bezanty—Cistercian Abbey at VALE ROYAL, Cheshire.

Gules, a crosier reversed in bend sinister, surmounted by a sword in bend dexter proper; on a chief argent a thistle leaved also proper—CHURCH, Hampton.

Argent, a bishop's crook in pale sable—M'LAURIN, Dreghorn.

The *pastoral staves* of Abbots resembled those of bishops, and were no doubt equally ornamented, especially when the Abbot was head of the Mitred Abbeys. However, it seems there was a custom to attach a small *pallium,* called also *sudarium,* or strip, to the crosier of Abbots to distinguish them from those of Bishops, though it was not generally adhered to; and this seems to be represented on the insignia of S. Benet's, HULME. Examples are also found of Abbesses represented with a pastoral staff, as on the brass of ISABEL HERVEY, Abbess of Elstow, Bedfordshire (ob. A.D. 1524).

Staff with Sudarium.

Sable, a crosier in pale or, garnished with a pallium crossing the staff argent [otherwise, having two ribbons entwined about it] between two ducal coronets of the second [otherwise between four crosiers or]—Abbey of S. BENET's, HOLME, Norfolk.

The following Abbeys, Priories, &c., bear the *crosier* in their insignia—

ALVINGHAM, Lincoln; BARDNEY, Lincoln; BYLAND, Yorkshire; BOXLEY, Kent; BUCKFESTRE, Devon; BURSCOUGH, Lancashire; BUTLEY, Suffolk; CUMBERMERE, Cheshire; DELACRE, Stafford; DEREHAM, Norfolk; FEVERSHAM, Kent; FURNESS; HALES; LLANDAFF; LANGDON, Kent; MALMESBURY, Wilts; MISSENDEN, Bucks; RICHMOND, Yorkshire (S. Agatha); Ditto, (S. Martin's); SHREWSBURY; STRATFORD, Essex; THAME, Oxon; THORNEY, Cambridge; THORNTON, Lincoln; VALE ROYAL, Cheshire; WARSOP, Notts; WENDLING, Norfolk; WESTMINSTER; WIRKSOPP, Notts.

The following Sees also bear the *crosier* in their insignia :—

ARGYLL; BARBADOS; CALCUTTA; CLONFORT and KILMACDUAGH; CORK and ROSS; ELPHIN; GALLOWAY; JAMAICA; KILLALA and ACHONRY; KILMORE; LLANDAFF; LEIGHLIN and FERNS; LIMERICK; QUEBEC, &c.

Cross, (fr. *Croix;* old fr. *crois, croyz,* &c.): the term *Cross* without any addition signifies, § 1, a *Plain* cross, which, it is said, should occupy one-fifth of the shield; but when *charged* it may occupy one-third. Its use as an heraldic ensign may be considered to be as early as any, and to belong to the time of the first crusades, in which the principal nations of Christendom are said to have been distinguished by crosses of different colours: and it is naturally found to be most frequently employed in the insignia of religious foundations.

Cross of S. GEORGE.

> " And on his brest a bloodie crosse he bore,
> The deare remembrance of his dying Lord,
> For whose sweete sake that glorious badge he wore,
> And dead, as living ever, him ador'd :
> Upon his shield the like was also scor'd."
>
> **Spenser's " Faerie Quene," bk. i.**

§ 1. The primary idea of the plain heraldic cross is that the four arms are equal, and that they meet in the fesse-point of the shield; from the shape of the shield, however, the horizontal bar is generally shorter than the vertical. This even-armed cross is frequently termed the *Greek* cross, to distinguish it from the *Latin* cross, in which the lower member is always longer than the other three. The plain cross of *gules* on a field *argent* is termed the *Cross of S. George,* having been assigned to S. George of Cappadocia, or S. George of England. (See *Union Jack* under *Flag.*) The *plain cross* was the most frequent amongst the early arms.

Le Conte de NORFFOLK, d'or a ung crois de goulez—Roll, temp. HEN. III.
Piers de SAUVOYE, goules ung crois d'argent—*Ibid.*
Robert de VEER d'argent a la crois de goulz—*Ibid.*
Argent, on a bull statant gules, armed or, upon a mount vert; a plain cross argent at the shoulder—RIDLEY.

As said above, the position of the cross is that the centre should occupy the fesse-point, but in those cases where there is a *chief* this ordinary must be *abased,* though it be not mentioned.

Argent, a cross gules, a chief chequy sable and of the first—SCOLYCORNE.
Argent, a cross and a chief sable—JOHN, Bishop of Exeter, 1185–91.
Or, a cross gules, a chief vert—VERE, Suffolk [granted 1584].

The *cross* admits of great varieties in outline and treatment,
and the inventors of heraldic devices have not been slow to
avail themselves of this, and heraldic writers have in their
ingenuity multiplied the forms. In giving a summary of the
chief forms only we are met with the difficulty of many synonyms occurring, for practically the same form is often much
varied by incorrect drawing, and much confusion has arisen
from blunders of heraldic writers in misreading or misunder-
standing the terms employed. The French terms are more
varied still than the English, and the correlation of the two
series can only be attempted approximately. It is the *plain*
cross which is most frequently made subject to the variations
described, § 1 to § 7, but it will be noted that other forms of
the cross are also at times subjected to the same treatment.

In the following classification the varieties have been, as far
as possible, restricted to cases of which examples can be found;
and an index at the end (see p. 179) will, it is hoped, render
reference easy.

§ 2. First of all it will be well, perhaps, to note that the
edges of the cross are subjected to the same variety of flection
as other ordinaries, namely, they may be *engrailed* (fr. *en-
greslée*), *embattled* (fr. *bretessée*), *indented* (fr. *denchée*), *invected*
(fr. *cannelée*), *wavy*, (fr. *ondée*) *raguly*, &c., and this treatment
is found at tolerably early dates.

Sire Thomas de YNGOLDTHORP, de goules a une crois engrele de argent
—Roll, temp. ED. II.

Sire Eustace de la HACCHE de or a une crois
engrele de goules—Roll, temp. ED. II.

Argent, a cross embattled sable—BALMANNO.

Ermine, a cross pattée invected gules CRAM-
DALE, Harl. MS. 1407.

Vert, a cross invected argent—HAWLEY, Clarenceux King of Arms, ob. 1577.

Argent, a cross wavy gules—LORAND.

Or, a cross raguly vert—ANKETEL, Co. Monaghan.

YNGOLDTHORP.

Sable, a cross flory raguly argent—BROTHERTON, Maidenhead.

Argent, a cross couped raguly and trunked sable—TYTHINGTON,Chester.

French works give a cross *émanchée*, but the application of this exaggerated form of *dancetty* to a cross must be somewhat difficult, and no figures of it have been observed. The *écotée* of French writers has the appearance of a coarse kind of *raguly*. In one case the term *slipped* is applied to a cross, which should probably have its edges adorned with leaves.

Argent, a cross slipped vert—RADELL, Harl. MS. 5866.

D'or, à la croix émanchée de trois pièces et deux demies d'argent sur gueules, cantonnée de quatre têtes de léopard d'azur—LE LYEUR DE LA VAL, Champagne.

§ 3. Next the crosses besides being of various tinctures may be diversified, as the field is diversified. A cross may be e.g. *chequy* (fr. *échiquetée*), *compony* or *counter-compony*, *fretty*, *trellised* (i.e. with a somewhat closer *fret*), *vair*, *maçonnée*, &c.

Sire Johan de KOCFELD, de azure a une crois chekere de argent e de goules—Roll, temp. ED. II.

Azure, a cross counter-compony argent and gules—Eustace de WITENEYE.

Ermine, a cross counter-compony gules and or; in the dexter chief a lion rampant sable—Richard LAUNDE.

Sire Robert de VERDUN, de argent, a une crois de azure frette de or—Roll, temp. ED. II.

Or, a cross vair—EXMYLE.

§ 4. A cross is frequently *charged* with other devices.

Sire Nicholas de VALERES, de argent, a une crois de goules e v escalops de or—Roll, temp. ED. II.

Sire Johan de BADDEHAM, de argent a une crois de goules; en la crois v molez de or—*Ibid.*

Sire Wauter de CORNEWAILLE, de argent, a une crois de sable besaunte de or—*Ibid.*

Sire Gelem de DUREM, de argent a une crois de goules e v flures de or—*Ibid.*

Nicholas de VALERES.

§ 5. The *Cross* may be of two tinctures, i.e. party *per fesse*, *per pale*, &c., or *per cross*, which is equivalent to *quarterly* (fr. *écartelée*), and in most cases it is so in connection with the partition of the field, and hence the tinc-

tures are counter-changed. Though some heralds would use
the term *counter-quartered*, the term *counter-changed* applied to
the cross is all that is needed.   The partition lines should meet
in the centre in a *cross* and not in a *saltire*.

> Gules, a cross per fesse or and argent—BROCKHALL.
>
> Gules, a cross moline per pale argent and ermine—FRISKENEY, Lincoln.
>
> Or, on a cross quarterly azure and gules five roses of the first—Thomas
> LANGTON, Bp. of S. David's, 1483 ; Salisbury, 1485 ;
> Winchester, 1493—1501.
>
> Per bend azure and argent, a cross moline per
> bend or and of the first—HAWTRE, Bedford.
>
> Per bend argent and sable, a cross potent coun-
> terchanged—ALMACK, Suffolk.
>
> Argent, a cross pattée, per saltire, gules and
> azure—INGHAM ABBEY, Norfolk.
>
> Per chevron, argent and gules, a cross counter-
> changed—CHAPMAN, York.

LANGTON.

> Quarterly azure and gules a cross patonce coun-
> terchanged ; in first and fourth quarters a rose gules barbed and seeded
> or ; in second and third quarters a sun in glory
> proper — Thomas BENTHAM, Bp. of Lichfield and
> Coventry, A.D. 1560-79.
>
> Quarterly argent and azure, a cross counter-
> changed—BEVERCOTT.
>
> Quarterly argent and gules, a cross botonny
> counterchanged—CROSLAND.
>
> Quarterly indented argent and sable, a cross
> counterchanged—GLENDINING.

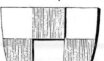

BEVERCOTT.

When, however, the cross is composed as it were, of five
pieces or divisions, the central being that
of the field, the term *quarter-pierced* is used.
Heraldic writers have, however, invented
various terms, e.g. *quarter-voided* and *square-
pierced*. And some have described the form
(taking the field into account) as '*chequy
of nine panes ;*' but it is to be noted that
as a rule the pieces are charged with some
device.   With the French, however, the
term *équipollée* describes the figure exactly.

BOISY.

Argent, a quarter-pierced cross moline sable between three crescents gules—MILWARD.

Sable, on a cross quarterly pierced argent, four eagles displayed of the first—BULLER, Bp. of Exeter, 1792-96.

Argent, five crosses croslet gules, over all on a quarter-pierced cross as the last, four crosses croslet like the second—BONWELL, London, 1601.

Ermine, on a quarter-pierced cross or four chevrons gules—City of LICHFIELD.

Cinq points d'argent, équipollés à quatre de gueules—BOISY, Ile de France.

§ 6. A cross is described as *voided* when the central portion of the four limbs is of the same tincture as the field, and only a narrow border is left, and this is found in ancient blazon described as ' *une fausse croix.*'

The term *voide* is used of a *Cross* in one or two ancient rolls in connection with *recercelé*, and it has been thought to imply that the voiding extends into the field, which may be described as *voided throughout,* and as is shewn in the illustration of the arms of KNOWLES. (See under § 32.)

Hamon CREVECEUR, d'or ung faulx crois de goules—Roll, temp. HEN. III.

Azure, crusily, a cross moline voided throughout [otherwise disjoined] or—KNOWLES, Barony, 1603.

Gules, a cross patty pointed voided argent; at each corner a bezant—Henry LE WALYS (Glover's Ordinary).

Argent, a cross flory voided gules—James PILKINGTON, Bp. of Durham, 1561-76.

Ermine, a cross voided sable—ARCHDEACON, Harl. MS. 5866.

Argent, a cross humetty voided azure—WASHBORNE.

Or, a cross humetty pointed, voided azure—BURR.

But as it is possible to superimpose one cross upon another (fr. *croix chargée,* or *remplie*), and the latter may be of the tincture of the field, the result would be the same as a cross voided. Modern heralds consider that the difference is to be shewn by the shading of the lines, as already noted in the case of the chevron, but such niceties were unknown in ancient heraldry.

De gueules, à la croix d'argent chargée d'une croix alaisée d'azur—NEUFVILLE, Limosin.

Further, there is a third way in which such arms might in some cases be blazoned, namely, as *fimbriated, bordured,* or *edged* (fr. *bordé*) of such a tincture.

And with this may be noted crosses which have *cotices,* though these are by no means common in English arms. One remarkable example, however, occurs, in which a *fleur-de-lis* serves as a *cotice* instead of a line.

Argent, a cross gules fimbriated or—BRADE-STONE.

Argent, a cross or bordured sable—TIPPET.

Quarterly or and azure, over all on a griece of three steps a holy cross, all of the first fulfylled sable [i.e. sable fimbriated gold]—Cluniac Priory at LYNTON, Notts.

Argent, a cross cottised with eight demi-fleurs-de-lis, their bottoms towards the fesse-point, sable, between four mullets pierced of the last—ATKINS, co. Cork.

ATKINS.

§ 7. As with other ordinaries, a cross may be *couped;* and then it is termed *humetty* (fr. *alaisée,* spelt sometimes *alésée*), though the term *coupée* seems to be occasionally used. Of course all the four arms are couped, un-less there is any distinguishing note to the contrary. It would also appear that this cross should be always drawn with its arms equal. When more than one cross or *crosslet* occurs in the same shield it stands to reason they must be *humetty,* so that it is not necessary to mention it.

D'argent, à la croix alaisée de gueules—XAIN-TRAILLES, Ile de France.

XAINTRAILLES.

A cross humetty between four plain crosslets—John de PONTISSARA, Bp. of Winchester, 1282—1304.

Azure, a bend wavy in the sinister chief a cross coupy argent—Arms assigned to William de CURBELLIO, Abp. of Canterbury, 1123-36.

The term *humetty* is sometimes used in connection with spe-cial terminations to the arms of the cross, but practically it is needless, for were the cross extended to the edges there would be no room for such terminations. See e.g. cross *annuletty*, § 11, and *fleuretty*, § 20 ; also *gringolée* and the like, § 21. To these might be added *anserated* and *ancetty* (from the French *anse*, 'a handle'), though the terms have not been observed in any English blazon.

Azure, a cross humetty terminated with four leopard's heads or— PECKHAM.

Argent, a cross humetty gules, the point in chief terminating in a crescent of the last—WANLEY.

Sable, billetty argent, a cross humetty at top, and there flory of the last—Sir John MORIS, co. Gloucester [Harl. MS. 1465, fol. 53].

On the other hand a cross *pattée* (which is naturally *humetty*) must be blazoned as *throughout* or *fixed*, if it is intended that the four arms of the cross should reach to the edges of the shield. See § 26.

See also *passant*, as meaning *throughout*.

The French term *tronçonné*, signifying that the cross is broken up into small cubes, is given by Edmondson, and others, but no examples have been noticed either in French or English arms.

One example only of a *demi-cross* has been observed.

Argent, a chevron between three demi-crosses gules—TOKETT.

§ 8. Beyond the variations to which the cross is subjected there are certain devices which are made up of charges arranged in the form of the cross, and so in some cases are blazoned as such. A cross, for instance, of *four ermine-spots*, with the heads meeting (fr. *aboutées* or *appointées*) in the fesse-point, has been blazoned by some heralds as a *Cross erminée*. A cross composed of *four escallop shells*, or of *four pheons*, would only be blazoned as such.

HURSTON.

Argent, a cross of four ermine-spots sable— HURSTON, Cheshire.

Vert, a cross of four escallops, the tops at the centre meeting, or—WENCELAUGH, co. York, 1584.

Quarterly, gules and azure, a cross of four pheons, the points to the centre argent—TRUBSHAWE.

With respect, however, to the formation of crosses from *lozenges*, *fusils*, and *mascles*, the device is so frequent that the terms cross *lozengy*, or cross *fusilly* (fr. *fuselée*), or cross *masculy* of such a tincture, are frequently adopted, though strict heralds consider these terms inadmissible, for lozengy, masculy, and fusilly require that two tinctures should be named, and that the cross or other ordinary be drawn entire, and treated just as if it was blazoned *chequy*, or *compony*, or any other form of diversification; they therefore contend, and with reason, that the proper expression for a cross of this description should be a *cross* of so many *lozenges*, *fusils*, &c.

But further than this, very strict heralds contend that a *cross fusil*, or *of fusils* (where no particular number is mentioned), should consist of nine, whereof five should be entire and four halved for the extremities, which touch the edge of the shield. If, however, the blazon runs, 'a cross of so many *fusils*,' especially of *fusils conjoined*, all the fusils should be entire, but need not necessarily touch the edge of the shield. If, however, they are intended to touch the edge of the shield, then the term *throughout* should be added. Practically, however, these rules are in ancient drawing never adhered to, and in modern drawing but seldom. What has been said of fusils applies of course also to *lozenges* and *mascles*.

Examples below will be found to illustrate sufficiently the variety of blazon, and it will be noted also that in some cases a cross composed of lozenges, or fusils, is terminated by some other device, e.g. *fleuretty*, or by a *bezant*.

Or, a cross of lozenges, and in the dexter chief an eagle displayed gules—FODRINGHEY.

Gules, a cross lozengy argent—STAWELL, Devon.

Gules, a cross of nine lozenges conjoined argent—STOWELL, Somerset.

Argent, a cross of five lozenges conjoined gules—Sr. de KESSELL.

Per pale or and azure, a cross lozengy counterchanged—HASLEFOOTE.

Quarterly or and sable, a cross lozengy counterchanged—HUNT.

Or, a cross of nine mascles gules—QUATERMAN, Leicester.

Gules, a cross masculy argent—BUTLER.

Azure, a cross of four mascles conjoined or—MILLER, Warwickshire.

Argent, a cross of nine mascles throughout gules—John de BREWES.

Argent, a cross of four fusils sable—Sir Thomas BANESTER, K.G.

Gules, a cross lozengy fleuretty or, a crescent for difference—FOTHERBY, Bp. of Salisbury, 1618-20.

Gules, a cross flory of nine fusils or—FOTHERBY, co. Lincoln, 1730.

Gules, a cross of four mascles argent, at each point a bezant—WALOIS.

In many cases, too, we find five or more charges arranged *in cross,* and in one case a cross is supposed to be formed of one *lozenge* with the *fleury* projections (see under *mascle*); and in another case a cross is formed of *bones.* While to a cross composed of two strings of beads the name of *cross pater-noster* has been given, although no example is cited.

Argent, fretty of six sable, five crosses crosslet fitchy in cross as the first—Sr. de BUGG.

Gules, a cross flory of one lozenge or—CASSYLL.

Sable, a cross of thigh bones, in dexter chief a bezant—RALPH BAYNE, Bp. of Lichfield and Coventry, 1554-59.

Another way of composing a cross is by crossing *bars,* or rather *barrulets* or *fillets,* as some heralds term them, for the horizontal line, with *endorses* or *batons* for the vertical line. When two of these occur the term *cross biparted* or *double parted* is used, and when three occur it is called a *cross triple parted.* By the following examples it will be seen how loosely the various terms are used.

Gules, a cross of one barrulet ermines, and an endorse ermine, both humetty--SPONNE.

Azure, a cross double parted argent—DOUBLER.

Argent, a cross triple parted and fretted sable—SKIRLAW, or SCYRLOW, Yorkshire.

Argent, a cross of six batunes interlaced sable—SKIRLAWE, Bp. of Lichfield, 1366; afterwards of Bath and Wells, 1386-88.

SKIRLAW.

Argent, a cross humetty triple parted azure—HURST, Salop.

Azure, a cross of three barrulets, and as many endorses fretted argent, dovetailed or—PICKFORD.

If a Cross *triparted* should be also *flory* heralds say that the fillets, &c., should terminate in the manner shewn in the margin, but no example is given in the works which lay down this rule.

Triple termination.

A cross *cabled* is given in English lists (in French lists *cablée*) and described as formed of a *cable* or twisted rope; but no arms bearing these devices, either English or French, have been noticed. And the fr. *cr. vivrée* probably consists of a *fillet* crossed by an *endorse*, both of them *nebuly* or *dancetty*.

§ 9. The expression *pierced* is applied to crosses, and is variously used. The term *pierced* (more frequently applied to *mullets* than similar charges) implies that there is a circular opening, and the field shewn through, and such opening would be in the centre of the cross. But the opening may be of a lozenge form or of a square form. When the whole of the centre is of the tincture of the field it is, as has already been described, to be blazoned *quarterly pierced;* but, farther, some heralds contend that if the aperture does not occupy the whole of the central portion where the arms meet, it is to be blazoned *quarter-pierced.*

Azure, a cross humetty pierced sable, a chief gules—KNOWLYS.

Azure, a cross moline, lozenge-pierced argent—GAILIE.

Azure, a cross moline square-pierced argent—MOLLYNS.

Argent, a cross moline quarter-pierced azure—SIBBALD, Scotland.

Argent, a cross moline quarter-pierced gules—CROKEYN, Ireland ; DOW-DALL, MILBORNE, SIBBALD, Balgony, Scotland.

Argent, a cross moline quarter-pierced sable—COLVIL, Ochiltry, Scotland; Robert COPLEY, called GROSSETESTE, Bp. of Lincoln, 1235-53; COPLEY, Batley, co. York; Sir Thos. MELBOURNE.

Gules, a cross moline rebated and lozenge-pierced or—FENEY.

Argent, a cross moline quatrefoil-pierced sable—MILBOURNE.

§ 10. In some few cases, but rarely in English heraldry, from the angles formed by the meeting of the arms there project certain charges, e.g. *rays, acorns, fleur-de-lis,* &c.; with rays the term *rayonnante* would be used. The French term is *anglé* of such a charge, but there is no English equivalent. Edmondson uses the expression " adorned at angles," but gives no example.

We now come to crosses which have special names, derived either from their general outline or from their termination.

§ 11. *Cross annuletty:* a cross which is *couped* and has rings at the four extremities is thus called, and not, as it might be supposed, a cross formed of *annulets* (q.v.), either conjunct or braced one with another. It is found blazoned also as ' humetty, ringed at the ends.'

WESTLEY.

Argent, a cross annuletty sable—WESTLEY, Harl. MS. 1405.

Argent, a cross flory voided and ringed gules—Monsire John MOLTON, Harl. MS. 1386.

§ 12. *Cross avellane:* so called from its resemblance to four filberts (*nuces avellanæ*); there seems to be no French representative (but see *otelles*); very few English instances have been observed.

SYDENHAM.

Vert, a cross avellane argent — SYDENHAM, Somerset, granted 1757.

Argent, two bars gules, on a canton of the second a cross avellane or—KIRKBY, Cumberland.

§ 13. *Cross barby* (fr. *barbée*): much the same probably as the French *croix tournée*, or the *croix cramponnée* (the *crampon* being the hook shape described under that term); it does not seem to be a very definite term, but may be represented as in the margin.

Cross barby.

Argent, a cross barby gules, in chief three griffin's heads sable—TILLIE, Cornwall.

§ 14. Cross *bottonnée* is derived from the French *bouton,* a bud or knob, though the name does not appear to be used by French heralds, who use the term *tréflée.* It is a cross ending in three lobes like the trefoil leaf, and is of rather frequent occurrence.

BRERLEGH.

Argent, a cross bottonnée gules—BRERLEGH ; Harl. MS. 1407.

Argent, a cross bottonnée sable—WINWOOD, Bucks.

Argent, a cross bottonny azure—EGMON.

Gules, a cross botonny argent, on a chief azure a lion passant or—CHAWNCY, Harl. MS. 1465.

Argent, a cross bottonny voided gules—PILKINGTON, Durham.

Argent, crusily and a cross botonny gules—RALEIGH, Warwickshire.

Monsire John de MELTON port d'argent a une crois patey et botone—Roll, temp. ED. III.

Monsire William de COLVILL port d'or a une fes de gules; trois crossiletts botones d'argent en le fes—*Ibid.*

Gules, a cross botonny and raguly argent—John le FROME, Harleian MS. 1465.

§ 15. *Cross Calvary,* (fr. *cr. de Calvaire*): is a *long* cross or *Latin* cross (that is with the lower limb longer than the other three, and raised upon three steps). It has been poetically said that the three steps are symbolical of the three Christian graces, Faith, Hope, and Charity, and it is suggested by theoretical writers that the bearer took the arms in consequence of having erected such a cross at Rome. It is also sometimes called a *Holy cross.*

ANWICKE.

Ermine, on a canton vert a cross calvary on three grieces or—QUAILE.

Quarterly or and azure, over all a cross calvary on three grieces or steps sable fimbriated of the first—LENTON Priory, Notts.

Argent, a cross calvary gules; on a chief azure five bezants—Stephen WESTON, Bp. of Exeter, 1724-42.

Argent, a long cross gules on a grice of three steps, the upper one azure, the second as the cross, and the undermost sable—ALMEARS or ALMEERS.

Ermine, on a pale between two roses gules a cross calvary argent—MOYSE.

Azure, a passion cross standing on a Catherine wheel argent—Augustinian Nunnery at FLIXTON, Suffolk.

Argent, a holy cross sable—ANWICKE.

The *Passion Cross,* or *Long Cross* (fr. *haute croix*), resembles the true *Latin* cross in form, but seldom occurs except when it is raised on three steps, and it is then called a *Cross Calvary.* See also *Crucifix.*

Barry of five argent and gules, over all a long cross (sometimes called a crosier) in bend sinister or — Gilbertine Priory at SEMPRINGHAM, Lincoln

A long cross mounted on three degrees ensigned on the top with a fleur-de-lis ; on each side the cross an escutcheon ; therein a chief and two chevrons—On seal of the Borough of HEYTESBURY, Wilts.

Long Cross.

Borough of HEYTESBURY.

But the steps or *degrees*, or *grieces* (spelt also *grices*), as they are variously termed, are sometimes referred to apart from the *Cross of Calvary*, and the term *graded* or *degraded* is employed. Consequently a *cross degraded* (fr. *à degrés*, and sometimes *enserrée de degrés* and *peronnée*) *and conjoined* signifies a plain cross, having its extremities placed upon steps joined to the sides of the shield. The number of the steps should be mentioned, as it is often four, and sometimes as many as eight.

Argent, a cross graded of three sable—WYNT-WORTH.

WYNTWORTH.

Argent, a cross degraded and conjoined (or issuing from eight degrees), sable—WOODHOUSE.

§ 16. *Cross clechée :* this signifies a cross with the ends as shewn in the margin. Some heralds contend that the true cross *clechée* should have the ends *voided*, but there seems to be no good authority for this, at least not in English arms, and in French arms it will be seen that it is often blazoned *vidée*. It appears also, when *voided* and *pommettée*, to bear the title with French heralds of *Cross of Toulouse*, from it appearing in the insignia of that city, though, as will be seen, an old blazon describes these arms as a *cross paté voided*.

BANASTER.

Argent, a cross clechée sable—Sir Thomas Banaster, K.G., ob. 2°
Ric. II. [as depicted upon his stall-plate at Windsor, elsewhere blazoned,
Argent, a cross patty pointed sable].

Or, on a mount between two lesser ones vert a lamb sable, holding
with the dexter foot a banner ermine charged with a cross clechée gules—
Grose, Surrey (1756).

Or, on a chevron between three crosses clechy sable a fleur-de-lis
between two stag's heads cabossed of the first—Carver.

D'azur, a la croix vidée, clechée et pommettée d'or—Comtat Venaissin.

De gueules, à la croix de Toulouse d'or—Oradour, Auvergne.

De gueules, à la croix vidée, clechée, pommettée et alaisée d'or, dite
Croix de Toulouse—P. Languedoc.

Le Conte de Tolosa, de goules a un croyz d'or pate et perse a une bordure d'or—Roll, temp. Hen. III.; Harleian MS. 6589, circa 1256-66.

§ 17. *Crosslet*, (fr. *croissette* or *petit croix*): two or more
crosses are sometimes borne in the same coat, and are then
termed *crosslets*. If only two or three are borne they may be
termed *crosses* or *crosslets*. If more, they must be termed *crosslets*. They are drawn couped, but it is not necessary to mention that circumstance, because they could not be otherwise.

William de Sarren, d'azur a trois crois d'or—Roll, temp. Hen. III.

Or, three crosses gules—De la Mayne.

Distinct, however, from the *crosslet* is the
cross crosslet, or, as it is sometimes, though
rarely, termed a *cross crossed* (fr. *croix
croisée*). By rights, however, a cross
crossed is equivalent to a *cross crosslet
fixed*, that is, the arms extend to the extremities of the escutcheon.

The *Cross crosslet* is often borne *fitched ;*
it may also have each extremity formed
like those of the cross pattée, and it is then
called a *Cross crosslet pattée.*

Cross crosslet.

But further, a *Cross crosslet* may be itself
crossed (fr. *recroissetée*), though there have been
differences of opinion as to its character. The
true signification of this term seems to be a cross
composed of four cross crosslets, but Gerard Leigh
represents it as shewn in the margin.

Cross crosslet
crossed.

Or, a cross crosslet fitchy azure—Gilbert IRONSIDE (Bp. of Bristol, 1689).

Argent, a cross crosslet pattée sable—WYKERSLEY.

Gules, a cross crosslet argent—CHRISTIAN, Ireland.

Or, a cross crosslet azure—CARROLL, Ireland.

Argent, a cross crosslet azure—BRITTON.

Gules, a cross crosslet crossed next the centre on the upper and lower limbs or—CHADERTON, Harl. MS. 1465.

Argent, a cross crosslet crossed (or, as Leigh expresses it, double-crossed) pattée [at all the extremities] sable—BARROW.

§ 18. *Cross entrailed:* is figured in the margin, and is borne by one family only, namely, that of CARVER. It appears to be only drawn in outline.

Or, on a chevron sable a fleur-de-lis accompanied by two stag's heads cabossed, between three crosses entrailed of the second— CARVER.

Cross entrailed.

§ 19. A *Cross fitchy* (fr. *fichée*) is a plain cross having the lower member *pointed*, but the term *fitchy* is very frequently applied to various kinds of crosses, and more especially to the crosslets, and sometimes to the cross crosslets.

Monsire John d'ARDERNE, port gules vi crois d'or fitche, le cheif d'or—Roll, temp. ED. III.

Monsire John D'ESTRIVELYN, sable a trois coupes d'argent croisele argent as peds agus— *Ibid.*

Argent, a cross crosslet fitched sable—SCOTT.

Cross crosslet fitchy.

Sable, a bend between six crosslets fitchy—LAKE, Bp. of Bath and Wells, 1616-26.

Gules, a cross patty fitched at foot or—Sir Gilbert HEYTON, Harl. MS. 6589.

Argent, a cross fitchy at base gules—POTES-FORD Church, Devon.

There is a cross of the peculiar shape in the margin which (for want of a better name) has been called a cross *double fitched*. It is not known to what family the representation found belongs.

Gules, a cross double fitched argent . . . . . [a coat existing at Quorndon, Leicestershire].

Coat at Quorndon, Leicestershire

§ 20. Of crosses with a floriated termination there are many varieties found in the actual emblazoning, but the nomenclature both of French and English heralds appears to be in a very unsatisfactory condition. The term most frequently employed is a *cross fleury*, and this is written also *flory*, *floretty*, and *fleuronny*, while the modern French heralds give us *fleurée*, *fleuronnée*, *florencé* (or *fleuroncée*), and *fleur-de-lisée*. It is not easy, however, to distinguish these from each other, or correlate them with the English terms, or with those used in ancient heraldry.

Cross flory.

The commonly-accepted distinction by English heralds is that *fleury* signifies the cross itself terminating in the form of the upper portion of a fleur-de-lis, but that *fleuretty* (which is seldom used) signifies the cross to be couped, and the flower, as it were, protruding from the portion so couped; but it is a great question whether there is the slightest authority

Cross fleuretty.

for such to be obtained from actual examples, or any such agreement to be found amongst the heralds of the seventeenth and eighteenth centuries. As to the French terms, *fleurée* seems not to be applied so much to the *cross* as to other ordinaries, and signifies rather the edges ornamented with flowers or trefoils, while *fleuri* is applied only to plants in flower. The French *fleur-de-lisée*, on the other hand, seems to be the equivalent of the English *fleuretty*, and is represented with the flower protruding from the couped ends of the cross. The *florencée* and *fleuronnée* seem to be practically the same term, and both to be the equivalent of the English *fleury*. On the other hand, *fleur-de-lisée* seems in English blazon to be applied to the edges of the cross rather than to the ends, and consequently to be synonymous with the French *fleurée*.

We find also confusion in drawings between the cross *fleury* and the cross *patonce*, which latter, it will be seen, may be said to lie between a cross *fleury* and a cross *patée*, according to some authorities, though drawn differently by others.

It will be observed that in the old blazon, the ends (*chefs* or *bouts*) are sometimes described as fleuretty. " Richard SUWARD, who accompanied those [at Caerlaverock], had a black banner painted with a white cross with the ends fleuretty."

John LAMPLOWE, argent ung crois sable florettee—Roll, temp. HEN. III.

Sire Johan de LAMPLOU, de or a un crois de sable les chefs flurettes—Roll, temp. ED. II.

Sire Roger de SUYLVERTONE, de argent a une crois de sable, les chefs flurettes—*Ibid.*

Monsire William TRUSSELL, port d'argent une crois de gules les bouts floretes—Roll, temp. ED. III.

Monsire de PAVELEY, d'asure a une crois d'or en les bouts floretes—*Ibid.*

Monsire le Suard D'ESCOZE port sable a une crois d'argent les bouts floretes—*Ibid.*

Richart SUWART, Re o cus converse Noire baniere ot aprestée

O crois blance o bouz flouretée.
Roll of Caerlaverock, A.D. 1300.

Argent, a cross flory azure—BEVERCOURT and LEXINGTON.

Argent, a cross flory voided azure—MELTON, Lancaster.

Argent, on a cross flory sable four bezants—WHITGIFT, Bp. of Worcester, 1577, afterwards Abp. Canterbury, 1583--1604. [Arms granted, 1577.]

Argent, a cross fleuretty sable—HOLMSHAW, Scotland.

Gules, a cross fleuronny argent—BROMFLET.

D'azure, à la crois d'argent, les extrémités fleur de lisées d'or—DUNOIS, Champagne.

Per pale azure and gules, over all a cross fleur-de-lis on the sides or—Gilbert IRONSIDE, Bp. of Bristol, 1661-71.

§ 21. *Cross gringolée*, is used only in French heraldry, but it is typical of a class of crosses which consist of a cross humetty, but with heads of animals or some such device issuing from the ends. (See under *Cross*, § 7.) In the case of gringolée the heads of snakes are implied. *Guivrée* possibly has the same signification, i.e. with *vipers'* heads.

KAER.

De gules, a la croix d'hermine gringolée d'or—KAER, Bretagne.

D'argent, a la croix de gueules gringolée d'or—MONTFORT, Bretagne.

§ 22. A *Cross hameçon* is given in heraldic books, but appears to be borne only by one family in England, and that probably of foreign origin. The name implies that the ends should be represented like fish-hooks.

Azure, a cross hameçon argent—MAGENS, SUSSEX.

§ 23. *Cross Maltese*, or *of eight points*. A cross of this form is the badge of the knights of Malta, and of some other religious orders. The points are imagined to symbolize the eight beatitudes.

A Maltese cross enamelled white and edged with gold—Badge of the Knights of MALTA.

Argent, a cross Maltese gules—Order of S. STEFANO, Pisa, 1561.

Maltese Cross.

A cross *of sixteen points* is also found noted in some heraldic works, but probably only used in modern French heraldry. The drawing appears as an ordinary cross *humetty*, with the extremities *indented*, each having four points.

§ 24. We next come to a cross having a great variety of nomenclature as well as of form. The ordinary and correct term is the Cross *moline*, and like the *fer-de-moline* or *mill-rind*, from which it derives its name, the ends are bifurcated. But they are usually made to turn over like the two side lobes of the *cross fleury*, the central lobe being absent.

Neither the *fer-de-moline* nor the *cross moline* occurs in the rolls of Henry III. In those of Edward II. the *fer-de-moline* occurs as a charge, and also the cross *recercelée* (q.v.), which may perhaps represent the Cross *moline*; but by some heralds the term *Cross recercelée*,

Cross moline (a).

q.v., is supposed to be confined to a *cr. moline voided*.

Moreover, with the author of the poem which describes the siege of Caerlaverock, the term *Fer-de-moline* appears to mean the *Cross moline*, as there is no doubt the arms of

Antony BECK, the warrior-bishop of Durham, 'who sent his banner of red, with a fer-de-moline of ermine,' were somewhat as represented in the margin, since a Bishop would be sure to bear a cross.

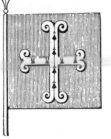

> Le noble evesque de Dureaume,
> Le plus vaillant clerk du roiaume ...
> Vermeille, o un fer de molyn
> De ermine, e envoia se ensegne.
> Roll of Caerlaverock, c. 1300.

Bp. of DURHAM.

The Cross *recercelée* too is found more frequently in the later rolls, e.g. in Edward III.'s reign, and then it will be seen that the *cross moline* occurs but in one instance.

The drawings vary in the extent to which the bifurcated end is curved, and either of those shewn in the margin may be followed. If they are much more curved, the term '*anchory*' may perhaps be given to the cross, a translation of the French term *ancrée*, which seems to represent the *cross moline;* but it is not a very happy description, as the ends are not drawn like the flukes of an anchor.

Cross moline (b).

Monsire Symon de CHAMBERLAYNE, quarterly, d'or et gules a une crois molin argent en la quarter devant—Roll, temp. EDW. III.

Azure, a cross moline or—MOLYNEUX, of Hawkley, Lanc. [Many other families of the same name bear crosses moline variously pierced and tinctured.]

Argent, a cross moline azure—MILLER, Scotland.

Azure, a cross moline or—Adam MOLEYNS, Bp. of Chichester, 1445-50.

Per fesse embattled gules and azure, in chief two pickaxes and in base a cross moline or—PICKWICK.

Argent, a cross moline pierced gules—MILBORNE.

Gules, a cross moline voided argent—BECKE.

Gules, a cross moline sarcelled argent—BEC.

Azure, a cross anchory or—BEAURAIN.

Sable, a cross anchory or—TATYNGTON, Suffolk, Harl. MS. 1449.

Cross anchory.

The cross called by French writers *anillée,* and varied in
spelling by French and English writers into *neslée, nyslée,
nillée,* &c., seems to be but another name for the cross *moline,*
the French *anille* being exactly the same as the *mill-rind.*
But because some French heralds have drawn the curved extremities more slender than is usual in English drawing, the
cross *anillée* has been described as a very thin *cross anchory.*

D'azur, à trois anilles ou fers de moulin d'or—GERESME, Brie.

Cross miller.

A severer form, and perhaps one more
akin to the original notion of the *fer-de-
moline,* is one with rectangular ends, which
heralds have named *cross mill-rind,* abbreviated into *cross miller*). But so far as has
been observed the title occurs only in
heraldic works, and is not applied especially
to any actual arms.

Under this head it may be well to include the Cross *fourchée.* It is found in
ancient blazon, particularly in the roll of arms of the time
of Henry III., and in one the term *fourché
au kanee* occurs, which has been itself a
crux to heraldic writers. The exact form
of the cross *fourché* is not known, but it
is supposed to be like that in the margin,
for which later heralds have invented
the term *cross miller rebated.* In French
heraldic works a distinction seems to be
made between *fourchée* and *fourchetée,* but
it is not clear what that distinction is.

Cross miller rebated.

Gilbert de la VALE, de la MARCH, d'argent ung croix fourche de goules—
Roll, temp. HEN. III.

John de LEXINGTON d'argent ung crois d'azure fourche *au kanee.—Ibid.*

Per pale or and vert, over all a cross fourchy gules   HINGHAM

Argent, a cross moline rebated engrailed, sable—COTES, Harl. MS. 6829.

In connection with the *cross fourché* may be noted the
erroneous blazon of the *shake fork* (q.v.) as a *cross pall;* it is

not, however, a cross at all; it is the forked character of the *pall* which has led to a combination of the two ideas.

A Cross *moline* is said to be sometimes used as a mark of *cadency*.

§ 25. *Cross nowy.* When the term is used by itself it is supposed to signify that the arms of the cross, instead of meeting and forming right-angles, stop at the edge of a circle, which, so to speak, cuts off the angles; at least, it is represented thus in the drawing given in Edmondson. Thence varieties are imagined, viz. *nowy lozengy, nowy masculy,* &c., with each of the angles filled by a projection of half a *lozenge, mascle,* &c., but no examples are named. *Nowy quadrate,* however, is applied when the projections appear to form a square, and an example will be found figured in the Arms of LICHFIELD under *cross,* § 31.

There is a term also said to be used, namely, *nowyed,* which means that the projection need not be in the centre but in each of the arms of the cross. Both *nowy* and *nowyed,* however, are quite distinct from *nowed* (fr. *noué*), applied to *serpents,* &c.

§ 26. The term Cross *pattée* (fr.), more often writen *patty,* primarily means that the arms of the cross become expanded, or opened out, as they approach the edge of the shield. Named by itself, it means that the extremities are bounded by a straight line, that is, they are couped before reaching the edge of the shield. If otherwise, that is if the arms are extended to the edge of the field, the word *throughout* must be added (or, as some prefer, *fixed, ferme,* or *entire*); or if they have any other termination, e.g. *flory, pometty,* &c., such termination must be named; but in this case they belong rather to the class of Cross *patonce* (q. v.). In one case the ends are indented by a hollow (see below, under DYMOCK), and Berry gives a figure of a cross patty *notched,* but gives no name of bearer.

Cross pattée.

As to the expanding sides of the cross there seems to be no

rule, but they are generally drawn slightly curved outwards, and not straight, as in the *Maltese cross.* Amidst the various forms which appear in the works of different authors it is difficult to define the line of demarcation between it and its kindred, cross *patonce,* which is described in the next article.

The extremities in French arms are sometimes so much curved that the outline of the four arms represent so many segments of a circle. With the French, however, the rule is for the Cross *pattée* to reach to the edge, and when it does not the term *alaisée* is introduced. It is not at all unusual in English arms for the lower extremity of the *cross patty* to be terminated in a point, and then it is blazoned cross *patty fitchy. Cross crosslets* may also be *patty,* and the device is then a very striking one. A Cross *patty* is also said to be used as a mark of *cadency.*

Le Conte d'AUMARLE, de goules, ung croix pate de verre—Roll, temp. HEN. III.

Sire William de LATIMER, de goules a un croys pattee de or—Roll, temp. ED. II.

Monsire Le LATIMER, port de gules a une crois patey or—Roll, temp. ED. III.

Sire Johan de BERKELEYE, de goules a iij crois patees de or, e un cheveron de argent—Roll, temp. ED. II.

Sire Moris de BERKELEYE, de goules a les crusules pates de argent, e un chevron de argent—*Ibid.*

Sire Johan de RESOUN, de goules a un lion de or, en la un quarter un crois patée de veer—*Ibid.*

Monsire de ROIOSBY, de gules a trois crois pateis de sable, eu une bend d'argent—Roll, temp. EDW. III.

Sable, a cross pattée, or—ALLEN.

Ermine, a cross patty invected gules—GRANDALE, Harl. MS. 1407.

Verte, a cross patee fitchy or—HARRIS, Bp. of Llandaff, 1729-38.

Sable, a cross patty throughout fitchy or—COLLIAR.

Argent, a cross patty throughout engrailed sable —PESHALL.

Argent, a cross patée fixed sable WOODHOUSE.

Gules, a cross patty crenelly at the ends argent— BATNYMERSH.

Argent, a cross pattée gules, in each end a small semicircle (otherwise a cross patée with one engrail) —DYMOCK.

DYMOCK.

Sable, on a chevron between three estoiles or, three crosses pattee fitchy gules—William LAUD, Bp. of S. David's, 1621; Bp. of Bath and Wells, 1626; Bp. of London, 1628; Abp. of Cant., 1633-45.

Argent, a cross patty elongated at the foot and pierced gules— MOLTON.

As to the synonym *formée* or *formy*, which appears to be used with modern heralds as frequently as *patty*, it is difficult to explain its origin or meaning. One example is found in a roll as early as Henry III., but no other till a roll of Edw. III., where certain small crosses are described as *formé de lis*, that is, made up of the four flowers united in the centre. This may therefore be the origin of the term, since it will be observed that the same arms are blazoned in the previous reign (see above) as bearing 'iij crois patées.' It will be noted also that, as read by NICOLAS, the word *lis* appears as *lij*, but there can scarcely be much room to doubt the true reading.

Le baucent del hospitale de goules a un croyz d'argent fourme—Harl. MS. 6589, *c.* 1256-66.

Monsire Morris de BERKELEY, port de gules, a une cheveron d'argent entre dis croises forme de 'lij [*forme de lis*]—Roll, temp. EDW. III.

Gules, a cross formée or—Simon ISLIP, Abp. of Cant., 1349-66.

Ermine, two rings interlaced sable, on a chief of the last three crosses formy argent—WYCHINGHAM, Norfolk.

Argent, two annulets linked together gules, between three crosses formy sable—THORNHAGH, Nottinghamshire, confirmed 1582.

Argent, a wolf statant sable, on a chief azure three crosses formee of the first—EWER, Bp. of Llandaff, 1761, afterwards of Bangor, 1769-74.

Per fesse or and argent, in chief a lion rampant holding in the paw a cross formy fitchy gules, a chief sable, in base a cross formy fitchy ermine, surmounted by a fleur-de-lis of the fourth—VAWDREY, Chester.

Argent, on a chevron, the upper part terminating in a cross formée, gules, three bezants—NEWLAND, Southampton. [See similar example under *Fesse.*]

Argent, on a chevron between three crosses formées gules, three doves of the field—W. SANCROFT, Abp. of Canterbury, 1678-91 [from MS. Lambeth, No. 555].

Abp. SANCROFT.

§ 27. Cross *patonce* is certainly an ancient term, as it occurs in the Roll of Arms, temp. Hen. III. Its definite origin or exact meaning cannot be determined; but the primary idea seems to be that the arms should expand, as a *cross pattée*, and that they should be terminated more or less like a *cross flory*.

The cross figured in the margin is taken from the glass in Dorchester Church, which is not later than the early part of the fourteenth century, and may therefore be said to be contemporary with the man whose arms they represent, viz. William LATIMER, Lord of Corby, who sat in Parliament 1289—1305. But if we look at the blazon of the Latimer arms in the earlier rolls we find the cross described as a *cross patée*, though in later times as *cross patonce*.

Cross Patonce.

William de VECEY, goules, a une croix patonce d'argent—Roll, temp. HEN. III.

Sire William de LATIMER, de goules, a un croys patee de or—Roll, temp. ED. II.

. . . . De Guilleme le LATIMIER.   Portoit en rouge bien pourtraite.
Ki la crois patée de or mier   Roll of Siege of Caerlaverock, A.D. 1300.

Gules, a cross patonce or—LATIMER, Northamp.

Sable, a cross patonce argent, pierced plain of the field, between four escallops of the second—Richard FLETCHER, Bp. of Bristol, 1589; afterwards of Worcester, 1593; and then of London, 1595-96.

Azure, an eagle displayed ermine, on his breast a cross patonce of the field—HOWLEY, Bp. of London, 1813; Abp. of Cant., 1828-48.

Argent, a cross patonce voided and pomelled at the four ends gules—Monsire John MELTON Harl. MS. 1386, fo. 34.

FLETCHER.

Azure, two bars, and in chief a cross patonce or—HOLTE, Warwick.

Vert, a cross patonce or between four crosses pattee argent—Town of ABINGDON, Berks, granted 1623.

Argent, a cross patty flory sable; over all a bendlet gules   SWINNER-TON, co. Salop.

Argent, two bars sable, over all a cross formy flory gules—BRERETON, co. Chester.

Or, a cross patty, and at each end flory gules—EVETT, co. Worcester.

§ 28. *Cross patriarchal* (fr. *cr. patriarcale*) is a cross which has two horizontal bars instead of one. It is said that the ancient Patriarchs of Je- rusalem bore this kind of cross, and that afterwards it was borne by the Patriarch of Constantinople, while the cross adopted by the Pope of Rome had three horizontal bars; but the historical evidence as to this adoption is very obscure. The name does not appear, so far as has been observed, in

Ralph de TURBINE.

any of the rolls of arms in the thirteenth, fourteenth, or fif- teenth centuries.

Sometimes the arms in the first-cited example are represented with the extremity of the lower limb and the extremities of the chief horizontal limb touching the edge of the shield, but the usual representation is as in the illustration, with all the limbs couped. It is often blazoned as a *cross Lorraine,* and in some cases it is termed an *Archiepiscopal cross,* though it may gene- rally in that case be taken to mean instead of the Ordinary a charge drawn like a *crosier* (q.v.), and surmounted by a cross instead of a crook.

Sable, a cross patriarchal argent—Arms ascribed to Ralph de TURBINE, Bp. of Rochester, 1108; Archbp. of Cant., 1114-22.

Argent, a cross patriarchal on a grice of three steps gules—Cluniac Priory, BROMHOLM, Norfolk.

Or, on a cross sable, a cross patriarchal of the field—VESEY, Visc. de Vesci.

A cross patriarchal gules fimbriated or—Badge of the KNIGHTS TEM- PLARS.

Argent, on a bend gules, over all a cross patriarchal sable—RORKE, Ireland.

Gules, a buck trippant argent, in chief two bees volant or, on a chief nebuly of the third a Lorraine cross as the field between two eagles dis- played sable—GOODHART, Kent.

An example is given by Palliot of a *cross Patriarchal,* viz. that of the bishopric of HERCHFELD, with the lower end ter- minating something like a cross *patonce,* to which he applies the term *enhendée.*

§ 29. *Cross pomel,* or *pommelly* (fr. *bourdonnée*). A plain
cross terminating in four round pomels,
e.g. like the knobs at the end of sword-
hilts, or in *bourdons,* that is, the knobs
at the top of the pilgrims' staves. But
there is much confusion arising from carelessness in writing the name in different ways. We find *pomy,* and very frequently *pometty* (fr. *pommettée*), and some
heralds contend that the latter means something different, i.e. that there are two *knobs*

WASTERLY.

terminating the arms of the cross ; others say that it means
a cross with a circular protuberance in the middle of each arm
(like the *escarbuncle*). Again, in some French blazoning, the
term *pomettée* signifies having knobs at several angles, as in
the case of the Cross of Toulouse, given under *cleché.*

Argent, a cross pomel sable—WASSELEY, or WASTERLEY.

Argent, a bend between two cotises gules and six crosses pomelly
fitchy sable—BOUDENELL.

Or, on a pale gules a cross pomy fitchy argent, on a chief azure three
bezants—WRIGHT, London.

Argent, a fesse dancetty between three crosses pomel fitchy gules—
SANDES, Bucks.

Gules, a fesse checquy or and sable between six crosses pomel argent—
KYNYSMAN.

Gules, a cross pometty voided or—BRAUNSTON.

D'azure, à la crois d'argent, le pied bourdonné ou pommetté et fiché
du même ; aux cantons quatre étoiles d'or—BAZAS, Guyenne.

The French term *Moussue, moussé,* or *émoussé,* appears to
mean a cross with the ends simply rounded at the extremities,
from an obsolete word equivalent to blunted, and is given in
some heraldic works, but without examples.

§ 30. *Cross portate* or *portante :* an ambiguous term which
Edmondson says is given by Randle Holmes to a *long cross
raguly.* Other heraldic writers give it to a peculiar form,
which is neither *chevron, bend,* nor *cross,* but an odd admixture
of the three, and is so drawn by Berry, who says that *double
portant* means a cross *patriarcale.* The idea seems to be a cross

'in bend,' as if being carried. Confusion has also, no doubt, arisen from bad drawing, hasty writing, and careless reading. One coat of arms only has a cross so blazoned.

Barry of six gules and argent, over all a cross portate in bend sinister azure (?)—St. GILBERT.

§ 31. *Cross potent,* written sometimes *potence* (fr. *potencée*): so called because its arms terminate in *potents* (q.v.), or like crutches. It is also called a *Jerusalem cross*, from its occurrence in the insignia of the kingdom of JERUSALEM, established by the Crusaders, the crosses being supposed by some writers to symbolize the five wounds of Christ.

Cross of Jerusalem.

Sable, a cross potent or—ALLEN, Finchley, Middlesex.

Sable, a cross potence argent—APRICE, Wales.

Argent, a cross potent between four plain crosslets or—Arms of JERUSALEM.

It is observable that in this coat metal is placed, contrary to the general rule, upon metal, a peculiarity which in this case is said to bear allusion to Ps. lxviii. 15.

A singular variety of the *cross potent* is called sometimes the Cross of S. Chad, because it occurs in the insignia of the episcopal see of LICHFIELD AND COVENTRY, of which S. Chad was the first Bishop.

Cross of S. Chad.

Per pale gules and argent, a cross potent quadrat in the centre (or nowy quadrat) per pale of the last and or, between four crosses pattée, those on the dexter side silver, those on the sinister side gold. (See of LICHFIELD and COVENTRY.)

The above arms are, however, sometimes blazoned as—

Per pale gules and argent, a cross potent quadrat between four crosses formy all counterchanged.

Some other curious varieties of the cross potent occur. When *engrailed* the term applies only to the inner edges, the outer edges remaining plain. When *crossed*, it is meant that each arm is crossed by another piece half-way between the potent and the centre, and seems to be the equivalent of what is called by some writers a *cross gemelle*, though, as is so frequent, no examples are adduced of the use of the term. In one case the term *batune* is said by Papworth to be applied to a cross *potent;* but we have little doubt the word is *botoné*, i.e § 14, where from another Harleian MS. he gives BRERLEGH as bearing such a cross.

CHEDERTON.

Azure, a cross potent fitchée or—Coat ascribed, in the sixteenth century, to King ETHELDRED.

Azure, a cross potent engrailed or——BRENCH-ESLEY.

Argent, a cross potent crossed sable—CROWCHER.

Gules, a cross potent crossed or—CHEDERTON.

Quarterly, first and fourth, gules, a crosslet potence or; second and third argent, a chevron between three crampirons gules—CHADDERTON, Bp. of Chester, 1579; Bp. of Lincoln, 1595—1608.

Argent, a cross batune (i.e. potent) gules—PRERLEY, Harl. MS. 1407.

The most remarkable, however, is what Palliot and others call a Cross *potence repotencée*, drawn with the *potents* starting off at different angles, and said to be borne by the family of SQUARCIAFICHI. The *potent rebated* of Edmondson appears to be the *Fylfot* (q.v.).

§ 32. *Cross recercelée :* of all the crosses perhaps this has been the most disputed by heraldic writers. We find the term *sarcelly* more frequently used, but there are so many varieties of spelling adopted by different authors of the seventeenth and eighteenth centuries, that it is a question whether there is one word or two; attempts, however, appear to have been made to distinguish different meanings attached to different modes of spelling. They are as follows, so far as printed works go (manuscript readings would add to the number):—*cercelée, re-cercellé, recersile, resarcelée, resarcelled, sar-*

KNOWLES.

celée, sarcelly. One writer speaks of *cerclée* being spelt *cercelée* and *recercelée*, and so confused with the *sarcelly*.

The term as applied to the *Cross* occurs twice in one of the
two rolls which are apparently of HENRY III.rd's reign. Also
in a roll temp. EDWARD II. two examples occur with the term
voided added and one without, though in the latter *voided* is,
no doubt, implied; hence, as the general outline was similar to
the *cross moline*, it may be considered as a *cross moline voided*,
or *disjoined*, and drawn as in arms of KNOWLES opposite. See § 6.

The appearance is just as if in order to strengthen his shield
the smith had taken four pieces of iron and bent them round,
as was done in the case of hinges and other ornamental iron-
work found remaining on church doors, &c., of the 13th and
14th centuries, primarily to add strength to the woodwork, but
at the same time ornamentation.

Modern heralds seem to use the term alike for the *cross
moline* and for the *cross moline voided*, and employ usually in
blazon the spelling sarcelly. But beyond this, in various books
on heraldry, both English and foreign, an attempt is made to
distinguish between *recercelé*, i.e. *cerclé* or circled, and *sarcelly*,
defined by Berry as 'a cross voided, or as it were, sawed apart.'
See more under *Recercelé*.

Hugh de BAUCOY, d'or a une croyz de goules recersele; a une labeu
de sable—Roll, temp. HEN. III.

Edwarde de PAVELEY, dazure a un croys dor recersele—*Ibid.*

Sire William de BASINGES, de azure, a une crois recercele e voide de
or, e un baston de goules—Roll, temp. ED. II.

Sire . . . de BASINGE, de azure, a un crois recercele et voide d'or—*Ibid.*

Sire Peres de TADINGTONE, de sable a un crois de or recersele—*Ibid.*

Monsire de WONNEDALE, port d'argent une crois recersele de gules—
Roll, temp. ED. III.

Monsire de BEKE, port le revers—*Ibid.*

Monsire de BRENNE, port d'asure a un crois d'or
recersele; une baston de gules—*Ibid.*

Monsire Oliver de INGHAM, port parte d'or et
vert, a une crois recercele gules—*Ibid.*

Quarterly, gules and sable, a cross sarcelle quarterly or and ermines, on a chief of the third a rose
en soleil between two pelicans of the first—Edmund
BONNER, Bp. of Hereford, 1539, afterwards of London, 1539-49, and 1553-59.

BONNER.

Ermine, a cross sarcelly sable—GODARD, Chester.

Azure, crusilly a cross sarcelly disjoined or—KNOWLES, Earl of Banbury, ob. 1632.

Argent, crusily gules a cross sarcelly sable—RALEIGH.

Argent, a cross sarcelly engrailed sable—COTTER.

Per fesse argent and gules, a cross sarcelly counterchanged—COLUMBERS.

Quarterly, argent and azure, a cross sarcelly counterchanged—JAMES, Surrey.

Azure, a cross sarcelly pierced argent—MELTON, Aston, York.

Gules, a cross sarcelly ermine—BECK, Yorkshire.

Argent, a cross sarcelly disjoined or—BASINGES.

Argent, a cross patty fitchy disjoined or—BROKENCROSS.

§ 33. *Cross recoursy* (fr. *raccourcie*) : a very doubtful term. Modern French heraldic works distinctly consider it to be the same as *couped*, but Berry, who appears to have based his definition on Edmondson and other English heraldic works, implies that it means *voided*.

Azure, a cross crosslet recoursy argent—BASING.

§ 34. *Cross tau*, or *of S. Anthony*, who is represented with

Friary of S. ANTHONY.

such a cross embroidered upon the left side of his garment. It is called cross *commisse* by some heraldic writers, with a somewhat fanciful allusion to Ezekiel, chap. ix. ver. 4, or as representing the token of absolution with which malefactors are said to have been stamped on the hand. It should be drawn like a Greek Tau.

Or, a cross tau azure—Friary of S. ANTHONY, London.

Gules, a cross tau surmounted by a crescent or—WANLEY.

Per chevron or and vert, in base on a hind trippant, argent, a cross tau, and in chief a cross tau between two crosses patonce fitchy gules—CROSSLEY, Ireland, 1725.

Argent, on a bend sable three taus of the first—BERD.

Ermine, on a chief indented gules, three cross taus or—THURLAND.

Argent, a cross tau gules, in chief, three crowns of thorns proper—TAUKE.

§ 35. *Cross urdée* (written sometimes *verdy*, fr. *aiguisée*), or *cross champaine*, should be represented as annexed. Sometimes it is drawn with the edges curved inwards, towards the centre, but it is then a *cross cleché*. It is also found blazoned simply as a *cross pointed*, and *humetty pointed* has also been used by some writers for the same.

Or, a bend vair between two crosses verdy voided sable—MANGLES, Surrey.

Argent, a cross pointed and voided sable—DUKENFIELD, Bart.

Cross urdée.

INDEX TO THE ARTICLE *CROSS.*

Cross-staff: this is a general term for any instrument for taking levels or altitudes. The *Mariner's Cross-staff*, now of course obsolete, was commonly called the *fore-staff*. One form of the cross-staff will be found under *Plumbers'* implements.

Azure, on a chevron between three mariner's cross-staves or five mullets of the first—EVINGTON, co. Lincoln.

Crown, (fr. *couronne*): this word occurring in blazon without any addition usually implies a *ducal coronet* without the cap. When blazoned *proper* it signifies that it is of gold.

Or, a crown sable garnished gold—BELLINGHAM.
Sable, three crowns or—LEE, co. York.

Crown royal of England, sometimes also called an *Imperial crown*. The forms of the crowns worn by the successive kings of England vary considerably, and will be found in architectural illustrations of the sculptured heads of kings from monuments and other stone carvings in churches [see examples in Rickman's Gothic Architecture, sixth and seventh Editions];

Royal Crown of England.

but in this place they must be considered only in their connection with armorial bearings. The earliest instance of the royal arms being ensigned with a crown is in the case of those of Henry VI. At this time the crown had attained its present form, with the exception of the number of arches. The arms of Edward IV. are surmounted by the rim of the crown only, adorned with crosses pattée and fleurs-de-lis. The crown of Richard III. shews five semi-arches, that of Henry VII. shews but four, and his successor's only three, although seldom met with until about the time of James II., before which five semi-arches were generally shewn. Several instances of *Royal crowns* are found on coats of arms.

Gules, a royal crown or—M'ALPIN, Scotland.
Gules, a regal crown, within a double tressure-flory counter-flory or—ERSKINE, co. Fife.
Azure, a royal crown of gold; in chief a quarter gironny of eight or and sable; on the sinister side three dexter hands couped fesswise, each holding a bunch of arrows proper—MACKONOCHIE.

Argent, an arrow fesswise piercing a heart surmounted with a royal crown proper, on a chief azure three mullets of the first—DOUGLAS, Kent.

Azure, a stag trippant argent, unguled, attired, and bearing between his horns an imperial crown or—OWAIN GETHIN.

Ermine, on a chief gules three imperial crowns proper—Company of FURRIERS, Edinburgh.

The *crown of Spain*, as used by King Philip II., consort of Queen Mary of England, was a circle of gold jewelled, supporting eight strawberry-leaves. Four ogee arches, pearled, were sometimes added, meeting under a mound and cross pattée. No cap.

The *crown of Scotland*, as borne by James VI. before his succession to the throne of England, exactly resembled the imperial crown of Great Britain. It is represented in the Crest of *Scotland* (q.v.). This differs essentially from the actual crown of Scotland, discovered in Edinburgh Castle in 1817.

The *crown of Hanover*. The electorate of Hanover having been constituted a kingdom, the bonnet which had hitherto been placed over the insignia of that state was exchanged for a crown, in pursuance of a royal proclamation dated June 8, 1816.

Crown of Hanover.

The *crown of Charlemagne*. This crown having been borne by five kings of England as Arch-treasurers of the Holy Roman Empire, claims a place in the armory of Great Britain. Its form is generally depicted as in the margin.

Crown of Charlemagne.

The *crown of a king of arms* is of silver gilt, and consists of a circle inscribed with the words 'miserere mei Deus secundum magnam misericordiam tuam' (i.e. Ps. li. 1), supporting sixteen oak-leaves, each alternate leaf being somewhat higher than the rest. Nine only of these leaves are shewn in drawing, two of them being in profile. The cap is of crimson satin, turned

Crown of the King of Arms.

up with ermine, and surmounted by a tassel of gold. The crowns of kings of arms formerly resembled that of the sovereign, or sometimes ducal coronets.

The other crowns used in British heraldry follow in alphabetical order.

Antique crown, or *Eastern crown*, as it is sometimes called, is supposed to represent the crown anciently worn by Oriental princes, as appears by their coins. The *unicorn* supporting the royal arms is gorged with this kind of crown, but it probably is here in fact only the rim of the *crown royal*.

Antique crown.

Argent, a bar wavy and a demi-otter issuant sable, armed, langued, and crowned with an antique crown, gules—MELDRUM.

Argent, a lion rampant gules, crowned with an antique crown or—ROCHE, Ireland, also SLOAN.

Ermine, on a chief engrailed sable three antique crowns or—EARLE, Bp. of Worcester, 1662; afterwards of Salisbury, 1663-65.

Argent, a lion rampant, tail nowed gules, gorged with an Eastern coronet or, in chief three falcons proper—BEWES, Cornwall.

Gules, a demi-Virgin couped below the shoulders, issuing from clouds all proper vested or, crowned with an eastern crown of the last, her hair dishevelled and wreathed round the temples with roses of the second, all within an orle of clouds proper—MERCERS' Company [inc. 1394, arms confirmed 1634].

Celestial crown: a crown resembling the *Eastern*, with the addition of a radiant star in the form of a mullet upon each point. This is frequently used as an ornament upon the *achievements* of deceased ladies.

Argent, three pastoral staves, two and one, each ensigned on the top with a crown celestial—WORTHINGTON.

Civic crown: a wreath of oak acorned, has been already noted under *Chaplet*.

Crook. See *Crosier*, also *Staff*.

Crossed, (fr. *croisé*,) used rarely of a charge having a cross on it; (2) more often having a bar across, e.g. a crossed-crosslet.

Cross-bow. See *Bow*.

Crouch, or *Crowche*: a crutch. See *Potent*.

Crow. See *Raven*.

Crusule, old fr. *crosslet*, § 17.

The *Prince's crown* should more properly be blazoned Prince's *coronet* (q.v.); still the term is found.

Ermine, on a chief gules three prince's crowns composed of crosses pattee and fleurs-de-lis or, with caps of the first tasselled of the third—SKINNERS' Company [inc. 1327, arms granted 1551].

Ducal crown: see *post*, under *Coronet*, but the term is sometimes used.

Imperial crown: is properly the crown peculiar to the German emperor, which forms part of the crest of STOKES of Cambridgeshire, though, as already said, in English arms the crown royal of these realms is often so called.

Imperial crown.

Or, an imperial crown gules — ROBINSON, Hertford.

Gules, an imperial crown supported by a sword in pale proper hilted and pommelled within a double tressure-flory counter-flory—SETON, Earl of Winton, 1306-29.

Mural crown: formed of battlements *masoned.* Fancifully said to have been given by the Romans to the soldier who first ascended the walls of a besieged fortress.

Mural crown.

Or, a mural crown gules, between two barrulets azure and three wolf's heads erased sable—SEALE.

Erminois, on a pile embattled azure a mural crown between two caltraps in pale or—WALKER, Herts.

Argent, three griffins passant in pale azure murally gorged of the first, within a bordure sable bezanty—WILLS.

Gules, three mural coronets argent masoned sable—JOURDAN.

Crown palisado is a name given to a form of crown with, as it were, palisades upon it, and hence fancifully said to have been given by the Roman generals to him who first entered the enemies' camp by breaking through their outworks. It is called *vallar*, or

Crown Vallary (a).

vallary, from the Latin *vallus*, which practically means the palisade surmounting the
vallum. It is sometimes (though less correctly) represented as the second figure,
namely, with a *champaine* border.

Crown Vallary (b).

Or, a crown vallery gules between three stags
trippant proper—ROGERS, Denbigh.

Naval crown: a circle, having upon its upper edge four masts
of galleys, each with a topsail, and as
many sterns placed alternately. Imagi-
native heralds say it was invented by the
Emperor Claudius as a reward for sea
service.

Naval Crown.

Gules, six ancient naval crowns or—CLYTON, Scotland.

Azure, a lion rampant argent charged on the shoulder with an eagle
displayed sable ; on a chief wavy ermine, an anchor erect of the third,
the shank surrounded with a naval crown, rim azure, sterns and sails
proper—LOUIS, Devon.

Azure, a naval crown within an orle of twelve anchors or—LENDON
[granted 1658].

Crown of Rue, (fr. *Crancelin*, from germ. *Kranslein*): the
ancient arms of the Dukedom of Saxony
were barry of eight, or and sable. The
story goes that the *bend vert* was added by
the Emperor Frederick Barbarossa, when
he confirmed the dukedom on Bernard of
Anhalt (*c.* 1156), who desiring some mark
to distinguish him from the dukes of the
former house, the emperor took a chaplet
of rue which he had upon his head, and
threw it across the shield. These were

Dukedom of SAXONY.

the paternal arms of the late Prince ALBERT. The bearing is
sometimes called a *ducal coronet in bend*, and sometimes a *bend
archy coronetty*.

Papal or *Triple crown:* see *Tiara*. *Crown* of *Thorns:* see
Thorns, Crown of. The *Crown Obsidional*, and *Crown Triumphal* (composed of grass and of laurel or bay-leaves) have
been already noticed under *Chaplet*.

Under the article *Crown* it is convenient to include *Coronet*, as the two terms are in some cases interchangeable.

From the reign of Edward III. coronets of various forms were worn (as it seems indiscriminately) by princes, dukes, earls, and even knights, but apparently rather by way of ornament than distinction, or if for distinction, only (like the *collar* of SS) as a mark of gentility. The helmet of Edward the Black Prince, upon his effigy at Canterbury, is surrounded

Helmet of EDWARD the Black Prince.

with a *coronet* totally different from that subsequently assigned to his rank.

The *coronets* at present in use in England are the following, but connected more frequently with the *Crest*.

1. The coronet of the PRINCE OF WALES only differs from the royal crown in the omission of one of the arches. Edward, the son of Richard III., is recorded to have worn a *demy crown* on the day of his father's coronation at York (June 26, 1483); and was that day created Prince of Wales. It was formerly only the rim of the crown; but the arch was added in pursuance of a warrant of King Charles II., February 9, 1661.

2. That of the PRINCESS ROYAL has a coronet composed of four fleurs-de-lis, two crosses, and two strawberry leaves; one of the crosses appearing in the centre. Within the circle is a cap of crimson velvet turned up with ermine, and closed at the top with a golden tassel.

3. That of other PRINCES and PRINCESSES, sons and daughters of a sovereign, resembles the coronet of the Prince of Wales, but without the arch. The cap as before.

4. That of PRINCES and PRINCESSES, sons and daughters of the above, is similar, except that strawberry-leaves are substituted for the fleurs-de-lis. The *Princes' crowns*, however, are usually drawn in heraldry after a somewhat conventional manner.

Azure, a prince's coronet . . . . between two ostrich feathers in chief, a garb in base, all within a bordure sable bezanté—Town of EVESHAM.

Ermine, on a chief gules three prince's crowns composed of crosses pattée and fleur-de-lys or, with caps of the first, tasselled of the third— SKINNERS' Company [incorporated 1327, confirmed 1395].

5. That of DUKES is a circle of gold richly chased, and having upon its upper edge eight strawberry-leaves; only five are shewn in the drawing, two of them being in profile. The cap is of crimson velvet lined with white taffeta and turned up with ermine. At the top is a gold tassel. A *coronet* without the cap, and shewing

Duke.

but three leaves, is called a *Ducal coronet*, and frequently a *Ducal crown*.

Azure, three ducal crowns two and one or, each pierced with two arrows in saltire of the last—Abbey of BURY S. EDMUNDS.

Gules, two lions passant guardant in pale or; in chief two ducal coronets of the last—Priory of S. BARTHOLOMEW THE GREAT, London.

Gules, three ducal crowns or—See of ELY.

6. That of the MARQUIS is a rim of gold richly chased, supporting four strawberry-leaves and as many large pearls (or rather balls of silver) upon short points. The cap as before, though in heraldic drawings it is usually omitted.

Marquis.

7. That of the EARL. A rim of gold richly chased, on the upper edge of which are eight strawberry-leaves, and the same number of pearls set upon high points, so that it is readily distinguished from the coronet of the marquis. The cap, if shewn, the same as the first.

Earl.

Sable, a roundle argent between three earl's coronets or—CORONA.

8. A VISCOUNT'S *Coronet* is a chased circle of gold supporting twelve, fourteen, or, as some say, sixteen pearls, but usually only seven visible. The cap resembles those of the other coronets. This coronet was appointed by King James I.

Viscount.

9. A BARON'S *Coronet* is a plain circle of gold having six large
pearls upon it, four of which are seen in
a drawing. The cap as before. This coronet was assigned to barons on their
petition to King Charles II., soon after
his restoration. Before that period they

Baron.

wore caps of crimson velvet turned up with ermine, and at
a still earlier period, scarlet caps turned up with white fur.

Crowned, (fr. *couronné*) Many cases occur of beasts, especially
the lion, and sometimes birds, especially the
eagle, being crowned. A ducal coronet is
implied unless some other be expressly mentioned, but birds and beasts are sometimes
described as crowned with a *diadem* (fr. *dia-
demmé*), i.e. a plain fillet of metal. Also
lions, dogs, and other animals are frequently
gorged with a crown.

HILTON.

Argent, a lion rampant gules, crowned or—HILTON, Lanc.

Or, a lion rampant azure, crowned gules—CLYVEDON, Essex.

Argent, a lion rampant azure, crowned with a coronet of four balls
azure or—Ralph de MAIDSTONE, Bp. of Hereford, 1234—1239 [MS. Add.
B. Mus. 12443].

Per pale argent and gules, three bars counterchanged, on a canton of
the second a rose crowned or—BARRETT, co. Cork.

Crucifix. Such a charge occurs in one or two arms.

Azure, a saint standing on three degrees of steps vested in a loose
robe, with rays of glory round his head, holding a crucifix before him
in pale, his hands extended to the extremities of the cross, and the foot
of the cross resting on the upper step, all or—Insignia of the See of
WATERFORD.

Argent, on a cross Calvary with a griece of three steps gules, the
Saviour or—BUTLER, Baron Caher, 1543.

Crusily, *Crucilly,* or *Crusuly* (old fr. *Crusule*), is used now
to signify semé of *cross crosslets,* but whether or not in the
older arms simply small crosses were used cannot be determined. Any ordinary or charge over a field crusily *debruises*

Crutch, or *Crutch-staff.* See *Pilgrim's-staff* and *Potent.*

portions of the crosses, which should be arranged diagonally,
as in the example given in the margin.

Gules, crusily or—ROHAN, Lord of Warwick.

Sire William de KYME, de goules crusule de or
a un cheveron de or—Roll, temp. ED. II.

Sire Henri de LEKEBOURNE, de argent, crusule de
sable a un cheveron de sable—*Ibid.*

Azure, crusily three bars or — BLACKENHAM,
Suffolk.

Monsire de PARIS, sable, cheveron, entrecrusule
argent—Roll, temp. ED. III.

ROHAN.

Sire ... de DEN, de argent ij barres de sable ; en les barres les crusules
pattées de or—Roll, temp. ED. II.

At the same time the term is used when the crosses are of
a different kind, and then they have to be named.

Azure, crusily bottony, a lion rampant argent—BRAYTOFT, co. Lincoln.
Gules, crusily fitchy or, a griffin segreant of the last—PAU.

Cubes, or *Blocks :* a somewhat indefinite term for squares
appearing on a shield. So uncertain is the intention of the
draughtsman, that sometimes the very same charges are blazoned
as *dice, delves,* which are elsewhere blazoned as *blocks,*or *gads.*

Or, on a chevron gules between three cubes pean as many horse-shoes
argent—WILLIAMS, co. Pembroke.

Azure, on a chevron engrailed three blocks or, each charged with
a cross of the second—HOBSON, Harl. MS. A.D. 1404.

Azure, on three blocks (or billets, or delves, or dice), argent, an annulet to each sable—PAYNTER, Cornwall.

Argent, on three blocks (or billets, or delves, or dice) sable, a mullet
to each of the first—AMBROSE, Lancaster.

Cuirass, or *Breastplate :* a charge but rarely
borne in coats of arms.

Vert, a bar counter compony argent and azure between
three cuirasses of the second ; on a chief silver as many
buckles of the third—BALDBERNEY, Scotland.

Argent, a chevron ermine between three breastplates
argent—SWALLMAN, Kent.

Cuirass.

Cuffed : used of an arm vested
with a sleeve, of which the *cuff*
is of another tincture.

Crystals. See *Diamond.*
Cubit arm. See *Arm.*
Culter, i.q. *Coulter* under *Plough.*

Cummin: used as a charge only for the sake of the name.

Azure, a chevron between three sheaves of cummin or — COMYN, Durham.

Gules, three comyn-sheaves or, two and one—REDCOMYN.

Cup, (old fr. *Coupe*) : the cup was rather a favourite device from the fourteenth century onwards, as shewn by several references to it in the Rolls of Edward II. and Edward III. The plain chalice-like cup without a cover was perhaps first emblazoned, such as is found figured on incised slabs, &c. ; but it is sometimes represented in modern heraldry ornamented, as shewn in the drawing of the arms of CANDISH.

Sire William le BOTILER de Wemme, de azure a une bende e vj coupes de or—Roll, temp. ED. II.

CANDISH.

Sir Johan DARGENTEM, de goules a iij coupes de argent—*Ibid.*

Monsire de ARGENTYNE, gules trois coupes d'argent—Roll, temp. ED. III.

Monsire Edmond le BOTELER, port d'asure a trois coupes d'or—*Ibid.*

Sable, a chevron or between three cups uncovered—CANDISH, Suffolk.

But many families, especially those of BUTLER and CLEAVER, bear *covered cups* (fr. *coupes couvertes*), which are frequently represented on their tombs, and which are similar in shape to that in the margin, which is taken from the tomb of Johan le BOTILER, *c.* 1290, in the church of S. Bride, Glamorganshire.

Covered Cup.

Argent, a standing cup covered sable—John CLUER, London, 1716.

Gules, a cross between four covered cups argent—Richard DE LA WYCH, Bp. of Chichester, 1245-53.

Argent, between two bendlets engrailed sable, three covered cups of the second—Joseph BUTLER, Bp. of Bristol, 1738 ; afterwards of Durham, 1750-52.

Gules, a bend between three covered cups or —John BUTLER, Bp. of Oxford, 1788—1802.

Quarterly, first and fourth, azure, a chevron between three covered cups or, second and third ermine, on a chief indented sable, three escallops argent—BUTLER, Bp. of Lichfield, 1836—1839.

CLUER.

Sable, three cups covered per fesse or and argent—Symonds.

Gules, three cups covered argent garnished or—M. Gilis D'Argentine.

Quarterly, gules and azure ; in the first and fourth a leopard's head or ; in the second and third a covered cup; and in chief two round buckles, the tongues fessways, points to the dexter, all of the third—Goldsmiths' Company [incorporated 1927].

Besides these ordinary forms are some with descriptive details, as also others under the different names of *drinking-pots, college-pots*, &c.

Gules, three cups covered, with one handle to each, argent—Reginald at Conduit, Lord Mayor of London, 1334-5.

Per pale azure and gules, a cup covered with handles argent between three catherine wheels or—Street, Middlesex.

Argent, three cups sable coronetted or—Brandishfield.

Argent, three drinking-pots sable—Geriare, co. Lincoln.

Gules, three college-pots argent—Argenton, Devon.

Sable, three covers for cups argent—Koverdaw.

The small cup sometimes found, and as borne in the arms of Athull, is probably intended for an *acorn-cup*.

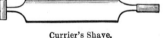
Cup.

Argent, three cups azure—Athull.

Currier's Shave, i.e. the *Curriers'*, or *Paring Knife*,

borne by the Curriers' Company, is represented as in the margin. In some drawings, however, both the handles resemble that on the dexter side of the figure.

Currier's Shave.

Azure, a cross engrailed or between four pairs of currier's shaves in saltire argent, handles of the second—Curriers' Company [incorporated 1605].

Curry-comb : this very rarely occurs in coats of arms, and there is no definite form of representation.

Argent, a chevron gules between three curry-combs proper—Harman.

Sable, three curry-combs argent, garnished or—Harmond, co. Oxford.

Culverin. See *Gun.*

Cuppa, or *Cuppy.* See *Potent counter potent.*

Cuppules (i.e. couples), e.g. *Bars gemelles.*

Curlew. See *Snipe.*

Curved-recurved : bent in the form of the letter S, synonymous with *flexed reflexed*, and *bowed embowed.*

Cushion: this charge is found in ancient arms under the name *oreiller* (old fr. *horeler*), or *pillow*, the latter term also sometimes occurring in modern blazon. It has, as a rule, four *tassels*, one at each of the corners, and it is not necessary to mention them unless of a different tincture. Cushions are sometimes *fringed*. They may also be charged with some device.

Cushion.

Maheu de REDMAIN, de goules a trois horielers d'or —Roll, temp. HEN. III.

Sire Mahteu de REDEMAN, de goulys a iij horilers de ermine—Roll, temp. ED. II.

Monsire John FLEMINGE, barre d'argent et d'asur a trois oreillers de gules en la sovereign barre—Roll, temp. Ed. III.

Monsire John de NORTON, port d'argent une cheveron entre trois oreilers de sable—*Ibid.*

Gules, on a fesse or, between three cushions ermine, tasselled of the second, three fleur-de-lys of the field—HUTTON, Bp. of Bangor, 1743; Abp. of York, 1747; Abp. of Cant. 1757-58.

Quarterly, first and fourth gules, three cushions tasselled ermine, second and third gules, a lion rampant argent—Richard REDMAN, Bp. of S. Asaph, 1491; afterwards Bp. of Exeter, 1496—1500.

Argent, three cushions lozengewise gules, tasselled or—BECARD.

Gules, three square cushions argent—GREYSTOCK.

Abp. HUTTON.

Gules, a cross argent between four cushions lozengeways ermine, tasselled or—William REDMAN, Bp. of Norwich, 1595—1602.

Sable, on a cushion a dog couchant or—ALABAND.

Or, on each of three cushions within a bordure gules, a crescent of the first—MELVILLE, Scotland.

Vert, three pillows ermine—HOPKINSON, co. York.

When the *tassels* appear as a separate charge they are to be represented as in the margin.

Gules, three tassels or —WOOLER.

Tassel.

Cutlas. See *Sabre.*

Cutting-knife. See (1) *Basket-makers*; (2) *Pattern-makers*; (3) *Plumbers.*

Cyclamor, fr.: a single large ring, not used in English arms.

Cygnet. See *Swan.*

Cypress. See *Pine.*

Dagger, (fr. *poignard*): Amongst weapons daggers are frequently borne, though blazoned under different names. Their position should be described, whether paleways or fessways. If not otherwise stated the points should be upwards. The hilts, pomels, &c., may be of a different tincture.

Gules, a fesse chequy argent and azure, a dagger paleways in base proper, [and in chief a mullet for difference]—LINDSAY, Pitscandly, Scotland.

Sable, two daggers in saltire, points upwards, between four fleur-de-lys argent—BARROW, Bp. of Sodor and Man, 1663, afterwards of S. Asaph, 1670-80.

Ermine, two bars within a bordure engrailed gules; on a canton of the last a dagger erect proper, pomel and hilt or—NUGENT, Berks.

Azure, a fesse or, between three dagger's heads of the last—LOCKYER, 1672.

Azure, a chevron between three daggers, with blades wavy, pointing downwards argent—CLEATHER, Cornwall.

The other names and varieties found are *dirk, rapier,* and *skean,* or *skene,* the last a Scottish word for a weapon, which perhaps may be best described as a short sword, and is borne mostly by various branches of the family of SKENE.

Argent, a chevron between three dirks azure hilted or, with those in chief pointing downward—GLASHAM, Scotland.

Gules, a dirk palewise argent, between two fleurs-de-lys in chief and a mullet in base or—MACAUL, Scotland.

Gules, a dexter hand fessways, holding a rapier erect, on the point a boar's head proper—BEATH.

Azure, a skean in fesse argent, hilted and pomelled or, between three boar's heads, couped of the second and muzzled sable—FORBES, Robslaw.

Gules, three skenes palewise in fesse argent, hilts and pomels or, surmounted of as many wolves' heads of the third—SKENE, Aberdeen.

Per chevron argent and gules, three skeans surmounted with as many wolves' heads counterchanged—SKENE, Newtile.

Daisy, (fr. *marguerite*): this flower appears but rarely.

Quarterly, argent and gules, on a cross between four half roses, a daisy counterchanged, stalked vert—George DAY, Bp. of Chichester, 1543 [Harl. MS. 1116].

Argent, three daisies gules, stalked and leaved vert—DAISIE, Scotland.

D'or, à trois marguerites [ou paquerettes] d'argent boutonnées d'or—PASQUIER, Orleanais.

Dacre's knot. See *Cord.*   **Daim,** (fr.). See *Deer.*

Dancetté or *dancetty*, and sometimes *dantelly*, (fr. *denché*) : a zigzag line of partition, differing from *indented* only in the indentations, being larger in size, and consequently fewer in number.

Dancetty per long is a term said to be used by some heralds to signify that the indentations are very deep; so deep as to be equivalent to *pily*. The terms *dauncet* and *dauncelet* are used evidently for a *fesse dancetté*, and there are various contractions found in the rolls, e.g. *daunce, daunze, dans*, &c. The *fesse dancetté* and the division called *per fesse dancetté* have but three indentations, unless particularly described otherwise.

Or, a fesse dancetté sable—Vavasour, York-shire.

Gules, four bars dancetty argent—Totten-ham.

Gules, a fesse dancetty in the upper part or—Thorelys.

Monsire John de Stonor, port d'azur une dauncelet d'or une chief d'or — Roll, temp. Ed. III.

. Azure, two bars dancetty or, a chief argent—Rt. Hon. Thomas Stonor, Baron Camoys. [The arms are painted as in the margin, in windows of Watlington and Pirton churches; also on the tomb ascribed to Sir John de Stonor in Dorchester church.]

Sire Richard Loveday, de azure, a iij daunces de or—Roll, temp. Ed. II.

Sire William Deyncourt, de argent, billette de sable e un daunce de sable—*Ibid.*

Sire Edmon de Kendale de argent a une bende daunce de vert, et ij coties daunce de goules—*Ibid.*

Argent, a fesse dancetty with a cross formy issuing in chief gules—Arms ascribed to Reginald Fitz-Jocelyn, Bp. of Bath and Wells, 1191.

Sire Johan de la Riviere, de azure a lj daunces de or—Roll, temp. Ed. II.

John Deyncourt, azure, ung danse et billety d'or—Roll, temp. Hen. III.

Sir Roger le Bred, de goules besaunte de or e un daunce de or—Roll, temp. Ed. II.

VAVASOUR.

STONOR.

FITZ-JOCELYN.

The term *downset* seems a barbarism for *dauncet*, and as applied to a *bend* signifies *fracted*, or broken. In a grammar or Glossary of Heraldry, Harl. MS., No. 1441, fol. 97, the figure of a bend is drawn as in the margin. A figure of a *double downset* has already been given under *bend*.

Per pale argent and azure, a bend downset counterchanged—ZORKE, Cotton MS. Tiberius D, 10, fol. 672.

Azure crusilly argent, a fesse double downset ermine—MOIGNE, co. Leicester.

ZORKE.

Debruised, (fr. *brisé*): 1. a term applied more especially to an animal having an ordinary or other charge over it, which also extends over part of the field as well. It is more usual to blazon an ordinary thus treated as *surmounted by*, though there does not appear to be any very definite rule followed as to the distinctive use of the two terms. It will be observed that this differs essentially from one bearing being *charged* with another, because in the latter case the sur-charge does not extend into the field.

Argent, a lion rampant gules, debruised with a ragged staff in bend throughout or—STUART, [being an augmentation given by King Charles VI. of France, to Sir Alexander STUART, knight, and since borne by the family upon an inescutcheon over their paternal arms.]

Azure, a lion rampant argent, debruised with a bend gules—WAYLAND, Kent.

Argent, a saltire sable, debruised of a pale gules—John CONEYBEARE, Bp. of Bristol, 1750-55.

Sable, a fesse debruised by a pile or—BRINGBURN.

STUART.

Or, a chevron gules surmounted by a bendlet azure—Robert de STAFFORD.

Damask. See *Rose.*

Danché, i.q. *denché* = *indented.*

Dancing: applied to *bears.*

Danish hatchet: see *Axe.* Ditto *warrior:* see *Man.*

Dart, (fr. *dard*). See *Spear.*

Dauncelet, (fr.): a *bar dancetty.*

Daw. See *Raven.*

Death's head. See *Achievements;* also *Bones.*

Debased: when arms are reversed. See *Abatement.*

Dechausse, written also *dehaché,* (fr.): *Dismembered.*

The terms *depressed* and *oppressed* seem to have practically the same signification as above.

Argent, five annulets, one within the other, azure, alternately oppressing a cross engrailed sable—Robert GIFFORD, Harl. MS., 6137.

Or, five annulets, one within the other vert, embracing and depressed by a cross engrailed gules—Robert GYFFARD.

Gules, a fesse ermine, depressed by a pale of the same within a bordure engrailed azure—SPONNE.

Another application of the word, but rarely and improperly used, is when a *bend* or *chevron* is *broken*.

Deeble, or, as commonly written, *dibble,* is the gardener's implement, and is borne for the sake of the name.

Azure, three deebles argent—DEEBLE.

Deer: the term deer (fr. *daim,* old fr. *deym*) is seldom used in blazoning, but it is convenient to employ it here as a general name under which to group several of the family of *Cervidæ.* First and most common is the *stag* itself (fr. *cerf*), but other names appear, frequently representing varieties of stags, and in some cases evidently used for the sake of the name, rather than for any difference which could be shewn in the drawing. They are *Hart, Buck, Roe, Roebuck, Doe, Fawn, Hind* (fr. *biche*), *Brocket.* The *Brocket* is a young stag up to two years, or (according to some authors) to three years, old; it becomes a *Buck* in its sixth year. With them may be classed the *Reindeer* (fr. *renchier*), which heralds distinguish from the stag by double attires, one pair erect, the other pendent, as shewn in the diagram in the margin.

Reindeer.

It may be added that the old name was simply *cerf,* and according to the rolls it is chiefly the *head* which appears on the ancient arms, but it will be observed that the two examples

---

Docked: sometimes said of feathers trimmed at their edges with a different tincture.

Declinant, said to be used of the *tail* of a serpent hanging down.

Decoupé, (fr.): with the edges cut out, or into shreds.

Decrement in, and *Decrescent.* See *Moon.*

Deer-goat: a monstrosity. See *Goat.*

given are probably both allusive. In the first the *biche* (fr. for *hind*) probably refers to the name BECHE; and in the second the 'hert' or 'hart' distinctly alludes to the name HERTFORD.

Sire Johan de BECHE, de argent, a une bende de goules a iij testes de cerfs de or en lo oantel un merelos de sublu Roll, temp. ED. II.

Monsire de HERTFORD port d'argent a une fes sable a trois testes de cerfs d'or en le fes—Roll, temp. ED. III.

Taking the stag as the typical beast of chase, it will be well here to note the terms which are especially applied in heraldry to the positions in which it may be represented.

It may be *statant* (fr. *arrêté*), which means that it is standing still, with all its feet touching the ground; while *statant at gaze*, or standing at gaze, means that it is the same, and *guardant* (which is the term used of beasts of prey). Further, it may be represented as *grazing*, or more correctly (of stags) *browsing*, that is, with its head touching the ground, in the act of feeding; or *at bay*, i.e. with head downwards.

Argent, a stag statant gules—HOLME.

Argent, a stag statant at gaze gules—GRYFFYDD GWR.

Gules, a stag standing at gaze argent, attired or—JONES.

Ermine, three stags at gaze gules—BLYTHE, Bp. of Salisbury, 1493–99.

Azure, on a mount vert a hind grazing argent—HENDLEY, Lancaster.

Or, two tilting spears in saltire sable, surmounted by a stag browsing proper; a chief azure . . . .—THORNHILL, Derby.

Or, again, a stag may be *trippant*, or *tripping*, that is *passant*, but in a leisurely manner (and when two, *counter-trippant*); while *courant*, or more properly, *in full course* (fr. *elancé*), means that the stag must be represented as if passing at full speed. Again, instead of the term *rampant*, which is applied to beasts of prey, the terms used for stags are *springing*, or *salient*.

Argent, a buck tripping upon a mound proper —STRAHAN.

Vert, three roebucks trippant argent, attired or —TROLLOP.

Azure, three stags trippant or—GREEN, Bp. of Lincoln, 1761–79.

Azure, a reindeer trippant ermine—WALSTONE.

STRAHAN.

Gules, a chevron between three hinds tripping or—HINDE.

Ermine, three bucks trippant gules, on a chief indented, party per pale or and azure, a cross patonce counterchanged between two roses dexter gules, sinister or—Geoffrey BLYTHE, Bp. of Lichfield and Coventry, 1503–31.

Sable, two hinds counter-tripping, in fesse argent [or as elsewhere blazoned, Sable, two hinds counter-passant, the one facing to the sinister, surmounting the other in fesse argent]—COTTINGHAM.

Sable, two bucks in full course or—BUCKSIDE.

COTTINGHAM.

Azure, a stag in full course or, pursued by a brace of dogs argent, all bendwise and at random—YARDLEY.

Vert, a stag courant argent, armed or—GETTHIN, co. Cork.

Azure, a hart springing or—STRATHALLAN.

Sable, on a mount vert, two stags salient affrontant argent, collared and chained or—FISHER, Bp. of Exeter, 1803; afterwards Bp. of Salisbury, 1807–25.

. . . Two does counter-salient . . .—DRYHURST.

Argent, a stag salient proper armed or—KIRCH.

FISHER.

Sable, two greyhounds rampant, regardant, addorsed argent; in chief between them a fawn's head cabossed or—BARNARD, Hants.

Or, lastly, the stag may be *couchant,* or more properly *lodged,* which latter is a term used specially of the stag. It may also be represented in a sitting posture, when the term *sejant* is applied, the same as that used for other animals.

Azure, (another sable,) a buck lodged argent—DOWNES, Cheshire.

Vert, three stags lodged argent, attired or, and langued gules—ANDERSON.

Vert, a hind couchant argent—PEYTON, co. Brecon.

Argent, a stag sejant gules attired or, in the mouth a trefoil slipped proper—BOWEN.

DOWNES.

Besides these the expressions applied to other animals are found sometimes used, e.g. *unguled* when the hoofs are of different tincture, *armed* (though this very improperly), to include both horns and hoofs, and also *langued ;* and so also the terms *passant, guardant,* and *reguardant,* and even *rampant,* are found.

Quarterly or and azure, four roebucks passant counterchanged—ROSIN-DALE, [4441].

Vert, a buck rampant proper—PARKER, Cheshire.

As already noted under *attires* the horns of the stag are considered as ornaments, and hence the term *attired* is more properly employed than either *armed* or *horned.* An old term for the stag's horns is *perches.* The number of *tynes* or projections from the *beam* is sometimes given, if not it is quite optional. Also it may be observed that *stags' heads* are very frequently adopted. In one case even the stag's *ears.* When the front only of the head, with the attires, but without the neck, is shewn, it may be called a stag's head *caboshed* (fr. *rencontre*); the French term *massacre* may also be used, though some think that only a portion of the cranium should in this case be shewn.

Or, a stag's head couped and attired with six tynes on every horn sable —CALDER, Scotland.

Azure, three stag's heads couped argent, attired with ten tynes or— PORTEOUS, Scotland.

Argent, a stag's head erased, armed with three tines gules—CRAWFURD.

Argent, a buck's head cabossed sable, the tips of all the attires or— SNOKISHULL.

Le Counte de WARTEMBERG, BARNARD, Hants, d'or a iij perches de deym de sable—Harl. MS. 6589.

Azure, a bend between a deer's head erased, and in base three crosses crosslet fitchy argent—PETREE.

Argent, three brocket's heads, couped azure collared or, thereto a bell affixed gules—HANNEY.

Argent, three reindeer's heads cabossed sable—BOWETT, York.

D'azur, a trois massacres de cerf d'or—LA FERTÉ.

One of the badges of Richard II. was a white hart couchant beneath a tree proper, gorged with a crown and chained or. The annexed cut is from a carving in Westminster Hall, and a similar representation is seen in the glass in the chapel of S. Michael in Canterbury Cathedral.

Badge of RIC. II.

Defamed, (fr. *diffamé*): a term applied to a *lion* or other beast (and perhaps also to an *eagle*) which has lost its tail. *Defamed looking backwards* is given by some writers for counter rampant regardant, the lion being supposed to be flying from an enemy, but it is doubtful if any example exists.

Delf, or *Delph,* (plural *delves*). This word (derived from the verb delve, to dig) is the name of a charge representing a shovelful of earth: the sides are sometimes drawn straight, sometimes curved inwards. When *tenne*, it is said to be one of the *abatements*, and it is then over the *fesse point*. See also *Gad.*

Delf.

Argent, a chevron between three delves gules—DELVES.

Or, a fesse wavy between three delves [elsewhere billets] sable—STANFORD.

The representations of this charge are sometimes very doubtful, and they have been blazoned *cubes, gads* (as in the insignia of the IRONMONGERS' COMPANY), *blocks,* &c.; but in the following examples the cubes are no doubt intended for *dice*, and should be drawn as such.

Azure, a chevron between three dice sable, each charged with four spots—ENGLOWES, Somerset.

Argent, a chevron between three dice sable, each charged with a cinquefoil [? 5 spots] of the first—FITZWILLIAMS, York.

Gules, three dice argent, on each five (six?) spots in front, two upon the top, and three on the sinister side, sable—MATTHIAS, London.

MATTHIAS.

The last of those given is supposed to be allusive to the election of S. Matthias to the Apostleship.

Defense, (fr.): used for the tusk of a boar, or of an elephant.

Degrees = *Steps*, as a Cross of three degrees, more frequently termed *grieces;* or *degraded.* See under *Cross,* § 15.

Demi-vol, (fr.): signifies a single wing of a bird.

Dejected: cast down, e.g. of a *garb;* or hanging down, e.g. of the head of an animal.

De l'un en l'autre, or *De l'un à l'autre,* nearly always means counterchanged, except in the case when applied to 'two bends *indented* de l'un en l'autre.'

Demi, or *Demy,* i.e. fr. for half: when applied to an animal, its upper or fore half is always intended; when any thing inanimate, generally the dexter half per pale.

Demi-fleur-de-lis. The fleur-de-lis may be divided either per pale or per fesse; the former is usually intended.

A *demi-lion* may be passant, rampant, or in any of the other positions.

Demi-vol : one wing. See also *demi-garter ;* and demi-*hull* under *ship.*

Argent, on a fesse gules between three demi-hinds couped azure as many bezants—HEYNES.

Argent (another or), a demi-lion rampant gules—DENNETT ; MALLORY.

MALLORY.

Device, (fr. *devise*): a motto, emblem, or other mark by which those who entered the lists were distinguished at tournaments, but especially a motto affixed to the arms, having some punning allusion to the name. It differed from a *badge* or cognizance only inasmuch as it was an arbitrary and generally temporary distinction, whereas the badge was often borne by members of the same house successively.

Dexter: the right-hand side of the shield, being that to the left of the spectator. A bend, if not otherwise blazoned, is supposed to be a bend dexter, but a *baston* is often described as a *dexter baston.* The term is frequently applied to the *hand.*

Argent, a lion rampant gules, over all a dexter baston compony or and azure—Piers LUCIEN.

Denché, (fr.) : perhaps something between *indented* and *dancetty.*

Denchure, (fr.) : a fillet indented at the top of the shield, not borne in English, and very rare in French, arms.

Denté, (fr.) : with *teeth,* when of a different tincture.

Dentelé, (fr.) : *indented.*

Denticulé, (fr.) : used of a bordure with very fine indentations.

Detriment, in; of the *Moon,* q.v.

Depressed by: sometimes used for *debruised* or *surmounted* by.

Develloped : unfurled, e.g. of a flag. Written also *disvelloped,* and *divelloped.*

Dextrochère, (fr.) : a dexter arm issuing from the sinister side of the shield, very frequently from clouds. It may be bare, or armed, or bearing weapons. It is only found in French heraldry.

Dez : old fr. for *dice.*

Diamond, (fr. *diamant*): this, the chief of precious stones, is sometimes represented in English, but more frequenﬡly in French, coats of arms, and with this may be associated both the *crystal* and the *brilliant*. The term, however, it may be added, has been chosen in the fanciful blazoning of the arms of peers in the seventeenth century for *sable*.

Argent, on a mount vert, a palm tree of the last thereon pendent a shield azure, charged with three mullets of the first pierced of the third; on a chief of the last a sun proper between two rings or, each adorned with a diamond—NORDEN, London, [1771].

Or, a chevron between nine links of a chain, each division consisting of three links sable. On a chief gules, a large diamond set in the midst of a triangle within a double row of brilliants proper—MIGNOT.

Argent, on a fesse gules, three Crystals . . . . in a bordure ermine—BOUSALL, Co. Cardigan.

De gueules, à trois diamants en lozanges tailleés a facettes d' argent, en fasces—AFFAGARD, Normandie.

Diapered, (fr. *diapré*): an ancient mode of relieving the plain tinctures of fields and charges by arabesque and other patterns, generally of a darker shade of the same colour, and left to the fancy of the painter or sculptor. Some species of diapering have been mistaken for fretty, as that on the tomb of Robert DE VERE, in the church of Hatfield-Broad-Oak, Essex.

At the same time it appears to have been recognised as a mode of tincture, as in the following :—

Diapered.

Le Counte CHAUMPAINE, d'azur a une bende d'argent a custeres d'or diasprez—Roll, temp. HEN. III., Harl. MS. 6589.

Le Counte DEL ILLE, de goules a treis barres dor diasprez—*Ibid.*

What is meant by *diapers* in the following arms as thus blazoned in Burke is not clear. Papworth suggests *didapper*, an aquatic bird.

Argent, on a chevron gules between three diapers azure, a crescent or charged with a mullet sable—BREDNELL, London.

Diademé, (fr.) : used of an eagle with a fillet of gold on its head.

Dibble. See *Deeble*.

Dice. See *Delf*.

Dimidiated, (fr. *mi-parti*) halved; applied to animals, birds (especially eagles), fleurs-de-lis, &c., of which only one half is shewn, in consequence of the field being *party per pale.* When only two half-charges are joined together, e.g. a rose and pomegranate, they may be blazoned as a demi-rose conjoined with a demi-pomegranate. See arms of BILSON under *Pomegranate,* and of CINQUE PORTS under *Ship.*

Party per pale argent, an eagle displayed sable dimidiated per pale, and argent a wolf salient sable —Laurence CAMPEGIUS, Bp. of Salisbury, 1525–34.

Gules, an eagle displayed double-headed or, dimidiated with chequy argent and azure—SWEETMAN, co. Kilkenny.

D'or, à l'aigle de l'empire mi-parti d'azur à la fleur-de-lis d'or—BASTARD, Berry.

CAMPEGIUS.

The expression impaling arms by *dimidiation,* will be referred to under *Marshalling,* when the whole coat of arms, both of wife and husband, is *dimidiated.*

Dish, or *standish;* this is represented as in the margin, in Bp. STANDISH's arms, and the charge is also found blazoned as a *platter.* Though in the second example the charge is blazoned as a dish, it was probably intended for a *bowl.*

Dish.

Sable, three dishes argent—STANDISH, Bp. of S. Asaph, 1518–35.

Azure, three boar's heads couped argent, within as many dishes or—BOLLES, Lincoln.

Dismembered, (fr. *demembré,* or *dechaussé*), is said by writers to be applied to beasts whose heads, feet, or tails are cut off, but left so near the parts whence they were severed that the outline of the animal remains the same, but the term has not been met with in actual use. The French term *tronconné,* or *trononné,* is said to be applied to various charges, and even to ordinaries when so severed. See *Cross,* § 7.

Dismembered.

Or, a lion rampant dechaussé [or couped at all the joints], within a double tressure flory counter-flory gules—MAITLAND, Earl of Lauderdale.

Or, a lion rampant couped in all the joints of the first—MAITLAND, Scotland.

Gules, a lion rampant the head argent divided by a line indented or erased from the body or—GRACE.

D'argent, au lion de sable accompagne de trois merlettes demembrées aussi de sable—PICARD, Bretagne.

Distillatory : this device, borne by the DISTILLERS' Company, and usually blazoned 'a distillatory double armed,' is represented on their arms as in the margin.

Distillatory 1.

Azure, a fesse wavy argent, in chief the sun in splendour encircled with a cloud distilling drops of rain all proper; in base a distillatory double armed or on a fire proper, with two worms and bolt receivers of the second—DISTILLERS' Company [Incorporated 1638].

Another 'distillatory,' or 'still,' is represented as the smaller engraving, and appears as the crest of the family of WYNINGTON, London.

Distillatory 2.

Dock-leaf : this leaf seems to be borne almost entirely by Scotch families, and is variously named *edock* (lat. *rumex*), *burdock* (lat. *arctium*), or simply *dock* leaf, or even *bur* leaf.

Argent, three dock-leaves vert—BRAINISS, Scotland.

Argent, a bishop's pall sable, between three dock-leaves vert—MARSHALL, Scotland.

Argent, a saltire humetty azure; between an edock-leaf in each flank and base vert—MARISHALL, Queensbury.

Argent, three burdock-leaves vert—NOBLE, Edinburgh.

Or, a chevron ermine between three bur-leaves proper ; (a crescent for difference)—BURWELL, Suffolk.

Dog, (fr. *chien*): occurs very frequently in armorial bearings, and under a variety of names; the drawing in most cases being made generally to suit the dog described. The oldest name is the *levrier*, spelt *leverer*, and amongst the arms of the last two or three centuries the *greyhound* is the most frequently chosen, the *bloodhound* and the *ratch-hound* but rarely.

The *talbot* is a hunting-dog, distinguished chiefly by the form of his ears; the modern *mastiff* occurs in one or two coats of arms, and we find also the *spaniel* and the *terrier*. The *Alant*, or *Aland*, [Span. *alano.*, med. lat. *Canes alani*], a mastiff with short ears, appears to be used only as the supporter of the arms of Lord DACRE.

"About his char ther wenten white alauns."—Chaucer, Knight's Tale. 2450.

In the following examples it will be seen that besides the ordinary position of the dog, which is *passant*, it may be represented *sejant*, *rampant*, *salient*, *skipping*, *questing* (i.e. pointing), *courant*, and *in full cry*. The *ears* may be of a different tincture, and it is frequently *gorged* or *collared*.

Sire William MAULEVERER, de argent a iij leverers de goules—Roll, temp. ED. II.

Sir Perez BURDEUX, porte d'or ou ung lev'er de gules, ou le collere de sable ou le bordure de sable besante dor—Harl. MS. 6589.

Per pale gules and azure, three hounds in full cry—TURNER [Lord Mayor of London, 1769].

Argent, a greyhound passant sable collared gules —HOLFORD.

Argent, a greyhound salient party per long sable and of the first—DE LA FORDE, Iver, Bucks.

Argent, a greyhound courant sable, in a bordure engrailed gules—Ralph BRIDEOKE, Bp. of Chichester, 1675–78.

Vert, three greyhounds argent, gutté de larmes; on a chief or a fox passant gules—WELDISH, Kent [granted 1542].

HOLFORD.

Argent, a greyhound skipping in bend sable—ATTWOOD.

Gules, two greyhounds salient affrontant or—DOGGET, Norfolk.

Argent, on a chief dancetty sable three bezants; in base a greyhound courant of the second collared or—Offspring BLACKALL, Bp. of Exeter, 1708–16.

Gules, two greyhounds salient counter-salient in saltire (the dexter surmounted by the sinister) argent, collared of the field between three fleurs-de-lys two and one; in chief a stag's head couped attired with ten tynes or—UDNEY, Scotland.

Sable, a bloodhound passant within a bordure engrailed argent—SUDBURY.

Azure, three bloodhounds argent—RAGON.

Argent, a ratch-hound courant between three hunting-horns sable—FORRESTER, Dundee.

Argent, a talbot passant gules—WOLVESLEY, Suffolk.

Argent, a talbot passant sable eared and collared or; to the collar a ring of the second; on a chief indented azure three crosses crosslet of the third—KENE, Norfolk.

Sable, three talbot's heads erased argent langued gules—Joseph HALL, Bp. of Exeter, 1627; afterwards of Norwich, 1641–56.

Or, a fesse wavy, between three talbots questing sable—ALLEN, Kent.

WOLVESLEY.

Azure, a talbot passant argent collared gules lined or; at the end of the line a knot—BURGOYNE.

Azure, a talbot seiant within a bordure engrailed azure—Simon SUDBURY, Bp. of London, 1362; afterwards Abp. Cant., 1375–81. [From glass at Trinity Hall, Cambridge.]

Argent, on a fesse between two mullets in chief gules, and a dove in base azure, a mastiff's head couped of the field—FUDDIE, Scotland.

Argent, a spaniel-dog passant proper; on a chief embattled azure, a key palewise, the wards upward between two crosses crosslet or—MAIRE.

SUDBURY.

Azure, a chevron argent between in chief two garbs or, and in base a spaniel passant proper; in the centre chief point a cross crosslet fitchy of the second—BURDEN.

Gules, a fesse ermine between three water-spaniels argent, each holding in the mouth a birdbolt or—RIGGS, Lincoln.

Sable, a chevron ermine between three terriers argent—BUTHER.

Sable, a chevron between three spotted dogs of the second—HARTHAM, co. Leicester.

Diffamé. See *Defamed.*

Differences. See *Cadency*, marks of.

Diminutive. See *Ordinary.*

Dirk. See *Dagger.*

Disarmed, (fr. *desarmé* and *morné*): rarely applied to lions without teeth, talons, &c., and eagles without claws, &c.

Disclosed. See *Wings.*

Displayed. See *Eagle;* also *Wings.*

Distilling *drops of blood:* said sometimes of a part of an animal, e.g. under *Deer*, i.q. *imbrued.*

Diverse: an irregular term applied to three *swords* or other charges posed in different directions, e.g. in arms of STAPLETON, Cumberland, under *Point.*

Divise, *fasce en* (fr.) = *bar.*

Doe. See *Deer.*

Dog-fish. See *Shark.*

Dog-hook. See *Horse-picker.*

Dolphin, (fr. *dauphin*): the Dolphin, which is not a true fish at all, according to the system of naturalists, was considered by the older heralds as the chief of fish, just as the lion was the chief of beasts, and the eagle the chief of birds.

It is even used in arms when it is supposed to be a play upon the name of *fish*, e.g.

Azure, a fesse wavy or between two crescents in chief, and a dolphin in base argent—FISH, Kempton, Middlesex.

Gules, a dolphin or; a chief ermine—FISHER, Whitlingham, Norfolk.

Azure, a dolphin embowed between three ears of wheat or—John FYSHAR, Bp. of Rochester. [From a facsimile of a Parliament Roll, 1515.]

In the Arms of the FISHMONGERS' Company of London, both the *Dolphin*, and the *Lucy*, or pike, are borne—intended, no doubt, the one as the type of the sea-fish, the other of those of fresh-water. It is probably due to the same reason that several Lord Mayors, who were members of the Fishmongers' Company, bore the dolphin in their arms; and perhaps also why some seaport towns also bear it, e.g. BRIGHTON.

Azure, three dolphins naiant in pale argent, finned and ducally crowned or, between two pair of lucies in saltire, the sinister surmounting the dexter proper; over the nose of each lucy a ducal crown of the third; on a chief gules three pair of keys endorsed in saltire or—FISHMONGERS' COMPANY.

Gules, a fesse or between three dolphins embowed argent—Sir William ASKHAM, Lord Mayor of London, 1404.

A chevron between three dolphins embowed—Sir John RAINWELL, Lord Mayor of London, and Fishmonger, 1426.

The badge of the County of Dauphiné in France appears from the thirteenth century onwards to have been a Dolphin, an early example of ' Armes parlantes.' It was subsequently borne

---

Doloire, (old fr.): the head of an adze, without the handle.

Domed. See *Tower.*

Donjonné, (fr.): of a castle which has turrets.

Door. See under porch of a *church.*

Door-bolt. See *Lock.*

Dorcers. See *Water-bouget.*

Doric column. See *Pillar.*

Dormant: sleeping, with the head resting on the fore-paws.

Dorsed: shewing the back, particularly of a hand, and so contrary to *apaumy.*

Dos a dos: old French term for *endorsed.*

Dosser. See *Water-bouget.*

by the Dauphins, who were sty ed Lords of Auvergne. In the
fourteenth century the title of Dauphin being adopted as the
style of the eldest son of the King of France, the charge frequently appears. The Arms of the Dauphin, son of Louis XIV.,
represent in the third and fourth quarters a dolphin, while the
crown which serves as the crest is ornamented also with
dolphins. The Dolphin is also used in other canting arms,
besides those of the DAUPHIN of France, i.e. the Venetian family
of DOLFIN, and the English families of DOLPHIN, DOLPHINLEY,
DOLPHINTON, and Lord GODOLPHIN.

Although the fish is in reality straight it is always represented *embowed*, i.e. curved, and this term is often added in the
blazon; in more recent drawings it is represented with a double
curve, i.e. *bowed embowed*, though the terms are not used. It is
blazoned either *hauriant* (i.e. upright), or *naiant*, i.e. in fesse;
sometimes also *erect*. It may be also *vorant* (i.e. swallowing a
fish). It may be *fimbriated* or *finned* of a different tincture.

Le Comte de FOREST, de goules a un dauffin de
mer dor—Roll, temp. HEN. III., Harl. MS. 6589.

Sire Johan de MAULEE de or, a une bende de
sable, en la bende iij daufins de argent—Roll,
temp. ED. II.

Sable, a dolphin hauriant or—DOLFINTON.

Azure, a fesse between three dolphins naiant
argent—BARNARD, Essex [also LEMAN].

Argent, two dolphins hauriant respecting each
other sable, chained together by their necks, the   DOLFINTON.
chain pendent or [otherwise an anchor between two dolphins proper]—
COLSTON, Essex.

Per pale or and azure, two dolphins erect
counterchanged; on a chief gules a covered cup
between as many dovecots of the first—COTES,
Lord Mayor of London, 1542.

Gules, on a chevron engrailed argent, three
dolphins embowed proper—Arms ascribed to Ralph
FLAMBARD, Bp. of Durham, 1099–1128.

Sable, a dolphin embowed argent fimbriated or
—JAMES.   BARNARD.

Argent, three dolphins hauriant azure, finned or—GILROY, Scotland.

Argent, a fesse gules oppressed with two dolphins haurient respectant in pale or, the space between them ermine—BUCKLAND.

Argent, three dolphins haurient azure, finned or—GILROY, Scotland.

Vert, three dolphins embowed naiant in pale argent—DOLFINLEY, Hants.

Quarterly, first and fourth; azure, a dolphin embowed argent; second and third; argent, a cross engrailed sable, in dexter chief an eagle displayed gules—Richard FITZ-JAMES, Bishop of Rochester, 1497, of Chichester, 1504, and London, 1506–22.

Argent, on a bend azure three dolphins of the field, [and Crest a dolphin embowed proper pierced through the sides with two fishing spears in saltire or]—William FRANKLIN, Hertfordshire, 1613.

Dolphins are also used very frequently both as *supporters* and *crests*.

Dove, (fr. *colombe*): the Dove is a very frequent device; sometimes the *turtle dove* and sometimes the *ringed dove* are specially mentioned. And also with the dove may be grouped the *Pigeon*, with its fellows the *Stock-dove* and *Wood-pigeon*. It is said to have been adopted as an emblem of purity, and sometimes it appears as the *Holy Dove*. The Dove is subjected to the usual terms expressing position, &c., applicable to birds (see *eagle*), but the more frequent are *volant, close, rising,* and often having an olive-branch or some sprig in the mouth, and in one case '*displayed in a glory,*' and also *nimbed*. It may be, of course, also *membered, legged, beaked, billed,* &c., of a different tincture.

It will be observed that the dove very frequently occurs in the arms granted to Bishops, and sometimes it is used evidently for the sake of the name.

Sable, three doves argent, beaked and membered gules, each holding an olive-branch proper—COLUMBALL [temp. RIC. II.]

Gules, on a fesse argent, between three doves proper, as many crosses formé of the field—Peter GUNNING, Bp. of Chichester, 1670; afterwards of Ely, 1675–84.

Argent, on a chevron between three crosses formy gules three doves of the field—SANCROFT, Abp. of Cant., 1678–91.

COLUMBALL.

Argent, on a pale azure between two crosslets gules, a dove displayed in a glory issuing from a chief of the first—Anthony KITCHIN, Bp. of Llandaff, 1545–65.

Azure, a cross patty between four doves argent—Thomas DOVE, Bp. of Peterborough, 1601–30.

Azure, on a chevron argent between three dove's heads erased of the second, each bearing in its beak a flower, two roses gules, stalked and leaved proper—HOLBECK, Bp. of Rochester, 1544 ; Bp. of Lincoln, 1547–57.

Argent, a cross gules between four doves, the dexter wings expanded and inverted azure—COLLEGE OF ARMS, or HERALDS' OFFICE.

Per fesse azure and argent, a pale counterchanged, three doves of the last, each holding in his beak an olive-branch or—TALLOW CHANDLERS' Company, Incorporated 1463.

Barry wavy of five argent and azure ; on a mount vert in the centre a dove rising nimbed gold, between three fishes naiant or—John HILSEY, Bp. of Rochester, 1535–38.

Argent, a cross azure between three ring-doves vert beaked and legged gules—DALTON.

Argent, a chevron between three turtle-doves azure—WINTOUN, Strathmartine, Scotland.

Gules, a cross engrailed between four stock-doves azure—ALBERY, Wickingham, co. Berks, 1590.

Argent, three pigeons azure—MOMPESSON.

Or, on a mullet sable a pigeon argent—DON, Ardonhall, Scotland.

Azure, on a chevron or three wood-pigeons proper, each charged on the breast with an ogress ; another chevron couped sable—PENFOLD, Cissbury, Sussex.

Argent, a chevron sable between three wood-doves proper—SCARELL, Thanks, Cornwall ; confirmed, June 16, 1602.

Dove-cot, or *Dove-house:* this is represented usually as in the margin, but other forms are found.

Dove-cot.

Vairy argent and sable, two bars or ; on a chief of the last three dove-cots gules—LYDCOTTE, Oxon.

Sable, a chevron or between three dove-cots argent—SHAPCOTT, Devon.

Sable, three dove-houses argent—SAPCOTTE, co. Huntingdon, Hertford, Cornwall, &c.

Doubling : the lining of a mantle : if *or,* or *argent,* supposed to be of cloth of gold, or white fur.

Downset : a corruption probably of *Dancetty,* q.v. See also *bend* and *chevron.*

Dovetailed: a line of partition of recent origin, derived from the form well known in carpentry. Edmondson says that it was first introduced into English heraldry in 1720. Some writers have used the term *lambeauxed*, *lambeau* being the old French for the *label*, q.v.

Quarterly per pale dovetailed, gules and or— BROMLEY, Horse-heath, Cambridgeshire.

Per bend sinister dovetailed or and azure, a lion rampant double queued ermine—STUCKEY.

Per chevron dovetailed or and vert; three lions rampant counterchanged—RIPLEY, Westminster, granted 1742.

Argent, a pelican in piety wings expanded proper ; a chief dovetailed gules — VOGUALL, London.

BROMLEY.

Ducks, (fr. *canard*): We find this very large family (*anatinæ*) represented in heraldry under several names. The *duck* proper, as also the *drake*. The shield-drake, or *sheldrake*, as it is written (*anas tadorna*). The *wild-duck* (*anas boschas*), with the *teal* (*anas crecea*) and the *mallard*. What is meant by the *sea-teal* is not certain. The sholarde, or *shoveller* (*anas clypeata*) may be distinguished by two small tufts of feathers, one on the back of the head, another on the breast.

Argent, a fesse gules between three ducks azure —CARTHEN.

Argent, a fesse gules fretty or between three ducks sable—HANKINSON, Middlesex.

Sable, a duck argent beaked or within a bordure engrailed of the last—MORE.

Gules, a fesse between three drakes argent—Philip ap RHYS.

Argent, a chevron sable between three drakes azure, beaked and membered or—YEO.

CARTHEN.

Argent, on a fesse gules, between three drakes proper, a rose or— DRAX Priory, Yorkshire.

Dragon. See *Griffin*.

Dragon's head. See *Tenné*.

Dragon's tail. See *Sanguine*.

Drake. See *Duck*.

Draught in : said of a bow and arrow. When *in full draught*, the bow is bent, just as if the arrow is about to fly.

Drawing-board. See *Grose*.

Drawing-iron. See *Wire-drawing* iron.

Drinking-pots. See *Cups*.

Argent, on a chevron gules three sheldrakes of the field ; on a canton of the second a rose or—SHELDON, Bp. of London, 1560; Abp. of Cant. 1663–77. [Founder of the Sheldonian Theatre; arms granted 1660.]

Azure, a fesse erminois between three sheldrakes proper—JACKSON.

Gules, a fesse between three sheldrakes argent—JACKSON (Bart. 1660).

Azure, a chevron between three wild ducks volant argent—WOLRYCH, Salop.

Quarterly per fesse indented sable and argent, in the first quarter a mallard of the last—BRESSY, Cheshire.

Argent, a chevron sable between three mallards proper—Joseph HEN-SHAW [Bp. of Peterborough, 1673].

Per chevron gules and sable, in chief two teals argent, in base a fish or—COBB, Norfolk.

Argent, a sea-teal gules winged or—ELCHAM.

Gules, a shoveller argent. Crest: a demi-shoveller argent—LANGFORD, London.

Sable, a shoveller argent—POPLER.

Gules, a fesse between three shovellers argent—William JACKSON, Bp. of Oxford, 1812–15.

Azure, three shoveller's heads erased or—Edmund LACY, Bp. of Hereford, 1417; afterwards Bp. of Exeter, 1420–55.

LANGFORD.

Quarterly, first and fourth; argent, a chevron sable between three mallards proper; second and third; argent, a cross between four fleurs-de-lys sable—HENSHARD, Bp. of Peterborough, 1663–79.

Gules, a bend nebuly between two shovellers argent—READE, Oxon.

The *Muscovy* duck (*cairina moschata*) and the *smew* (*mergellus albellus*) are found named. The *white nun* is another name for the smew, while the term *cannet* (fr. *canette*) seems to be an old heraldic name for a duck, which is to be represented drawn in profile, and is to be used when several appear in the shield.

Argent, a chevron azure between three muscovy ducks proper—STOCK.

Azure, a smew or white nun proper—ABNOTT.

Argent, a chevron gules between three cannets sable—DUBISSON.

Argent, in chief two cannets, and in base an annulet gules—KENNAWAY, Scotland.

Argent, seven cannets, 3, 3, and 1 sable—CANNETON.

Ducally gorged. See under *Collar* and *Crown*.

Ducipers See *Cap* of maintenance

Drops. See *Gouttes ;* but the term has been used erroneously for the *ermine* spots.

Dyke. See *Wall.*

Duke (from latin, *dux;* fr. *duc,*) is the highest title recognised in the British peerage. Whatever may have been the date of the introduction of the term in foreign countries, and however ancient the name, and whatever be its origin, the chief fact to be recorded is that the first dukedom created in England was that of Cornwall, which king Edward III. in the eleventh year of his reign, A.D. 1337, conferred upon the Black Prince his son, since which every eldest son of a sovereign has been duke of Cornwall from his birth. A special *Coronet* q.v. is assigned heraldically to the title.

Eagle, (fr. *Aigle*): the eagle being the recognized king of birds, it is natural that it should form a favourite device. With the Romans, it will be remembered, it was adopted as their ensign, no doubt as symbolical of the courage and power attributed to that bird. It is found very frequently in the earlier rolls of arms, and is very common throughout the Middle Ages. In the roll, for instance, of the time of Edward II., to which reference has already been made, over forty coats of arms bear eagles. In that, however, of Henry III. there are only two or three, and in that of Edward III. not so large a number in proportion. From the following selection it will be observed that amongst the earliest examples the *beak* and *claws* are blazoned of a different tincture from that of the body; and in Edward the Second's reign we find the *double-headed eagle*, and in Edward the Third's reign we get the term *espanie*, signifying *displayed*, or spread out; (conf. modern fr. *épandre*). The mention, too, of the eagles being tinctured *barry* implies rather that they were represented displayed, even where not so described.

John de BEAUCHAMP, noir ung egle d'argent, beke et les pees d'or—Roll, temp. HEN. III.

Dru de BARANTINE, noir a trois egles d'or—*Ibid.*

Sir Johan de CASTRE, de sable a un egle barre de argent e de goules—Roll, temp. ED. II.

Sire William de GRAUNSON, pale de argent e de azure a une bende de goules e iij egles de or—*Ibid.*

Sire Johan PLUET, de or et un egle de goules a iĵ testes—*Ibid.*

Monsire Edward de MONTHERMER, port d'or une egle espanie de vert beke et pedes gules—Roll, temp. ED. III.

Monsire de WANTY, port d'argenta une egle espanie d'asur beke et peds gules—Roll, temp. ED. III.

Monsire de SIGESTON, port d'argent a une egle espanie de sable a double teste beke et pedes de gules—*Ibid.*

Monsire John CHANSCYRE, port d'azur a un egle barre di sis peeces d'argent et gules—*Ibid.*

In later arms also, an eagle is more frequently rendered displayed (mod. fr. *eployé*), and it may be drawn in two different ways. The first figure shews an eagle with its *wings elevated*, which is what is generally intended by the phrase 'an eagle displayed,' and the second with its *wings inverted*. The difference appears,

Eagle Displayed.
Wings elevated.

Eagle Displayed.
Wings inverted.

however, to be an accidental one. The term *expanded* is also found sometimes used, which implies, perhaps, that the wings are displayed more than usual. Unless otherwise appointed, the eagle is to be drawn with the head looking towards the dexter.

Or, an eagle displayed vert, armed sable—MONTHERMER.

Or, an eagle displayed gules, armed azure—PEVENSEY.

Or, an eagle displayed wings downwards sable—FREDERICK II., Emperor of Germany, and EDMUND, E. of Cornwall, son of Richard, the King of the Romans.

Azure, an eagle displayed wings downwards argent, crowned or—(Part of the arms of) DIEPHOLZ.

Argent, an eagle displayed reguardant sable armed or—BOKELAND.

Argent, an eagle wings expanded sable, armed or—HILTOFTE.

Azure, an eagle reguardant, wings expanded or armed gules—CANVILL.

But there are various terms which, though not confined to the eagle, are more frequently applied to it than to other birds, namely, as regards its wings, and the several positions in which it is represented.

It may be with wings *close*, i.e. closed, or it may be with its wings *elevated*, or it may be with wings *disclosed*, i.e. somewhat open, but *inverted*, and pointing downwards (and this is practically the same as the expression *overt*, written sometimes *overture*).

Sable, an eagle close or—ROPER, Derby.

Sable, a chevron ermine between three eagles close argent—GAMES, Leicester, granted 1614,

Sable a chevron between three eagles close argent—JERVOISE.

Azure, an eagle with wings elevated argent—COTON, Ashill, Norfolk.

Argent, a bendlet (or baston) sable, between in chief an eagle rising overt vert, and in base a cross crosslet of the second—RICSWORTH.

If it is *recursant*, it means the head is turned back towards the sinister, the term *reguardant* being used for the same. If *in full aspect*, it is facing the spectator; if *in trian aspect*, something between that and facing towards the dexter.

Or, a bendlet (or baston) gules between three eagles close in trian aspect sable—Robert WILTRAM, co. York.

Azure, an eagle reguardant to the sinister, rising wings overt and inverted or, beaked gules—Richard CANVILL.

Again, an eagle may be *rising*, that is, about to fly; *volant*, that is, flying; or *eyrant*, that is, sitting, as it were, on its nest; or it may be *statant*, i.e. standing in an ordinary position; and if so, generally *perched* upon some branch or other object, or holding something in its mouth; or it may be represented as *preyant;* or, again, *pruning* its wings. These are a few for which examples are readily found; but to judge of the varieties which might be adopted, the reader is referred to those noted under *Bird*, and to the article *Wings*.

Argent, an eagle recursant wings overture sable—BACK.

Argent, an eagle rising, wings overt inverted gules, standing on a baston raguly in bend vert—William PORTER.

Sable, an eagle volant argent—STAYLTON or STALTON.

Gules, an eagle ayrant or—BARDOLPH, Norfolk.

Azure, an eagle eyrant or, armed gules—BYGBERY, Devon.

Per pale or and argent, an eagle displayed perched on a ragged staff sable—PYNELL.

Azure, an eagle with wings endorsed standing on a branch of laurel all or—Priory of Austin Canons at CAERMARTHEN.

Quarterly, gules and vert, an eagle displayed holding in the beak a slip of oak proper—GREAVES.

Argent, an eagle preyant sable, upon a child swaddled gules—CULCHETH.

Azure, an eagle pouncing on a hare courant or—DENSKINE, Scotland.

Or, an eagle displayed pruning its wings azure, armed gules—ROUS, co. Devon, and HALTON, co. Cornwall.

Again, *Eagles,* whether in any of the positions above named, or *displayed,* may have their beaks, talons, or legs of a different tincture from that of the body. Of the talons the term *armed* is most frequently used, though *unguled* (fr. *onglé*) is sometimes used; of the legs, *membered* (fr. *membré*); of the beak, *beaked* (fr. *becqué.*) It is not unusual, too, to find an eagle *crowned,* or having a *collar.*

Argent, an eagle displayed sable, armed purple—EAGLESTON.

Or, three bars azure, over all an eagle displayed gules, beaked and armed or—JERNEGAN, Fitz-Hugh.

Argent, an eagle displayed sable, armed and langued gules—BRUYNE, Harl. MS. 1603.

Argent, an eagle displayed sable crowned or—ESTE.

Azure, an eagle displayed argent armed or, collared with a ducal coronet gules—WILCOCKS.

Or, an eagle displayed azure, holding in the dexter talon a rose slipped in pale proper—CARNEGIE.

When three or more eagles occur in the same shield they are generally represented *displayed,* though occasionally they are found blazoned otherwise. If they are more than three they are generally blazoned as *eaglets.*

Argent, three eagles displayed gules, armed or—Robert de EGLESFIELD, [Founder of Queen's College, Oxford, and borne by the college].

Vert, three eagles displayed in fesse, within a bordure or—WILLIAMS, London.

Argent fretty and four eagles displayed gules—Priory of Austin Canons at MARTON, Yorkshire.

Sable, five eagles displayed in saltire argent—ROGER, Abp. of York, 1154–81. [Similar arms (excepting the tinctures) are also ascribed to Roger, Bp. of Salisbury, 1107–30, and to Alexander, Bp. of Lincoln, 1123–47.]

EGLESFIELD.

Azure, seme of eagles displayed or—FITZSYMON, Hertfordshire.

Vert, three eagles statant, wings displayed argent collared or—SMITH-ERMAN.

The *double-headed eagle* was borne by the German emperors (who claimed to be considered the successors of the Cæsars of Rome), and hence the term frequently applied to it is the *imperial eagle*. The wings of the imperial eagle are always drawn by German heralds with a small feather between each pair of large ones. An eagle is also borne by the emperor or czar (that is Cæsar) of Russia. In the Bulle d'or of Charles IV. (A.D. 1323) the eagle is there represented with but one head, and it is not until Sigismund his son began his reign that we find the eagle represented double headed.

German Empire.

The eagles in the arms of many English families can be traced to some former connection between those families and the German empire. The Eagle of France dates from Napoleon Bonaparte.

Or, an eagle with two heads displayed sable— GERMAN EMPIRE.

Argent, an eagle displayed double-headed sable —ATHESON, Scotland; BOWCEGAULT, Brin, co. Chester; BROWNE, Ireland, &c.

Or, an eagle displayed with two necks sable— MILLINGTON.

MILLINGTON.

One *monstrosity* may be mentioned, viz. *Eagles' heads* with hounds' ears.

Or, an eagle's head with hound's ears azure—AERBOROUGH.

Eagles occur sometimes as *supporters;* e.g. two Eagles are the supporters to the Arms of CLARKE of Courie Castle, co. Perth.

Eagles' wings are also borne by themselves; also the *legs,* which are frequently blazoned as erased *a-la-quise,* q.v.

Sire Wauter le BAUD, de goules a iij eles [i.e. ailes] de egles de or— Roll, temp. ED. II.

Azure, three eagle's legs couped argent—GAMBON.

Gules, three eagle's legs erased, talons in chief or—BAWDE, Essex.

Eaglets, (fr. *aiglettes* and *aiglons*): the diminutive of *Eagle*, and the term is more properly used when two or more appear upon the same coat of arms. They may have all the attributes of Eagles. [See also *Allerion.*]

Or, six eaglets displayed, three two and one proper—BAXTER.

Ear: the *ear* is seldom borne separately, but it is not uncommon in some animals, e.g. *dogs*, to find the ears blazoned of another tincture.

Argent, three hind's ears gules—AUDICE.

Earl: the third order in the British Peerage, corresponding with the French Comte, and the German Graf. The name is of Saxon origin, an eopl having been in the early history of this country the governor of a shire. The first hereditary earl in England is said to have been Hugh of Avranches, surnamed Lupus, to whom William the Conqueror gave the county palatine of Chester.

Eels. These are not very common on English Arms, and generally adopted, as will be observed by the examples, on account of the name. Neither the *anguille* or the *congre* have been observed on French arms. Eels may be represented *naiant* and *hauriant*, terms usually applied to fish; also *nowed*, a term which is applied to snakes, and *embowed*, which is applied to dolphins. The small eels are termed *grigs*.

Argent, three eels in pale, naiant barwise sable— Antony ELLIS, Bp. of S. David's, 1752–61.

Argent, three eels naiant in pale sable—ELLIS, Cornwall.

Argent, three eels embowed in pale sable— EALES.

Five arrows or entwined by an eel—Crest of family of ELWES, Suffolk.

A hand gauntletted grasping an eel—Crest of family of ELLEIS, Southside, Scotland, and of ELLIOT, Clothall, Hertfordshire.

ELLIS.

Ears of wheat, barley, rye, &c. See under *Wheat ;* (2.) Of beasts, the *ears* are sometimes of a different tincture.

Earn : a hawk (Nisbet).

Earth. See *Colour.*

Ebranché, (fr.): of a tree of which the branches have been lopped.

Argent, two eels hauriant confronty vert between two etoiles gules—ARNEEL, Scotland.

Azure, a saltier between four eels naiant or—FLEURY, Ireland.

Argent, three eels naiant in pale azure—DUCAT, Scotland.

Gules, a chevron between three grigs with tails in their mouths argent—GRIGG.

Gules, an eel nowed argent—MATHILLY.

The *Conger eel*, a large eel found upon the British coasts, is as frequently adopted as the eel of the rivers. The head is perhaps more frequently found in heraldry than the whole fish, and also *demi-congers*.

Argent upon a pale sable, a conger's head couped and erected or—GASCOIGNE, Bedford.

GASCOIGNE.

Azure, three congers hauriant [also blazoned erased] or—CONGHURST.

Ermine, on a bend engrailed sable three conger-eel's heads erased argent, collared with a bar gemel gules—CLARKE, Ipswich.

Sable, three conger's heads erased and erect argent—HOTOFF, Notts.

Argent, a chevron between three conger's heads erased—CANBROOK.

A tun floating on waves between two congers respecting each other, and upon the tun a lion statant—Town Seal of CONGLETON.

Gules, on a fesse argent between three congers [or sea-dragons' heads] erased or as many trefoils slipped sable—CONGLETON, Northamptonshire.

Azure, three conger-eel's heads erased and erect or ; in the mouth of each a cross crosslet fitchée of the last—Town of KING'S LYNN, Norfolk.

Argent, a chevron between three demi-congers naiant gules—SHAMBROKE.

KING'S LYNN.

At the same time, it should be noted that there seems to be often a confusion between *lucies*' heads and eels' heads, from the similarity of drawing.

Ecaillé, (fr.) : of fish having scales when of another tincture.

Ecartelé, (fr.) : *quarterly* and *ecartelé, en sautoir = per saltire*.

Echiqueté, (fr.) : *chequy*.

Ecimé, (fr.) : of a tree which has had its top cut off.

Eclaté, (fr.) : broken, applied by French heralds to a lance.

Echalas = *Vine-stick*.

Echelle, (fr.) : a *ladder*.

Eclipse. See *Sun*.

Ecorché, (fr.) : of animals flayed, either in part or wholly.

Eel-spear: a kind of fork (fig. 1) used in taking eels; is represented on one or two coats of arms, while a charge in the bearings of the company of SOAPMAKERS, called an eel-spear, is represented as in the second figure.

With the eel-spear may be associated the *Harpoon, Harping-iron,* or *Salmon-spear,* represented as in figs. 3 and 4. The ordinary position of the charge is with the points downwards.

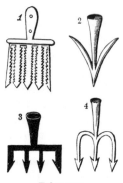

Sable, a chevron between three eel-spears, points downwards, argent—STRATELE, or STRATLEY.

Argent, three eelpicks sable—WORTHINGTON, Lancashire.

Azure, a dolphin naiant between three eel-spears or—Company of SOAPMAKERS (Inc. 1638.)

Argent, three harpoons sable [otherwise blazoned as Argent, three salmon-spears, point downwards, sable]—GLYNN, Cornwall.

Eel-spears.

Effets: these in heraldic drawing are perhaps hardly to be distinguished from *lizards,* and hence the same arms are sometimes variously blazoned. The *asker,* which is a water-lizard, and the *newt,* are also found.

Azure, three effets in pale proper—COTTER, Ireland.

Azure, three asker's heads couped or—ALSACHER, Chester.

Azure, an asker's head erased or—ALSARIN.

Or, a newt vert, in chief a lion rampant gules, all within a bordure of the last—SUTTON.

Eclopé: used by French heralds to describe a charge couped by a line of partition.

Ecoté, (fr.): of a trunk of a tree, of which the branches have been lopped.

Ecrevisse, (fr.): *Crab* (not crayfish). *Ecrevisse de gueules* is sometimes blazoned by French heralds, *écrevisse cuite.*

Ecureuil, (fr.): *Squirrel.*

Ecusson, (fr.): *Escutcheon.*

Ecuyer, (fr.): title of *Esquire.*

Edged: See under *Fimbriated.*

Edock leaf. See *Dock.*

Eel-pot. See *Weel,* or fish-basket.

Effaré, (fr.): same as *Effrayé.*

Effarouché, (fr.): of a *cat* when scared.

Effrayé, (fr.): applied to a *horse* when rearing.

Egret. See *Heron.*

Egyptian's head. See *Head.*

Eight-foil. See *Foil.*

Elder-leaves appear in one coat of arms on account of the name, but neither the elder-tree nor the elder-berry seem to occur unless the *alder berry*, q.v., is intended for the latter.

Argent, a fesse wreathed of five pieces gules and vert ; in chief two elder-leaves of the third, and a crescent in base azure—ELDERSHAW, Scotland.

Elephant, (fr. *éléphant*): occurs in a few insignia of cities, and in the arms of some families. The *trunks* or *probosces* (fr. *proboscides*) occur separate in some few cases. The *tusk* in French blazon is called the *defense,* and *tusked* is described as *defendu* of such a tincture. In one example the elephant is represented carrying a howdah, and in two examples a castle. Elephants sometimes appear as supporters, e.g. to the arms of OLIPHANT of Gask, co. Perth, and to the city of OXFORD, &c. They are not unfrequently used as crests.

Argent, an elephant statant, and carrying a howdah containing three persons with a driver proper ; a bordure or—The Rajah KALEE KRISHNA Bahadin, [granted in India, Ap. 3, 1833].

Per pale gules and vert, an elephant, on his back a tower triple towered all or—City of COVENTRY.

Or, an elephant azure, on his back a quadrangular castle argent, masoned proper ; on the sinister tower a flag-staff and banner gules, on the dexter corner of the banner a canton argent charged with a cross gules ; on the dexter corner of the escutcheon a canton quarterly of France and England—Royal AFRICAN Company, [Inc. 1662].

Gules, a chevron or between three elephant's heads erased proper —HUSKISSON, Sussex.

Argent, two elephant's trunks reflexed endorsed gobony or and gules, fixed upon a hairy scalp with two ears sable—BOSIN.

Ermine, on a pale vert between two daggers, points downwards, azure hilted or, three elephant's probosces of the last—HUTCHINS.

Also borne in the insignia of the Burgh of DUMBARTON, and by the families of SUTCLIFFE, BUTTON, and ELPHINSTONE ; and the *heads* of elephants by the families of JEWE, SANDERS, FOUNTAINE, PRATT, SUCKLING, BRODRICK, &c.

Elancé, (fr.): of a stag at full speed.

Elbows: sometimes mentioned in describing portions of the *arm.*

Elevated: when applied to *wings* signifies that the points are upward.

Email, (fr.): *tincture* (pl. *emaux*).

Elm-tree: this tree is found, and the leaves also, the latter rather frequently.

Per fesse azure and argent, a fesse counter embattled or; in chief a mullet of six points of the second; in base on a mount vert an elm tree proper—OLMIUS, London.

Ermine, on two bars sable six elm leaves or, three and three—ELMES, Lincolnshire.

Sable, three bars engrailed between ten elm leaves erect or—ELMSALL, Yorkshire.

The leaves are also borne by the families of WALLER, Devon ; FOLLI-FARD, Suffolk ; MURVESSE, Suffolk ; ELLAMES, and several branches of the family of ELMES.

Emanche, (fr.) : a term about which English heralds seem to differ. It is, however, confined to French and German heraldry, and appears to be a piece partitioned off from the shield by a dancetty line, but often so much exaggerated as to be like two or three piles; they may be upright or fesswise; the indentations appear not to be always drawn uniform.

The adjectival form *emanché* is perhaps more common than the substantive, an *emanche.* When there is only one projection the term *embrassé* seems to be employed by French heralds.

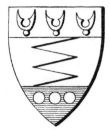

Emanché d'or et d'azure de trois pieces, à trois besants d'or en pointe ; au chef d'argent chargé de trois bouterolles de gueules—BRUYSEL DE SURE.

D'argent embrassé de gueules de sénestre a droite—DOMANTZ, Silesia.

BRUYSEL DE SURE.

Embattled, *battled, battelly, crenelled,* or *kernelied :* a line of partition resembling a row of battlements, (from which it derives its origin and its name) across the shield; the term may also be applied to the edge of an ordinary.

When a *fesse* or *bend* or *chevron* is said to be embattled, it implies that it is so upon the upper side only, though sometimes this is mentioned (fr. *crenellé*), and the term *super-embattled* is occasionally found. When a fess or a chief is embattled on the under side only, the French use the term *bastillé.*

The "crenelles" are properly speaking the embrasures or open spaces between the "merlons," which are the upright solid pieces.

If the ordinary is crenellated on both sides it may be said to be *embattled counter embattled*, and this is properly used only when the crenelles on one side are opposite to the merlons on the other, and *vice versâ*. It may also be said to be *bretessé*, and this is properly used with English heralds, to signify that the crenelles are opposite to each other. With French heralds, however, the word *bretessé* is frequently used for counter embattled, and these terms do not seem to be used with their respective meaning very strictly even by English heralds.

ABBERBURY.

Battled embattled, or *battled grady*, is a name given to a figure having, as it were, an extra battlement, but, as usual for these fanciful names, no examples are given. And the same may be said of *battled arrondi*, i.e. with the tops of the battlements rounded instead of straight. The term *double embattled*, however, does occur, and it is possibly the same as *grady*.

Battled grady.

Or, a fesse embattled [on the upper side only] sable—ABBERBURY, Oxon, and ADDERBURY, Sussex.

Sire Johan de PENZRET de goulys a une bende batille de argent—Roll, temp. ED. II.

Monsire Henry de SANTON d'argent a une bend bateley sable—Roll, temp. ED. III.

Or, a chevron embattled at the top gules — ASLYN, Harl. MS. 1386.

Argent, a bend embattled counter embattled azure —SANDILANDS, Scotland.

Azure, a bend bretessed or—BRESCETT.

Or, a fesse bretessed gules—CREBBOTT, Sussex.

Argent, masonny ; a chief embattled sable — REYNALL, Devon, 1716.

Argent, three bendlets embattled sable—Hadrian de CASTELLO, Bishop of Hereford, 1502; Bath and Wells, 1504-1b.

Per bend embattled argent and gules—BOYLE, Middlesex.

Argent, a saltire counter embattled sable—Richard KIDDER, Bp. of Bath and Wells, 1691—1703.

Sable, a fesse counter embattled between three Catherine wheels or—Thomas de BRENTINGHAM, Bp. of Exeter, 1370–94.

Or, a fesse double embattled at the top sable; a label of three points gules—M. Richard ABBERBURY, [Roll, A.D. 1392–97].

BOYLE.

Azure, three bendlets embattled counter embattled or—FREYNES.

Embelief, a word of doubtful origin, but of which *enhanced* is the probable signification, as will be seen by comparison of the two blazonings of the arms of GREILLI. Sir Harris Nicolas suggests that it is a misreading of *en le chief.* Confer with *derechief* in arms of S. AMANT, from Roll of Carlaverock, under *roundle.*

Thomas GREILEY, de goules a trois bendes d'or embelief—Roll, temp. HEN. III.

[Johan de GRELLI, gules, three bendlets enhanced or—Roll, temp. EDW. I.; Harl. MS. 6137.]

Robert de MERE, gules, a lion 'rampant sautant embelif' d'argent—Roll, temp. EDW. III.; [Harl. MS. 6589.]

Embowed, (fr. *courbé*): bent, or bowed; applied to the *arm* of a man, and still more frequently to *dolphins.* The term *flected* or *flexed* is also used of the arm of a man, to signify the same.

On a wreath or and sable, a dexter arm embowed vambraced proper, the gauntlet holding a sword below the hilt, in bend sinister, point downwards, argent, hilt and pomel gold—Crest of GWIN, Wales and Berks.

Crest of GWIN.

Sable, three dexter arms vambraced, couped at the shoulders, embowed to the sinister, two and one, the upper parts in pale, the lower fesswise, each holding in the gauntlet a sword erect, all proper garnished or—STRONGITHARM.

Sable, three dolphins embowed argent—KENDALL, Exeter.

Emblazon: to draw out in full and colour a coat of arms from a description. Reverse of to *blazon.*

With French heralds the word *courbé* is more frequently applied to the fesse, bend, &c., when either are slightly bent upwards. English heralds also speak of the bend, &c., as *arched, enarched,* or *embowed,* but such devices, though common in French arms, and more so still in German arms, are very seldom, if ever, found in true English heraldry. An example of a bend embowed is given under *Crown* of *Rue,* from the Dukedom of SAXONY.

Bend embowed.

Argent, three bars enarched in the middle gules—HENCKELL, London.

Bowed embowed, and *flexed reflexed,* are terms used to signify the form of the letter S : the terms also *annodated, torqued,* &c., are used irregularly for the same : and *bowed counter embowed* is said of two arms bowed in opposite directions.

Embroiderers' *Broaches, Trundles,* and *Quill.*

The *broach* is an instrument used by embroiderers, and borne by their several companies; it is represented as in the margin, but as a rule two are borne together in saltire.

Embroiderer's broach.

The *Trundle* represents a quill of gold thread, two of which are represented in the arms of the London company, as in fig. 1, though in the drawing there appears to be some confusion between the *trundles, fusils,* and *quills* when full.

Trundle.

Embouté, (fr.) : knobbed ; used when the end of a handle or staff is of a different tincture.

Embordured : a term given, but not used, in British heraldry, signifying that the bordure is of the same tincture as the field, and only distinguished from it by the shadow.

Embraced, (fr. *entrelacé*) ; e.g. of *Annulets.*

Embracing : hands are sometimes so described ; also improperly used of *annulets* when *braced.*

Embrassé. See *Emanche.*

Embrued : bloody, or rather, dropping with blood, and so different from *ensanglanté.* Weapons are thus blazoned (e.g. *spearheads, swords*), and also sometimes an animal, especially a *wolf.*

Quill (or *wheel quill*) *of yarn*, if full, would be represented as in fig. 2 ; an *empty quill* as in fig. 3 ; but there are many varieties of drawing of the same arms. See also *Fusil*.

Paly of six, argent and azure ; on a fesse gules between three lions passant guardant or, two broaches in saltire between two trundles (i.e. quills of gold thread) or—EMBROIDERERS' COMPANY of London [incorporated 1562].

Quills.

Gules, two broaches in saltire argent, between as many trundles or, on a chief of the second a lion passant gules—EMBROIDERERS' COMPANY at Bristol and Chester.

Argent, three weaver's shuttles sable, topped and furnished with quills of yarn, the threads pendent or—SHUTTLEWORTH.

Emerasses, or *ailettes ;* also written *alettes* and *alerons* (all fr.) : small escutcheons affixed to the shoulders of an armed knight. They are named in the inventory of Humphrey de Bohun, taken 1322.

iiij peire de alettes des armes le Counte de Hereford.

They are sometimes shield-shaped, as those of Sir Simon de FELBRIGGE, K.G., on his sepulchral brass at Felbrigge, Norfolk, which are charged with the cross of S. George, and sometimes circular, as those of the TUR-VILE family at Wolston, Warwickshire, which are charged with the arms of the knight himself.

Square emerasses with the arms of the bearer generally denote that he was a *knight banneret,* as in the figure of one of the HOWARD family at East Winch church, Norfolk, and in that of Sir Roger de TRUMP-INGTON, which is shewn in the margin.

Ailettes shewn in the brass of Sir Roger de TRUMPINGTON.

Emerald. See *Vert.*

Emmanché, (fr.) : of hatchets, or hammers, and the like, having handles of a different tincture.

Emmet. See *Ant.*

Emmuselé, (fr.) : muzzled, e.g. of a *bear.*

Emoussée, (fr.) : of an arrow, if the point is couped or blunted.

Endorse, *endorce,* or *indorse :* a diminutive of the *pale,* of which it is one-fourth, or according to some authorities, one-eighth. It bears exactly the same relation to that ordinary as the cottice does to the bend. See *Cross,* § 8.

Argent, a pale engrailed between two indorses sable—BELLASIS, Scotland.

Enfiled, (fr. *enfilé*). When a sword is drawn with the head of a beast, a coronet, or any other object so placed that the blade pierces it through, the sword is said to be *enfiled* with such an object; or in the case of rings, crowns, or fillets, through which a sword or crosier is passed, the term may also be used.

Gules, three keys enfiled with as many crowns or—Robert ORFORD, Bp. of Ely, 1303–10.

Azure, a sword palewise argent, enfiled in chief by a dexter hand couped fessways gules, all between two mullets pierced or—MAC MORUN.

Per pale azure and gules, over all a lion passant guardant holding a crosier enfiled with a mitre or; all within a bordure argent charged with eight text B's sable—BERMONDSEY, Cluniac Priory, Surrey.

Argent, on a cross patty gules a crosier enfiling a mitre or—Bishopric of CORK and Ross.

ORFORD.

Empenné, (fr.) : *feathered;* of arrows.

Empiétant, (fr.) : of birds, *preying.*

Empoigné, (fr.): = *banded;* used e.g. of arrows when three or more are tied together.

Enarched. See *Embowed.*

Enaluron. See *Bordure.*

Encensoir, (fr.). See *Censer.*

Enceppé : girt or collared about the middle, as of apes or monkeys, e.g. the supporters of the arms of the Duke of LEINSTER, which are said to have reference to a family legend.

Enchaussé, (fr.): only occurs in French arms, and that rarely ; it refers to a portion of the shield obscured, and seems to be the reverse of *chapé.*

Enclavé, (fr.) : a rarely-used term of French heralds, describing a peculiar partition of the shield, when one portion enters another like a mortise.

Encoché, (fr.) : of an *arrow* notched or *nooked.*

Endented, (fr. *endenté*). See *Indented.*

Endentures, (old fr.): indentations.

Endorsed : often used in the sense of *addorsed,* q.v.

England, *Armorial insignia of.* The Insignia of England are said to have had originally only two lions, but that on the marriage of Henry II. with Eleanor of Aquitaine, another lion for that duchy was then added. They thus appear for the first time on the Great Seal of RICHARD I.; the Seals of the two Williams, as well as of the two preceding Henries, shewing only the reverse side of the shield, and that of Stephen being to all appearance plain. From this time

Royal Arms of ENGLAND.

forward they have been recognized as the Arms of England.

Le roy DENGLETER, de goules a treys lepardes de or—[Harl. MS. 6589, temp. HEN. III.]

Le Roy d'ANGLETERRE, porte goules trois leopards d'or—[MS. L. 14, College of Arms, temp. HEN. III.]

Gules, three lions [properly leopards] passant guardant in pale or— Royal Arms of ENGLAND.

Engrailed, or *Ingrailed,* (fr. *engrélé*): a term applied to the cutting of the edge of a border, bend, or fesse, &c., into small semicircular indents, the teeth or points of which being outward enter the field: it is the contrary of *invected,* in which case the points are inwards. The term, as will be seen from the examples, is an old one, and is very frequently applied to the bordure; when applied to crosses and saltires heralds contend that they ought not to be engrailed at their ends. The term *counter engrailed* is found, but it is seldom employed; as when a fesse chevron or bend is blazoned *engrailed,* it implies that the ordinary is to be so on both sides. With French heralds the term *engrelure* signifies a narrow *chief,* so to speak, engrailed on the lower side.

Englanté, (fr.): of an oak-tree with the acorns on it.

Engoulant, or *Ingullant:* swallowing or devouring. See *Vorant.*

Engrélé, (fr): engrailed.

Engrossing block. See Crest of *Wire-drawers.*

Engoulé, (fr.): in French arms ordinaries are found terminated with heads of animals, in the act of swallowing them, e.g. *sauton engoulé de quatre têtes de* leopards.

Enguiché, (fr.): of ends of horns, when of different tincture.

Adam de NEWMARCHE de goules ung fece engrele or—Roll, temp. HEN. III.

Sire Johan de PENBRUGE de argent, od le chef de azure e une bende engrele de goules—Roll, temp. ED. II.

Monsiere Philip do DABENNHY, port gules une fesse engrele d'argent de quatre peces—Roll, temp. ED. III.

Monsire BOTEVILL, port d'argent une fesse engrele gules de iiij points, trois feuilles de sable en le cheif—*Ibid.*

Argent, a bend engrailed sable—RADCLIFFE.

RADCLIFFE.

Gules, six annulets or, three, two, and one, within a bordure engrailed compony argent and azure—CROUMWELL.

Argent, on a pale voided engrailed counter engrailed three crosses patty, all within a bordure sable—CROWCHE.

De sinople, à trois fasces d'argent à l'engrelure du même—SAINT CHAMANS DU PECHER, Limosin.

Ensign, or *Insignia,* (fr. *enseigne*): the more correct term for the armorial bearings of a Kingdom, of an Office, or of a Community. In common parlance, however, the Arms of England, or the arms of this or that town, are spoken of.

The term *ensigned* has a different signification, and is used of a charge having a cross, or mitre, or crown, placed above it, and the term *supporting* such a charge is sometimes used also with the same signification. It is to be distinguished from *enfiled.* A staff also may be ensigned with a flag.

Sable, a chevron ensigned with a cross patty argent—FAIRFIELD.

Azure, an annulet ensigned with a cross patty, and interlaced with a saltire, couped and conjoined at base or—Borough of Southwark.

Argent, an oak tree eradicated in bend sinister vert, surmounted by a sword in bend dexter azure, hilted or, ensigned on the front with a royal crown of the last—M'GREGOR.

Enhanced, (fr. *enhaussé*): applied to an ordinary borne higher than its usual position.

Enlevé, (fr.): raised or elevated; synonymous with *enhanced.*

Enquerre, (fr.), *Armes à,* q.v.

Enraged, (fr. *fier*): applied to the *horse* when *saliant;* also to a *boar,* and rarely to a *lion.*

Ensanglanté, (fr.): of the pelican and other animals represented bleeding, i.q. *vulned.*

Enty: a word adopted but by few writers from the French *enté*, a graft, and applied to the base of the shield when parted off by a line chevronwise: written by some heralds *ampty*. See *Point*: also *Gusset*.

Argent, on a chief enty [in more recent blazon 'indented'] azure five crosses croslet or—Raphe de WILSHERE.

Enveloped, *enwrapped, entwisted, entwined, environed* (fr. *environné*), *entoured* (fr. *entouré*), are all terms used in blazoning with much the same signification. *Enveloped* and *enwrapped* are used when any charge is entwisted or entwined about something else, e.g. of boys' *heads*, (q.v.) when enveloped about the neck by a snake.

Or, a pillar sable enwrapped with an adder argent —MYNTER.

Sable, a crosier in pale entwined with a ribbon between two coronets ... S. Benet's Abbey, HULME.

Azure, three boy's heads affronty couped at the shoulders proper, armed or, each enveloped (or enwrapped) about the neck with a snake vert—VAUGHAN, Wales.

Enveloped.

Environed is more frequently applied when the charge is surrounded by wreaths, and *entoured*, perhaps, when other charges are placed around *in orle*: also used of a shield which is decorated with branches.

Entire, *throughout, fixed,* or *firm*: used of *Crosses* (see Cr., § 7), or other charges, to signify that they are extended to the sides of the escutcheon.

Entoured. See *Enveloped*.

Entoyer, *Entoire,* and *Entier.* See under *Bordure*.

Entrailed: outlined, with black lines. See *Cross*, § 18, and *Adumbration*.

Entrelacé, (fr.): *interlaced*.

Entrevaillé: a French term applied to fish when interlaced in bars or bendlets.

Entwined. See *Enveloped*.

Enurney. See *Bordure*.

Enwrapped. See *Enveloped*.

Envecked. See *Invected*.

Environed. See *Enveloped*.

Epanoui, (fr.): of fleur-de-lis, &c., the top flower being open with buds between.

Eperon, (fr.): *Spur*.

Epervier, (fr.): sparrow - hawk, under *Falcon*.

Epieu, (fr.): a kind of halbert used in the chase.

Epis, (fr.): used for ears of corn, &c., with stalks erect.

Azure, an annulet environing a barrulet, between two bars, and in chief a cross patty fitchy or—HOLTE.

Sable, an annulet environing a crosier, the foot enwrapped by a snake; in chief two coronets argent—Benedictine Abbey, BARDNEY, co. Lincoln.

Erased, *eraced,* or *erazed* (fr. *arraché*); violently torn off, leaving a jagged edge. The term is chiefly applied to the *heads* and limbs of animals. When applied to birds' legs the expression *à-la-quise,* i.e. *à la cuisse,* is often added to signify that the upper part of the leg is shewn. A head *erased close* signifies that it is torn off without any part of the neck remaining attached to it.

HUGH DE ABRINCIS.

Azure, a wolf's head erased argent—HUGH DE ABRINCIS (or LUPUS), Earl of Chester.

Argent, an elephant's head erased gules—BRODRICK.

Ermine, a goat's head erased gules—GOTLEY.

Azure, three eagle's legs erased a la quise or—GAMBON.

Gules, a lion rampant, the head argent, divided by a line of erasure from the body within an orle of seven 5-foils or—GRACE.

Erect: the term used by heralds for upright, as of *heads* of animals, fishes, &c.; also of lions' *tails,* placed perpendicularly; and of the *hand* in the baronet's badge. The word should not be used with relation to any charge, the natural position of which is upright, as a flower or a tree; it is very properly used for leaves and fruit, of which the natural position is pendent. The word is also supposed to be more properly used of certain animals and reptiles instead of *rampant,* and of *crabs* and *lobsters* instead of *haurient;* it is sometimes applied even to *fish,* though perhaps improperly. Insects also are found blazoned as erect, e.g. *bees,* q.v.

Episcopal staff. See *Crosier.*

Equartilé: i.q. *quarterly.*

Eployé: the French term for *displayed,* applied to wings of birds. It seems in some cases to imply the double-headed *Eagle,* q.v.

Equipped, (fr. *equipé*): of a vessel, with all its sails, ropes, anchor, &c., complete.

Equipollé, (fr.): *chequy* of nine squares, five of one tincture, four of another. See *Cross,* § 5.

Argent, three boar's heads erased erected sable—John BOOTHE, Bp. of Exeter, 1465–78.

Gules on a sinister hand couped and erect proper, a human heart of the field charged with a cross argent—MULENCAR, Amsterdam.

Argent, three crabs erect sable — ALLYM or AUDLYM.

Sable, three salmons erect argent, two and one; a chief or—KIDSON, Bishopwearmouth, Durham.

Gules, three fishes erect or, two and one— O'CAHANE, Ireland.

BOOTHE

Ermine, or *Ermin,* (old fr. *armine,* fr. *hermine*): the fur most frequently used in heraldry. It derives its name from the Ermine or *mus Armenicus* (so called from being found in the woods of Armenia), a small white animal whose fur it is. The

black spots are supposed to represent the tails of ermines, sewed to the white fur for its enrichment. When a bend is ermine, the spots (like all other charges placed upon a bend) must be bendwise, but on a chevron, saltire, &c., they are drawn upright.

The term *ermyn* is frequently found in the ancient rolls of arms, and is very often applied to a *quarter* or *canton.*

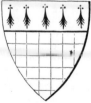

BRITTANY.

Ermine is practically used like any other tincture, and so any animals, e.g. *lions,* may be blazoned ermine. Also a *crescent,* q.v., and even *martlets* may be blazoned *ermine,* both occurring in the arms of Frank DE BOUN.

A coat of arms of *ermine* only has been ascribed to the dukes of BRITTANY, but more frequently to the province.

Robert de TATESHALE, escheque d'or et de goules, ung chief d'ermyne—Roll, temp. HEN. III.

Robert de TATISHALE eschequere d'or e de goules al chef armine— Roll, temp. HEN. III. Harl. MS. 6589.

John de NEVILLE, COWERDE, mascule d'or et de goules ung quartier de hermyne—Roll, temp. HEN. III.

Hugh BOLEBEK, vert ung lion d'ermyn rampand—*Ibid.*

TATESHALE.

Le Counte de Bretaine eschekere d'or e dazur a une kantelle dermine
a un bordure de goules—Harl. MS. 6589, temp. HEN. III.

Cele de TATESHALE a oun   De or e de rouge eschequeré
Por sa valour o eus tirée   Au chef de ermine outréement.

Roll of Carlaverock, A.D. 1300.

The arms, too, which in some rolls are tinctured *blanc* are
supposed to represent this fur, as they are in others tinctured
ermine, the tincture representing rather the white skin of the
animal than the metal. For instance, at the siege of Carlaverock the arms of Morice de BERKELE are described as—

Vermeil . . . croissilie o un chevron blanc,

though the arms of the Berkley family are elsewhere blazoned—

Gules, crusilly argent, a chevron ermine.

Again, while numerous instances occur of "gules with a fesse
ermine," it is doubtful if an example is to be found of "gules
with a fesse argent." And the Carlaverock poet possibly in-
tends ermine when he writes :—

Bien doi mettre en mon serventois   Baniere ot rouge ou entaillie
Ke Elys de AUBIGNI li courtois   Ot fesse blanche engreelie.

The same poem also gives

BADELSMERE, Ki tout le jour   Portoit en blanc au bleu label
Iluec se contint bien e bel   Fesse rouge entre deux jumeaux.

Again, the waterbougets in the arms described there as

Guillemes de Ros assemblans   I fu rouge o trois bouz blans

appear afterwards, blazoned of different tinctures, sometimes
as *argent*, sometimes as *ermine*.

Although the form shewn in the illustrations is used in all modern emblazoning, there were ancient forms of the ermine spot,
as shewn in the margin. No. 1 is from
the surcoat of Sir Robert du BOIS,
upon his tomb in Fersfield Church,
Norfolk, — he died 1311 ; No. 2,
from the stall-plates of Sir Walter
PAVELEY, one of the first knights of
the Garter, and Sir Thomas BANASTER,
his successor in the stall,—the first

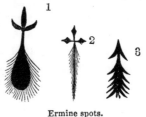

Ermine spots.

died 1376, the other, 1379 ; and No. 3, from the stall-plate of
Sir Simon DE FELBRYGG, K.G., who died A.D. 1422.

An *ermine spot*, (fr. *hermine*, or *moucheture*, whence the word *mouchetor* in some heraldic works) is occasionally found to occur by itself; sometimes more than one are named, and sometimes, when there is only space for a few spots, the term *spotted* is used.

Azure, three plates, on each an ermine spot sable—NEWALL.

Or, on two bars azure as many barrulets dancetty argent; a chief indented of the second charged with an ermine spot or—SAWBRIDGE.

Argent, a chevron between three crows sable, in each beak an ermine spot—LLOYD, Bp. of S. Asaph, 1680, Lichfield, 1692, and Worcester, 1700-17.

Argent, a fesse gules between three ermine spots sable—KILVINGTON.

Argent, two bars sable, spotted ermine, in chief a lion passant gules—HILL, co. Wexford.

D'argent, à cinq hermines de sable posées 2, 1 et 2—BROUILHAC DE LA MOTHE COMTAIS, Poitou.

D'azure, à trois besants d'argent chargés chacun d'une moucheture d'hermines—VENCE, Orleanais.

A *cross erminée* or of four ermine spots.—See Cross, § 8.

Ermines (fr. *contre hermine*), and *counter ermine*, as given by Nisbet: a fur resembling ermine in pattern, but having the tinctures reversed, the field being sable, and the spots argent.

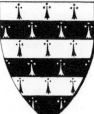

Barry of six ermine and ermines—BRADWARDINE, Archbishop of Canterbury, 1349.

Argent, a chevron engrailed ermines; on a chief sable three martlets of the first—WILDE, co. Leicester.

Ermines, simply—MIGNON.

ABP. BRADWARDINE.

Per chevron ermine and ermines, a chevron per chevron sable and argent; on the first three estoiles or—WIGSTON.

Erminites, or *erminetes* and *erminois*. These are varieties of ermine, i.e. of the fur of the same form but of different colours. The first is supposed to be distinguished by having a red hair on the side of each spot, and it is doubtful if a case occurs in true English heraldry; *erminois* is used when the field is or,

---

Er: contraction of the word *ermine*, often used in *tricking*.	**Eradicated,** (fr. *arraché*): used of a *tree* (q.v.) which has been torn
Ermine, (the animal). See *Weasel*.	up by the roots.

and spots *sable*. The *pean* is said to be *sable* with spots *or*. This name was derived from the old fr. *pannes*, or square pieces of fur of different tincture sewn together. The French call all the above furs *hermines*, adding the names of the tinctures.

Quarterly indented erminois and gules, in the first quarter a lion passant guardant gules—Croft, co. York.

Sable, a chevron erminois; on a chief indented argent an estoile between two mullets gules—Keirll, co. Hereford.

Per bend sinister ermine and erminois, a lion rampant or—Eddowes.

Pean, a cross quarter pierced erminois—Groin, Watlington, Norfolk, Harl. MS., 1177.

Per bend sinister ermine and pean, a lion rampant or gorged with a wreath of oak vert, and supporting in the dexter forepaw a sword erect proper pomel and hilt gold—Lloyd, Lancing, Sussex.

Per bend sinister ermine and ermines, a lion rampant reguardant erminois; on a chief azure three mullets of six points argent—Davis.

Or, a cross gules, semée of ermine spots argent—Deobody, Ireland.

De gueules, a six hermines d'argent 3, 2, et 1—Roux.

D'argent, semé d' hermines de sable—Berry, Poitou, Languedoc.

Escallop, or *escallop shell*, (fr. *coquille*). This is the badge of a *pilgrim*, also a symbol of the Apostle S. James the Great, who is generally drawn in the garb of a pilgrim. As it is found in ancient heraldry as early as Henry III.'s time, it was probably suggested by the eastern pilgrimages. It is borne in various ways, often surmounting an ordinary or other charge, especially a *cross*, *chief*, or *bordure*, &c. It is clear that the old French term *coquille* (from which we derive our modern *cockle shell*), is the same, though heralds pretend that when this is used the shell should have the edge upwards.

The shell is always represented with the outside of the valve towards the spectator; but in French arms the interior is sometimes shewn, and then the term *vannet* is used. See *fan* under *basket*.

PRELATE.

Argent, an escallop gules—Prelate, Glouc.

Azure, three escallops or—Abbey of Reading, Berks. [Under the patronage of S. James Abbey.]

Per pale argent and gules, an escallop or—Augustinian Abbey of S. James, Northampton.

Gules, two lions passant guardant or, oppressed by a bend azure, within a bordure of the third semé of escallops argent—HOLLAND.

Quarterly argent and gules, in the second and third a fret or, over all a bendlet sable, charged with three escallops of the first—SPENCER, of Althorpe, Northamp. [The mullet or is a mark of cadency.]

SPENCER.

Argent, a lion rampant gules; on a chief sable three escallops of the first—RUSSELL, Duke of Bedford.

Herbert de CHAMBERLEYNE, de goules a trois escallops d'or—Roll, temp. HEN. III.

Rafe BIGOT, d'or ung crois de goules a les escalops d'argent en le croix—*Ibid.*

Warin de MONCHENSY, d'or ove trois escocheons barres de verre et de goules—*Ibid.*

Sire Thomas de SEIN LOY, de goules a une fesse e iij escalops de argent—Roll, temp. ED. II.

Duke of BEDFORD.

Monsire de ST. LOE, port de gules a une fes d'argent entre trois cokils d'argent—Roll, temp. ED. III.

Le Sire de HALTON, port d'argent deux barres d'asur a trois escalops gules en la chief—*Ibid.*

Monsire Richard de HOWLAND, port de sable a une lyon rampant d'argent a une urle des cokelles d'argent—*Ibid.*

Monsire Robert INGHAM, port d'ermin a une fes de gules trois cokils d'or en le fes—*Ibid.*

Barry of four argent and azure semé of cockleshells—Silesian family of VON STRACHWITZ.

D'azur, a trois vannets d'or—BEAUSSIER DE LA CHAULANE, Provence.

The escallop, it will be noted, is sometimes used to denote a *difference,* but it does not occur amongst the recognised charges for this purpose. See *Cadency.*

Pale of six argent and vert an escallop for "difference," as the first —HOPWOOD, Lancaster.

Or, an escallop for "difference" between three crescents within a double tressure flory counter flory gules—SEATON, Pethoder, Scotland.

Escallopped is used in a remarkable case, forming a kind of vair, in which the scallops represent scales.

Barry of four, counter escallopped argent and gules, each scale nailed sable—ARMOURER.

Escarboucle: since the earliest form which we find of this word is *charboucle*, which only in very much later times was corrupted into *carbuncle*, we must look for its origin in a buckle of some kind. The present form seems to owe its origin to the metal-work on the shield, such as is exhibited on the monumental effigy (commonly ascribed to Geoffrey of Mandeville, Earl of Essex, who died in 1144,) now existing in the Temple church. The effigy, however, can scarcely be earlier than 1185, the date of the consecration of the church. The device being so exactly of the character of the metal-work of the thirteenth century it was no doubt intended by the sculptor to pourtray the ornamental iron-work, which was added to strengthen the shield, the protuberances representing bosses or rivets. That they were not intended for the arms of DE MANDEVILLE is clear, as in the contemporary Rolls of Arms we have his shield blazoned thus

Ascribed to MANDEVILLE.

Le Comte de MANDEVILE, quartele d'or et de goulez—Roll, temp. HEN. III.

Nor is there any reason to attribute them especially to any knight who is likely to have been buried there. The special figure appears afterwards to have been assumed as a regular device, and it is found amongst the historical arms painted on Queen Elizabeth's tomb in Westminster Abbey, but it is of more ornamental a character than the one on the supposed tomb of Geoffrey Mandeville.

Having become a regular device, and borne by several families, it came to have varied nomenclature, and the number of rays was reduced to six and extended to twelve, so that the number came to be mentioned. Some authors have called the rays *staves*, nor is this altogether needless, as examples are to be found with the *staves* blazoned *nowyed*, or *pometty*, and others *floretty*. In some of the cases, however, the device thus blazoned may be intended for a wheel, but badly drawn.

The name *charboucle* is the old form, as will be seen, since it is used in the earliest rolls as well as by Chaucer.

"His shield was all of gold so red,   A charboucle beside."
And therin was a bores hed,   *Chaucer, Rime of Sire Thopas, 13798.*

Le Counte de CLEVE, de goules a un eschochon d'argent a un charbocle d'or flurte—Roll, temp. HEN. III.; Harl. MS. 6589.

Gules, a chief argent over all an Escarbuncle or—Arms ascribed to the Counts of Anjou. [Painted on Queen's Elizabeth's tomb.]

Argent, an escarbuncle or, over all an escucheon sable—CLEVE.

Argent, an escarbuncle sable—BOTHOR.

Gules, an escarbuncle of six points or—NAVERNE.

Argent, two bars azure, over all an escarbuncle of eight points gules, pometty and floretty or—BLOUNT. [In another family an escarbuncle gules nowed or, and in another of eight rays or.]

Arms on ELIZABETH's tomb, Westminster.

Argent, on a bend gules three escarbuncles or—THORNETON.

Gules, a cross within a bordure or, over all an escarbuncle of eight staves sable—Benedictine Abbey of S. JOHN, COLCHESTER.

Sable, an escarbuncle or, but with twelve rays—RUTHFIO, Cornwall.

Argent, an escarbuncle of eight rays argent, over all a fesse as the second—PHEIPOWE, Ireland.

Quarterly gules and argent, over all an escarbuncle sable oppressed by a quatrefoil quarterly argent and gules—Sir Geoffrey MANDEVILLE, Earl of Essex. [Only in a very late MS.]

Escroll, or *Scroll:* a long strip of parchment bearing the motto. It is for the most part placed below the arms, but sometimes, especially in Scotland, above the crest. Scrolls are occasionally found in both these positions.

Escrolls occur rarely as charges.

Or, on a bend sable, three ostrich feathers argent, the quills transfixed through as many escrolls gold—Sir Roger de CLARENDON, [natural son of Edward the Black Prince].

Azure, a lion rampant or between three escrolls argent—GOULD.

Escroll.

Gules, a coronet or, ensigned by a demi swan without wings argent; from the mouth a scroll compassing the neck in form of a rein sable—BUCKHILL.

Argent, a lion rampant azure, holding in his dexter paw a chaplet of laurel vert in chief a scroll sable, thereon the word Emmanuel or—EMMANUEL COLLEGE, Cambridge.

Esculapius' Rod is borne in coats of arms.

Per fesse or and sable, a lion rampant counterchanged, armed and langued gules, on a canton of the last an Esculapius' rod palewise entwined with serpents argent—M'WHIRTER.

Sable, on a chevron between three spear heads argent, two staves of Esculapius, chevron wise, each ontwined by a serpent proper—JONES, co. Carnarvon.

Escutcheon, (fr. *écusson*): (1) The *shield* itself whereon arms are emblazoned, (2) more especially of a small shield of which more than one (generally three) are borne on the shield. A single one so borne is called an *inescutcheon.* The term is found in early rolls spelt in various ways. Where there is a single inescutcheon the arms might be blazoned as with a *bordure* of such a tincture as the arms of DARCY shew. While the *pierced* or *false escutcheons* of the old rolls would be now blazoned as *orles.* As a rule the escutcheon is drawn much smaller than the space enclosed by a bordure.

Argent, three escutcheons gules—HAY.

Warin de MONCHENSY, d'or ove trois escocheons barres de verre et de goules—Roll, temp. HENRY III.

Le Counte de WHITINGWEN veire dor e de goules a une escuchon dazur a un sautour dargent—*Ibid.*

Sire William de VAUS, de argent, a un escuchoun de goules, od la bordure de merelos de goules—Roll, temp. ED. II.

Sire Johan DARCY, de argent, a un escuchon de

HAY.

sable, od les rosettes de goules assis en la manere de bordure—*Ibid.*

Sire Robert DARCY, de argent a iij roses de goules, od la bordure en-lente de sable—*Ibid.*

Sire Thomas de BAYLOLF, de argent a une es-cuchoun de goules percee e un label de azure—*Ibid.*

Sire Bertelmehn de A WYLLERS, de argent a iij escoucheons de goulys—*Ibid.*

Or, an inescutcheon gules—CONSTABLE.

Eustace de BALIOLL, d'azur au faus escocheon d'or crusule d'or—Roll, temp. HEN. III.

Sr Alexandre de BAYLOLFZ, porte d'argent ou ung faux eschue de gulez—Roll, temp. ED. I. [Harl. MS. 6589.]

CONSTABLE.

Or, two bars gules; on a chief azure an inescutcheon ermine—NORTON, London, 1611, and STRELTON, co. Salop.

Or, three bends wavy azure; on an inescutcheon three fusils—Simon MONTACUTE, Bp. of Worcester, 1337–45.

Gules, crusily and a lion passant gardant or, a canton argent, charged with an eagle displayed sable, on the breast an escucheon gold charged with three bars azure—ASTELL, Leicester.

. . . . a castle with five towers, over the port, an escucheon argent on a cross gules a fleur-de-lis or—Seal of City of LINCOLN.

Or, on a lion rampant sable an antique escutcheon or, charged with a cross patty gules—POWNALL.

MONTACUTE.

Gules, on a rock proper a castle triple-towered argent masoned sable, surmounted by an escucheon gules, three lions passant guardant in pale or—Town of DORCHESTER, Dorset.

Escutcheon of Pretence: a shield containing the arms of an heiress, placed in the centre of her husband's arms instead of being impaled with them, is so called.

Argent, on a fesse dancetty azure, between three mullets sable as many bezants, over all an inescutcheon of pretence or, a sinister wing erect sable—DIMSDALE, Herts.

Esquire, *equire, esquierre,* or *squire* (fr. *esquerre,* or *équerre*): a figure similar in form to a gyron. The chief examples are those in the arms of MORTIMER (earls of March), which are variously blazoned, each successive heraldic writer attempting to improve upon his predecessor. The following is the description in the Siege of Carlaverock, and it has been thought well to give the English in a parallel column.

Epuis Rogiers de Mortemer,	And next Roger de Mortimer,
Ki, deca mer e dela mer,	Who, on both sides the sea,
A porté quel part ke ait alé	Has borne wherever he went
L'escu barré au chief palé	A shield barry with a chief paly
E les cornieres gyronnées,	And the corners gyronny,
De or e de asur enluminées,	Emblazoned with gold and blue,
O le escuchon vuidie de ermine.	With the escutcheon voided of
Roll of Carlaverock.	ermine.

Next are given the varieties of blazoning, the same, or nearly the same, arms in different rolls of arms, as well as one or two more recent examples.

Roger de MORTIMER, barre, a cheif palee a corners gerone, d'or et d'azur, a ung escuchon d'argent—Roll, temp. HEN. III.

Sire Rog. de MORTIMER, barre de or e de azure od le chef palee les corners geroune, a un escuchon de argent—Roll, temp. EDW. II.

Sire Rog. de MORTIMER, lo oncle, meyme lou armes, od le escuchon de ermyne—*Ibid.*

Roger de MORTYMER, barre dor et dazur al chef pale al chantel gerone a un escochon dargent—Roll, temp. HEN. III., Harl. MS. 6589.

Per pale azure and argent, two bars, and in chief a pale between as many esquires based dexter and sinister all counterchanged; an escutcheon of the second—MORTYMER [as bla-

MORTIMER.

zoned by York Herald, Harl. MS. 807, from Hagley Ch., Worcester].

Barry of six or and azure, on a chief of the first, three palets, between two based esquires [some say *gyrons* or *gyronnies*] of the second; over all an inescutcheon argent—MORTIMER.

On a chief azure between two cantons per bend or and the last, dexter and sinister, as many palets gold—MORTIMER.

Barry of five azure and or, on a chief as the first two palets between so many based esquires like the second, over all an escucheon argent—BLANCFRONT.

Barry of five gules and or, on a chief as the first two palets between so many based esquires like the second, over all an escucheon or—HOGELEY.

Barry of five sable and or, on a chief as the first two palets between so many based esquires like the second, over all an escucheon barry of six gules and ermine—BUTTELER.

HOGELEY.

Barry of seven azure and argent on a chief as the first two palets between so many based esquires like the second, over all on an escuchon a cross croslet fitchy argent—Benedictine Abbey at WINCHCOMBE or WINCHELCOMBE, Gloucester.

Per fesse; the chief part quarterly indented per fesse or and ermine; the base argent charged with squires [cantons voided] sable—BARLAY.

Theoretical heralds say that the *esquire* may be drawn across the whole shield, but no examples are found; while the expression *based* or *bast esquire* has probably arisen from some error, but it is found used by more than one writer. It would have been better if heralds had been content with the old form, *corners gyronny.*

Esquire, (lat. *armiger*, fr. *escuyer*): a title of a gentleman of the rank immediately below a knight. It was originally a military office, an esquire being (as the name *escuyer*, from *escu*, a shield, implies) a knight's attendant and shield bearer.

Esquires may be theoretically divided into five classes: 1. The younger sons of peers and their eldest sons. 2. The eldest sons of knights and their eldest sons. 3. The chiefs of ancient families are esquires by prescription. 4. Esquires by creation or office. Such are the heralds and serjeants at arms and some others, who are constituted esquires by receiving a collar of SS. Judges and other officers of state, justices of the peace, and the higher naval and military officers are designated esquires in their patents or commissions. Doctors in the several faculties, and barristers at law, are considered as esquires, or equal to esquires. None, however, of these offices or degrees convey gentility to the posterity of their holders.

5. The last kind of esquires are those of knights of the bath; each knight appoints two to attend upon him at his installation and at coronations.

A special *helmet* was appropriated to *esquires*.

Estoile, or *star*, (fr. *étoile*): is as a rule represented of six points and wavy. Estoiles sometimes occur with a greater number of points, as eight, or sixteen. Where the rays are represented straight this has been probably by accident, as the figure would then more properly be described as a *mullet* of so many points; but there has, no doubt, been some confusion between the estoile and mullet, the latter

INGILBY.

with English heralds being of five points, and with French heralds of six. See *Mullet*, also *Star*, and *Rowel*.

Sable, an estoile argent—INGILBY, Yorkshire. [Other branches of the same family bear the estoile with eight and sixteen points.]

Azure, an estoile of sixteen points or—HINTSON, Yorkshire.

Gilbert HANSARDE, de goules a trois estoiles d'argent—Roll, temp. HEN. III.

Monsire John de COBHAM, gules sur une cheveron d'or, trois estoilles de sable, entre trois lis le asur—Roll, temp. ED. III.

Le Count d'OXFORD, port quarterly, d'or et gules, a un estoiele d'argent en le quarter gulus devant—*Ibid.*

Argent, a chevron between three estoiles sable—MORDAUNT, Earl of Peterborough, 1628.

Ermine, on a canton sable a five-pointed estoile argent—Sir William de STROUD, Somerset.

Argent, a chevron between three estoiles of eight points wavy or—WISEMAN, Scotland.

Gules, a chevron engrailed between three six-pointed estoiles argent—PUISON, London.

Azure, a nine-pointed estoile or—ALDHAM.

MORDAUNT.

A star within a crescent appears as the *badge* of RICHARD I., JOHN, and HENRY III., and was possibly intended to signify the ascendancy of Christianity over Mahomedanism, and so emblematic of the Crusades.

Badge of RICHARD I.

Evangelistic Symbols : These four symbols, which have their origin in the mystical interpretation of the first chapter of Ezekiel (ver. 10) compared with the fourth chapter of Revelation (ver. 6, 7), occur on at least one coat of arms.

Azure, on a cross or between the symbols of the four evangelists of the last, five lions rampant gules, armed and langued azure—REYNOLDS, Bp. of Worc. 1309, afterwards Abp. of Cant. 1314—1327.

Abp. REYNOLDS.

Espanié, (old fr.): of an eagle, *displayed.*

Espaule, (old fr.): for shoulder.

Esquartelé = *quarterly.*

Essorant, (fr.): *Soaring, or rising.*

Essore, (fr.): of the tincture of roofs of houses (?).

Estendart, (fr.): *standard.* See *Flag.*

Estroict, (old fr.): used of a lion's *tail* when *straight.* See under *Tail.*

Etête, (fr.): used by French heralds when an animal is headless.

Etincélant, (fr.): of coals when emitting sparks.

Etincelé, (fr.): semé of sparks.

Etrier, (fr.): *stirrup.*

Ewer, or *laver-pot*, (fr. *aiguierre*, also *burette*): this and similar charges, such as *jug*, and *beaker*, are variously represented. The *laver-pot* in the FOUNDERS' Company is represented as below, but the more ordinary form is that given in the margin. The handle (fr. *corniere*) should be sinister, and the lip dexter. This charge does not appear to be represented in any of the ancient rolls of arms by name, but perhaps some of the ancient *pots*, q.v., were represented like pitchers. The term *flagon* also occurs (fr. *flacon* probably answers to the same).

Ewer.

Azure, on a chief or between two ewers [or beakers] in chief, and a three-legged pot with two handles in base, of the second three roses gules seeded gold, barbed vert—Company of BRAZIERS, incorporated temp. HEN. VI.

Azure, a laver-pot between two taper candlesticks or — FOUNDERS' Company [arms originally granted, 1590].

Gules, on a fesse wavy argent, between three pitchers double eared or, as many bees volant proper—CONDUITT, Westminster [granted 1717].

Sable, on a chevron ermine between three jugs argent, as many martlets of the first—WHITE.

Argent, three ewers gules—BLAND.

Argent, three water-pots covered gules within a bordure sable bezanty—MONBOUCHER.

Laver-pot.

Gules, three pitchers argent—CONDUIT.

Argent, a bend engrailed between six ewers sable—WOOD.

Argent, on a bend sable three ewers of the first—LEWER.

Sable, three ewers argent—BUTLER; also TOTEWHILL, Cornwall.

Sable, on a chevron ermine between three flagons, the two in chief with spouts argent, as many martlets gules—WHITE, Kent.

The old French *pichier*, the modern *pitcher*, is found as early as the roll of the Siege of Carlaverock, but it appears to be a solitary example, and the name of the bearer seems rather to suggest its connection with the *water bouget*.

Le bon Bertram de MONTBOUCHIER,　　En son escu de argent luisant
De goules, furent trois pichier　　　　En le ourle noire le besant.
　　　　　　　　　　　　　　　　Roll of Carlaverock, A.D. 1300.

Per bend gules and azure, a pitcher in bend or; on a chief of the last a beast's head erased between two mullets sable—WHEELER [Harl. MS., 1404; but probably meant for the arms of Wheeler, which are a fish-wheel in bend or, on a chief of the last a wolf's head erased sable between two ogresses].

Azure, a fesse ermine between three pitchers or—PITCHARD, co. Breck-nock.

Ewers are borne by families of TODWELL, REGINALD, &c.

Eye: The human eye is sometimes represented in arms; the eyes of animals are rarely referred to, and only when they are of a different tincture.

Vert, on a canton argent, an eye proper—WALKER, Barbadoes.

Argent, an oak-tree growing out of a mount in base vert; in chief a human eye eradiated proper, all within a bordure gules—WATT, Edinburgh.

Barry of six azure and argent, on a chief of the second three eyes gules—DELAHAY, Ireland.

Barry of six or and sable, on a pale gules an eye argent weeping and dropping or—DODGE, Suffolk.

Azure, a chevron or between three eyes argent—LEGIER.

Argent, three cows passant sable, eyes gules, collared or—Benedictine Alien Priory at COWICK.

Faces: in French arms the human face is sometimes represented on charges, such as *roundles*, &c., and in English arms the *sun* is generally represented as having such a face. Leopards' and bucks' *faces* also occur, signifying that the head is *caboshed*, i.e. shewing only the front portion, and badly expressed. *Bacchus' faces* is a term also found, but in this case it would have been more correct if they had been blazoned *heads*.

Argent, a fesse humetty gules: in chief three leopard's faces of the second—BRABANT.

Argent, a fesse dancetty gules; in chief three leopard's faces sable—Sir John POUNTNEY [Lord Mayor of London, 1330, 31, and 33–36].

Expanded, or *expansed*, i.q. *displayed*. Some writers would confine the term *displayed* to birds of prey, and apply that of *expanded* to tame fowls.

Extendant: also used in the sense of displayed, and likewise to signify that some charge generally found *curved* (as a serpent), is borne straight.

Eyrant, or *Ayrant*: applied to *eagles* and other birds, as if sitting on their nests.

Eyry: the nest of a bird of prey.

Argent, on a chevron engrailed sable, between three estoiles gules streaming on the dexter side downwards in bend or, three buck's faces of the first—AYLIFF, co. Wilts.

Argent, three Bacchus' faces, couped at the shoulders clothes gules—BROMALL.

Faggot: This was borne by the now extinct Company of WOODMONGERS, of London, as shewn in the margin, and very similar to the bundle of *laths*, q.v., so much so that in a Cottonian MS. the arms are blazoned as charged with a bundle of laths vert. In another coat of arms the faggots are sometimes blazoned as the military *fascines*.

Faggot.

Gules, a sword erect argent, hilt and pommel or, enfiled with a ducal coronet of the last between two flaunches of the second, each charged with a faggot proper; [elsewhere blazoned, argent, a chevron sable between faggots of the second]—WOODMONGERS' Company, London, 1716.

Argent, on a chevron between three bundles of faggots (or *fascines*) sable as many bezants—STALWORTH.

Falcon, (fr. *faucon*), is found as an heraldic bearing as early as Edward the Second's reign, if not earlier, and with it it will be convenient to associate other birds of prey, such as the *hawk* and *sparrow-hawk* (fr. *epervier*), the *goshawk* (which has not been observed in French arms), the *kite* (fr. *milan*), of which the heads occur in one English coat of arms, and the *merlion*, of which the wings are mentioned (the *emerillion* being still a French term used for a species of falcon). The French names occur of *gerfaut* in the arms of LA VALETTE Guyenne (old fr. *girfauk*), and the *fauconnet* in the arms of MOUCHET Franche Comté. A *crowned falcon* with a sceptre was the badge of ANNE BOLEYN, and was also afterwards adopted by her daughter, Queen ELIZABETH.

Badge of ANNE BOLEYN.

There are no conventional ways of representing the difference of the species of birds of prey in heraldic design, and they are fre-

---

Failli, (fr.): of a *chevron*, when broken into one or more pieces.

Falchion. See *Sabre*.

Falot, (fr.). See *Lantern*.

quently blazoned with the same descriptive terms as are applied to the eagle. They may be *close,* or *preying* (**fr.** *empiétant*), and this is also described as *lolling,* or *trussing;* they may be *surgerant,* or *rising, overt, hovering, volant,* &c.; also the wings are often described. When the beak and talons are of a different tincture, they are said to be *armed* of that tincture.

A hawk trussing.

Sire Thomas de HANVILE, de. azure a iij girfauks de or e une daunce [i.e. fesse dancetty] de or—Roll, temp. ED. II.

Sir Johan le FAUCONER, de argent a iij faucouns de goules—*Ibid.*

Argent, three sparrow-hawks close gules—HAYDOE, Lancaster.

Azure, a goshawk argent—MICHELGROVE.

Sable, three marlion's sinister wings displayed argent—ATCOMB, Devon.

Ermine, a milrind sable; on a chief azure, two marlion's wings or—MILLS, Kent.

Sable, a marlion's wing in fesse argent, between four crosses formy or, two and two—DYNE, Norfolk.

Azure, on a chevron or between three falcons close argent, three roses gules—Nicolas CLOSE, Bp. of Carlisle, 1450; of Lichfield, 1452.

Gules, a chevron between three falcons close argent—RIDLEY, Bp. of Rochester, 1547; of London, 1550–53.

Sable, a falcon rising overt or—Sir Nicolas PECHE.

CLOSE.

Gules, a falcon rising, wings expanded argent—HOWELL, Bp. of Bristol, 1644–46.

Sable, a falcon hovering with bells proper over a castle with four towers argent—LANYON, Cornwall.

Or, a falcon surgerant azure beaked or—CARWED, Llwydiarth.

Gules, a hawk reguardant, trussing a bird all argent—GOODWIN.

Gules, a hare argent seized by a goshawk or—DENSKYN.

Sable, a falcon or preying on a duck argent; on a chief of the second a cross botonny gules—MADAN, or MADDEN, Wilts.

Azure, a hawk volant argent seizing a heron also volant or—FOURNIER.

But more especially a *falcon,* as also a *hawk,* is represented with the appurtenances which belong to the art of falconry, that is, it is blazoned frequently as *belled* (fr. *grilleté*) and *jessed* of such a tincture.

The *bells* (fr. *grillets*) are little hollow circular bells, of metal, having a slit on one side, and some hard substance within, which produces a jingling sound when they are shaken; this is attached to the hawk's legs by *jesses* (fr. *jets*), or thongs of leather.   To the jesses, it is said, are attached the *varvels*, sometimes written *vervels*, or rings.

Sable, three hawk's bells or—BELLSCHAMBER.

Hawk's Bell.

The *leash* is the line by which a hawk is held (an example is noted under *heron*).

The *hawk's lure* is a decoy used in falconry, consisting of two wings joined with a line, to the end of which is attached the ring.   The line is sometimes nowed.

Gules, a hawk's lure argent—WARRE.

The *perch* (fr. *perche*), to which a hawk is sometimes borne chained, or fastened by the *leash* (fr. *lié*), generally consists of

WARRE.

two cylindrical pieces of wood joined in the form of the letter T.

The bird also may be represented *hooded* (fr. *chaperonné*); whilst the *hood* itself also appears as a separate charge. The hawker's *glove* is also found mentioned.

Sable, a goshawk argent, armed, jessed and belled or—BOLTON.

Sable, two bendlets between three hawk's bells argent —BRADSHAW.

Gules, a lion passant ermine, between three hawk's lures argent—CHESTER, co. Gloucester.

Gules, on a fesse argent, a hawk's lure of the first; in chief a cinquefoil, and in base a hawk's leg, erased, jessed and belled of the second—SHANKE, co. Fife.

Argent, on a bend wavy sable an arm issuing from the sinister of the last; perched on a glove of the first a hawk or—HAWKERIDGE, co. Devon.

D'azur, au faucon d'argent chaperonné de gueules perché sur un tronc d'arbre d'or accompagné en chef de trois tiercefeuilles du même—FAUCON, Auvergne.

SHANKE.

D'azur, à un faucon d'or grilleté d'argent empiétant une perdrix aussi d'or, becqueé et ongleé de gueules—VARLET, Bresse.

Argent, a fesse between three hawk's hoods gules—A quartering of KIRTON, Northampton.

D'argent, à trois chaperons d'oiseaux liés de gueules—RAPOUEL, Ile de France.

Sable, a hawk standing on a perch argent, beaked and legged or—HAWKER, co. Wilts.

Sable, a goshawk perched on a stock argent, armed, belled and jessed or—WEELE, Devon.

The heads also of the birds are some-times borne alone.

WEELE.

Azure, on a chevron between three kite's heads erased or, three roses gules—John KITE, Bp. of Carlisle, 1521-37.

Argent, a chevron between three falcon's heads erased gules beaked or—CASSEY.

Argent, on a fesse gules three falcon's heads of the field—BAKER, Bp. of Bangor, 1723; of Norwich, 1727-33.

[Two hawks proper are the supporters to the arms of ROSE of Kilravock.]

BAKER.

Fan: besides the *fan* or *shruttle* already noted under *basket*, there is the ordinary *fan*, which occurs in the insignia ascribed to the FANMAKERS. The device also seems to occur in the arms ascribed in one MS. to the company of HABERDASHERS.

Or, a fan displayed with a mount of various devices and colours, the sticks gules; on a chief per pale gules and azure, on the dexter side a shaving-iron over a bundle of fan-sticks tied together or; on the sinister side a framed saw in pale of the last—FANMAKERS' Company [inc. 1709].

Argent, on a chevron between three fans (?) gules as many Catherine wheels or—Company of HABERDASHERS, anciently called HURRERS and MILANERS, Cottonian MS., Tiberius, D. 10.

Fanon, (fr.): this ecclesiastical term, i.e. the ornamentation of the sleeve, or cuff of a priest's vestment, is only found (like the *censer*) in French heraldry, no English example having been met with.

D'argent, a trois fanons de gueules, doublés et frangés de sinople—CLINCHAMPS, Normandie.

False heraldry, (fr. *faux armoiries*) : offending against rules.

Farriers' Implements. See *Butrices*.

Fasces, (fr. *faisceaux*) : the Roman fasces, consisting of a bundle of rods bound round the helve of a hatchet, are found in some arms, but more frequently as a crest.

Azure, a fasces in pale or, with axe argent ; over all on a fesse gules three estoiles of the second—Cardinal MAZARIN, 1601.

Argent, a Roman fasces and sword saltirewise proper ; in chief a pair of balances held by an armed arm azure—HOSEASON, Zetland.

Per pale vert and azure, a lion rampant argent crowned or ; on a canton ermine two swords in saltire surmounted by a fasces impaled within a wreath all or—DOBEDE, co. Cambridge.

Ecartelé aux 1 and 4 d'argent ; aux 2 and 3 d'azur ; le 2 à deux faisceaux d'armes antiques, le 3 à un faisceau de même à une bande de gueules brochante sur le tout chargée de trois étoiles d'argent—NADAULT DE BUFFON.

Fer-de-moline, or *fer de moulin* (fr.), also *inkmoline, mill-ink, millrind, millrine,* (fr. *anille*), is, according to Gibbon, "that piece of iron that beareth and upholdeth the moving millstone." Perhaps no charge has a greater diversity of forms found in ancient drawings ; so much so that it may be reckoned amongst the conventional charges of heraldry. It is, indeed, generally drawn like one or other of the first two, but sometimes it appears like the third. The ordinary position of the fer-de-mouline is erect, but it may be borne fesswise, or bendwise.

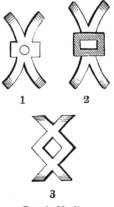

Fers-de-Moulin.

Sire William SAUNSUM, de or a un fer de molin de sable—Roll, temp. ED. II.

Sir Robert de WYLEBI, de goules a un fer de molin de argent—*Ibid.*

Sire Rauf le MARESCHAL, de or a un fer de molin de goules—*Ibid.*

Paly of six argent and azure, a milrind of the second—PRICHET, Bp. of Gloucester, 1672–81.

Fascé, (fr.) : a *fesse.*

Fasce en divise, (fr.) : a fesse of half its usual width, i.e. a *bar.*

Fascé, (fr.) : is equivalent to the English *barry.*

Fascines. See *Faggot.*

Faucille, (fr.) : *Sickle.*

Faux, *false,* e.g. *faux armoiries* = false heraldry ; also in old rolls applied to *crosses, escutcheons, roundels,* &c. = *voided.*

Fawn. See *Deer.*

Gules, a fer-de-mouline argent—FERRE.

Or, a fer-de-mouline azure—MOLYNERS.

Ermine, a fer-de-moline azure pierced of the field—MOLINS, London.

Argent, on a milrind sable five estoiles of the field—VICOREY, co. Derby.

Azure, fifteen fers-de-molines or; on a chief of the second a lion rampant purpure—Insignia of LINCOLN's INN [according to Guillim].

Gules, a mill ink pierced argent—FERE, co. Stafford.

Gules, two bars argent; over all an inkmoline argent—PAUNERTON, co. Stafford.

Gules, a millrind bendways argent between two martlets in pale or —BURNINGHAM, Hants.

Fern, (fr. *fougère*): fern-leaves are found on one coat of arms, and the *Adder's-tongue* fern in another, but no third instance has been noticed.

Argent, three fern-leaves vert—VERNAI, Devon.

Azure, a fesse between three adder's-tongue leaves or—BROUNESLANE.

Ferris: the old-fashioned means employed in striking a light is found as a charge on one coat of arms.

Per pale argent and azure, a ferris counterchanged—BOGNER.

Fesse, sometimes spelt *fess*, (fr. *fasce*) : one of the ordinaries, and though not found so frequently perhaps as the bend, it is used as much as the chevron, and if its kindred charge (for this is not allowed to be a diminutive), the *bar* is taken into account more so. It is the most natural form to be produced in the construction of a shield, though fanciful heralds find an origin for it in the military girdle. It should occupy, according to heraldic rule, one third of the height of the escutcheon, but this proportion is almost always considerably diminished in practice. Its position is across the centre of the shield, unless it is described as *enhanced,* or *abased.*

COLEVILLE.

Walter de COLEVILLE, dor ung fece de goulz—Roll, temp. HEN. III.

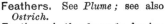

Feathers. See *Plume ;* see also *Ostrich.*

Feathered, (fr. *plumeté*): having feathers or plumage [of an arrow, fr. *empenné*].

Feez, *fez,* &c., old fr. *fesse.*

Feon. See *Pheon.*

Fencock. See *Heron.*

Fer de cheval = horse-shoe : *de fleche* = arrow-head : *de javelot* or *de lance,* lance-head.

Le Counte de WARWICK de goules crusule de or, a une fesse de or—
Roll, temp. ED. II.

Monsire Symon de COLVIL, porte d'or a une fes de gules.

The *fesse* is subjected to the same series of variations as to its
margin as have already been noted under the *bend*, &c., and this
from earliest times; the *fesse dancetty* was called a *dauncet*, and
when *indented* q.v. the number of indentations is sometimes
given. It is also found *humetty* (q.v.) and even with the ends
botonny.

Piers PERCY, d'or ung fece engrele d'azur—Roll, temp. HEN. III.

John de DEYVILLE, d'or ung fece flourey de l'un en l'autre—*Ibid*.

Argent, a fesse botonny gules—ABIBSON.

There cannot properly be more than one fesse in a single coat
of arms; if more they are *bars;* but still, in rare instances, in
old blazoning the term *fesse* is used where *bar* would be used
now; the term a *demi-fesse* occurs also when it is joined with
a canton. (See under *Canton*, arms of PYPARD.)

Sir John de WAKE, port d'or ov ij fesses de gulez ov iij torteus d'or en la
chef.—Falkirk Roll, A.D. 1298, HARL. MS. [But in the Roll in the Cottonian MS. Caligula, A. xviii. A.D. 1308–14, these arms are blazoned, Sire
Johan WAKE, de or, a ij barres de goules, en le chef iij rondels de goules].

Sir Rauff PIPART, porte d'argent ov ung fees et demy fees et le cantell
d'azure; et en le cantell quint foyl d'or—Falkirk Roll, Harl. MS. 6589.

Again, like the *chevron*, the *fesse* may be *abased, enhanced,* &c.

Argent, a fesse enhanced and a chevron gules—MACK.

And it may be *debruised* or *broken*, when it
would probably be represented as in the margin; though there is much doubt as to the
practical application of such terms as de-
bruised, fracted, &c., as has been shewn under the terms *bend,
chevron,* and *downset.*

Gules, a fesse removed or debruised in the centre argent—BROKROSE.

It may be charged with various devices, and very rarely is it
depressed by other ordinaries, but such cases do occur.

Gules, a fesse ermine depressed by a pale of the same within a bordure
engrailed azure—SPONNE.

Or, a fesse chequy azure and argent, over all a bend engrailed gules
within a bordure of the third charged with eight mullets of the second—
STUART, CO. OXon.

Party per fesse (fr. *coupé*) is very rare in comparison with *party per pale*. While the division into three horizontal portions (fr. *tiercé*), though comparatively common in French arms, is seldom if ever found in English examples. See *Party*.

Fesswise, or *fessways*, is used to signify that a charge, the normal position of which is upright, is placed lengthways.

Gules, a sword lying fesswise proper, hilt and pomel or, the hilt towards the sinister between three fleurs-de-lis of the last—BROWNE, Scotland.

Fesse-wards signifies that the charge, or charges, are to be placed with the heads or points towards the centre of the shield, i.e. the *fesse-point*.

Sable, a close helmet between three spear-heads, points fesse-wards—DOLBEN, Bp. of Bangor, 1632.

DOLBEN.

Fetterlock: this, so far as heraldic drawing is concerned, appears to be the same as what is elsewhere blazoned as *shackle-bolt*, *shackbolt*, or *manacle*. It is, in fact, a 'handcuff,' or prisoners' bolt, and generally represented as shewn in the margin, though sometimes represented of a square form. In the arms of SHAKERLY, Worcestershire, they are sometimes represented more like oval rings, while in the crest of WYNDHAM the semicircular part is generally represented as a chain, and in the badge of PERCY it is made to resemble the *swivel*, as in the arms of the IRONMONGERS. A double bolt also occurs in the arms of ANDERTON.

Fetterlock.

The device does not seem to occur in the more ancient rolls, but it is found very widely spread among several ancient families.

Argent, a shack-bolt sable—NUTHALL, Nuthall, Lancashire.

Gules, five shackles in fesse argent—SHAKERLEY.

Argent, a heart gules, within a fetterlock sable—LOCKHART, Scotland.

A lion's head erased or, within a fetterlock of the last—Crest of WYNDHAM, Earl of Egremont.

NUTHALL.

Azure, a fetterlock and key argent—MABEN.

Sable, on a bend between two pair of mana-cles argent three pheons bendwise in bend gules; a chief or charged with a demi-lion rampant issuant enclosed by a pair of lozenges azure—Thomas JOHNSON, co. York.

Argent, a fesse between three fetterlocks [? padlocks] gules—GRIERSON, Dumfries.

Sable, two single shack-bolts and one double one argent—ANDERTON, Chesh. and Lanc. [also blazoned three double shack-bolts].

Argent, an anchor in pale azure, the ring or; the anchor surmounted with a fetterlock of the

ANDERTON.

second, within the fetterlock on the dexter side of the anchor a sword erect of the last, hilt and pomel or; on the sinister side of the anchor a rose gules—Insignia of the town of BEWDLEY, Worcestershire.

A falcon *displayed* within a closed fetter-lock was a *badge* of King Edward IV. for the dukedom of York. The example is taken from the brazen gates of King Henry the Seventh's chapel at Westminster.

Badge of EDW. IV.

Fig-tree, (fr. *figue*): the tree and the leaves occur, but no instance of the fruit being borne in English arms has been ob-served.

Per fesse wavy gules and argent, in chief a lion passant guardant erminois, in base on a mount vert a fig-tree proper—MIRTLE.

Per chevron argent and gules, three fig-leaves counterchanged—GREVES.

Fermaile, (i.e. *fer de maille*). See *Buckle.*

Fettered: used in one case of a *lion's* forefeet. In the case of a horse the term *spancelled* is used.

Feuillé, (fr.): *leaved,* i.e. of a tree or plant having leaves.

Fiché, (fr.): *fitchy.*

Fiddle. See *Violin.*

Field, (fr. *champ*): the ground or surface of the shield on which all charges are placed. See *Blazon.*

Field, a, is represented in one case with a river of *water,* q.v.

Field-pieces. See *Guns.*

Fier, (fr.): of a lion enraged.

Fierte, (fr.): applied to the teeth of *whales.*

Fifes. See *Pipes.*

Figured, (fr. *figuré*): the sun, moon, and some other charges are so termed when drawn with human countenances, as if re-flected in them.

Fimbriated, (fr. *bordé*): said by strict heralds to be applied only to an ordinary or other charge having a narrow edging of some other tincture *all round it*, so that if any part touches the outer edging of the shield without the border being continued in that part the term should not be applied, but the term *edged* instead. This distinction, however, is never adhered to in practice. The crosses, for instance, in what is termed the Union Jack (see *flag*) are always blazoned as fimbriated, and many other examples might be cited. When applied to the *dolphin* it probably only extends along the dorsal ridge.

Argent, on a fesse engrailed sable, fimbriated or, between two grey-hounds courant of the second, three fleurs-de-lys of the third—BAKER.

Gules, on a bend sable fimbriated or, two pierced mullets and as many ducks argent membered of the first alternately—Sir Robert RUSSELL.

Finches: beneath this term it has been thought well to comprise a number of birds of the *finch* tribe, examples of which are found in heraldic blazon. In many cases only single instances have been met with, and some appear to have been adopted only for the sake of the name. They are as follows, and for the sake of reference to foreign arms the scientific names according to Linnæus have been added to each: The *Goldfinch* (*carduelis*); the *Bulfinch* (*pyrrhula*); the *Chaffinch* (*fringilla cælebs*); the *Brambling* (*fringilla montifringilla*); the *Canary* (*fringilla canaria*); the *Linnet* (*fringilla cannabina*), and the *Pinzon*. This last is the only one of the series which occurs in any of the old rolls, and it has evidently been chosen for the sake of the name. It is not quite certain what is the bird meant, but it has been supposed to be the *chaffinch*, i.e. the modern fr. *pinson*. It has not, however, been found possible to fix upon the equivalents of the above in the French lists of arms.

Filberts. See *Hazel*.

File: See *Label*. A file with three labels is more properly called a label of three points.

Filet, (fr.): a narrow band; but the term is used irregularly. See *Chief* and *Cotice*.

Filière, (fr.): a very narrow border not used in English arms.

Fillet. See *Chief*. It is also used as a band round the *head* of a person.

Finned, of *dolphins* or *fish*, when the fins are of another tincture.

Argent, a chevron sable between three goldfinches proper—MOLENICK, Cornwall.　[Borne also by GOULDSMITH, Kent, and GOOLD, co. Cork.]

Or, a fesse between three bulfinches proper—ALPIN.

Azure, on a bend invected argent between three crescents, each surmounted by a mullet of eight points or as many chaffinches proper—CHAFFERS, Liverpool.

Argent, three bramblings proper; a chief gules—BRAMBLEY.

Sable, on a bend or, three canary birds proper—KINNEIR of that Ilk.

Azure, a chevron argent between three linnets proper—CARDALE, Hagley, 1590.

Sire ... MOUNPYNZON, de argent a un lion de sable a un pinzon de or en le espandle [i.e. on the shoulder]—Roll, temp. ED. II.

Vert, on a chevron argent, between three plates, each charged with a pyncheon (i.e. goldfinch) proper, as many pansies, stalked proper—MORGAN, Bp. of S. David's, 1554–59 (grant A.D. 1553, College of Arms).

Fire: flames of fire (fr. *flammes*) are not at all a rare device in coats of arms, though not observed to occur in arms before the sixteenth century; sometimes by themselves, but more frequently in connection with other charges, e.g. *Altar, Beacon, Bush, Fireball, Firebrand*, &c., when the term *flammant*, or *flaming*, is used. When emblazoned the flames may be represented by *gules* and *or* alternating.

Flames.

Or, on a fesse dancette, between three flames of fire gules, a lamb couchant, between two estoiles argent—Ascribed to HOOPER, Bp. of Gloucester, 1550–54; also of Worcester, 1552–53.

Azure, a book open between three flames of fire proper, within a bordure argent, charged with four mullets and so many crosses crosslets as the first —SMITH, Edinburgh.

Ermine, two flames in saltire gules—LEIGHT, Hants.

Azure, flames of fire proper—BRANDER, Hants.

Argent, a chevron voided azure between three (another two) flames of fire proper—WELLS, co. Monmouth.

WELLS.

Argent, a bend between three crescents flammant proper—PADDON, Hants [granted 1590].

Argent, three hearts flammant gules—HEART, Scotland.

Argent, two billets raguled and trunked placed saltirewise, the sinister surmounted of the dexter azure, their tops flaming proper—SHURSTABLE.

S. Anthony's Fire is named in the following singular coat of arms :—

Or, on a fesse chequy azure and argent, in chief two stars of the second ; quartering argent a galley, oars in action sable with S. Anthony's fire on the topmast, and in the centre of the quarters a crescent for difference—STEWART, Innernytie, Scotland.

Fire-ball, (fr. *bombe*): a *bomb-shell*, or *grenade*, with fire issuing from a hole in the top, or sometimes from two or more holes. For *Firebrand*, see *Torch*.

Azure, a fire-ball or flamed proper—DAN-CASTER, co. Berks, granted 1556.

Argent, a fire-ball proper held in the dexter paw of a lion rampant sable — BALL, co. Chester.

Fire-balls.

Argent, an eagle displayed or ; in chief a naval crown between two bombs of the last fired proper—GRAVES.

Sable, on a fesse ermine between three mullets of the last a bomb-shell bursting proper—BENSLEY, London.

Argent, a chevron between three fire-balls sable fired in four places—BALL, Devon [but it is also blazoned elsewhere as between three balls sable with four tassels].

Argent, on a fesse gules between three grenados sable fired proper a plate—SILVERTOP, Northumberland.

Ermine, a lion rampant sable between in chief two torteaux, and in base a hand grenade exploding proper—BALL, Norfolk.

Paly of six or and gules, on a chief engrailed ermine three hand grenades proper—BOYCOTT, Norfolk.

Fire-chest: a figure resembling an iron box used to contain fire to warm a hall is drawn as in the margin in Berry's Heraldry, and attributed as a crest to one of the families of PRYCE. It is said to have been blazoned as a *fire-beacon*, but probably its use was domestic, not military.

Fire-chest.

Fired : the term is especially used of a grenade, or *fire-ball*, when represented bursting, or of a *cannon* with flames of fire issuing from the mouth. See *Gun*. It is also sometimes used for flammant or inflamed, e.g. of a *beacon*.

Fish, (fr. *poisson*): in the earlier arms (as in the case of beasts) very few varieties of fish indeed are found mentioned in heraldic bearings. In the four rolls of arms referred to under the summaries of *beasts, birds,* &c., viz. of Henry III., of Edward I., II., and III., the only fish represented are the *Lucies* or Pikes, and the *Barbel*. But in later arms we find named between thirty and forty varieties of fish, as will be seen by referring to the Synopsis. As in the case of the *birds,* a large proportion are selected for the sake of the name, as *lucie* for LUCY, *eels* for ELLIS, and *chub* for CHOBBE; hence, too, we find many local names of fish introduced, some of which it has been difficult to identify, such as the *birt* fish (see under *turbot*), the *cob* and the *sparling* (see *herring*), the *spalding,* and the *tubbe* fish. The last, however, borne by the family of TUBBE, are usually blazoned *gurnets,* q.v.

It must not, however, be forgotten that the term *fish* had a much wider meaning than we now give it. In unscientific days not only the *Dolphin* was considered a fish, but, as already said in the notice of this mammal, it was looked upon as the king of fishes. At the same time the *Whale* was classed as a fish, being an inhabitant of the sea. Also the *crustacea,* such as crabs and lobsters, and the *mollusca,* such as the escallop and whelk, were considered as fish, or at least what were called shell-fish.

When a fish is mentioned without any definite name, it may be drawn perhaps like a trout or herring.

Per fess gules and or, in base a wolf passant reguardant vert, holding in his mouth a fish of the third; in chief . . . KYERKWALD.

Azure, three otters passant in pale or, each holding in his mouth a fish argent—PROUDE, Kent.

Vert, three fishes hauriant or, spotted gules—DOGGE.

Argent, a bend engrailed between six fishes hauriant argent—COOPER.

Argent, on two bars wavy azure, three fishes naiant two and one, or in fesse a mount vert, charged with a dove rising, nimbed of the third—HILSEY, Bp. of Rochester, 1535–1538.

Fir-tree.   See *Pine*.   Fish-hook.   See *Hook*.
Firm.   See *Throughout*.   Fish-weel.   See *Weel*.

As has been already pointed out under dolphin several Lord Mayors of London bore this supposed fish in their arms, by reason of the flourishing condition of the FISHMONGERS' Companies. The two Companies of SALT and STOCK-FISH MONGERS were united in 1536, when they obtained a charter from Henry VIII. In their old Hall, destroyed by the fire of London, there were arms in the windows of twenty-two Lord Mayors, who had been chosen from the Fishmongers' Company.

Fish are, as a rule, borne upright, when the old French term *hauriant* is used, i.e. the heads are supposed to be just above the water, and to be taking in air; but they are also often borne extended, when the old term *naiant*, or swimming, is applied: and so it is generally stated which of these two should be the position of the fish, though if not, the first must be assumed. If two fish are '*respecting one another*,' or *endorsed*, the upright or hauriant position is implied, or *in fesse* the naiant position. Two fish may also be drawn *in saltire*, &c. The term *embowed* appears to be applied only to the Dolphin, and the same of *vorant*. The term *urinant*, i.e. diving, is sometimes applied to a fish with the head downwards. Besides the above, the terms *allumé* (fr.), when the eyes are of some bright tincture, and *pamé* (fr.), when the mouth is open, and the fish is as it were gasping, are applied by French heralds, but seldom, if ever, by English writers. Dolphins and sometimes other fish may be *finned* of another tincture than that of the body.

In French heraldry the following have been observed: *truite, hareng, saumon, brochet* (pike), *carpe, tanche, eperlan* (smelt), *lamproie, rosse* (roach), and *rouget* (gurnet).

Per pale azure and purpure, a fish hauriant or—VAUGHAN, Wales, [Granted 1491].

Gules, a fish naiant argent—HARBRON, co. Chester.

Gules, three fish conjoined at their tails, in triangle or, heads sable—BERNBACK.

Argent, three fishes' heads meeting in the fess point argent—TWYNKYN.

Gules, a fish in bend argent—NEVE.

Argent, two fishes in saltire azure—GEDNEY, co. Lincoln.

Vert, a dolphin urinant (or in pale, tail in chief) or—MONYPENNY, Kent.

Fitché (fr. *fiché*), *fitchy*, or *fitched*, are terms signifying pointed at the lower end, they are chiefly applied to *crosses*, or crosslets. See *Cross*, § 19, where several examples will be found. Crosses may be simply *fitchée*, that is, from the middle downwards, or only *fitchée at the foot*. Crosses *fitchée of all four* are mentioned by theoretical writers, but it is doubtful if examples occur. The *pale* has sometimes the tower terminated *pointed*.

Crosses fitchy.

Crosslets fitchy.

Argent, a pale pointed in base gules between two cinquefoils of the second—ARCHDALL, Ireland.

The terms *double fitched and treble fitched* have been awkwardly applied by heraldic writers to crosses, the ends of which terminate as shewn in the margin. See *Cross*, § 19.

Double and treble fitched.

Flag, (fr. *drapeau*): the flag, like the shield, was ornamented with heraldic devices, &c.; and further than this, it appears itself sometimes as a charge: a few notes on the names of flags are therefore appended. As already pointed out, a distinction has been made between a *banner* which is a *square flag*, and a *flag* proper, though it is rather a theoretical than a practical one.

Azure, a chevron between three flags displayed argent—DRUMSON.

Argent, a saltire between four laurel leaves vert, on a chief embattled azure two French flags in saltire, surmounted by a sword erect all proper; over the sword Bourbon in gold letters—Sir Henry KEATING, Justice of the Common Pleas, 1859.

Argent, a lymphad with sail furled on a sea in base proper, at the poop a flag flying towards the bow argent fimbriated vert, charged with a pomme in fesse, on a chief gules three bezants each charged with a mullet—UTTERSON, Sussex.

The *Standard*, (fr. *estendart*), is a long flag, gradually becoming narrower towards the point, which, unless the standard belong to a prince of the blood royal, must be split.   The

---

Fizure: a name given in the 'Boke of S. Alban's' to a *baton*.

Fixed. See *Throughout*.
Flagon. See *Ewer*.

following figure is taken from a pedigree of the WILLOUGHBY family, c. temp. Eliz. It may be described as follows:—

In the chief, the cross of St. George, the remainder being parted per fesse or and gules [the livery colours], divided into three portions by the white scroll containing the motto. In the first the cognizance a griffin passant argent, armed blue. In the second crest, an owl crowned proper, upon a wreath of the family colours. The fringe green and white, the colours of the royal house of Tudor.

WILLOUGHBY.

Standards of different dimensions are assigned by heraldic writers to each rank, from an emperor's standard of eleven yards long, down to a baronet's of four yards.

What is now called the *Royal Standard*, namely a *square flag* bearing *the royal arms*, is, properly speaking, a *banner*, for a standard cannot be square, and ought only to contain crests, badges, mottoes, and ornaments, and not the arms, but custom has sanctioned the name. The royal standards, how-ever, were anciently of the true form, though the devices have varied; that of Edw. III. may be described as follows:—

In the chief the cross of S. George, the remainder party per fesse azure and gules, and divided into three portions by a white scroll, bearing —DIEU ET MON DROIT.

In the first, a Lion of England between in chief a coronet of crosses patés and fleurs-de-lys between two clouds irradiated proper; in base, a cloud between two coronets. In the second, in chief a coronet; in base, an irradiated cloud. The third, quarterly 1 and 4, an irradiated cloud, 2 and 3 a coronet.

Standards are sometimes named in coats of arms.

Gules, on a standard argent, fringed or, in saltire, with a broken spear of the second, a cross of the first—SMYTH, Scotland [granted 1765.]

Argent, three standards (another vanes) sable in an orle gules—VYRNEY.

The *Union Jack*. The national flag of Great Britain and
Ireland is also, properly speaking, a *banner* and not a flag, but
as custom has sanctioned the name, it is given here instead of
under *banner*. It was the banner of S. George (argent, a cross
gules), to which the banner of S. Andrew (azure, a saltire
argent) was united (instead of being quartered according to
ancient custom) in pursuance of a royal proclamation dated April
12, 1606. It would then have been blazoned as follows:—

Azure, a saltire argent, surmounted
by a cross gules, fimbriated (more accurately edged) of the second.

The white edging was no doubt
intended to prevent one colour
from being placed upon another,
but this precaution was hardly necessary, for the mere contact of the
red cross and blue field would
have been authorized by numerous
precedents. This combination was

Union Jack, 1707.

constituted the national flag of Great Britain by a royal proclamation issued July 28, 1707.

No further change was made until the union with Ireland,

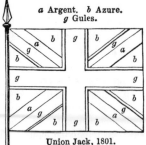

a Argent. *b* Azure.
g Gules.

Union Jack, 1801.

Jan. 1, 1801, previous to which instructions were given to combine
the banner of S. Patrick (argent,
a saltire gules) with the crosses of
S. George and S. Andrew. In obe-
dience to these instructions, the
present national flag of Great Britain and Ireland was produced,
which may perhaps best be blazoned
thus (though there is difference of
opinion as to the correct manner). It must be drawn with
upper quarters of the saltire argent towards the staff, and lower
quarters argent away from it.

Azure, the saltires of S. Patrick and S. Andrew quarterly per saltire,
counterchanged argent and gules; the latter fimbriated of the second;
surmounted by the cross of S. George of the third, fimbriated as the last.

The word *Jack* is of doubtful origin, possibly some trifling incident may have given the name. Philologists have derived it from the surcoat, charged with a red cross anciently used by the English soldiery, which was once called a jacque (whence the word jacket): but it is doubtful whether the name Union Jack ever appears before the name Jacque had quite gone out of use. Others suggest that the name of *Jacques* was given by the French in allusion to King JAMES, in whose reign the union took place. But these are mere guesses.

The *Gonfanon* is said to differ from a banner in this respect that instead of being square and fastened to a transverse bar, the gonfanon, though of the same figure, was fixed in a frame made to turn like a modern ship's vane, with two or three streamers, or tails.

Guidon, or (fr. *Guidhomme*), is a flag resembling the standard in form, but less by one third, and generally ending in a point. An *ancient* was a name given to the guidon carried at funerals.

Quarterly sable and argent, the first quarter occupied by a lion rampant of the second, over all a representation of the guidon of the Thirty-first Regiment (. . . . two laurel leaves saltirewise . . . . below the Union Jack) in bend sinister—BYNG, Earl and Baron Strafford.

Pennon : a flag resembling the guidon in shape, but only half the size. It is not to be charged with arms, but only with crests, heraldic and ornamental devices, and mottos.

La ot meint richa guarnement	Meint beau penon en lance mis
Brodé sur sendaus e samis	Meint banier deploié.

Roll of Carlaverock, A.D. 1300.

Argent, two lances in saltire sable, pennons gules, surmounted by an esquire's helmet azure—CLINKSCALES.

Or, three pennons in chief sable—LOGIE, Scotland.

A kind of pennon seems also to have been called an *ancient*, but many of these names appear to be loosely used. See *Banner*.

The *Pennant* in ships is probably the same. It sometimes ends in a point, more often it is forked. In the former case it is also called a *streamer*.

Argent, a saltire wavy sable between two human hearts gules in flanks a dexter hand gules holding a cross crosslet azure in chief, and a ship (square rigged) proper with pennants gules in base—John TAYLOR, Orkney.

Pennoncelle, or *Pensell:* the diminutive of the pennon, supposed to be carried at the end of a lance. As used at funerals, they are very small pointed flags charged with crests and ornaments.

Forked pennon.

A demi-lion argent issuing from a ducal coronet, and holding a pennoncelle gules charged with a lion passant gardant or, the staff of the last—Crest of BROMLEY, Staff. and Warw.

Pavon: a triangular flag about four or five yards long, tapering from about half a yard in width to a point, the lower side being at a right-angle to the staff.

Banderolle, a narrow but long flag or streamer sometimes attached to the staff beneath the flag itself.

Vane, sometimes written *wyn,* also signifies a little flag.

Flag-stone: a charge in the insignia of the London Company of PAVIOURS, and probably nowhere else. It is represented as in the margin.

Argent, a chevron between three flag-stones sable—Company of PAVIOURS.

Flag-stone.

Flaunches, *flanches, flanks,* or *flanques,* sometimes also written *flasques,* are always borne in pairs, though by some writers the last are considered rather as diminutives of the flanches, i.e. not projecting so far into the shield. *Voiders* are said to be of similar form, and with still less projection, and incapable of being charged, though it is doubtful if cases occur in any ordinary blazon. The *square flaunches* are drawn like two projecting triangles, the outer edge of each side of the shield forming the base respectively.

Or, two flaunches gules—LANERCOST PRIORY, Cumberland.

Sable, two talbot's heads couped or, between as many flaunches ermine — BEVAN, London, 1687, and Norfolk.

LANERCOST Priory.

Flambeau, (fr.): *torch.*

Flambant, (fr.): flaming; e.g. of a pale wavy, and ending in a point like a flame.

Argent, three palets azure between two square flaunches gules—MOSYLTON.

Or, three palets, over all two square flanks gules—MOSELTON.

Azure, two talbot's heads erased or, between as many flasques ermine—HERVARE, Marshland.

Argent, three martlets in pale; on two flaunches sable three lions passant of the field—Thomas BROWN, Bishop of Rochester, 1436-1445.

In flank, or *in the flaunche*, is also used to signify at the side; e.g. in a quarterly per *saltire* in the flanks would be equivalent to the quarters two and three; the French term *flanqué* is sometimes used instead of *accompagné*, or *accosté*, but the *flanc* is especially used for the extreme edge of the shield, from which, when any charge issues, it is said to be *mouvante*.

Azure, a saltire between in chief an arrow point upwards argent, in the flaunches and base three hunting horns of the last—POTTOCK, Scotland.

Argent, two eels paleways waved, between two stars in the flanks azure—ARNEEL, Scotland.

D'azur, au pal d'argent chargé de trois tours de gueules, et accosté (ou soutenu) par quatre jambes de lion d'or mouvantes des flancs de l'ecu—BRANCAS Comtat Venaissen.

Fleam, *Fleme,* or *Flegme :* a form, as shewn in the margin, representing an ancient *lancet* borne by the Company of BARBER-SURGEONS.

Fleam.

Quarterly first and fourth sable, a chevron between three flemes argent [i.e. arms granted, 1452], second and third per pale argent and vert, a spatula in pale argent surmounted of a rose gules charged with another of the first, the first rose regally crowned proper; between the four quarters a cross of S. George gules, charged with a lion passant gardant or—BARBERS' Company, London, [Barbers' Company incorporated, 1461 ; then Barbers and *Surgeons* united, 1540; conferred, 1630; union dissolved, 1745].

Ermine, two surgeon's fleams in saltire gules—TYTHERLEY, Hants.

Sable, three fleams argent—RENDACY.

Argent, a chevron gules between three fleams or—CHETHAM, co. Derby.

Gules, two dirks in saltire argent, points downwards, hilts and pomels or, in base a lancet open proper—M'KAILE, Aberdeen.

Flames and *Flammant.* See *Fire.*

Flank. See *Flaunch.*

Flask. See Fish-*Weel.*

Flasque. See *Flaunch.*

Flax-breaker. See *Hemp-break.*

Flax-comb. See *Wool-card.*

Fleece : the *Golden Fleece*, (fr. *Toison d'or*), owes its celebrity to the classical fable of Jason's expedition to Colchis in the ship Argo to obtain it. This fleece gave name to the very celebrated order of knighthood in Spain and Austria, and was afterwards borne by certain families.

Azure, a toison or, within a double tressure fleury counterfleury of the last—Sir Robert JASON (Baronet 1661).

Azure, a chevron engrailed ermine between three golden fleeces—JENNINGS, Dover.

The Golden Fleece.

Per chevron ermine and gules, in base a golden fleece—FUNEAUX.

Fleur-de-lis, (fr.). Although there has been much controversy concerning the origin of this bearing, no doubt it represents the lily, but in a conventional form, such as was produced by the workers in metal. It is essentially the Royal Badge of France, having been adopted by King Louis VII. in the twelfth century, in allusion to the name *lois*, or *lys*. It appears amongst the Royal Badges in England in the time of the STUARTS.

Badge of the Stuarts.

From some of the following examples it will be seen how variously the name is written in ancient rolls of arms. It will also be observed that the fleur-de-lys is subject to certain variations, e.g. *stalked, slipped, leaved, seeded,* and even *fitchy.*

Robert AGULON, de goules ov ung fleur-de-lis d'argent—Roll, temp. HEN. III.

Robert AGEUYN, de goules a une florette dor—*Ibid.*, Harl. MS. 6585.

William de CANTELOWE, de goules a trois fleurs *delices* d'or—*Ibid.*

Sire Johan DEYVILE, de or a iij flures de goules e une fesse de goules a iij flures de or—Roll, temp. ED. II.

Sire Henri de COBHAM, de goules a un cheveron de or a iij frures (*sic*) de azure—*Ibid.*

Sire Gerard de OUSFLEI, de argent a une fesse de azure a iij flures de or—*Ibid.*

Flected, or *flexed :* used instead of embowed, e.g. of an *arm.*

Flêche, (fr.): *arrow.*

Flesh-pot. See *Pot.*

Monsire de UFFLET, port d'argent a une fess d'asur trois lis d'or en le fes—Roll, temp. ED. III.

Monsire Robert DEYVILL, port d'or a une fes de gules a vi lis—*Ibid.*

Per pale, sable and argent; a fleur-de-lis between two flaunches, each chargen with a fleur-de-lys all counterchanged—John ROBYNS, co. Worc.

Azure, on a bend between three fleurs-de lys or, un manny pierced mullets gules— Tnawius, Herringfleet, Suffolk.

Azure, two lions rampant supporting a tower with three fleurs-de-lys out of the battlements—KELLY Castle, Kelly, Ireland.

Barry of six argent and gules, fifteen fleurs-de-lys, three, three, three, three, two and one all counterchanged—BRANKER.

Gules, three fleurs-de-lis stalked and slipped argent—WADSWORTH, co. York.

Gules, a bar between two fleurs-de-lis stalked and leaved in chief and an annulet in base—KELLOCK, Scotland.

LEATHES.

Per fesse gules and azure, three fleurs-de-lis seeded or; a crescent for difference—PAUNCEFOOT, Somerset.

Monsire CONSTANTINE DE MORTYMER or, flourté de fleure de lis sable as peds agus—Roll, temp. ED. III.

Besides the ordinary occurrence, as above, of perfect fleur-de-lis, the upper portion is frequently employed for the termination of other devices, or combined with them. The cross *fleury*, or flory (see *Cross*, § 20) is the most frequent. A singular example of a *mascle* so treated in the arms of MAN will be found further on, and the more singular combination of a fleur-de-lis with another charge has already been given under *Cross*, § 6. The terms *fleury* (fr. *fleuré*), *flory*, *fleurty*, *floretty*, *flourite*, or *flurte*, and similar variations, also signify adorned with, or ending in, *fleurs-de-lis*.

The term *fleur de lisé* is also sometimes used in the sense of *fleurs-de-lis* being conjoined with the charge. At the same time it is said to be used also in the sense of a field or charge being *semé* of *fleurs-de-lis*, and so also the terms *fleury*, *flory*, and *floretty*. The modern French *fleuri* (to be distinguished from *fleuré*) is applied to plants, and signifies having flowers of another tincture, i.e. flowered. See under *Hawthorn*.

In French heraldry the *fleur-de-lis* is drawn sometimes with a 'fleuron,' that is, it has buds added to the flowers; it is then described as *epanoui*, or *florencée*. When it is couped, so that only the upper portion is visible, it is said to be *nourrie*. Fleurs-de-lis are blazoned *naturelles*, or *au naturel*, when they are represented as natural *lilies*.

William PEYVER, d'argent a ung chevron de goules florettz d'or en le chevron—Roll temp. HEN. III.

Le REY DE FRAUNCE, de asur poudre a flurette de or—*Ibid.*, Harl. MS. 6589.

Le ROY DE CECYLE [Sicily] dasur poudre a florettes de or, a un lambeu de goules—*Ibid.*

Sire Mostas de LATIMER, ove la bende d'aszure flourite d'or—Roll, temp. EDW. II.

Sire Robert de HOYLANDE, de azure flurette de argent a un lupard rampaund de argent—*Ibid.*

Argent, two bars azure, over all an escarbuncle of eight rays gules pometty and floretty or—BLOUNT.

Per fesse dancetté argent and sable, each point ending in a fleur-de-lis—WOODMERTON.

D'azur, a une fleur-de-lys d'or au pied nourri; deux lis au naturel sortant d'entre les cotes—BOSCHIER, Bretagne.

WOODMERTON.

Fleury counter fleury, or *flory counter flory*, signifies adorned with fleurs-de-lis alternately placed, as in the *tressure* of Scotland, and the annexed example. In the case of a tressure, or any other ordinary borne double or *cottised*, no part of the fleurs-de-lis is seen in the space between the pieces.

Or, a bend fleury counter fleury azure—GOLD-INGTON.

Argent, a bend fleury counterfleury gules—BROMFLETT.

GOLDINGTON.

Or, three bars wavy gules quartering or, a lion's head erased within a double tressure flory counter-flory gules as a coat of augmentation—DRUMMOND.

Flighted: applied to an *arrow*.

Flint-stone. See *Shot*.

Floatant, (fr. *flottant*): floating, either in the air as a *bird*, or flag, or more especially of a *ship* or sometimes of a *fish*, but then = *naiant*, i.e. supposed to be swimming in the water.

Float: a tool used by Bowyers, and borne by their Company. Two forms occur.

Sable, on a chevron between three floats or, as many mullets of the first—BOWYERS' Company [Incorporated, 1620].

Sable, three flotes in pale argent—BIRONE.

Float.

Flowers, (fr. *fleurs*) : flowers, as will be seen by the Synopsis, find a varied expression in heraldry, but the *rose* and the *lily*, or *fleur-de-lis*, are the most frequent; both of these, however, are usually represented in the conventional form, though the natural forms of each also occur. Of others the *planta genista* has been brought into note from being the badge of the Plantagenet kings; the *trefoil*, or rather the *shamrock*, from being the badge of Ireland; and the *thistle*, from being that of Scotland. The *daisy*, the *primrose*, the *nettle*, the *violet*, the *columbine*, and the *honeysuckle*, so common in our lanes, and the *poppy* and *bluebottle* in our fields, and the *marigold* in our marshes, naturally find a place. The *tulip, narcissus, silphium* (or chrysanthemum), *sunflower, carnation, gilly-flower,* and *pansy* are the garden-plants which have been introduced into arms; but by what chances the choice has fallen on these few is most probably beyond discovery. The most singular of all, perhaps, is that selected by Dr. Caius—the *sengreen*. These and one or two more will be found noted in their proper places.

In the French coats of arms it is much the same. The *rose* and the *lily*, in both the conventional and the natural forms stand at the head of the list; and we find rarely the *marguerite, violette, ancolie, gesse, pavot,* and *souci*, which represent the daisy, violet, columbine, vetch, poppy, and marigold amongst wild flowers, while the *œillet* and *pensée*, or *pink* and *pansy*, amongst garden-plants, complete a very short list.

In some few cases the term *flowers* occurs, i.e. where a ground is to have flowers scattered over it, and these can be only repre-

Flook. See *Turbot*.
Flounder. See *Turbot*.

Flory, *floretty, florencé, &c.* See *Fleury;* also *Cross,* § 20.

sented by dots of gules and azure, sprinkled over what is supposed to represent the green grass. But such devices, if not
false heraldry, are nearly approaching it.

The field a landscape, the base variegated with flowers ; a man proper
vested round the loins with linen argent, digging with a spade all of the
first—Company of GARDENERS, London.

Argent, a cedar-tree between two mounts of flowers proper ; on a chief
azure a dagger erect proper, pomel and hilt or between two mullets of
six points gold—MONTEFIORE, Sussex.

Flowers, also, are referred to in the bearing a *chaplet of
flowers*, but as they are, as a rule, blazoned gules, they are intended for roses. In rare cases the *stem* is referred to.

Gules, semy of nails, argent, three stems of a flower vert—ASHBY.

Flower-pots are occasionally named. See also *Lily-pot.*

Or, on a chevron gules, between three columbines argent, as many
flower-pots of the first—COLNET, Hants.

Fly, (fr. *mouche*): this generic name when standing alone
is probably intended to represent the common *house-fly*. Other
flies will be found under the headings respectively of *gadfly,
silkworm-fly*, and *butterfly*. Flies and *bees*, however, seem to be
much confused in heraldic drawing. See also *Beetles.*

Azure, three flies or—Geoffrey de MUSCHAMP, Bishop of Lichfield and
Coventry, 1108—1298.

Per chevron sable and argent, in chief two flies of the second—
LAMBERBY.

Argent, a chevron between three flies sable—MUSKEHAM.

Ermine, a leopard rampant regardant, and in chief three flies volant
proper—PEARCE, Bp. of Bangor, 1742, afterwards of Rochester, 1756-74.

The French coats of arms add to the list the *demoiselle* and
the *cousin*, that is, the dragon-fly and the gnat.

Flying-fish, (lat. *esocetus*, a branch of the genus *esox*,
established by Linnæus, which includes the *pike*). Until

Fluke: of an *anchor*, q.v.

Flute. See *Pipe.*

Foi, (fr.). See *Hands* joined.

Foile: old fr. = leaf.

Foine. See *Weasel.*

Force: a particular kind of *shears*
used in French factories.

Forcené, (fr.): furious, applied
to a *horse* rearing.

Fore-staff. See *Cross-staff.*

a comparatively recent period this fish was drawn, not as it appears naturally, but more like a herring with the wings of a bird. Foreign examples are more frequent than in England, only two families here having been noticed bearing this device.

ROBINSON.

Azure, a flying-fish in bend argent, on a chief of the second a rose gules between two torteaux— Henry ROBINSON, Bp. of Carlisle, 1598—1616.

Vert, three flying-fishes in pale argent—GARMSTON, co. Lincoln [granted 1758.]

Foil, (lat. *folium*, fr. *feuille*), but borne only in compounds.

Unifoil: a charge which probably never existed anywhere but in the fancy of Randle Holme, who says that it is like a single leaf of the trefoil. The *twyfoil* no doubt derived its origin from the same or a similar source. Under their heads are given *Trefoil, Quatrefoil, Cinquefoil, Sexfoil.*

Huit-foil, Eight-foil, or *Double quatrefoil:* said to be used as a mark of *cadency,* but no example has been met with.

Foot. The human foot occurs but rarely. In the case of the TREMAILE arms it is no doubt intended to be covered with a *boot,* as the alternative blazon shews.

Argent, a fesse between three feet gules—TRAMAILL, co. Devon.

Argent, a fesse gules between three brogues of the second—TREMAYLE, co. Devon.

Azure, a human foot in base argent; on a canton gules a grappling iron or—BLAAUW.

The feet of birds and animals occur, but generally with a portion of the *leg,* q.v.

Fork, (fr. *fourche*). *Forks* of various shapes, and varying in the number of their prongs, are borne as charges, such as *pitch-fork, dung-fork,* and *hay-fork.* The *shake-fork* is a conventional charge, and will be found in its alphabetical order. The *forks* used for fishing, &c., have been noted already under *eel-spear.* There do not appear to be any special rules in depicting the various forks above named.

Argent, three dung-forks two and one, prongs in chief, sable—Worth-ington, Yorkshire.

Argent, three dung-forks gules—Sherley or Shorley.

Sable, three pitch-forks in pale argent—Pyke, co. Somerset.

Argent, three two-pronged forks sable, two upwards and one down-wards—Walley, Harl. MS. 1396.

Argent, three three-pronged forks gules—Chorley.

Argent, three five-pronged forks sable—Worthington.

Forked, (fr. *fourché*), is also an heraldic term applied to the cross, § 24, and to lions' *tails,* &c.

Founders' *closing-tongs, melting-pot,* and *furnace* are seen only in the crest of the Founders'
Company. An illustration of the *laver-pot* which occurs in the coat of

Founders' closing-tongs.

arms has been given under *ewer,* and the *candlestick* also in its order in the alphabet.

A fiery furnace proper, two arms of the last, [i.e. or] issuing from clouds on the sinister side of the first, [i.e. azure], vested of the last, holding in both hands a pair of closing-tongs sable, taking hold of the melting-pot in the furnace proper—Crest of the Founders' Company.

Founders' melting-pot and furnace.

A laver pot between two taper candlesticks or—The Founders' Company.

Fountain: this conventional device is supposed to represent a well or spring of water, and might generally be blazoned as a roundle barry wavy of six argent and azure. That this is so is evidenced from so many families of Wells bearing it. The family of Sykes also bear it in allusion to the old name of *sykes* for a well. Guillim also says that the six fountains given to the family of Stourton represent six springs, whereof the river Stour in Wiltshire hath its beginning.

Forest. See *Wood.*

Forest-bill: i.q. Wood-*bill.*

Formé and *formy.* See *Cross,* § 26.

Fort, *Fortress,* and *Fortification.* See *Castle.*

Fouine, i.e. *foine.* See *Weasel.*

Foudre, (fr.): in French arms is represented by a thunderbolt in the midst of lightning.

Argent, three roundles barry wavy of six argent and vert—THEMILTON.

Argent, a chevron sable, between three fountains—SYKES, Kirkella, co. York.

Argent, three fountains—WELLER.

Sable, a bend or, between six fountains proper—STOURTON.

Azure, three moor's heads couped argent on a bordure of the last three fountains proper—EDINGTON, Glasgow.

Argent, on a chevron sable three fountains—CASSHE.

THEMILTON.

Per fesse gules and argent; a pale counterchanged, thereon three fountains proper—LAVENDER, co. Herts.

Or, three bars wavy gules; on a canton argent a fountain azure—DRUMMOND, Innermay, Scotland.

Vert, a lion rampant argent within a bordure or, charged with nine fountains or wells proper—HOME, Whitfield, Scotland.

Or, on a pile engrailed sable, three crosslets of the first in base two fountains barry wavy of six argent and azure—HALIFAX, Bp. of Gloucester, 1781, afterwards S. Asaph, 1789–90.

Practically the *well* is sometimes mistaken for the *fountain*, but the former should properly be *masoned*, i.e. should shew the stone-work, while the heraldic *fountain* is supposed to represent the water in the well only. *Fontaine* with the French, however, is used for a fountain, i.e. masonry, with a jet of water.

Fox: occurs somewhat frequently as an heraldic charge. The *tod* is a local name; hence borne by the family of TODD.

Argent, two foxes salient counter salient in saltire, the sinister surmounted of the dexter gules—WILLIAMS, Wynnstay, co. Flint.

Ermine, on a fesse gules, a fox passant or—PROBY, Elton Hall.

Sable, on a fesse argent, between three helmets close a fox courant proper—KENNEDY.

Argent, three fox's heads couped gules—TODD.

Quarterly, first and fourth, argent, on a bend gules, three dolphins embowed or, second and third

WILLIAMS.

or, a chevron between three fox's heads erased gules—Edward Fox, Bp. of Hereford, 1535–38.

With the *fox* may be classed the *genet*, an animal somewhat resembling it, but considerably smaller, and usually grey spotted with black. It was highly valued on account of its skin, and is made to be the badge of an order of knighthood said, according to the legend, to have been instituted by Charles Martel, king of France, in the year 726. The chief instance known of its use is in the Plantagenet *badge* of a genet passing between two broom-trees (or *Plantæ genistæ*), given by Edward IV. to his illegitimate son, Arthur Plantagenet, the badge thus providing a double pun.

France: *Fleurs-de-lis* have long been the distinctive bearings of the kingdom of France, and it is to the almost constant wars between that country and our own that its frequent use in English armory is to be attributed.

Early arms of FRANCE. Later arms of FRANCE.

From the time of King Charles V., 1364-80, the royal insignia of France had but three fleurs-de-lis or. Before his time the escutcheon was *semé de lis*, which bearing was probably assumed by King Louis (Loys) VII., 1137-80, in allusion to his name.

The *Label of France* is a frequent expression occurring in old genealogical works; it may signify a label azure semé of fleur-de-lis gold, or charged with three fleurs-de-lis, or again, with three fleurs-de-lis upon each of the five points.

D'azure, semé le lis d'or—Ancient arms of FRANCE.

D'azure a trois fleurs-de-lis d'or—Later arms of FRANCE.

De France, au lambel de trois pendants d'argent—Ducs d'ORLEANS.

England, a label of five points azure, each charged with three fleurs-de-lis or—Edmund PLANTAGENET, [surnamed Crouchback, Earl of Lancaster, &c., second son of Hen. III]

Fret: a charge consisting of two narrow bendlets placed in saltire, and interlaced with a mascle. It has been supposed to represent the meshes of a fishing-net. Being borne by the

family of HARRINGTON it is found called a *Harrington's knot;*
and riddle-makers see a connection be-
tween the Herring-town and the net.
Whatever may be the origin, the term
fret, or rather *fretté,* occurs frequently in
the ancient rolls, but in many cases probably only a single *fret* is intended. When
two or more frets are borne in the same
arms they must be couped, unless each
occupies an entire quarter.

HARRINGTON.

Sable, a fret argent, charged with nine fleurs-de-lis gules—HARRINGTON
of Honington Sibble, co. Essex.

Sable, a fret or—HARRINGTON, Essex.

Ermine, a fret gules in chief a lion passant guardant sable—HUD-
DLESTON, Upwell Hall, Cambridge.

Gules, three lions rampant or; on a chief of the
second a fret of the first—JONES, co. Kent.

Or, a pale gules, in chief two frets and in base
another counterchanged—BOAK.

Du bon Hue le DESPENSIER . . . .

Fu la baniere esquartelée

De une noir bastoun sur blanc getté

E de vermeil jaune fretté.— Roll of Carlaverock.

DESPENCER.

Aymer de ST. AMONT, d'argent frette de sable ung chef de sable—Roll,
temp. HEN. III.

Sire Johan de HOORNE, de goules a une frette de veer—Roll, temp.
ED. II.

Hue le DE SPENSER quartele d'argent et de goules, ung bend de sable;
les quartres frette d'or en le goules—Roll, temp. HEN. III.

Sire Laurence de HAMELDENE de argent fretté de goules e les flures de
or e les nowe de la frette—Roll, temp. ED. II.

Monsire TRUSSELL le Cousin, port d'argent, fret gules, les joyntures
pomelles d'or—Roll, temp. ED. III.

Fourché : applied to a *cross,*
(§ 24); also to a lion's *tail.*

Fourmie, and *Fourmilière,* (fr.) :
ant and ant-hill.

Fourrures, (fr.) : *Furs,* q.v.

Fracted, broken. See *Fesse, Chevron,* and *downset* (*dancetty*).

Frame. See *Knitting-frame.*

Framed-saw. See *Saw.*

Franc-quartier. See *Canton;* also
Quarter.

Frasier. See *Strawberry.*

Fret : a name applied to the *wine-
piercer.*

Fretty, (fr. *fretté*) : is now understood to mean a continuous *fret*, and forms a pattern for diapering the field, or some ordinary. Very many instances are found, and sometimes the points of junction are ornamented, at others the fret itself is charged with roundles, &c. The fr. *treillissé* is only to be distinguished from the *fretté* from the mesh being smaller.

CAVE.

Azure, fretty argent—CAVE, Kent.

Azure, fretty of eight pieces raguly or—BROADHURST.

Argent, a cross azure, fretty or—VERDON, Warwick. [See also under *Cross*, § 3.]

Azure, fretty ermine—MELBORNE.

Sable, fretty or ; flory argent—STOCKWOOD.

Argent, fretty gules ; on the points thereof fleurs-de-lis or—HAMELDEN.

Argent, fretty gules ; on each joint a bezant ; all within a bordure azure —TRUSSELL.

VERDON.

Fretted, or *interlaced*, (fr. *entrelacé*) : is also sometimes used when three or more charges are so placed that a portion of one overlaps and is itself overlapped by an adjoining one. An example will be seen of three *fish fretted in triangle*, under *salmon*, and of fillets *interlaced* under *cross triparted*, § 8, and of chevrons under *braced*. All *knots* are more or less *interlaced*, and *annulets, serpents*, &c., when there are more than two, are generally so. Even ordinaries are sometimes so represented.

Azure, eight arrows interlaced in bend dexter and sinister argent, headed and feathered or, fretting a bowstring in fesse of the second—Town of SHEFFIELD.

Argent, a fesse and chevron interlaced sable—KEMPSING, Kent.

Fringed, (fr. *frangé*) : edged with fringe, said of flags and of other charges, e.g. the pall of the see of Canterbury.

Frighted : applied by some to a horse rearing upon his hind-legs, the same as *forccné*.

Fronde, (fr.) : a sling.

Frogs, *toads, tadpoles,* and *powets* are all named, though rarely in English heraldry. They have not been observed in French examples.

Or, a chevron between three frogs displayed gules— TREVONECK, Sancreed, Cornwall.

Ermine, a fesse between three toads sable— REPLEY.

Argent, three toads erect sable—BOTREAUX, Cockermouth, Cumberland.

Argent, a cheval gules between three tadpoles haurient sable—RUSSELL [quartered by RAMSAY].

Argent, a cheveron gules between three powets haurient sable—RUSSELL [quartered by RAMSAY].

BOTREAUX.

Fruits and *fruit-trees* of various kinds are found as charges, as the synopsis shews. The *apple,* perhaps, is the most frequently used, but it will be seen the *pear* and the *plum,* the *fig* and the *quince,* the *strawberry* and the *cherry,* the *pineapple,* the *orange,* and the *pomegranate,* are all found; and to these may be added the *hazel-nut* and the *walnut,* as well as one or two others. As a rule the fruit should be drawn in its natural position, i.e. pendent. When *fruits* are named without any description, probably apples are intended. The term *fruited* or *fructed* (fr. *fruité*) is often used, and applied not only to ordinary fruit-trees, but to the *oak, almond, pine, thorn, cotton-tree,* &c.

Argent, a tree eradicated vert fructed gules—Sir Humfrey ESTURE [elsewhere blazoned an apple-tree].

Gules, three fruits in fesse argent, in chief two cinquefoils or—COL-WYKE.

An oak-branch slipped vert fructed or—BOBART, Brunswick.

Furs, (fr. *fourrures,* also *pannes*): there are several varieties. *Ermine, ermines, erminites,* and *erminois* have already been noted

---

Fructed, (fr. *fruité*): bearing fruit, but generally used when fruit is of another tincture.

Fruttle. See *Basket.*

Fumant: smoking, e.g. of a *brick-kiln.*

Fulgent: with shining rays.

Furieux, (fr.) : of a bull, &c., when enraged.

Furnace. See *Founders' Furnace.*

Furnished: a horse completely caparisoned is so termed.

with *pean* under *Ermine*. *Vair*, and an irregular fur named *Potent counter potent*, will be described in their alphabetical order. All these are conventional representations of skins of divers animals, or portions of the skins sewn together in divers forms. Being mixed tinctures, that is, consisting both of metal (although not considered as such) and colour, they may be placed upon either, and conversely metal and colour may equally be placed upon them.

The furs recognised in French heraldry are *hermine* proper, *contre hermine* (which is the reverse), and *hermines* of different tinctures (which are described), and the *vair*. The *pannes* is rather a general name for mixed fur; perhaps in its origin having a reference to the lining of mantles, &c.

Fusil, (fr. *fuseau* and *fusée*), in its natural form and sense, is a spindle belonging to a distaff; but in its conventional form it is an elongated lozenge, and very often the one charge is mistaken for the other. In different arms they are differently drawn, and in the same arms at different dates they are variously represented. In an ordinary way the conventional fusil is the one to be drawn. In French armorial blazon the name *fuseau* seems to be reserved for the true spindle, while the *fusée* is used for the conventional form. In its primitive form, as in the arms of BADLAND, afterwards assumed by HOBY, it is represented as in the margin (fig. 1). The family of TREFUSIS bear another variety of the fusil (fig. 2); but the usual term for such is *spindle*, q v.; while the heraldic fusil is drawn as fig. 3. The fusil does not appear in the rolls of arms, so far as has been observed, before the time of Edward III.

Fusils.

Monsire de MONTAGUE, Count de Sarum, port d'argent trois fusilles gules—Roll, temp. ED. III.

Monsire DAWBENEY, port de sable a une fes fusile de v points d'argent —*Ibid.*

Argent, three fusils (or spindles) in fesse gules threaded or—HOBY, Bisham.

Argent, a chevron between three ancient fusils (or wharrow spindles) sable—TREFUSIS.

Compared with the *lozenge* and the *mascle* the fusil should always be represented narrower in proportion to its height, but, whatever rules may be laid down, they are seldom adhered to, as the disposition of the fusils and shape of the shield oblige modifications.

Fusils are most frequently borne conjoined in the form of a *fesse*, a *bend*, a *cross*, or of a *saltire*.

The *bend fusil* should consist of about five entire fusils, and two halves, each individual fusil being placed bend-sinister-wise. The *fesse fusil* should have five perfect fusils, and the cross, as already pointed out (see *cross*, § 8), should consist of nine, five of which should be entire. But, as will be observed, an ordinary is often described "of so many fusils."

In the *fesse* the fusils are naturally all upright; in the *bend* they are drawn at right angles to the diagonal line passing across the shield; in a *cross* of fusils all the fusils are placed upright; while in a *saltire* they diverge from the fesse point.

Or, five fusils conjoined in fesse azure—PEN-NINGTON, Muncaster, Cumb.

Further, there is much inconsistency in nomenclature. A fesse, bend, or cross *fusil*, is used instead of a fesse, bend, or

PENNINGTON.

cross, composed *of so many fusils: fusilly* also is often written with the same meaning, but, as pointed out under *cross*, § 8, it is incorrect.

Fusilly (fr. *fusilé*) is a well-defined term applied to the field, and the two tinctures must be named, as in the arms of PATTEN given below. The application of this term to a series of fusils (with one tincture only named) is consequently entirely wrong, but custom has so completely sanctioned it (no doubt through carelessness in the first instance) that the error has become almost the rule.

Fuseau, (fr.) : *spindle*. See *Fusil*.

Fusée, (fr.) : *fusil*.

Fusté, (fr.) : of the handle of a weapon, or trunk of a tree, when of another tincture.

Futé of shafts of *arrows* q.v.

Monsire William de MONTAGUE, Counte de
Sarum, port d'argent trois fuselles gules—Roll,
temp. ED. III.

Monsire Edward de MONTAGUE, port d'ermine
a trois fuselles de gules—*Ibid.*

Argent, four fusils in fesse azure—PLOMPTON.

Argent, a fesse fusily gules—NEWMARCH.

Ermine, five fusils in fesse gules pierced—
HUTTON.

MONTAGUE.

Or, on a fesse gules, five fusils argent; in chief
three mascles azure, in base a fret of the second;
all within a bordure of the fourth, entoyre of bezants—Thomas BURGESS, Bp. of S. David's, 1803;
of Salisbury, 1825–37.

Argent, a fesse of two fusils conjoined gules—
CHAMPENEY, co. Devon.

Argent, within a bordure sable, three fusils in
fesse gules—James MONTAGUE, Bp. of Bath and
Wells, 1608; then of Winchester, 1616–18.

BURGESS.

Per chevron or and azure, a bar fusily of the
first, each fusil being charged with an escallop
gules; in chief two fleurs-de-lis of the last—EDGAR.

Argent, two bars fusilly gules—Rauf RAUL.

Vert, a bend fusil or—KNIGHT.

Argent, three fusils in bend gules—MAL-
MAYNES.

Argent, a bend of four fusils conjoined gules—
BRADESTONE.

Argent, four fusils in cross sable—Sir Thomas
BANESTER, K.G.

Argent, five fusils in cross—ARCHARD.

KNIGHT.

Vert, a saltire fusilly or—FRANKE.

Argent, four bars gules; on a canton ermine
as many fusils in bend of the second—WALEYS,
Dorset.

Argent, six fusils in pale sable—DANIELS.

Gules, five fusils in fesse quartered argent and
sable, between six crosses flowered of the second
—BOALER.

Fusilly, ermine and sable — PATTEN, Stoke
Newington, Middlesex.

Fusilly, gules and or—CRONE.

PATTEN.

No case has been noticed in which when the term *fusilly* is applied to an ordinary two *tinctures* are named; as all the examples appear with one tincture, the term *fusilly* must be read '*of so many fusils.*'

Fylfot, [suggested to be a corruption of A.-S. *fier-fóte* (for *fyðer fote*) four-footed, in allusion to the four limbs]: an ancient figure to which different mystic meanings have been applied. All that can be said as to the occurrence in England is that it possibly was introduced from the East as a novel device; for a similar form is said to have been known in India and China long before the Christian era. It is called in the Sanskrit 'swastica,' and is found used as a symbol by the Buddhists.

Fylfot.

It is curious that the same kind of device appears in the Catacombs, and at the same time it is found on a coin of Ethelred, King of Northumbria, in the ninth century. It is probably similar to the ornament which is mentioned by Anastasius as embroidered on sacred vestments during the eighth and ninth centuries in Rome under the name of *gammadion*, which was so-called on account of the shape resembling four Greek capital Gammas united at the base. There is no reason to suppose that all these are derived from a common source, as such a device as this would readily suggest itself, just as the Greek pattern is frequent on work of all ages. It was on account of its supposed mystical meaning perhaps introduced into mediæval vestments, belts, &c.; and though several instances of this use are found on brasses, only one instance occurs on coats of arms, namely, in those of CHAMBERLAYNE.

One instance only of the name also has been observed in any MS. or book anterior to the eighteenth century, namely in the directions given by Francis Frosmere, *c.* 1480, apparently to designate his monogram F. F. (See MS. Lansdowne, No. 874.)

Argent, a chevron between three fylfots gules—Leonard CHAMBERLAYNE, Yorkshire [so drawn in MS. Harleian, 1394, pt. 129, fol. 9 = fol. 349 of MS.]
[N.B. In Harl. MS. 1415 this coat seems to be tricked with what are meant distinctly for three escallops.]

Gad : A plate of steel for hammering iron upon, borne by the London Company of IRONMONGERS, and represented as in the margin.

Argent, on a chevron gules three swivels or (the middle one paleways, the other two with the line of the chevron) between three steel gads azure—IRONMONGERS' Company [Incorp. 1463, but arms granted 1435, and confirmed 1530].

Gad.

Another form is borne by a Lincolnshire family, and has been blazoned sometimes as a demi-lozenge.

Argent, a chevron between three steel-gads sable—BELLESBY, or BILLESBY, of Bylesby.

Gad.

As said before under *delf*, there is great laxity in the blazon of charges of this shape, and the same arms are variously described.

Argent, three gads [or billets, or delves] sable—Richard GADDES.
Ermine, on a chief gules two gads [or billets] engrailed or—WATTYS.
Or, a fesse wavy between three gads [or delves] sable—STANFORD.

Gad-fly, more frequently blazoned *Gad-bee*, is the Brimsey, or Horse-fly.

Sable, three gad-bees volant en arrière argent—BUNNINGHILL.

Sable, three gad-bees volant argent—GARLINGTON, co. Hereford.

Vert, three gad-bees argent—BODRIGAN.

Argent, two bars and in chief three gad-flies sable—FLEMING, co. Lancaster.

Gad fly.

Per pale azure and gules, three gad-flies or—DORRE.

Argent, a saltire between four gad-bees sable—TRAVERS.

Gambe, or *Jambe :* the leg of a beast. If couped or erased at the middle joint it is not a jambe but a *paw,* as in the example given under *Seal,* q.v.

Or, a lion's jambe inverted and erased in bend gules—POWIS.

Gules, three lion's jambes erased and inverted argent—NEWDIGATE, Surrey.

Azure, a lion's gamb erased in fesse between two chains or; on a canton of the last a rose gules barbed and seeded proper—Brian DUPPA, Bp. of Chichester, 1638 ; of Salisbury, 1641 ; of Winchester, 1660–62.

G : in *tricking* is the proper abbreviation for the word *gules.*

Argent, a lion's gamb erased in bend sinister, claw in base, sable; a canton gules—
RIGAUD.

Azure, two lion's gambs issuing out of the
base of the escutcheon, and forming a chevron
argent; between the gambs a fleur de lis or—
CHIPPENDALE, Leicester.

Azure, on a bend between six mullets or, a
bear's gamb couped at the knee sable—BRE-
TOBON.

Gules, on a bend argent three lion's paws
erased azure—SPARMAN, Suffolk.

POWIS.

Sable, a maunch argent within a bordure or, charged with eight pairs
of lion's paws saltireways erased gules—Philip WHARTON.

Monsire Thomas de VERDON, port sable, a une lyon dargent; en le
paw de lyon une rouke de gules—Roll, temp. ED. III.

Garbe, or *Garb,* (fr *gerbe*): a wheat-sheaf. When a sheaf
of any other grain is borne the name of the grain must be expressed; e.g. the *barley-garbs* in the Company of BREWERS
(see *Tun,* and examples under *Wheat*).

From early times they are found of various tinctures. When
the stalks are of one tincture and the ears of another, the term
eared must be used with reference to the
latter.

Azure, a garbe or [sometimes banded gules is
added]– GROSVENOR, Cheshire.

Le conte de CHESTER, d'azur a trois garbes
d'or—Roll, temp. HEN. III.

Gilbert de SEGRAVE, noir trois gerbes d'argent
—*Ibid.*

Sire Johan COMYN, d'argent crussile de goules
a iij garbes de goulys—Roll, temp. ED. II.

GROSVENOR.

Gai, (fr.): of a horse without harness careering.

Galley. See *Lymphad.*

Gallows: *Man* hanging on.

Galthrap, i.q. *Caltrap.*

Gamecock. See *Cock.*

Gammadion. See *Fylfot.*

Gannapie. See *Cormorant.*

Gar-buckle. See *Buckle.*

Gardant, (fr. *guardant*): of beasts,
&c., having the face turned towards the spectator. See under
Lion.

Garde-visure: the visor of an
helmet.

Gardener. See *Man*

Azure, a chevron between three garbes or—Sir Christopher Hatton [Chancellor, temp. Elizabeth].

Garlick: this singular device is borne on one coat of arms, for the sake of the name.

Argent, three heads of garlick proper—Garlick.

Garter: the garter, as represented around the escutcheon of a *knight* of that order, but usually without the motto. It occurs as a charge in the official insignia of the king of arms so named. An ordinary garter also occurs, as does the *demi-garter*, or lower half of the same, which is called 'the perclose of a demi-garter, buckled and nowed.'

Azure, a boar's head couped, over which a knot within a garter all or —Newton.

Per fesse gules and azure, a man's garter fessewise argent, fimbriated and buckled in the centre or, between in chief a rosary and in base three bells of the last—Beadnell.

Sable, a man's garter buckled in orle . . . . between three square buckles, tongues erect or—Bockland.

Argent, three demi-garters azure, buckled and garnished or—Peter Narborne, Granted by King Henry VII.

Garter, or *Gartier*, is occasionally applied to the bendlet.

Vairy, a garter [i.e. bendlet] gules—Hebmines, France.

Garter, King of Arms. See *Heralds.*
Garter, Order of the. See *Knighthood.*

Gate, (old pronunciation, *yate*): a charge rarely borne, and then generally for the sake of the name.

Argent, a fesse between three gates sable — Yates, Lyford, Berks.

Per pale crenelly argent and sable, three field-gates counterchanged—Yate, Buckland, Berks.

Per fesse crenelly sable and argent, three five-barred gates counter-changed—Yeates, Bristol.

Gate.

Gules, a gate between three goats passant or—Portnowe.

Garnished, (fr. *garni*): ornamented; as an esquire's helmet argent, garnished or; or of a sword when the hilt and pomel are of another tincture.

Garland: See *Chaplet.*

Garvin. See *Herring.*

Gastelles, (fr. *gâteaux*). See *Tourteaux.*

Gaze, *Stag at.* See under *Deer.*

Gateway: distinguished from the field-gate is the *gateway*, which sometimes occurs, called also *port* or *portal*. See *Castle*.

Sable, a gateway between two towers argent, standing on the upper part of a base, barry of four as the second and azure—Richard Rawson [Alderman of London, 1746].

Azure, a double-leaved gate, triple towered on an ascent of five degrees [steps] flanked by two towers, all argent; the towers arch-roofed and masoned sable—Sanquhan, Scotland.

Gauntlet: a glove of mail. The ancient form is shewn in the margin, but it is more often represented shewing the fingers. In blazon it is necessary to distinguish be-tween the dexter and sinister; that given in the margin being a *sinister gauntlet*. Gauntlets some-times occur with separate fingers, and thus they may perhaps be represented as in the arms of Vane. An arm *vambraced* is not in general understood to have a gauntlet unless it be specially mentioned.

Gauntlet.

Azure, three dexter gauntlets or—Vane, Rasell, Kent.

Azure, three sinister gauntlets or—Vane, Lord Bernard.

Argent, two bars azure, on a canton gules a gauntlet grasping a broken sword proper, hilt and pomel gold—Stamford, Derby.

Azure, a lion passant argent goutté d'or between three dexter gauntlets of the second — Conway, Callis.

Vane.

Gules, three dexter gauntlets pendent azure; a canton chequy or and azure—Denvers, Norfolk.

Sable, three pairs of gauntlets clipping argent—Purefoy, Lancaster.

Geai, (fr.): a jay. See *Magpie*.

Ged, (a fish). See *Lucy*.

Gemel, written also *gymile* and *gimyle* = double, e.g. a *bar*, (q.v.). A *collar gemel* = two narrow col-lars.

Gemeus, (written also gymiles) = *bars gemel*.

Gemmed: used of a *ring*.

Gem-ring. See *Ring*.

Genet. (1) See *Fox*; (2) See Planta-genista under *Broom*.

Genuant: kneeling.

George, The: a badge represent-ing the figure of S. George on horseback, attached to the collar of the *Order of the Garter*. See *Knights*.

George, Cross of S. See *Cross*, § 1.

Gilly-flower, *Gillofer,* or *July-flower,* (fr. *Girofre*): this flower, resembling a pink or carnation in form, and of a bright crimson colour, occurs more frequently than might have been expected. The gilly-flowers so blazoned in the insignia of OUR LADY'S INN, London, were no doubt originally *lilies.* See *Lilypot.*

Gilly-flower.

Argent, three gilly-flowers slipped proper—JORNEY.

Or, on a chevron azure, between three gilly-flowers gules, slipped vert, a maiden's head of the first ducally crowned of the third; on a chief sable a hawk's lure double-stringed or, between two falcons argent, beaked and legged of the last—JEWEL, Bp. of Salisbury, 1560–71.

Argent, on a bend argent three gilly-flowers proper—WADE, co. York.

Argent, a chevron gules between three gilli-flowers azure—BOTHELL.

Argent, a chevron sable between three gilli-flowers proper [elsewhere pinks]—Thos. PACE, alias SKEVINGTON, Bp. of Bangor, 1510–33.

Borne also by the families of SPURLING, DE LISLE, LISTON, LIVINGSTON and SEMPLE.

Glaziers' Nippers: called also *grazier, grater,* and *grosing-iron:* a tool used by glaziers, and borne by their company. It occurs also in other arms, and is figured as in the margin.

Figures of the Glazier's nippers, or Grosing-iron.

Argent, two grosing-irons in saltire sable, between four closing-nails of the last; on a chief gules a lion passant guardant or—GLAZIERS' Company [incorporated 1637].

Argent, two grazier's [elsewhere glazier's nippers, grosing-irons, and also spokeshaves], in saltire sable between four pears gules, in a bordure engrailed of the second—KELLOWAY, co. Wilts.

Gules, two glazier's nippers in saltire between four lions rampant argent—STERLING.

Ermine, three glazier's cripping-irons in saltire gules—TITHERLY.

Gerattie: ancient word for *semé.*

Qorbo, (fr.): garbe.

Gimbal rings, or *Gimmal rings,* may be double, triple, or of a greater number. A triple gimbal ring consists of three *annulets* interlaced in triangle.

Geronny. See *Gyronny.*

Gimlet. See *Awl,* also *Winepiercer.*

Girfauk, i.e. *Ger-falcon.* See *Falcon.*

Giron. See *Gyron.*

Gironné, (fr.): *gyronny.*

Givre. See *Adder.*

Glove: the glove occurs in early arms, and is supposed to be meant for the *Falconer's*, or *Hawking-glove*, as in many later arms it is referred to as such.

Sire William de WAUNCY, de goules a vi gaunz de argent —Roll, temp. ED. II.

Argent, a bend wavy sable, an arm issuing from the sinister of the last, on a glove of the first a hawk or —HAWKERIDGE, co. Devon.

Sable, three gloves in pale argent—VANCEY, Northants.

Sable, three falconer's sinister gloves pendent argent tasselled or—BARTLETT, Sussex.

Hawking-glove.

Sable, three dexter hawking-gloves (fingers downwards?) tassels pendent, argent—VAUNEYE.

Goat, (old fr. *chever*, fr. *chèvre*), is not infrequent as a charge. It may be *statant, passant, clymant* (which is sometimes used instead of *salient*, or *rampant*), and where there are two, frequently *combatant*. It may be described as *bearded, crined, unguled, attired* (as to its horns), and even *armed* is sometimes so used. French heralds also use the word *bouc*.

Gules, a goat statant argent, armed and crined or, between three saltires of the last [elsewhere attired or]—BAKER.

Azure, on a mount in base vert, a goat statant argent, armed, hoofed, and bearded or—Burgh of HADDINGTON, Scotland.

Sable, a goat passant argent, attired, bearded, and unguled or—CARNSEW.

Gules, a goat climant argent, attired or—BARWELL.

BAKER.

Gules, a goat salient argent, armed or—BENSTED.

Argent, a goat rampant sable, the head and part of the neck of the first armed vert—DE BUCKTON.

Azure, two goats salient, combatant argent—KIDD.

Sable, two goats statant affrontant or—Quartering in the insignia of the LEATHERSELLERS' Company, granted 1505.

Argent, a fesse gules between three goats passant sable, bearded, unguled, and armed or—HANDLEY, Newark.

Gules, a fesse between eleven goats argent, four, four, two and one—DREELAND, Kent.

Gland, (fr.): *acorn.*
Gletver leaf. See *Leaves.*

Gliding: used sometimes of *Serpents.*

Goats' heads are also frequently found employed as charges.

Sire Richard de CATESBURI, de goules a une fesse verree de or e de azure a iij testes de chevers de argent—Roll, temp. ED. II.

Ermine, a goat's head erased gules attired or— GOTLEY.

Gules, a goat's head couped or—BALLENDEN.

Azure, a chevron or between three goat's heads erased argent, attired of the second—CORDWAINERS' Company [incorporated 1410].

Quarterly gules and ermine; in first quarter a

MORTON.

goat's head erased armed or—John MORTON, Bp. of Ely, 1486—1500 (MS. Lambeth, 555). [Similar arms are ascribed to MORTON, Bp. of Chester, 1616; and of Ely, 1619.]

The *Assyrian* or *Indian Goat* is nearly like the common goat, but has horns more curved, and ears like a talbot's.   Two such goats *argent, attired,* and *unguled or,* support the escutcheon of the HABERDASHERS of London.

There are two monstrosities derived from the goat found in heraldic bearings, viz. the *lion-goat* and the *deer-goat.*   Only the heads, however, appear.

Or, three lion-goat's heads proper—BLOORE.
Vert, a deer-goat's head argent—ABELADAME.

Gobony, *goboné, gobonated,* and *compony* (fr. *componé*) : said of an ordinary composed of small squares of two tinctures alternately in one row.   If there be two rows it is called *counter compony* (or *compony counter compony*), but if more, it comes under the term *checquy.*   A bordure compony should consist of sixteen pieces or gobbits gyronwise.

The name *gobony* is a corruption of some word (possibly even of *compony*), but Gibbon fancifully suggests it is "a word used in carving, as to Gobon a lamprey, or the like, into seven or eight pieces."   It is certainly an ancient term, and found, as will be seen, in early rolls of arms.

MI MIR BILEBATID de Trie dor a une bende gobone dargent et dazure— Roll, temp. HEN. III. (Harl. MS. 6589).

Globe.   See *Sphere.*   **Glory.**   See *Nimbus* and *Sun.*

Sire Henri de LEYBURNE, de azure a vi lioncels de argent a un label goboune de or e de goules—Roll, temp. ED. II.

Sire Nicholas de GREY, les armes de Grey a un baston goboune de or e de goules—*Ibid.*

Sire Henri de BEUMOND, de azure flurette de or a un lion rampaund de or e un baston goboune de argent e de goules. *Ibid.*

Monsire de BEAUMONT, port d'asure a un lyon rampant d'or floret d'or: une baston goboune d'or et de gules de six peeces—Roll, temp. ED. III.

Monsire John de SUTTON, port les armes de Percy [i.e. or, une lyon rampant d'asure] a une baston gobonnie d'argent et de gules—*Ibid.*

Or, a bend compony, sable and ermine [elsewhere compony ermines and ermine]— STYLE.

Argent, a fesse counter compony, or and gules— HILLARY, Norfolk.

STYLE.

Argent, a fesse gobonated argent and gules between three owls of the second—HARWORTH, Norfolk.

Ermine, four bars gemel, compony or and sable —HORWOOD.

Argent, on a bend sable three bars [otherwise three gobbons] of the first, each charged with a saltorel gules—WORSYCKE.

Gules, a saltire argent; a label gobony argent and azure — NEVILLE, Earl of Salisbury, *c.* 1450.

NEVILLE.

Gules, a saltier argent, and a label compony of the second and azure— NEVILLE, Bp. of Exeter, 1456; afterwards Abp. of York, 1465-76.

Quarterly, France and England within a bordure gobony argent and azure—S. JOHN'S COLLEGE, Cambridge [Founded 1508].

Golpe: an heraldic term used for the *roundle,* when it is of the tincture of *purpure.* It is supposed to be derived from *golpa,* an old Spanish word for a wound. It is scarcely ever used.

Or, a chevron gules between three golpes—GLENHAM.

Goose, (fr. *oie,* lat. *anser*): geese are rarely represented in coats of arms, and beyond the *Barnacle* goose already noticed, it is not easy to identify any species meant by the terms used.

Gold. See *Or.*
Golden fleece. See *Toison.*

Goldfinch. See *Finch.*
Gonfanon· See *Flag.*

The Gray-lag, or *Wild-goose*, is considered the progenitor of our farm-yard goose. The *Magellan* is possibly Mergellan, i.e. the *Mergellus,* and if so, allied to the *Smew* rather than the goose proper. The gander (fr. *jars*) occurs in French arms.

Three geese passant close—WALTON, Bp. of Chester, 1660–61.

Quarterly, indented gules and vert, a goose rising argent—LOVENHAM.

Gules, a wild-goose close, argent, a crescent for difference—LANGFORD, Alington.

Or, on a mount vert, a Magellan-goose sable, head argent—ASHFIELD.

De sable, à trois jars d'argent becqués et membrés de gueules—LESQUIN, Bretagne.

Bp. WALTON.

Gore : a portion of the shield obliterated, so to speak, as represented in the margin ; it may be either on the dexter or sinister side. If the former, it is supposed to be an honourable charge, but if the latter, and when tenné, it is an abatement for cowardice in battle ; but though writers descant upon their use, they give no examples, probably because there are none. Guillim calls it "one of the whimsical abatements." See also *Gusset.*

The Gore.

Gourd : in only one coat of arms does this fruit occur.

Argent, three gourds or, stalks upwards—STENKLE.

Gouttes, (fr. *larmes*), drops : i.e. a figure of an elongated pear-shape, with the sides wavy. They are seldom, if ever, used singly, and generally the number is enumerated.

Per chevron argent and sable, three gouttes counterchanged—CROSBY.

Argent, a fesse dancetty or between three gouttys of the last—INGLEDEN.

Azure, on a saltire argent five gouttys gules—GOOSELIN (also GOVOR).

Gules, a fesse between six gouttys or—WYKE.

Barry of six, sable and ermine, nine gouttes argent, three, three, and three—BRADWARDINE.

Argent, fifteen gouttes gules [de sang], five, four, three, two, one—LEMMING, Essex.

Argent, a saltire gules between twelve gouttes sable—KERCEY.

In the case of a *lion* with a *goutte de sang,* the blazon of *vulned* seems to be more properly used. At the same time there are many cases of lions represented with *gouttes d'or,* &c.

Monsire HAMLYN, port gules une lyon d'or goute sable—Roll, temp. ED. III.

Argent, on a lion rampant sable a goutte d'or streaming at the shoulder —LUDLOW.

Azure, on a lion rampant argent gouttes de sang—BERESFORD.

Azure, on a lion rampant argent gouttes purpure—FOSTER, Essex.

The more frequent form is *gutté, or gutty, goutty, gouté* (that is, *semé* of an indefinite number of drops. They may be of various tinctures, and in English heraldry a distinct term is used for each, though this was probably of late introduction.

When argent, *gutté d'eau :* representing drops of water.

When or, *gutté d'or* or *auré :* representing drops of gold.

When azure, *gutté de larmes :* representing tears.

When sable, *gutté de poix :* representing drops of pitch.

When gules, *gutté de sang :* representing drops of blood.

When vert, *gutté d'huile,* or *d'olive :* representing drops of oil.

WINTERBOTTOM.

Azure, gutté d'eau—WINTERBOTTOM[Lord Mayor of London, 1752].

Argent, a lion rampant sable gouttée d'eau— MORTIMER, Vamouth, Scotland.

Barry of six ermine and sable, gutty d'eau— Thomas BRADWARDINE, Abp. of Canterbury, 1349. [But this is blazoned in the Lambeth MS. as barry of six ermine and ermines.]

Monsire John HALOU [HANLOW], port d'argent une lyon rampant d'azure goutte d'or—Roll, temp. ED. III.

Argent, on a talbot passant sable gouttes d'or—SHIRINGTON.

Sable, goutty de larmes, a lion rampant argent—CHANTRY.

Argent, goutty de poix and a lion rampant sable—Jake de la PLANCE, Roll, temp. ED. I. [Harl. MS. 6137].

Gordian knot. See *Cords.*

Gorge, (fr.): the neck. Leigh, however, uses this term for a water-bouget.

Gorged. See *Collar.*

Gorgé, (fr.) : is used when the neck is of a different tincture, e.g. of a *Peacock* (not to be confused with *gorged*).

Gorget. See *Helmet.*

Argent, goutty de poix, a chief nebuly gules—ROYDENHALL.

Gules, a bend or guttée de poix, between two mullets argent pierced of the field—See and City of BANGOR.

Sable, guttée d'eau three roses—John STILL, Bp. of Bath and Wells, 1593—1608.

Argent, gutty de sang, two darts points upwards gules feathered of the first piercing a heart of the second—YEOMAN.

In modern French blazon the term *larmes* is used for *gouttes*, and *semé de larmes* for *gouttée*. The tincture is always given, though *larmes d'argent* seems to be the most frequent.

D'argent, semé de larmes de sable—POILLOT, Ile de France.

When the *goutte* is reversed the term *icicle* is used by heraldic writers, that is, the charge is of the same shape, but the thicker portion is upwards, and the point downwards. Some heralds, however, call these figures *Clubs*, others *Gouttes reversed*, and others *Locks of hair*. The bearing seems to be confined to branches of one family.

HARBOTTLE.

Azure, three icicles bendwise in bend sinister or—HARBOTTLE, Brecon.

Azure, three locks of hair in bend or—HARBOTTLE.

Grain-tree: a tree, the berries of which are used in the process of dying.

Upon a wreath argent and sable, three sprigs of grain-tree erect vert, fructed gules—Crest of the DYERS' Company.

Grain-tree.

Grappling-iron, or *Grapnel*, (fr. *grappin*): an instrument used in naval or army engagements, and is distinct from the *anchor*. As the number of *flukes* varies it should be noticed. Some grappling-irons have double rings.

Argent, two grappling-irons in saltire sable, between four pears gules—STOFORD, Devon.

Grappling Iron.

Azure, a chevron or between three grappling-irons, each of as many points and double-ringed argent—STEWYNE [Harl. MS. 1386]

Grass is always represented in *tufts ;* also the old botanical terms of *spires* and *piles* applied to grass are employed in one example of blazon.

Azure, three pillars argent ; out of each a tuft of grass or—Boscoe.

Argent, three tufts of grass vert—Tylflmy, on York

Gules, three tufts of grass or—Sykes.

Argent, a fleur-de-lis, on the top three grass spires, each containing seven piles gules—Bernheim.

The term *graminy* is also found, which signifies made of grass, and is applied to the *chaplet,* under which an example is given.

Grasshopper, (fr. *sauterelle*) : is only occasionally found on coats of arms :—

Gules, on a bend engrailed argent a grasshopper sable—Louis, Colyton House, Devon.

Argent, three ravens sable between two bars dancetty gules ; in chief a griffin segreant between two grasshoppers of the second—Griffiths.

Argent, a chevron sable three grasshoppers proper [vert]—Woodward Kent.

D'azur, à une sauterelle d'argent, accompagnée de trois coquilles d'or —Moulins, Normandy.

Gridiron : this device is represented as in the margin, but is rarely borne. In the first of the three instances named below it has been chosen for the device of the Company of Girdlers (in whose arms the grid-iron is figured somewhat differently from the ordinary shape). The reason of the Company bearing this device was no doubt that S. Laurence was

Gridiron.

Goshawk. See *Falcon.*

Gothic work. See *Church.*

Goules. See *Gules.*

Gournet, i.q. Gurnet.

Gousset, (fr.) : *Gusset.*

Gradient : walking, e.g. of the *tortoise.*

Grady. See *Cross,* § 15, *Degraded* and *Embattled.*

Graft. See *Gusset.*

Graminy : used of a *Chaplet* made of grass.

Granada, Apple of. See *Pomegranate.*

Grapes. See *Vine.*

Grappe de raisin, (fr.) : a bunch of grapes.

Grapples. See *Cramp.*

Grater. See *Glazier's nippers.*

Gray. See *Badger.*

their patron saint. Sir Thomas Scott may
have been a member of the Company.

Per fesse azure and or, a pale counterchanged ;
three gridirons of the last, the handles in chief—
GIRDLERS' Company [arms granted, 1454].

Argent, a chevron between three gridirons
erect handles downwards sable—LAURENCE.

Argent, a chevron between three gridirons
dexter bendwise, handles upward sable — Sir
Thomas Scott [Lord Mayor of London, 1458].

Company of GIRDLERS.

Griffin, or *Gryphon*, (fr. *griffon*) : the Griffin is the most
frequently represented of the imaginary animals introduced into
coats of arms. Although variously drawn, the great principle
is that it is a compound of the *Lion* and the *Eagle*. The lower
part of its body, with the tail and the hind-legs, belong to the
lion ; the head and the fore-part, with the legs and talons, to
those of the eagle, but the head retains the ears of the lion.
It has large wings, which also closely resemble those of the
eagle. Its ordinary positions are *rampant segreant* (generally
blazoned segreant only), and *passant segreant*.

It may be represented as without wings, and then with rays or
spikes of gold proceeding from several parts
of its body. Sometimes it has two long
straight horns. The term *Alce* is given,
as if used by writers for a kind of griffin, but
no example can be quoted.

Azure, a griffin segreant or—READ, Herts.

Gules, a griffin segreant, or—RIVERS, Earl of
Devon.

The representation on the shield of READ
is, according to the mode of drawing the

READ.

Grazier. See *Glazier's nippers.*

Greaves : armour-plates for the
leg ; seldom used as it is implied
by the term 'a leg in armour.'

Grelier, (fr.) : a kind of hunting-
horn.

Grelot, (fr.) : the round bell on
collars of dogs, mules, &c., and
sometimes used for the *grillet* on
the feet of *falcons*, q.v.

Grey. See *Colour.*

Greyhound. See *Dog.*

griffin, sometimes seen, but the example taken from the supporters to the arms of Alexander ANNAND
of Elton is the more usual way of drawing
the animal.

Griffins' heads are also represented in
some coats. They are readily distinguishable
from the eagles' heads by the presence of
the ears.

ANNAND.

Argent, a griffin segreant gules, beaked and
legged or—CATERALL and GRIMSHAW, Lancashire.

Sire Geffrey fitz WYTHE, de azure a iij grifons
de or—Roll, temp. ED. II.

Sire Robert de BRENTE, de goules a un griffoun de argent—*Ibid.*

Sire Rauf de CORT' de goules a un griffoun de or—*Ibid.*

Monsire John GRIFFEN, sable a une griffin argent beke et peds or—Roll,
temp. ED. III.

Argent, a griffin segreant, coward sable—GODFREY.

Azure, a griffin segreant volant or, supporting an oak-branch vert,
acorned of the second—REDE.

Vert, a griffin segreant or, beaked, legged, and ducally gorged argent—
COLLINS, Kent.

Or, a gryphon segreant sable, in chief two mullets of six points gules,
pierced of the field—Nelson Smith MORGAN, Sussex.

Or, a griffin segreant sans wings sable, fire issuing from the mouth and
ears proper; on a chief argent, three quatrefoils vert—SAMLER.

Per chevron or and ermine, in chief two griffin's heads erased proper—
NEED, Nottingham.

Argent, three griffin's heads erased sable, beaked gules—TRENTHAM,
Stafford.

Sable, a chevron or between three griffin's heads erased argent—
Robert SKINNER, Bp. of Bristol, 1637; afterwards of Oxford, 1641-63.

The *Dragon* (fr. *dragon*), the next in importance to the griffin
amongst the fictitious animals, seems perhaps to have had its
origin in the stories brought by travellers who, on their way to
the Holy Land, may have seen the crocodiles on the banks of the
Nile, and exaggerated or idealized the form; and probably the

---

word, in some of the instances in which it is used in the Bible, means the *crocodile*.

Represented usually like the griffin, that is, rampant, its head is that of a serpent, of which an essential addition is the forked tongue. It has also, like the griffin, ears. The body, as to its proportions, is that of a lion, but it is represented scaled, and the large wings, instead of being those of an eagle, are webbed and pointed, and resemble rather those of the bat. The legs are also scaled, and the feet are represented usually with webbed talons, instead of those of the eagle; a spur, however, is often added. The tail, instead of ending like that of a lion, in a tuft, is always represented as *barbed* in English arms, but in French arms it is sometimes represented as with a fish-tail, and twisted. The dragon may be also represented ' *sans* ' wings.

Dragons' heads frequently occur as charges: the presence of the ears and of the barbed tongue distinguishes them from the heads of eagles or serpents.

Argent, a dragon rampant sable—DAUNEY.

Argent, a dragon volant in bend sable—RAYNON, Kent.

Or, a dragon segreant vert, on a chief gules three spear-heads argent—SOUTHLAND, Kent.

Vert, a dragon sejant with wings expanded between three escallops or—CARMALT, Cumberland.

Or, a chevron between three dragons sable—FOLBORNE.

DAUNEY.

Argent, a chevron gules between three demi-dragons couped, erect, vert —HEYGEYS.

Argent, three dragon's heads erect and erased azure without ears—HORSKE.

Argent, three dragon's heads erased, fire issuing from their mouths proper—HOLSALL.

The Dragon, like the Griffin, is often used as a crest, or as one of the supporters. The illustration here given is from one of the supporters to the arms of William HUGHES, of Gwerclas.

HUGHES.

A *Sea-Dragon* appears on the crest of Sir Jacob Gerrard, Bart. 1662.

The *Opinicus* is allied more nearly to the dragon in the forepart and in the wings; but it has a beaked head and ears, something between the dragon and the griffin. The hind part and the four legs are probably intended to represent those of a lion, but the tail is short, and is said to be that of the camel.

Two opinici vert, beaked sable, wings gules, are Supporters to the Insignia of the PLASTERERS' Company.

An opinicus, with wings endorsed or, is the Crest of the Company of BARBER SURGEONS.

Opinicus.

Lion-Dragon : the foremost part of a lion conjoined to the hinder part of a dragon.

Rouge Dragon : a favourite badge of King Henry VII. and assumed as the dexter supporter of his arms. It was also the title of a *pursuivant* established by that monarch. See *Herald.*

See also *Sea-Dragon.*

Grose, or *Drawing board :* a tool used by COOPERS. It forms part of the insignia of their companies in London, Chester, and Exeter.

Gyronny of eight gules and sable; on a chevron between three annulets or, a grose between two adzes azure; on a chief vert three lilies slipped and leaved argent—COOPERS' Company, Incorporated 1501.

Grose.

Griggs. See *Eels.*

Grilleté, (fr.): of a *falcon*, &c., having bells on its feet.

Gringolé, (fr.). See *Cross*, § 21, but with French heralds *saltires fers de moulin*, &c., are sometimes so named when terminated with serpents' heads.

Grimpant: a French term rarely applied to animals, to signify the attitude of *climbing*, and so somewhat differing from *rampant.*

Griotte, (fr.) : a *Cherry-tree.*

Grittie: a fanciful name for a field composed of colour and metal in equal proportions, should such exist.

Grouse. See *Moorcock.*

Grove. See *Wood.*

Grosing iron. See *Glazier's nippers.*

Gudgeon, (fr. *goujon*, lat. *gobio*) : belonging to the order of the *cyprinidæ*, occurs in some rare instances on account of the name.

Quarterly, first and fourth or ; third and fourth barry argent and gules, all within a bordure sable, charged with eight gudgeons fesswise argent —GOBYON [from Glover's ordinary].

Argent, three gudgeons hauriant within a bordure engrailed sable— GOBION, Waresby, Hunts [also GOBYON, or GOBYNS].

Argent, three gudgeons within a bordure sable—French family of GOBAUD.

Azure, two gudgeons in saltire argent, in base water waved proper— French family of GOUJON.

Gules, (fr. *gueules*) : the heraldic name of the tincture red. The term is probably derived from the Arabic *gule*, a red rose, just as the *azure* was derived from a word in the same language, signifying a blue stone. The word was, no doubt, introduced by the Crusaders. Heralds have, however, guessed it to be derived from the Latin *gula*, which in old French is found as *gueule*, i.e. the "red throat of an animal." Others, again, have tried to find the origin in the Hebrew word

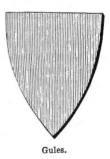

Gules.

gulade, which signifies red cloth. Gules is denoted in engravings by numerous perpendicular lines. Heralds who blazoned by planets and jewels called it *Mars*, and *Ruby*.

The name variously spelt *goules, goulez, goulz, gowlys*, occurs frequently in ancient rolls of arms, as will have been observed by the examples given throughout the Glossary.

In the Siege of Carlaverock, as has been noticed under *Colour*, the terms both *rouge* and *vermeile* are poetically used, and to these may be added *rougette*.

"Mes Eumenions de la BRETTE   La baner ot tout rougette."
Siege of Carlaverock.

Grue, (fr.) : *crane*.

Gryphon. See *Griffin*.

Guardant. See *Gardant*.

Gui, (fr.) : mistletoe, only found in French coats of arms.

Gu don. See *Flag*.

Guns: the *cannon* should be represented mounted, unless otherwise expressed. The *field-pieces, chamber-pieces* (or *chambers*), as they are sometimes called, are varieties, but no special variation in drawing seems to be recognized, except that they are represented, as a rule, unmounted. The *culverin* is a cannon with a wide bore in proportion to its length. The smaller *guns* will be found referred to under *Musket*.

Argent, two guns in saltire proper, in chief the letter G, and in base the letter V, each crowned with a regal crown ; on the dexter side in fesse a barrel, and on the sinister three balls all of the second—GUNSMITHS' Company [but doubtful if these arms are of any authority].

Gules, three cannons barways in pale, argent—GOUNING, Mayor of Bristol [granted 1662].

Azure, three field-pieces in pale or, on a chief argent as many pellets [or cannon-balls]—BOARD of ORDNANCE.

Argent, a chevron ermine fimbriated sable, between three chamber-pieces of the last fired proper—DE LA CHAMBRE, Radmill, Sussex.

Argent, a chevron sable surmounted of another ermine ; three chambers, placed transverse of the escutcheon of the second fired proper—CHAMBERS, co. Worcester.

Argent, a culverin dismounted in fesse sable —LEIGH.

Argent, three bars wavy sable, each charged with as many plates ; on a chief gules a culverin between two anchors or—GONSTON, Essex.

LEIGH.

Gurges, or *Whirlpool:* as the gurges (like the *fountain*) represents water, argent and azure are its proper tinctures. Instances, however, occur in which other tinctures are employed.

In an ancient roll of arms the whirlpool is represented not as a continued line, but as a number of rings one within another, and it is probable that, by the term *roelé* in the arms of GORGES in the early roll, the same charge is meant, though the term *rouel* is found in other rolls with a different signification.

GORGES.

Rauf de GORGES, roele dargent et dazur—Roll, temp. HEN. III.

Argent, a gurges azure—GORGES, Wilts [Baronet, 1612].

Or, a cross engrailed gules, a whirlpool intertwined vert—Robert GYFFARD.

Gusset, (fr. *gousset,* the armpit): this truncation of the shield, like the *gore,* occurs usually on either the dexter or sinister side. In the former case (when sanguine) it is imagined to be an abatement for adultery, in the latter for drunkenness. *Gussets,* however, occur as honourable charges. When in base, the term graft seems preferable.

CONINGHAM.

Sable [another gules], two gussets argent—CONINGHAM.

Or, over a gusset invected purpure two barbels countersalient—ZORNLIN, Clapham.

Gules, a lion rampant or, between two flaunches and a gusset in base ermine—CELY, Havering, Essex.

Gules, a lion rampant or, between two flaunches ermine, and a graft in point of the last—CEELY [Glover's Ordinary].

Gurnet, *gournet,* or *gurnard* (lat. *trigla*): this fish, found on our coasts, occurs in the crest of one Norfolk family and in the arms of one Cornish family; in the latter case on account of the local name by which it is known, namely, *tubbe* fish. With it may be associated the *mullet,* which is sometimes found blazoned in the arms of WAYE, and the French *rouget,* which appears to include both kinds of fish.

On a chapeau gules turned down ermine, a gurnet fish in pale with the head downwards—Crest of GURNEY, Norfolk.

Argent, a chevron sable between three gournets [or tubbe fish] hauriant gules—TUBB, Trengoff, Cornwall, granted 1571.

Argent, a cross engrailed gules, between four mullets of the second [probably the fish]—GORNEY.

Azure, three mullets hauriant argent [elsewhere three fish, and in one case three lucies]—WAYE, or WEYE, Dorset.

D'or à trois rougets de gueules en pals bien ordonnés—ROUGET, Guyenne.

Guivre, (fr.): a viper, or serpent.

Gull. See *Sea-gull.*

Gumène: cable of an *anchor.*

Gun-stone, or *Gun-shot.* See *Pellet.*

Guttée, or *gutty.* See *Gouttes.*

Guze, (Turkish, *Guz,* an eye): represented by a roundlet sanguine.

Gypsy's, or *Egyptian's head.* See *Heads.*

Gymile = *gemel.* See especially under *bar.*

Gyronny, (fr. *gironné*), (from the Spanish *Gyron,* a triangular piece of cloth sewed into a garment). The usual number of pieces is eight, but there may be six, ten, or twelve. Party per saltire has been erroneously called gyronny of four, but in English armoury one of the lines forming the pattern must be *in fesse.* It will be observed that the term is an ancient one. The gyron with which the tinctures begin is the uppermost upon the dexter side.

ACTON.

Warin de BASSINGBORNE, gerony d'or et d'azur—Roll, temp. HEN. III.

Roger de MORTIMER, barre, a cheif palee, a corners gerone d'or et d'azur, a ung escocheon d'argent—*Ibid.* [See under *Esquire*].

Sire Omfrey de BASSINGBOURNE, geronne de argent e de goules—Roll, temp. ED. II.

Monsire Humphrie de BASINGBORNE, port gerone de vi peces argent et gules—Roll, temp. ED. III.

Monsire BRINZON, port gerone d'argent et d'azur de xij peeces—*Ibid.*

Gyronny of eight, argent and gules—ACTON.

Gyronny of eight engrailed, or and sable (points of engrailing towards the dexter)—CAMPBELL.

Gyronny of eight (*quarterly,* Cole's MS.) argent and sable, four fleur-de-lys counterchanged; on a saltier or, five cinquefoils gules—Edward VAUGHAN, Bp. of S. Davids, 1509–22.

VAUGHAN,

Gyronny of ten, or and azure—BRYASNON.

Gyronny of twelve, vair, or, and gules—BASSING-BORNE.

The term *gyron* rarely occurs in blazoning English heraldry, but there are instances. In the arms of MORTIMER the *esquire* is practically a gyron.

Argent, three cinquefoils gules, and a gyron issuing from the dexter side in chief azure—CHIVERS.

Azure, three bars argent, on a chief of the second a pale between two gyrons [elsewhere piles] of the first; over all an escutcheon gules charged with a cross croslet fitchy as the bars—Benedictine Abbey of WINCHCOMBE, Gloucester.

Or, three bars azure, in chief a pile between a gyronny of two pieces [or two gyrons] of the second; over all an escutcheon ermine—MORTYMER.

Hair: a lock of hair is rarely found, but a head, &c., is often blazoned as having the *hair* of a particular tincture, and more frequently the term *crined* (fr. *chevelée*) is used. In the case of the arms of HARBOTTLE, however, the locks should more properly be blazoned *icicles*. See under *gouttes*. A head proper would naturally have the hair; and if no tincture is named, brown may be used. In one case the head is blazoned *bald*. See *head*.

Sable, a comb argent on a lock of golden hair—BLOUD.

Azure, three locks of hair in bend or—HARBOTTLE.

Gules, three boy's heads couped argent, crined or, with snakes round about their necks azure—VAUGHAN, Hargest, Wales.

Gules, three maiden's heads couped argent, crined or—MADESTON.

See example also under *boar, colour.*

Hame, or *Heame:* the collar by which a horse draws a waggon. A hame (or, as some call it, a pair of hames) was the badge of the family of SAINT JOHN, supposed, in consequence, by heraldic writers to have held the office of master of the baggage-waggons. It has not been observed actually borne in any arms.

Hame.

Two eagles with wings expanded or, ducally crowned gules, each charged in the breast with a pair of horse-hames tied at the top and bottom proper, the inside per pale argent and of the second—Supporters of the Arms of Viscount BOLINGBROKE and ST. JOHN.

Habergeon. See *Hauberk.*

Habick. See *Clothiers'* habick.

Habillé, (fr.): clothed; said of men when habited, and also of a ship when the sails are of another tincture.

Habited: clothed or vested.

Hache, (fr.): hatchet. See *Axe.*

Haddock. See *Cod.*

Hafted, (fr. *emmanché*): with handle (of a different tincture), e.g. of an *axe, hammer,* &c.

Haie, (fr.): in French arms an enclosure of any kind, either of brambles and branches, or of military *fascines.*

Hake. See *Cod.*

Halbert, (fr. *haillebarde*). See Pole-*axe.*

Hameçon. See *Cross,* § 30.

Haméide, (fr.): signifies a figure formed by three *bars humetty* chamfered at the ends and set one above the other

Hammer, (fr. *marteau*): hammers of several kinds occur as charges. There are the Plasterers' and the Wrights' hammer especially named. The device is usually represented as if clawed (as shewn in the margin), although it be not so specified. It will be seen that it occurs in the ancient rolls under the term *martel*, and one or two French families of the name of MARTEL still bear this charge.

Hammer.

Sir Adam MARTEL de sable a iij martels de argent — Roll, temp. ED. II.

Azure, on a chevron engrailed or, between in chief two plasterer's hammers argent handled of the second, and in base a treble flat-brush of the third handle upward like the third; a rose gules seeded or barbed vert, enclosed by two fleurs-de-lis of the first; in chief a trowel fesswise, handle to the sinister as the third—Company of PLAS-TERERS, London [Inc. 1501].

London Plasterers' Company.

Sable, a chevron or between three hammers argent handled of the second, ducally crowned of the last — Company of BLACKSMITHS and SPURRIERS [Inc. 1579].

Azure, a hammer erect in pale argent ensigned with a ducal coronet or—Company of HAMMERMEN, Edinburgh.

Sable, a chevron argent between three hammers or ducally crowned of the last — SMITHS' Company, Exeter.

London Blacksmiths' Company.   Edinburgh Company.

Azure, a chevron between three lathing-hammers argent, handled or —SLATERS' Company, Newcastle-on-Tyne.

Or, three hammers sable—HAMERTON.

Gules, a fesse between three hammers or—PIGOTT.

Gules, three hammers with claws argent—MARTELL.

Argent, a bend of six lozenges conjoined between as many mattocks, with the clawed ends to the dexter, sable—BOLRON, co. Chester.

Gules, three wright's hammers clawed argent—PURSER.

Gules, a dexter hand couped proper holding a sword paleways argent between two broken hammers or—NASMYTH.

D'or, a trois marteaux de gules—MARTEL, Normandy.

With the *hammer* may be associated the *mallet*
(fr. *maillet*), used by masons and others. It is
usually figured as in the arms of FORTE, but sometimes with a square head, while a figure like that
in the margin above is found in the insignia of
the MARBLERS' Company. (See the arms given
under Chipping-*axe*).

Mallet.

Argent, three mallets gules—FORTE, co. Somerset
[ancient arms of DE FORTIBUS].

Gules, a chevron between three mallets or—
SOAME, [Bart., 1684].

Sable, three square hammers [i.e. mallets] argent
—BROWNE, co. Rutland.

Argent, a fesse between three mallets sable—
BROWNE.

Argent, a fesse between three mallets, the handles reversed gules—BLOODMAN.

FORTE.

Hand, (fr. *main*): the human hand is often borne in coat
armour, though only one instance has been
observed in the early rolls, and that only
incidental. When no other position is mentioned it is understood to be *apaumé*, as in
the arms of ULSTER, which came to be the
badge of a baronet of Great Britain; it is
borne either on an *escutcheon* or *canton*. See
Baronet. Otherwise the hand may be
borne *dorsed* (or, as it is sometimes called,

Badge of ULSTER.

aversant); or it may be *in fesse*, or with *the fingers downwards*,
or *clenched*, or *holding* some object; the hand is generally *couped*
at the wrist, and is so represented if no other description is
given; sometimes, however, the blazon runs *couped below*, or
above the wrist; generally a *dexter* hand is named, and it is so
understood unless a *sinister* is specified; hands in armour should
rather be blazoned *gauntlets*. See also *Gloves*.

Sometimes hands are represented as *clasping* or *embracing*; and with French heralds two hands joined thus are simply blazoned *une foi*. In connection with this the arms of PUREFOY and PUREFEY should be noted.

Argent, a sinister hand erect couped gules.   Province of Ulster.

Sire Johan de COYNERS dazure ov la maunch dor e ove la meyn [i.e. a maunche or, a hand proper]—Roll, temp. ED. II.

Azure, a dexter hand [in some instances, a sinister hand] apaumé, couped, argent—BROME.

Gules, a fesse between four dexter hands couped argent—QUATERMAIN, Oxford.

Gules, a dexter hand couped barways argent—BAREMAINE.

Or, on a chief gules a hand couped barwise [otherwise extended transverse the chief] argent—MAINSTONE.

QUATERMAIN.

Gules, three hands, fingers downwards argent; a quarter chequy azure and or—SUTTON.

Or, on a bend azure three dexter hands couped at the wrist and clenched, argent—ESINGOLD.

Azure, a dexter hand couped at the wrist and clenched, in pale argent—FEAST, Middlesex.

Sable, a close hand [i.e. clenched] argent—POWNSE.

Sable, three sinister hands erased argent—MAYNARD.

Gules, three hands holding a crown a key and a purse or—Arms ascribed to NIGELLUS, Bp. of Ely, 1133–69; and to RICHARD DE ELY, Bp. of London, 1189–98.

Gules, in a maunch ermine a hand proper holding a fleur-de-lis or—BRUTON Priory, Somerset, [also MOHUN].

Purpure, a sinister hand couped and erect argent—MANLEY.

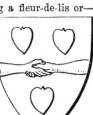

Gules, two arms and hands clasped in fesse proper between three hearts or—WARTON, Bp. of S. Asaph, 1536, and of Hereford, 1554–57.

Gules, three pairs of hands back to back argent—PUREFOY, co. Buckingham.

Sable, three pairs of armed hands embracing argent two and one—PUREFOY, Caldecot, co. Warwick.

WARTON.

Sable, three pairs of dexter hands conjoined or ruffled argent—PUREFEY.

Gueules à la foi d'argent—COUSIN de la TOUR FONDUE.

D'azur, a une foi d'argent vêtue de pourpre posée en bande et mouvante d'une nuée d'argent—ARENE, Provence.

As the *Badge of Ulster* has been referred to under this article, it is thought well to give one or two examples.

Per pale argent and sable, a chevron between three talbots passant counterchanged; on a chief gules as many leopards' heads or. On the fesse-point the badge of Ulster—Gooch, Benacre Hall, Suffolk.

Gules, a fret argent, a canton of Ulster—Sir George Fleming, Bp. of Carlisle, 1735–47.

Gules, a fesse between six mullets argent; a canton of Ulster—Sir William Ashburnham, Bp. of Chichester, 1754–97.

Gooch.

Argent, a chevron sable, a canton of Ulster— Sir Jonathan Trelawney, Bp. of Bristol, 1685; afterwards of Exeter, 1689; and last of Winchester, 1707–21.

Hank: Hanks of *cotton*, of *silk*, and of *bowstrings* are found in heraldry. The cotton-hank is the most frequent, and it occurs in the arms of very many families of the name of Cotton.

An example of hanks of *silk* will be found under that term, and one of bowstrings is given below. The position of the *hank* is usually upright, as shewn in the margin.

Azure, a chevron between three hanks of cotton erect argent— Hugh Cotton, co. Stafford.

Cotton-hank.

Azure, three cotton-hanks argent—Cotton, Combermere.

Argent, three bars sable, over all as many cotton-hanks or—Cotton.

Barry of six argent and sable, three cotton-hanks or—Haywood.

Azure, on a fesse argent between a bee-hive surrounded by bees volant in chief, and in base a mill-wheel or, a hank of cotton of the field between two roses gules barbed and seeded proper—Calron, co. Lancaster.

Azure, a hank or knot of bowstrings in pale or; on a chief argent three bows—Long Bowstring Makers' Company, London.

Hare: the Hare (fr. *lièvre*), as also the rabbit (fr. *lapin*), always blazoned *coney* (and in one case the *leveret*), are not infrequent in coats of arms, but, so far as has been observed, there are no rules followed as to distinct drawing of these varieties.

They are more frequently represented as *sejant*, and if no description is given they would be drawn so; but they are found

---

Hareng, (fr.): herring.　　　　Harnysed: clad in armour.

blazoned *courant, boltant, passant, salient,* and (though wrongly) *rampant;* also *feeding,* and issuing from their burrows; the most remarkable of all is the hare playing upon the *bagpipes* (q.v.). Hares' *heads* occur in one case.

Argent, three hares (elsewhere *conies*) courant in pale azure—Aunos-wood, Lancashire.

Azure, a chevron ermine between two hares courant in chief, and a sun in base [elsewhere in chief three suns argent, in base a hare courant]—WATSON, Bp. of Winchester, 1580–84.

Azure, a hare salient guardant argent with a hunting-horn hanging about the neck vert garnished gules within a bordure counter-compony of the second and first—CLELAND, Edinburgh.

Azure, a hare rampant between three mullets or—MARCHANT.

Argent, a chevron gules between three leverets courant sable—LEYVER, or LEVER, co. Lancaster.

Azure, three leverets courant in pale—LEVER-INGTON.

Gules, three conies sejant argent within a bordure engrailed sable—Sir Humphry CONESBY, co. Hereford, and CONINGSBY, co. Norfolk.

Argent, [otherwise or,] three conies passant sable—CONYSTON.

Argent, on a chevron azure a coney passant between two fishes hauriant of the first; on a chief

CONESBY.

checky of the first and second a rose or on a pale of the second—CHEY-NEY, Bp. of Bristol, 1562–79.

Argent, a saltire gules between four conies feeding sable—CONY, co. Hertford.

Per fesse argent and vert, a pale counterchanged, three conies issuing from their burrows of the first—BROWGHE.

Argent, on a fesse nebuly sable three hare's heads couped or—HARE-WELL, Bp. of Bath and Wells, 1366–86.

Harp, (fr. *harpe*): this charge is best known as the ensign of the kingdom of IRELAND, but is borne also by one or two families. It first appears crowned amongst the royal badges on the accession of the Stuarts. The head and wings of an angel have been added in late examples, but without authority. The Irish name *cloyshackes* seems to be applied in one

Badge.

MS. to the harp (see under *Ireland*).   We also find the *Jew's harp* mentioned, but it is doubtful if it is not meant (as the name of the bearer implies) for a *scoop*.

Azure, a harp or stringed argent—IRELAND.

Gules, three cloyshackes or stringed argent—IRELAND, Harl. MS. 304.

Azure, three harps or—DOBBIN, Ireland.

Argent, three harps sable stringed or—HARPSFIELD.

Azure, two lions rampant combatant supporting a garbe or; in dexter base a crescent argent, in sinister base the harp of Ireland—FOGARTY.

Insignia of IRELAND.

Argent, a Jew's harp [or a scoop] in bend sable between six laurel-leaves of the last—SCOPHAM, co. Lincoln.

Harrow, (fr. *herse*) : two forms of the harrow occur in armoury, the first is square, the other triangular.   The former might be mistaken for the portcullis, and in fact the French term *herse* is applied to both.

Azure, a chevron between three harrows or—HARROWER.

Harrow.

Argent, three harrows sable two and one [otherwise argent, a chevron between three harrows sable]—HARVY, Hale, Cornwall.

Erminois, an annulet interlacing three triangular harrows conjoined in the fesse point—REDMAYNE, co. York.

Ermine, three triangular harrows gules, toothed or, and conjoined in the nombril point of the escutcheon gules by a wreath argent and of the second [otherwise, Ermines, the harrows or, the wreath argent and or]—HARROW, or HARWE.

HARROW.

Hat, (fr. *chapeau*) : one similar to the figure in the margin is borne by the FELTMAKERS' Company, but various forms occur depending on date, &c.

Hat.

Harpoon. See *Eel-spear*.	**Hart.** See *Deer*.
Harpy. See under *Sphinx*.	**Harvest-fly.** See *Butterfly*.
Harrington's Knot. See *Cords*, also *Fret*.	**Hatchet.** See *Axe*.
	Hatchments. See *Achievements*.

Ermine, on a chevron between three felt hats with strings sable as many escallops argent—Company of HATTER MERCHANTS, London.

Argent, a chapeau or hat azure, with a plume of ostrich-feathers in front gules—John KINGE-STON, 1390 [Harl. MS. 1178].

For the Cardinal's hat, see *Cap.*

Hat-band.

Hat-band.   Two forms of this bearing occur.   The first is wreathed, as in the arms of BURY; and the second that borne by the Companies of FELTMAKERS and HATBAND-MAKERS.

Sable, a chevron argent between three hat-bands wreathed of the second and azure—BURY.

Argent, a dexter hand couped at the wrist gules between two hat-bands nowed azure, in chief a hat sable banded of the third—FELT-MAKERS' Company [Inc. 1604].

Hat-band.

Azure, on a chevron between three hat-bands or as many merillions sable—HATBANDMAKERS' Company [Inc. 1664].

Gules, a chevron between three hat-bands argent—MAYNES.

Hawthorn : this bush is used in some few instances on account of its name. It was also adopted as a *badge* by Henry VII., and described as a hawthorn-bush regally crowned.   The *white-thorn* is found on the arms of Bishop ALDRICH, and the *may-flowers* probably represent the flowers of the bush.   It may be *fructed*, or *flowered*, and the *leaves* also occur.

Badge.

Argent, a hawthorn-tree eradicated proper—SYLVESTER.

Argent, three thorn-trees vert—THORNHOLME [granted 1653].

Per pale argent and gules, a chevron between three lion's heads erased counterchanged; on a chief or a thorn-tree proper—THORNTHWAITE, Cumberland.

Argent, a thorn-tree fructed proper on a chief gules a lion passant guardant or—O'MURCHOE.

Argent, a hawthorn-tree erased vert, flowered gules—BRETLAND, co. Chester.

Argent, a chevron sable between three hawthorn-leaves vert—THORN-TON, co. York.

Verte, on a fesse argent between three garbs or, banded gules, two boughs of whitethorn saltier-wise enfiled with a crown proper, between a mound royal azure and a robin redbreast proper, all within a bordure engrailed of the third [pometty?]—ALDRICH, Bp. of Carlisle, 1537–56.

Gules, a cross ingrailed ermine between in chief two may-flowers slipped or—MAYFIELD, co. Cambridge [granted 1684].

Hauberk, or *Hauberg:* a name which appears to be given to the *cuirass,* from the German Hals=berg, i.e. a protection for the neck, but it has only been observed in one coat of arms.

The *Habergeon* is given in books as a diminutive of Hauberk, and is a short coat of mail without sleeves, but no example has been noticed in blazon. [The word, it may be added, is used in the Authorized Version, 2 Chron. xxvi. 14.]

Per pale azure and gules, a tilting-spear in pale proper surmounted by a hauberk [or coat of mail] or—AUBERT.

Hazel: the *tree,* the *leaves,* the *nuts,* are all represented in different arms; the *filberts* also. A *chaplet* is sometimes composed of *hazel,* and a *squirrel* is sometimes represented cracking *nuts.* A bunch of filberts is in French blazon called *coquerelles.*

Argent, on a fesse gules between three owls sable as many lozenges ermine; on a chief azure three nut-trees [or hazel-boughs] proper—HASLEWOOD.

Argent, a hind's head couped azure collared or, between two hazel-boughs vert fructed or—ALFORD, Suffolk.

Argent, a chevron sable between hazel-leaves vert—HESILRIGGE.

Or, on a fesse azure between three hazel-slips proper as many crescents argent—HASELL, Cumberland.

Or, a chevron sable between three hazel-nuts erect slipped gules—TARSELL.

Argent, a fesse gules between three hazel-nuts or husks and stalks vert—HASELEY, Suffolk.

Argent, on a chevron between three filberts sable two cats combatant of the first—GIBBS.

Haurient: breathing, a term applied to a fish in an erect position. See under *Fish.*

Haussé, (fr.): of a chevron fesse, &c., when *enhanced.*

Haut, (fr.): sometimes used of a sword when *erect.*

Hautboy. See *Trumpet.*

Hawk, *Hawk's Bell,* and *Hawk's Lure.* See *Falcon.*

Hawmed, i. q. *Humetty.*

Hay-fork. See *Fork.*

Hay-hook. See *Horse-picker.*

D'argent, à la rose de gueules cantonnée de quatre coquerelles de sinople—LA BORDE.

Head, (fr. *tête*): as will have been noticed, the heads of beasts, birds, and fishes are very frequently represented by themselves, being *couped*, or *erased;* but it has been thought well to group under one article the various forms of the *human head* as they appear in heraldic design, and it has been observed they are very frequent in the arms of Welsh families. It may be said generally that, unless otherwise specified, the human head (as well as heads of beasts) should be drawn in profile. In English arms the heads are usually blazoned *proper;* in French arms the tincture is usually named, i.e. *carnation.* The following are the representative types of these charges, of which it is thought well to give examples. Besides *men's heads* proper, which are generally represented as those of old men with hair (fr. *chevelée*), and bearded (fr. *barbée*), and *young men's* heads (see example under *mascle*), we find various heads specified, as of *Englishmen*, of *Saxons*, of *Princes*, of *Saracens* (as in the crest of DRAYTON), of *Turks*, of *Moors*, or *blackamoors* and *negroes*, of the *gypsy* or *Egyptian*, and finally of *savages'* heads. In one case a *bald head* is given. There

Crest of DRAYTON.

seem to be no very defined rules for drawing the respective heads, much being left to the ingenuity of the artist; still in many of the arms as exhibited in sculpture or in glass the heads are very characteristic.

Azure, three broad arrows or, two and one feathered argent; on a chief of the second as many men's heads couped sidefaced proper—WATTES, Somerset.

Gules, a chevron ermine between three Englishmen's heads in profile proper — LLOYD, co. Denbigh.

[Similar arms seem to be borne by Abp. WILLIAMS of York, and Bp. GRIFFITH of S. Asaph.]

Gules, a chevron between three Saxon's heads in profile, the two in chief couped and one in base erased argent—GRIFFITH.

LLOYD.

Ermine, three prince's heads crowned and mantled proper couped at the breast—ENFANTLEROY.

Gules, a chevron between three Saracen's heads couped at the shoulders argent—SARES, Middlesex.

Gules, a Saracen's head erased proper hair and beard or, round the temples a fillet nowed argent and azure; on a chief or three roses gules —HUGHES, Bp. of S. Asaph, 1573—1600.

Vert, a chevron gules between three Turk's heads couped proper turbaned or—SMITH, granted 1623.

D'azur, à trois têtes de Turcs de carnation, le turban parti et tortillé d'or et de gueules—BELO, Manche.

Argent, three moor's heads couped at the shoulders proper filleted or and gules— TANNER, Bp. of S. Asaph, 1732–35.

Or, on a fesse between three Moor's heads erased sable as many crescents argent— BLACKMORE.

Or, a blackamoor's head couped sable— BINNS.

Or, a cross gules between four blackamoor's heads affrontee, couped at the shoulders proper, wreathed about the temples gold—JUXON, Bp. of London, 1633; Abp. of Cant. 1660–63.

TANNER.

Per fesse argent and sable, a pale counterchanged three negro's heads proper—GERARD.

Per fesse gules and argent, three Egyptian's heads counterchanged— ASHPOOLE.

On a wreath a cubit arm erect grasping a dagger, enfiled with a gypsy's head couped proper—Crest of MACLELLAN, Lord Kircudbright.

Azure, a bird's leg couped at the thigh or, conjoined to a savage's head argent, hair sable—PETRE.

Vert, a lion rampant or; on a chief argent a man's head couped at the neck and bald proper between ducal coronets of the second—MULTADY, Ireland.

Gules, a chevron argent between three St. Paul's heads proper— PAULSWORTH, or PILSWORTH.

Amongst peculiar examples may be named *Moses' head* and the head of *John the Baptist in a charger*. The former, however, is borne only as a crest, that is to say, by the family of HILTON, and the engraving is taken from the carving on the

---

Headpiece.　See *Helmet.*
Heaume, (fr.), *Healme,* (old fr.) : *helmet.*

eastern front of Hilton Castle, Durham. The latter appears
as the crest of the London Company of TALLOW-
CHANDLERS, adopted, no doubt, in consequence
of S. John the Baptist being chosen as their
patron Saint; it is also borne by the town of
Ayr in Scotland (see the arms given under *Lamb*).
Again, a peculiar head appears as the crest of
Sir Sandich de TRANE, knight-founder of the
Garter (that is to say one of the first knights of
the order); it is blazoned sometimes as a *Satyr's*
head, and the device appears also in a coat of
arms. Other fanciful heads occur as crests, e.g.
a *Fiend's head* (blazoned also '*Satan's head*'),
i.e. a man's head with ears like a dragon's wings,
and a *Whittal's head*, said to be a man's head
with short horns, and called by Anstis 'the head
of *Midas*, with asses' ears.'

Crest and Arms of
HILTON.

The head of Moses proper, with two rays or horns or—Crest borne by
HILTON. [The arms are argent, two bars azure.]

On a wreath a demi angel issuing from clouds, proper, vested azure,
wings expanded or, crined of the last; on
his head a cap; thereon a cross patée of the
third, holding a dish argent, glorified or;
therein the head of S. John the Baptist proper—TALLOW-CHANDLERS' Company, London.
[Arms and crest granted, Sept. 24, 1463.]

Head of S. John the Baptist.

Argent, on a bend sable, three satyr's heads
couped at the shoulders of the first, horned or
—WHEYWELL.

Sable, three Midas's heads erased argent, crowned or—JAY.

Of *Women's* heads there are also several varieties. As a rule
they are drawn with dishevelled hair. The *maidens' heads* are
drawn as the head and shoulders of a woman *affronty*, couped
below the breasts, her hair dishevelled, and usually wreathed
with a garland of roses; sometimes also crowned with an *eastern
crown*. The term *bust* is also sometimes used in English, but
more frequently in French blazon. The term *lady's head* is also
found, as also *nun's head*, the last being generally veiled.

Azure, a fesse or, in chief three women's heads couped at the breasts proper and crined of the second; in base a leopard's face of the last—SUGDON.

Sable, a fesse enhanced argent; in chief three nun's heads couped at the shoulders proper, vested of the second, crowned or; in base an ox passing a ford proper—S. FRIDESWIDE'S PRIORY, Oxford, afterwards the arms of the Bishoprick of OXFORD.

Azure, on a chevron argent between three maiden's heads of the second, crined or, three lilies slipped gules; on a chief of the third a cross tau sable between two roses of the fourth—TAYLOR, Bp. of Lincoln, 1532–54.

Azure, three lady's heads in fesse between as many fleurs-de-lis or—COLLARD.

Argent, a chevron sable between three nun's heads veiled couped at the shoulders proper—DAVENEY, Norfolk.

Argent, on a bend between six billets gules three veiled nun's heads couped bendwise of the first—WEDNISSON.

Gules, a maiden's head proper crined or—MAYDENSTUN, Bp. of Worcester, 1314–17.

Gules, three bars ermine; on a canton argent a maiden's head proper—BARETTI, India.

. . . . A quadrangular castle surmounted with another, over the battlements the bust of a queen, her hair dishevelled and (ducally) crowned . . . .—Seal of Corporation of QUEENBOROUGH, Kent.

D'azur, a trois bustes de reine de carnation couronnées à l'antique d'or—GRANDMONT, Comtat-Venaissin.

Infants', and *children's*, and *boys' heads* are also found named, frequently with a snake twisted around the neck.

Argent, a boy's head proper, crined or, couped below the shoulders, vested gules, garnished gold—BOYMAN.

Gules, three boy's heads couped argent crined or—INFANT.

Sable, three infant's heads couped at the shoulders proper crined or—BONYFANT.

APJOHN.

Sable, a fesse or between three children's heads couped at the shoulders proper; about each neck a snake vert—APJOHN, Surrey.

Sable, a chevron argent between three children's heads couped at the shoulders proper crined or; about each neck a snake vert—VAUGHAN.

The *Seraph's head* is said to be represented as the head of an infant with six wings, two above it in saltire, two below it in saltire, and one on each side, but so far as has been observed no example occurs. *Death's heads* are but rarely borne (see under *Bones*).

Heart, (fr. *cœur*): the human heart when blazoned ' proper'
is to be gules. It is sometimes borne *flammant ;* also *crowned ;*
but the latter not before the sixteenth century.

Argent, a heart imperially crowned proper [i.e. gules, crowned gold]
on a chief azure three mullets of the field—
DOUGLAS.

[This crowned heart is said to be an *augmentation* in memory of Sir James Douglas, who
undertook to carry the heart of King Robert,
called the Bruce, to the Holy Land to be buried
there in the year 1328.]

Argent, a chief sable in fesse a human heart
gules—Edmund SCAMLER, Bp. of Peterborough,
1561 ; Bp. of Norwich, 1585-94.

DOUGLAS.

Gules, a body-heart, between two wings displayed or—Henry de WENGHAM, Bishop of London, 1259-62.

Argent, a heart gules within a fetterlock sable ; on a chief azure, three
boar's heads erased argent—LOCKHEART.

Per fesse wavy or and vert ; in chief a human heart emitting flames of
fire proper between two crosses crosslet sable ; in base an anchor erect
of the last—WADE, co. Durham.

Azure, a fesse or ; over all on a pile argent three hearts gules, two and
one—KEAN, Ireland.

Argent, three hearts flammant gules—HEART, Scotland.

Or, three bars wavy gules ; over all a human heart counterchanged
—DRUMMOND, co. Perth.

Heath-cock, or *Black-cock*. This bird, which differs from
the common cock, is represented as in the
annexed figure. It is frequently confounded
with the *moor-cock* (q.v.).

Argent, a heath-cock proper [i.e. sable], comb
and gill gules—Sir Francis MORE, Serjeant-at-
law, 1619.

Sable, a buck lodged reguardant argent ; between the attires a heath-cock volant or—MOR-
TOFT, Norfolk.

Sable, on a mount in base vert a buck salient

MORE.

or ; a chief of the third charged with a black-cock proper—MARTOSET.

Argent, on a fesse wavy sable between five heath-cocks of the second
six plates—Sir John EBRINGTON [ob. A.D. 1477].

A demi heath-cock with wings expanded azure, powdered with annulets
or ; in the beak a lily argent—Crest of the COOPERS' Company.

Hedgehog, (fr. *hérisson*) : this animal is chiefly borne allusively to its French name by families whose names are varied forms of HARRIS. The *urchin,* as well as the *porcupine,* are no doubt sometimes blazoned instead of it, from the drawings being mistaken one for the other.

Argent, three hedgehogs sable—HARRIES, Scotland [also HERIZ].

Argent, a thistle vert flowered gules between three hedgehogs sable—HARRIS, Cousland.

Azure, three hedgehogs argent—HERYS.

Azure, three hedgehogs or—HERIZ, co. Leicester.

Or, three hedgehogs azure—HARRIS, co. Salop.

Or, three hedgehogs passant in pale gules—HERCY.

Azure, three hedgehogs statant or—Sir Roger SWELYTON.

D'argent, à trois herissons de sable—HERICY, Normandy [also HERISSON, Bretagne].

Helmet, (fr. *casque,* old fr. *heaume,* but applied to a close helmet) : the covering for protection of the head in warfare has varied in form from the earliest ages onwards, but an account of the various shapes belongs to the history of armour.

In heraldry the *Helmet* assumed an important place as an appendage to the shield, for on this was fixed the *crest* (q.v.). Originally there seems to have been no special distinction as regards the forms of the helmet; they simply followed the customary shape of the period, and were drawn sideways; but in Elizabeth's reign it would appear that certain kinds of helmets were assigned to different degrees of nobility.

I. *The sovereign's* was to be of burnished gold, *affronty,* i.e. full-faced, with six *bars,* or *grilles,* and lined with crimson.

II. The helmets of *dukes, marquesses, earls, viscounts,* and *barons,* were to be composed of silver or polished steel, with five gold bars, and

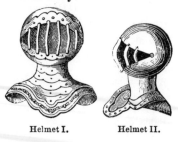

Helmet I.　　　　Helmet II.

Heights : used of rows of feathers. See under *Plumes.*

Heliotrope. See *Sunflower.*

Helved : with handle or haft of a different tincture, used e.g. of a *Pole-axe.*

lined with crimson. According to some authorities they should be placed neither *affronty* nor *in profile*, but between those positions; but there seem to be conflicting directions, and the practice varied.

III. *Baronets'* and *knights'* helmets were to be *affronty* and *open*, but supplied with a *visor*. They are supposed to be formed of steel ornamented with gilding, and usually lined with crimson.

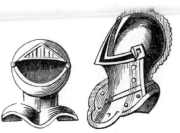

Helmet III.　　　Helmet IV.

IV. The helmets of *esquires* and private gentlemen were to be placed *in profile*, with the *visor* or beaver *closed;* to be of steel, but enriched with gold. These are drawn after various patterns however, the only point being that the visor should be closed, whence they are termed *close helmets*.

The French *timbre* includes the *helmet* and all that belongs to it. For the appurtenances it is supposed we are indebted to the tournaments, and they consist of the *crest*, the *wreath*, the *supporters*, the *mantle*, ribbons or *feathers*, and the *scroll*.

It should be added that helmets are seldom, if ever, found over the shields of bishops (except over that of the Bishop of Durham, to represent his temporal dignity), the *mitre* taking its place; or over that of women, except in the case of a sovereign. More than one helmet may be placed over the same shield, but it is rare.

Helmets, however, are also occasionally borne as charges, and generally the *esquire's* or *close* helmet is intended. In blazoning, however, there is frequently a reference to the *visor* (fr. *viziere*, or *garde vizure*), or *beaver* (old fr. *beauvoir*); the modern fr. *mezail* is also used. When this is up it is supposed to be a *knight's* helmet, when down an *esquire's*.

The portion which rests upon the shoulders, and protects the neck, is termed the *gorget*.

The helmet has sometimes *plumes* of feathers (q.v.).

Sable, a close helmet between three spear-heads, points fessways argent —David DOLBEN, Bp. of Bangor, 1632 ; also John DOLBEN, Bp. of Rochester, 1666, Abp. of York, 1683–86.

Azure, two bars argent between three close helmets or—ARMIGER, Norfolk.

Sable, a lion passant guardant or between three helmets argent— COMPTON, Bp. of Oxford, 1674 ; of London, 1675—1713.

Argent, three helmets with open vizors adorned with plumes of feathers azure—MYNYOT, Kent.

Argent, three knight's helmets azure lined gules—GOODACRE, Ireland.

Gules, three helmets argent, vizors and garnishing or—BASSET, [Lord Mayor of London, 1475].

Gules, three men's heads in profile armed with head pieces and gorgets argent—O'KENNEDY.

Or, three front-faced helmets proper—ELLICE, Herts.

Azure, a knight's helmet with snake entwined round it between three lion's heads erased or—ADOLPHUS.

Argent, a lion rampant gules, on his head a helmet azure—CLAPHAM, Scotland.

Hemp-break, or *Hemp-hackle* (also *Flax-breaker*), was the device of Sir Reginald BRAY, and is seen upon the vaulting of S. George's chapel at Windsor. This machine for pounding the hemp seems, like many other devices, to be borne on account of the name, the old word *bray* signifying to bruise or pound (see Proverbs xxvii. 22). From the form it has been confused with the *breys* or *barnacles*, q.v.

Hemp-break.

Argent, three hemp-breaks sable—HAMPSON.

Sable, on a fesse between three bugle-horns stringed and garnished argent a hemp-break gules—BRAINE.

Azure, on a fesse between three bugle-horns stringed argent a hemp-hackle gules—BRAYNE, co. Gloucester.

Herald, (fr. *héraut,* old fr. *herault*): the duties of heralds were originally of a military and diplomatic character, but in

---

time were transferred to granting and regulating armorial bearings, investigating genealogies, and superintending public ceremonies.

From the thirteenth century there seem to have existed certain officers of arms known as *Heralds* and *Pursuivants*, the latter being noviciates and candidates for the superior offices. They were eventually incorporated by King Richard III., and received further privileges from Edward VI. Queen Mary, on July 18, 1555, gave the society Derby House, in the parish of S. Benedict, Paul's Wharf, now called Heralds' College.

The COLLEGE OF ARMS.—The corporation consists of thirteen persons, namely,

The three KINGS of Arms,—*Garter, Clarenceux,* and *Norroy.*

Six HERALDS, and

Four PURSUIVANTS, whose precedence is regulated by seniority of appointment.

The *Insignia* of the college are:—

Argent, a cross gules between four doves, their dexter wings expanded and inverted, azure. Crest: in a ducal coronet proper, a dove rising azure. Supporters: two lions rampant gardant argent, ducally gorged or—COLLEGE OF ARMS.

The Lyon Office, Edinburgh, and the Office of Arms, Dublin, have cognizance of the heraldry of Scotland and Ireland respectively, as the College of Heralds has of that of England and Wales.

KINGS OF ARMS. The principal herald of England was of old designated *King of the heralds,* a title which seems to have been exchanged for *King of arms* about the reign of Henry IV. The kings of arms at present existing in England are three; Garter, Clarenceux, and Norroy, the two latter called *provincial kings of arms,* besides Bath, who is not a member of the college. Scotland is placed under an officer called *Lyon King of arms,* and Ireland is the province of one named *Ulster King of Arms.*

Garter King of arms was instituted by King Henry V. A.D. 1417, for the service of the most noble order bearing that name, which had hitherto been attended by Windsor herald. He was also made chief of the heralds, and had apartments within the castle of Windsor assigned to him. His official costume as *principal king of arms of the English* is a surcoat of velvet, richly embroidered with the arms of the sovereign, a crown, and a collar of SS, while the insignia belonging to the office are,—

Argent, S. George's cross ; on a chief azure, a ducal coronet encircled with a garter, between a lion of England [ducally crowned] on the dexter side, and a fleur-de-lis on the sinister, all or. [Guillim, 1632.] [Formerly, 1559, a dove in the first quarter.]

Clarenceux is the second in rank of the kings of arms, and the establishment of his office has been traced to the reign of Henry V. His ancient title was *Roy des armes des Clarenceux*, that is of the people of Clarence, a district which comprehends the castle and town of Clare, in Suffolk, but his province is all England to the south of the Trent. Clarenceux has a crown, collar of SS., and surcoat like those worn by Garter, and the insignia of his office are,—

Argent, S. George's cross ; on a chief gules, a lion of England [ducally crowned] or. [Formerly, 1595, a fleur-de-lis in the first quarter.]

Norroy is the most ancient of the three kings of arms, but the lowest in order of precedence. The name first occurs in the reign of Edward II., and the province assigned to this officer is that part of England which lies north of the river Trent, whence his title, *Roy des armes des Norreys*, a word used by Peter of Langtoft and other old historians in the sense of Northmen. His crown, surcoat, and collar, resemble those of the other kings. His official arms are,—

Argent, S. George's cross ; on a chief [per pale azure and] gules, a lion of England [ducally crowned] between a fleur-de-lis on the dexter side, and a key, wards in chief, on the sinister, all or.

Bath king of arms, although not a member of the college, takes precedence next after Garter. His office was created in 1725 for the service of the order of the Bath, and he was constituted *Gloucester king of arms* (an office originally instituted by Richard III., in whose reign it also became exslnct), and *principal herald of the parts of Wales*. He was likewise empowered to grant arms (either alone, or jointly with Garter) to persons residing within the principality

Lord Lyon king of arms is the chief heraldic officer for Scotland. The title is derived from the lion in the insignia of the kingdom.

Ulster king of arms has Ireland for his province. A king of arms called *Ireland* existed at least as early as the reign of Richard II. There is reason to believe that the succession remained uninterrupted for about a century, after which it probably became extinct. Ulster was created to supply the vacancy by Edward VI. on Candlemas day, 1551. His official arms are,—

Or, a cross gules; upon a chief of the last a lion passant guardant between a harp on the dexter side and a portcullis on the sinister, all gold.

HERALDS: there are at present six *heralds*, who rank according to their seniority in office. They derive their titles from certain districts, with which, however, they have no official connection. They are as follows.

Chester herald: whose office is said to have been instituted in the reign of King Edward III.

Lancaster herald: perhaps instituted by King Edward III. in the 34th year of his reign, when he created his son John of Gaunt duke of Lancaster.

Richmond herald: probably instituted by King Edward IV., in the 12th year of whose reign this herald was made Guienne king of Arms.

Somerset herald: is said to have been instituted by King Henry VII., in the 9th year of his reign.

Windsor herald: instituted by King Edward III. in the 38th year of his reign, at which time he was in France.

York herald: of the establishment of this office there does not appear to be any record.

The official costume of a herald consists of an embroidered satin surcoat of the royal arms, and a collar of SS.

There have been at different periods several other heralds, whose titles are now laid aside. Such were *Falcon*, first appointed by King Edward III., and *Blanch sanglier* by Richard III. Heralds extraordinary have also been occasionally created, as Edmondson was by the title of *Mowbray*, in 1764.

PURSUIVANTS: the follower or messenger attendant upon the superior officers at arms was regarded as a noviciate, and candidate for the offices of *herald* and *king*, and called the *Pursuivant*. There are at present four, distinguished by the names following:—

Rouge croix, generally considered to be the most ancient. The title was doubtless derived from the cross of S. George.

Blue mantle, instituted by Edward III. (or, according to some, Henry V.) and named from the robes of the order of the Garter.

Rouge dragon, founded by Henry VII., on the day before his coronation, the name being derived from the supposed ensign of Cadwaladyr.

Portcullis, instituted by the same monarch, from one of whose badges the title was derived.

The ancient costume of the king's pursuivants was a *surcoat*, embroidered with the royal arms, and worn sideways, that is, with one sleeve hanging down before, and the other behind. Their *tabards* are of damask silk.

There were also *Pursuivants* of the nobility who wore coats of their lords' arms, in the same manner as the king's pursuivants did, but they had no connection with the College of Arms.

Heraldry (fr. *armoirie*, or *La science des armes et de blason*): the name of *Heraldry* has been applied to the Art, or (as some with reason contend that it should be called) the Science which deals with observing, deciphering, and recording the coats of arms borne by the ancestors of the nobility and gentry of the present day; because in the sixteenth and seventeenth century this became an important part of the duties of the *Heralds*. It will be seen that a series of *Visitations* (q.v.) were commanded to be made throughout the country for this purpose, namely, to collect and register, as far as possible, all armorial and genealogical information. These visitations extend from 1528 to 1686, and then it is that we find the term *Heraldry* applied to the study, instead of '*Armorie*' and the like. At the same time, too, it may be said to have a wider signification.

There was, however, an extensive literature bearing on the subject going on simultaneously with these visitations. One of the earliest, if not the earliest book on the subject, is "The Boke of S. Alban's," first printed in 1486, the third part of which relates to 'coot armuris' beginning, "Here shall shortlie be shewyd to blase all armys if yo entende diligently to your rulys."

The following titles of books, with the date of their first publication, will shew perhaps more clearly the attention paid to the study, and the light in which it was viewed, than any general remarks. It is probable that the visitations gave considerable impetus to the study.

Gerard Leigh's "Accedence of Armorie," London, 1562.
John Bossewell's "Works of Armorie," London, 1572.
Sir John Ferne's "Blazon of Gentrie," London, 1586.
Sir William Segar's "Book of Honour," London, 1590.
William Wyrley's "The True Use of Armorie," 1592.
William Camden's "Discourse of Orders in Britain," [in his Britannia, 1594; also, "The Discoverie of certain Errors in the 'Britannia' ed. of 1594," by Ralph Brooke, 4to., 1596, reprinted in 1724].
Edmund Bolton's "Elements of Armories," London, 1610.
John Guillim's "Display of Heraldry," first published 1611.
Thomas Milles, "The Catalogue of Honour, or Treasure of true Nobilitie," London, 1610 (chiefly compiled by Robert Glover, his uncle).
Andrè Favine's "Theater of Honour and Knighthood," London, 1623.
James Yorke's "Union of Honour," London, 1640.
Nicholas Upton's "De Studio Militari Libri Quatuor;" cum notis Ed. Bissæi, Lond. 1654. [Upton, however, wrote c. A.D. 1450.]
Sylvanus Morgan's "The Sphere of Gentry," London, 1661.
John Selden's "Titles of Honour," London, 1614, (later ed. 1672).
Sir George Mackenzie's "Science of Heraldry," Edinburgh, 1680.
John Gibbon's "Introductio ad Latinam Blasoniam," Lond. 1682.
Randle Holme's "Academie of Armorie," Chester, 1688.
Samuel Kent's "Grammar of Heraldry," London, 1716.
Alexander Nisbet's "System of Heraldry," 2 vols., Edinburgh, 1722-42.
Joseph Edmondson's "Complete Body of Heraldry," 2 vols., London, 1780.
James Dallaway's "Inquiries into the Origin and Progress of Heraldry," Gloucester, 1793.
"Anecdotes of Heraldry," Worcester, 1795.

It will be seen by the above titles of books (representing

the chief works published at the time) that, with the one exception of Guillim's work, the term *Heraldry* is not used till quite the end of the seventeenth century; while in the next century it appears to be used exclusively in describing the study of coat-armour and all that belongs to it.

The greater part of the early treatises, and much of the later works, is taken up with fanciful disquisition, based on the guesses of the meaning of arms adopted, and attempts to adopt a scientific method in blazoning ; so much so, that a large number of forms are described in very technical language, which were never borne on any coat of arms at all. A fashion had arisen also of ascribing arms not only to the early Saxon kings, and also to the imaginary British kings of the Arthurian romances, but also to the chief personages of sacred and classical history. In Sylvanus Morgan's book we are gravely told that "to Adam was assigned a shield *gules*, and to Eve another *argent*, which latter Adam bore over his as an inescutcheon, his wife being sole heiress." Again, "that Adam after the fall bore a *garland of fig-leaves*, which Abel *quartered* with ' *Argent, an apple vert*,' in right of his mother." From Gerard Legh we learn that the arms of Alexander the Great were—

Gules, a golden lyon sitting on a chayer and holding a battayle-axe of silver.

In some instances the writers invented the arms themselves, in others they took idle gossip; but the worst part was that these legendary arms were not confined to the literature, but were carved in wood and stone, and such has been the extent that with respect to personages of the thirteenth and fourteenth centuries the fictitious arms cannot be distinguished from the genuine ones; thus the science has been obscured, and it is not too much to say, in consequence of some of their extravagancies, brought into ridicule.

The material, however, for the study of *Heraldry* is still very extensive. Apart from a very large number of monuments remaining in cathedrals and churches, a considerable amount of sculpture on domestic as well as on ecclesiastical buildings, and some stained glass in church windows, and in those of old manor-houses, as well as here and there paintings on panels, &c., go to supply our store of documentary evidence. A large number of the Visitations were taken happily before the Puritans had their way, when, as William Dowsing's Journal shews, as well as other evidence, superstition was made the excuse for pure havoc. It was only necessary to say that a monument was superstitious, or a coat of arms in a window was profane, and the axe and hammer shattered it. The work, however, done during these Visitations does not appear to have been so complete or so accurate as it might have been: certainly it would be much more satisfactory to have the originals before us now.

But the most important material we have are the rolls of arms, beginning as early as Henry III.'s reign. The following is a list of the chief rolls, only a few of which have been as yet printed:—

circa

.... Acre roll, MS.Harl. 6137, and MS. Ashmole, 1120 [dated 1192, but probably later].

1245. Roll MS. in the College of Arms, L. 14.

1260. Roll, MS. Harl. 6589.

1280. ,, MSS. Harl. 6137, 6589.

1286. ,, MS. Harl. 6137.

1290. ,, MS. Harl. 6137.

1296. ,, MS. Harl. 6137.

1298. Falkirk Roll, MS. Harl. 6589.

1299. Roll, MSS. Harl. 6137, 6589.

1300. ,, MSS. Harl. 6137, 6589.

1300. Carlaverock Poem, MS. Cotton, Caligula, A. 18.

1308. Dunstaple Roll, MSS. Harl. 6137, 6589.

1310. Roll, MS. Harl. 6589.

1312. ,, MS. Queen's Coll. Oxon,

circa

No. 158 MS.; Dodsworth, 145, 5086; MSS. Harl. 4033, 5803, 6137, 6589.

1322. BoroughbridgeRoll, MS.Ashmole, 831.

1338. Roll, Grimaldi's MS.

1346. ,, MS. College of Arms; MS. Harl. 6589.

1348. Calais Bannerets MS. Ashmole, 1120, Cotton MS. Tiberius E. 9, MSS. Harl. 6589, 6595.

1348. Calais Knights MS. Harl. 6589.

1395. Roll, Newling's MS.

1418. Rouen Roll, MS. Ashmole, 1120; MS. Harl. 6137.

1512. Parliament Roll, MS. Cole, 30.

A history of the origin and first actual instances of the use of armorial bearings, clearly distinguishing between true and regular coat-armour, and the classic devices and badges, symbols and the like, borne by tribes in warfare, or carved on their shields, and, above all, clearing it of the fancies and fictions with which the study has been surrounded in the sixteenth and seventeenth centuries, and by which it has been obscured, still remains to be written.

Hercules: this figure occurs on one coat of arms, and one only, so far as has been observed. He is repesented as holding a *quadrant*.

Azure, the figure of Hercules [in one blazon 'a savage'] wreathed about the head and middle with laurel-leaves, holding in the dexter hand a quadrant, and therewith looking towards a star in the dexter chief; and in the sinister hand holding a club all proper—OSWALD, Scotland.

Heron, (fr. *héron*): this and its allies the *hernshaw*, *bittern*, and *fencock*, are borne by several families; but, as will be seen in most cases, allusively. Probably no great distinction can be made in the several drawings except, perhaps, in the case of the *spoonbill;* indeed, there appears to be some confusion in blazoning the arms bearing these devices, and a further confusion between such and those bearing the *crane* and the *stork*. It will, however, be seen that the *Heron* proper is found in arms of ancient date. It is generally drawn *standing* but rare examples occur of it being blazoned volant.

Odinel HERON d'azur a trois herons d'argent—Roll, temp. HEN. III.

Sire Odynel HERON de argent a iij herons de azure—Roll, temp. ED. II.

Sire Roger HERON de goules a iij herons de argent—*Ibid.*

Sire Johan HEROUN de azure a iij herouns de argent—*Ibid.*

Sable, a heron within a bordure argent—MATTHEWS.

Azure, a bendlet between two herons [otherwise blazoned cranes] argent—HYGHAM.

MATTHEWS.

Gules, three herons argent, a bend engrailed or—HERON [in Canterbury Cathedral].

Sable, a bend argent between three heron's heads erased of the second —GLOVER.

Gules, three heronshaws [otherwise blazoned storks, and perhaps really pewits] or—TYRWHITT, co. Lincoln.

Or, on a chevron engrailed sable between three heronshaws [otherwise blazoned storks] argent, a plain chevron or—LYMINGTON, co. Chester.

Argent, a bittern [otherwise blazoned ' a fencock'] sable, membered gules—MATTHEW.

Sable, a bittern argent—ASBITTER.

Gules, three bitterns argent—BITTENNECK, or BITTERER.

Azure, on a bend or, within a bordure argent, three bitterns sable, membered gules—READE.

Gules, on a fesse or between three mascles ermine, each charged with three drops sable, a trefoil slipped azure between two bittern's heads erased of the field beaked argent, and about their necks a leash of the last—THACKER, co. Derby, granted 1538.

Or, a fesse wavy sable between three fencocks proper—FENCOTE, co. York.

Or, a heron volant proper; on a chief sable three escallops of the first —GRAHAM, Scotland.

With these may be associated the *spoonbill* (*platalea*), of which the head occurs only, and the French *aigrette*, with its remarkable tuft, but no example of an *egret* has been noted in English arms.

Argent, three spoonbill's heads erased argent beaked or—Sir John LACY, Cornwall.

D'azure, à trois aigrettes d'argent becqueés et membreés de sable— ALLIGRET, Champagne.

Herring, (fr. *hareng*, old fr. *hairaing*), is found more especially for the sake of the play upon its name, and this from the earliest period. The *cob*, which also supplies a convenient pun, is probably meant for a young herring, though the term is used for the young of other fish.

Sire Johan HERINGAUD, de azur crusule de or a vi harengs de or—Roll, temp. ED. II.

[On seal of John HERINGOL, of Westwell, Kent, temp. HEN. III., is a shield with a border charged with six herrings.]

Sable, three herrings hauriant argent, a chief or—Sir Thomas KYRTON, Sheriff of London, 1533.

Vert, a herring hauriant argent—Benjamin HARENC [Sheriff of Kent, 1777].

Azure, semee of crosslets, three herrings hauriant two and one argent—HERRING, Bp. of Bangor, 1738; Abp. of York, 1743; Abp. of Cant. 1747-57.

Sable, a fesse between six herrings [or sprats] hauriant or—SPRATTON.

HERRING

Sable, a chevron argent between three cob-fish naiant or; a chief of the last—Cobb, Sandringham. [A monument in Adderbury church, Oxfordshire, where a branch of the family resided.]

Gules, a chevron wavy between three cob-fish naiant argent, on a chief of the last two sea-cobs [or gulls] sable [and in one case given as two shovellers sable beaked and legged or]—Cobb, Sharnbrook, Bedfordshire.

Party per chevron sable and argent, in chief two sea-cobs [i.e. gulls] respecting each other, and in base a herring naiant or—Cobb, Snetisham, Norfolk.

Per chevron gules and sable, in chief two swans respectant, in base a herring proper [otherwise blazoned a herring-cob]—Cobb, co. Oxford, [Baronet, 1662].

Of the same family (*clupeidæ*) as the herring are other fishes which are named in heraldry, viz. the *sprat*, the *garvin*, and, on account of the name of the bearer, the *spalding*, which is perhaps, after all, but a local name. There is also the *pilchard* (Germ. *pelzer*, lat. *clupea pilchardus*) of the same family.

Argent, a chevron sable, between three sprats naiant proper—Thomas Spratt, Bp. of Rochester, 1684—1713.

Azure, three garvin fishes naiant fessways in pale argent—Garvie, Scotland.

Argent, a chevron sable between three spaldings azure—Spratt [or Sprott, Harleian MS. 1404].

Gules, a chevron or between three pilchards naiant argent—Job Militon [Governor of S. Michael's Mount, temp. Hen. VIII.]

Argent, a chevron gules between two roses in chief and a pilchard naiant—Roscarreck, Cornwall.

Hinge, (lat. *cardo*): hinges occur but in one coat of arms, affording a characteristic example of the play upon the name.

Hinge.

Sable, a fesse between three door-hinges argent— Cardinall, Hadley, Suffolk [in the arms of the Essex branch of this family the fesse is engrailed].

Hérissonné: used in French examples of a cat 'with its back up.'

Hermine, or *semé d'hermines*: the French manner of spelling *Ermine* (q.v.).

Heronshaw, or *Hernshaw*. See *Heron*.

Herse, (fr.): a *Portcullis*, also a *Harrow*.

Hersée, l.q. *coullssé*. closed with a portcullis.

Hibou, (fr.): *owl*.

Heydodde. See *Bluebottle*.

Hew = pick-*axe*.

Holly, (fr. *houx*): this is found rarely as a tree or bush; but the branches and sprigs often occur; still more so the leaves.

Gules, a boar argent, armed, bristled, collared and chained or, tied to a hollybush on a mount in base both proper—OWEN, co. Pembroke.

Argent, a holly-tree eradicated proper; on a chief engrailed azure a lion passant between two trefoils slipped or—DOWLING, Kilkenny [granted 1662].

Argent, a sheaf of arrows gules between three holly-branches [otherwise blazoned branches of holly, or sprigs of holly, and bundles of holly] each of as many leaves proper banded of the second—IRVINE, Scotland.

Argent, a holly-branch between three bay-leaves slipped vert—FOULIS, Edinburgh.

Argent, a chevron pean between three hollen-bushes [*sic*] fructed proper—BUSHNAN, co. Essex [granted 1784].

Argent, three holly-leaves pendent proper — INWYNE, Cumberland.

INWYNE.

Argent, a battle-axe between three holly-leaves in chief and a bugle-horn in base vert garnished gules—BURNET, Scotland.

Gules, on a bend argent six holly-leaves, two, two, and two bendwise in fesse sable—RYON.

Hone-stone: this singular device is found in one coat of arms only, and that on account of the name.

Argent, two bars wavy between three hone-stones azure—HONE, Devon. [Quartered by BODLEY.]

Hone-stone.

Honeysuckle: this, or the *woodbine*, is found but rarely in coats of arms.

Sable, on a fesse or between three honeysuckles argent two lions passant azure—MASTER, co. Wilts.

Azure, three woodbine leaves argent—BROWNE.

Argent, three woodbine leaves bendways vert two and one—THEME

Hie, (fr.): the paviour's beetle drawn like a fusil with rings.

Hill and *Hillock*. See *Mount*.

Hilt and *Hilted*. See *Sword*.

Hind. See *Deer*.

Hirondelle, (fr.); *Swallow*.

Hog. See *Boar*.

Hogsheads. See *Tun*.

Holy Lamb. See *Lamb, Holy*.

Homme d'armes: i.q. man in *armour*.

Honoured: occasionally used by heraldic writers in the sense of *crowned*.

Honour point. See *Point*.

Hook: it will, perhaps, be better to group under one head the chief varieties of hooks, though they are used for various purposes. They may be enumerated as follows:—

Boat-hook: this occurs in but one coat of arms.

Or, an annulet beset with three boat-hooks in triangle sable—BROBACH.

Fish-hook: this occurs in at least two coats of arms, and the cross hameçon, (see *Cross,* § 22), is supposed to have its termination in the form of fish-hooks.

Sable, a chevron between three fish-hooks argent—MEDVILLE.

Argent, a fesse sable between three fish-hooks gules—PENKERCH, co. Lincoln; also BOSDON.

Fish-hook.

Flesh-hook: a fork for the purpose of taking meat from the cauldron. The first figure is perhaps the more correct in form. The second figure is sometimes erroneously blazoned a *Pike-staff.*

1   2

Argent, a fesse between three flesh-hooks sable—PENKERIDGE.

Argent, three flesh-hooks (fig. 2) sable, two and one—WALLEY.

Flesh-hooks.

Pot-hooks, which appear to be the same as the *hangers* are borne only by German families; at least no example with a true English name has been observed. One of the forms it takes is given in the margin.

Argent, a hanger, or kettle-iron, expanded gules—KETTLER.

Argent, a double-hooked hanger closed in pale sable—ZERTSCHEN.

Rope-hook: this occurs in but one coat of arms.

KETTLER.

Argent, a chevron azure between three rope hooks sable—ROPE-MAKERS' Company, Newcastle-on-Tyne.

Hood: *Falcons* are sometimes borne *hooded.*

Hoofed. See *Unguled.*

Hooped: having iron hoops or bands of another tincture, e.g. *Buckets, Water-bougets.*

Tenter-hook: two forms of this charge occur, as shewn in the margin.

Sable, three tenter-hooks argent—CLARKE, or CLERKES.

Argent, three tenter-hooks sable—CLARK.

Argent, a fesse between three tenter-hooks sable —PENERECHE.

Tenter-hooks.

Argent, two tenter-hooks [elsewhere harts' horns] in saltire sable—LACHAULT.

Thatcher's-hook: this appears to be borne by two branches of the family of CHOWNE, according to the blazon. But the drawing is so vague, that they have been blazoned in one case as stag's *attires.*

Gules, three thatcher's hooks in fesse argent—CHOWNE, Kent.

Sable, three thatcher's hooks in pale argent—CHOWNE, Berks.

See also *Sickle,* called sometimes a pruning-hook ; *Horsepicker,* called erroneously a hay-hook. The shave-hook is given under *Plumbers'* implements.

Hop : this plant occurs under the form of *hop-vines, hop-bines,* and *hop-poles.*

Argent, on a bend engrailed gules, between two hop-vines with poles proper growing out of mounts vert, three stag's heads cabossed or—BOORMAN, Kent.

Argent, on three mounts vert as many hop-poles sustaining their fruit proper [otherwise as many hop-vines with their poles proper]—DARKER, London.

Argent, three hop-poles sustaining their fruit proper [otherwise three hop-bines fructed on their poles proper]—HOBILLION, London. [The same from a base vert ; HOUBLON.]

Horns of animals, (fr. *cornes*): the *horns* of *stags* (*attires,* q.v.), though generally affixed to the head or the scalp, are at times borne separately, but such arms appear to be, as a rule, of foreign origin. Of other animals only the cow's horns have been noticed as borne separately.

Hopper. See *Mill*-hopper.

Hopping : in one case used of a lion.

Horeler, i.q. *Oreiller.* See *Cushion.*

Horn. 1. See *Bugle-horn* and *Trumpet.* 2. Ink-horn under *Penner.* 3. Stags' horns under *Attires* and Deer. 4. Of a *mullet.*

Horned, (fr. *acorné*) of the *Bull, Unicorn,* and *Owl,* when the horns are of another tincture.

Hornet. See *Bee.*

Argent, a stag's horn in bend gules—REINSTEIN.

Argent, a hart's attire sable—ZAKESLEY.

Argent, two hart's horns in saltire sable—LACHAULT.

Argent, three stag's horns barways sable, the top to the dexter side—COUNTESSE.

Azure, two cow's horns endorsed or between four crosses crosslet fitchy argent—BURDON.

Horse, (fr. *cheval*): the *horse* does not occur in ancient rolls of arms, and less often than would be expected in modern coats. It is represented as *standing* (or *upright*), as *trotting*, as *courant*, or in *full career* (fr. *galoppant*, or *échappé*), and as *salient*, or *rearing* (fr. *acculé* and *cabré*, also *effaré*): it may be *saddled* (fr. *sellé*), and *bridled* (fr. *bridé*); also the general terms for *harnessed*, and with *trappings*, are found in French *bardé*, *houssé*, and *caparaçonné*, while the French term *gai* is used when the horse is at liberty, without any harness whatever.

In English arms the horse is sometimes represented as *spancelled*, a term used when two of its legs are fettered to a log of wood. Very frequently only horses' heads are given. The term *nag* is sometimes used for a *horse*, and *colt* also appears as a charge. A horse is borne in the insignia of the House of Hanover, and is found blazoned as the *White horse of Hanover*.

Argent, a horse standing sable—BROMFALING.

Sable, a horse upright argent bridled or—CAVELL, Devon.

Argent, a horse passant sable bridled and saddled or—ROSTLINGS.

Argent, on a mount in base vert a horse trotting sable furnished gules; in chief a star of the third—TROTTER, Scotland.

Argent, a fesse between a horse courant in chief, and a water bouget in base sable—COULTHARD, co. Lancaster.

Gules, a horse [argent] in full career—House of HANOVER [ancient SAXONY].

Sable, a horse passant argent, spancelled in both legs on the near side gules — PERCIVAL, Hants.

Gules, three horse's heads couped argent bridled sable—HORSLEY, Bp. of S. David's, 1788; of Rochester, 1792; afterwards of S. Asaph, 1802–6.

Sable, three nag's heads erased argent—JONES, Bp. of S. Asaph, 1692—1703.

PERCIVAL.

Gules, on a bend engrailed or, between two nag's heads erased argent, three fleurs-de-lys of the field; in chief a mullet for difference—PEPYS, Bp. of Sodor and Man, 1840; of Worcester, 1841–46.

Argent, a fesse between three nags passant sable —CULLIFORD, co. Dorset.

Gules, three colts courant argent, a fleur-de-lis or in the centre for difference—FRY.

Argent, a fesse azure between three colts in full speed sable—COLTE, Essex.

Sable, a fesse ermine between three colts passant argent—STAMP, co. Berks and Oxon.

PEPYS.

Horse-shoe, (fr. *fer-de-cheval*): the horse-shoe is found as a charge amongst the earliest arms we have. There are usually six or eight nail-holes, which should be of the tincture of the field; but when of another tincture probably it is intended for that of the *nails* (fr. *cloué*).

Argent, a horse-shoe azure—The burgh royal of DORNOCH, Scotland.

Argent, six horse-shoes sable, 3, 2, 1 [also, Gules, seven mascles conjoined or; on a label azure, nine horse-shoes argent] — FERRERS [Planché writes, "Three or six horse-shoes are said to have formed the early coat of the FER-RERS, Earls of Derby, who afterwards bore 'Vairy or and gules, and the horse-shoes as a border.'"]

Burgh of DORNOCH.

Gilbert de UMFREVILE, d'or ung quintefoile de goules, ung bordure d'azur ferrs de goulz—Roll, temp. HEN. III.

William de MONTGOMERY, d'ermyne a la bordure de goules et les fers en la bordure—*Ibid.*

Sire Johan de BAKEPUCE, de goules a ij barres de argent en le chef iij fers de cheval de or—Roll, temp. ED. II.

Argent, three horse-shoes sable pierced of the field—FARRIERS' Company [Inc. 1670].

Or, on a bend engrailed sable, three horse-shoes argent—ROBERT FERRAR, Bp. of S. David's, 1548–54.

Argent, five horse-shoes in saltire gules, nail-holes or—FERRERS.

Vert, on a pale gules between two horse-shoes, each horse-shoe between three nails, two in chief and one in base, all meeting with their points to the shoe, argent; a sword in a scabbard azure, hilt, pommel, and studding of the scabbard or; on the point of the sword a cap of maintenance gules turned up ermine; on a chief per pale of the fifth and purple, a boar's head couped of the third between two demi-roses, the dexter of the second barbed of the first, the sinister argent barbed vert each issuing rays from its centre pointing to the boar's head gold—City of GLOU-CESTER. [Arms obtained by Sir Richard Bell, temp. HEN. VIII., replacing the more simple and original arms, " Or, three chevrons gules between ten torteauxes three, three, three and one."]

Argent, six horse-shoes sable, three, two and one studded with gilt nails—Augustinian Priory of LITTLE DARLEY, Derbyshire.

[Horse-shoes are borne also by families of ENDESORE; HODSON; PITT; SMITH, Eastbourne; SOUTH, Wilts; COOK; VYTAN-GIMPUS; BOHEM; BOOTH; besides the various families of FERRERS, FERRIER, FERRARS, and FARRAR. Borne also by the town of OAKHAM, and the Cistercian Abbey of FOUNTAINS, Yorkshire.]

Horse-picker, or, as it is called also, *Dog-hook,* or *Hay-hook:* a very singular charge, and probably peculiar to the arms of METRINGHAM.

Vert, a chevron between three horse-pickers argent—METRINGHAM. [From Glover's Ordinary and MS. Harl. 1386.]

Horse-picker.

Horse-leech: one coat of arms only has this device.
Azure, three horse-leeches—PREEDE, co. Salop [MS. Harl. 7570].

Hose: these are apparently borne on one ancient coat of arms.
Argent, three hose gules—HESE, Roll, temp. ED. I., penes Soc. Ant.

Hour-glass, or *Sand-glass:* this device is borne only on two or three coats of arms. In connection with the Bible, it has possibly a reference to the preaching by the hour.

Horse-fly. See *Gad-fly.*

Houce des armes, (old fr.): a surcoat embroidered with armorial bearings.

Houlette, (fr.): a shepherd's crook.

Hound. See *Dog.*

House-fly. See *Fly.*

House-leak. See *Sengreen.*

Housing : the embroidered caparison of a horse. See *Caparison.*

Houssé: of a *horse* having a *housing,* or horse-cloth.

Housseau, or *Housette:* described as a kind of medieval boot, and appears somewhat equivalent to the English buskin. Used in several cases in French arms.

Houx, (fr.): *holly.*

Hovering. Of a bird: see *disclosed* under *Wings.*

Howdah. See *Elephant.*

Party per chevron embattled or and gules, three roses counterchanged slipped vert; on a chief of the second three hour-glasses argent framed of the first—John WHITE, Bp. of Lincoln, 1534; of Winchester, 1557–59.

Vert, in chief the holy Bible expanded proper; in base a sand-glass running argent—JOASS, Scotland.

Vert, on a chevron between three hour-glasses argent as many trefoils slipped of the first—SHADFORTH, Northumberland.

WHITE.

Vert, three hour-glasses in bend proper between two bendlets argent—ANDERTON, co. Lancaster.

Humetty, (fr. *alésé*), is a term applied to certain ordinaries instead of *couped*, which is applied to charges, and especially those of animals. Applied to the *fesse* and the *bar*, humetty signifies that both ends are cut off so as not to reach to the edge of the shield. Applied to *crosses* (see *Cross*, § 7) and *saltires*, all four ends are so treated; and when there is more than one of either of these in the same shield they are to be drawn *humetty*, though it be not expressed. It does not appear that a *bend* is ever *humetty*, and the single *bendlet* so treated would be blazoned a *baton*, q.v. Nor has any example been observed of a *pale* or *pile* so blazoned; the chevron and the pallet are sometimes *couped*, but the term *humetty* seems not to be applied to them.

Sable, a fesse humetty argent—BOSTOCK, Cheshire.

Argent, a fesse engrailed humetty sable, between three chaplets of holly-leaves proper—Nicholas BUBBEWYTH, Bp. of London, 1406; Bp. of Salisbury, 1407; afterwards of Bath and Wells, 1408–24.

Ermine, on three bars humetty gules, nine escallops or three, three, and three—John de DABRICHECOURT, Roll, temp. RIC. II.

BOSTOCK.

Huchet, (fr.): a *bugle*.
Huit: an old term used for *owl*.
Huitfoil. See *Foil*.
Hulk and *Hull*. See *Ship*.

Hulotte, (fr.): *owlett*.
Human figure. See *Man*.
Human skull. See *Bones*.
Hunting-horn. See *Bugle-horn*.

Argent, two bendlets humetty purpure—KEYE, Oxon, (gr. 1688).

Gules, a fesse humetty ermine; over all a pale couped ermines—
SPONNE.

Per fesse or and argent; in chief three palets couped in base gules—
KEITH, Scotland.

Per pale argent and or, three palets couped gules—BARNARDER.

Gules, five palets raguled, trunked, and couped or—SOMERVILLE.

The *Humet* is a term sometimes, but seldom, used for a *fesse*,
or *bar humetty*, i.e. couped at each of the extremities.

Or, three humets sable, charged with as many annulets argent—
AMBROSE, Lancashire.

Hurt, (fr. *heurte*, but more frequently *tourteau d'azur*):
a *roundle azure*, said to be named from the hurtle or whortle-
berry. The term does not appear to be used before the seventeenth century. In old arms the '*rondels de azure*' and *pellets
de azure* signify the same thing. See also under *roundle*. The
term *hurty*, signifying *semé* of *hurts*, is also employed.

Sire Walter BASCREVILE, de argent a iij rondels de azure e un cheveron
de goules, crusule de or—Roll, temp. ED. II.

Monsire de BASKERVILE, d'argent a une cheveron gules charge de trois
lis d'or; entre le cheveron trois pelletts d'asur—Roll, temp. ED. III.

D'argent, a trois tourteaux d'azur—LANCESSEUR,
Normandie.

Argent, a fesse sable in chief three hurts—LANG-
LEY, co. Gloucester.

Or, a hurt—HURTLE [Randle Holmes' MS.]

Argent, six hurts, two, two, and two—SHIELDS.

Argent, two bars azure; in chief three hurts
—CARNABY.

Argent, three bars azure; in chief as many hurts
—BASSETT.

LANGLEY.

Gules, fretty argent; on each joint a hurt—WYMESWOLD.

Azure, a buck trippant or between three pheons argent; within a bordure engrailed of the second hurty [or better 'charged with eight hurts']
—PARKER, co. Cambridge.

Huppu, (fr.): a *Pewit*. See under
  Lapwing.

Hure, (fr.): the name given to
  the head of the wild *boar* when
  couped or erased.

Hurst. See *Wood*.

Husked; when the husk is of a
  different tincture—e.g. of an
  acorn. See under *Oak*.

Hyacinth. See *Tenné*.

Hydra. See *Cockatrice*.

Impaling: the meaning and object of the impaling or setting side by side two coats of arms or more in the same shield will be found explained under *marshalling*, as well as some of the chief rules laid down by heralds respecting the process. An example is here given from a monument which once existed in Dorchester Church, Oxon, which is thus blazoned by Antony à Wood.

YOUNG.

Lozengie argent and vert; on a chevron gules three bezants; on a chief gules a goat's head erased between two cinquefoils or; *Impaling*, (1) Or, on a chevron between three choughs gules, a crescent or; (2) Azure, three hatchets or—William YOUNG and Alicia his wife, which died, May 15, 1430. [Wood does not give the name of the second wife.]

It will be observed that the ordinaries, or charges, have to be drawn, as a rule, smaller, or at least narrower, than when the whole shield is occupied; and what is particularly to be noticed is that when a *bordure*, or an *orle*, or *tressure* occurs, it is, as a rule, not continued round the side where the impaling takes place; it may be said to be (but not blazoned as) *couped* by the line of impalement. The example given in the margin represents the arms of John KEMP, Abp. of Canterbury, 1452.

Azure, a pastoral staff in pale or, ensigned with a cross pattée argent, surmounted by a pall of the last, edged and fringed of the second, charged with four crosses pattée fitchée sable, for CANTERBURY; impaled with Gules, three garbes within a bordure engrailed or, for KEMP.

John KEMP.
Impaling CANTERBURY.

Other illustrations of *Impaling* will be found under *Marshalling*. It will, as a rule, readily be distinguished from *Party per pale*.

Ibex. See *Antelope*.

Icicles. See *Gouttes*.

Imbattled. See *Embattled, Imbowed, Imbrued*, &c.

Immole: misreading of *jumellé*.

Incontrant: of two aquatic birds, e.g *Sea-pies, Geese*, or *Swans*, swimming towards one another.

Indented, (fr. *denché*), sometimes written *endented :* signifies
that the edge of the ordinary, or the line of partition, is notched
after the manner of *dancetty*, but with smaller teeth. It is applied most frequently to the fesse, though the bend, the pale, and
the chevron are sometimes thus treated; also the chief, the indentation of course being in this case only on the under side.
When the indentations are so deep as that the points touch the alternate edges of the ordinary, they are said
to be *indented point in point,* or *throughout.*

Azure, a chief indented or—DUNHAM, Lincolnshire.

Sire Roger de BAVENT, de argent, od le chef
endente de sable—Roll, temp. ED. II.

Sire Elys DAUBENY, de goules a une fesse endente de argent—*Ibid.*

Azure, a chevron indented gules—BRIGHTELEY,
Devon.

DUNHAM.

Azure, a bend indented point in point or
and gules between six escallops of the second—CRUSE, Devon.

Argent, a fesse per fesse indented throughout
vert and sable, cottised counterchanged [other-
wise, a fesse indented point in point vert and
sable]—HODY, Dorset.

Argent, a fesse indented point in point or and
gules; three trefoils slipped in chief sable—TYLL,
Devon.

When the indentation of two ordinaries
intersected one another the term ' *de l'un
en l'autre* ' was employed. The number

HODY.

of the *endentures* (or *indents*) is also sometimes given, and

---

Incensed, (fr. *animé*) : said of
panthers and other wild beasts
borne with fire issuing from their
mouths and eyes.

Increment, or *Increscent.* See
Moon.

Inde. See *Azure,* and examples
under *Cadency* and *Colour.*

Indian. See *Man.*

Indorse, i.q. *endorse,* and *Indorsed.*

See *Endorsed.* Similarly *Ingrailed, Inhanced,* &c.

Inescutcheon. See under *Escutcheon.*

Infant. See *Child,* also *Head.*

Infamed; i.q. *Defamed.*

Inflamed, (fr. *ardent*): burning
with fire. See *Altar, Beacon,* &c.

Infula. See *Cap.*

Ingots of gold. See *Metal.*

it is clear the old *endenté* answers rather to the modern *dancetty*.

Sire Walter de Fresnes, de goules à ij bendes endentes de or e de azure le un en le autre. Sire Hugh de Fresnes, de argent e de azure les bendes endente. [The first might be blazoned 'Gules, a bend per bend indented or and azure;' the second is intended to have the same field] —Roll, temp. ED. II.

Sire William de MONTAGU, de argent, a une fesse endente de goules a iij endentures—*Ibid*.

Interlaced, (fr. *entrelacé*): of any three charges so arranged, such as *angles*, *annulets*, or fish (see *Salmon*); two ordinaries also may be so arranged, e.g. two *chevrons* or a *fesse* and *chevron* may be so treated. But the term is not a very definite one, being used in the place of *braced, embraced, fretted,* &c.

Gules, a chevron argent interlacing another reversed or—SHEDAN, Scotland.

Argent, a fesse and chevron interlaced sable—KEMPSING, co. Kent.

Invected, *invecked, envecked,* or *invecqued :* the reverse of engrailed, the points being turned inwards. Although *engrailed* occurs frequently in ancient rolls of arms, no case has been observed of *invected*, and, indeed, it is somewhat rare in modern arms, and it is doubtful if it occurs in French arms.

Invected.

Gules, a pale invected argent—VECK, Scotland.

Ermine, a fesse invecked azure between two bees volant in chief proper, and a damask rose in base gules barbed vert—KEET, Canterbury.

Or, two bars invected above and engrailed below gules—BOXLE.

Argent, a fesse azure voided invecked of the field; in chief a martlet sable—WIGGON.

Ingulphant, *ingullant,* or *engulphant,* swallowing, e.g. of a *Whale* swallowing a fish. See *Vorant*.

Ink-horn. See *Penner.*

Ink-moline. See *Fer-de-moulin.*

Inraced, i.q. *Indented.*

Inter. Some heralds have used this word for *between*.

Interchangeably posed : said of three arrows, *swords,* q.v.

fishes, or other long charges, placed over one another, but not fretted.

Interchanged : erroneously used for *Counterchanged.*

Inverted, or reversed; used when the charge is turned upside down.

Involved : said of a serpent when twisted round in a circular direction (fr. *arrondi*).

Argent, two bendlets invecked sable; a mullet in the sinister chief point for difference—RADCLIFFE, [Somerset Herald, 1543].

Or, three bars azure, over all a saltire counterchanged within a bordure invecked gules—DIPFORD, London.

Interstices : a somewhat awkward expression used in cases where awkward arms have to be blazoned, similar to the following.

Argent, semy of annulets, within each a lion rampant and an eagle displayed alternately sable; in the interstices a lesser annulet of the last —YVAIN.

Ireland, *Insignia of.* These have been very differently described by early heraldic writers; indeed so much doubt has prevailed concerning them that in the reign of Edward IV. a commission was issued to enquire what they were.

Azure, three crowns in pale proper—According to the commission, temp. ED. IV.

Gules, three ' old harpes ' [cloyshackes] or, stringed argent, two and one—MS. Harl. 304. [*Three* harps occur as the arms of Ireland upon certain coins of Elizabeth, A.D. 1561.]

Gules, a castle argent, a hart issuing out of the gate in his proper colour, horned or—*Ibid.*

" [The armes of Yrland] as by the description of strangers is per pale gules and argent, in the gules an armed arme w̄ the poldron arg. holding a sword in the gantlet, garnished gold; in the silv'r a demy splayed egle sable, membred gules."—*Ibid.*

On a field vert a harp or stringed argent—The [unauthorized] national flag of Ireland.

Although our kings were styled lords of Ireland from the time of its conquest, and even though Henry VIII. was in 1541 declared king of that island by an Act of Parliament, its armorial ensigns were not quartered with those of England until the accession of James I. They are now held to be—

Azure, a harp or, stringed argent. *Crest:* upon a wreath or and azure, a tower (sometimes triple-towered) gold, from the port, a hart springing argent [also a harp or stringed argent, but this is properly the badge].

See also under *Badges.*

Iris. See *Lily.*

Irish brogue. See *Boot.*

Iron, a Basket-maker's, see *Basket.*

    Grossing-iron and cripping-iron,

see *Glaziers.* Cutting-iron and soldering - iron, see *Plumbers.* Also *Wiredrawer's* iron.

Irradiated : surrounded by rays.

Issant, or *Issuant:* arising from the bottom line of a field or chief, or from the upper line of a fesse, or from a coronet. *Naissant,* a term with which *issuant* is often confounded, has a somewhat different signification, namely, when the figure rises from the midst of the *chief,* or *fesse,* or other charge. *Issuing from the side of the shield* is also found; and this is perhaps the same as the French *mouvant.* See under *Arm, Aspect,* &c.

Azure, on a chief or, a demi-lion rampant issuant gules—MARKHAM, Notts.

Argent, a fesse gules, a demi-lion issuing therefrom sable—CHALMERS, Scotland.

MARKHAM.

Ivy branches: so far as has been observed, only two examples occur, and then on account of the name.

Argent, a bend sable between three ivy branches proper—IVETT.

Argent, an ivy branch overspreading the whole field vert—The town of SAINT IVES, Cornwall.

Jessant, (fr. *issant*), shooting or giving forth: is often used for *issuant,* and sometimes, though erroneously, for *naissant.* The term is chiefly applied to the *fleur-de-lis,* and the phrase *jessant-de-lis* is used with respect to a leopard's head having a fleur-de-lis passing through it, as in the insignia of the See of HEREFORD; though there seems to be some doubt whether the *reversing* of the leopard's head was not by accident, since

---

Jacob's staff. See *Staff.*

Jacynthe, or *Hyacynthe.* See *Tenné.*

Jambe, (fr.): a leg. See *Gambe.*

Jar. See Fish-*weel.*

Jars, (fr.): a gander. See *Goose.*

Jaune. See *Or.*

Javelin, (fr. *javelot*). See *Spear.*

Jaw-bone. See *Bones.*

Jay. See *Magpie.*

Jellopped, *Jowlopped:* used to describe the *wattles* or *gills* of a cock when of a tincture different from his body.

Jersey-comb. See *Wool-comb.*

Jesses: the thongs by which bells are fastened to the legs of a *falcon,* q.v. Hence *jessed.*

Jew's harp. See *Harp.*

John, S., the Baptist. See *Heads.*

Joinant: i.q. *conjoined,* or *conjunct,* e.g. of *annulets,* &c.; but seldom used.

Jowlopped, i.q. *Jellopped.*

in the reign of Edward III. the blazon makes no mention
of the fact.

Sable, a leopard's head [or face] argent, jessant
a fleur-de-lis or—MORLEY, Hants, &c.

Argent, a lion passant guardant gules royally
crowned or, between two chess-rooks in chief
sable and a cup in base gold, jessant a flame
proper; a bordure azure— OGILVIE, Ruthven,
Scotland.

Sable, in chief a lion passant guardant, in base
a leopard's head jessant - de - lis or. [Another,
Argent, on two bars sable three leopard's heads
or jessant fleurs-de-lis of the first]—MORELAND.

MORLEY.

Sire Johan de CAUNTELO, de azure a iij flures de
or od testes de lupars yssauns—Roll, temp. ED. II.

Gules, three leopard's faces reversed jessant-
de-lys or—Walter de CANTILUPE, Bp. of Worcester, 1236–66; and Thomas de CANTILUPE, Bp.
of Hereford, 1275–82; and afterwards the Insignia of the See of HEREFORD.

Gules, ten crescents each jessant a quatrefoil
argent—RONGROLLIS.

DE CANTILUPE.

Or, a fesse chequy argent and azure between
three crescents jessant as many crosses-croslet fitchy gules—ROWANS,
Scotland.

Justice: the figure of 'Justice' is borne on one coat of
arms thus,

Azure, a female figure representing Justice habited in white holding in
the dexter hand a pair of scales and in the sinister a sceptre, both or—
WIRGMAN, London.

Key, (fr. clef): is a very common bearing in the insignia
of sees and religious houses, especially such as are under the
patronage of S. Peter; in other arms they are supposed to
denote office in the state.

Jug. See Ewer.

July-flower. See Gilly flower.

Jumelle, (fr.): a Bar gemelle.
Jumelle, (fr.), is also used when
chevrons, bends, &c., are doubled.

Jupiter: the planetary term for
Azure. See also Thunderbolt.

Katherine-wheel. See Wheel.

Kene, (and qu Kanee), old fr.:
supposed to be chêne. See Oak
and Cross, § 24.

Kernellated, i.q. crenellated. See
Embattled.

Keys, Ashen. See Ash.

Keys borne singly are usually in pale, and as two keys can be placed in a variety of ways the particular way must be expressed. More frequently the two are borne in *saltire* (fr. *passées en sautoir*), but they may be *addorsed* (fr. *adossées*). Further, it is necessary sometimes to state on which side the wards (fr. *panne- tons*) of the keys should be drawn. When no direction is given, the key is drawn *erect:* i.e. with the *bow* in base. Keys may be *interlaced* in the *bows*, or *rings*.

Azure, two keys in saltire or—See of GLOU-CESTER.

Gules, two keys in saltire or—CHAMBERLEYN.

Gules, three pairs of keys in saltire or; on a chief as many dolphins naiant argent—Company of SALT-FISHMONGERS [in stained glass at Canterbury].

Azure, three pairs of keys, two in chief and one in base or; each pair addorsed and conjoined in the rings, the wards in chief—ABBOTSBURY Abbey, Dorset.

See of GLOUCESTER.

Gules, two keys endorsed in saltire between four cross crosslets fitchy or—See (and Deanery) of PETERBOROUGH.

Gules, on a chevron between three keys argent as many estoiles of the field—Matthew PARKER, Abp. of Cant. 1539–75.

Gules, three keys, enfiled with as many crowns or—Robert ORFORD, Bp. of Ely, 1303–10.

Argent, two bends nebulé within a bordure gules charged with twelve pairs of keys addorsed and interlaced with rings or, the wards in chief—EXETER College, Oxford [i.e. Arms of Bp. STAPLEDON, founder, A.D. 1314],

Argent, a bend sinister sable in chief an annulet gules, in base a griffin's head erased of the second, holding in his beak a key azure—KAY, co. Durham; also Scotland.

Gules, three keys fessways in pale, wards downwards or—GIBSON, Scotland.

Per chevron dovetail ermine and gules, three keys erect or—KEY, co. Gloucester; also KEY, Lord Mayor of London, 1830–31.

Per chevron gules and sable, three keys or, the wards of the two in chief facing each other, those of the one in base to the sinister—Roger KEYS, Clericus [granted by HEN. VI. 1449].

Azure, three fleurs-de-lis, two and one, and as many keys, one and two, or—SHELLETOE.

Azure, three fleurs-de-lis or, one and two, and as many keys of the last two and one—SHILECORNE, co. York.

Azure, flory and a lion rampant or; over all on a bend gules three keys gold—Benedictine Priory at HOLLAND, co. Lancaster.

Keys occur in the insignia of the following Sees : CASHEL ; DOWN AND CONNOR ; DROMORE ; GLOUCESTER ; EXETER ; JAMAICA ; KILLALOE ; OSSORY ; PETERBOROUGH ; QUEBEC ; SAINT ASAPH ; WINCHESTER ; YORK.

Of the following Abbeys and Religious Houses : ABBOTSBURY, Dorset ; BATH ; BOURNE, Lincolnshire ; BROMME, Hants ; CHERTSEY, Surrey ; ELY ; S. Peter's, GLOUCESTER ; HYDE, near Winchester ; HOLLAND, Lincolnshire ; S. Mary de MENDHAM, Yorkshire ; MUCHELNEY, Somerset ; PENWORTHAM, Lancashire ; PETERBOROUGH ; PLYMPTON, Devon ; THURGARTEN, Norfolk.

Of the following Cities and Towns : MONTGOMERY ; PETERBOROUGH ; SALISBURY ; SAINT ASAPH ; BATH ; GUILDFORD ; TOTNES.

The Deaneries of ST. ASAPH, WELLS, and YORK. (Peterborough Deanery bears the same arms as the See.)

King: the title and position of the *King* has given rise to much discourse by heraldic writers, but there is nothing very practical to be derived from such discourses. The *King's arms* have already been treated of under *Arms royal*, the *Kings of arms* under *Heralds*. It should, however, be observed that on one or two coats of arms a *King* is borne as a charge, and generally a full description is given.

Argent, on a mount a bear standing against a tree all proper, the bear collared and chained or, between two escutcheons in fesse, each charged with the arms of France and England quarterly ; on a chief argent a king crowned and habited proper holding in his dexter hand a mound and in the sinister a sceptre both or—Town of BERWICK-UPON-TWEED.

Sable, a king enthroned proper—IRELAND ; Harl. MS. 4039.

Kings of Cologne, *The Three*. The three Magi, or Wise Men, in the legendary account, are changed into three Kings, and their bodies were supposed to have been brought by the Empress Helena to Constantinople, afterwards transferred to Milan, and in 1164, on the taking of Milan, presented by the Emperor Frederick to the Abp. of Cologne. No doubt the

---

Kidneys. See *Lambs'* kidneys.
Kings of Arms. See *Heralds*.

Kite. See *Falcon*.
Knee-holly. See *Brush*.

offerings given at this shrine which enclosed them went a long way to erect Cologne Cathedral. The names usually ascribed to them are Jaspar, Melchior, and Balthasar.

Gules, on three bezants the Kings of Cologne [elsewhere blazoned as three bezants each charged with a crowned king, his robes sable doubled ermine, holding in his right hand a covered cup and in his left a sword of the second]—LYLDE, Thomas DE LISLE, or DE INSULA, Bishop of Ely, 1345–61.

DE INSULA.

Kingfisher: this bird seems to be borne by at least two families, and in one branch of the second family it is, oddly enough, blazoned *gules*.

Per fesse argent and azure a pale counterchanged three kingfishers of the second—HONYTON.

Or, three kingfishers proper—FISHER, London.

Or, a kingfisher close gules—FYSHER, co. Bedford.

Knife: knives are not unfrequently borne in arms, but they have generally some precise designation, e.g. the shoemaker's *knife*, the pruning *knife*, and the shredding *knife*, but it is difficult to find good examples to shew the correct drawing. In the insignia of CROWLAND Abbey they are sometimes blazoned as S. Bartholomew's *knives*.

The *plumber's* cutting-knife, and the *patten-maker's* cutting-knife, and the *currier's* paring-knife, will be found beneath their respective heads.

Pruning-knife.

Butchers' *knives* are borne by the foreign families of KOHLER, KROSIG, and WINCKEL in Saxony, but no English examples have been noticed.

Gules, a knife argent, haft or—BLOOD.

Azure, three knives argent, hafted gules—KNYVETT.

Gules, three knives argent—WORSYCKE.

Quarterly first and fourth gules, three knives erect in fesse argent handles or, second and third azure, three scourges erect in fesse or with three lashes to each—CROWLAND, Benedictine ABBEY, co. Lincoln.

Argent, three shoemaker's knives gules—HACKLET.

BLOOD.

Azure, a cutting-knife proper ensigned with a marquess's coronet or—
CORDNERS' Company, Edinburgh.

Argent, three shredding-knives sable—ABBOT, co. Salop.

Knights : Knight is a title of honour derived from the old
English Cniht, a servant or attendant, which refers to those
who attended kings upon horseback, whence the name by which
the knight is distinguished in other languages, e.g. chevalier,
ritter, &c. In medieval Latin, however, the term *miles* is used
instead of *eques*.

There are many orders and kinds of knighthood, but only
those need here be noticed which have been connected with
Great Britain and Ireland.

I. *Knight Bachelor* is the most ancient, though lowest, rank
of knighthood. Every holder of a knight's fee, that is, of
a certain quantity of land, varying at different periods, was,
from the introduction of knight-service by William the Conqueror to its abolition in the 12th of Charles II. capable of receiving knighthood; indeed, early in the sixteenth century it
became usual to compel every such holder either to receive
knighthood, or make a composition with the sovereign for the
loss of his services; for every knight was bound to attend the
king in war for forty days, reckoned from the time of arrival in
the country of the enemy. Since the abolition of knight-service
knighthood has been conferred without regard to property, as
a mark of the esteem of the sovereign, or a reward for service.

The arms of a knight bachelor are only distinguished from
those of an esquire by the full-faced and open helmet, and this
distinction is not ancient.

II. *Knight Banneret* is not known to occur in England previous to the reign of Edward I.; and about the commencement
of the sixteenth century the title seems to have been almost
entirely laid aside: still occasionally, i.e. in 1547, 1642, 1743,
and 1764, and so late as 1773, instances occur. As to the last
creation, however, great doubts were raised as to regularity.

III. *The Order of the Bath*, (lat. *Ordo de Balneo*, fr. *Ordre du
Bain*). The institution of the Society of the Bath does not seem
to be of greater antiquity than the reign of Henry IV., who at

his coronation gave the title to forty-six esquires. It was at first not strictly an *order*, although the dignity was conferred at coronations and other great national ceremonies, such as the marriage of the sovereign, or the creation of a prince of Wales. Forty-six knights of the Bath were made at the coronation of Queen Mary, and sixty-eight at that of King Charles II. They were anciently distinguished by an *emerasse* or escutcheon of azure silk upon the left shoulder charged with three crowns proper, with the motto, *Trois en un.*

From the coronation of King Charles II. the dignity was disused until revived by letters patent of George I. dated May 18, 1725. It was then directed to be a military *Order* consisting of the sovereign, a grand master, and thirty-six companions, besides a dean, register, king of arms, genealogist, secretary, usher, and messenger. The office of dean was annexed to the deanery of the collegiate church of S. Peter at Westminster, but the other officers were directed to be appointed by the grand master.

In 1725 the collar and badge are thus described :—

Collar of the Order of the BATH.

Nine imperial crowns of gold (five demi arches visible, no caps) and eight roses and thistles [the shamrock has been added subsequently] issuing from a sceptre, all enamelled proper, linked together with seventeen white knots.

Badge of the Order of the BATH.

An oval plate azure, charged with a sceptre in pale, from which issued a rose and a thistle, between three imperial crowns proper ; the whole within the circle of the order.

Collar and Badge of Knights of the Bath.

A banner of arms was also directed to be suspended over the stall of each Companion in King Henry VII.'s chapel at Westminster.

The order continued in this form until January 2, 1815, when the Prince Regent, in commemoration of the termination of war, ordained that the order should henceforward consist of the three following classes.

. (*a.*) *Knights grand cross* (G.C.B.), corresponding with the late companions. These were never to exceed the number of seventy-two, of whom twelve might

Circle and Badge of the Order of the Bath.

be nominated for civil services. The arms of knights of this class are distinguished by supporters, and by being placed within the red circle of the order edged with gold, and having the motto *Tria juncta in uno*, in gold letters. This is surrounded with a wreath of laurel, and has the badge of the order pendent by a red ribbon; over this badge is an escroll azure, with the words *Ich Dien*, or. Knights who have received the order for civil services omit the wreath of laurel and the escroll.

Or, on a chief indented sable, three crescents argent—Adm. Sir Eliab HARVEY, G.C.B.

(*b.*) *Knights commanders* (K.C.B.), who must be officers holding commissions in the British army or navy. They are not permitted to use supporters, but may place their arms within the red circle, with a similar, but somewhat smaller *badge* pendent. The number was originally fixed at 180, exclusive of ten honorary knights, who were to be foreigners holding commissions in the English service.

(*c.*) *Companions* (C.B.), who are unlimited as to number, and take precedence of all esquires, but not authorized to assume the style of knighthood. This class was at first exclu-

sively composed of naval and military officers, but afterwards
included civilians. They may bear the *badge* belonging to their
class pendent by a red ribbon below their arms, which are not
otherwise distinguished from those of esquires. The *Stars*,
like the badges, vary in several particulars according to the
class by which they are to be worn.

IV. *The Order of the Garter*, (fr. *Ordre de la Jarretière*):
Froissart fixes the date of the institution of this order to the 18th
year of King Edward III., though, perhaps, it was not actually
bestowed till some few years later. Edward had lately assumed
the title of King of France, and seems to have instituted the
Order of the Garter to reward some of the most distinguished
persons by whose assistance he accomplished the conquest.
Hence the colour of the garter is blue,—the royal livery of
France, and the motto, HONI SOIT QUI MAL Y PENSE, which
should be translated, *"Dishonoured be he who thinks ill of it,"*
may be reasonably understood to refer to the order itself.
Why the garter was chosen as the badge of the order is not
known, since the singular story respecting the Countess of
Salisbury does not deserve consideration. It is worn by
knights buckled below the left knee, and it encircles the left
arm of her Majesty. The order originally consisted of the
sovereign and twenty-five companions, of whom the Prince of
Wales was first. The original statutes of the order are lost.
Others were given by Henry V. and Henry VIII., and a few
trifling alterations have been made since.

The principal officers of the order are,

(*a.*) The PRELATE, who has always been the bishop of Winchester. He may encircle his arms (impaled with the insignia
of the see) with the garter. The badge of his office may be
suspended beneath by a dark blue ribbon.

(*b.*) The CHANCELLOR. An office fulfilled by one of the companions, until Edward IV. annexed the chancellorship to the see
of Salisbury. In Edward VI.'s reign it passed into lay hands,
but in 1669 the chapter of the order re-annexed the office to the
see of Salisbury, and recent alterations (1836) having placed
Windsor in the diocese of Oxford, the Bishop of Oxford is now

Chancellor of the garter. His arms are arranged in a similar manner to those of the prelate.

(*c.*) The REGISTRAR, whose office was instituted at the foundation of the order, was annexed to the deanery of Windsor, 8 Hen. VIII. His arms (with the insignia of the deanery,—argent, a cross gules) may be encircled by the garter, the badge being appended below.

(*d.*) GARTER KING OF ARMS, an office instituted by Henry V., the order having hitherto been attended by Windsor herald. See *Kings of arms*, under *Herald*. His badge (which may be suspended below his arms) consists of the arms of S. George and the royal arms impaled within the garter, and ensigned with the imperial crown.

(*e.*) THE GENTLEMAN USHER OF THE BLACK ROD, who is required to be a natural-born subject of England, and a knight bachelor. This office was instituted by the founder. His badge is a knot (like those in the collar) within the garter.

The *Garter* does not appear to have been commonly placed around the arms either of the sovereign, companions, or officers, until the reign of Henry VIII., the earlier stall plates in S. George's chapel at Windsor being without it. The colour of the garter is blue, the motto and edging being of gold. The motto was anciently in the old English character, but for some centuries past it has usually been in Roman.

The Garter.

Or, a chevron gules—Edw. STAFFORD, Duke of Buckingham (ob. 1521).

The collar (which may be placed around arms, outside the garter) consists of twenty-six garters enclosing red roses, barbed and seeded proper, upon a blue ground, and as many golden knots, i.e. in reference to the sovereign and twenty-five companions. To one of the garters the *George* is suspended. This is a figure of S. George on horseback, piercing the fallen dragon, which lies upon a mount.

This *Collar* was ordained by King Henry VIII., whose arms occur within it; and the *Star* was devised in 1664, i.e. of eight points formed by silver rays surrounding the badge, which con-

The Collar of the Order of the Garter.

sists of a cross of S. George, surrounded by the motto.

Although there are precedents to justify surrounding the impaled arms of a knight and his lady with the garter, it is not usual, and certainly must be laid aside by the lady should she survive her husband.

The Order of the Garter in Ireland was instituted in 1466 by King Edward IV., but was abolished by parliament in 1494.

V. *The Hanoverian, or Guelphic order.* This order was instituted by King George IV. when Prince Regent, Aug. 12, 1815, but it is no longer connected with the British empire.

VI. *Knights Hospitallers of S. John of Jerusalem;* often called *Knights of Rhodes,* and afterwards *of Malta,* from their temporary occupation of those islands.

In the year 1048, almost half a century before the first Crusade, some merchants of Amalfi, in the kingdom of Naples, were permitted by the infidels to erect three religious edifices in Jerusalem: a church, called S. Mary ad Latinos; a convent for women, dedicated to S. Mary Magdalene; and an hospital for pilgrims, dedicated to S. John the Baptist. From the latter sprung the most celebrated order of knighthood that ever existed in Christendom. At the close of the eleventh century the brethren of the hospital of S. John, under Gerard, their first superior, materially assisted the crusaders by affording relief to their sick and wounded; and in gratitude for their services many of the European princes gave them considerable property in their respective states. A few years afterwards the brethren assumed a long black habit, with a cross of white cloth of the form since called *Maltese* [see *Cross*, § 23], upon the left breast. The rule which they adopted was that of S. Augustine, and the arrangements were ratified in 1113 by Pope Paschal II. The first body of statutes were given, in 1121, by Raymund du Puy, and confirmed by Pope Calixtus II. in the same year.

The order, having become military as well as religious, was soon joined by many persons of very high rank, and rapidly increased in wealth and influence. Upon the downfall of Christian power at Jerusalem (1187) the Hospitallers were forced to move from place to place, till, in 1310, they besieged and conquered Rhodes, with seven smaller islands adjacent, hence they have been sometimes called by this title. Their newly-acquired territory was frequently attacked by the Saracens, and eventually, in 1523, they were compelled to surrender the islands to an immense army under the Sultan Solyman, called the Magnificent. Upon the 24th of March, 1530, the emperor Charles V., to whose neglect to assist the knights the loss of Rhodes was attributed, ceded to the order the sovereignty of the island of Malta, whence their later title.

An important branch of the order was established in England in the magnificent hospital of S. John of Jerusalem at Clerkenwell, founded by Jordan Briset, a baron, about 1110, and the prior of this Hospital had a seat in the Upper House of Parliament, and was commonly styled first Baron of England. This hospital, with all its dependencies, was dissolved by Act of Parliament, 32 Hen. VIII. (1540), but restored by charter of Queen Mary in 1557. About a year afterwards the knights being called upon to take the oath of supremacy to Queen Elizabeth, chose rather to surrender into her hands all their possessions.

The ensign of this order of S. John is gules, a *cross* argent, and while in official seals, &c., the Grand Masters quartered this cross in the first and fourth, the knights bore it upon a *chief*. A *Maltese cross*, enamelled white, and edged with gold, is worn by all the knights as a *badge*, with certain variations denoting their several countries.

The annexed woodcut represents the arms of Sir Thomas DOCWRA, the last prior but one of S. John of Jerusalem in England before the dissolution, as sculptured upon the gateway of S. John's, Clerkenwell (1504), which has recently been restored.

Sable, a chevron engrailed argent, between three plates, each charged with a pallet gules; on a chief of the last a cross argent—Sir Thomas DOCWRA.

DOCWRA.

VII. *The most distinguished Order of SS. Michael and George.* An order which was founded by King George IV. when Prince Regent, April 27, 1818, in commemoration of the republic of the Ionian islands being placed under the protection of Great Britain. The Sovereign of Great Britain being protector of the United States of the Ionian islands, was also Sovereign of the order of SS. Michael and George. The Grand Master was the Lord High Commissioner of the United States of the Ionian islands for the time being. The order has been much modified of late, and is now used as a reward for services in the colonies. It consists of three classes, Knights Grand Crosses, Knights Commanders, and Knights Companions. The principal officers are two Prelates, a Chancellor, a King of arms, and a Registrar.

The ribbon of the order is blue, with a red stripe of one third of its width down the centre. The badge appended to it is a white star of seven double rays, edged with gold and ensigned with the royal crown. Upon its centre is a circular plate, upon which is a representation of the archangel Michael overcoming Satan. In his right hand is a flaming sword, and in his left a chain. This is surrounded by a blue fillet edged with gold, and inscribed AUSPICIUM MELIORIS ÆVI in letters of the same.

VIII. *The Order of the Passion of Jesus Christ* was founded by Richard II. of England and Charles VI. of France in 1380, for the recovery of the Holy Land. It was to have consisted of one thousand knights, each attended by one esquire and three men-at-arms, and its officers were a Grand Justiciary and a Grand Bailiff, but the duration of this order appears to have been very brief.

The *badge* of the order was as follows :—

A plain red cross fimbriated with gold, upon the intersection an eight-foiled compartment (composed of four pointed leaves in cross, and four round ones in saltire) sable, edged or, and charged with an agnus Dei proper

IX. *The Order of S. Patrick.* An order instituted by King George III. for his kingdom of Ireland, Feb. 5, 1783. It consists of the Sovereign, the Grand Master, who is the Lord Lieutenant of Ireland for the time being, and knights, originally fifteen in number, but at present more, the first of whom is always a prince of the blood royal. Each knight has three esquires. The first investiture took place at Dublin Castle, March 11, 1783, and the first installation in the cathedral of S. Patrick on the 17th of the same month.

The officers up to 1870 were the Prelate, viz. the Archbishop of Armagh; the Chancellor, viz. the Archbishop of Dublin; the

Registrar, which office was annexed to the deanery of S. Patrick's; Ulster king of arms, Athlone pursuivant, the Genealogist, Secretary, and Usher of the black rod.

The *collar* is of pure gold, and is composed as follows :—

Six harps and five roses (each rose with a bordure charged with trefoils) alternately disposed, and connected by twelve knots. The central place is occupied by a royal crown, to which the badge is appended by another harp.

An oval plate argent, charged with a saltire gules, surmounted by a trefoil slipped proper, on each to be an imperial crown of the last. The oval plate has two borders, the innermost or,

Order of S. PATRICK.

with the motto QUIS SEPARABIT, MDCCLXXXIII., the outer argent, charged with about sixteen trefoils proper—Badge of the Order of S. PATRICK.

When the collar is not placed around the arms of a knight, this badge may be suspended below them by a light blue ribbon. The *Star* is of chased silver, similar to that of S. Patrick, but with the badge in the centre, surrounded by a circle, which bears the motto.

X. *Knights of the Round Table*. an imaginary order of knighthood, the institution of which is attributed by the legend to King Arthur, when he entertained twenty-four of his chief warriors at a table, which, in order to prevent disputes about precedency, was made circular. The names and arms of these warriors, supplied of course by the fancy of after ages, are given by writers of the sixteenth century.

On the first of January, 1344, King Edward III. kept a great festival at Windsor, in the *domus quæ 'Rotunda tabula' vocaretur*, 200 feet in diameter; which probably referred to the large Round Tower at Windsor. It is considered that this was rather a grand commemoration of the supposed order than in any sense an actual revival of it. A painted table also, of about the time of Henry VII., and made on some commemoration of the order, is preserved in the county hall at Winchester.

XI. *Knights of the Royal Oak.* This was to have been the designation of an order contemplated by King Charles II. Six hundred and eighty-seven baronets, knights, and gentlemen, were selected as its recipients, but the project was relinquished.

XII. *Knights Templars.* An order founded in the Holy Land in or about 1119, to guard the supposed site of the Temple of Solomon, and to protect pilgrims who resorted thither. The original number of knights was only nine. They received a rule from Pope Honorius II., who directed them to wear a white dress, to which they afterwards (by order of Pope Eugenius III.) added a red cross. The order of Templars, like that of S. John, consisted of three classes, Knights, Priests, and Serving brothers. As a religious order they conformed themselves to the rule of S. Augustine. Their first settlement in England was in Holborn, London, which was soon eclipsed in splendour by their house in Fleet-street, still known as the

Temple. The round church erected by them here in imitation of the Church of the Holy Sepulchre at Jerusalem was dedicated by Heraclius, patriarch of the Church of the Resurrection in that city, Feb. 10, 1185. The chancel was consecrated in 1240.

Early in the following century, the Templars were charged with many great crimes, perhaps with the view of seizing their vast possessions. However this may be, they were on the Wednesday after Epiphany (Jan. 10), 1308, arrested throughout England by command of the king (Edward II.), and by authority of a papal bull; and a council held at London, A.D. 1309, having convicted them of various crimes, the king seized all their possessions. In 1312 a council held by Pope Clement V. at Vienne in Dauphiné, condemned the order throughout Christendom, and gave their property to the knights of S. John. Their English possessions were formally transferred to the said order, by an Act of Parliament made in the 17th year of King Edward II., A.D. 1323.

The badge of the order was a red patriarchal cross edged with gold, and their *banner* (called *beauseant*) per fesse sable and argent, signifying terror to the enemies of Christianity, and peace to its friends.

XIII. *The Order of the Thistle*, or *of S. Andrew*. The charter of King James VII., dated May 29, 1687, by which the order was restored, and the chapel of Holyrood-house appointed for installations, gives a traditional account of its origin. It has been supposed to be at least coeval in its origin with the order of the Garter, inasmuch as certain coins of Robert II. of Scotland (A.D. 1370-90) bear on the reverse the figure of S. Andrew supporting his saltire; but this is very weak evidence. Nothing can be said of the order with any degree of certainty until the time of King James V., in or about the year 1540. It was again brought into notice by Queen Anne, Dec. 31, 1703, and has flourished ever since. Simple knighthood is a necessary condition of admittance into the order of S. Andrew. The officers of the order are a Dean, a Secretary, Lyon King of Arms, and an Usher of the Green Rod.

The *collar* and *badge* of the order are composed as follows:—

Golden thistles and sprigs of rue enamelled proper—The Collar.

A radiant star of eight points, charged with a figure of S. Andrew proper (his gown green and surcoat purple), standing upon a mount vert, and supporting his cross argent—The Badge of the Order of the THISTLE.

The jewel, worn attached to a green ribbon, consists of an oval plate argent, charged with the same figure proper, within a border vert, fimbriated (both internally and externally) or, and inscribed, in letters of the same, NEMO ME IMPUNE LACESSIT.

Order of the THISTLE.

In the base of this border is a thistle of the last. The ribbon of the order may encircle the arms of knights instead of the collar, the jewel being appended to it.

XIV. *The most exalted Order of the Star of India.* Instituted by her Majesty, February 23, 1862; consisting of a Sovereign, a Grand Master, and twenty-five Knights, with such honorary Knights as her Majesty shall choose to appoint. The first class of twenty-five are styled Knights Grand Commanders, and there are now a second and a third class. The collar and badge are as follows:—

The *Collar* is composed of a Lotus-flower of four cusps, two palm branches set saltire-wise, and tied with a ribbon; alternating with an heraldic rose; all of gold, enamelled proper, and connected by a double chain, also of gold. In the centre, between two Lotus-flowers, is placed an imperial crown enamelled proper, from which by a small ring depends the badge.

The *Badge* is a chamfered mullet set with brilliants, below which is an oval medallion of onyx cameo, having a profile bust of her Majesty; the whole encircled by a band enamelled azure fimbriated with brilliants, bearing the motto of the order, 'Heaven's light, our Guide.'

XV. With the above should perhaps be classed *The Royal Order of Victoria and Albert.* This illustrious order also was instituted by her Majesty on Feb. 10, 1862, in commemoration of her marriage with the late Prince Consort, but it is conferred *solely* upon Ladies. The institution was primarily for conferring an order upon her Majesty's female descendants, and the wives of her male descendants, as well as upon queens and princesses of foreign houses connected by blood or amity, but consists now of three classes.

XVI. *Various Orders.* The above, perhaps, complete the list for Great Britain, but there are, besides, certain Orders of Knights which appear to have held but a brief existence; and others of a mythical character, though they are found referred to in books of reputation. The *Knights of S. Antony*, supposed to have been established in Ethiopia by the famous Prester John, *c.* A.D. 370: an order called the *Knights of the Swan*, said to have been instituted in Flanders, *c.* A.D. 500: an order called the *Knights of the Dog*, said to have been established by King Clovis in France about the same time: and an *Order of S. Lazarus*, said to have had its existence at Jerusalem long before the Crusades, and to have had a hospital there for lepers, and the *Knights of S. George* in Italy, said to have been incorporated by Constantine, rest upon little or no foundation whatever.

The *Knights of S. James* are said to have been founded by Ramira, the Christian King of Leon, in A.D. 837; but according to others by Ferdinand the First, King of Castile, to expel the Moors from Spain.

The *Knights of S. Catherine* at Mount Sinai, instituted to protect and guard the sepulchre of that virgin in A.D. 1063, are said to have been founded at the same time as the Knights Hospitallers of S. John of Jerusalem. Also at this time the *Knights of the Holy Sepulchre* are said to have been established, but very soon to have merged into the *Order of the Knights Hospitallers.*

The *Teutonick Knights* are said to have been established also in Jerusalem by wealthy travellers from Bremen, Lubeck, and other German cities. The *Knights of the Martyrs* in Palestine are also found mentioned, as well as the *Knights of S. Blaise*, and of *Jean d'Arc.* The subject, however, of Knights errant requires a book to itself.

Knitting-frame: this is borne only by the FRAMEWORK KNITTERS of London, a company incorporated 1663. The *knitting-needle* is borne only by one of the supporters.

Argent, a knitting-frame sable garnished or, with work pendent in base gules. Supporters: the dexter a student of the University of Oxford vested proper; the sinister a woman proper vested azure, handkerchief, apron, and cuffs to the gown argent; in her dexter hand a knitting-needle, and in her sinister a piece of worsted knit gules—Company of FRAMEWORK KNITTERS.

Label, (fr. *lambel,* in old fr. *lambell, labell,* and *labeu*): a charge generally considered to be a temporary mark of *cadency,* q.v. In the ordinary system of differences a label of three points (which has also been termed *a file with three labels*) is the distinction of the eldest son during the lifetime of his father. In the oldest rolls of arms the labels are all of five points; but labels of three points were at an early period used interchangeably. The theories respecting two extra points being borne to mark the surviving generations will not hold.

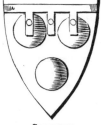

COURTENY.

Labels have been supposed by some to represent the collar and cape of a garment, with several pendent labels or tongues, which were worn hanging from the back part of the neck, over the surcoat or tabard.

King EDWARD I. before his accession differenced his arms with a label azure, sometimes of five points, and sometimes (even on the same seal) of three points.

EDMUND Plantagenet, called Crouchback, earl of Lancaster, the second son of Henry III., bore England with a label, sometimes (as his seal testifies) of three points, and at other times of

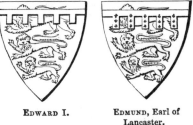

EDWARD I.　　　EDMUND, Earl of Lancaster.

five points, as upon his monument at Westminster. In both instances each point is charged with three fleurs-de-lis.

The earliest instances on record of the use of the label in England appear to be the following:—

England, with a label of five points azure—Geoffery PLANTAGENET, earl of Anjou, Poictiers, Britanny, and Richmond, fourth son of King Henry II., born 1159, and died 1186.

After this date the label is frequently noticed.

Le ROY D'ANGLETERRE, porte goules trois lupards d'or.

Son fitz, teile, ovecque ung labell d'azur—Roll, temp. HEN. III.

Le Counte de LANCASTRE, les armes de Engleterre od le label de France —Roll, temp. ED. II.

JOHN OF GAUNT,
Duke of Lancaster

Quarterly France and England, a label of three points ermine — JOHN OF GAUNT, third son of Edward III., created Earl of Derby and Duke of Lancaster, 1340. [In the roll of arms, however temp. ED. III., in the College of Arms the arms are thus given :—Le Count de Darby, port les armes d'Engleterre a une baston d'asure.]

Monsire Richard de GREY, de Sandiacre port les armes de Grey [i.e. barre de vj peces d'azur et argent] a une labell gules besante—Roll, temp. ED. III.

Besides being used as mere temporary marks of cadency, labels are also employed as permanent distinctions, that is to say, they are borne by every member of some particular branches of certain families, just as any other charge is borne.

Sire Hue de COURTENY, de or a iij rondeus de goules e un label de azure—Roll, temp. ED. II.

Or, three torteaux; on a label azure, three mitres of the field—William COURTENAY, Bp. of Hereford, 1374 ; of London, 1375 ; Abp. of Canterbury, 1381-96.

Or, three torteaux ; with a label of three points ; azure, on each point a bezant—COURTENAY, Devon.

Gules, a saltire argent a label of three points azure—NEVILL.

NEVILL.

[Richard NEVILLE, Earl of Salisbury in Henry VIth's reign, as well as his son, Richard, Earl of Warwick, bore a label of three points, compony, argent and azure.]

Argent, three chevrons gules; a label of three points azure—Shute Barrington, Bp. of Llandaff, 1769; of Salisbury, 1782; of Durham, 1791—1826.

[Several other families appear also to bear a saltire, with a label, e.g. Bafford; Barksworth; Belesby [or Helesby, spelt Halusby]; Beroun; Botetort; Bounorter; Charnelly; Clubblaw, Cookfield, Gurney; Fitzgerald; Kerdestone; Maxwell; Shouldham; Typtoft, &c.

The points were first straight, then pattée, and at last labels were formed as they generally are at the present day, without any connection with the sides of the shield, the points dovetailed.

A label.

In later times the shape of the label was sometimes varied, nor was it confined to three or five points (or *drops*, as they are sometimes irregularly called). The labels were terminated also in other charges, e.g. *bells*. And one of three points, each formed as a plain cross and charged with five escallops argent, was borne by John de Foix, Earl of Kendal, 1449. The label also was borne at times on an ordinary, or in different positions.

Or, a fesse gules and label of eleven points azure—Saher de Quincy, Earl of Winchester [*c.* 1210].

Sable, three crescents; in chief a label of two drops, and in fesse another of one drop argent—Fitzsimon, Harl. MS. 1441.

Or, three files borne barways gules, the first having five points, the second four, and the last three—Liskerke, Holland [Gwillim].

Or, a lion rampant sable; on a chief gules a label of five points argent—Thomas Dampier, Bp. of Rochester, 1802; of Ely, 1808–12.

Argent, a file of three points in bend sable—Goffe, Ireland.

Argent, a label of five points in bend gules—Morten [ascribed in Guillim, 1632, to 'one Morien, an alien'].

DAMPIER.

Or, a file gules with three bells pendent azure clappers sable—Belfile.

Labels, (fr. *lambeaux*), is a term also applied to the pendent ribbons at the side of the *mitre* (q.v.).

Knowed. See *Nowed.*

Knots. See *Cords.*

Knotted. See *Raguly ;* also *Nowed.*

Lacs d'amour: a true lover's knot.

Ladder, *Scaling,* (fr. *échelle*): the military ladder, with the curved top, is what is intended. The charge is perhaps more frequent in Welsh arms. In French arms the number of *rounds* (fr. *échelons*) are occasionally named.

Argent, three scaling-ladders bendwise, two and one, gules—KILLINGWORTH.

Argent, a tower sable, having a scaling-ladder raised against it in bend sinister or—MAUNSELL.

Or, three double scaling-ladders sable—ASHLIN.

Ladder.

Azure, three beacons with ladders or, fired gules—GERVAYS.

Azure, a lion rampant between in chief two castles triple towered, and in base a scaling-ladder argent, a bordure or charged with four roses gules, and as many spear-heads sable alternately—JAMES.

Sable, a spear-head between three scaling-ladders erect argent—Sir Robert DE LA VALE.

D'or à l'aigle éployée de sable portant en ses serres une échelle de cinq échelons d'argent—L'ESCHELLE.

Lamb, (fr. *agneau*): when represented *passant*, the face is shewn in profile; but when the *Holy* or *Paschal Lamb* is intended then the face should be *guardant* or *reguardant*.

This bearing varies considerably in different examples, particularly in the shape of the flag, but the annexed figure may be considered as a fair type. The nimbus should be gold, with a red cross: the flag argent, cross and ends gules. The Holy

The Holy Lamb.

Lamb is, however, not unfrequently borne all of one colour.

Argent, a chevron engrailed gules between three lambs passant sable—LAMB.

Azure, three paschal-lambs or—LAMB.

Argent, on a cross gules a paschal-lamb or carrying a banner argent, charged with a cross of the second—The Honourable Society of the MIDDLE TEMPLE.

Ladies' heads. See *Heads.*

Lambeaux: dovetails; used also of the files of the *label.*

Lambel, (fr.): e.g. *Label.*

Lambrequin: the *Mantle* placed upon a helmet: also the point of a *Label.* The word is sometimes applied to the wreath.

Gules, three holy lambs argent [elsewhere, or] —Rowe, Devon.

Argent, on a base wavy azure, a lamb triumphant [i.e. with the banner] sable—John de Oxford, Bp. of Norwich, 1175–1200.

Argent, a paschal-lamb couchant, with banner argent, staff and nimbus or, in base the letters P P of the last—Town of Preston, co. Lancaster.

Azure, a chevron argent, over all a bend or, on a canton of the last a holy lamb gules—Eynell.

Gules, a castle triple towered argent, between a holy lamb passant with cross-staff and banner of S. Andrew on the dexter, and the head of S. John the Baptist in a charger on the sinister, both proper; in base the sea of the last—Burgh of Ayr, Scotland.

Argent, on a saltire gules two keys in saltire or; on a chief of the second a holy lamb proper—See of Ripon.

Two families in France, and one or two in England, of the name of Pascal, or Paschal, bear the Holy Lamb.

Amongst the examples of the worst style of English heraldry occur the two charges, a *lamb* with three heads, and a *lamb's kidneys.*

Vert, a lamb passant, with three heads guardant and reguardant argent—Trippet.

Azure, on a chevron or between in chief two lambs, and in base a ram argent, three lamb's kidneys gules—Kidney, London; and Market Harborough, co. Leicester, granted 1765.

Lamp, (fr. *lampe*): several forms of this charge are found in arms; one drawn after the Roman model occurs in the insignia of the Society of Antiquaries. Some are borne as in fig. 1, e.g. by the family of Farmer, while the Company of Tin-plate-workers bear their lamps like urns with covers. (fig. 2.)

Lamp, fig. 1.

Sable, a chevron argent, between three lamps of the same, inflamed proper—Farmer, Leic. (granted 1663).

An antique Roman lamp or, over it 'Non extinguetur'—Crest of Society of Antiquaries.

Sable, a chevron or between three lamps (the two in chief one light each, facing each other, the lamp in base with two lights) argent garnished or, illuminated proper—Company of Tin-plate workers [Inc. 1670].

Argent, on a fesse sable three lamps or—Periond.

Argent, three lamps sable—Lamplow.

Lamp, fig. 2.

Lamprey, (fr. *lamproi*) : this fish occurs but rarely in coats of arms.

Sable, three lampreys in pale argent—RADFORD, Devonshire.

Azure, on a bend or three lampreys of the first—CASTLETON, Suffolk.

Or, three lampreys proper—LAMPRELL, Flanders.

D'azur, a trois lamproies d'argent mouchetées de sable, posées en fasce—HELYE, Languedoc.

Landscapes: several views and landscapes, with skies and sea, have been gradually introduced into modern heraldry, but it is needless to say that their introduction is an absolute departure from the principles by which the choice of ancient devices was guided. Perhaps one of the first to adopt the innovation was the Trinity House ; but other companies did the same, and then Indian and naval officers followed suit, with scenes in India or sea pieces. See also under *Flowers.*

Azure, a cross gules, between four ships of three masts each under full sail all proper ; on each sail, pennant, and ensign, a cross gules, and each quarter painted as a sea-piece with sky, sea, &c., all proper—TRINITY HOUSE Guild or Confraternity [Inc. 1515].

Azure, a globe whereon are represented the Straits of Magellan and Cape Horn, all proper ; in the sinister chief point two herrings hauriant in saltire argent, crowned or; on a canton the united arms of Great Britain of the second—SOUTH SEA Company, established by Act of Parliament, 1712.

Lantern, *Ship,* or *Globular lamp.* Such a lantern, ensigned with a royal crown, all proper, is the crest of the Company of TIN-PLATE-WORKERS of London. The fr. *Falot* is somewhat similar, being a sort of lantern borne on a pole or handle.

Ship's Lantern.

De gueules, au falot d'or—DURANT, Burgundy.

D'azur, a trois falots d'argent, emmanchés d'or, et garnis de sable—LANTERNIER, Normandy.

Lamp, *Globular.* See *Lantern.*

Lampago. See under *Satyr.*

Lampassé, (fr.) *langued,* is used by French heralds with reference to the tongue of a lion, or other quadruped, when of a different tincture.

Lance, (fr. *lance*). See *Spear.*

Lancel. See *Fleam.*

Langue, (fr.) *langued :* but used especially of the tongues of eagles, dragons, &c., and all winged animals.

Langued. See *Lampassé.*

Lapwing (or *pewit*) : this bird is frequently found blazoned by name; also the *Tyrwhitt*, which appears to be another name for it.

The French *huppe* (signifying crested) is the same as the *pewit*.

Azure, a bend between three lapwings argent—HYHAM.

Azure, a fesse engrailed ermine between six lapwing's heads erased argent—SPENCER.

Gules, three lapwings close or—TYRWHITT, Lincolnshire.

TYRWHITT.

Gules, three lapwings or—TERRICK, Bp. of Peterborough, 1757; Bp. of London, 1764–77. [The name is probably a corruption of TYRWHITT.]

D'azur, a une huppe d'or; au chef d'argent chargé de trois hermines de sable—PELISSIER, Bourgoyne.

The *sea-pye* seems also to be associated with it, which is a maritime bird of a dark brown colour with a white breast.

Gules, a cross patonce or, between four sea-pyes proper (i.e. sable winged argent)—S. Edmund de ABBENDON, Abp. of Cant. 1233–40.

Argent, three sea-pyes proper—WALDEN.

Argent, two sea-pyes incontrant sable—TRELAWNEY, Cornwall.

Sea-pye.

Lapwings are also borne by the families of ISPRED, CRULE, HERBERT, HEWITT, &c., while *Sea-pyes* are borne by families of SAWYER, TREVENOM, TYRWHITT, WILKINS, &c.

Larks : very few coats of arms appear with this bird named.

Argent, three larks proper—BARKER.

Laths : a bundle of laths is borne by the BRICKLAYERS' Company, and also by the WOODMONGERS' Company, but not by any family.

Azure, a chevron or; in chief a fleur-de-lis argent, between two brick axes paleways of the second, in base a bunch of laths of the last—BRICKLAYERS' and TILERS' Company, incorporated 1508.

Bundle of laths.

Larmes, or *Larmettes, Gutté de.* See *Goutes*.
Lapin. See *Rabbit* under *Hare*.

Argent, a chevron sable between three bundles of laths vert [as the second, in 1716]—Company of WOODMONGERS, London, V. Cotton MS. Tiberius, D. 10, fo. 885.

Latticed, (fr. *treillisé,* or *treillé,* also fancifully called *portcullised*): a pattern said to resemble fretty, but placed crossways, and closer; also that it may be interlaced or not, and that it is sometimes *cloué* or nailed at each intersection, but the term is seldom, if ever, used by English heralds.

D'argent, treillisé de gueules, cloué d'or—BARDONNENCHE.

Laurel, (fr. *laurier*): branches of this plant have been granted for military services, and *sprigs* of laurel are also found named. The wreaths of *laurel,* or *bay,* have already been noted as 'crowns triumphal' under *Chaplet.* But the *leaves* only (q.v.) occur most frequently, and these often blazoned as *bay-leaves.*

Gules, the stump of a aurel-tree eradicated proper on a chief or an Eastern crown of the field between two annulets azure—BURROUGHS, Castle Bagshaw, co. Cavan, Baronetcy.

Gules, a fesse between in chief a mullet and in base a dove or holding in the beak a sprig of laurel vert—WALKER.

Argent, a chevron gules between three bay-leaves vert—BOYFORD, or BYFORD.

Gules, three ducal coronets or, on a chief of the second as many bay-leaves vert—BIRKENHEAD.

Laurel branches have been granted to the families of GAITSKILL, BYNG (Earl and Baron Stafford), &c.

Leaves, (fr. *feuilles*): such as *oak, holly, laurel,* or *bay,* and more especially the last, are the more usual ; but it will be seen that many other leaves are borne, and besides those which are mentioned by name, sometimes *leaves* simply, when probably laurel-leaves are meant. The leaves on the arms of LYNDE-WODE are blazoned *linden-leaves,* and are supposed to be those of the lime-tree. What leaf is meant by the *gletver* named in the Roll of Arms as borne by SIR JOHN DE LISLE is very doubtful:

Laurier, (fr.) *laurel.*

Laver : (1.) See *Plough.* (2.) See *Seaweed.*

Laver-pot. See *Ewer.*

Leash, the thongs of leather. See under *Falcon.* Also a line fixed to the collar of a greyhound.

possibly the cleaver-leaf (a name given to the *galium aperinum*) may be intended. Care should be taken accurately to describe the position of the leaf, which is generally erect. In French arms leaves are sometimes *veined* (*nervés*) of another tincture.

Azure, a fesse nebuly argent between three leaves or—LEVESON, Warwick.

Sr Walter de Lytm pnrl d'un en ung chevron de gulêz, iij foules de gulcz ou ung label d'azur—Harl. MS. No. 6589.

Azure, a water-leaf argent—MORIENS, Suffolk.

.... a chevron .... between three linden-leaves—JOHN LYNDEWODE (on a brass 1421 at Linwood, co. Lincoln).

Argent, four leaves in pairs pendent sable; on a canton azure three crescents or—GROVE.

Sire Johan DEL ILE, de or a un chevron e iij foilles de gletvers de goules —Roll, temp. ED. II.

Leg, (fr. *jambe*): The legs of men are not unfrequently borne, but generally in armour. The knee is always embowed.

Three legs conjoined in the fesse point in armour proper, garnished and spurred or—Insignia of the ISLE OF MAN.

[The motto belonging to these insignia is QUO-CUNQUE JECERIS STABIT.]

Le ROY DE MAN de goules a treys gambes armes o tutte le quisses et chekun cornere seyt un pee—From Harl. MS. 6589, temp. HEN. III.

Isle of Man.

Gules, a leg in pale, armed and couped at the thigh between two spears proper—GILBERT, Bp. of Llandaff, 1740; afterwards Bp. of Salisbury, 1748; Abp. of York, 1757–61; also GILBERT, Bp. of Chichester, 1842.

Gules, a fesse argent between a bow and arrow in full draught in chief, and three men's legs couped at the thighs in fesse paleways of the second—BIRNEY, Broomhill, Scotland.

Argent, a fesse between three legs couped at the ankle of the first fretty gules, the toes to the sinister side—TREMAYLL.

GILBERT.

Legs of beasts and birds with the *paw, foot,* &c., are also

Legged: when the legs of a bird are of a different tincture. The more usual term is *membered.*

Leopard. See under *Lion.*

Leopardé. For *passant,* see *Lion.*

borne as charges apart from the animal or bird itself: but the term most used is *gambe*, q.v. The fr. term *à la quise*, i.e. at the thigh, is also frequently found in connection with *erased*.

Argent, a black bear's dexter hind-leg erect couped at the thigh, shewing the bottom of the foot all proper—PLANTA, Sussex.

Argent, two lion's gambes in saltire azure—NERT, co. Worcester.

Gules, two lion's gambes couped under the knees, the claws endorsed or—BAREFOOT.

Sable, two lion's gambes bended issuing from the dexter and sinister sides meeting foot to foot in the chief point [or simply 'issuing from the sides of the escutcheon and meeting chevronwise'] argent between three annulets or—MARKEBY.

Gules, three eagle's legs a la quise or—BAND, co. Worcester.

Argent, three raven's legs erased sable meeting in the fesse point, talons gulee, extended in the three acute corners of the escutcheon—OWEN AP MADOC, Wales.

Letters of the Alphabet (fr. *lettres*) are occasionally employed as charges. The following instances will suffice to shew the different ways in which they have been used. The letters may be old Text, or Greek, or Roman, and hence the type should be stated.

The signification of the letters of the charge is not always apparent. When an 𝕸 occurs it is no doubt as a rule intended for MARIA or MARY.

Sable, on a fesse between two cinquefoils in chief argent, and on a mount in base three sprigs of oak proper, acorned or, the text letters 𝕬 𝕭 𝕮 𝕯 𝕰 𝕱 of the field—LANG.

Gules, three text 𝕾's or—KEKITMORE.

Argent, a chevron (another two chevronels) between three text 𝕿's sable—TOFTE.

Azure, a cross argent charged with the letter 𝕏, in the fesse point, and the letter i, in the honour point, both sable—CHRIST CHURCH PRIORY, Canterbury. [These letters were evidently intended as a contraction of the word *Christi*. Since the Reformation the above insignia have been used for the Deanery, the ancient letters having generally been changed to x and i.]

Argent, a cross gules with a letter r in the centre—City of ROCHESTER.

Party per chevron argent and sable, in chief the Greek letters A and Ω of the second, in base a grasshopper of the first; on a chief gules a lion passant guardant or—Greek Professorship at CAMBRIDGE, granted 1590.

Sable, on a pale argent a Greek upsilon gules—CLARK, London, granted 21 Jan. 1604.

Argent, on a cross azure the letter 𝔐 crowned or—Arms ascribed to William de ST. MARY'S CHURCH, Bishop of London, 1199—1221; Simon MEPHAM, Archbishop of Canterbury, 1328-33; Simon SUDBURY, alias TYBOLD, Bishop of London, 1362; Archbishop of Canterbury, 1875-81.

Per chevron or and vert, in chief the letter M sable, in base a falcon of the first—John MARSHALL, Bishop of Llandaff, 1478-96.

Gules, on a fesse argent a Roman A—ALTHOUN.

Per pale, sable and argent, three Roman B's counterchanged—BRIDLINGTON PRIORY, Yorkshire.

Or, a capital Z gules—DE ZEDDES.

Argent, a fesse between three S's sable—SHUGLEY, co. Chester.

Azure, a lion rampant argent resting his dexter hind-foot on the letter H—Town of HORSHAM, Sussex.

Sometimes figures and astronomical signs are used.

Azure, three figures of 7 two and one—BERNARD.

Per fesse argent and or, a fesse wavy azure between a sword and a branch of aurel in saltire proper passing a ring of the astronomical character of Mars [♂] sable in chief, and the stump of a tree, one branch sprouting from the dexter side thereof issuing from water in base proper—STOCKENSTORM, Maasstrom, Cape of Good Hope, Baronet, 1840.

Azure, on a fesse between three mullets of six points or two characters of the planet Venus sable—THOYTS, Sulhamstead, co. Berks, and London; granted 1788.

Sometimes a combination of letters are used, and this especially in canting arms and in *Rebuses*. Names of various kinds, both of places and persons, are found inscribed sometimes with, at others without, *scrolls*. See e.g. ACRE, under *Sphinx;* NAKSIVAN, under *Ararat;* EMMANUEL, under *Escroll,* &c.

Argent, on a chevron between three cock's heads erased, the two in chief respectant sable, an escallop-shell or, in chief the letters A L azure —ALCOCK.

Azure, a paschal lamb couchant with the banner all argent; round the head a nimbus or, in base the letters P P of the last—Town of PRESTON, co. Lancaster.

Azure, in chief a scroll argent inscribed B R E, in fesse a tun of the second—BRETON.

Gules, a bugle-horn stringed and garnished within the word RIPPON in orle [i.e. in pale the letters I and N, in chief the letters R and P, and in fesse those of P and O]—Town of RIPON.

The word *eye* under an antique ducal coronet—Town of EYE, Suffolk.

Per chief embattled azure and gules; in chief the letters JOHES or; in base a tun of the last thereon the letters BRIT sable—The late John BRITTON, F.S.A.

Sable, a lion rampant argent holding between the paws a mural crown or, a canton ermine thereon pendent by a riband gules fimbriated azure a representation of the medal presented for services subinscribed WATERLOO in letters sable—CHURCHILL.

Levels and *Plummets* are borne by some few families, but the most notable instance occurs in the insignia of the PLUMBERS' Company, London, where the level is reversed, and figured as in the margin. [See the blazon given under *Plumbers' Implements*.]

Level.

Argent, three levels with their plummets or—COL-BRAND, Chichester, Lewes, and Burnham, Sussex.

Argent, a chevron gules between three plummets sable—Sir Stephen JENINGS, Lord Mayor of London, 1508.

Level reversed.

Argent, a fesse gules between three plummets sable—JENNINGS, Old-castle, co. Chester; and co. Salop.

Argent, on a fesse dancetty gules a plummet of the first between two anchors or—STANMARCHE.

Quarterly ermine and gules, in the dexter chief a cross croslet of the second, in the sinister base a plummet sable—CROSS, quartered by Starkey, CROSS, Wrembury Hall, co. Chester.

Plummet.

A *Level staff* occurs in one coat of arms already referred to under *Axe*, where it is associated with a compass-dial and two *Coal-picks* in the arms of FLETCHER.

Levé, (fr.) : used of a *bear* when erect.

Lever. See *Cormorant*.

Leveret. See *Hare*.

Levrier, (fr.) : *Greyhound*, also *Levron*. See *Dog*.

Lezard. See *Cat*, also *Lizard*.

Libardo, or Lybbarde: an ancient form of the word *leopard*.

Licorne, (fr.). See *Unicorn*.

Lié, (fr.) : joined or tied together.

Lièvre, (fr.). See *Hare*.

Lighthouse : a representation of the Bell Rock Lighthouse appears in the arms of STEVENSON.

Argent, on a chevron between three fleurs-de-lis azure as many mullets of the first ; a chief silver, on the base thereof the sea and rocks, thereon the Bell Rock Lighthouse with temporary lighthouse, men at work and ships in offing proper—STEVENSON, Edinburgh.

Lily : next to the rose the lily is perhaps the most frequently borne of all the flowers, and there is probably little question that this flower is the original of the *fleur-de-lis*, which took a conventional form. By some the figure so frequently found is supposed to represent the *Iris* and not the *Lily*.

Lily.

Argent, on a fesse sable between three roses gules a lily of the first—Richard MAYO, Bishop of Hereford, 1504-16.

Sable, three lilies slipped argent, a chief per pale azure and gules, on the dexter side a fleur-de-lis or, on the sinister a lion of England—ETON COLLEGE.

Fusilly ermine and sable a chief of the second, charged with three lilies slipped argent—MAGDALEN COLLEGE, Oxford. [William PATTEN, commonly called WAYNFLETE, Bishop of Winchester, the founder, added the chief to his family arms.]

Argent, in base a rock with nine points issuant, from each a lily all proper, on a chief azure a crescent between two mullets of the first—ROMILLY, Baron Romilly, 1865.

Gules, a lion rampant between eight lilies argent —DENVILE or DEVILE.

MAGDALEN COLLEGE.

Gules, on a fesse or, between three wolf's heads erased pean five lilies slipped and inverted—LEDIARD, Cirencester.

Azure, three roses two and one in base or ; in chief as many lilies argent stalked and leaved vert ; all within a bordure gules charged with eight plates—BARKING Abbey, Essex.

The three *lilies* represented on the chief in the arms of the COOPERS' Company (see under *Grose*) are figured usually as in the margin. The French heralds use the term *Lis de jardin*, or *au naturel*, to distinguish the natural *lily* from the conventional *fleur-de-lis*.

Lily.

Lily-pot, or *flower-pot.* Although the example figured in the margin is blazoned as if holding *gilly-flowers,* they were, no doubt, meant for lilies.

Vert, a flower-pot argent, with gilly flowers gules, leaved of the first — NEW INN, or OUR LADY'S INN, London.

Gules, three lily-pots [? covered cups] argent —ARGENTYNE.

Azure, a pot of lilies argent — The Royal Burgh of DUNDEE.

Limbs: the Seal of the city of Lichfield (= field of the Lich, or dead body)

NEW INN.

has a curious representation, in which the disjointed limbs of three men are scattered over the field.

A landscape, on the dexter side several trees on a hill, on the sinister a view of the cathedral, on the ground the bodies, heads, and limbs of three men all proper [no doubt in allusion to the Lichfield martyrs], with crowns, swords, and banners dispersed all over the field—City of LICHFIELD, co. Stafford.

Limbeck, or *Alembick:* the charge represented in the annexed cut is so termed by numerous heraldic writers, but the connection between the name and the figure is not very apparent. The word seems to be an old name for a kind of distilling vessel, and occurs only in the arms of the PEWTERERS' Company. In one instance they are blazoned ' cross-bars.'

Limbeck.

Azure, on a chevron or, between three antique limbecks argent, as many roses gules, seeded of the second, barbed, slipped, and leaved proper—The PEWTERERS' Company, London, granted 1479. [Elsewhere the arms of the PEWTERERS appear to be thus blazoned:—Gules, on a chevron argent between three silver single-handled cups each containing so many sprigs of lilies proper, the Virgin accompanied by four cherubs or enclosed by two pair of limbecks as the second.]

Limacon. See *Snail.*

Limb. See also *Tree.*

Linden leaves. See *Leaves.*

Lined: this word is used in two senses, as (1) a mantle gules,

lined ermine, and (2) a *bear* or *greyhound* gorged and lined, that is, with a line affixed to his collar.

Lines *of Partition.* See *Party per.*

Ling. See *Cod.*

Lion, (fr. *lion*): this beast is perhaps the most frequent of all bearings. In early heraldry it is generally represented *rampant*, while leopards are represented *passant guardant,* and hence the arms of England, no doubt, are more correctly blazoned *Leopards.* Practically, however, the same animal was intended, but different names given according to the position; in later times the name *lion* was given to both. The chief evidence is that the first entry in one of our earliest rolls of arms runs:—

Le Roy d'Angleterre porte goules, trois lupards d'or—Roll, temp. HEN. III.

Son filz teile, ovecque ung labell d'azur—*Ibid.*

And in the early roll of Edward II. the royal arms are thus blazoned:—

Le Roy de Engletere porte de goules, a iij lupars passauns de or.

And it will be observed that in the former it is taken for granted that the term 'lupar' involves passant.

Again, as a general rule more than two lions are seldom represented in the same shield, and, on the other hand, seldom less than two leopards. The commonest bearings are one lion or three leopards. The lions are drawn conventionally, and the design is suited to the material or character of the work into which they are introduced.

As already said, the position of *rampant* is the one most common, as it was thought to be the most natural for the lion. It signifies rearing, but with the sinister hinder leg and the sinister fore leg lower than the two dexter legs respectively. The lion is rarely represented rearing with both its hind legs touching the ground and its fore legs even; when it is so it is blazoned *salient.* A lion rampant, like all other animals, is always understood to be facing the dexter side of the shield.

FITZ ALAN,
Earl of ARUNDELL.

Le Conte de Arundell de goules, ung lion rampand d'or—Roll, temp. HEN. III.

Linnet. See *Finch.*   Lioncel. See *Lion.*

Le Conte DEL ILE, d'or, ung lion d'azur rampant—Roll, temp. HEN. III.

Sire Roger FELBRIGGE, de or, a un lion salient de goules—Roll, temp. ED. II.

Or, six lions [or lioncels] salient sable—DATELING.

Azure, a lion salient or—Robert SNOWDEN, Bp. of Carlisle, 1616-21.

Argent, a lion salient gules—LIGHTON, Scotland.

Argent, a lion salient guardant gules—JERMY.

SNOWDEN.

The head may be, however, turned to face the spectator, when it is said to be *rampant guardant*, or it may be turned completely round, when it is said to be *rampant reguardant*. Two lions rampant facing each other are blazoned *combatant*.

Argent, a lion rampant guardant or—FITZHAMON, Gloucester.

Argent, a lion rampant guardant gules—CATTESBY, Suffolk.

Azure, semy de lis a lion rampant guardant or—HOLLAND, Earl of Kent.

Or, a lion rampant reguardant sable—JENKINS, Cornwall.

Gules, a lion rampant reguardant argent—MORGAN, Bp. of Bangor, 1666-73.

Argent, a lion rampant reguardant gules—AGINAL, Cresseley.

FITZHAMON.

Argent, a lion rampant gules facing the sinister side—VIVIAN, Cornwall

Ermine, two lions rampant combatant gules—LUCAS, Cornwall.

The lion *passant* is more frequently represented *guardant* than not, but it ought rightly to be expressed: rarely is it represented passant *reguardant*. As already said, the term *leopard* was the ancient term used, and this in some cases evidently implied a *lion passant guardant;* so much so that with the French heralds the expression *lion leopardé* signifies a *lion passant guardant*, and conversely a *leopard lionné* a *lion rampant guardant*. When blazoned spotted the leopard itself is meant.

PALGRAVE.

Azure, a lion passant argent—LYBAND; PALGRAVE &c.

Gules, two lions passant guardant in pale or—Arms ascribed to WILLIAM I., WILLIAM II., and HENRY I. [But on no early authority.]

Sire Robert DE LA MARE, de goules, a ij lupars passanz de argent—Roll, temp. ED. II. [Engraving from arms in March Baldon Church, and blazoned Gules, two lions passant guardant in pale argent.]

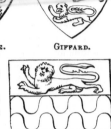

DE LA MARE.   GIFFARD.

Sire Johan GIFFARD, de goules, a iij lyouns passauns d'argent—*Ibid.*

Monsire de LITTLEBERY, d'argent, sur une bend vert trois egles d'or entre deux leopards gules passants—Roll, temp. ED. III.

Barry nebuly of six argent and azure; on a chief gules a lion passant guardant or—Company of STAPLE MERCHANTS [Inc. temp. ED. III.]

D'Azure, a deux lions leopardés or—PUISAYE, Normandie.

MERCHANTS OF THE STAPLE.

Gules, two leopards passant in pale argent spotted sable—MARE, Chester.

Lions may also be blazoned as *couchant* (fr. *couché*); they then should be represented with their heads erect, to distinguish them from *dormant* (of which no actual example occurs; though Guillim ascribes to the Tribe of Judah, 'Azure, a lion dormant or'). The term *lodged* is equivalent to *couchant*, but should only be applied to deer, &c., not to beasts of prey. The term *statant* (fr. *posé*) is also found occasionally applied to the lion, that is standing with both the fore legs touching the ground, and thus distinguished from *passant*, in which case the right gamb is raised. It may also be *séjant*.

Gules, a lion couchant between six cross crosslets, three in chief and as many in base argent—TYNTE, Somerset.

Gules, a lion couchant or—EILEWORTH.

Ermine, a lion statant guardant gules—Simon de SEGRE.

Per pale sable and gules, a lion statant argent—NEALE, co. Bedford.

Argent, a lion sejant sable—MEGGISON.

Lions are very frequently *crowned;* they are subject also to various treatments, sometimes being *charged* with some device

on the shoulder, sometimes col*l*ared. A lion may also be represented as supporting some other charge, that is, holding it
between its paws, but this is more frequently the case in crests
than in coats of arms. Lions may also be of any tincture, and
even party-coloured, in fact they are in this respect treated just
as any *ordinary*.

Sire Johan de SEGRAVE, de sable, a un lioun rampaunt de argent
courone de or—Roll, temp. ED. II. [The engrav-
ing is from arms in Dorchester Church, Oxon.]

Sire Johan de BEAUCHAMP de Fifelde, de or, a un
lion de sable corone de goules—*Ibid.*

Gules, a lion passant guardant argent crowned
with an antique crown or, and girt round the waist
with an annulet of the last—OGILVIE.

Sire Nicholas de ESTLEE, de argent, a un lion de
goules; en le espaudle del lion un quintefoil de
argent—Roll, temp. ED. II.

SEGRAVE.

Monsire Jerves de CLIFTON, port d'azure, a une lyon rampant d'argent
en lespau une fleur-de-lys de gules—Roll, temp. ED. III.

Argent, three bars gemel sable, and over all a lion rampant gules
charged on the shoulder with a crosslet fitchy or—Roger de MOHAUT, co.
Lancaster.

Argent, a lion rampant vert vulned proper at the mouth—TYRWHITT-
JONES, co. Salop.

Gules, on a leopard passant guardant or spots sable—ARLOTT.

Argent, five barrulets gules, over all a lion rampant crowned and sustaining a battle-axe or—ALEXANDER.

Gules, a lion rampant holding in the dexter paw a pen argent—GREY.

Argent, a lion passant sable, the fore-feet fettered or—Madoc ap ADDA
MOEL.

Or, a lion hopping in a tun gules [otherwise, Gules, a demi-lion erect
issuing from a tun argent]—HOPTON [a Rebus].

Azure, a lion rampant vairy argent and gules—HULTON.

Gules, a lion passant ermine—HEREFORD, Norfolk.

Gules, a lion rampant, per bend ermine and ermines—TIMBERLEY.

Gules, a lion rampant guardant per fesse or and argent—Priory
HOUNSLOW, Middlesex.

Sir Thomas de WOKINGDONE, de goules, a un lion barre de argent et
de azure—Roll, temp. ED. II.

A lion may be *armed*, or *armed* and *langued*, of a different tincture (i.e. with its tongue, claws, or teeth, &c., of such tincture);

or *disarmed*, that is deprived of claws and teeth; also *enraged* or *incensed*, that is with fire issuing from the mouth and ears.

Ermine, a lion rampant azure, crowned and langued or—PICKERING.

Ermine, a lion rampant gules, crowned or, armed and langued azure—TURBERVILLE, Bp. of Exeter, 1555-9.

Argent, three bars gemel gules, a lion rampant sable armed and membered azure—FAIRFAX.

Argent, a lion rampant gules enraged azure—ETHRICK.

Azure, a lion rampant argent, maned or, collared sable—LOKYER.

Azure, a lion rampant guardant argent the feet gules—HUM.

Argent, a lion passant disarmed sable—SMITH.

Argent, a lion unarmed gules—ALBONE.

Argent, a lion rampant gules incensed azure—Morgan ap MEREDITH, Lord of Tredegar, co. Monmouth.

But beyond this heralds frequently describe the *tail* of the lion in the blazon; for instance, the animal may be represented as *coward*, that is, with its tail hanging down between the hind legs (whence the English word); it may also be represented with the tail erect, but this is rare, the ordinary position for the tail being as if curved over the back; it is very often *forked* (*queue fourché*), that is a double tail, and this is sometimes represented *nowed* or knotted. An illustration of *fourché* is seen in Woodford Church, Northants, on the brass of Symon MALORY, who died in 1580. Without a tail a lion is said to be *defamed*.

MALORY.

Argent, a lion passant coward sable—HERWELL.

Le Conte LEICESTER, goules ung leon rampand d'argent, le cowe fourchee—Roll, temp. HEN. III. [i.e. Simon DE MONTFORT, Earl of Leicester, temp. King JOHN. The annexed engraving represents a common form found in early drawing.]

Sire Adam de WELLES, de or, a un lion rampand de sable od la couwe forchee—Roll, temp. ED. II.

In the same Roll of Arms, Sire Johan de KYNESTONE; Sire Johan de KYNGESTONE; Sire Walter de KINGESTONE; Sire Nicolas de KINGE-STONE; Sire William de CRESCI; Sire Roger de CRESCI; Sire Johan de

DE MONTFORT.

HAVERINGE; Sire Bertilmeu de BOROVASH; Sire Johan de SEINCLER; Sire Robert le VENOUR; Sire Felip de WELLES; Sire Felip de BARING-TONE; Sire Roger de CHAUNDOS; Sire Robert de HASTANG; Sire Robert de STAPELTONE; Sire Edmon WASTENEYS; Sire . . . de MORLEE; also bear lions 'rampaund, od la couwe fourchie.'

Sire Richard de BREOUSE, de ermyne a un lion rampaund de goules, od la couwe forchie e renouwe—Roll, temp ED. II. [Sire Giles de BREOUSE and Sire Pere de BREOUSE bear lions similarly forked and nowed.]

Gules, a demi-lion rampant argent tail forked— STOKES.

Argent, two bars gules, over all a lion rampant, double queued or pelletty—BRANDON, Chamberlain of London.

Or, a lion rampant, tail forked gules—MALORY.

Argent, a lion rampant, tail forked and double nowed purpure—Sir William STOREY.

Purpure, a lion rampant, tail forked and nowed or, crowned argent—Sir Richard PASHLEY.

Argent, a lion rampant sable, the tail introverted, the head, paws, and brush of the tail of the field—LLOYD, co. Carmarthen.

Argent, a lion rampant, the tail elevated and turned over the head sable—BUXTON, Norfolk.

Argent, a lion rampant reguardant purpure, the tail flexed from between his legs over the back—Sir Amand de ROUCH.

Argent, a lion rampant, tail nowed purpure—STOREY.

Gules, a lion rampant, tail erect argent—Randolph de GERNONIIS, fourth Earl of Chester.

Lions also may be represented couped, when they are called *demi-lions* (q.v.), and there are besides this some singular combinations of two or several lions' bodies, but with only one head.

NORTHAMPTON.

Gules, a bicorporate lion guardant rampant counter-rampant coward or, ducally crowned azure—John NORTHAMPTON, Lord Mayor of London, 1381 and 1382.

Gules, three demi-lions rampant argent—BENNETT.

Gules, two lions sejant conjoined under one head guardant or, crowned azure—COMBERTON.

Or, a lion rampant with two heads azure—Simon MASON, co. Huntingdon, 1730.

Gules, two lions rampant conjoined with one head or, crowned azure within a bordure argent—KELLHAM.

Gules, a tricorporated lion issuing out of the three corners of the escucheon, all meeting under one head in the fesse point or, armed and langued azure— Edmond PLANTAGENET (Crouchback), Earl of Lancaster, temp. ED. I.

Argent, a lion guardant with two bodies counter rampant per pale gules and sable—Dayr Howell. [The same charge, azure in a field or, is the coat of NASHE.]

Earl of LANCASTER.

Lions' heads sometimes occur in blazon, but more frequently leopards' heads. A *leopard's head* should shew part of the neck, but the phrase is sometimes used for what should be termed a *leopard's face*. See *Caboshed.*

Monsire William de REDNESSE, sable une cheveron entre trois testes du leopard arrasht d'argent —Roll, temp. ED. III.

Monsire LUGHTBURGH, de gules a une cheveron d'argent entre trois testes de leopardes d'or— *Ibid.*

Azure, a leopard's head affronté erased or— MITCHELL.

MITCHELL.

Azure, three leopards' faces argent—BARNES, Linc., and BARNEY, Kent.

Azure, a fesse between three leopard's faces or— DE LA POLE, Earl of Suffolk.

Sable, a fesse between three leopard's faces argent —GIBBONS, Ireland.

Or, a fesse between three leopard's heads sable— FARINGDON, co. Lancaster.

Argent, a bend between two lion's heads erased sable—MELL [or MELLS.]

Azure, a fesse ermine between three lion's heads erased or—HAMMOND, Kent.

DE LA POLE.

Azure, two bars argent, in chief a leopard's face or—WRIGHT, Cranham Hall, Essex.

Argent, a fesse humetty gules, in chief three leopard's faces of the second—BRABANT.

Argent, a fesse dancetty gules, in chief three leopard's heads cabossed azure—John de POULTNEY.

Sable, in chief a lion passant guardant, in base a leopard's head jessant-de-lis or—MORLAND.

See also examples under *jessant-de-lis*. Lions' *gambes* (q.v.) and *paws* are also often borne as separate charges, as likewise, but rarely, the *tail*.

Lioncels, (fr. *lionceaux*). When two or more lions occur in the same coat not separated by an ordinary, they are more properly blazoned (except in a royal coat, or except in the case of two lions combatant or addorsed) as *lioncels*, the dignity of a lion being supposed not to allow a competitor in the same field. Practically, however, in modern blazon the term lioncel is only used when there are five or six. The arms of LONGESPEE, Earl of Sarum (natural son of Henry II.), and of Humphrey de BOHUN, Earl of Hereford, are found very frequently in old glass, &c., and present good examples of lioncels. The first engraving here given is from the seal attached to the will of Humphrey de Bohun (the son), who died 1319.

Le Conte de HEREFORD, azure six lionceux d'or, ov ung bende d'argent a deux cotises d'or ·—Roll, temp. HENRY III.

Humphry de BOUN, d'azur ung bend d'argent entre six leonceux d'or cotisee d'or, ove ung la-bell de goules—*Ibid*.

Seal of HUMPHREY DE BOHUN.

Le Counte de HEREFORD, de azure, a vi lioncels de or a une bende de argent e ij cottes de or—Roll, temp. ED. II.

Azure, six lioncels rampant three, two, one, or—William LONGESPEE, Earl of Sarum, ob. 1226. [The arms are varied from those of ANJOU, the ancient inheritance of his father's family, which were azure, eight lioncels (or perhaps lioncels sans nombre) or.]

LONGESPEE, Earl of Salisbury.

ANJOU.

Sire Edmon TALEBOT, de argent a iij lioncels de pourpre—Roll, temp. ED. II.

Lion poisson. See *Sea-lion*.
Lisiere. See *Achievements*.
Lis, *Lys*: for Fleur-de-lis.

Liste, old fr. for *Cottice*.
Liston: a French term for the ribbon containing the motto.

Sable, six lioncels couchant coward argent three, two, and one—BATE-MAN, Essex.

Argent, on a bend engrailed between six lioncels gules, a rose of the first between two arrows proper—SAWREY, co. Lancaster.

Argent, on a cross gules five lioncels rampant or—AUDYN, Dorchester.

Liveries of servants and retainers should in general be of the principal colour and metal of their lords' arms. The liveries adopted by the kings of England have been as follows :—

The later Plantagenets, white and red. The House of York, murrey and blue. The House of Lancaster, white and blue. The House of Tudor, white and green. The House of Stuart, yellow and red. William III. the same; but before his accession blue and orange.

The House of Hanover, scarlet and blue. Before their succession to the English throne they used yellow and red.

Lizard, (fr. *lézard*): the reptile so called is used but rarely on English coats of arms. Its proper tincture is vert.

Two scaly lizards erect on their hind feet combatant proper [i.e. vert], each gorged with a plain collar or, the collars chained together; a chain with a ring at the end pendent between the two lizards of the last—Crest of the IRONMONGERS' Company.

Argent, three lizards in pale vert—LOVYS or LUVYS, Cornwall.

Azure, three lizards or—COTTER, Ireland.

Lobster : this crustacean seems not to occur entire in any known examples of English heraldry ; but the *claws* occur in more than one coat of arms, and these are represented as in the margin ; allied to it is the *crevice* (fr. *écrevisse*), or crayfish.

TREGARTHICK.   GRILLA.

Argent, two lobster's claws in saltire gules, the dexter surmounting the sinister—TREGARTHICK.

Litvit's skin: a pure white fur used for lining mantles. See under *Argent.*

Loach. See *Gudgeon.*

Loaves of bread. See under *Basket* and baker's *Peel.*

Argent, a chevron between three lobster's claws gules—KERNE.

Barry wavy of six argent and gules, six crevices or two and one—ATWATER.

Gules, on a bend or, a lobster sable—GRILLA, Spain.

Lock: the form of this charge varies; it is generally blazoned as a *padlock* (fr. *cadenas*), sometimes a *quadrangular lock*. The more frequent form, however, is the *fetterlock*, of which drawings have already been given.

Per fesse or and sable, a bend wavy between two padlocks counterchanged—WHITLOCK, co. Devon.

Per fesse azure and or, a pale and three falcons two and one with wings addorsed and belled, each holding in the beak a padlock all counterchanged—LOCK, Norbury Park, Surrey, V.

Argent, a cross moline azure placed in a lock proper and in chief two mullets of the second.—MILLER, Gourlebank, Scotland.

Argent, a fesse engrailed voided gules between three square padlocks of the second—GREIVE.

Gules, a fesse or between three quadrangular locks (or fetterlocks) argent—GRIERSON, Lagg, co. Dumfries; baronetcy, 1685.

Sable, three square padlocks argent—LOVELL, or LOVETT, Bucks.

With this may be associated the single example of the *door-bolt* (fr. *verrou*).

Argent, three door-bolts gules—BOLTON, Yorkshire.

Lozenge, (fr. *losange*): this charge is of a diamond shape, the diameter being about equal to each of the sides; in the *fusil*, which is similar in shape, the diameter is less than each of the four sides, thus giving it a narrower appearance. When a *lozenge* is voided, or *percée*, it is always in modern heraldry blazoned as a *mascle*, q v.

FREEMAN.

Sire Gerard de BRAYBROK, de argent a vij lozenges de goules—Roll, temp. ED. II.

Monsire Henry de FERRERS, port de gules a vj lozenges perces d'or [i.q. mascles] Roll, temp Ed. III.

Loch. See *Water*.

Lock of hair. See *Hair*, also *Gouttes*.

Lochabar-axe. See *Axe*.

Lodged: said of a stag when couchant. See *Deer*.

Argent, three lozenges conjoined in fesse gules, between three ogresses, in chief a mullet—Richard MOUNTAGUE, Bp. of Chichester, 1628; afterwards of Norwich, 1638—1641.

Azure, three lozenges or—FREEMAN, Hereford.

Azure, three lozenges in fesse argent—FREEMAN, co. York.

Azure, three lozenges in triangle ermine—HALTOFTS.

Azure, three lozenges in bend argent—MARTYN.

Azure, three lozenges in pale argent—GRAVILLE, Suffolk.

Argent, three lozenges lying fess-ways sable—LEE.

Paly of six sable and or, two lozenges in pale counterchanged—HILLINGE.

Lozenges are frequently conjoined in the form of ordinaries, and in all such cases the number of the lozenges should be given, and care taken that each lozenge be drawn entire; otherwise the blazon should be *lozengy*. When more than three are named they should be drawn with the points touching. The lozenges also are themselves frequently charged with some other device.

DE BURGO.

Gules, seven lozenges conjoined vaire, three, three, and one—DE BURGO, Bp. of Llandaff, 1244-53.

Gules, four lozenges conjoined in fesse ermine—OLIVER DINANT.

Gules, four lozenges in fesse ermine—DENHAM.

Argent, five lozenges conjoined in bend sinister gules; on a canton of the last a crosier in pale or—BOXLEY Abbey, Kent.

Argent, five lozenges in saltire, between four others gules—ACHENEY.

Gules, ten lozenges argent, conjoined, three, three, three, and one—LALAIN, 1433.

Gules, three lozenges conjoined in fesse argent, each charged with a rose of the first—WELBECK Abbey, Notts.

Ermine, three lozenges meeting in the fesse point—HALTOFT.

Lolling: a name rarely used for *Preying.* See under *Falcon.*

Long, *Per. Indented per long* is a phrase implying that the indents are deeper than usual.

Lopped, or *Snagged.* Said of a limb of a tree, couped in such a manner that the transverse section is exposed to view.

Loopholes. See under *Castle.*

Lorraine, *Cross* of, § 28.

Lou, (old fr.) *Loup :* the wolf.

Lowered : a term signifying an ordinary is placed below its usual position, same as *Abased.*

Loup cervier, (fr.) : *lynx.*

Lorré, (fr.) : of fishes, finned ; used when of different tincture.

Argent, on a lozenge sable a lion rampant of the first—Put.

Gules, on a lozenge or a chevron azure—Brocke.

Gules, a lozenge flory at the points or—Cassyl, or Calshill.

Sable, a sword in bend sinister argent, hilted or, surmounted of a pastoral staff in bend dexter of the last, between two lozenges of the second, one in chief, the other in base, each charged with a pall ensigned of a cross patée gules—Roger Le Noir de Beleye, Bp. of London, 1229-41.

Lozengy, (fr. *losangé*): entirely covered with lozenges of alternate tinctures. The lines are variously drawn, but as a rule they should produce lozenges narrower in breadth in proportion to their length than in the example drawn to illustrate what *bendy, dexter* and *sinister* would produce, yet not so narrow as *fusilly.*

Lozengy, argent and gules — Fitz-William, co. Northampton.

Lozengy, gules and or—Crome, London.

The term *lozengy,* however, has come to have the meaning of ' composed of lozenges,' that is when only one tincture is given (see what has been said under *Cross,* § 8). It is

Lozengy.

contended that this is legitimate, and thus some writers use the term *lozenge* instead of *lozengy,* e.g. a *fesse lozenge ;* further it is laid down that in this case care should be taken that the lozenges at the termination are *not* drawn entire so as to distinguish the bearing from a fesse of so many lozenges. It is doubtful, however, if these distinctions have been much regarded in practice.

Gules, a bend lozengy argent—William de Raleigh, Bp. of Norwich, 1239—1242; Bp. of Winchester, 1244—1250.

Argent, a pale lozengy sable—Savage, Bp. of Rochester, 1493; of London, 1496—1501.

Lozengy may also be combined with other lines of diversity, e.g. *bendy lozengy* (q.v. under *Bendy*); *barry bendy lozengy* also occurs (see under *Bar*), but the word is redundant since *barry bendy* produces the lozenge form. So also *paly lozengy* is not needed since *bendy paly* produces the lozenge form. At the same time the diagonal lines may be drawn less acutely, and the result may give more the idea of *paly lozengy.* [See figure under *paly bendy.*]

Lucy, or *Luce,* (old fr. *luc* and *luz*) : the fish now commonly called a pike. The *merlucius,* or pike of the sea, is the *hake.* See under *Cod.*

> "And many a breme, and many a luce in stew."
>
> Chaucer, Prologue, 352.

It is, as will be seen, found frequently in ancient arms, where it plays upon the names. The large head and long mouth distinguish it in the drawing from other fishes. In early arms *lucies* seem to have been always *haurient;* as they are not so now it is necessary to note the position.

Geffrey de LUCY, de goules a trois lucie d'or—Roll, temp. HEN. III.

Sire Ammori de LUCY, de azure crusule de or a iij luys de or—Roll, temp. ED. II.

Sire Thomas de LUCY, de azure crusule de argent a iij luys de argent—*Ibid.*

Lucy.

Monsire LUCY, seigneur de Dalington, gules a trois lucies d'or crusele—Roll, temp. ED. III.

Monsire de FITZACRE, port d'asure a vj luces d'or —*Ibid.*

Azure, two lucies in saltire argent, with coronets over their mouths or—STOCK-FISHMONGERS [united with the SALT-FISHMONGERS, 1536. Note also FISHMONGERS' Company under *Dolphin.*]

Gules, a chevron between three lucies haurient argent—BROUGHAM, Brougham, Westmoreland.

Ermine, on a bend engrailed sable, three lucy's heads erect erased or, collared with bars gemels gules—GILLET or GILLOT, Broadfield, Norfolk. GILLET, Ipswich, Suffolk.

Azure, three lucies haurient argent—WAY, Essex; also Dorset.

Gules, a luce naiant between three annulets argent—PICKERING, Alconbury, Hunts.

Argent, on a pale sable a demi luce or [though probably intended for a demi-conger-eel]—GASCOIGNE, Gawthorp.

The *Ged* is but another name for the *lucy,* and is equally used as a canting charge.

Azure, three geds haurient argent—GED of that Ilk.

Azure, two geds in saltire argent—GEDNEY, Hudderley, Linc. [Crest, two geds as in the arms.]

Luna. See *Argent.*
L'un sur l'autre = surmounted.

Lupar (old fr.) : *Leopard.* See under *Lion.*

Argent, two geds in saltire azure—Gedney of Enderby.

Gules, an escutcheon between three luce's heads couped argent—Geddes, Tweeddale. [Elsewhere, between three ged's or pike's heads couped or.]

The name *Pike* (fr. *brochet*), though not properly used by heralds, is obviously intended by the following canting coats of arms.

Gules, three luces [or pikes] naiant within a bordure engrailed argent—Pike, London.

Per pale argent and gules, on a chevron between three trefoils slipped a luce naiant all counterchanged—Pyke, Devonshire.

Per chevron wavy, argent and vert; in chief two luces chevron-wise respecting each other proper; in base a hind statant of the first—Picke.

Argent, three luces naiant in pale gules—Piketon.

Azure, three luces naiant within a bordure engrailed argent—Pikeworth.

D'azur, au brochet d'argent surmonté d'une étoile d'or—Luc-Fontenay.

Possibly the Sea-pike or *Gar*-fish may be intended in the crest of the Garling family. The two Sea-lucies borne on arms of the Stock-fishmongers' Company are probably meant for *Hakes* (q.v. under *Cod*).

Lymphad, or *Galley:* an ancient ship with one mast, not unfrequent in the heraldry of Scotland. The accompanying figure is copied from a Scottish MS., circ. 1580, in which it is given (sable, in a field or) as quartered by the Earl of Argyll. It is the feudal ensign of the lordship of Lorne; but it is usually drawn in a different form, and in a field argent. See also under *Ship.*

LORNE.

Or, an eagle displayed gules surmounted by a lymphad sable; in the dexter chief a right hand couped gules—Macdonald.

Argent, on a fesse sable three cinquefoils of the first on a canton azure a lymphad within a tressure flory counterflory or—Boswell, Auchinleck, co. Ayr, baronetcy; [descended from Thomas Boswell, who fell at Flodden]—Boswell, Crawley Grange, co. Bucks.

Lure, (1) *Hawk's* lure. See under *Falcon.* (2) In lure. See *Wings.*

Lybbarde: found written for *Leopard.*

Lynx. See *Panther.*

Vert, a lymphad, her oars in action, sails furled argent, flags gules—MACKINDER, or M'KINDER, England.

Argent, a stag passant gules, on a canton azure a galley or—PARKER.

Lyre : this device has been observed but upon one coat of arms, and it would be drawn in the usual classical way.

Argent, a saltire between four holly leaves vert within a bordure of the last, on a chief azure a lyre between two talbot's heads erased or—BRAHAM, Finchley.

Mace, (Civic): this device, derived from the insignia of the office of the Mayor, is borne occasionally in coats of arms.

BIRDE.

Per chevron ermine and azure; in chief a plume of three ostrich feathers argent between two chaplets vert with roses gules; in base a civic mace, enclosed by the collar of the Lord Mayor of London, or—Sir James DUKE, Lord Mayor of London, 1848.

. . . . . A [? verger's] mace in bend dexter surmounted of a pastoral staff in bend sinister. . . . . BIRDE, Bp. of Bangor, 1539; afterwards of Chester, 1542-54.

The fr. *Masse d'armes* is a weapon, and somewhat similar to the *club* called *Massue*, the latter term being in French armory more frequently employed. See under *Staff*.

D'or à deux masses d'armes en sautoir de sable liées de gueules—GONDI.

Mackerel, (fr. *mackereau*: the *scomber* of Linnæus): this fish is borne chiefly for the sake of the name.

Gules, three mackerel, haurient argent—MACKEREL, Somersetshire. [Also by a family at Norwich.]

Argent, on a chevron between three mackerel [haurient] gules, a rose of the field; a chief chequy of the first and second—MACBRIDE.

Macle, i.q. *Mascle*.

Madder-Bag. See *Bag of Madder*, under *Bale*.

Magellan Goose. See *Goose*.

Maiden's head. See *Heads*.

Maintenance, *Cap of*, q.v.

Maison, (fr.): a house, occurs only in French arms.

Majesty, *In his*: said of an eagle crowned and holding a sceptre.

Mallard. See *Duck*.

Mallet. See *Hammer*.

Magnet, or rather *Magnetic needle,* is represented in one instance, and a *Compass-Dial* in another. A compass also occurs in the hands of the *demi-miner,* which serves as the crest of the Company of MINERS ROYAL [Inst. 1568].

Ermine, on a bend azure, a magnetic needle pointing to the pole-star or—PETTY, Ireland.

Argent, on a cross engrailed sable a compass-dial between four pheons or; a chief gules charged with a level staff enclosed by two double coal-picks of the third—FLETCHER, Derby.

PETTY.

Magpie, (fr. *agace* or *pie*): the *Magpie* and the *Jay* (fr. *geai*) are blazoned in several coats of arms, and in nearly all cases *proper.*

Argent, a chevron azure between three magpies proper—HORLEY.

Argent, a fesse wavy gules between three magpies proper—OVERTON, co. York.

Magpies are also borne by the families of PLUMESDON; OTHEWELL; CARIGS; CANHEYS; PEYTON, co. Lancaster; WATERS, Ireland; KINGDON, Cornwall; PIPER, *Ibid.;* JACKSON, co. York; HEWETT, London and York.

Ermine, on a chief sable three jays or—TREGEAN, Cornwall.

Argent, a fesse between three jays sable—CRAIK.

Argent, a chevron azure between three jays proper—JAY, Devon.

D'or, a trois agaces, on pies au naturel, au soleil de gueules posé en abîme—DURSUE, Normandie.

Mallow: this plant occurs in one coat of arms, perhaps on account of the name: sometimes, however, they are blazoned nettle leaves.

Gules, a chevron between three sprigs of mallow-leaves argent—MALHERBE.

Man: although not found in early arms, in later arms the human figure is found represented in all varieties. The man *in armour* has already been noted as frequent, especially as a sup-porter: no less frequent is the *Savage,* or, as he is indifferently termed, the *Wild-man,* or *Wood-man,* a man wreathed about the head and loins with leaves, and generally carrying a club.

The man is frequently represented *naked,* or sometimes only vested round the loins, as in the case of the *Savage.* The

Watchman, in the arms of the town of WARWICK, would be represented as a soldier. In the arms of the MINERS' COMPANY the *miner* is described (see *Mine*), but more minutely in the description of the *supporters* of the arms of that Company (see below). Men are also frequently referred to by their nationality, e.g. an *African,* a *Negro* (see under *Cinnamon*), a *Moor,* a *Blackamoor,* an *Indian,* a *Beloochee* Soldier, a *Danish Warrior,* &c., &c. A man may also be represented in various positions, e.g. in one coat *hanging on a gallows.* See under *Armour,* also under *Head.*

Azure, three woodmen [sometimes blazoned men of Kent] in fesse proper holding in their right hands clubs argent, in their left escutcheons of the second each charged with a cross gules—WOOD.

Sable, three bars or ; on a canton gules a demi woodman holding a club over the dexter shoulder gold—WOOD, Devon.

Sable, a wild man holding a club argent—EMLAY, co. York; Harl. MS. 1404, fo. 154.

Argent, a savage shooting an arrow from a bow gules—BONNIMAN.

Per fesse azure and argent ; on the first a demi-savage issuing wielding a wooden mallet proper ; on the second three branches of oak vert —KIRKWOOD, Scotland.

The field a landscape, the base variegated with flowers, a man proper vested round his loins with linen argent, digging with a spade all of the first—GARDENERS' Company [Inc. 1616].

A castle triple towered, on the dexter side the sun in its glory, on the sinister a crescent, on the top of the two front towers a watchman—A Seal of the Town of WARWICK.

Argent, on a mount vert an African proper wreathed round the middle with feathers, holding in the dexter hand a bow, and in the sinister three arrows both of the third—ROUPELL, Chartham Park, East Grinstead, Sussex.

A man habited as an Indian, on his head a cap, in the dexter hand a long bow, in the sinister an arrow—Ancient Seal of Town of PORT-PIGHAM or WEST LOOE, Cornwall.

Argent, goutty de sang, a Danish warrior armed with a battle-axe in the dexter and a sword in the sinister hand all proper—BLACKER, Carrickblacker, co. Armagh.

Per chevron azure and argent, six crosses patty four and two or ; in base a Beloochee soldier habited and armed, brandishing a sword proper, mounted on a bay horse caparisoned ; on a chief silver the fortress of Khelat; a canton charged with a Dooranee badge—WILTSHIRE, 1840.

Sable, a naked man with arms extended proper—DALZELL, Earl of Carnwath.

Sable, a naked man hanging on a gallows proper—DALZIEL.

As already said, the different varieties of men are more frequently exhibited in the *supporters* of coats of arms, a few examples, therefore, are here given, which speak for themselves: a remarkable one, viz. a student of the University of Oxford will have been noticed under *Knitting-frame.*

An armed man with a drawn sword—RALSTON.

Two men in armour—EYRE.

A European soldier of the 40th Bengal native infantry and a Bengal native artillery-man—Major-General KNOTT.

A Chinese Mandarin, and a Scinde soldier—POTTINGER.

Two Highlanders—MACKENZIE of Kilcoy, co. Ross.

Two Indians wreathed about the head and middle vert—JOHNSTON, Aberdeen.

Two savages wreathed about the loins and resting their exterior hands on clubs—SPOTTISWOOD, co. Berwick.

A miner, his face, legs, and arms of a brownish colour, vested in a frock argent tied above his knees as at work, cap and shoes of the last, holding in the dexter hand erect a hammer azure handled proper (for dexter supporter). Another miner proper, the cap, frock, and shoes argent, the frock loose and down to the ankles; in the sinister hand a fork azure handled proper (for sinister supporter)—Company of MINERS.

A Russian habited in the dress of the country (for dexter supporter). An Indian vested round the waist with feathers of various colours (for sinister supporter)—DISTILLERS' Company.

In French heraldry the *homme d'armes*, i.e. Man in *Armour*, occurs, but the variety of men does not seem to be so large, only *Sauvage* having been observed.

Mandrake, (fr. *mandragore*): this only occurs on one English coat of arms.

Gyronny of eight gules and sable three mandrakes argent [another or] —BODYHAM.

D'azure à cinq plantes de mandragore d'argent mal ordonnees; au franc quartier d'hermine—CHAMPS, Nivernals.

Manacles. See *Fetterlock.*

Manchets: a name for small loaves or cakes. See under *Peel.*

Manche, (fr.). See *Maunch.*

Manche (fr.): more usually *emmanché* hafted; of an *axe*, &c.

Mancheron: used (chiefly by the French) for any kind of sleeve.

Mantle, (*Mantling,* or *Cappeline,* fr. *Lambrequin*): this device of the painter to give prominence to the coat of arms and crest

is considered in theoretical heraldry to represent the *lambrequin,* or covering of the helmet, to protect it from the sun or rain. Some authorities contend it should be of the principal colour and metal of the bearer's arms, but red and white have most frequently been used in England. The Royal *mantling* should be of gold and ermine;

Mantle.

that of peers is often of crimson (representing crimson velvet), lined with ermine. This kind of mantle cannot be used by ladies, being inseparable from the helmet.

The *Robe of estate,* however, may be used as a mantle (fr. *manteau*), in which sense it may be borne by all ranks of gentlemen, and by peeresses, and it is represented as encircling the crest, if any, and the whole of the shield or lozenge with

Mantle.

its external appendages. The mantle may be embroidered on the outside with the arms, or be powdered with heraldic objects.

No man of lower rank than a knight (or perhaps than a peer) should double his mantle with ermine.

Maned, of a *Horse:* rarely of other animals, e.g. of an *Antelope,* &c., as the term *Crined* is more frequently used.

Mangonel. See *Sling.*

Mantelé, (fr.): while the *Chapé* (q.v.) is supposed to obscure, as with a hood, a part of the shield, so mantelé is supposed to obscure the same with a mantle, i.e. a greater part is so obscured: (according to some = party per chevron extending to the top of the escutcheon). Not, however, used in any English arms.

Man-tiger. See *Satyr.*

Maple-tree: this has been observed but in one coat of arms.

Argent, three maples sable—BAY.

Marigold, (fr. *fleur de souci*): this is more frequent than might be supposed. It is equally common in French arms. It will be observed that in one coat of arms a *French* marigold is specified.

Pean, on a fesse engrailed or, between three squirrels sejant argent, each holding a marigold slipped proper, a stag's head erased azure between two fountains also proper— SMITH, Lydiate, co. Lancaster.

Azure, a horse passant argent bridled gules between three marigolds or —MORECROFT, Churchill, co. Oxford.

Gules, a chevron or between three marigolds of the last stalked and leaved vert—GOLDMAN, Sandford.

Or, on a chevron azure between three French marigolds slipped proper two lions respectant of the first—TYSSEN, London, 1687.

D'azur, a trois soucis d'or—HERTES, Picardie.

D'argent, au chevron de gueules accompagné de trois soucis de même feuillés et soutenus de sinople—ROBIN.

Marquess: the second order in the peerage of England, being below a duke, but above an earl. The title seems to have been originally given to certain officers to whom was committed the government of the Marches, or borders of Wales. We find the word *Marchio* used in this sense as early as the reign of Henry III. The first Marquess in the modern sense of the word was Robert de Vere, Earl of Oxford, whose elevation for life to the marquisate of Dublin by King Richard II. (in the year 1386) gave no small offence to the earls, who were obliged to yield him precedence. In Sept. 1397, the same king made John Beaufort, Earl of Somerset, Marquess of Dorset, which title was taken from him in the next reign. The oldest existing marquisate is that of Winchester, created by King Edw. VI. in 1551. A special *coronet* belongs to the Marquess.

Marcassin. See *Boar*.

Marché, (old fr.) : for the cow's hoof.

Marined, (fr. *mariné*): a term fancifully applied to any beast having the lower parts of a fish, e.g. a *Lion marined* for *Sea Lion*, q.v.

Marlet, *Marlion, Merlion*. See *Martlet*.

Marshalling is the art of arranging several coats of arms in one shield, for the purpose of denoting the alliances of a family.

Before marshalling was introduced rare instances occur of *arms composed,* i.e. when an addition of a portion of the arms of a wife has been made to those of the husband. The instance usually quoted (though of most doubtful authority) is that of Henry II. taking an additional lion upon his marriage with Eleanor of Guienne.

a. Impaling. The simplest and earliest way of placing the arms of a husband and wife was side by side. Shields thus placed are said to be *accolées,* or in *collateral position.* Contemporary with this practice, but continuing much longer, was the custom of *impaling* arms by *dimidiation,* the dexter

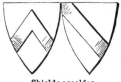

Shields accolées.

half of the husband's arms being joined to the sinister half of the wife's.

This was much practised about the time of King Edward I. The arms of Aylmer de Valence, Earl of Pembroke and Montgomery, and Mary his wife, daughter of Guy de Chastillon, may be taken as an example. They are borne by Pembroke Hall, Cambridge, founded by the latter in 1343.

VALENCE—CHASTILLON.

Barry of ten argent and azure, over all ten martlets in orle gules, for VALENCE.

Vair, three pallets gules, on a chief or, a label of three points azure, for arms borne by CHASTILLON.

In some cases the husband's arms only were dimidiated, the wife's being borne entire. The impalement, whether of whole or dimidiated arms, was referred to by Heralds as *Baron et Femme.*

Marqueté, (fr.): spotted, used of a *trout.* See under *Salmon.*

Mars. (1.) The planetary name for *Gules.* (2.) Astronomical sign of. See *Letters.*

Marshal: a title formerly granted

by the Sovereign at will. William the Conqueror appointed the Earls of Hereford and Arundel Marshals of England, but in 1672 the office of Earl Marshal was annexed to the Dukedom of Norfolk.

An early instance of dimidiation, though rudely represented, occurs on a brass in Stanton Harcourt Church, Oxfordshire, which commemorates Sir Richard Harcourt (ob. 1330), who married Margaret, daughter of Sir John BEKE of Eresby.

Gules, two bars or (for HARCOURT) impaled with gules, a cross moline [or sarcelly] argent (for BEKE).

HARCOURT—BEKE.

Dimidiation in many cases, however, was found inconvenient, and was exchanged for *impaling* the coats entire, though bordures, tressures, and orles were usually omitted (as they are still) on the side next the line of impalement.

As an instances of *impaling* an example from the arms in Dorchester Church, Oxfordshire, is given.

Sable, a lion rampant argent crowned or, for SEGRAVE.

Or, a saltire engrailed sable, for BUTTETOURT.

SEGRAVE—BUTTETOURT.

In a few early instances, in which the wife was of much higher rank than the husband, her arms were placed upon the dexter side; a seal of John of Ghent, as King of Castile and Leon, is an example.

When the wife is an heiress (even in expectation) it is now customary for the husband to bear her arms upon an *escutcheon of pretence;* but it is evident that until the husband has issue by the heiress, and until the death of her father, he should merely impale her arms; because until then he cannot transmit her inheritance to his posterity. Instances might be cited of husbands bearing their wives' arms both upon an escutcheon of pretence over their own, and also as an impalement.

Many modern heralds condemn the practice of a knight impaling the arms of his wife within the garter or collar of his order, but there are many precedents for so doing. The widow of a knight, though she continues to impale the arms of her deceased husband in a lozenge, must of course relinquish his insignia of knighthood.

When a man marries a second wife, he should certainly cease to impale the arms of the first. Some, however, have thought

proper to impale both, which may be done in two ways, as shewn
in the annexed cuts (figs. 1, 2), the bend shewing the position of

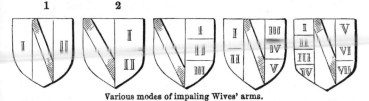

Various modes of impaling Wives' arms.

the man's arms, and the numerals those of his wives. The
other figures shew how the arms of three, five, and seven wives
might have been borne, or at least represented. When a widow
of a peer marries a second time, her second husband impales
her paternal arms only.

Bishops, deans, heads of colleges, and kings of arms, impale
the insignia of their offices with their own arms, giving the
dexter, as the place of honour, to the former.

b. Quartering. Arms may be *quartered* for several reasons.
First, a sovereign quarters the ensigns of his several states,
generally giving the precedence to the most ancient, unless it
be inferior to some other. The first English monarch who
bore quartered arms was Edward III., who assumed,—

Azure, semée of fleur-de-lys or (for FRANCE)

in 1340, three years after his taking the title of King of France,
his mother, in whose right he claimed the crown of France,
being daughter and heiress of Philip the Fair. He is said to
have set the example to others.

The arms, however, of Castile and Leon are quarterly (see
ante, under *Castle*), and are sculptured on the tomb of Eleanor,
Queen of Edward I., who died 1296, and thus afford an earlier
example. Again, in the Inventory of the goods of Humphrey
de Bohun, Earl of Hereford, taken in 1322, we find—

"j. autre [quintepoint, i.e. quilt,] quartelé des armes Dengleterre et
de Hereford."

An early instance of quartering arms is that of John Hastings,
earl of Pembroke, who married King Edward's youngest daugh-

ter Margaret, and died 1375. Their arms are emblazoned upon the north side of the king's tomb at Westminster :—

Quarterly, 1 and 4, or, a maunch gules, HASTINGS. 2 and 3, barry of twelve, argent and azure, over all eight martlets in orle gules—VALENCE, impaling 1 and 4 France ancient, 2 and 3 England, being the arms of his wife.

Feudal Arms are sometimes quartered by subjects, as arms of dominion are by princes ; and an augmentation is sometimes so borne. But the most common reason for quartering is to shew what heiresses have married into the family.

An elected king, or one succeeding under any special arrangement, generally places his hereditary arms upon an inescutcheon over the insignia of his dominions, as did the Emperors of Germany, and as William of Orange did, when raised to the throne of Great Britain. This has been the usage in the kingdom of Greece.

It was a frequent practice from the reign of Edward III. to that of Henry VIII. for the husband, if he acquired any great possession through his wife, to quarter her arms with his own, and even to place them in the first quarter ; or sometimes to give her arms alone ; or, reversing modern usage, to give her arms and others, bearing his own in an escutcheon surtout.

The rules attending the *Quartering* of arms are somewhat complicated, and vary according to the attendant circumstances. The general principle is that when a man marries an heiress, all the issue of that marriage are entitled to bear both the maternal and paternal coat quartered ; also the quarterings to which the mother may be entitled, so that an escutcheon may be charged with the arms of any number of families. Indeed in an achievement of the KNIGHTLEY family, in the hall at Fawsley, Northamptonshire, there are 334 quarterings.

The manner in which quarterings are acquired will be best shewn by an example. One is therefore given in the three plates annexed, and the frontispiece, which are derived from a pedigree of the WILLOUGHBY family drawn up in the reign of Queen Elizabeth. By attention to the following examples a clearer idea of the system will be obtained than by printing any code of regulations.

I

Sir Philip Marmion = Joan, daughter of Sir
Hugh, Baron Kilpeck.

II

Sir Alexander Frevile = Joan, daughter of
Sir Philip Marmion

III

Sir Baldwin Frevile = Maude, daughter
of . . . Devereux

see p. 397

IV

Sir Baldwin Frevile = Elizabeth, daughter of
Sir John Mountforte

V

Sir Baldwin Frevile = ... daughter of
Lord Strange

I.

Sir Philip Marmion, Knt., nat. circa temp. R. Jo.
= Joan, daughter and coheiress of Sir Hugh, Baron of Kilpeck.

Sir P. M. bore the paternal arms alone, viz. Vair, a fesse gules, fretty argent. The arms of his wife (which, according to modern practice, would be borne upon an escutcheon of pretence) were Sable, a sword in pale, point downward, argent, hilt and pomel or. The lady being an heiress, this coat descended to her children.

II.

Joan, daughter and coheiress of Sir Philip Marmion
= Sir Alex. Frevile, Knt.

The arms of Sir A. F. were Or, a cross patonce gules. His wife being a coheiress of the families of *Marmion* and *Kilpeck*, bore, or by later usage might have borne, their arms quarterly.

III.

Sir Baldwin Frevile, Knt. son and heir
= Maude, daughter of . . . . Devereux.

He inherited the arms of *Frevile* from his father, and those of *Marmion* and *Kilpeck* from his mother. As his wife was not an heiress, the coat of *Devereux* (Argent, a fesse gules, in chief three torteaux) was impaled by him during her lifetime only, after which the family of Frevile had nothing further to do with it.

IV.

Sir Baldwin Frevile, Knt., Baron of Henley in Arden, son and heir
= Elizabeth, d. and coh. of John de Mountforte, Baron of Beaudesert.

The quarters belonging to this Sir B. F. were the same as those of his father, without any addition. His wife inherited the arms of *Mountforte* (Bendy of ten, or and azure), *De la Plaunche* (Argent, billetté sable, a lion rampant of the last, crowned or), and *Haversham* (Azure, a fesse between six cross crosslets argent).

V.

Sir Baldwin Frevile, Knt., Lord of Henley in Arden, son and heir
= . . . daughter of . . . Lord Strange.

This Sir B. F. was entitled by inheritance to the following quarters—*Frevile*, *Marmion*, *Kilpeck*, *Mountforte*, *De la Plaunche*, and *Haversham*. His wife's arms (Argent, two lions passant gules, armed and langued azure) were borne in the same manner as those of *Devereux*.

Marteau, (fr.): a large hammer used by smiths.

Martel. See *Hammer.*

Marten. See *Weasel.*

Martin. See *Swallow.*

Martre, (fr.): the marten. See *Weasel.*

Martyr. See *Saint.*

VI.

Sir Baldwin FREVILE, Knt., Lord of Henley in Arden, son and heir.
= JOICE, d. and coh. of John, Lord BUTTETOURT, of Welley Castle.

His mother not being an heiress, he bore his father's quarters without any addition. His lady inherited the arms of *Buttetourt* (Or, a saltire engrailed sable), *Dudley* (alias *Somerie*, or, two lions passant azure, armed and langued gules), and *De la Zouche* (Gules, ten bezants, 4, 3, 2, 1), which descended to her posterity.

VII.

MARGARET, daughter and coheiress of Sir Baldwin FREVILLE, Knt.
= Sir Hugh WILLOUGHBY, of Willoughby on the Wold, Knt.

Sir H. W. bore the paternal arms (Or, on two bars gules, three water-bougets argent) alone. His lady inherited *Frevile*, *Marmion*, *Kilpeck*, *Mountforte*, *De la Plaunche*, *Haversham*, *Buttetourt*, *Dudley*, and *De la Zouche*.

VIII.

Richard WILLOUGHBY, Esq., son and heir, ob. s. p. 1471.

He bore the arms of *Willoughby*, followed by the quarters which he inherited from his mother. His arms, as represented in the plate (see frontispiece), afford an example of the achievement of an esquire complete, viz. shield, helmet, mantle, crest, and motto.

Stained glass in the windows and brasses on the floors of churches often afford much assistance in determining family connections through the marshalling of the arms. Annexed are the arms as emblazoned upon the brass at Winwick, Lancashire, of Sir Peter Legh, who died 1527; but who, on the death of his wife, had relinquished his secular position for the priestly office, so that he is represented wearing a chasuble over his armour, but over the former a shield is represented bearing seven quarterings. They are respectively :—

LEGH.

1. Argent, a cross sable, in the dexter chief quarter a fleur-de-lis of the second—HAYDOCK.

2. Gules, a cross engrailed argent—NORLEY [afterwards taken by LEGH.]

3. [? Azure] a chevron between three cross crosslets [? or]—Unknown.

4. Argent, a mullet sable, charged on one point (?) with a bezant—ASHTON.

VI

Sir Baldwin Frevile = Joice, daughter of
Lord Buttetourt.

VII

Sir Hugh Willoughby = Margaret, daughter of
Sir Baldwin Frevile

5. Vert, a cross flory or—BOYDELL.

6. Lozengy argent and sable—CROFT of Dalton.

7. Azure, a chevron argent between three covered cups or—FRECK-ELTON.

I.

Robert Leigh of Adlington, on Chorlton

= Maud (second wife) daughter and coheiress of Sir Thurston NORLEY, Lord of Norley, &c., and heiress to BOYDELL.

The arms of this Robert Leigh were Azure, two bars argent, over all a bend compony or and gules. His marriage was so great a match that the family, now or later, relinquished their own arms, and took those of (2) *Norley* instead. It seems that by this marriage were brought in the arms of —— (3), *Ashton* (4), and *Boydell* (5).

II.

Piers LEIGH of Hanley, beheaded 1399

= Margaret (first wife), daughter and heiress of Sir Thomas Daniers, Lord of Grappenhall and Brone, widow of Sir John Savage.

The Leighs did not quarter the arms of Daniers. Probably they never got the lands.

III.

Sir Piers LEIGH, slain at Agincourt, 1415.

= Jane, daughter and heiress of Sir Gilbert Haydock, Lord of Haydock and of many other manors.

This match was deemed of so much importance that the Leighs gave the arms of *Haydock* the first place in their shield.

IV.

Sir Piers LEIGH, knighted by Richard Duke of York, at Wakefield, 1460, = Margaret, daughter (not heiress) of Sir Richard Molineux.

V.

Piers LEIGH, ob. 1468, in his father's lifetime.

= Mabel, daughter and heiress of James Croft, Lord of Dalton and Claghton, and heiress to her mother, who was heiress of . . . Freckelton.

By this match came in the arms of *Croft* (6), and *Freckelton* (7). Their arrangement in the shield upon the brass is anomalous; but such anomalies are not unfrequent.

"Ladies often," says Haines (p. cxiii.), " bore arms on their dresses, usually those of their husbands on their mantles or

cloaks, and their own on their kirtles or gowns, as at Cardington, Beds, *c.* 1530; but after the fifteenth century their
own are more frequently on the sinister side of the mantle,
their husbands' bearings occupying the
dexter. The brass of Elizabeth KNEVET,
1518, at Eastington, Gloucestershire, is
a good example of a lady in an heraldic
mantle." The six quarters represent the
families of 1. KNEVET, 2. CROMWELL, 3.
TATERSHALL, 4. CAYLEY, 5. BASSET, and 6.
BISHOPSDON.

KNEVET.

When the number of coats to which
a person is entitled is an odd one he
usually fills up the last quarter by re-
peating the first. The royal arms brought
into any family by an heiress (and there
are more such cases than might be supposed) are sometimes placed in the first
quarter, so e.g. they were borne by Cardinal Pole.

If a man marries two or more heiresses
successively, the arms of each will descend only to her own
children.

When a man bears a double surname (e.g. DYKE-ACLAND)
it is the practice for his first quarter to contain the arms pertaining to those names quarterly, and for the second to contain
his own paternal coat. This, however, is a modern usage, and,
as it seems, not a very good one.

It is not uncommon, to avoid confusion by marshalling too
great a number of coats in one escutcheon, to select a few of
the principal, leaving out, for example, the secondary quarters
brought in by heiresses. Many families entitled to a hundred
or more quarters use but four, e.g. Howard, Duke of Norfolk,
has done so for many generations.

In conclusion, it may be observed that quartered arms may
be borne on banners, surcoats, and official seals, just as single
coats are.

Martlet, (fr. *Merlette,* possibly the diminutive of the *merula, merle,* or blackbird): a bird resembling a swallow, with thighs but no visible legs. They form a very common bearing, being found in early Rolls, and are as common in French arms as in English. They may be of any tincture, even of *ermine* (see example under *Crescent*), and are very frequently represented in *orle* (q.v.). It is used also as the *difference* of the fourth son.

ADAMS.

Gules, a fesse between six martlets or—BEAUCHAMP, Powick, co. Worc.

Sable, a martlet argent—ADAMS, co. Pembroke.

Roger de MERLEY, barrée d'argent et de goulz, a la bordure d'azure et merlots d'or en la bordur—Roll, temp. HEN. III.

Sire Roger de WATEVILL, de argent a iij chevrons de goules, a un merelot de sable—Roll, temp. ED. II.

Sire Henri de APPELBY de azure a vj merelos de or—*Ibid.*

Monsire TEMPEST d'argent une cheveron de gules entre trois merletts du sable—Roll, temp. ED. III.

Argent, five fusils conjoined in fesse gules, in chief two martletts respecting each other—DAUBENE.

BEAUCHAMP.

Monsire de FENWIKE, port d'argent, chief gules, a vj merletts de l'une et l'autre [i.e. counterchanged]—*Ibid.*

Mascle, (fr. *macle*): a lozenge voided: indeed in a roll temp. Henry III. they are blazoned as *faux lozenges.* Mascles are supposed to represent the links which composed chain armour. When the mascles touch each other, as shewn in the engraving annexed, they should (now) be blazoned as conjoined. Mascles so arranged generally extend to the edges of the escutcheon, or nearly so. The first three examples shew the variation of blazon for the same arms.

DE QUINCY,
Earl of Winton.

Le Conte de WINCHESTER, de goules a six mascles d'or voydes du champ—Roll, temp. HEN. III.

Le Comte de WINCHESTER, de goules poudre a faux losenges d'or—
Another Roll, temp. HEN. III.

Le Counte de WINCESTRE, de goules a vii lozenges
d'or—Roll, temp. ED. II.

Gules, seven mascles conjoined, 3, 3, 1, or—
Roger DE QUINCY, Earl of Winton.

Sir Johan de GYSE, de goules a vi mascles de
veer e un quarter de or—Roll, temp. ED. II.

Azure, on a fesse argent, between three mascles
or, as many cinquefoils of the first—PURVIS, Suffolk [Comptroller of the Navy, 1735].

PURVIS.

Masculy would appear in some few cases to have been used
as synonymous with *lozengy;* since the form 'o mascles voidies'
occurs, and a comparison of the different blazoning of the same
arms in one case points in this direction; nor is it probable
that the charges in the arms of the 'Earl of KENT' were drawn
as *mascles.* Still in many cases the term probably had its present meaning.

Guillemes de FERIERES. . . de armes vermeilles ben armés, O mascles
de or del champ voidiés—Roll of CAERLAVEROCK.

Sire Allisandre de FREWYLLE, d'or, a une croys mascle de ver e de
goulys—Roll, temp. ED. II.

Sire Baudewyne de FREWYLLE, d'or, a une croys de goulis a les
mascles de ver—*Ibid.*

Monsire Baldwin de FREVILL, port les armes de Latymer [i.e. gules a
une crois patey or] a cinq loisanes de verre en la crois—Roll, temp. ED. III.

William le BLOND, mascule d'or et de noir—Roll, temp. HEN. III.

Le Conte de KENT, masculée de verrée et de goules—*Ibid.*

Sir Toham de BEZOM, mascle d'argent e de sable—Roll, temp. ED. II.

Le bon Richart de la ROKELE . . .   Mascle de goules et de ermine.
Cil ot son escu fait portraire   Roll of Carlaverok.

Crosses and other ordinaries may be formed of mascles as of
fusils and lozenges, and although some contend that a *fesse
mascle* or *masculy* should begin and end with a half, and that
otherwise it will be so many *mascles conjoined in fesse,* the
distinction can scarcely be sustained by facts.

Sire Geffrey de AUBEMARLE, de goules crusule de or a une bende mas-
clee de ermyne—Roll, temp. ED. II.

Sire Henri FAUCONBERGE, de argent a ij barres mascle de sable—*Ibid.*

Ermine, a fesse masculy gules [elsewhere five mascles in fesse gules;
and five fusils in fesse gules pierced]—HUTTON.

Masculyn: there is a curious figure composed of a single mascle with the ends terminating in fleurs-de-lis, to which the name seems to have been given in one instance of a *masculyn fleur-de-lisé* (i.q. *fleury*).

Azure, a masculyn fleur-de-lysé or, within and without five young men's heads couped argent crined or—Henry MAN, Bp. of Sodor and Man, 1546–56 [Harl. MS. 5846].

MAN.

Masoned, (fr. *maçonné*): a term used to describe the lines formed by the junction of the stones in a building. It is sometimes applied to the field, but more frequently to a *castle, tower,* or *wall,* q.v.

Argent, masoned sable, a chief embattled of the last, [otherwise sable, an embattled wall throughout argent, masoned of the first]—REYNELL, Devon.

Argent, masonné and on a chief azure, a demi-lion issuant or—BEAW, Bp. of Llandaff, 1679–1706.

Gules, a fret sable masoned argent—SCHEERLE.

REYNELL.

Matches, roll of : the match formerly used for the discharge of fire-arms was kept in a roll, as exhibited in the margin.

Argent, a fesse gules between two rolls of matches sable, kindled proper—LEET, co. Cambridge.

Argent, on a fesse gules between two rolls of matches sable fired proper a martlet of the field—LETE, Hunts.

Matchlock: a doubtful figure which has been blazoned *matchlock, bill-head, ploughshare,* and *crescent.* Probably what was intended by the figure is a rest for the gun when firing it, and not the gun itself, to which that name is given.

Roll of Matches.

Argent, a chevron between three matchlocks sable—LEVERSEGE.

Argent, a bend engrailed and in chief a matchlock sable—COSANCE, Higham Barrow.

Sable, on a chevron argent, between three matchlocks [pistols] or, as many roses gules barbed vert seeded or—HOPKINS.

Matchlock.

Maunch, (fr. *manche*) : an ancient *sleeve* found as a frequent device in the earliest rolls of arms. Sometimes in French arms it is called *manche mal taillée*, to distin-guish it from an ordinary sleeve. Generally but one *maunche* is borne. No doubt the three little *manches* [*manchelles*] are allusive to the name of MANSEL.

Reinauld de MOUN, de goules ov ung manche d'argent—Roll, temp. HEN. III.

Sire Robert THONY, de argent a une maunch de goules—Roll, temp. ED. II.

R. DE MOUN.

Monsire de HASTINGS port d'or a une manche de gules—Roll, temp. ED. III.

Monsire de MOUN, gules a une manche d'ermin —*Ibid.*

Gules, a maunch ermine, with a hand proper, holding a fleur-de-lis or—MOHUN, Earl of Somerset.

Or, a maunch gules—HASTINGS, Oxfordshire.

Argent, a maunch sable—HASTINGS, Leicester.

Argent, three sleeves erect sable—BLAKE.

Sable, a hand proper holding a fleur-de-lis and

MOHUN.

vested in a maunch issuing from the dexter side of the shield or—CREKE.

Argent, an anchor azure surmounted by a maunch sable charged with three crosses patty of the field—COLPOYS.

Argent, three maunches sable; [another Argent, a chevron between three maunches sable]—MANSEL.

D'or à une manche mal taillée de gueules—DASTING, Normandie.

D'or à trois manches mal taillées de gueules — CONDÉ DE COEMY, Champagne.

Medal : in later coats of arms of very debased heraldry special medals or *medallions, clasps,* &c., granted for services in war have been frequently adopted. Sometimes a coin is in-troduced, e.g. a *pagoda* (i.e. a Madras coin), and in one old

---

Massacre, (fr.) : a stag's head and horns affronty. See *Deer.*

Masse, (fr.) : *Mace.*

Massue, (fr.) : a large club or *Mace.* See also *Club* under *Staff.*

Mastiff. See *Dog.*

Mast. See *Ship.*

Masuré, fr. = *in ruins.*

Mattock ; i.q. *Hammer.*

May-flowers. See *Hawthorn.*

Medallion. See *Medal.*

Meiré, or *Meirée.* See *Potent.*

Melting Pot. See *Founder's fur-nace.*

instance what is called a *penny-yard penny*. This is a coin which is said to have been struck in Penyard Castle, near Ross, Herefordshire.

Or, a lion rampant gules, a canton of the last, thereon pendant from a mural crown of the first a riband of the second fimbriated azure, a representation of the gold medal and clasp presented for services in the Peninsular War—MACDONALD, Perth.

Erminois, on an eagle displayed double headed gules an eastern crown or; a chief vert charged with pendant from a chain two oval medallions in pale, the one bearing Arabic characters and the other a dagger in fesse, blade wavy, point downwards, the dexter in relief gold —Sir Thomas S. RAFFLES, Lieutenant-Governor of Java, &c.

Gules, two estoiles, in chief argent a lion passant; in base or on a chief of the second a wreath of laurel vert, enclosing two swords in saltire proper, pomels and hilts or; in chief the medal for Waterloo— McINNES, Charlton Kings, co. Gloucester.

Argent, three palets gules on a chief azure as many martlets of the first with a canton of the second charged with the medal presented to him by the East India Company proper—MARTIN, Wivenhoe, Essex.

Azure, two swords in saltire argent .... on a chief ermine a bee volant between two star pagodas proper—BLADES, Sheriff of London, 1812.

Azure, three penny-yard pence proper [i.e. argent]—SPENCE.

Penny-yard penny.

Merchant's Mark: since those engaged in trade were not formerly allowed to bear arms, the merchants adopted 'marks,' often composed of their initials or other special letters intertwined, and sometimes other devices intermingled; and, though contrary to rule, they placed them in shields and sometimes marshalled them with arms. The subject of merchants' marks,

---

Membered, (fr. *membré*): refers to the legs of birds argent, and to the talons and tongues of beasts of prey.

Même, De, (fr.): of the same tincture. In English blazon, however, to avoid repetition, usually the expression 'of the first' or 'of the second' is employed.

Menu, fr. = small and fine, e.g. *menu*-vair, the old form of *miniver* applied to a fur. See *Vaire;* also a *menue burlure* is found = *barrulet* (q.v.) as distinguished from *grose burlure*, used in the same roll and = *bar*.

Mercury. The planetary name for *Purpure*.

found as they are frequently in stained glass, on brasses and
carved in wood and stone, is too wide a
subject to treat in a short article; besides
which they scarcely come under the head
of heraldry. One example is given, which
is characteristic of very many others. It is
from stained glass in S. Michael's Church,
Oxford.   The letters may possibly signify
Thomas R . . . Merchant of Oxford. From
the white roses (barbed and seeded or) we
may infer that he was attached to the
House of York.

A Merchant's Mark.

Merillion: an instrument used by Hatband-makers, and borne by their Company.
It is figured as in the margin.

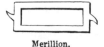

Merillion.

Mermaid, (fr. *siréne*): composed of the upper half of
a woman (with dishevelled hair) joined to
the lower half of a fish. It occurs but very
seldom as a charge upon true English arms.
The *Siren* seems to be only another name for
the mermaid.

Argent, a mermaid gules, crined or, holding a
mirror in her right hand, and a comb in her left,
both gold—ELLIS, Lancashire.

Vert, three mermaids two and one, each holding
comb and mirror or—WOLLSTONECRAFT, Essex and London, granted 1765.

ELLIS.

Azure, a siren with comb and glass argent within a bordure indented
gules—French family of POISSONNIERE.

A mermaid is found on the Seal of Sir William Bruvire, or
Bruere, temp. Richard I., and probably had its origin in the
tales told by travellers who joined in the crusades.

Mermaids occur frequently as supporters; e.g. to the arms of
the Burgh of MONTROSE, as also as crests, e.g. of Lord BYRON;
and Sir John WALLOP, temp. Henry VIII., who bore a black
mermaid with golden hair.

Merlette, (fr.), or *mertlet*.   See   Merle, (fr.), *blackbird*.
　　Martlet.   Merlion, or marlion. See *Falcon*.

The German family of DIE ERSTENBERGER bear as their crest a mermaid, but with wings instead of arms.

Metal : (1.) The metals employed as tinctures in heraldry are two in number, that is to say *or* and *argent*. See *Tinctures.*

(2.) Blocks of metal are frequently introduced into heraldry, and are called by different names, and are generally conventionally represented. We find *ingots* of gold, *cakes* of copper, *blocks* of tin, and *pigs* of lead. We also find a mineral named, viz. the calamine *stone.*

Ingots of gold.

Argent, on a chevron between three mullets gules a crescent or ; on a chief azure three ingots of gold palletwise, fretted with another in bend proper—WILSON, Sneaton Castle, Yorkshire.

Azure, on a chevron engrailed three blocks [of metal] or, each charged with a cross of the second—HOBSON.

Ermine, three cakes of copper proper ; on a chief gules a chamber [i.e. a chamber-piece] or—CHAMBERS, London, granted 1723.

Cake of Copper.

Or, on a cross gules between four Cornish Choughs proper five blocks of tin marked with the letter W.— KNAPMAN, co. Devon.

Vert, on a fesse or between three doves close argent beaked and legged gules, each with an ear of wheat in the bill of the second, as many pigs of lead azure—GREENSMITH, Steeple Grange, co. Derby, granted 1714.

Two arms embowed proper, both hands holding a calamine stone argent spotted with red, yellow, and blue—Crest of the Society of MINERAL and BATTERY Works, incorporated 1568.

Calamine stone.

Mill, (fr. *moulin*) : portions of the mill machinery are represented on coats of arms. We find first of all the *Mill-stone*, and this is generally borne with the *mill-rind* or *fer de moline* upon it.

Azure, three mill-stones argent, on each a mill-rind sable—MILVETON, Cheshire.

Mill-stone.

Next the *Mill-wheels* are sometimes found, as also the *cogs* of the same, and *mill-clack*. See under *Tremoile.*

Meslé : mingled. Used by a few old writers in describing a field of metal and colour in equal proportions, as gyronny, paly.

Azure, on a fesse argent, between a beehive surrounded by bees volant in chief, and a mill-wheel in base or; two roses gules barbed and seeded proper—CALROW, co. Cheshire.

Gules, three mill-wheels or—CHAWCERS.

Sable, on a bend between three cogs of a mill-wheel or as many elm leaves vert—COGGS, London.

Azure, a mill-clack in fesse or—MILLS, London; (descended from MILLS of Cornwall).

The *Mill-rind*, or *Mill*-rine, has already been noticed under *Fer-de-Moline*. See also *Wind-mill*, and Water-mill under *Wheel*, *Silk-throwers-mill*, &c.

Mill-pick: a tool used by millwrights. It is drawn differently from the *pickaxe*, *paviour's pick*, &c. (q.v. under *Axe*).

Sable, a chevron between three mill-picks argent—MOSELEY, Moseley, Staffordshire.

Gules, a fesse chequy argent, and of the first between three mill-picks (or pickaxes) or—PIGOTTS.

Argent, three mill-picks gules—PICKWORTH.

Mill-pick.

Argent, a chevron between three mill-picks sable—MILLERS' Company, Newcastle-on-Tyne.

Mine: this is shewn but in one coat of arms, and it is characteristic of the extraordinary details which were introduced into coats of arms in the sixteenth century.

Argent, a mine open of earth colour, the upper part variegated with various shrubs vert; within the mine a miner proper vested sable, on his head a cap argent, round his body a belt of the last, and in the attitude of working the dexter side of the mine with two hammers; on the sinister side a candle of the first lighted proper in a candlestick azure fixed in the mine: on a chief brown a square plate or, between a bezant on the dexter and a plate on the sinister—Royal MINERS' Company [Inc. 1568].

Meubles or *meubles d'armoires*: charges generally of whatever kind.

Mew. See *Sea-Gull*.

Michael, (S.) and S. George, Order of. See *Knights*.

Midas. See *Heads*.

Miner. See *Man*.

Mineral. See *Metal*.

Miniver, i.q. Menu Vair. See *Vair*.

Mi-parti, (fr.). See *Dimidiated*.

Miraillé: a French term signifying variegated of several tinctures, applied e.g. to butterflies.

Mitry: this awkward word is suggested to a bordure charged with eight mitres.

Mitus. See under *Pheasant*.

Mirror, (fr. *Miroir*) : is represented as a small circular looking-glass with a handle when borne by a *Mermaid* (q.v.). In French arms it is more frequent, and is described as *de toilette, ovale, arrondi,* and *pommeté,* i.e. the frame adorned with knobs.

Argent, a tiger statant reguardant, looking down into a mirror in base, handle to the dexter all proper—[From old glass in Thame Church, impaled after the arms of Hadrian de BARDIS, Prebendary of Thame.]

Argent, a tiger reguardant at a mirror azure—SIBELLS. [But Qy.]

D'Azur, à trois miroirs arrondis d'argent—MIRAMBEL, Limosin.

Mitre, (fr. *Mitre*) : one of the principal insignia of the episcopal office, although not belonging to it exclusively. There were three kinds of Mitres recognized by old writers—the precious, the 'aurifraged,' and the simple.

The privilege of wearing a mitre was first conceded to abbots and priors about the eleventh century. Soon afterwards it was decreed that mitred abbots exempt from episcopal jurisdiction should wear the second mitre mentioned above, the third being assigned to non-exempt abbots and priors. These rules do not appear to have ever been very strictly observed or enforced. It is the first which is always represented in heraldic drawing.

ABP. LAUD.

Though the use of the mitre as a part of the episcopal costume had, until quite recently [a], become obsolete in the Anglican Church, its prelates have continued to bear it above their arms. The mitres of the two archbishops, and the Bishop of Durham, are sometimes encircled with ducal coronets, which, however, is, at least in the two former cases, a practice of late origin, and without authority. The Bishop of Durham might (until lately) with propriety enjoy this mark of temporal dignity, as he was Count Palatine of Durham. His mitre in the sixteenth century was represented with a plume of ostrich feathers issuing from the sinister side and with the coronet.

---

[a] In recent days a mitre was worn by an Anglican Bishop for the first time on June 28, 1885, at S. Andrew's, Lincoln.

The annexed figure of a mitre is taken from a roll of the peers of England, dated 1515. The abbots' mitres drawn in that document are
precisely similar in form, but differ in the
colour of the enclosed triangular spaces.
Earlier mitres were generally lower: in
later times they have usually been represented much higher and more acutely
pointed. In all cases they should be represented with the *labels*, or pendent rib-
bons at the sides of the mitre. Sometimes the term *stringed*
is applied to these when denoting their tincture.

Mitre.

As *charges*, mitres occur in the insignia of several English sees
and abbeys, and previous to the introduction of the practice
of bishops impaling the insignia of their sees, they often differenced their paternal arms by the addition of mitres, keys, or
other official insignia within the shield.

Gules, three mitres or—See of CHESTER.

Azure, three mitres or—See of NORWICH.

Azure, a saltire argent; in chief a mitre of the last garnished or—See
of EDINBURGH.

Or, three torteaux, with a label of three points azure, charged with
a like number of mitres gold [for difference]—William COURTENAY,
Archbishop of Canterbury, 1381.

Checky or and azure, on a fesse gules, a mitre stringed argent; all
within a bordure of the second—CLIFFORD, Bp. of Bath and Wells, 1401;
Worcester, 1401; afterwards of London, 1407–21.

Argent, on a fesse azure, a mitre or; in chief three buck's heads
caboshed gules; in base as many pheons sable—Thomas de BECKINGTON,
Bishop of Bath and Wells, 1443.

Sable, three mitres or—Robert MASCALL, Bp. of Hereford, 1404–16.

Very few families bear mitres, but the family of BERKELEY
bears for a crest (without any wreath) a mitre gules, labelled
and garnished or, charged with a chevron between ten crosses
patee six in chief and four in base the family arms. Similar
crests are used by some families of HARDING.

Azure, three mitres or—MYTERTON, Newcastle.

Or, on a bend between two cotises and as many garbs azure a mitre
of the first—TYLSON.

Mole, (fr. *taupe*): this occurs more frequently than might have been expected. With it may be classed the *mole-hill*, though this is perhaps used to signify any small *hill* or *hillock*. See also under *Mound*.

Azure, on a cross patonce or fretty gules in the dexter chief a plate charged with a mole sable—MOLLE.

Argent, three moles sable—NANCOTHAN, Cornwall.

Argent, three moles sable, snouts and feet gules —NANGOTHAN, Scotland.

Argent, a chevron between three moles sable —TWISTLETON.

Argent, a mole-hill in base sable—ASCHAW.

Argent, three mole-hills proper—ILSLEY.

Moles are also borne by the families of NEVELE, MEDPATH, QUICK, co. Devon, and MITFORD, Earl of Redesdale.

TWISTLETON.

Mogul, Fish of, (lat. *Cyprinus Rohita*): this fish, which is allied to the *Carp* (of which there is no English representation as an armorial bearing, though it is not un-frequent on the Continent) is used as a badge of dignity called the MAHI MARATIB, which dignity is said to have originated with the Mogul dynasty founded in 1206. General (created in 1807 Lord) LAKE had this dignity or order conferred upon him, and bore it on his arms.

Fish of Mogul.

Sable, a bend between six cross crosslets fitchy argent; on a chief of the last the fish of Mogul per pale or and vert, banded vert and gules surmounting the Goog and Ullum honourable insignia in saltire—Viscount LAKE of Delhi, 1807.

Monastery: a curious device, the following being a unique example, and evidently chosen on account of the name.

Per fesse purple and vert; on a fesse sable a monastery with two wings argent; in base three monks, the centre one affronty the other two confronting him habited, all proper—MONKHOUSE, Newcastle-on-Tyne.

Moile. See *Bull*.

Mole or Molet: old form of *Mullet*.

Molette d'éperon, (fr.): *Mullet*.

Moline. See *Cross Moline*, § 24. Also *Mill*.

Monsters, (fr. *monstrueux*): bearing in mind how much, in the way of devices, heraldry derived from the crusades and pilgrimages to the Holy Land, and what a taste seems to have been created for romance at the beginning of the twelfth century, as evidenced by the rapid expansion of the stories surrounding the exploits and death of King Arthur, it is no wonder that tales of travellers suggested remarkable animals for the varieties of distinguishing charges. The *Griffin*, and with it the Dragon, the one a compound of the Lion and Eagle, the king of beasts and of birds, the other an imaginary Crocodile, with the head of a serpent and the wings of a bat, were the two favourites. From the latter the forked tongue, painted of a different tincture (generally gules), added to the terrible appearance of the monster.

Somewhat similar to these was the *Cockatrice*, and with it the Wyvern; these animals having but two legs instead of four, and partaking more of the character of the reptile than of the beast. Examples of each will be found under the respective heads of *Griffin* and *Cockatrice;* beneath the first of these heads are grouped the *Dragon, Alce,* and *Opinicus;* beneath the other the *Wyvern, Basilisk, Amphistera,* and *Hydra.*

Another class of monsters arose from adding wings to beasts, i.e. to the *Horse, Stag,* and *Bull,* and the *python* or winged serpent may be classed with them; these will be found noticed under the heading of *Pegasus,* the winged horse. In the same way the *Lion* and the *Ox,* amongst the symbols of the Evangelists, are always represented winged.

After adding birds' and bats' wings to some animals it was only a step to add fishes' tails to others, and such appears to be simply the origin of such monsters as those to which the name of *sea-horse, sea-lion, sea-dragon,* and *sea-dog* have been applied.

Montant, (fr.): used when a charge (which has of itself no definite direction) is directed towards the chief, e.g. insects crustacea and the like: nearest English equivalent perhaps *erect.*

Montjoie, a hill composed of six hillocks. See *Mount.*

But next we find a group in which men appear combined with portions of animals; the old *Satyr* from Roman story, with the Satyral and Centaur (or Sagittarius), which last was one of the signs of the Zodiac and King Stephen's badge; also the *Lampago*, and man-tiger, the last two being probably but one figure. All these appear on shields. Nor is the representation of mythical forms of women overlooked. The *Sphinx* with the woman's head standing at the head of them, and the classical *Harpy*, follows on one side, the *Mermaid* and *Siren* on the other. The mystery of fire was associated with the *Phœnix* and the *Salamander*. These latter will be found noted under the respective headings of *Satyr*, *Sphinx*, *Mermaid*, and *Phœnix*.

Lastly, combinations of animals will be found in the examples of the *Unicorn* and *Apre*, the one a horse with the tail of a lion, the other a bull with the tail of a bear: the *Allocamelus*, partly an ass and partly a camel; the head of the *Goat*, which has been varied according to fancy, forming the lion-goat, and the deer-goat; and even the *Eagle* is in one case represented with hound's ears.

Moon, (fr. *lune*, lat. *luna*): the moon is a common device. It is occasionally borne full, when it is termed *in her complement*, and it is then figured with a human face. It may also be illuminated, that is, surrounded with very short rays. It proper tincture is argent. When sable it is supposed to be eclipsed.

When a half moon is represented with the horns towards the dexter side of the shield it is supposed to be *increscent*, and is described as *in her increment;* when the horns are turned to the sinister side it is supposed to be *decrescent*, and is described as *in her decrement* (or, as some blunderingly write it, *in her detriment*). But these terms are chiefly found in theoretical works, and not often in practical blazon. When the horns are repre-

---

Montegre = *Man-tiger.*
Moor hen. See *Coot.*
Moor's head. See *Head.*

Mooted (or *Moulted*) up by the roots: used by an old writer for *eradicated.*

sented uppermost the charge is simply a *Crescent*, and this from the earliest times was the special ensign of the Turks.

Azure, the sun, moon, and seven stars or, the two first in chief, the last in base; [otherwise Azure, seven estoiles in orbicular form, in chief the sun and full moon or]—John de FONTIBUS, Bishop of Ely, 1220–25.

Gules, two flaunches ermine on a chief azure a sun between two moons or—DAY, co. Derby.

Azure, a cross calvary on a griece of three steps argent between a sun in splendour and a moon in her detriment proper—MARTIN, Ireland.

Azure, a moon descrescent or—DELALUNE [or DELALYNE].

(Decrescent.)
DELALUNE.

Azure, an increscent [i.e. a moon increscent] or—BALSWILL.

Gules, a moon increscent or—DASTURES [or DESTURES].

Azure, three increscents or, each enclosing a mullet—GREGORIE, co. Devon.

Ermine, three increscents gules—SYMMES, co. Northampton.

Increscents are also borne by the families of BUNNELL; BAIRD, co. Haddington; FALLON, &c.

(Increscent)
BALSWILL.

The term *luna* is used to signify *argent* in the fanciful system of planetary tinctures.

Moor-cock, *(tetrao scoticus)* or *Grouse* is borne by several families in allusion to their names.

Argent, a moor-cock proper—MOORE, Fawley, Berks, Bart. 1627.

Argent, on a fesse between three moor-cocks sable as many mullets or—MOORE, Pendridge, co. Dorset; MORE, co. Hants.

Or, on a fesse humetty between three moor-cocks proper, a garb of the field—MORRIS or MORRS, Coxwell, co. Berks.

Sable, on a mount proper a stag lodged or, a chief of the third charged with a moor-cock of the second—MORTOFT, co. Norfolk; confirmed October, 1606.

MOORE.

Or, a falcon sable preying on a moor-cock proper, on a chief of the second three birdbolts argent—KNOLLES, co. Devon.

Argent, a chevron azure between three moor-cocks proper—John Luxmore, Bishop of Bristol, 1807; Hereford, 1808; St. Asaph, 1815–30.

Azure, on a fesse dancetty between eight garbs or banded gules three grouse of the field beaked and membered of the third—Downam, co. York.

Borne also by families of Highmore, Middlemore, Moor and More, and Fitz-Moore, and many families of Morbwin Moммон, Пыли, Kindwood, &c.

The bird occurs also frequently as a crest. For *Moorhen* see under *Coot*.

Mortar: the guns so called do not seem to be blazoned by this name in any arms, unless those borne by the family of Goter are meant to represent them: but the ordinary *pestle* and *mortar* for some reason has been chosen as an armorial bearing by two families, of one of which there appear to be several branches which bear the pestle and mortar differently.

Azure, three mortars and pestles or—Broke, co. Warwick.
Sable, three pestles in mortars argent—Wakley; Harl. MS. 1404.
Sable, three mortars argent, in each a pestle or—Wakerley.
Azure, a fesse between three mortars or—Wakerley.
Gules, billetty and three ringed mortars argent—Goter.

Mortcour (so spelt, but qy. an error for *Mortarium*, or fr. *Mortier*): a candlestick used at funerals. It occurs only in the insignia of the Company of Wax Chandlers. In some drawings the ornamental foliage accidentally resembles small snakes.

Azure, on a chevron between three mortcours argent as many roses gules (but another Azure on a chevron argent between three mortcours or as many roses gules seeded of the third barbed vert) — Company of Wax-Chandlers, London; Incorporated 1484. Arms granted by Holmes, Clarenceux, 1487.

Mortcour.

Morailles, (fr.). See *Barnacles*.
Morion. See *Cap of Steel*.
Morné, (fr.): of a lion without teeth, tongue or claws.
Morse. See *Seal*.

Mortier, (fr.): a round cap worn by chancellors, &c., and placed above the *crest* in some French arms; somewhat similar to the Lord Mayor's *Cap*.

Motto : a word or sentence upon a scroll, generally placed below the shield, but sometimes, especially in Scotland, above the crest. The family motto should never be inscribed (as it too often is) upon a garter or circle, nor should it accompany the arms of any woman except the sovereign. In the case of William of

WYKEHAM'S arms here given it will be seen the garter is reserved for the motto of the ' order.' His personal motto, adopted by his two colleges, is *manners makyth man;* and that is always found beneath. Bishops, as a rule, do not use mottoes.

Many ancient mottoes were war-cries. Such it is probable were the following :—

WILLIAM OF WYKEHAM.

Forward. DOUGLAS, Duke of Queensbury. *Crom a boo.* (I will burn). FITZGERALD, Duke of Leinster. *Courage sans peur.* GAGE, Viscount Gage.

Many mottoes refer obviously to the name of the bearer, as—
Cavendo tutus—CAVENDISH. *Per se valens*—PERCEVAL. *Pie repone te*—PIERREPONTE, Earl Manvers. *Scuto amoris divini*—SCUDAMORE. *Time Deum, cole regem*—COLERIDGE.

Some have reference to a charge in the arms to which they are annexed, or to the crest above it, e.g.—

Soyes sage et simple—SPRY; the crest being: on a wreath a serpent nowed, thereon a dove.

But the generality of mottoes express a sentiment, hope, or determination. Such are the following :—

Dum spiro spero—DILLON. *Garde la foy*—COX, POULET, RICH, &c. *Spero meliora*—CORY. *Toujours prest*—CARMICHAEL.

Mottoes are often borne by several successive generations, but may be changed at pleasure. The languages most in use are Latin, French, and English; but in Scotland they are often in the old Lowland dialect, and in Wales, in the language of the principality. A few peers use Italian mottoes, and some recent ones are even in Oriental languages.

The present royal motto, *Dieu et mon Droit*, was certainly used as early as the reign of Henry VI. It was probably a *war-cry* long before, as King Richard I. is recorded to have said, " Not we, but *God and our right* have vanquished France at Gisors." The *Cri de guerre* of the kings of France was *Mon joye Saint Denis*. Scottish heralds term such war-cries *Slogans* or badly spelt *Sloghorns*.

Mount, (fr. *montagne*); in later heraldry it is not unusual to separate the lower portion of the shield by a curved line, and by tincturing the same *vert* to represent therein a *mount* supposed to be covered with grass. The French heralds use a specific term for this device, viz. *terrassé*. On this some other device is placed, most frequently a tree, but often an animal grazing, e.g. a stag (see one or two examples under *Deer*). It may be covered with *flowers*, or be *burning*, &c. The *mount* is sometimes incorrectly written *mound*, which is a very different device. [See under *Orb*, and note arms of BERWICK below.] It is sometimes blazoned as a hill, or hillock, (fr. *tertre*), or even mole-hill where there is more than one mount represented. A *mount mounted* is said to mean a large mount with a smaller one upon it. The French use the term *coupeaux* for a series of hills.

Hillock.

The *mountain* also occurs, and perhaps may be distinguished somewhat in the drawing from a *mount*.

Argent, in chief a gem-ring gules; out of a mount in base three trefoils vert—DORRIEN, co. Herts.

Argent, a mountain vert—DOUGAL, Scotland.

Moulin, (fr.), *Mill*. See also *Windmill*.

Moulin, Fer de. See *Fer de Moline*.

Moussu or *mossu*, old fr. = *emoussé* or blunted, said to be applied by French heralds to a *Cross* with ends rounded. See § 29.

Moucheté, (fr.): spotted with small leaf pattern like on lace, and in one case used of black spots on the lamprey.

Mouchetor, (fr.), *moucheture*: said to be an *Ermine spot* without the three specks usually placed at its upper end.

Mound. See *Orb*, also *Mount*.

Mounting : a term used for *rampant*, applied to beasts of chase and sometimes to reptiles.

Argent, on a mount inclining to the sinister an oak-tree proper, acorned or, debruised of a fesse azure—Richard WATSON, Bp. of Llandaff, 1782—1816.

Or, a mountain [couped in base] azure inflamed in several places proper—MACLEOD, Lord of Lewis.

Gules, a chevron ermine between in chief two mounds and in base a talbot passant or—DAVIS, Bristol.

Argent, three hills in base azure—BRINCKMAN, Baronetcy, 1831.

Vert, three hillocks argent—HILLS, Middlesex.

WATSON.

Per fesse argent and chequy argent and gules, a hill of three mounds azure—HOHEBURG.

Argent, three mountains issuing from the base, one in front and two behind vert ; on the top of each a cross Calvary gules—HILL, Ireland.

Argent, a chevron sable between three mole-hills with grass proper, each charged with an annulet of the first [otherwise three hillocks of rushes vert, on each an annulet]—TYLDESLEY.

D'or, à l'arbre arraché de sinople posé sur un tertre de même parti dor, au rocher de sinople—MONTOLIEU, Languedoc.

De sable, à une montagne d'argent semée de flammes de gueules—MOUSTOULAT, Guyenne.

D'Argent, à l'arbre terrassé de sinople, au cerf de gueules passant au pied de l'arbre—LOURMONT, Normandie.

D'or, à une montagne de trois coupeaux d'azure—CAUDECOSTE, Dauphiné.

The French have also a mount of six hillocks (*à six coupeaux*), which is called a *Montjoie*.

De gueules, à deux bourdons d'or posés en chevron accompagnés de trois montjoies d'argent [1st and 3rd Quarts.]—GUILLART DE FRESNAY, Poitou.

Mouvant: a term peculiar to French heraldry, and signifying that a portion of a charge only is visible, as if issuing from one of the sides or corners of the shield. (See e.g. under *Cloud.*) The following examples explain the use of the term.

D'azur, à un lion d'argent regardant un soleil d'or mouvant de l'angle dextre de l'écu—DU GARDIER, Dauphiné.

De gueules, à lavant bras gantelé d'argent mouvant du flanc senestre de l'écu et tenant une bride de sable—DE L'ESCAILLE, Brabant.

Mourned: used for blunted, but (fr.) *morné* = disarmed.

Mouse. Rere-mouse only found. See under *Bat*

Mulberry, (fr. *mûre*, old fr. *moure*) : the leaves of this plant occur on arms as early as temp. Henry III. as well as in recent arms. One example only of a branch has been noticed on arms, viz. on those of BASSANO (see under *Silkworm*), but it was used as a device or cognizance by MOWBRAY.

Sire Huge de MORIENS, de azure a iij foiles de moures de or—Roll, temp. ED. II.

Vert, three mulberry leaves or—WOODWARD, co. Norfolk, 1806.

Vert, a wolf salient argent ; impaling argent three mulberry leaves vert two and one—GAMBOW.

Azure, three mulberry leaves or—MOREYNE, Suffolk.

Azure, a Spanish merchant-brig under sail proper ; on a chief invected argent two mulberry leaves, the points opposed to each other ; on each leaf two silkworms also proper—FAVENC, London.

Mullet, (fr. *molette*) : this bearing is generally taken to represent the rowel of a spur, and in modern French heraldry is called *molette d'éperon*. In old French blazon it is sometimes termed *rouwell*, q.v. It might, however, when not pierced be taken to represent a star, and, as will be seen by the examples, it appears originally to have been interchangeable with the *estoile*. It usually has five points, and this number is always to be understood when no other is mentioned. In French heraldry the normal number of points is six.

Le Conte de OXFORD, quartele d'or et de goules [*sic*], ung molet d'argent ent le quarter devant—Roll, temp. HEN. III.

Le Counte de OXENFORD, quartile de or e de goules ; a un molet de argent—Roll, temp. ED. II.

Le Counte d'OXFORD, port quarterly d'or et gules ; a une estoiele d'argent en le quarter gules devant—Roll, temp. ED. III.

Quarterly gules and or, in the first quarter a mullet argent—VERE, Earl of Oxford.

William de ODINGSELES, d'argent a la fece de

DE VERE.

goulz a deux molets en le cheif goulz—Roll, temp. HEN. III.

William DODINGCELES, dargent a une fesse de goules a deus roueles de gules—Another Roll, temp. HEN. III.

Sire Johan DODINGSELES, de argent a une fesse de goules ; en le chef un molet de goules—Roll, temp. ED. II. [Similar in Roll, temp. ED. III.]

Mule. See *Ass.* **Mullet,** (a fish). See *Gurnet ;* also *Sea Urchin.*

Nicholas de MOELES, dargent a deux barres de goules a trois molets; en le cheif goules—Roll, temp. HEN. III.

Rauf DELAHAYE, dargent, a ruell de goules—Another Roll, temp. HEN. III.

Robert de HAMSART, tout apreste' . . . . Rouge o trois estoiles de argent—Roll of Carlaverock, A.D. 1300. [Cf. Gilbert HANSARDE under *Estoile*.]

Sire Robert HANSARDE de, goules a iij moles de argent—Roll, temp. ED. II.

Monsire HANSTED, gules a trois mulletts argent —Roll, temp. ED. III.

Sir Renaud de COBHAM [de goules a un cheveron de or]; en le cheveron iij moles de azure—Roll, temp. ED. II. [Cf. John de COBHAM under *Estoile*.]

LENTHALL.

Sire Johan de WIGKETONE, de sable, a 3 moles de or, od la bordure endente de or—Roll, temp. ED. II.

Le bon Baron de WIGNETONE . . . portoit bordure endentee O trois estoiles de or ensable—Roll of Carlaverock.

Argent, on a bend cotised sable, three mullets or—LENTHALL, Haseley, co. Oxon.

Argent, on a mullet sable an annulet or—ASHTON, co. Lancaster.

Mullets besides having for the sake of variety more than five *points* (or, as they are termed in one instance, *horns*), may be *pierced* of the field, or *voided* of some other tincture, and this is found to be the case with very early examples. Sometimes. though *pierced* is not mentioned, it may be understood.

Sire William de HARPEDENE de argent a un molet de goules percee—Roll, temp. ED. II.

Argent, a mullet of six points pierced sable —HARPDEN, Gloucestershire.

Monsire de BRADBOURNE, port d'argent a une bend gules trois molletts d'or percés— Roll, temp. ED. III.

Monsire John de HOTHAM, d'or, sur une bend sable trois mulletts d'argent voyde gules—*Ibid.*

HARPEDENE.

Monsire de KNEVILLE, gules a trois molletts d'or voyde vert—*Ibid.*

Muraillé, (fr.), also *mureld*, walled; i.e. masoned and embattled.

Mural, applied to a *Crown.*

Murr. See *Auk.*

Murrey. See *Sanguine.*

Muscovy Duck. See *Duck.*

Monsire œ Bonville, d'or, sur une bend sable, trois molets d'argent voyde du champ—Roll, temp. Ed. III.

Sire Miles de Hastynges, de or une, fesse de goules ; en le chef ij moles de goules—Roll, temp. Ed. II.

Or, a fesse, and in chief two mullets of six points pierced gules—Hastynges, Oxfordshire.

Argent, on two bars sable six mullets of as many points or, three and three—Hopton, co. York.

Azure, three crescents each enclosing a six-pointed mullet [or rather estoile] argent—Hobhouse, co. Somerset.

HASTYNGES.

Argent, three bars sable; in chief two mullets pierced of the last, the horns barry of the first and second—Houghton, London.

Edmondson has blazoned these as *star-fishes*, for which Guillim pretends that *mullet* was the ancient name.

A mullet is used for a *difference* of the third house. (See *Cadency*.)

Mushroom, (fr. *champignon*): not observed in English arms, but found in French arms.

D'azur, à un chevron d'argent accompagné de trois champignons d'or —Guyot d'Anfreville, Normandie.

Musket. The Musket is found amongst bearings as well as the *Potgun*, and the *Pistol*. They appear to have been drawn from the objects themselves. The *Petronel*, a kind of pistol used by the French, is given in heraldic books, but no case has been observed.

Gules, two muskets in saltire within a bordure argent; a chief or charged with a lion passant guardant of the field—Gunn.

Per fesse wavy gules and azure ; [in chief] a lion passant gardant or, beneath the feet a musket lying horizontally proper; [the base] semy of fleurs-de-lis confusedly dispersed of the third—Hockin, co. Devon, 1764.

Sable, on a chevron erminois between three pistols or, as many roses gules barbed and seeded proper—Hopkins, 1773.

Or, on a cross azure five pairs of pistols saltirewise of the first—Toulson, co. Lancaster.

Per saltire azure and or a lion rampant guardant of the first on a canton argent two pot-guns azure (another sable)—Gold.

Musimon: described by Guillim as resembling a ram with goat's horns as well as its own.

Music. See under *Book*.

Muzzled, (fr. *emmuselé*). Of bears and other animals so provided.

Nails are of various kinds; the ordinary nail has a square head; those in the insignia of the GLAZIERS' Company are called *closing* nails, and are drawn as in the margin; *tilers'* nails have larger heads than ordinary nails. *Horse-nails* are also found named. The term *spike* is sometimes used for nail, and the drawing is sometimes mistaken for the *wedge*. (See also *Passion-nails*.)

Closing Nail.

Ermine, three nails meeting in point sable—CADE.

Argent, a bend gules between six tiler's nails sable—John TYLER, Bishop of Llandaff, 1706–24.

Argent, on two chevrons sable ten horse-nails or—CLOUVYLE, Essex.

Argent, three spikes gules, closing towards the points in base—BALMAKIN, Scotland.

Gules, semy of nails or, a lion rampant argent—BRYN.

Naissant (fr.), sometimes written *nascent* : issuing from the middle of an ordinary, as shewn in the illustration. It is sometimes confused with *issuant,* which should be restricted to charges which rise from the upper line of a fesse or bar, or the lower line of a chief.

Or, a demi-lion rampant gules, naissant from a fesse sable. Sir Henry EAME, or ESME, K.G., temp. ED. III.

Argent, a demi-stag gules naissant out of a fesse tortilly of the second and first—McCORQUODELL, Scotland.

EAME.

Narcissus : the heraldic form of this flower is practically a *sexfoil*.

Gules, three narcissuses argent pierced of the field—LAMBART, *Earl Cavan.*

Vert, a fesse vairy argent and erminois between three narcissus flowers of the second—WHITE, Hursley, co. Northampton, 1750.

Nag. See *Horse.*

Naiant : written sometimes *Natant,* swimming : applied to a *fish* borne fesswise.

Nailed. See under *Latticed.*

Nascent. See *Naissant.*

Natte, (fr. for *mat*) : used for the sake of the name in two coats of arms of French families

Naturel, (fr.): *au naturel* is equivalent to the English heraldic term *proper,* q.v.

Nebuly, (fr. *nebulé*) : an undulating line of division, which being intended to represent clouds is drawn horizontally; when applied to the field, however, it is usually described as *barry nebuly*, q.v. But it may also be applied to ordinaries such as the fesse and chevron; but not to an ordinary so as to interfere with its horizontal position. It is liable to be confused from careless drawing with *undy* or *wavy*, and in ancient armoury with *vair;* but though the term does not occur in early blazon, it was in later blazon no doubt intended to denote a different form from either.

GOLAFRE.

Argent, four bars nebuly [otherwise barry nebuly of six argent and] gules; a bend sable charged with three bezants—GOLAFRE, Fyfield, Berks.

Gules, a fesse nebuly argent—APPLEDORE.

Argent, two bars nebuly gules—John CHAMPION, Kent.

Ermine, on a chief nebuly azure three escalops or—NEGUS, Norfolk.

Per bend nebuly argent and gules—FOLKSTAYNE.

Or, a chevron barry nebuly argent and azure [now vair] between three roebucks courant proper—SWYFT.

Needle: needles are named only in the arms of the Company of needle-makers. Tailors' *bodkins* are also borne.

Vert, three needles in fesse argent, each ducally crowned or [otherwise, Vert, from three crowns in fesse or as many needles pendent argent]—Company of NEEDLEMAKERS [Est. 1656].

Azure, three tailor's bodkins argent handles or—BODKINES.

Neptune. One coat of arms has the figure of Neptune thus minutely described, believed to have reference to an escape from shipwreck.

Argent, a Neptune crowned with an Eastern crown of gold, his Trident sable headed or, issuing from a stormy ocean, the sinister hand grasping the head of a ship's mast appearing above the waves as part of the wreck, all proper; on a chief azure, the arctic polar star of the first between two water bougets of the second—HEARD, co. Somerset [Lancaster Herald, afterwards Garter King of Arms, granted 1762].

Navette, (fr.) : *shuttle.* See under *Weaver's.*

Navire, (fr.) : *Ship.*

Navel, i.q. *nombril.* See *Points.*

Nest: birds' nests are introduced into some coats of arms, and birds are frequently represented as on their nests, especially the *Pelican*. In the arms of RISLEY a *child* (q.v.) is represented lying in a nest.

Argent, on a mount vert a tree of the last with two bird's nests pendent by strings gules—AURIOL, London.

Argent, three Pelicans in piety or, nests vert ; on a chief azure a mitre of the second between two mullets of the first—PATERSON, Scotland.

Net, (fr. *reseau*, old fr. *rets*) : in one Scotch coat a fisherman's net occurs, but it is suggested by heralds that the term fret, or rather *fretty*, should be used to represent the nets.

The field a sea proper, a net argent suspended from the dexter chief point and the sinister fesse point to the base ; in chief two and in base three herrings entangled in the net—Burgh of INVERERA, Scotland.

Sable, fretty [otherwise a fret] argent—HARINGTON.

Nettle: in one or two coats of arms the leaves of the nettle occur, and in one a bunch of nettles.

Or, a chevron gules between three nettle leaves proper—NETTLES, co. Cork, also MALHERBE, co. Devon.

Argent, a saltire gules between four nettle leaves vert—KEATING or KECHING, London.

Gules, on a saltire argent five nettle leaves vert—KEATING, Ireland.

Or, [otherwise argent] a bunch of nettles vert—MALLERBY, co. Devon.

Nimbus, or *Circle of Glory*, represents the ring of light placed around the *heads* of Saints, the Holy *Lamb* (q.v.) and other sacred subjects. Modern painters often represent it as a circle of sun-rays, as around the *head* of S. John the Baptist, (q.v.).

Azure, a book gules with gilt edged leaves supporting a Lamb couchant argent with nimbus and staff or and banner argent, a cross gules—

Negro. See *Man ;* also *Head.*

Nerved, (fr. *nervé*): when a leaf is veined of a different tincture.

Nippers. See *Glazier's.*

Noded: knotted, used of a *cable.* See example under *Ring.*

Nombril point. See *Points.*

Nooked, (fr. *encoché*): of *arrows*

and birdbolts when notched of a different tincture.

Norroy king of arms. See *Herald.*

Noueux, (fr.) : with knots ; applied to the stump of a tree, (to be distinguished from *noué* = nowed).

Arms attributed to the Company of STATIONERS, London. [See the Arms of the Company given under *Book*.]

Gules, two lions passant gardant or; on a chief azure the Virgin Mary, a circle of glory over her head, sitting on a tombstone issuant from the chief; in the dexter arm the Infant Saviour, Head radiant; in her sinister hand a sceptre all as the second—The See of LINCOLN.

Argent, upon a mount vert a dove rising . . . . nimbed gold, all between two bars wavy azure charged with three fishes naiant two and one or— John HILSEY, Bishop of Rochester, 1535–8.

Noah's Ark, (fr. *Arche de Noé*): this device is singularly chosen for more than one coat of arms, both of English and French families. It is generally represented floating on the waters of the deluge, and in chief a dove flying, bearing in its beak the olive-branch.

Argent, an ark in the water proper surmounted by a dove azure standing thereon and holding in the beak an olive-branch vert, all between three gilly-flowers gules stalked and leaved of the fourth—JOLLY, Scotland.

Argent, in a sea in base the Ark of Noah, and in chief a dove volant with an olive-branch in the beak all proper—GALLIEZ, Scotland.

Azure, an antique hulk, the stern terminating with the head of a dragon; in the hulk the ark with three doors in the side; from the ark against the side a stepladder all or; on a chief argent the Cross of S. George gules; charged in the centre with a lion passant gardant of the second—SHIPWRIGHTS' Company [Inc. 1605].

Nowed, (fr. *noué*, old fr. *renowé*): twisted so as to form a knot; applied chiefly to *serpents*, q.v., and the *tails* of lions. A *garter* also is sometimes said to be nowed and buckled. (See under *buckle, adder*, &c.)

Gules, a serpent nowed or—MANTHELBY [i.q. NATHELEY].

Argent, a lion rampant tail forked and nowed gules collared of the first—HAVERING, co. Dorset.

Nourri, (fr.): of a plant when no root appears.

Nowy, applied by certain heralds to a *Cross*, q.v., § 25.

Nuagée, (fr.): nebuly.

Nuée, (fr.): with a cloud passing over it, e.g. of a mountain.

Numerals. See *Letters*.

Nun: a *white nun* or *smew*. See under *Duck*.

Nun's head. See *Heads*.

Nut. See *Hazel*.

Nylle or **Nisle.** See *Cross Moline* § 24.

Oak, (fr. *chêne*): this tree very frequently finds a place in arms, especially in those in which the bearer's name admits of a meaning connected with it. Sometimes the whole *tree* is borne, sometimes the *branches*, sometimes *sprigs*, *slips*, *leaves*, &c., sometimes the *acorns*, q.v., and more frequently the tree is *fructed*, i.e. with the acorns of a different tincture.

In one of the earliest rolls of arms the term *kene* occurs, which has been thought to be *chêne*, from the name of the bearer being OK- STEDE. In the same Roll *fourché au kanee*, in the arms borne by LEXINGTON, has been supposed to be forked like an oak branch. See *Cross*, § 24.

FOREST.

Argent, on a mount an oak-tree all proper —FOREST.

Argent, on a mount in base an oak-tree fructed all proper—WOOD, Devon.

Rouland de OKSTEDE, ov ung Kene de goules —Roll, temp. HEN. III.

Argent, a three masted ship under sail in sea proper between three oak-trees eradicated and fructed of the last—DAROCH.

Argent, a greyhound courant gules in front of an oak-tree on a mount vert—LAMBERT, Norfolk.

Argent, the trunk of an oak-tree sprouting afresh sable—HERE.

WOOD.

Argent, out of a well gules an oak-tree growing vert—WELLWOOD, co. Fife.

Argent, a horse passant gules holding in the mouth an oak sprig vert, acorns or—ASHTON.

Azure, on a cross or an oaken slip vert—BRAYNE

Argent, a lion passant gules; on a chief three oak sprigs bearing acorns proper—JOHNSON.

Argent, a chevron engrailed sable between three oak leaves vert—SMITHSON.

Argent, three oak leaves in pale all proper— MILFORD, co. Devon.

Argent, a bend, and in the sinister chief an oak leaf azure—COX, co. Salop.

SMITHSON.

Or, semy of oak leaves vert a lion rampant azure; on a canton gules a buglehorn stringed of the first—PATCH, Tiverton, co. Devon.

Argent, an oak branch with three [oak] apples proper—APPLOCK.

Argent, a sinister hand in base issuing out of a cloud fessways, holding an oaken baton paleways proper, with a branch sprouting out at the top thereof surmounted of a bend engrailed gules—AIKMAN, Cornie

The holly-oak (fr. *chêne rouvre*) does not appear in English arms, but is sculptured on one of the pillars of the church at ROUVRAY, Burgundy, in the arms of that town. The oak often occurs as a *wreath*. (See under *Chaplet*, the *civic Crown*.)

Ocean: the waves of the ocean, or *sea*, are occasionally painted on the base of the shield in modern heraldry, but can scarcely be considered as an heraldic charge.

Azure, the sun in splendour or; in base the ocean proper; on a canton argent an escucheon gules charged with a lion passant gardant of the second—ROYAL INSTITUTION OF GREAT BRITAIN, established 1800.

Sable, on the waves of the sea proper a lion passant or; in chief three bezants—HAWKINS, co. Dorset.

Azure, a bend sinister or; in base the end and stock of an anchor gold issuant from waves of the sea proper; in chief two estoiles in like bend as the second—SHIFFNER, co. Sussex, 1818.

Olive-tree, (fr. *olivier*). The tree is occasionally borne, but more frequently *slips* and *branches* of it, the latter especially in the *dove's* mouth (q.v). The fruit seems only to occur in French arms.

Argent, on a mount in base an olive-tree proper—OLIVIER, co. Beds.

Or, a fesse gules between three olive branches proper—ROUNDELL, co. York.

Or, two olive branches in saltire vert—VANHATTON, London.

Argent, a fesse azure, two eagles displayed in chief and in base through an annulet gules a slip of olive and another of palm in saltire proper —KENNAWAY, co. Devon: Baronetcy, 1791.

O in tricking stands for *Or*. Sometimes in old blazon o=*ove*, or fr. *avec*, eng. *with*.

Oar. See *Boat*.

Oats. See *Wheat*.

Oeil, (fr.): eye.

Oge: one of the numerous terms for *water-bouget*.

Ogles: the eyes.

Ogress. See *Pellet*, also *Roundle*.

Argent, on a pile azure, a dove close bearing in her beak an olive branch proper; on a chief sable a cross potent between two escallops of the first—GRAHAM, Bp. of Chester, 1848.

Argent, on a bend azure three doves of the first with olive branches in their mouths proper—THOMASON, co. Chester.

D'argent, a trois olives de sinople—DE BREHIER, Bretagne.

Or, (fr. from Latin *aurum*): the chief of the tinctures, i.e *gold*. It is called *Sol* by those who blazon by the sun and planets, *Topaz* (or *Carbuncle*) by those who have fancifully taken the names of precious stones. Engravers represent it by an indefinite number of small points. The term *Gold* is not unfrequently used by heralds to avoid repetition, and the French word *Jaune*, i.e. yellow, is met with in old heraldic poetry. For instance, at the Siege of Carlaverock instead of Or, a lion azure, we find:—

Or.

HENRI DE PERCI, son nevou ...   Fu sa baner bien vuable

Jaune o un bleu lyon rampant   Roll of Carlaverock.

Jaune, o crois rouge engreelie—EUSTACE DE HACHE—*Ibid.*

Orange: both the tree and the fruit are found amongst heraldic bearings, but when by themselves they may be meant for *roundlets tenné*, q.v.

Argent, on a mount vert a lion rampant looking to the sinister gules supporting an orange tree leaved and fructed proper—DE LA MOTTE.

Azure, three oranges slipped proper within an orle of thistles or—LIVINGSTONE, Viscount Tiviot.

Argent, on a mount vert an orange tree fructed proper; on a chief embattled gules three roses of the field barbed and seeded also proper—SWEETLAND, co. Devon.

Ombre, (fr.): in French arms a shadowy outline of the charge with the tincture named; but where *ombré* is used it seems to signify that the charge is shaded with a black line. See *Adumbration*.

Ondé, (fr.). See *Undy*.

Onglé, (fr.): *unguled*, or having claws.

Opinicus. See *Griffin*.

Oppressed, i.q. *depressed*. See *debruised* and *surmounted by*.

Orange colour. See *Tenné*.

Orb, or, as it is also called from the French *Monde* a *Mound royal*, is supposed to represent the Universe, and then it is usually surmounted by a cross. This device is said to have been first used by the Emperor Justinian, and to have been introduced into England by King Edward the Confessor, upon whose seal it appears as a plain orb; but it is surmounted by the cross on the seal of William the Conqueror. The cross signifies the ascendancy of Christianity over the whole earth, and is referred to in our Coronation Service thus:—

CHAWLAS.

"And when you see this orb set under the cross, remember that the whole world is subject to the power and empire of Christ our Redeemer."

Or, a mound sable, encircled gules, ensigned with a cross avellane of the last—CHAWLAS.

Azure, a mound or—LAMONT.

Quarterly gules and azure, a royal orb argent banded and crossed or—Arms assigned to GILBERT UNIVERSEL, Bp. of London, 1128-34.

Or, on an orb [qy. a torteau] gules a raven proper—RAVEN, Richmond Herald, temp. JAMES I. d. 1615.

Ordinaries are certain charges in common use in arms, and in their simple forms are bounded by straight lines, so that they may well be supposed to have had their origin in the bars of wood or iron of different shapes used for fastening together or strengthening the portions of which the *Shield* might be composed. Their number has never been precisely agreed upon, but most heralds reckon nine principal ones which they call honourable, namely, the *cross*, the *chief*, the *pale*, the *bend*, the *bend sinister*, the *fesse*, the *bar*, the *saltire*, and the *chevron*. The following charges are generally reckoned as *subordinaries*, namely, the *bordure*, the *canton*, *flanches*, the *gyron*, the *inescutcheon*, the *orle*, the *quarter*, the *pile*, and the

---

Orbicular, said to be used of a number of stars arranged in a circle.

Orders of Knighthood, (fr. *Ordres de Chevalerie*). See *Knights.*

tressúre, all of which appear to encroach, as it were, on the field. To these are added the *fret*, the *label*, the *pall*, and others, but there seems to be little reason to separate them from several other rectilinear charges. The *diminutives* of the ordinaries (which are never charged) may be reckoned as follows :—*Fillets* and *Barrulets, Pallets, Bendlets, Scarpes, Closets, Cotises, Chevronels, Crosslets,* and *Saltorels.* But there is much diversity; some consider the *bar* to be but a diminutive of the fesse. [See *Synoptical Table.*]

An *Ordinary* of arms is sometimes used in the sense of a collection of coats of arms, arranged under the various bearings.

Orle, (fr. *orle*): an ordinary in the form of a *bordure*, but detached from the sides of the shield, or, as it appeared to the more ancient heralds, an *escutcheon voided,* (old fr. *faux escuchon*). Double and triple orles are sometimes spoken of, and when one within the other they are spoken of as being concentric, but this term seems out of place in armoury ; they should rather be blazoned *tressures* (q.v.). The *orle* like the *bordure* is usually dimidiated when impaled.

John de BALLIOLL, de goules, ove ung faux escochon d'argent—Roll, temp. HEN. III. [Founder of BALLIOL COLLEGE, Oxford, which has adopted the same arms.]

Roger BERTRAM, de goules et ung faux escucion et croisele d'or—Roll, temp. HEN. III.

Sire Gilberd de LYNDESEYE, de goules, crusules [crosslets] de or a un escuchon de veer percee— Roll, temp. ED. II.

BALLIOL.

Sire Wauter de MOLESWORTHE, meisme les armes, les crusules de argent —*Ibid.*

Gules, an orle argent ; over all a bend ermine—Town of RICHMOND, co. York.

Gules, two concentric orles in a bordure argent—BURDON.

Argent, two concentric orles gules [elsewhere two orles in fesse gules] BAGWAY.

Azure, three concentric orles or—LANDLES.

Oreillé, (fr.) ; of the ears of dolphins, shells, &c.

Oreiller, (old fr. for *pillow*). See *Cushion.*

An *orle of martlets* should rather be blazoned *eight martlets in orle*, although, as seen below, the term is quite legitimate, and has ancient authority. The number of charges placed in orle is generally in later heraldry understood to be eight, unless some other number is mentioned. (See also under *Bordure*.)

Though some few other charges are borne *in orle*, the *martlets* are the most frequent in the ancient coats of arms.

AYLMER DE VALENCE,
Earl of Pembroke.

William de VALENS, burelee d'argent et d'azur, ung urle des merlotts de goules—Roll, temp. HEN. III.

Le Conte de VALENCE, burle d'argente et d'azur a merloz de goules bordears [i.e. in bordure]—Another Roll, *Ibid.*

De Walence Aymars li vaillans
Bele baniere i fu baillans
De argent e de asur burelée

O la bordure poralée
Tout entour de rouges merlos.
Roll of Carlaverock.

Le Counte de PENBROC, burele de argent e de azure od les merelos de goules—Roll, temp. ED. II.

Walter de FAUCOMBE, noir ung quinte-fueile d'argent et les merlotts d'argent entour—Roll, temp. HEN. III.

Monsire de HARDESHILL, port d'argent a une cheveron sable, et une urle des merletts gules—Roll, temp. ED. III.

Monsire de VAUX, port argent, a une urle de merletts gules a une eschochion gules—*Ibid.*

Monsire de PIERPOINT, port d'argent a une lyon de sable rampant, et une urle de cinqfoiles gules—*Ibid.*

Argent, two annulets conjunct sable within an orle of trefoils slipped vert—John ETON.

An *orle*, like the ordinaries, may be *indented, engrailed,* &c., but does not seem to occur charged, as is the case with the *bordure.*

Or, an orle indented on the inner edge azure—LEND, Scotland.

Gules, an orle engrailed on the inner side or, within a bordure also engrailed of the last—RUTLAND, co. Surrey.

Argent, an orle gules, flory and counter flory on the outer edge vert, in the centre a dagger in pale azure, hilt and pomel or—CONSIDINE.

Organ pipe. See *Pipe.*   **Organ rest.** See *Rest.*

     Oriflamme. See *Banner.*

Ostrich, (fr. *autruche*) : this bird occurs but in one or two coats of arms.

Sable, an ostrich argent—MATTHEWS, Cornwall.

Sable, a fesse between three ostriches argent membered gules—BOYTON.

Argent, an ostrich sable holding in the beak a horseshoe or (otherwise gules)—MACMAHON, Ireland.

Per fesse argent and gules, three ostrich's heads erased, each holding in the beak a horseshoe, all counterchanged—RYED.

More frequently, however, the *ostrich feathers* are named, a *plume* of which (q.v.) is now the *cognizance* of the Prince of Wales. (See also *Escroll.*)

Azure, semy of fleur-de-lis a lion rampant guardant argent; on a bend gules an ostrich feather of the second between two bezants—HOLLAND, London.

Azure, two ostrich feathers in saltire between three boar's heads, couped at the neck, argent, bristled and tusked or—NEWTON, co. Kent.

Otelles, (fr.) : a term used by some French heralds for four figures described as resembling four peeled almonds, the thickened portion meeting in the centre, something after the fashion of the filberts in the *Cross avellane*, § 12, but in saltire instead of in cross, and the ends pointed instead of *fleury*.

De gueules, a quatre otelles d'argent adossés en sautoir—COMMINGES, Guienne and Gascoigne.

Otter, (fr. *loutre*) : this animal was more frequent in streams than now, and otter-hunting was once a favourite pastime. The stream near Hexham was called the *Otterbourne,* from which the family mentioned below derive their name. Otters are borne in the arms of several families. The two otters borne as supporters to the arms of NORREYS are represented *collared* and chained, each devouring a fish, as may be seen in the stained glass at Ockwells in Berkshire. As supporters to the arms of the SALTERS' Company they are represented sable *bazanty, ducally collared* and chained, each devouring a fish. Two otters rampant proper are the supporters to the arms

---

Osier.   See *Willow.*

Ounce.   See *Panther.*

Ounde de long.   See under *Paly.*

Oundy, or *Ondé.*   See *Wavy.*

of BALFOUR of Orkney, and of KINLOCH. The family of LUTTRELL
bear *otters* in allusion to the French name; possibly by the
sea dogs (q.v.) otters are intended.

Azure, three otters passant in pale or, each holding in the mouth
a fish argent—PROUDE, Kent. [The arms are
sculptured in the cloisters of Canterbury Cathedral.]

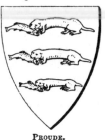

Argent, a fesse between three otters sable,
[*Crest :* an otter sable, in his mouth a fish proper]
—LUTTRELL, co. Warwick.

Argent, a fesse sable between three otters of the
last; in each mouth a fish proper—LUTTRELL,
Luttrelstown, Ireland.

Argent, three otters passant sable—WORSELL.

Sable, a chevron between three otters passant
ermine—HARTOPP, co. Leicester [Granted, 1596].

PROUDE.

Argent, on a mount vert in base an otter proper; a chief gules charged
with a dove of the field between two crosses patty fitchy or—COLERIDGE.

Argent, a demi-otter sable issuing out of a loch in base proper—
LITHGOW, Scotland.

Argent, three otters issuant out of a fesse wavy sable—MELDRUM,
Tyvie, Scotland. [Another branch of the family bears one otter. See
also under *Crown* antique.]

Ermine, a chevron between three otter's heads couped sable; a chief
vert—OTTERBOURNE.

Gules, an otter's head erased argent between two crosses crosslet
fitchy in fesse or; on a chief of the second as many mullets azure—
ROWAND, Ireland.

Argent, an open boat proper between three otter's heads erased sable;
on a chief vert as many crescents of the field—M'NABB.

Over all, *surtout,* (fr. *sur-le-tout*): said of a charge placed
over several other charges or over a particoloured field, as also of
an *escutcheon* placed over four or more quarters. French heralds
also employ the term *brochant sur le tout* (see example under
fasces). In the first example given below, i.e. in the arms of

Ours, (fr.): *Bear.*

Ousel, or *Oysel* (?): supposed to be
intended for the black bird.

Outstickers, Basket-maker's. See
Basket.

Ov and Ove, old fr. = *avec.*

Overt, (fr.), or *ouvert*: open, of
gates, doorways, &c.: it is also
applied to birds, and is synonymous with *disclosed.* See *Wings.*

GREY, and in similar instances of particoloured fields, the words *over all* are understood, and therefore may be omitted, but in the other examples they are almost indispensable.

Barry of six argent and azure, [over all] a bend gules (as a mark of cadency)—Lord GREY, of Rotherfield Greys, Oxon, (c. 1300).

Argent, three bars gemelles gules, over all a lion rampant sable, crowned or—FAIRFAX, Yorkshire.

GREY.

Sable, a chief gules, over all a lion rampant or—WOOD, Bp. of Lichfield and Coventry, 1671-92.

Or, a bull passant gules; over all a pale ermine—Sir Thomas BROKE, Temp. HEN. VIII.

Azure, a pale sable, over all a fesse gules voided of the first, cotised of the second—AKELAND, co. Devon.

Or, two pallets azure; surtout on a fesse checky azure and sable three martletts or—Richard CURTEYS, Bp. of Chichester, 1570-82.

WOOD.   CURTEYS.

Coupé d'argent et d'azur, a la croix ancrée de l'un en l'autre; à la bande de gueules brochante sur le tout—DU PUY or DE PODIO.

Owl, (fr. *hibou*): this bird is frequently found in armorial bearings, and it is always depicted full-faced. It is found in an old roll of arms (as is supposed) under the name of *huit*. In one coat the *horned owl* is named. An owlet, fr. *hulotte*, is only borne in French arms: the French also have the *chouette*, which is the screech-owl. The *chat-huant*, also a kind of owl, is borne by the family of D'HUC DE MONSEGOUT.

Sable, a chevron between three owls argent—PRESCOTT, co. Hertford.

Argent, three owls sable, beaked and legged or—BRIGGE, Norfolk.

Or, three owls in fesse sable—OULRY.

Gules, three huits [owls in margin] argent—Sir Richard BERINCHAM, Roll, temp. 1308.

PRESCOTT.

Sable, a chevron between three owls argent; on a chief three roses gules—OLDHAM, Bp. of Sodor and Man, 1481–86.

Ermine, on a canton gules an owl or—FOWLER.

Vert, a lion rampant between three owls argent—HOLGRAVE.

Azure, a bend engrailed or between three owls argent, each on a tun lying fesswise of the second—CALTON, co. Cambridge, 1567.

Argent, on a mount a tree, on the top an owl proper, in chief two mullets gules—BOUCHIER, London.

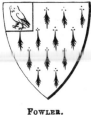

FOWLER.

Sable, three horned owls argent—FESTING.

Owls are borne also by the families of APPLEYARD, co. Norfolk; ATLOW; BURTON, co. Buckingham; BRIDGES, (Bp. of Oxford, 1604–18); BROUGHTON, co. Salop; FINN, Ireland; FORD, co. Devon; FORSTER; GOSSETT; HERWART, 1730; HEWETT; HOOKES, co. Denbigh; LEMARCHANT, Guernsey; OLDGRAVE, co. Chester; ROWTON; SKEPPER, co. Lincoln; THURCASTON; TREWOLA, co. Cornwall; WAKEFIELD, co. York; WESTERDALE.

Pale, (fr. *pal*, pl. *paux*, old fr. *pel*): considered as one of the honourable ordinaries, and may occupy one third of the width of the shield. It has two diminutives, the *palet*, which is one half, and the *endorse* (q.v.), which is by some said to be one eighth of its breadth, by others one fourth.

The term *vergette* is said by French writers to be one third the width of their *pal*. The term occurs in one or two ancient coats of arms, but it is comparatively rare.

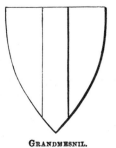

GRANDMESNIL.

Gules, a pale or—Arms ascribed to HUGH DE GRANDMESNIL, Lord High Steward of England, temp. HEN. I.

Sire ROBERT DE FORNEUS, de argent a un pel engrele de sable—Roll, temp. ED. II.

Oyster-dredge is given as the badge of the family of GOLDINGHAM [Harl. MS. 4632].

Ox. See *Bull*.

P. in *tricking* is sometimes used for *purpure*.

Pack-saddle. See *Saddle*.

Packs. See *Woolpacks*.

Padlock. See *Lock*.

Pagoda. See *Medal*.

Pails. See *Bucket*.

Paillé, (fr.): used for *diapré*.

Sire Richard de WELLES, de or, a iij paus [i.e. pales] de goules; a un quarter de argent, et un molet de sable—Roll, temp. ED. II.

Argent, three pallets azure—THORNTON.

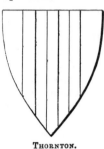

Or, two bars sable; on a chief of the second a palet between as many base esquires of the first; an inescucheon charged with a fesse and chief ermine—BUTLER.

Sable, on a fesse or two palets argent—Sir Richard MALINS, Vice-Chancellor, 1866.

D'azur, à quatre vergettes d'ermine—RICHER, Orleanais.

De sinople, au pal d'or chargé, d'une vergette de gueules; au chef d'argent chargé d'une épée contreposée de sable—JULIANIS DU ROURET, Provence.

THORNTON.

Pales and *palets* are subject to the same kind of variations as the other ordinaries, such as the *bend, fesse,* &c., but not to so many, being far less frequently employed.

Argent, a pale chequy azure and or—BRICKWOOD.

Azure, a pale or goutty de sang—PLAYER, Middlesex.

Argent, a pale fusilly sable—DANIEL, co. Chester.

Gules, a pale lozengy [elsewhere of five lozenges] or—NIGEL, co. Chester.

Gules, a fesse depressed by a pale—DYRBYNE.

Argent, a chevron sable surmounted by a pale ermine—ENDERBY.

Gules, three palets vair; on a chief or a lion passant azure—Simon PATRICK, Bp. of Chichester, 1689; of Ely, 1691–1707.

Argent, a pale dancetty gules—STRANHAM, Kent·

Azure, a pale engrailed sable—DANIEL, co. York.

Gules, a pale invecked argent—VECK.

Argent, a pale nebuly sable—KAYNTON.

.... On a chief argent a pale quarterly azure and gules; on the first and fourth a fleur-de-lis; on the second and third a lion passant gardant all of the second between two roses gules, seeded or, barbed vert—EAST INDIA COMPANY, 1600.

PATRICK.

Argent, a pale bretessed sable cotised; three torteaux in pale on each side—UNKNOWN, Ireland.

Pairle, (fr.).   See *Pall.*

Pairs, (fr.): = Peers [of France].

Pair of, sometimes used e.g. of wings, keys, crescents, &c.

Paissant, or *Pascuant*, = grazing.

Pales, or *Palings.*   See *Park.*

Palisade.   See *Crown palisado.*

Pallet, or *Palet.*   See under *Pale.*

Argent, a pale pointed in base gules—DEVEY.

Argent, a pale furche, between two cotices sable—CUNNINGHAME, Scotland.

The *pale furché* in the last example is probably intended for the *Shakefork*, q.v.

In pale, (fr. *l'un sur l'autre*), is used when charges are arranged beneath one another, as in a pale. The term is frequently used, and often when not so it is implied, e.g. in the case of the three lions of England.

Azure, three escallops in pale or—SYMMES, Somerset.

Argent, three anchors sable in pale between two palets vert; a chief gules—DARWELL.

Palewise, (fr. *en pal*), is more accurately used of some one charge of which the position is not determined, such as of a *key,* which may be upright or lengthways, and would be described as *palewise* or *fesswise* accordingly.

Argent, a spaniel dog passant proper; on a chief embattled azure a key paleways, the wards upward between two crosses croslet or—MAIRE.

Argent, a bend gules; in chief two broad arrows, shods conjoined by an annulet, palewise azure—COMRIES, Scotland.

Per pale or *Party per pale* is very frequent. See under *Party.*

Paly, (fr. *palé*): when the field is divided by perpendicular lines into an even number of equal parts, the first of which is generally of a metal, and the last of a colour. An uneven number (see *barry*) would be blazoned as of so many *pales.* The French term *vergetté* is used when the pales, or rather palets, are above ten in number.

Paly of six, or and azure—GOURNAY, or GURNEY, Devon.

Paly of four pieces argent and vair—William de LONGCHAMP, Bp. of Ely, 1189–97.

Le Comte de HUNTINGDON, pale d'or et de goules, ung bende noir—Roll, temp. HEN. III.

Monsire FITZNELE, pale argent et gules de vi peeces—Roll, temp. ED. III.

GOURNAY.

Palmer's Staff, Scrip, &c. See *Pilgrim's Staff,* &c.

Paly. See under *Pale.*

Pampre, (fr.) : a *vine-shoot.*

Monsire de STRELLE, pale de vj d'argent et d'asure—Roll. temp.
ED. III.

Monsire Hugh MENILL, per pale de xij peces argent et gules a une
bend d'asure a trois fers de chevall d'or en la bend—*Ibid.*

Monsire William de MENILL, port pale de viij peeces argent et gules
a une bend d'asur a trois fers de chevall d'or en la bend—*Ibid.*

Le Sire de GOUSHILL, port d'argent et gules pales, au cheif de asur
en le cheif une damez (? daunce) or—*Ibid.*

Again, in the same way as *barry* so may *paly* be diversified,
e.g. the lines may be *undy*, and in
respect of this a curious expression
occurs in the ancient rolls of arms, viz.
oundée de long, which means *paly wavy*,
as is evidenced by the ancient arms both
of the GERNON and VALOYNE family.

William GERNON, oundee de long d'argent
et de goules—Roll, temp. HEN. III.

Sire William GERNOUN, d'argent a iij peus
[=pales] undes de gulys—Roll, temp. ED. II.

Paly wavy of six, gules and argent—GERNON.

GERNON.

Sire William de VALOYNES, oundee de long de argent e de goules— *Ibid.*

Monsire Warren de VALOINES, port pale de vi peeces unde d'or et gules
—Roll, temp. ED. III.

Paly dancetty of six or and gules, all per saltire counterchanged—
POUGES.

Paly embattled of eight argent and gules—WIGLEY, co. Derby.

Paly nebuly of six gules and or—MOLEYNS.

But further, in the combination with the *bend*, &c., a diversity
is produced, which has already been referred to under *bendy paly*,
more frequently called *paly bendy*. One
coat of arms is blazoned *paly bendy lozengy.*
And though the term lozengy may seem
redundant it appears drawn as in the
margin in the note-book of the late Mr.
Wyatt Papworth, and varying somewhat
from the figure of *paly bendy*. *Paly pily*
is only another name for *pily*, but not
necessary since the piles are drawn palewise, unless otherwise expressed. *Paly*

Paly bendy lozengy.

saltiery is only a fanciful and vague way of blazoning the arms of Pouges, given above.

Paly bendy lozengy, or and sable—Calvert, Lord Mayor of London, 1749.

Paly bendy or and gules—Croone, London.

Pall, (fr. *pairle*, which is also occasionally used by English heralds):

1. As a *charge* it represents an ecclesiastical vestment known as the *pallium*, and symbolical of Archiepiscopal authority, e.g. the Pall was sent by Pope Gregory to Augustine in 601; see Beda, Bk. I. cap. 29. Also to Abp. Justus in 624; Ibid., Bk. II. cap. 8. In the East, however, it occurs as an episcopal ornament.

When borne as a *charge*, e.g. in the arms of archbishops, the lower end is always *couped* and *fringed*.

CANTERBURY—
CHICHELE.

Azure, a pastoral staff in pale or, ensigned with a cross pattée argent surmounted by a pall of the last, edged and fringed of the second, charged with four crosses pattée fitchée sable—The Archiepiscopal See of Canterbury.

Impaled with argent, a chevron between three cinquefoils gules—Henry Chicheley, Archbishop of Canterbury, 1414–43.

Sable, a cross argent in the dexter chief the archiepiscopal pall proper—Benedictine Abbey of St. Augustin at Canterbury.

Argent, a bishop's pall sable; in chief a stag's head erased gules—Cunninghame, Scotland.

Similar insignia to those borne by the See of Canterbury were formerly borne by the See of York, but with the field gules. Those of Armagh are the same as Canterbury, and those of Dublin have one more cross.

2. As a *sub-ordinary* the pall may be described as a figure of the shape of the letter Y.

All three arms are to be drawn *throughout*. The figure with the three arms *couped* and *pointed* would be blazoned as the *Shakefork*, q.v.

Argent, a pall sable; on a chief or, a dragon passant gules, between two chaplets of the last leaved vert—Sheriffe, London, 1761.

A *pall* is but rarely subject to modification like the ordinaries. In one case it is *reversed* in another *patonce*. The term *cross pall* also occurs which cannot be a cross at all, but is supposed to mean merely the pall used as a subordinary, that is with the members drawn *throughout*.

Gules, a pall reversed ermine—KELVERDON, or KELDON, Essex.

Gules, a pall [ending in points] patonce between three estoiles argent—HARROLD.

Gules, a cross pall, argent—DEYCHETER, Germany.

The terms *per pall* and *in pall* also occur, but they are written with the French form *per pairle* and *in pairle*.

Per pairle reversed or gules and ermine over all a tau azure—LYLSEY, Harl. MS. 1386, fo. 66.

Gules, three swords in pairle hilts meeting in the centre argent—BRISAC.

Palm, (fr. *palme*), and *Palm-tree*, (fr. *palmier*): the branches are symbols of victory, though not frequently used in English heraldry: in French heraldry they are common. With this may be associated the *Cocoa-nut* tree, and the *China Cokar*.

In a landscape field a fountain, thereout issuing a palm-tree all proper—FRANCO, St. Catharine Coleman, London: granted 1760.

Argent, an ape sejant on a heart holding a palm branch proper—VAULT.

Argent, a mural [i.e. embattled] fesse gules, charged with three palm branches of the field between six Cornish choughs proper—MORRALL, co. Salop.

De gueules, à six palmes d'or, les tiges ajoutées en cœur—MESSEMÉ, Poitou.

Argent, a cocoa-nut tree fructed proper growing out of a mount, in base vert on a chief azure a shakefork between a martlet in the dexter and a salmon naiant in the sinister holding in the mouth an annulet or—GLASGOW, Mount Grenon, recorded 1807.

Quarterly, azure and ermine, on a bend or, three cocoa-nut trees eradicated proper—BRAM, Bongul.

Argent, a China cokar-tree vert—ABANK.

A palm-tree is borne in the arms granted to Earl NELSON, also in those of the family of CORNFOOT, and palm branches in families of MONTGOMERY, KENNAWAY, &c.

Panes: pieces or rather squares [as we say a pane of glass]. Some heralds have blazoned a *cross* quarterly pierced, (q.v.) § 5, as 'checquy of nine panes.' But the word is an old word, occurring as it does in the siege of Caerlaverock signifying the large square of the banner. Cf. also *pannes*, i.q. pieces of *fur*. See under *Ermine*.

Guillemes de LEYBOURNE aussi   Baniere i ot o larges pans
Vaillans homs, sanz mez et sans si, De *inde*, o sis blans lyouns rampans.

Roll of Carlaverock, A.D. 1300.

Pansy, (fr. *pensée*): occurs in both English and French arms.

Vert, on a chevron argent between three plates each charged with a pyncheon (or goldfinch) as many pansies slipped proper—Henry MORGAN, Bishop of St. David's, 1554–59 ; granted 1553.

Argent, three fleurs-de-lis vert on a chief azure a pansy between two fleurs-de-lis or—WOOLBALL, London.

Gules, on a bend or three pansy-flowers proper, stalked and leaved vert—PASKIN.

D'argent, à trois fleurs de pensées d'azur—BABUT, Bourbonnais et Nivernais.

Panther, (fr. *panthère*): this beast is always borne gardant, and generally *incensed*, that is to say, with flames issuing from its mouth and ears, as in the case of the dexter supporter of the Earl of Pomfret. With the panther may be grouped the *lynx* (fr. *loup cervier*) and the *ounce*, both of which occur in several arms, the latter being found at an early date.

Or, on a fesse azure between three panthers passant proper a pansey of the first between two lilies argent—NORTHEY, Bocking, Essex.

Per fesse ermine and sable, in base a panther passant of the first, in chief two mascles of the second—DANIELL, Truro, Cornwall.

Azure, three panther's heads erased proper—SMITH.

Sire Johan de HAMME, de azur, a un cheveron de or e iij demy lyns de or—Roll, temp. ED. II.

Pamé, (fr.): of a fish with a *gaping* mouth, and as if gasping.

Panache, (fr.): a *plume*, q.v.

Panettes, (fr.): Poplar leaves.

Pannes. See *Furs*.

Paon, (fr.): *Peacock*.

Papal Crown. See *Tiara*.

Papegay, i.q. *Popinjay*. See *Parrot*.

Papillon, (fr.): Butterfly, and *Papillonné* (fr.): scaled, as of a Butterfly.

Sable, three lynxes passant gardant argent—LYNCH.

Argent, on a chevron azure between three lynx's heads erased sable as many crescents ermine—NICOLLS, Mershland, Norfolk.

Sable, three ounces statant in pale or, spotted of the first—Sir James BOURCHER, 1610.

Argent, on a bend sable three ounces passant or—WATONE.

Sable, on a fesse argent between three ounces [otherwise cat a-mountains] passant gardant or as many escallops gules—HILL, co. Berks.

Argent, on a pile azure three ounce's heads erased of the first—JOHNSON, Milton-Brian, co. Bedford.

Paradise: the device of Adam and Eve on either side of a tree, occurs in two coats of arms.

Argent, on a mount vert a representation of the Tree of Life [? Knowledge] environed with a serpent, on the dexter side thereof a male figure, and on the sinister a female (representing Adam and Eve); at the bottom of the tree a rabbit all proper—MACKLEAN, Scotland.

Azure, on a mount in base vert the tree of Paradise environed with the serpent between Adam and Eve all proper—Company of FRUITERERS, London.

Park: the idea of a park is a circular space enclosed with pales, and having a gate in front. *Park pales* are usually represented as in the margin.

Argent, a mount vert, a stag lodged within park pales and gate all proper—Town of DERBY.

Ermine, on a mount vert issuing from park palings with gate proper a lion rampant or holding in the

Palings.

dexter paw a scimetar all proper; on a chief indented sable two lions rampant argent—BURE ; quartering Davis, Higford, and Scudamore.

A pine-tree or, leaved vert, fructed proper, enclosed with pales argent and sable, nails counterchanged—Crest of PINFOLD, co. Bedford.

Parrot, (fr. *perroquet*): is found in a few modern arms, but the more usual term is the old name *Popinjay* or *Papegay*, (fr. *Papegaut*, ital. *Papagallo*): the parrot when blazoned *proper*

Paradis, *Oiseau de:* Bird of Paradise, found only in French arms (e.g. family of PARADIS, Limosin).

Parapet: mentioned in one case under *Castle*.

Parcel: sometimes used instead of bundle, e.g. of spears, of bird bolts, of ears of *wheat*, &c.

Pard. See *Leopard*.

Paring-knife. See *Currier's Shave.*

Parliament Robe. See *Robe.*

should be vert, beaked and membered gules. The old form *papegai* occurs very frequently in the old rolls of arms from Hen. III. onwards. One coat bears *wood wallises*, by which some consider parrots to be meant, but possibly *doves*. In one case the *wings* only occur.

Per pale argent and gules, in the dexter fesse point a parrot russet beaked and legged or—SENHOUSE, Cumberland [also Richard SENHOUSE, Bp. of Carlisle, 1624–26].

Richard le FITZ MARMADUKE, de goules, ung fece et troys papegeyes d'argent a ung baston d'azure sur tout—Roll, temp. HEN. III.

Sire Richard FITZ MARMADUKE, de goules, a une fesse e iij papingais de argent e un baston de azure—Roll, temp. ED. II.

Sire Johan FIZ MARMADUC, de goules, a une fesse e iij papingays de argent—*Ibid.*

Marmaduk de TWENGE, d'argent, a trois papegayes de vert ung fece de goules—Roll, temp. HEN. III.

BP. SENHOUSE.

Sire Marmaduc de TUENGE, de argent, a une fesse de goules e iij papingais de vert—Roll, temp. ED. II.

Monsire de THWENGE, port d'argent, a une fes de gules entre trois popageis vert—Roll, temp. ED. III.

Sire Robert de LOMELEYE, de goules, a une fesse e iij papingais de argent; en la fesse iij moles de sable—Roll, temp. ED. II.

Argent, a fesse gules between three parrots proper, gorged with collars of the second—LUMLEY, Middlesex; and co. York.

Or, a parrot close vert, legged gules—POYNER, co. Salop.

Or, three parroquets vert—CHAUNCELER, Brafferton, co. Durham.

D'argent, à trois perroquets de sinople becqués et membrés de gueules —CHAMPS, Normandie.

Azure, two chevrons or between three wood wallises [? doves] proper— PINFOLD, Dunstable, co. Bedford; granted 1601.

Argent, on a fesse engrailed gules between three parrot's wings expanded and addorsed azure as many bezants each charged with a parrot's head erased sable—GEORGE.

Parroquet. See *Parrot.*

Parted. See *Party.*

Partition, lines of. See *Party per.*

Paschal Lamb. See *Lamb.*

Pascuant, (fr.) or *Paissant :* applied only to cattle grazing with the head touching the ground. If the head is in the usual position *statant* would be employed.

Parsley leaves seem to be used in a solitary example.

Or, a lion rampant sable between three parsley leaves vert—CLAP-PESON.

Parted is not strictly a heraldic term, but it is used by some writers in compounds such as *biparted*, *triparted*, &c. The term is applied to the *Cross*, see § 8. *Biparted* has also been used to signify notching, as in the margin, and *triparted* has been used for the French *tiercé*, but none of these terms are needed, and do not occur in any correct blazon.

Biparted.

Partridge, (fr. *perdrix*): occurs tolerably frequently both in English and French arms. In the arms of GREGOR there is a play upon the name, it being Cornish for Partridge.

Gules, on a fesse argent between three lions rampant or as many part-ridges proper—PARTRIDGE.

Argent, a chevron gules between three partridges proper—GREGOR, Tre-warthenick, Cornwall.

Gules, a fesse between three partridges argent a bendlet azure—FITZ-MARMADUKE, Nottingham. [See *ante* under *Parrot*.]

Vert, a garb between three partridges or—SAXBY, Chafford, Kent; granted 1751.

Argent, a chevron sable between three partridges proper—ELD, co. Stafford, 1574.

Azure, a hawk seizing a partridge argent; on a chief of the last three bolts of the first—KNOWLES.

D'azur, à trois perdrix d'or—RAMBOUILLET, Lorraine.

Party, (fr. *parti*): signifies that the field is divided, the name of some ordinary being added to shew in what direction; the term, however, may be applied also to ordinaries and to charges of all kinds, and even to crests and supporters. Many heralds say *per bend*, &c., considering the word party to be un-necessary. The term *party per pale* is perhaps the most used, and very frequently the charge superimposed is party also, the tinc-tures being *counterchanged*. But besides these *party per fesse, per chevron,* and *per saltire* are not infrequent. *Party per pile* is some-what rare, while instead of *party per cross* the term *quarterly* (q. v.) is nearly always used. But the *party* may be considerably varied, as the *per pale, fesse, bend*, &c., may be subjected to the same variations as the ordinary itself, i.e. it may be *per bend indented, per fesse nebuly*, &c. Again there may be a combination, such as *party per pale and per chevron*. In the Earl of PEMBROKE's arms, in the second roll, the term *en lung*, i.q. *en long = palewise*. Cf. arms of GERNON under *Paly*. See also under Lincoln.

Le Conte MARESCHALL, party d'or et de vert, ung lion rampant goules —Roll, temp. HEN. III.

Le Count de PENNBROK, party d'or e de vert, a un lion rampant, party de or e de goules en lung—Another roll, temp. HEN. III.

Herbert le FITZ MAHEWE, party d'azur et de goulz, ove trois leonseux rampants d'or—*Ibid.*

Le Conte de LEISTER. . . Et le Banner party endentee d'argent et de goules—*Ibid.*

Sire Richard de AUNTESHEYE, parti de or et de argent, e oundee de goules—Roll, temp. ED. II.

Monsire Richard PLACE, port parte d'or et de gules, une lyon passant d'argent—Roll, temp. ED. III.

Party per bend, or and vert—HAWLEY.

[Party] per bend sinister ermine and ermines, a lion rampant or—Matthias MAWSON, Bp. of Llandaff, 1740; of Ely, 1754–70. [Also in several other Welsh coats of arms].

Party per fesse or and

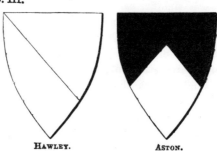

HAWLEY.   ASTON.

gules, in chief a demi-rose gules with two eagle's heads issuing therefrom sable, and from each side an eagle's wing of the last, in base a demi-sun or—KNIGHT, Bp. of Bath and Wells, 1541–47.

Party per chevron, sable and argent—ASTON, co. Lancashire. [An example of the colour being uppermost and the metal below, contrary to the usual practice.]

Party per saltire, ermine and gules—RESTWOLD, Bucks.

Passé en sautoir, (fr.): of tails of lions, or any other like charges, crossed in saltire.

Passion-nail. See *Nail.*

Pastoral Staff. See under *Crosier.*

Party per pale nebuly azure and or, six martletts counterchanged ; a crescent for difference—Fleet-wood, Bp. of S. Asaph, 1708; afterwards of Ely, 1714–23.

Per bend sinister, embattled argent and gules—Byles.

Per bend indented, gules and or—Ferne, co. Stafford.

Per fesse wavy argent and barry wavy of four azure and or—Barle.

FLEETWOOD.

Per fesse dancetty argent and sable, each point terminating in a fleur de lis—Woodmerton.

Party per pale and per chevron, counterchanged or and azure —Henry de Braundeston, Bp. of Salis-bury, 1287–88.

The French heralds employ special terms for some of the varieties of their partitions, (fr. *partitions*). *Parti* alone signifies *pary per pale; coupé* signifies *party per fesse; tranché* signifies *party per bend;* and *taillé*

BRAUNDESTON.

signifies *party per bend sinister ;* while the two together produce *party per saltire.* They also employ a term *tiercé,* which sig-nifies the division of the field either *per fesse* or *per pale* into three parts. This division does not seem generally to be used in English arms, though sometimes in rare cases three coats are *marshalled,* one above the other. Also something at first sight like "*parti et tiercé en fasce*" occurs in the arms of Chris-topherson, which, however, is differently blazoned.

Argent, a lion rampant gules langued azure—Armenia, impaling Jerusalem and azure, three bars argent, over all a lion rampant gules langued azure; all tierced. —Harl. MS. 6829, fol. 46.

Quarterly, first and fourth azure a cross botton-née gules second and third gules, three suns in splendour or—Cyprus; On a chief party per pale gules and azure three cinquefoils counter-changed — John Christopherson, Bp. of Chiches-ter, 1537–58.

Coupé de sable et d'or—Houtteville, Nor-mandie.

CHRISTOPHERSON.

Parti, au 1 d'argent coupé sur sinople ; au 2 de gueules—Ferrus, Dauphiné.

Tranché d'or et de sable, diapré de l'un en l'autre—Allamanon, Provence.

Tranché taillé d'argent et d'azur—Blanc, Dauphiné.

Tiercé en fasce ; au 1 d'or au lion leopardé de gueules ; au 2 de sinople ; au 3 d'hermine plein—Le Roy de Barde, Flandre.

Tiercé en pal ; au 1 d'hermine ; au 2 de gueules à une étoile à dix rais d'argent ; au 3 de contre-hermine—Le Goux, Bourgogne.

Passant: a word used to express the position of a beast walking past, most frequently applied to the *Lion*, q.v.   If gardant be not added, his head must look straight before him.

Counter passant, or *repassant* : passant towards the sinister.

Passant counter passant, or *Passant repassant* : is used of two animals passing each other in contrary directions.   The beast passing towards the sinister, should be in front.

Passant applied to the *Cross* (see under *Banner*) is thought to be equivalent to *throughout*, but probably means rather *over all*.

Walter de Berg, eskartile dargent et de goules a une croyz de goules passant—Roll, temp. Hen. III.

Baudewin de Friville, de veyr a une croyz passant de goules—*Ibid.*

Le roy de Chipre, de vert besanté de goules a un croyz dor passant —*Ib.*

Passion, Implements of the : so many coats of arms were connected directly or indirectly with religious institutions, that it is not surprising that the Implements of the Passion were pressed into the service of heraldry.   The most frequent, how-ever, are the *Passion nails* (fr. *clous de la Passion*): they are generally drawn square and with a pyramidical head. The *Cross of Calvary* has already been referred to, § 15. In carvings, both in wood and stone, the Implements of the Passion are very frequently represented on shields, but as religious, not heraldic, symbols.   It may be added that some heralds have gone so far as to ascribe coat-armour to our Lord, in which all the various implements of the Passion are pourtrayed.   But such is an instance only of the abuse of heraldry, not its use.

Passion Nails.

.... a cross between the instruments of the Passion—Seal of Philip de Repingdon, Bishop of Lincoln, 1405–20.

Argent, three Passion nails gules meeting in point—Wishart, Brechin, Scotland.

Argent, three Passion nails pileways in point embrued—Robert Guot-
hart, M.D., 1750.

Sable, two bars argent, on a canton of the second a garb between four
Passion nails or—Dedwood.

Gules, a lion rampant argent within an orle of eight Passion (or Calvary) nails or—Breedon, 1783.

Argent, nine Passion nails sable meeting in point in threes, two, and
one—Tonyn.

D'argent, à trois clous de la Passion, deux en chef et un en pointe—
Gonandour, Bretagne.

Pattens are borne only by the Company of Patten-makers,
in whose arms they are associated with
the *cutting-knife*, an implement used in
the manufacture, and which is shewn in
the margin.

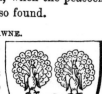
Cutting-knife.

Gules, on a chevron argent between three pattens or, tied of the second,
the ties lined azure, two cutting-knives conjoined sable—Company of
Patten-makers, London [Inc. 1670].

Peacock, (fr. *paon*): a few families bear this bird in their
arms. It is usually borne affronté, with the head turned towards the dexter and with the tail expanded, when the peacock
is said to be *in his pride*. The *pea-hen* is also found.

Argent, three peacocks in their pride proper—Pawne.

Argent, three peacocks in pride proper—Munt;
Pawne, 1716; Peacock, Bridge End, Scotland.

Argent, on a fesse gules between three peacocks
in their pride proper a castle of the first, inter two
bezants—Smyth, Dublin.

Argent, a fesse vair between three peacock's heads
erased gules collared or—Ridgeway, co. Devon.

Argent, a Cross gules between four peacocks
close proper—Smith, Baron Carrington, co. Warwick, 1643.

Pawne.

Sable, a bend between three peacock's heads and necks erased argent
—GELOUER.

Quarterly argent and azure, a cross quarterly ermines and gold between four peahens collared counterchanged—Edmund GRINDALL, Bp. of
London, 1559; Abp. of York, 1570; Canterbury, 1576–83; granted 1559.

Pear, (fr. *poire*): this, like other fruits, may be pendent,
erected, or barwise. The kind called the *Warden-pear* is borne
by the family of WARDEN, of WARDON Priory, Bedfordshire;
but it is not to be distinguished in the drawing from any other
species of pear. The *Pear-tree* (fr. *poirier*) is also found.

Gules, a chevron between three pears stalked or—George ABBOT, Bp.
of Lichfield, 1609; Bp. of London, 1610; Abp. of
Cant., 1611–33.

Argent, a fesse between three pears sable—City
of WORCESTER.

Vert, a fesse or, in chief three pears slipped pendent of the second—PARINCHEFF.

Argent, a saltire sable between four pears pendent
gules— KELLOWAY.

Argent, three warden-pears leaved vert—WARDEN.

Or, a pear-tree vert fructed proper—PERITON.

ABBOT.

Peascods appear in one or two coats of arms. Those of
HARDBEAN seem to arise from an error in blazon (see *Bean*).
The term *pea-rise* for pea-stalk with leaves and flowers is given
by heraldic writers, but its use in blazon has not been observed.

Argent, on a fesse azure between three roses in chief gules and as
many peascods, in base vert a sword barways of the first hilt and pomel
or—COLLISON, Auchloumes; COLLISONE, Scotland.

Argent, a crescent gules between three peascods fesswise vert —
HARDBEANE or HATBEANE.

Pattée, (fr.): spreading; chiefly
   applied to the *Cross*, § 26.

Pattes, (fr.): paws. See *Gambes*.

Paumy. See *Apaumy*.

Paus. See *Pale*.

Pavier's Pick. See *Pick-axe*.

Pavillion. See *Tent*.

Pavon. See *Flag*.

Paw. See *Gambe*, and examples
   under *Ape*, *Lion*, and *Seal*.

Pean. See *Ermine*.

Peantré, (fr.): of tails of fishes
   of a particular tincture.

Pearl. See *Argent*.

Peel: a baker's shovel.   This occurs chiefly in the arms belonging to the several families of PISTOR It is blazoned sometimes as bearing three *manchets* or small cakes, at others three loaves, and at others (wrongly) three *plates*.

Argent, on a baker's peel in pale sable three manchets of the first, two and one—PISTOR, Linc. and Suff.

Argent, on a baker's peel sable a crescent or between three plates—PISTER.

Sable, three oval peels or—KILL, Kill, Scotland.

PISTOR.

Pegasus: a representation of the winged horse well known in classical mythology.   The old seal of the Knights Templars is said to have borne the device of two knights on one horse, and it is not improbable that to some rough representation of this device the members of the Society had given the name of the classical Pegasus, and so adopted it in their arms.   It is frequently used as a *crest*.

Azure, a pegasus salient or—Society of the INNER TEMPLE, London.   [Assumed temp. Elizabeth.]

Azure, on a bend argent, a pegasus in full speed sable—MILDMAY, Essex (granted May 20, 1552).

Azure, goutty argent, a pegasus of the second —Michael DRAYTON the poet [ob. 1631, from his tomb in Westminster Abbey].

INNER TEMPLE.

The pegasus also appears in the arms granted to the family of CAVALER in 1554; and appears in that of BIRCHENSHAW-QUIN; MACQUEEN, Bedford; and QUIN-WYNDHAM, Earl of Dunraven, &c.

Two pegasi argent, wings endorsed maned and crined or; on the wings three bars wavy, form the supporters to the arms of the city of EXETER.

Pecking, sometimes used of *Birds*.

Ped, (old fr.) : foot.   See arms of MORTYMER under *Fleur-de-lys;* also under *Eagle*.

Pedestal.   See *Pillar*.

Peel, i.q. *Pile*.

Pee, (old fr.) : foot.   See arms of MAN under *Leg*.

Peer.   See *Duke, Marquess*, &c.

Peg.   See *Wedge*.

Peg-top.   See *Top*.

Peigne, (fr.) : *Combe*.

In connection with the *Pegasus,* or winged horse, may be named other *monstrosities* composed of animals with wings, such as the *winged lion,* the *winged bull,* the *winged stag,* and the *winged snake* or *python.* The first two of these occur amongst the *Evangelistic symbols,* q.v. in arms of REYNOLDS.

Azure, a winged bull rampant or—CADENET.

Argent, a stag trippant with wings attached to the buttock and hind legs proper; between the attires an antique crown or—JONES, co. Brecon.

Argent, a python regardant; in chief three teals proper—TEALE, London (granted 1723).

Pelican, (fr. *pelican*): this bird is usually drawn with her wings *endorsed,* and wounding her breast with her beak, i.e. *vulning* herself. When in her nest feeding her young with her blood, she is said to be *in her piety.*

Fox.

Azure, a pelican in piety or, vulned proper— Richard Fox, Bishop of Bath and Wells, 1492; afterwards of Durham, 1494, and then of Winchester, 1501–1528. [Founder of Corpus Christi College, Oxford.]

Argent, a pelican in piety sable—CANTRELL, Monsall, co. Lancaster; and BURY, Suffolk.

Sable, a pelican in piety wings displayed inverted argent vulned gules, nest or—LYNDE.

Azure, a cross between in dexter chief and sinister base a pelican and her nest, but in sinister chief and dexter base a cinquefoil argent— FOWLER, Scotland.

Gules, a fesse or; in chief two pelicans vulning themselves of the last —LECHMERE, Rhyd, co. Worcester; Baronetcy, 1818.

Argent, on a chevron azure between three pelicans in piety sable, three cinquefoils or—CRANMER, Abp. of Canterbury, 1533.

Azure, a bend or between three pelicans feeding their young argent— CRAMOND or CRAWMOND, Auldbar, Scotland.

A pelican's head erased or otherwise detached from the body

Pencell, *Pencil,* or *Pensell.* See *Pennoncelle,* under *Flag.*

Pendent: hanging down, as a leaf or fruit with the stalk up-

wards: in one case applied to a *crescent* (q.v.) it would seem to imply that the horns are to be drawn downwards.

must always be drawn in the same position. It must therefore be separated as low as the upper part of the breast.

Or, three pelican's heads erased sable; on a chief azure, a fleur-de-lys between two mullets of the first — John SCORY, Bp. of Rochester, 1551; of Chichester, 1552 ; of Hereford, 1559-85.

Party per pale argent and gules, three pelican's heads in piety counterchanged; on a chief azure three fleurs-de-lys or—DAVIES, Bp. of S. Asaph, 1560; afterwards of S. David's, 1561-81.

SCORY.

Pellet, or *gunstone,* (fr. *ogresse,* but more frequently *torteau de sable*) is a *roundlet sable.* The term *pellet,* spelt in various ways, is found in ancient rolls, and is used by Chaucer, e.g. ' as suyfte as a pellet out of a gonne.' Hence, perhaps, the later name *gunstone.* The word *ogress,* borrowed from the French, is also found used by English heralds. In the ancient rolls the tincture of the *pellet* is not confined to *sable,* being used in the sense of *roundel,* q.v.

Argent, on a bend gules between three ogresses as many swans proper—CLARKE, co. Northampton.

CLARKE.

Monsire Olyver de DYNHAM, gules a trois pelots d'or; labell d'azure—Roll, temp. ED. III.

Monsire de HUNTINGFELD, port d'or, sur fes gules trois pelotts d'argent—*Ibid.*

Monsire William de WISTOWE, d'argent a une cheveron et trois pellets de gules en le chief—*Ibid.*

Argent, three bars sable ; in chief as many pellets—HUMBERSTON.

Argent, six gunstones sable—LACYE.

Argent, a fesse sable ; in chief three ogresses—LANGLEY, co. Gloucester.

Argent, a battle-axe gules between three ogresses—MORSE.

D'argent, à trois tourteaux de sable—BURET, Normandie.

Pellotty is used sometimes for *semé* of pellets.

Gules, a hind courant argent, between three pheons or, within a bordure of the last pelletty—HUNT.

Argent, two bars gules; over all a lion rampant double queued or pelletty—BRANDON, Chamberlain of London.

Pen: this device is found in few coats of arms. In one ancient roll the word *penne* is used for *feather*, drawn as in the margin, e.g. in Arms of COUPENNE.

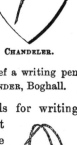

.... three pens two and one, points towards the base—CHANDELER, Bp. of Salisbury, 1417–26.

Sire Renaud de COUPENNE, de goules a vi pennes de argent—Roll, temp. ED. II.

Gules, three writing pens argent—COWPEN.

Or, a bend sable between three pens gules—RIDELL.

CHANDELER.

Per pale argent and sable a chevron between in chief a writing pen fesswise and in base a crescent counterchanged—ALEXANDER, Boghall.

Penner and Ink-horn: that the materials for writing should find a place in heraldic devices is not extraordinary. The most marked example is the *penner* as exhibited in the insignia of the SCRIVENERS' Company. The *Sand-box* is also found in one coat.

Azure, an eagle displayed holding in the beak a penner and inkhorn, standing on a book fesswise closed, the clasps downwards or—Company of SCRIVENERS, London, [Inc. 1616].

Gules, a chevron between three writing sand-boxes reversed issuing sand or—SANDON, Horton.

A penner
and ink-horn.

Pepper-pods: one instance only of this device has been observed.

Argent, three pepper-pods sable—BITLEY.

Perch, (1.) (lat. *pertica*): this fish is scarely found in any English arms. The French *Chabot*—our Miller's Thumb—(lat. *cottus gobis*) is found in the arms of a French family connected with England.

Penne, (fr.): a feather of a bird borne in a cap. See *Pen*.

Pennon. See *Flag*.

Penny yard penny. See *Medal*.

Pensées, (fr.): *Pansies*.

Perched, (fr. *perché*): of a bird resting on a perch or on a tree.

Perche de daym; *attires*.

Argent, a perch azure—BERSICH.

Or, three chabots gules—CHABOT, France [Philip Chabot, Lord High Admiral of France, was elected Knight of the Garter at Calais, 1532].

(2.) *Perch.* Birds are sometimes represented perched (fr. *perché*), i.e. standing on a perch. See under *Falcon.*

Petiz beestez occurs so written in a roll, but the meaning is uncertain.

Azure, three herons argent 'petiz beestez' (*sic* in orig.) or—Sir Godard and Sir Roger HERON, Roll, temp. HEN. III.

Pheasant, (fr. *faisan*): this bird is by no means an uncommon bearing in English arms, and is subjected to the same variations as birds generally. The *Mitus* heads have been thought to represent a bird of the pheasant kind (fr. *mitou*).

Azure, three pheasants or, membered and beaked gules—FESIANT.

Azure, three pheasant cocks or—READE.

Or, on a pale vert, on a chief gules a pheasant argent, all within a bordure azure charged with eight estoiles of the last—PAYZANT.

Azure, on a fesse between three pheasant cocks or as many crossbows sable—READ.

Argent, on a bend azure three pheasants or in chief a crescent (? for diff.) of the second—OGILL, Poppill, Scotland.

Ermine, a chevron gules between three cock pheasant's heads erased azure—PETYTT, Suffolk.

Argent, three mitus' heads (of the pheasant kind) proper—BROWNE-SHAUGH.

[Pheasants also appear to be borne in the arms of the following families, but there are often variations in the blazon as to the kind of bird intended. STANNICH, co. Chester ; CHOPIN ; TOMKINS, co. Hereford ; ZE-KETH ; JERVEIS, co. Worcester ; O'COWICK ; PHESANT ; NORTH, co. Hants ; BRYSILLY, &c.]

Perclose. The perclose of a *garter* is the lower part with the buckle, &c.

Perforated. See *Pierced.*

Peruke: erroneously used in the blazon of the arms of HARMAN, Kent, for *Ostrich* feathers. See *Plume.*

Pery, (fr. *peri*): this term is said by some heralds to be used to signify that a charge (a chain for instance) does not reach to the sides of the shield. With French heralds it seems to be applied especially to fillets where *couped* might be used with us.

Pheon, or *Pheon head,* written also *feon :* the head of a dart, barbed, and engrailed on the inner side ; the *broad arrow* being in this respect plain. Its position is with the point downward, unless otherwise blazoned. The French synonym is perhaps *fer de fleche,* but *fer de lance, fer de javelot,* and *fer de hallebarde* are also similar.

Pheons are occasionally borne shafted and feathered.

Or, a pheon azure—SYDNEY, Earl of Leicester.

Azure, a pheon argent, a bordure or, entoyre of torteaux—SHARP, Abp. of York, 1691–1714.

Argent, three escutcheons sable, on each a pheon or—PARKER.

Or, three escutcheons sable, on each a broad arrow-head [pheon] of the field—Henry PARKER, Fryth Hall, Essex [granted Feb. 21, 1537].

Sable, three pheons, their outer edges engrailed argent—LOTHAM.

Argent, a bend vair between three escutcheons sable, each charged with a pheon of the field ; a bordure engrailed gules bezanty—BRIGGS, Halifax.

Sable, a pheon inverted argent ; a canton or —JACKSON.

PARKER.

Sable, two pheons in saltire argent—PEARLE.

Sable, three pheons shafted rompu argent—NICOLLS, Middlesex.

Argent, nine pheons meeting in point, six in chief and three in base, sable—JOHNSON, co. Chester.

The term *pheoned* is also used of arrows to describe the tincture of the heads.

Azure, on a chevron gules between in chief two sheaves each of six arrows interlaced saltirewise of the second flighted and pheoned argent, and in base a bow stringed fesswise of the last, three bezants—SHOTTER, Farnham, Surrey.

Azure, a chevron between three sheaves of five arrows or, flighted and pheoned argent, pointed and banded gules—BRICKDALE, co. Somerset.

Pestle. See *Mortar.*
Petronel : a small gun.
Peuz, i.q. *Pales.*

Pewit. See *Lapwing.*
Phare, (fr.) : *Beacon.*
Phillip : a *Sparrow,* q.v.

Phœnix, (fr. *phenix*); an imaginary bird resembling the eagle, represented issuing from flames. See badge of JANE SEYMOUR, under *Castle*.

Sable, a phœnix argent—CAINE.

Gules, a phœnix argent, in flames proper—FENWICK, of that Ilk, Scotland.

With the Phœnix may be noted the *Salamander*, (fr. *Salamandre*) : a fictitious reptile represented as a lizard in the midst of flames.

Argent, a lion rampant gules on a chief sable a salamander in fire proper—DUNDAS.

Azure, a salamander or in a flame proper—CENINO, Italy.

Pick-axe: it has been supposed that the old French *pieces* in the following arms may mean *picks* or *pick-axes*, in allusion to the name of the bearer rather than to the natural meaning of the expression, viz. silver coins. See also under *Axe*.

Monsire de PICKWORTH, gules, a une bend entre vj pieces d'argent— Roll, temp. ED. III.

Pierced, (fr. *percé*) : applied to any bearing which is perforated, the tincture of the field or charge on which it is placed being seen through the aperture, (fr. *ajouré*). If a different tincture be seen it should be blazoned as *voided*. See e.g. examples under *Mullet*.

As to the form of the aperture it is doubtful as regards the ancient arms whether it should be circular, or should follow the outline of the charge. In modern arms *pierced* implies a circular aperture, though *Crosses* are sometimes *square pierced*, and *lozenge pierced*. See § 9, and § 5; and *voided* is used when the aperture follows the outline.

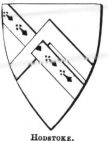

Pierced with an arrow generally means the same as *transfixed*. A singular, and perhaps single, instance of an ordinary *piercing* or perforating another is—

Or, a chevron gules pierced with [or perforated by] a bend ermine [otherwise a bend ermine perforating a chevron gules]—HODSTOKE, or HADSTOCK, Suffolk.

HODSTOKE.

Pile, (fr. *pile*): an ordinary which has been supposed to represent a stake used in the construction of a military bridge, but may well have had its origin like the pale, fesse, or bend in the constructive details of the shield. As will be seen, there are various forms of the name, and it is subjected also to difference in outline. The charge is found frequently in the old rolls of arms.

CHANDOS.

Or, a pile gules—CHANDOS, Baron Chandos. [Summoned to Parliament, 1337.]

Rauf de BASSETT, d'or a trois peles de goulz, ung quartre de ermyne—Roll, temp. HEN. III.

Guy de BRIAN, d'azur a trois piles d'or— *Ibid.*

Sire Rauf BASSET, de or a iij peus de goules e un quarter de ermyne—Roll, temp. ED. II.

Sire Johan MAUDUT, de goules a iij peuz daunces de or—*Ibid.*

Sire William GERNOUN, d'argent, a iij peus undes de goulys—*Ibid.*

Sire Robert de FORNEUS, de argent a un pel engrele de sable—*Ibid.*

Sire Johan de CHAUNDOS, de argent a un peel de goules e un label de azure—*Ibid.*

Monsire Rafe BASSET, port d'argent a trois piles gules a une quarter d'ermine—Roll, temp. ED. III.

Monsire Edward SHANDOS, argent a une pile gules une labell asure— *Ibid.*

According to the somewhat arbitrary rules of later heralds, a single pile uncharged should occupy one third of the breadth of the chief, but if charged it may be double that width. Piles are to be drawn in a perpendicular position, with the points downwards, reaching to, or nearly to, the *base point*, unless otherwise directed; but they are to be found *in bend* and *in fesse*, and it is not uncommon to designate some point in the edge of the shield from which they should start, and one at which they

---

Pie. See *Magpie;* also *Seapie,* under *Lapwing.*

Pieces, (old fr. *peeces*): used of bars, &c. ; e.g. 'undé d'or et gules de six peeces.'

Pied coupé, (fr.): of charges of which the lower part is wanting.

Pied, en : = (1) upright, (2) at the base of the shield.

Piety, *In her.* See *Pelican.*

Pigeon, (fr. *pigeon*): see *Dove.*

Pignon, (fr.): gable.

Pike, (the fish). See *Lucy.*

Pike-staff. See *Staff.*

should end, unless they are to be drawn *throughout*. The blazon is consequently often very intri-
cate, as will be seen from the examples. If the pile is simply reversed, i.e. with the point upwards, it is blazoned as *trans-posed*. When a pile is *pierced* it is said that a lozenge shape is intended.

HULSE.

Argent, two piles sable—HULSE, Cheshire.

Ermine, two piles in point [i.e. meeting in or near the middle base point] sable—HOLLES, co. Lincoln.

Sir Guy de BRYAN.

HACKET.

Or, three piles [meet-ing] in point azure—Sir Guy de BRYAN, (ob. 1390).

Or, three piles azure—Reginald BRIAN, Bp. of S. David's, 1350; of Worcester, 1353–61.

Sable, three piles in point azure; on a chief gules a lion passant gardant or—John HACKET, Bp. of Lichfield, 1661–70.

Azure, a pile issuing from the base in bend sinister or—KAGG.

Argent, a pile between two others reversed [or three piles, one issuing from the chief between two others transposed sable—HULLES, Cheshire and Berkshire. [Another branch of the family from one before named.]

Argent, three piles; two issuant from the chief and one from the base gules, each charged with an antique crown or—GRANT, Bishops Waltham, co. Hants.

Sable, a chevron ermine between three piles—CATER, London.

Argent, out of the dexter base side a pile flected and reflected sable —BOIS.

Azure, a pile wavy in bend [otherwise issuing bendwise from the dexter chief] or—ALDAM, Kent and Sussex.

Pilia pastoralia. See *Cap*.

Pillow. See *Cushion*.

Pink. See *Carnation*.

Pinzon. See *Finch*.

Pistol. See *Musket*.

Pitcher. See *Ewer*.

Pitchfork. See *Fork*.

Placque: a name given to the *tabard* of a herald in distinction from those of kings of arms, and pursuivants.

Plain point. See *Point*.

Argent, a fesse wavy azure; in chief three piles issuing from the chief gules—BLAMSCHILL.

Argent, three piles [rather a triple pile, or a pile triple pointed] flory at the points, issuing from the sinister base bendwise sable —WROTON.

Or, a pile masoned in bend triple flory sable WROTON. [Another branch.]

Or, a triple pile flory in bend sable [i.e. issuing from the dexter chief]—NORTON.

Gules, three piles issuing out of the sinister side argent; on a chief of the last a crescent

WROTON.

azure between two ermine spots—HENDERSON, Fordell, Scotland.

Argent, three piles issuing from the dexter side throughout gules; on a chief of the first a crescent between two ermine spots sable—HENDERSON.

Sable, three piles fesswise argent; on a chief gules a crescent between two ermine spots or, and in the centre a rose for difference—HENDERSON, co. Chester.

Or, on a fesse, between three fleurs-de-lis azure, as many bezants; a pierced pile in chief—SAINTHILL, co. Devon.

The terms *in pile* and *per pile* are both used: the former in reference to a number of charges, six at least, being arranged in the shape of a *pile*, though with so few, the formula of 'three, two, and one,' really amounts to the same thing; the latter involves the shield being divided into three parts by the two lines being drawn pilewise.

Sable, six swallows in pile argent—John ARUNDEL, Bp. of Lichfield, 1496; of Exeter, 1502-4.

Azure, ten torteaux in pile; a pile of three points azure—Gervais BABINGTON, Bp. of Llandaff, 1591; Exeter, 1595; Worcester, 1597–1610.

Barry of six or and sable per pile [otherwise a pile] counterchanged—William ENGHAM.

ARUNDEL.

Pily, or *Paly pily*, or *Pily counter pily* : is a division of the field into a certain even number of parts by piles placed perpendicularly and counterposed. The number of *traits*, i.e. pieces, should be mentioned, and both the pile and the interval are reckoned in the counting.

In *pily* the piles are ordinarily drawn *throughout*, unless blazoned otherwise, as in the arms of POYNTER.

Pily counter pily of seven traits (or pieces) or and sable, the points ending in crosses pattée, three in chief, and two in base—POYNTER.

Pily wavy of six traits in point or and gules; over all a fesse of the first—JOHAM, Kent.

Pily of six traits sable and argent, over all a fesse wavy gules—LOVELL, Scotland.

Some heralds use the term *dancetty per long* instead of *pily*.

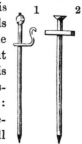

POYNTER.

Pilgrim's or **Palmer's Staff,** (fr. *bourdon*): this was used as a device in a coat of arms as early at least as Edward II.'s reign, as will be seen. The *Staff* and the *Escallop shell* (q.v.) were the badges of the pilgrim, and hence it is but natural it should find its way into the shields of those who had visited the Holy Land. The usual form of representation is like figure 1, but in some the hook is wanting, and when this is the case it is scarcely distinguishable from a pastoral staff as borne by some of the monasteries: it is shewn in figure 2. While, too, it is represented under different forms, it is blazoned, as will be seen also, under different names, e.g. a *pilgrim's crutch*, a *crutch-staff*, &c., but there is no reason to suppose that the different names can be correlated with different figures. The *crutch*, perhaps, should be represented with the transverse piece on the top of the staff (like the letter T) instead of across it. See *Potent*, also *Staff*.

Sire Johan BORDOUN, de goules a iij bordons de argent—Roll, temp. ED. II.

Argent, three pilgrim's staves (fig. 1) sable; the heads, ends, and rests, or—PALMER, Lincoln.

Gules, three water-bougets or, in pale a pilgrim's staff of the last enfiled with a water-bouget in base—KIRKHAM Priory, Yorkshire.

Barry of six argent and gules [otherwise argent, two bars gules]; over all in bend sinister a pilgrim's crutch or—Priory of SEMPRINGHAM, Lincolnshire.

Argent, a lion rampant sable between three palmer's staves or—PALMER.

Or, three pilgrim's staves sable. [Another branch of the family bear Azure, three pilgrim's staves or]—PILGRIM, Hertfordshire.

Gules, a lion rampant or, over all a long cross or pilgrim's crutch in bend siniстes of the last—Augustinian Priory at NEWBURGH, co. York.

Argent, three bars gules ; over all a crutch [otherwise blazoned crosier] in bend or—Gilbertine Abbey at ALVINGHAM, co. Lincoln.

Sable, on a point wavy a lion passant or ; in chief three bezants ; on a canton an escallop between two palmer's staves sable—HAWKINS.

Or, a bend between two bull's heads couped sable ; on a chief argent two bars gules, surmounted by a crutch-staff in bend azure—HOLGATE, Bp. of Llandaff, 1537 ; Abp. of York, 1545-54.

D'azur, à un bourdon d'or posé en bande, accompagné de trois coquilles du même, deux en chef et une en pointe—DE PELERIN, Languedoc.

Closely connected with the Pilgrim's Staff was the Pilgrim's *Scrip*, called also *pouch* or *wallet*, and sometimes *postscrip*.

> " Give me my *scallop-shell* of quiet,   My *bottle* of salvation ;
> My *staff* of faith to walk upon :   My *gown* of glory (hope's true gage)
> My *scrip* of joy, immortal diet ;   And thus I'll make my pilgrimage."
> *Sir Walter Raleigh.*

This device is usually represented as in the margin, and is sometimes pendent from the staff.

Pilgrim's scrip.

Argent, a chevron sable between three palmer's staves, with pouches hanging on them of the last garnished or—TASBOROUGH, Suffolk.

Argent, a chevron between three postscrips (or palmer's scrips) sable, tassels and buttons. Also PALMER, Wood Court, co. Somerset.

Azure, a chevron or between three open wallets argent, buckles and buttons of the second—TOWGOOD, Axminster, co. Devon ; granted 1770.

Argent, a bend between six pouches sable—WOLSTON, co. Cornwall.

Sable, a bend between six pouches argent—WOLSTON, co. Devon.

Pillars : details of buildings are but rarely introduced into heraldry, but when pillars occur they somewhat resemble *columns* of the Tuscan order ; plain Norman shafts with cushion capitals, however, are sometimes to be found. The *capital*, the *base*, and the *pedestal* are sometimes mentioned in the blazon. See also *Arches*.

Azure, a fesse argent over all a pillar gules issuant out of the base wavy azure—UDWARD, Longcroft, Scotland.

Azure, three pillars of the Corinthian order [?] two and one; on the top of each a ball of the last—MAJOR, Suffolk.

Argent, an eagle displayed sable resting each claw on a column with capital and base azure—BARTOLOZZI.

Barry of six argent and gules, on a canton as the first a column sable—DEALE.

Gules, a boy's face couped below the shoulders between two demi-pillars argent—BILERHEIT.

Gules, two lions rampant gardant or supporting a column marked with lines chevronwise proper, all standing on a base of the same;

MAJOR.

[a garter surrounding the whole with the inscription, "INSTITUTE OF BRITISH ARCHITECTS, anno salutis M DCCC XXXIV,"] above a mural crown proper, and beneath the motto "Usui Civium, Decori Urbium." Seal of that SOCIETY.

Sable, three Doric columns [?] palewise argent [elsewhere three columns in fesse] —TREMENHEERE, Cornwall.

Gules, three door-arches argent, capitals and pedestals or (another the arches also or)—ARCHES, co. Devon.

Pincers have been observed only in one coat of arms, and that of a private family; not of a company.

Argent, a fesse between three pair of pincers gules—RUSSELL.

Pincers.

Pine-tree, (fr. *pin*): this tree occurs in some few coats of arms, and more frequently the Pine-apple (fr. *pomme de pin*), or rather the *cone* of the pine-tree. In some modern instances the fruit of the tree is represented, but then the term *ananas* ought to be employed to prevent confusion.

Argent, on a mount in base a pine-tree fructed all proper—PYNE.

Argent, in base on a mount proper a pine-tree vert, a talbot tied thereto proper, and from one of the branches a buglehorn pendent of the second within a bordure of the third—LOUTHIAN, Edinburgh.

Argent, three pine-trees erased proper, fructed or—BRAYE, Cornwall.

Argent, three pine-apples [i.e. cones] gules—DYCHFIELD, Essex.

DYCHFIELD.

Argent, a chevron between three pine cones slipped erect gules—APPURLEY.

Argent, between two chevrons sable three pines [i.e. pine cones] pendent vert—ASHFORD.

Azure, a dolphin embowed naiant between three pine cones erect or—FISHER.

Azure, on a chevron argent between in chief two roses of the last and in base an ananas leaved or, a pair of palm branches vert—PAULMIER, co. Devon.

Argent, a negro cutting with a bill a sugar-cane proper, on a chief azure two pine-apples [i.e. ananas] or leaved and crowned of the last—CHAMBERS, Hanover, Jamaica; granted 1771.

Besides the pine, the *fir* (fr. *sapin*) the *cedar* and the *cypress* are sometimes mentioned; the sprig of the latter appears occasionally with that of laurel.

Argent, a fir-tree growing out of a mount in base vert, surmounted by a sword bendwise azure ensigned on the point with an imperial crown proper—MACGREGOR.

Or, a lion rampant gules, in chief three fir-trees eradicated vert, on a canton argent a flag azure charged with a saltire of the fourth—FARQUHARSON, co. Aberdeen.

Argent, on a mount a grove of firs proper—WALKINSHAND, Scotland.

Argent, a cedar-tree between two mounts of flowers proper on a chief azure a dagger erect proper, pomel and hilt or between two mullets of six points gold—MONTEFIORE, Ramsgate, Sussex, and London; Baronetcy, 1846.

Azure, three cypress sprigs or—BIRKIN.

MACGREGOR.

Pipe: musical instruments occur but rarely : we find the *pipe* or *fife*, the *flute*, and what is more remarkable the *Organ-pipe*, the latter being represented as on the next page.

Sable, three pipes two and one, the broad ends in chief, argent—PIPER.

Vert crusily, two fifes or sackbuts or—PIPE, Bilston, co. Stafford.

Azure, two pipes between ten crosses crosslet or—PYPE.

Gules, on a bend invecked argent a shepherd's flute azure, in chief a lion passant guardant of the second royally crowned or—ELLIOT, Woolie. [Several families of ELLIOT bear flutes and pipes together with other charges].

Plaited, i.q. *fretted.*

Planta genista. See *Broom.*

Azure, semy of crosses crosslet, or two shepherd's pipes chevronways of the second—PYKE, temp. HENRY VI.

Gules, two organ-pipes pilewise, the wide ends in chief, or [elsewhere two pipes in pile or, small ends conjoined in base, extending themselves in chief]—NEVILL.

Azure, semé of crosses croslet and two organ-pipes in chevron or — DELAPIPE, co. Derby.

Azure, two organ-pipes in saltire between four crosses patty argent—Lord WILLIAMS of Thame.

NEVILL.

Plain: it is sometimes found useful for the sake of distinction to introduce this word, e.g. in the following example

Argent, on a chevron plain within a bordure engrailed gules three pierced cinquefoils of the first—GILBERT.

Planet: the names of the planets are sometimes introduced under the astronomical signs which are used to note them. (See under *Letters*.) The planet *Venus* occurs in the crest of CHAMBERS, but has not been observed in any coats of arms.

Blazoning by the name of Planets was invented by certain fanciful heralds in the seventeenth century, and the names employed will be found under *Tinctures*.

Plates, (fr. *besant d'argent* also *plates*): a term applied by heralds to the *roundle argent*. In the old rolls of arms the term *rondeaux d'argent* is more frequently used, but *torteaux d'argent*, *gastelles d'argent*, and *pelotes d'argent* are all found. (See respectively *torteaux, pellet,* and *roundle*.)

Or, on a fesse gules three plates—HUNTINGFIELD. [See also under *Pellet*.]

Sable, two broad arrows in saltire argent feathered or; in chief a plate—PEARLE, Harl. MS. 1458.

Sir Rauf de CAMOYS, de or od le chef de goules a iij rondels de argent—Roll, temp. ED. II.

Sire Johan DE LA PENNE, de argent a une fesse de sable; en la fesse iij rondels de argent—*Ibid.*

Sire Johan de BABINGTONE, de goules a les pelotes de argent—*Ibid.*

HUNTINGFIELD.

Sable, a lion rampant argent between eight plates [otherwise within an orle of bezants]—PRENNE.

De gueules, à trois besants d'argent—ERMAR, Bretagne.

The term *platy* is also sometimes used for *semé* of *plates*.

Argent, a chevron gules within a bordure sable platy—Sir John BAVENT, Norfolk.

Sable, platy between two flaunches argent—SPELMAN.

Azure, platy three dual coronets or—LEIGH, co. Chester.

Or, fretty sable platy—PLATT, London.

Plough: the form of this bearing varies in different ex amples. In one coat an *antique plough* is named. The *Plough paddle* is carried by the sinister supporter of the arms of HAY, earl of Kinnoul, and is represented as in the margin, while the *Ploughshare* or *Coulter,* or as it is called by some heralds *laver cutter* is represented below.

Azure, a plough in fesse argent—KRAGG.

Azure, a fesse between three ploughs or—SMETON, Harl. MS. 1045, fo. 56.

Plough paddle.

Gules, on a fesse argent between two garbs in chief or, and an antique plough in base of the last, three trefoils vert DREGHORN, Scotland.

Argent, a chevron between three laver cutters (or ploughshares, also called scythe blades) sable—LEVERSEDGE, co. Chester.

Ploughshare.

Per pale dancetty argent and sable; on the sinister side a coulter of the first—STEVENTON.

Or, three coulters of a plough fessways in pale azure—KOEHLER.

Argent, a chevron between three coulters sable—DOE, Langhall, co. Lancaster, 1749.

Plover: this bird has been observed named but in two coats of arms.

Argent, a chevron ermine, between three plovers proper—WYKE.

Azure, a chevron argent between three plovers or—WYCHARD.

Plum: in one case has the fruit of the plum-tree been observed.

Sable, a cross engrailed between four plums argent—BUTTERWORTH.

Platter. See *Dish.*

Plenitude, i.q. *complement.* See *Moon.*

Plumby, i.q. *Purpure.*

Plumed—of an arrow—when the feathers are of another tincture.

Plumbers' implements consist of five or six kinds. There is first of all the *cutting-knife;* next the *shave-hook;* next the *soldering-irons;* and next the *cross staff.* These are shewn in the margin as they are usually represented in the insignia of the PLUMBERS' Company. The *level* and the *plummet* from the same arms have already been figured under *level.* The *soldering-irons,* it will be seen, were borne by two branches of the family of SHRIGLEY (unless the variation in the

Cross Staff.

Cutting-knife.

blazon arises from error), as well as by the family of BIDDULPH.

Or, on a chevron sable between a cross staff fessways of the last, enclosed by two plummets azure, all in chief, and a level reversed in base of the second, two soldering-irons in saltire, between a cutting-knife on the dexter, and a shavehook on the sinister argent—Company of PLUMBERS, London [Inc. 1612].

Shavehook.

Argent, a chevron between three plumber's soldering-irons sable—SHRIGLEY, Harl. MS. 1386, fo. 95.

Argent, three soldering-irons sable—BIDDULPH, co. Stafford, Erdeswick.

Soldering-irons.

Argent, a fesse between three plumber's irons sable—SHRIGLEY.

Plume. *Feathers* were naturally employed more frequently as badges and crests than as charges on coats of arms, and when three or more occur they are termed a *plume,* fr. *panache.* The best known example is the plume of ostrich feathers borne by the PRINCE OF WALES, a cognizance peculiar to members of the royal family. The favourite legend that Prince Edward received the ostrich feathers from the casque of John of Luxembourg, King of Bohemia, at the battle of Cressy, Aug. 26, 1346, will scarcely bear investigation, or that the motto *Ich Dien* referred to the Bohemian King serving the French King as a stipendiary; still the true origin has not been satisfactorily

Badge of the
PRINCE OF WALES.

ascertained. Since the time of Henry VIII. the ostrich feathers have been encircled by a coronet. An illustration is given from the Prince's Primer, printed by Richard Grafton, London, 1546.

Argent, a chevron sable between three ostrich feathers (erroneously called *perukes*)--HARMAN, Kent.

Argent, on a cross moline gules a feather of the first between two annulets in pale or—VIDAL, co. Devon.

Argent, a steel cap proper with a feather in front gules—KINGSTON, temp. RICH. II.

Argent, six ostrich feathers, three, two, and one sable—JERVIS.

When a *plume* consists of more than three feathers the number must be stated, but a very common device is to place the feathers in rows, and the rows are by some heralds blazoned as so many *heights*. When more than three heights occur, the term *pyramid* of feathers is used. The crest of MORTIMER supplies an example of this, though some heralds blazon this device as a *pyramid of leaves*.

Crest of
MORTIMER.

Gules, a fesse between three plumes argent—COLVELEY, co. Hants.

Sable, three plumes of ostrich feathers, three in each, argent—TUFFLE.

Per fesse gules and azure a griffin argent armed or seizing on a dragon vert holding a plume of the third—KIRKSWOLD.

Gules, on a horse courant or with a plume to the head, bridle, saddle and trappings of the field between three garbs as the second, a 5-foil at the shoulder like the first, the hip covered by an escucheon .... charged with a cross—MALT.

Sometimes a single feather is borne, and this not unfrequently is passed through an *escroll*, e.g. in the *badge* of JOHN OF GAUNT, as well as on his shield. See also *Pen*.

In case the quill should differ in tincture from the rest of the feather, the term *penned, quilled,* or *shafted,* may be employed.

Sable, three ostrich feathers ermine quills or, transfixed through as many scrolls of the last—JOHN, Duke of Lancaster.

Argent, three feathers in pale, each bending from the other in the tops gules, shafts [or quills] or—BROBRACH.

Badge of
JOHN OF
GAUNT.

Plumeté, (fr.): of scales, &c., when of another tincture.	Plummet. See *Level*.
	Poignard. See *Dagger*.

Point, (fr. *une partie de l'écu*).　(1.) The chief use of this term is to denote a position in the escutcheon.　Nine points are reckoned by heralds, but practically two of these (viz. Nos. 4 and 6) are needless, and are not recognized by the French heralds.　The following diagram will readily explain the terms. The most frequently used are *in chief* and *in base*, the word point being understood.

1. *In Dexter chief* point, (fr. au canton dextre du chef).

2. *In Middle chief* point, (fr. au point du chef).

3. *In Sinister chief* point, (fr. au canton sénestre du chef).

4. *In Honour,* or *Collar* point.

5. *In Fesse* point, (fr. au centre de l'écu, or 'en l'abîme,' or 'en cœur.')

6. *In Nombril* point.

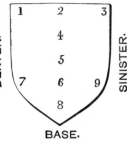

7. *In Dexter base* point, (fr. au canton dextre de la pointe).

8. *In Middle base* point, (fr. à la pointe).

9. *In Sinister base* point, (fr. au canton senestre de la pointe).

Party per bend indented or and azure; in sinister chief a pelican in piety between two fleurs-de-lys; in dexter base the same, all counterchanged—Poynet, Bp. of Rochester, 1550; of Winchester, 1551–53.

Vairy or and gules in the dexter corner [i.e. dexter chief point] a lion passant gardant of the last—Ferrers.

Argent, semy of trefoils two annulets braced in the nombril point sable—Eaton.

Quarterly gules and vert, four pheons in cross, points to the nombril of the escucheon argent—Trubshawe.

Gules, three swords conjoined at the pomels in fesse point, the blades extended to the dexter and sinister chief points, and middle base of the escutcheon argent—Stapleton.

Poix. See *Goutté de.*

Pole-axe. See *Axe.*

Pole-star or **Polar.** See *Star.*

Poles. See *Hop-poles* or *Hopbines.*

Pomel: the knob upon the hilt of a *sword*, q.v.

Pometty: applied to the *Cross*, q.v. § 29, terminated in pomel shaped knobs.　See also arms of Trossell, under *Fret.*

Pometty: also of a *Cross*, q.v. § 29, or *escarboucle* (q.v.) having a rounded excrescence on each arm.

Popinjay. See *Parrot.*

Gules, a bar engrailed argent between three suns or; in the collar point a demi-salmon naiant from the fesse, of the second—AULD, Scotland.

The expression *in point*, e.g. of swords meeting, is supposed, when no further description is added, to mean the *middle* base point, i.e. No. 8, but it is very unsatisfactory.

Argent, three swords conjoined in point [in pile would be better] gules—BARDEN.

In the old rolls these points are not recognized, but the term *en le cauntel* or *corniere* is sometimes used, which is equivalent to the *dexter chief point*.

Hugh Fitz [de John de BALLIOL], de goules ove ung escochon d'azur ove ung lion rampant d'argent coronne d'or en la corniere—Roll, temp. HEN. III.

Sire William de TRACY, de or a ij bendes de goules; en le cauntel un escalop de sable—Roll, temp. ED. II.

Point, (2.) (fr. *la pointe*): the term is sometimes used to signify a portion of the shield parted off at the base by a plain or compound line, just as the upper portion is treated when a *chief* is borne. If the partition line is drawn straight across it forms a *plain point*, but the line may be *wavy*, *indented*, &c.: if it is chevron shaped the point may be described as *pointed*, or *in point* or *enty* (q. v.) (which is sometimes badly spelt *ampty*). The best known example occurs in the Royal Arms of GEORGE I.

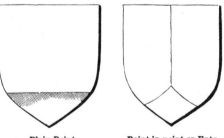

Plain Point.   Point in point or Enty.

At the same time the French *pointe* frequently signifies a figure rising up quite to the chief point, like a *pile* reversed, and so the term *pointé* is used to signify that the shield is divided by lines forming that figure.

D'azur, à la pointe d'argent—SAINT BLAISE DE BRUGNY.

D'azur, à l'aigle naissante d'or coupé d'argent, a quatre pointes de gueules—DE LANGLOIS DE SEPTENVILLE, Normandie.

The reason, perhaps, why the term *point* is not more frequently used is probably that when the field is parted off at the base, it is so by a *mound* (q.v.), or some similar device to which a definite name is applied.

Per pale barry of six, ermine and gules dexter, and azure sinister; a chief engrailed of the third; a point indented argent—Ac- TONLEY.

Sable, on a point wavy a lion passant or; in chief three bezants—HAWKINS, Plymouth.

Per pale or and gules, a point in point ermine; over all a cross tau azure—LISLE.

Argent, a chief gules; in base a point in- dented sable [otherwise per fesse indented argent and sable]—BLETHFIELD, or BLUFIELD.

ACTONLEY.

Gules, two lions passant gardant in pale or [for BRUNSWICK]; impaling or, semée of hearts gules, a lion rampant azure [for LUNENBURG]; on a point in point gules a horse courant argent [for SAXONY]. On the centre an inescutcheon gules charged with the Crown of Charlemagne or [for ARCH TREASURER of the Holy Roman Empire]. The fourth quarter of the Royal Arms of GEORGE I.

In French coats of arms this kind of encroachment on the shield is much more frequent and more varied than in the English, but the English heraldic writers have adopted the French names, and in their disqu'sitions have not used them very consistently. The French term *champagne* is said to occupy one fourth of the shield, while the '*plaine*' only one eighth of the shield, both being divided off the base by a line only slightly depressed in the centre. English heraldic writers describe the names *champion, champaine,* and *shapourne*, the last term being applied to any portion curved, but as there are no actual examples in English arms, their descriptions are quite valueless.

D'or, à l'olivier de sinople accosté de deux croissants de gueules; à la champagne d'azur chargé d'un brochet d'argent—BROCHANT DU BREUIL, Ile de France.

Point Champion.

Some heralds also include under the term '*point*' all the various partitions of the shield which are imagined to be *abatements* (q.v.), and describe dexter chief corner parted off by a line bendwise as a *point dexter*, and in a similar way they make a *point sinister*; also an imaginary *point dexter base*, and a *point sinister base*. Added to these are *gussets*, the *gore*, and perhaps the *flaunches* (q.v.).

The examples from German and Italian arms provide a still more varied field for the exercise of ingenuity in blazon; e.g. the arms of CORRARO [or Karraro]. Venice, (though Holme states that a similar coat was borne by the English family of HINXLEY). One or two instances are added as further specimens of extraordinary divisions of the shield.

Coupé d'argent et d'azur, vêtu de l'un à l'autre, (ou, coupé d'argent et d'azur à une grande lozange de l'un à l'autre aboutissante aux quatre flancs de l'écu); [in English, Per fesse argent and azure a lozenge throughout counterchanged]—CORRARO, or KARRARO, Venice.

Per fesse argent and vert, four points counterchanged [otherwise 'Per fesse vert and argent; a lozenge in point [or throughout] counterchanged']—HINXLEY.

HINXLEY.

Mi-coupé mi-parti vers la pointe et récoupé d'argent et de gueules—FROMBERG, Bavaria.

Mi-coupé en chef failli en taillant et récoupé vers la pointe de gueules et d'argent—D'ARPO, Italy.

Mi tranché audessous du chef, mi taillé en remontant vers le chef, et retaillé au flanc de l'écu d'or et de gueules—KAWSENGEN en Misnie.

The term *point* is used also in other ways. Irregularly for *pane* or *pièce* in the *Cross quarterpierced*, § 5, q.v. (where the French '*cinque points d'argent equipollés*' has been literally translated); and it has been even used for the squares of *chequy*. Again for a shield *tiercé* or triparted fesswise the term *three points* has been used for the three divisions. Custom has sanctioned the use of the word for the termination of the *label*, (q.v.), and there are also charges having points, e.g. *swords*, *spears*, &c., in blazoning which the direction of those *points* has to be stated. There is also the *Wire-drawer's* point.

Pomegranate, (lat. *Pomum granatum,* fr. *grenade*), i.e. the Apple of Grenada : the tree, the branch, and the fruit are all found borne in arms, the last generally represented as slipped. The *badge* of CATHARINE of ARRAGON affords a good illustration of the manner in which the fruit is represented.

Argent, on a mount a pomegranate-tree fructed proper—WILKES, Harl. MS. 6169.

Sable, a hand proper vested argent issuing out of the clouds, &c. [see *Clouds*] ; in base a pomegranate or between five demi-fleur-de-lis bordering the edge of the escutcheon of the last—College of PHYSICIANS, incorporated 1523.

Or, a pomegranate-tree erased vert fructed gold, supported by a hart rampant proper crowned and attired of the first —Dr. LOPUS, Physician to Queen Elizabeth, 1591.

Sable, a pomegranate branch slipped and fructed or— FORD, co. Devon.

Badge of
CATHARINE
of Arragon.

Or, a fesse indented ermine between three pomegranates leaved proper —BARR.

Gules, a pomegranate in pale slipped or—GRANGE, or GRANGER.

Gules, a demi-rose argent charged with another of the field, conjoined in pale with a demi-pomegranate or, seeded proper [i.e. gules] both slipped vert—BILSON, Bp. of Winchester, 1597–1616.

Or, a saltire between four martlets sable, on a canton argent a pomegranate proper seeded gules —GUILFORD.

Argent, a chevon gules between three pomegranates proper—Richard GARDENAR, Himbleton, co. Worcester. The pomegranates leaved vert— GARDINER, co. Worcester, 1592.

BILSON.

Pomeis, (fr. *volets,* but more frequently *torteaux de sinople*) : the name given to roundles *vert,* but of comparatively modern origin : the *pomey* is no doubt intended for the apple. In one blazon the term *pomme* seems to be used for this. (See Arms of UTTERSON, under *Flag.*)

Argent, a fesse cotised gules between three pomeys—TARPLEY, co. Northampton.

Argent, five pomeis in saltire ; a chief indented gules—FARMARY, granted 1611.

Ermine, three pomeis, each charged with a cross or—HEATHCOTE

Gules, on a fesse argent three pomeis—RANSON.

D'or, a trois chevrons de sable accompagne de trois torteaux de sinople
—DESCHAMPS.

Poplar-tree, (fr. *peuplier*): this has been observed but in
one instance. The *aspen* leaf is more frequent.

Argent, a mount vert, thereon a poplar-tree between two lions combatant proper ducally crowned or—GANDOLPHI, Richmond, Surrey.

Argent, a fesse between six aspen leaves vert—FENINGLEY.

Argent, an aspen leaf proper—ASPINALL.

Argent, three aspen leaves gules [another branch of the family, Gules,
three aspen leaves argent]—COGAN.

Poppy, (fr. *pavot*) : one instance of this has been observed
in English arms.

Gules, three poppy bolles on their stalks in fesse or—BOLLER.

D'or, à trois têtes de pavots de sinople—PAVYOT.

Porcupine, (fr. *porc-épic*): three instances of this device
have been observed. It may be *quilled* of another tincture.
There is some danger of it being confused with the *hedgehog*, q.v.

Argent, three porcupines sable—BYRON, Byron, co. Lancaster.

Gules, two porcupines argent—MERICKE, Wigmore Castle, Hereford,
1560, and co. Radnor.

Gules, a porcupine salient argent quilled and chained or—EYRE, Lord
Mayor of London, 1445.

Portcullis, or *Portquilice*, (fr. *coulesse* and *herse*, also
sarrasine): a frame of wood strengthened and
spiked with iron, used for the defence of the
gate of a castle. It occurs as a badge of the
house of Tudor in allusion to their descent
from the Beaufort family. The illustration
is taken from the east window of the Chapel
founded by the king at Westminster. Besides
being borne separately it is often referred to
in the descriptive details of the *castle*, q.v.

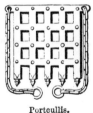

Portcullis.

Porc. See *Boar*.

Porch. See *Church*.

Porprin and *Porpre*. See *Purpure*.

Porridge-pot. See *Pot*.

Port or *portal*, i.q. a *porch* of a
Church, or a *gate* of a *Castle*.

Portcullis: the name of one of
the pursuivants. See *Herald*.

Argent, a portcullis sable, chains azure—REIGNOLD, or REYNOLDS, Devon.

Argent, a portcullis gules, chains azure—Burgh of ABERBROTHOCK, Scotland.

Ermine, on a chief azure three portcullises lined and ringed or—SNAPPE, Standlake, co. Oxford.

Or, a fesse embattled between three portcullises gules—YETTS, Teviotdale, Scotland.

[Portcullises are borne by the Society of TRADESMEN and ARTIFICERS; by LANGMAN, York Herald, temp. 2nd Elizabeth ; and by the families of PORT, co. Dorset, O'GRADY, Viscount GUILLAMORE, LUDGATE, JURY, REEVES, Somerset, WINDYGATE, WINZIET, WINGATES, NEWMAN, and the Borough of HARWICH.]

Pot, (fr. *pot*): there are several kinds of pots, and they are variously represented. The more usual is an iron vessel or cauldron standing on three legs, and with two handles, such as is found in the base of the arms of the BRAZIERS' Company (afterwards incorporated with the Armourers'). See for blazon under *Ewer*. It is the same probably as the *flesh-pot*, and as such the pots in the ancient arms of MONTBOUCHER were afterwards blazoned.

Flesh-pot.

Sire Bertram de MONBOCHER, de argent a iij pos de goules od la bordure de sable besante de or—Roll, temp. ED. II.

Argent, three flesh-pots gules—MOUNBOWCHIER.

Argent, on a chief azure two flesh-pots or—POTTER.

Gules, a chevron between three flesh-pots or—WETHERED, co. Buckingham, and co. Hertford.

Argent, on a chief azure two flesh-pots (or porridge-pots) without handles or—POTTER.

Several arms have simply *pots*, but whether intended for placing on the fire or standing on the table seems to depend on circumstances. The *porridge-pots* of DERLING are blazoned elsewhere *ewers ;* the *pewter pots* of DELVES are probably table pots. The arms of MONTBOUCHER, given above, are found blazoned as three *water-pots*, and also as three *possenets*, in different rolls.

Portholes or *loop-holes.* See under *Castle* and *Tower.*

Posé, (fr.) : of a lion *statant* with its four feet touching the ground.

Also see under *Cup* for *drinking-pots* and *college pots*, and under *Ewer* for the *laver-pot*, under *Founders* for *melting-pot* respectively: also *Lily-pot* and *Flower-pot*.

Argent, a pot sable with fire issuant proper—HAYWOOD.

Argent, a chevron between two pots sable within a bordure engrailed gules—BRAY.

Argent, a chevron between three porridge pots (elsewhere ewers) sable—DERLING.

Argent, on a chevron gules between three pewter pots sable fretty or—DELVES, co. Chester.

Potent: this was the name anciently given to a *crutch*, or walking staff. Thus Chaucer, in his description of 'Elde,' that is, old age, says,—

"So olde she was, that she ne went   A fote, but it were by potent."

In English blazon the term *Pilgrim's crutch*, q.v., is more frequently used than *crutch*, but in some French arms the word *potence* seems to be used in this sense, or perhaps for a *tau cross*.

Argent, three bars gules; over all a crutch in bend sinister or—Gilbertson Priory at MALTON, co. York.

D'or, à trois potences de gueules—MARCHALACH, Bretagne.

1. The term is most frequently used in connection with the Cross, where the four arms end in a crutch-like form. See *Cross potent*, § 31.

2. But it also gives its name to one of the heraldic *furs*, composed of any metal and colour: this is, however, usually blazoned *Potent counter-potent*. Some writers call it *Vairy cuppy*, *Vairy tassy*, and *Meirré*, and there is every reason to believe that it is nothing but an accidental variety of *Vair*, q.v., with fanciful names given to it.

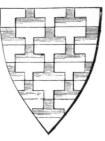

Potent counter-potent.

Potent counter potent, argent and sable, a bend gules—MANCHESTER, co. Stafford.

Potent counter potent gules and argent, a chevron or—AMOS or AMES.

Azure, a chevron potent counter potent or and gules between three ewers with handles of the second—BUREAU.

3. The term *Potent* is also applied to the edge of an ordinary or to a line of division, though the latter but rarely.

Azure, a bend argent between four cotises potent or—SANXER.

Azure, a bend argent two cotises potent on the upper side or—CHAMPAGNE.

Argent, on a plain bend between two cotises potent on the outer edge sable, a tilting spear of the first — CARMICHAEL [afterwards COULTHART].

Gules, a tower between three cinquefoils argent, within a bordure potent ermine—HAMILTON.

Ermine, a chief potent quarterly or and gules—PECKHAM.

Prester (or *Presbyter*) JOHN : this singular figure is represented as seated on a stone (described as a tombstone), and forms the insignia of the *See* of CHICHESTER, the only instance in which the bearing occurs. The origin of the figure is obscure. In 1180 the seal represented the Figure of Christ seated on a Tomb, with perhaps a symbolical reference to Rev. i. 16, and Rev. v. 1. Early in the next century the

CHICHESTER.

mythical story of Prester John, a supposed King of central Asia, was current, a certain Franciscan monk, by name Carpini, who went out as a Missionary in 1206, having brought home or invented the story, and this being very popular was afterwards, perhaps, applied to the device.

Azure, a Presbyter John hooded sitting on a tombstone, in his sinister hand a book open, his dexter hand extended with the two forefingers erect, all or ; in his mouth a sword fessways gules, hilt and pommel or, the point to the sinister—Bishoprick of CHICHESTER.

Possenet. See *Pot.*

Postscrip. See *Pilgrim's Scrip.*

Potgun. See *Musket.*

Pothook. See *Hook.*

Pouch. See *Pilgrim's Staff;* also *Purse.*

Pouncing : said of a faloon seising his prey.

Pourpre, fr. *Purpure.*

Powdered, fr. *poudré.* See *Semé.*

Powets : an old name for tadpoles. See *Frog.*

Primrose: this flower occurs in some few instances. Though the colour varies, the shape of the natural flower should be retained.

Or, three primroses within a double tressure flory counterflory gules —PRIMROSE.

Argent, on a fesse azure between three primroses gules as many mullets or—PRIMROSE, Scotland.

Argent, on a fesse azure three primroses of the field—PRIMROSE.

Or, a lion rampant vert armed and langued gules—PRIMROSE, Dalmeny, Scotland ; [quartering argent on a fesse azure between three primroses vert as many mullets or].

Azure, a chevron argent between three primroses slipped proper— CARSTAIRS, Kilconquhar.

Azure, on a saltire between a mullet in chief and base and a decrescent and increscent in fesse argent a primrose slipped proper—HAGNE, Scotland.

Proper, (fr. *au naturel*): when a charge is borne of its natural colour it is said to be *proper;* the word is sometimes used also as to shape, when there is a conventional or heraldic form of the charge, and when the natural form has to be adopted. It is not good blazon to say a rose proper in regard to tincture, because some roses are red and others white, and the same remark will apply to any object whose colour varies at different times, or in different examples.

The use of the term, however, often involves practically a disregard of the heraldic rules as to tincture. It is used to denote *colours,* and mixture of colours, and shading, and the like, quite unknown in all early coats of arms. A glance at the examples given throughout the present Glossary will shew how freely the term is used. Applied to the human figure it involves the use of flesh colour (fr. *carnation*), as well as of the colours of costumes of various kinds. It will be found that *Kings, Bishops,* figures of *Saints* and *children* are blazoned *proper,* as also such mythical beings as *Neptune,* a *Triton,* and a *Sagit-*

Ppr: an abbreviation of the word ' proper.' See *Trick.*

Prasin: green. See *Vert.*

Prawns. See *Shrimps.*

Preen. See *Clothiers.*

Press. See *Winepress.*

Pretence. See *Escutcheon of.*

Pretension. See *Arms of.*

tarius. Limbs and parts of men are also blazoned proper, e.g. *arms, hands, legs, eyes,* and even *bones.* Numerous animals also will be found so blazoned, e.g. *elephant, camel, panther, badger, otter, bat,* &c., and of different kinds of *deer,* and of *dogs.* Birds are still more frequently so blazoned, and examples will be found of the following : *peacock, parrot, kingfisher, finches* of various kinds, including the canary and the linnet, *owl, heron, stork, partridge, snipe, moorcock, heathcock, lark, eaglets, auk, blackbird, raven, magpie, cornish chough, swan, ducks* of several kinds, *seagull,* and *seapie.* Of fish examples will be found of the *salmon,* the *lamprey,* the *whiting,* and the *herring,* besides the heraldic *dolphin* so blazoned. Amongst reptiles the *alligator, snakes, serpents,* and *effets,* the *lizard,* and even the *chamelion;* while amongst insects are found *bees, ants, beetles,* and *grasshoppers,* blazoned 'proper.'

That Trees, Fruits, and Flowers should be so blazoned is less extraordinary, but it is not easy to decide whether *vert* only should be used. Examples of the *oak tree,* the *elm tree,* the *holly tree,* the *hawthorn tree,* the *hazel tree,* the *ivy* and the *rowan tree* occur, as well as of the *pine,* the *palm,* the *orange,* the *cherry,* and the *fig tree:* and the Fruit also in some few cases is found separately blazoned as proper, e.g. *apples, pine-apples, pomegranates, alderberries,* and *mulberries;* while the term *fructed proper* is not unfrequently applied to several trees; and in one case '*a basket of fruit, proper*' occurs. Amongst Flowers will be found the *primrose, lily, pansy, marigold, columbine, pink, gilly-flower, silphium, marigold, bluebottle,* and *thistle,* and in one or two cases the ground is blazoned or strewed with *flowers* generally. The term *leaved* or *slipped* proper is of frequent occurrence, and various kinds of leaves are blazoned proper; but for all these *vert* may be used.

Preying: applied to *birds.* See under *Wing* and *Falcon.*

Pride, *In his:* said of a *peacock affronté,* with his tail expanded. Also applied to the *Turkeycock.*

Pricket. See *Candlestick.*

Primo. See *Dasket*-maker's.

Profile in: used sometimes in describing *heads* of men.

Pruning-hook. See *Sickle.*

Pruning its wing: used of birds, especially the *Eagle.*

The term is also frequently applied to the *landscape* generally, and to the objects in a landscape; especially to *water* under its various forms, e.g. the *stream*, the *river*, the *ford*, the *sea*, the *waves*, &c. When applied, however, to the *fountain* it probably implies the use of the conventional heraldic tinctures of that *roundle*. Examples also may be found of the term applied to a *mount*, a *rock*, a *mine*, a *cave*, and even to a *mole-hill*. *Fire* and *flaming* are almost always blazoned proper. Buildings, which are quite out of place in true heraldic arms, occur so blazoned, e.g. a *Castle*, a *Monastery*, *Ruins*, and sometimes special buildings, e.g. the *Royal Exchange*, the *Bell-rock light-house*, the *Virginia College*, &c. Ships again are blazoned thus, as in *full sail* proper, or with *sails furled* proper. Armour and various kinds of weapons are also frequently blazoned proper, e.g. the *helmets*, *morions*, &c., *swords*, *daggers*, *muskets*, *guns*, &c. Various tools also are found so blazoned, e.g. *saw*, *wimble*, *fleam*, *cutting-knife*, *currycomb*, &c. Also such household articles as *mirror*, *hour-glass*, *globe*, or *astrolabe*, *books*, *rolls of parchment*, *cards*, &c. Besides these, other devices, oddly introduced into later coats of arms, such as a *rainbow*, *Noah's ark*, a *Caduceus*, and a *diamond*, are all found blazoned '*proper*.'

Purpure, (fr. *pourpre*): this colour, as it is considered by some, but tincture as it is allowed to be by others, is found but rarely in early rolls of arms. It is expressed in modern engravings by lines in bend sinister. The terms *plumby* and *porprin* occur. In the fanciful blazoning by planets it was called *Mercury*, and in that of precious stones *Amethyst*. It is not common in recent arms, still some hundred examples or so may be found.

Purple.

Sire Felip de LYNDESHEYE, de or a un egle de porpre—Roll, temp. ED. II.

Sire Nicholas MALEMEIS, de argent a une bende engrele de pourpre—*Ibid.*

Sire Johan de DENE, dargent a un lyoun raunpaun de pourpre—*Ibid.*

So also Henry, the good Earl of Lincoln, at the siege of Carlaverock bore a banner of yellow silk with a purple lion.

Enris li bons Quens de Nicole [i.e. Count
   of Lincoln]. . .

Baner out de un cendal safrin
O un lioun rampant purprin.

Purse, (fr. *bourse*), stringed and tasselled, is represented as in the margin. The *purse of state*, in which the great seal is kept, is of similar form, but more richly adorned. Very similar to the purse is the *pouch* or *scrip*. See under *Pilgrim's* Staff.

Purse.

Argent, a purse overt gules—CONRADUS.

Argent, a chevron between three dexter hands clenched sable, each holding a purse of the first—STEVENSON.

Or, a fesse chequy argent and azure between three purses gules—SPREWELL, Cowdon, Scotland.

Argent, two lion's gambes erased in saltire gules; on a canton of the second three purses or—ANDESLY.

Argent, a chevron between three swords point downwards, each supporting a purse sable, the pomels and tassels or—TASBOROUGH, Suffolk.

Quadrature: four charges placed in a square have been described as *in quadrature,* or in *quadrangle,* instead of *two and two,* which is more correct; but this is seldom necessary, as four charges would naturally so be placed.

Azure, a circular wreath plaited argent and sable with four hawk's bills or, appended thereto in quadrature—JOCELYN.

Punning Arms. See *Canting Arms.*

Purfled, or *Purflewed :* garnished: a term applied to the studs and ornaments of armour, the trimmings of robes, arrows, birdbolts, (q.v.) Some call a border of ermine, or any other fur, a bordure purflew ermine, &c., but this is needless, and indeed unintelligible.

Pursuivant. See *Herald.*

Pyncheon, i.q. *Pinzon.* See *Finch.*

Pyot : said to be used for *Magpie.*

Pyramid of *feathers.* See *Plume.*

Pyramide, (fr.) : a pyramid only used in one or two French arms.

Python, a winged serpent. See *Pyynotto.*

Quadrangular, used sometimes of *Castles,* rarely used of other charges, but see under *Fetterlock.*

Quadrate : square. See *Cross,* § 25 and § 31.

Quarter: an ordinary occupying one fourth of the field, and situated (unless otherwise directed) in the *dexter* chief. The term *quarter* is used also in referring to the divisions when the shield is quarterly, or when in addition to a cross there is a charge in one of the divisions; and in old arms we find the word *cauntel* used for this as well as *quarter*.

Vairy, argent and sable, a quarter gules—Estanton.

Bertram de Crioll, d'or a deux cheverons et ung quartier de goules—Roll, temp. Hen. III.

William de Lancastre, d'argent a deux barres de goules; ung quartier de goules et ung leopard en la quartier d'or—*Ibid.*

Sire Edmon de Pagenham, quartile de or e de goules, e un egle de vert en lun quarter—Roll, temp. Ed. II.

ESTANTON.

Sir Symon de Montagu, quartile de argent e de azure; en les quarters de azure les griffons de or; en les quarters de argent les daunces de goules—*Ibid.*

Monsire de Bradston, argent, a une quarter de gules, une cinque foille d'or—Roll, temp. Ed. III.

Monsire Philip le Despencer, port barre d'or et d'asur de vi peeces, a une quarter d'ermin—*Ibid.*

Sable, fretty argent on a quarter gules a cross forming flory or—Henry Wakefield, Bp. of Worcester, 1375–95.

Argent, two chevrons and a quarter gules—Crielle, Kent.

Argent, on a quarter sable, three cronels in bend or—Hulson, co. York (granted 1571).

Argent, on a quarter gules, three lions of England in pale—The Royal Society, London (Inc. 1663).

As already pointed out, it seems in ancient arms to have been practically synonymous with the *Cauntel* or *Canton.*

Rafe Basset, pale dor et de goules a une cantel dargent a une croys de sable paté—Roll, temp. Hen. III.; Harl. MS. 6589.

Rauff de Bassett, d'or a trois peles de goulz, ung quartre de ermyne—Another Roll, temp. Hen. III.; Transcript in College of Arms.

Sire Rauf Basset, de or a iij peus de goules; e un quarter de ermyn—Roll, temp. Ed. II.

It may be observed, perhaps, that in modern English arms the *quarter* is comparatively rare, the *canton* having superseded it.

In the French arms, however, the term *franc-quartier* is frequently used, which appears to be neither so large as a *quarter* nor so small as a *canton*, but like the latter has its definite position in the *dexter chief*. The name *franc-canton* is synonymous with it. The term *quartier* by itself is seldom, if ever, employed except in connection with quarterly (fr. *ecartelé*).

D'or, à la croix ancrée de sinople; au franc-quartier de gueules—LA SABLE, Bourbonnais.

D'argent, fretté de gueules; au franc-canton d'azur—GRIMONARD, Poitou.

Whatever be the number of coats of arms comprized in one shield (see *Marshalling*) the term *quarter* may be used for them, though *quartering* is the more accurate term.

Quartered : is the more correct term to be used when an escutcheon is divided into four or more squares for the reception of *different* coats of arms; the term *quarterly* being generally used when the quarters belong to the same coat of arms, though the phrase 'France' and 'England' quarterly is often found.

Compare *impaling* as distinguished from *party per pale*.

DRAYTON-SEGRAVE.

Quartered : 1 and 4; azure, a bend between six cross crosslets fitchée or, DRAYTON; 2 and 3, ermine, two bars gules, in chief a demi-lion issuant of the last—SEGRAVE.

Quartered first and fourth or; a lion rampant azure [being the ancient arms of the Duke of BRABANT and LOUVAIN]; second and third azure five fusils joined in fesse [for PERCY]—PERCY, Earl of Northumberland, temp. HEN. IV.

Quarterly, (fr. *ecartelé*): when a coat of arms is divided into four parts, which is usually *party per cross* (rarely *per saltire*). The term *quarterly* is found in ancient rolls, and the

PERCY.

Quadrant. An example given under *Hercules*.

Quarter Staff. See *Staff*.

Quarrel, (fr. *quarreau*): the arrow used with the Cross-bow.

Quarter pierced. See *Cross*, § 5.

lines of partition are subject to many of the variations to which ordinaries are subject.

The divisions are numbered 1, 2, 3, 4, beginning at the dexter chief, and most frequently Nos. 1 and 4 are alike, as also Nos. 2 and 3; and when the quarter is charged its number must be always specified.

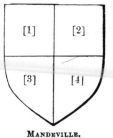

MANDEVILLE.

Le Conte de MANDEVILE, quartele d'or e de goulez—Roll, temp. HEN. III.

John de BERNERS, esquartile d'or et de vert ung labell de goules—*Ibid.*

Sire Fouk FIZ WARIN, quartale de argente de goules endente—Roll, temp. ED. II.

Monsire Foulk FITZ WARREN, quarterly endente per fes d'argent et gules—Roll, temp. ED. III.

Monsire le Conestable, Seigneur de FLAMBURGH, quarterly, gules et verre; une baston d'argent parmy le gules—*Ibid.*

Quarterly, per fesse indented azure and argent, in first quarter a lion passant gardant or —Herbert CROFT, Bishop of Hereford, 1662–91.

Quarterly, per fesse dancetté, or and azure— PEROT, Beds.

Quarterly, per fesse indented, argent and azure a bend gules—BLOMFIELD, Bp. of Chester, 1824; of London, 1828–56.

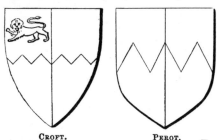

CROFT. PEROT.

Quarterly, per fesse dancetté, gules and or—BROMLEY, co. Salop.

Quarterly, per pale dovetailed, gules and or—BROMELEY, co. Cambridge.

Quarterly, embattled argent and sable—CAYLE, Cornwall.

Quarterly, wavy or and sable—SANDON, co. Lancaster.

Quarterly, per fesse wavy or and gules, a bend counterchanged— AUNCEY.

Quarterly, argent and sable; a pale and saltire ermine and ermines counterchanged—STUTVILE.

When there is a *bordure* the quarters should be within such bordure, but a quarter may contain a bordure. See under *Bordure*, examples of HUGH DE VERE and STAFFORD respectively.

Quarterly, or and gules, on a bordure engrailed sable eight escallops argent—HEVENINGHAM, Suffolk.

Quarterly; first and fourth gules, three cinquefoils, in fesse point a mullet argent; second gules, three cinquefoils argent, in fesse point a heart or; third gules, within a border argent, three doves close of the second—Walter Ker HAMILTON, Bp. of Salisbury, 1854.

HEVENINGHAM.   HAMILTON.

Quarterly, azure and argent, a cross or. In first and fourth quarters five mullets of the second; in second and third an eagle displayed sable.— Arms ascribed to Hubert WALTER, Abp. of Canterbury, 1193–1205.

Quarterly, ermine and azure, over all a cross or —OSBORNE, Earl of Danby, 1674; [also Duke of Leeds, 1794].

WALTER.   OSBORNE.

Ordinaries are sometimes made *quarterly*, e.g. a *chief* is found so, and in those cases suitable charges seem to be chosen for the compressed quarters. The *fesse* and *chevron* are rarely found quarterly: the *Cross* is more frequently so; and in some cases the four quarters of the shield may be of different tinctures as well, and the Cross is then blazoned *counterchanged*, (sometimes, but erroneously, *counterquartered*). See *Cross,* § 5.

Quarterly; first and fourth argent, a canton sable; second and third or, two bars azure, a chief quarterly of the last charged with two fleurs-de-lys or, and gules a lion of England—Charles Manners SUTTON, Bp. of Norwich, 1805; Abp. of Canterbury, 1828–48.

Barry nebulee of six argent and azure; a chief quarterly gules and or; on the first and fourth quarters a lion passant [gardant] of the fourth; on the second

MANNERS SUTTON.

and third two roses gules barbed vert—Company of MERCHANT ADVEN-
TURERS, London.

Argent, a fesse quarterly sable and or—
MACREERY, Dumpender, Scotland.

Argent, a fesse quarterly azure and or—
MAINHARD, Rooxston.

Vert, a chevron quarterly or and gules between three garbs gold; a balance or suspended
by a hand proper issuing from a chief wavy
argent and azure, charged with an anchor proper, fesswise, the stock to the sinister—Company of BROWN-BAKERS, London, Incorporated
1621.

MERCHANT ADVENTURERS.

Azure, a chevron quarterly gules and argent between three garbes or;
on a chief argent a S. Julian's Cross sable—Company of INNHOLDERS,
London [granted 1438, altered 1634].

Quarterly, argent and azure, a cross engrailed counterchanged—
HAYDON, Oxley, co. Hertford.

Quarterly, sable and argent, a cross counterchanged [awkwardly blazoned counterquartered of the field]—LORRAYNE, Bart., 1664.

The term *quarterly* is also sometimes used in connection with
the partition of the shield *per saltire* (fr. *ecartelé en sautoir*); but
it is not needed, *per saltire* being sufficient.

Per saltire, argent and azure—BANE; also PYPARD.

Per saltire, ermine and erminois, on a chief gules
a martlet between two roses or—GOLDRIND, Baronetcy, 1841.

Per saltire, argent and vert a pale counterchanged
—STABLES.

BANE.

Quarterly quartered, when applied to a *saltire* means *parted per cross* and *saltire*: but
the arms might, perhaps, with equal propriety be blazoned as a *saltire gyronny* of
eight. Another blazon is given of this
coat in the arms of Bp. MONTAGUE after
the Sees of BATH and WELLS were united,
viz., *per saltire* quartered. See *Saltire*.

Azure, a saltire quarterly quartered or and
argent [i.q gyronny of eight] or and azure—
See of WELLS [also united Sees of BATH AND WELLS].

See of WELLS.

Quatrefoil, (fr. *quartefeuille*): a charge the design of which may have been derived from some four-leaved flower, but more probably produced in the course of the ordinary workman's craft. It should be drawn *pierced*, unless described as *blind;* and when quatrefoils are *slipped*, the stalk should join the lower leaf. It is sometimes spelt *caterfoil*.

Though *quintefoils* are common in the ancient rolls, *quatrefoils* have not been observed. A *Double qua-*  *trefoil* is simply a *Huitfoil*. See *Foil*.

Gules, a quatrefoil or—ROE, Middlesex.

Azure, three quatrefoils slipped argent—HATCLIFFE, Hatcliffe, Lincoln.

Per pale argent and gules, a quatrefoil counterchanged—MULGRAVE.

Vert, three quatrefoils argent, each charged with a lion's head erased sable—PLOTT, Sparsholt, co. Berks.

Gyronny of eight argent and gules, on each a quatrefoil counterchanged—PORTAL.

ROE.

Quince: this fruit, drawn like a pear, is found blazoned according to Glover's Ordinary on one coat of arms.

Argent, a chevron between three quinces lying fessewise or [otherwise, pendent bendwise dexter or]—BONEFELD.

Questing (of a hound) represented as searching. See examples under *Dog*.

Queue, (fr.) : *Tail*.

Queue d'ermine : an ermine spot.

Queued : written also *cowed*, &c. (old fr. *cowe*) : used of lions and other animals whose tail is of a different tincture to the body, or placed in some other position than bending over the back. *Double queued* also is frequent. See *Lion*, also *Tail*.

Quill. See *Embroiderers' Quill*.

Quilled : 1. in describing a *feather* when the quill differs in colour from the rest. See *Plumes*. 2. Also applied to the *Porcupine*.

Quintaine, (fr.) : the Quintaine, i.e. the post, &c., against which the tilting took place, occurs only on one or two French coats of arms.

Quintefeuil. See *Cinquefoil* under *Foil*.

Quinysans, old fr. spelling for *Cygnisance*.

Quise, A la, or *A la cuisse* : said of the leg of an eagle or other bird (and sometimes of other living things) torn off at the thigh.

Quiver: in connection with *arrows* there are several examples of the *quiver* to be found.

Or, on a bend azure an annulet and two pheons conjoined in bend as the first; in chief a quiver full of arrows proper—COMRIE, Scotland.

Azure, on the sinister a bow erect, on the dexter a quiver erect holding three arrows or—MOLONY, Kiltanon.

Checky, argent and sable, on a chief or, three quivers gules, banded of the third, in each five arrows of the first—John COLDWELL, Bp. of Salisbury, 1591-96.

Rack: it is not clear what kind of *rack* is here intended to be represented *couped*. It appears to be a solitary instance, but perhaps some device badly drawn, e.g. a *gridiron*.

Argent, in base a rack couped sable; in chief two crosses crosslet fitchy gules—HOLDSWORTH.

Raguly, (fr. *noueux*): is a term properly applied to trunks of trees and the like, but occasionally to an ordinary, e.g. to a *Cross* (see § 2), having pieces like couped boughs projecting at the sides in a slanting direction, *ragguled* being an old word signifying chopped off.

Argent, a cross raguly gules—LAWRANCE, Gloucester.

Argent, on the trunk of a tree raguly vert an eagle with wings expanded gules—PORTER.

Argent, three trunks of trees raguled or, erect and inflamed proper—SUBSTON.

LAWRANCE.

Argent, two billets raguled and trunked placed saltirewise, the sinister surmounted of the dexter azure, their tops flaming proper—SHURSTABB.

Gules, a chevron raguly of two bastons couped at the top or—Christofer DROUNSFELD [*Ibid*, argent Christopher DRAIESFIELD, Harl. MS. 1386].

Argent, two bends raguly sable, the lower one couped at the top—WAGSTAFF, Derbyshire.

WAGSTAFF.

Argent, a fesse raguly and trunked between eight pellets—VYELL.

Gules, a bar or surmounted by a staff raguly argent—DRUITT.

Azure, three bars raguly humetty argent between as many estoiles or—TESHMAKER.

Rainbow, (fr. *arc en ciel*): is represented usually *in fesse,* but examples are very rare. The proper tinctures are gold, red, vert, and silver.

Argent, a rainbow, in fesse throughout proper—PONT, Scotland.

Azure, a rainbow in fesse proper, between two estoiles in chief, and the sun in base or—CLARET.

D'azur, à l'arc-en-ciel en bande; au soleil couchant d'or—DEYDÉ DE MURVIEL, Languedoc.

Rake, (fr. *rateau*): is drawn in the usual form of that used by haymakers.

Sable, two rakes (?) in pale argent—BROMLE.

Argent, on a bend sable three rakes of the first—BRAMBERT.

The *thatch-rake* or *thatcher's rake* is drawn as in the margin; but it is liable to be confused with the *wool-comb* and *thatch-hook*.

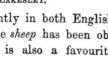

Thatcher's Rake.

Argent, three thatcher's rakes barwise sable—ZAKESLEY.

Ram, (fr. *belier*): this is found frequently in both English and French arms, while no example of the *sheep* has been observed in the former. The *Ram's head* is also a favourite device.

Argent, three rams passant sable—SYDENHAM, Brimpton, co. Somerset; Baronetcy, 28 July, 1641.

Azure, a chevron between six rams accosted countertrippant two, two and two argent attired or —HARMAN, Rendlesham.

Per fesse wavy azure and argent, in base on a mount vert a ram couchant sable armed and unguled or, in chief three doves proper—PUJOLAS, Middlesex; granted 1762.

On a woolpack a ram couchant argent—Crest of the town of BOSTON, Lincolnshire.

SYDENHAM.

Rabbit. See *Hare.*

Raccourcie, (fr.): *Recoursy.*

Radiant. See *Ray.*

Raft. See *Boat.*

Ragged. See *Raguly.*

Ragged Staff. See *Staff.*

Raisin. See *Vine.*

Ramé (or *chevillé,* fr.): of the horns of a stag when of a different tincture; also *ramure,* i.e. *Attire.*

Rampant, (old fr. *rampand,* &c.), of an animal, and especially of a *lion* = rearing. See examples under *Lion;* also *Bear, Tiger,* &c.

Per fesse sable and argent, a pale counterchanged, three rams salient
of the second two and one, armed and unguled or—
Glovers' Company [Arms granted 1464].

Argent, on a bend engrailed sable, three ram's
heads cabossed of the field attired or—Lampen,
Cornwall.

Argent, on a chevron gules three ram's heads
affronty of the field, attired or — Cirencester
Abbey.

Or, on a bend azure, three ram's heads couped
argent, attired of the first—Ramsey Monastery,
co. Huntingdon.

LAMPEN.

Rat, (fr. *rat*) : This rodent occurs only in one or two coats
of arms.

Paly of six or and gules, on a canton argent a rat salient sable—Trat,
Cornwall.

Argent, a fesse gules in chief a rat of the last—Bellet.

Ermine, a fesse engrailed between three rats (? weasels) passant gules
—John Islip, Abbot of Westminster.

Raven, (fr. *corbeau*): probably in heraldic drawing no difference would be detected in the drawing of the *raven*, the *rook*,
or the *crow;* and perhaps even the old names *Corbie, corby-
crow, corbyn, corf,* and the other variations of the Latin *corvus*
were not marked by any nice distinction. As will be seen,
the bearing occurs on several ancient arms for the sake of the
play upon the name. It may be blazoned as *croaking.* It will
be seen the *daw* also as well as the *rook* is adopted for the
same reason.

Thomas Corbet, d'or deux corbeaux noir—Roll, temp. Hen. III.

Sire Johan de Cormaxles de argent a iij corfs de sable—Roll, temp.
Ed. II.

Sire Peres Corbeht, de or a ij corbils de sable—*Ibid.*

Sire Peres Corbet, de or a un corbyn de sable—*Ibid.*

Random, at : used of dogs in a
chase. See example under *Deer.*

Rangé, (fr.) : arranged in a line.

Rangier, (fr.) : the blade of a
scythe.

Raphael. See under *Ararat.*

Rapier. See *Dagger.*

Rapin : said to mean devouring,
or feeding upon.

Rased, (old fr. *rasé*). See *Erased.*

Ratch-hound. See *Dog.*

Rateau, (fr.) : *Rake.*

Ravissant, (fr.): of a wolf with his
prey.

Sire Thomas CORBET, de or a iij corbyns de sable—Roll, temp. ED. II.

Per fesse or and argent, three ravens in chief proper— CORBYN.

Monsire Thomas de ROKEBY, port d'argent a une cheveron de sable entre trois corbins sable—Roll, temp. ED. III.

Or, a raven proper—CORBET, of Morton Corbet, Salop, and Richard CORBET, Bp. of Oxford, 1628; of Norwich, 1632–35.

Or, on a torteau a raven sable—RAVEN.

Argent, on a chief or, a raven proper—HURD, Bp. of Lichfield, 1774; of Worcester, 1781–1808.

Argent, a raven croaking proper—The ancient arms of HAMPDEN, Great Hampden, co. Buckingham.

Or, three ravens volant proper—WORCELEY, co. Hants.

CORBET.

Argent, in chief a lion passant azure, in base two ravens pendent from an arrow fesswise sable—MACKIE, Bargally, Scotland.

Or, a hog lying fesswise, a raven feeding on his back sable—DANSKINE, Scotland.

Argent, a fesse counterflory gules between three rooks sable—ROKES, co. Bedford.

Argent, a chevron between three rooks volant sable—CROWMER.

Argent, on a fesse gules between three crows proper as many crosses patty or—DEANE, Essex.

Argent, a crow sable between three fountains—CRAIGDAILLIE, Aberdeen.

Quarterly, first and fourth, argent, a saltier and chief, both engrailed gules; second and third, argent, two crows paleways, both transfixed through the neck by an arrow in fesse proper—Archibald Campbell TAIT, Bp. of London, 1856; Abp. of Canterbury, 1868–82.

Azure, a bend between three crow's heads erased argent—CASSIE.

Azure, on a bend engrailed argent three daws proper—DAWSON, Newcastle.

Argent, a chevron between three daw's heads erased sable beaked or— DALSTON, Westmoreland.

Ray: a ray of the sun is found in one or two cases in early rolls, and in each case is blazoned gules, but in later coats of arms rays are found only issuing from the clouds or round a *sun*, q.v. In the case of the *Badge* of RICHARD II. "The Sun behind a Cloud" is represented only by the *rays* being visible. When the rays issue from a charge they are generally

Badge of RICHARD II.

described by the term *radiated* being applied to that charge.

Rauf de la HAY, blank ung rey de soleil de goules—Roll, temp. HEN. III.

Sire Fraunceys de ALDAM, d'aszure a un ray de soleil d'or—Roll, temp. ED. II.

Azure, one ray of the sun issuing bendways from the dexter chief, proper [but blazoned otherwise a pile waved]—ALDAM.

ALDAM.

Radiant, or *rayonnant*, (fr. *rayonné*): is applied to ordinaries, as well as to charges such as the *Sun* and *Clouds*. The terms *radiated*, *irradiated*, *rayony*, or '*with rays*,' are also used, but all meaning the same thing.

Gules on a bend rayonated between two eagles displayed or three roses of the first—BODEN, Middlesex.

Azure, on a pale radiant or, a lion rampant gules—COLMAN, co. Suffolk.

[The same, but the field vert, and the lion sable—O'HARA, Ireland.]

COLMAN.

Azure, a pale rayony or—LIGHTFORD.

Argent, two chevrons sable, in chief a file of eight points of the last enclosed by a garter irradiated by sixteen rays of a star or; the garter azure bearing these words in gold letters, "Viditque Deus hanc lucem esse bonam"—[A quartering in the arms of] RUNDLE.

Gules, a chief argent, on the lower part thereof a cloud [otherwise a chief nebuly] with rays proceeding therefrom proper — LEESON, Earl of Miltown.

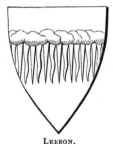

Rebus : defined by Dr. Johnson as "a word represented by a picture." It is not a true heraldic term, and ought not to be

LEESON.

applied to *canting* arms, but rather to those devices which are

---

Rayonnant: used of the sun, stars, &c., with *Rays*, q.v.

Razorbill. See *Auk*.

Rearing, (fr. *acculé*): said of a horse or stag standing upon his hind legs.

frequently found carved on buildings or painted in glass in reference to the name of the founders or benefactors. Such, for instance, are the following. Upon the Rector's lodgings at Lincoln College, Oxford, as well as on buildings at Wells, the rebus of a *beacon* and a *tun* is found in allusion to Thomas BECKYNTON, Bishop of Bath and Wells, 1443-65 : and on a gateway at Canterbury, erected in 1517, a *flint stone* (supposed to be *or*) ensigned with a mitre is carved in allusion to Thomas GOLD-STONE, the second Prior of Christ Church :

BECKYNTON.

while on a boss in the north transept of the Cathedral an eagle (for John) an *ox* and '**ne**' stand for John OXNEY.

In a window in the lady-chapel in Gloucester Cathedral a *comb* and a *tun* appear in allusion to Thomas COMPTON, Abbot of Cirencester, 1480; and in one of the windows in the chapel at Lullingston, Kent, the arms of Sir John PEECHE are encircled by the branches of a peach-tree bearing *peaches*, each one of which has the letter **e** on it.

Again in books, Richard GRAFTON, the printer, in 1547, puts as his rebus on the last page, a *tree* or *graft* rising from a *tun ;* and a copy of the " De Antiquitate Britannicæ Ecclesiæ," presented to Queen Elizabeth by the author, Matthew PARKER, Archbishop of Canterbury, has on the outside a *park* enclosed with pales embroidered on the green velvet binding.

Lastly, on seals a rebus very often appears, e.g. on that of Thomas WOODSTOCK, sixth son of Edward III., whose arms are engraved suspended from the *stock* of a *tree*.

Reaping-hook. See Sickle.

Rebated : having the points cut off, as a *mullet*, or a *sword rebated*. See under *Cross*, § 24, and *Fylfot*.

Rebatements : *Abatements*, i.q.

Rebent : bowed embowed, or flexed reflexed, like the letter S.

Reboundy : used only in heraldic treatises ; same as *re-vent*.

Recouped, (fr. *recoupé;* also *recourci*) used by earlier heralds, appears to be the same as *couped*.

Recoursy, (fr. *raccourci*) : same as *alaisé* applied to a cross. See under *Cross crosslet*, § 33.

Recercelé: a term which seems to have been inconsistently used by later writers from not understanding its original meaning. It occurs in ancient blazon, as will be seen, applied only to the *cross* and the *bordure*. In its application to the *cross* the early instances have already been given under *Cross*, § 32, and it will be found also referred to under § 6 and § 24.

In the Roll of Henry III.'s reign, in the College of Arms (from which most of the examples with that date quoted in the present work have been taken) the word does not occur at all. In a somewhat later roll, but still ascribed to Henry III.'s reign (viz. that of which a transcript is preserved in Harl. MS. 6589 and by Leland) two examples of the term occur, and both applied to the *cross* (see § 32). In the roll ascribed to Edward II.'s reign three examples occur of the term applied to the *cross;* two with the word *voided* added, and one without (see also § 32). When we come to the roll, temp. Edward III. there are some four or five examples of a *cross recercelée* (see § 32), and we find *recercelé* also for the first time applied to the *bordure,* and as will be seen, in the same arms in which the bordure in the previous reign had been blazoned as *indented:* possibly *recercilé* was used in these later instances to signify *engrailed,* with reference to the half circles which form that line of partition. In the following examples the varieties of the spelling in the roll have been adopted.

Monsire de ECHINGHAM, port d'asur, fret d'argent, a une border recersele d'or—Roll, temp. ED. III. [od la bordure endente de or—Roll, temp. ED. II.]

Monsire TALBOT, de gules, une lyon rampant d'or, une border recercele d'or—*Ibid.* [od la bordure endente de or—Roll, temp. ED. II.]

Monsire de GLOUCESTRE, argent, a trois lyonceux rampant gules, a une border cersele d'asure—*Ibid.* [od la bordure endente de azure—Roll, temp. ED. II.]

Monsire William RIDELL, port de gules, a une lyon rampant d'argent, a une border cersele d'argent—*Ibid.* [od la bordure endente de argent—Roll, temp. ED. II.]

Monsire de TETFORD, quarterly, d'argent et gules, a une border sercele sable—Roll, temp. ED. III.

Monsire Thomas WAKE de Blisworth, d'argent, a deux barres, et trois roundels de gules, a une border recersele de sable—*Ibid.*

Monsire Bartholomew de FANACOURT, port sable, a une crois patey d'argent, une border d'or recercele—*Ibid.*

Monsire Thomas de GREY, port de gules a une lyon rampant d'argent, a une border cersele d'or—*Ibid.*

[In the same roll also bordures are borne "*recersele*" by Walter de PERCENAY, William de PERCY, Rafe de LASCELES, Monsire de TETFORD, John de BAVENT, Monsire de ECHINGHAM, and Monsire de BILKEMORE.]

With respect to its application to the *Cross*, perhaps enough has been said to shew that the probabilities are it was a figure similar to, if not identical with, the *cross moline*, or the *fer-de-moulin*, but with the extremities perhaps more bent round, as shewn in the illustration of the banner of Bishop BECK of Durham, from the Carlaverock roll under *Cross*, § 24, and again from the brass where a dimidiated coat of the BEKE family is impaled with the arms of HARCOURT, q.v., under *Marshalling*. It may, however, be further added to this evidence that in Nicolas Charles' transcript of the Roll, from which the above are taken, (the original of which must be attributed to Edward III.'s reign,) one of the headings is "*Les Croisées Sercelées et Fer-de-mollyns.*" One figure at the side serves for both the terms thus employed, and it is drawn similarly to the *Cross anchory* given *ante*, under *Cross moline*, § 24.

English heraldic writers seem, however, to have made two words, *recercele* and *sarcelly*, and have implied that they are of different origin and meaning; but there is no agreement as to what those meanings were. The French heralds seem equally at fault. M. Bachelin-Deflorenne, in his "Science des Armoiries" (1880), gives under his list of terms as applied to the cross both *recerselé* and *resarcelée*, as two different words; in his Glossary he gives only one, spelt *resercelé*, which he defines thus :—

Terme de blason. Se dit des croix, bandes, fasces, etc., chargées d'un filet qui forme également fasce, bende, ou croix et dont l'émail est particulier.

Recrossed: (fr. *recroisetté*) : a cross recrossed is properly called a cross crosslet.

Recursant: said of an *eagle*, close, in trian aspect, the back to the spectator.

Recurvant : bowed embowed, that is, bent in the form of an S.

In M. de Grandmaison's "Dictionaire Héraldique, 1861," the two terms are defined thus :—

Recercelée. De la croix ancrée tournée en cerceaux, et de la queue des cochons et liévres.

Resercelée. Des croix qui en ont une autre conduite en filet d'autre email.

What is meant by these descriptions seems to be that while a cross with its ends turned over, or a tail of an animal twisted, might be blazoned *recercelée*, a cross charged with a filet of the same form being of another tincture would be blazoned *resercelée*.

As has been pointed out, the probabilities are that the term was derived from the metal-work on the shield added partly for strength and partly for ornament (in the same way as the *escarboucle*). Applied to a *bordure* this would, if voided is understood, mean thin bars of iron strengthening the shield, and if not so one thick bar, with the edges *engrailed* or possibly *invected*. But the word at this time had not become technical, or received any definite signification. It has been pointed out that in some of the examples given from the roll of Edward III.'s reign, in which a border *recersele* is used, the bearer's ancestor bore the same *indented*, but in the earlier blazon probably little distinction would be made between *indented, engrailed,* or *invected*. It will be noted also from the same series that the terms *recercele, cersele,* and *sercele* seem to be used indiscriminately.

The term is also found applied to the saltire in later times.

Argent, a saltire gules recerselly engrailed azure; a canton chequy erminois and of the last—GREGSON, co. Durham.

Reeds, (fr. *roseaux*) : reeds are represented in *bundles, sheaves* or *tufts,* and with them may be grouped *rushes* and *bulrushes.*

Red. See *Gules.*

Redorte, (fr.): a branch of a tree twisted into circles, either with or without leaves. Used only in foreign arms.

Reed. See *Weaver's Slea.*

Reel, Carpenter's. See under Carpenter's *Square.* See also *Turnstile.*

Reflected or *reflexed :* bent back, e.g. of a chain to a collar; a lion's *tail* is *reflected* over the back, but the term is seldom, if ever, needed.

Regardant or *reguardant:* looking back, e.g. of a *lion* (q.v.), or of any other animal; often combined with *passant.*

Argent, two bundles of reeds in fesse vert—JANSSEN, Wimbledon, Surrey; Baronetcy 1714; quartering second and third, per fesse or and azure a swan naiant proper, and fourth argent, one bundle of reeds vert.

Gules, a chevron engrailed between three reed sheaves argent— REDHAM.

Gules, three tufts of reeds vert—SYKES, late of Basildon, co. Berks.

Argent, on a chevron gules between three bundles of rushes vert, banded or a mullet of the last—SHAKERLEY, co. Derby (Temp HEN. VI.).

Argent, on a mount of bulrushes in base proper a bull passant sable, a chief pean billety or, with a canton of the last—SCOFF, co. Worcester.

Argent, on a mount with bulrushes proper stalked and leaved vert a bull passant gules—RIDLEY.

Regalia: a name given to the crown, orb, sceptre, &c. The blazon of Earl MANDEVILLE's arms, however, is perhaps erroneous.

Per pale or and gules; the regalia sable—MANDEVILLE, Earl of Essex, [according to Burke].

Reptiles: the reptiles are scarcely represented at all in ancient rolls of arms. Even the serpents are only referred to under the *Bisse's* head (see under *Serpent*). But in later times it will be found that *serpents* and *snakes* are not uncommon, as well as *adders, asps,* and *vipers*. As will be seen by the Synoptical Table, *frogs* and *toads, effets* and *newts,* and *lizards,* and the *cameleon* are found, but they are rare. While of the *tortoise, alligator,* and *crocodile* only solitary instances have been observed.

Rest: this is a puzzling device, but the more probable interpretation is that it represents a *spear* rest, though possibly in one or two cases a horn, from bad drawing, has been mistaken for it. The device is called by Leigh and others *Sufflue,* and

---

Reindeer. See *Deer.*

Remora: said by one writer (Henry Peacham, 1630) to be borne, but no example found.

Removed out of the usual place i.e. a fesse *removed* might be a fesse *enhanced*: in one case it appears as if it was used to signify the fesse was broken.

Rempli, (fr.): filled in with, e.g.

of ordinaries, &c., which have been voided and filled with another tincture.

Rencontre, (fr.). See *Gaboshed.*

Rènne, (fr.) : *reindeer.*

Renoué, (old fr.) : of a tail *nowed.*

Repassant. See *Passant.*

Replenished with: an odd expression = *Semé.*

Reremouse. See *Bat.*

by Guillim *Clarion*, though he hints that it may be a *rudder*. Gibbon proposes the term *Organ-rest*, but mentions a MS. wherein it is called *Claricimbal*, or *Clavecimbal*. Morgan terms it a *Clarendon*, obviously a mistake for Clarion. It is otherwise called a *Clavicord*. *Rest*, however, is the term generally used for the device.

BESSYNG.

Azure, three rests or—BESSYNG, Staffordshire.

Gules, a chevron ermine between three clarions or—HICKES.

Gules, three clarions [or rests] or—CARTERET, GRANVILLE.

Per saltire gules and vert, three clarions or—GREENFIELD.

Gules, a chevron argent between three organ-rests proper—MYLES, Dartford, Kent.

Or, a fesse bendy of eight, sable and argent between three rests gules —LINGARD.

Gules, a chevron argent between three rests or—Sir Thomas ARTHUR.

Rhinoceros: this animal has only been observed on one coat of arms.

Azure, on a fesse or between three rhinoceroses argent as many escallops gules—TAPPS-GERVIS, co. Hants, 1791.

[On a wreath a Rhinoceros statant is the Crest of APOTHECARIES' COMPANY, London.]

Riband or *Ribbon*. (1.) The term *Ribbon* is used by one or two heraldic writers for a diminutive of the *bend*, of which it is one-eighth in width; if *couped* at each end it would represent a *baton dexter*, but this does not occur.

Argent, a ribbon traverse sable—TRAVERS.

Or, a lion rampant gules surmounted by a ribbon [or bendlet] sable —ABERNETHY of that Ilk, co. Fife.

Reseau, (fr.): appears to be a net for ladies' hair, and appears on one or two coats of arms.

Resignant: concealed; applied to a lion's tail.

Retrait, (fr.): couped at one end only.

Respectant, or *Respecting each other*: used in describing two animals, or even birds and fishes (see *Dolphin*), borne face to face. Rampant beasts of prey so borne are more usually said to be *combatant*.

Azure, an eagle displayed or, a ribbon gules—GUERIET.

Argent, on a fesse humetty gules, three leopard's faces or, over all a ribbon sable—BRABANT.

(2.) The *Riband* in its usual sense is sometimes found mentioned in blazon, where a *medal* or the like is suspended by, or *arrows* and the like tied with, one.

Argent, three bars gules on a chief embattled of the last the representation of a castle with broken walls of the field; on a canton of the last a medal of Talavera or, suspended from a red ribbon with blue edges —FULLER.

Per fesse embattled azure and gules, in chief a lion passant argent, in base two faulchions in saltire blades of the third, hilts and pomels or, on a canton ermine a mural crown or, and suspended therefrom by a ribbon gules edged azure, the Corunna medal gold—DARLING.

Azure, a fesse dancetty in chief a bow bent in fesse and three arrows, two in saltire and one in pale, tied with a ribbon in base all or—BUDD, Willesley, co. Devon.

Ring: the most important bearing of this name is the *Gem-ring*, that is a finger-ring (fr. *bague*) set with a jewel, and this is sometimes described as *stoned*, *gemmed*, or *jewelled* of another tincture: sometimes the name of the gem is mentioned.

Gem-ring.

Gules, three rings (or annulets) or, gemmed azure (or enriched with sapphires proper)—EGLINGTOUN, Scotland.

Argent, in chief a gem-ring gules; out of a mount in base three trefoils vert—DORRIEN, co. Herts.

Per fesse gules and or, a pale counterchanged, three gem-rings of the second stoned azure—LAWDER.

Gules, three gem-rings argent stoned azure—MYCHILSTAN.

Azure, three fleurs-de-lis or, quarterly with gules three rings gold gemmed azure; over all a cross wavy or charged with a mullet between four crescents likewise azure—MONTGOMERY, co. Peebles, 1801.

Revers, le: the expression *Porte le revers* is often found in the ancient rolls of arms, when similar descriptions follow one another as to bearings but with *reversed* tinctures.

Reversed, (fr. *renversé*): i.q. *inverted*, q.v. as of a *chevron*, q.v.

See also arms of CANTILUPE under *Jessant*, &c. The coat of arms *reversed* = an *abatement*, q.v.

Revertant: bent and rebent.

Reynard, (fr. *renard*): used sometimes for fox.

Rigging. See *Ship*.

Ring-dove. See *Dove*.

Azure, a dove proper on a chief ermine three annulets or, each enriched with a ruby—Bevan, Carmarthen.

Rings of other kinds are incidentally mentioned, but they are more properly termed *Annulets*, q.v. An *anchor* also should be represented with its *ring* and *grappling-irons*, q.v. ; and the *rings* of *keys* are also sometimes named, but usually termed *bows.* See also ring of Mars under *Letters.*

Barry of six argent and azure, over all an anchor with two cables fixed to the ring noded and pendent or—Allen, London.

Robe : this is seldom borne singly. A king is found in his *robes;* the Merchant Taylors bear two *Parliament Robes,* which are faced with *ermine.* This is sometimes blazoned as a *mantle.*

Or, on a fesse between three doves azure, a robe between two garbs of the first—Fulmerston, Norfolk.

Argent, a royal tent between two parliament robes gules lined ermine, the tent garnished or, tent staff and pennon of the last, on a chief azure a lion passant gardant or—Company of Merchant Taylors [Inc. 1466].

A mantle or parliament robe of estate azure lined ermine, the collar tied with a string and tassel attached or—Town of Brecknock.

Parliament Robe.

Argent, on a cross gules a bezant; thereon a demi-king in his robes all proper ; in the dexter quarter a key in pale of the second—Priory of S. Mary de Mendham, Yorkshire.

Rock, (fr. *rocher*): is generally borne *proper,* and issuing from the base of the shield: it only occurs in comparatively late coats of arms, and is chiefly found in Scotch examples. It must not be confused with the *roe* or chess rook which occurs in the older arms.

Ringed. See *Annuletty.*

Rimmed : a collar may be thus blazoned, having an edging of another tincture.

Rising; of a bird. See under *Wings.*

River. See *Water.*

Rizom. See *Wheat.*

Roach. See *Chubb.*

Robin Redbreast. See *Wren.*

Roc or Rok. See *Chess Rook.*

Roe-buck. See *Deer.*

Roel, i.q. *rowell,* q.v.

Roll. See *Wreath,* also of *Matches.*

Rompu : broken. Said of a *Chevron,* q.v.

Argent, a castle triple towered and embattled sable, masoned of the first and topped with three fanes gules, windows and portcullis shut of the last situated on a rock proper—Burgh of EDINBURGH.

Argent, a fesse gules between three rocks sable—SWANTON.

Argent, on a bend sable three rocks of the field—BONERY.

Azure, a sea in base, in it a rock proper, on which stands a lion rampant argent gorged with an open crown or—M'DOWALL, Scotland, 1604.

Per fesse wavy argent and sable; in base three fleurs-de-lis argent; in chief the Rock of Gibraltar surrounded by fortifications and the sea proper; on a canton gules a sword erect proper, hilt and pomel or, entwined with a palm branch—CURTIS, co. Hants. [Baronetcy 1794.]

Rolls of parchment occur in one coat of arms.

Gules, three rolls of parchment proper—CAVEL or LOCAVEL.

Rosary: the chain of *beads* so called seems to occur but in two coats of arms. See BEADNELL under *Garter*.

Vert, eleven round beads in chevron, surmounted in the centre by a cross; pendent to the two end beads a tassel, all or, between three cinque-foils argent—WIMBUSH.

Rose, (fr. *rose*): this flower is very frequently employed in coats of arms, and more frequently still in badges. In the very ancient rolls, however, it is chiefly borne by branches of the one family of the D'ARCYS. The flower is not to be drawn with a *stalk* unless blazoned *stalked*, or *slipped*. The *heraldic rose* should consist of five foils as drawn in the example; though examples are to be found with six foils, and perhaps with four. The word proper applied to the *barbs* (or five leaves of the calyx) and central seeds, implies that the former are green, and the latter gold or yellow. A rose is the *difference* of the seventh house. Sometimes roses are arranged in a *chaplet*, q.v. and they are sometimes *crowned*.

Ermine, a rose gules, barbed and seeded proper—BEVERLEY, Yorkshire.

Phelip DARCY, d'argent a trois roses de goules —Roll, temp. HEN. III.

Sire Robert DARCY, de argent a iij roses de goules od la bordure endente de sable—Roll, temp. ED. II.

Sire Johan DARCY, de argent a un escuchon de sable od les rosettes de goules assis en la manere de bordure—*Ibid.*

BEVERLEY.

Sire Felyp DARCI, de argent a iij roses de goules—Roll, temp. ED. II.

Sire William de COSINGTONE, de azure a iij roses de or—*Ibid.*

Monsire de ROSTLES, gules vi roses argent—Roll, temp. ED. III.

Argent, on a bend azure three roses of the first —CAREY, co. Oxford.

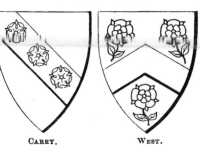

CAREY. WEST.

Or, a stag trippant azure on a chief of the last three roses argent — FRUID, Scotland.

Argent, a cross engrailed gules between four mullets azure, on a chief or three damask roses of the second seeded gold barbed vert—ALLGOOD, Nunwick, Northumberland.

Argent, a chevron sable between three roses gules slipped vert—Nicholas WEST, Bp of Ely, 1515-33.

Argent, on a fesse vert between three damask roses barbed and seeded proper four ermine spots of the field—WILLAUME, Tingrave, co. Bedford; granted 1767.

Argent, on a mount vert three heraldic roses gules stalked and leaved proper—Dr. PEARCE, Dean of Ely.

A *double rose* also occurs, that is one within another, and they are thus conjoined, either by placing a white rose upon a red one, or a red one upon a white. The term *rosette* is employed in one case where there are several.

Azure, a saltire argent charged in the centre with a double rose gules —OPPIN, Saxony.

Argent, a cross gules; in the dexter canton a dagger [probably meant for the sword of S. Paul] of the second; on a chief azure a double rose red and white barbed vert between two fleurs-de-lis or—CHRIST'S HOSPITAL, London.

Symon FRESEL, de cele gent   Le ot noire à rosettes de argent.
                                                           Roll of Carlaverock.

It will be seen also that *rose branches, slips,* and *leaves* are occasionally borne separately; and one early instance has been bserved in which the phrase ' 3 *rosers* ' occurs.

Argent, two bars azure, over all a lion rampant or, holding in the dexter paw a rose branch gules—TUDMAN.

Argent, on a mount vert three rose sprigs, the roses gules, the leaves and stalks proper—ROSECREEG, Cornwall.

Argent, a rose and thistle conjoined paleways proper—Ashton.

Or, a rose leaf in bend sinister vert—Bendlise.

Gules, a chevron argent between three rose leaves of the second (another, or)—Sir John Rose.

Le Counte de Rampsuile dor a treis rosers; sur chekune roser une rose; chekune roser verte—Roll, temp. Hen. III. (In another copy, possibly of the same original Roll, "Le Countee de Rummesville, dor trois roses [c]harges ove 3 roses vert.")

The use of the *Rose* as a political emblem may be traced to the wars between the rival Houses of York and Lancaster, the former of which used the device of a white rose, while a red one was the *badge* of the other, and these came to be blazoned

The Rose of Lancaster.   The Rose of York.   The Tudor Rose.

occasionally as the *Rose of* York and Lancaster respectively. They are said to have been first assumed by John of Gaunt, Duke of Lancaster, and his brother Edmund, Duke of York. Both these roses were sometimes surrounded with rays, and termed *en soleil*, and later on they were frequently *conjoined*.

A red rose en soleil—Badge of Lancaster.

A white rose en soleil—Ditto of York.

Red and white rose quarterly—Ditto of House of Tudor.

One of the badges of Katherine of Arragon (see also under *Pomegranate*) contains the Rose, and one of Katherine Parr also, but in both cases treated singularly, as shewn in the margin.

A pomegranate burst open conjoined with a red and white rose one within the other — Badge of Katherine of Arragon.

Badge of Katherine of Arragon.

Badge of Katherine Parr.

A maiden royally crowned proper, crined and vested or, conjoined to a part of a triple rose red, white, and red—Badge of Katherine PARR.

Again later on, Queen MARY adopted a badge in which the Rose figures, but later still the Rose appears amongst the badges of the *Stuarts*, and then it is crowned.

A dexter half of a double rose, gules and argent, barbed and seeded proper, impaled with a semicircle per pale vert and azure, therein a sheaf of arrows or, armed and fea-

Badge of QUEEN MARY.　　Badge of CHARLES I.

thered of the second, and tied together with a tasselled cord, forming a knot of the first; the whole rayonnant, and ensigned with a royal crown without arches proper—Badge of Queen MARY.

The two roses united one within the other royally crowned—Badge of the House of STUART.

Roundles, (old fr. *rondels, rondeus,* &c.) : this is a general name given to the circles borne on shields, and to which specific names are given according to their tinctures.　There seems to have been, however, in the earlier times an indifference to employing the same term to the same tinctures, as will be seen by the examples given :—

The *roundel or.*　In the rolls of Henry III.'s reign, though bezanté occurs three or four times, no case is observed of the "bezant."　In Edward II. we have *bezans d'or,* in the poem of the Siege of Carlaverok, and in Edward III.'s reign, *besant* (the *d'or* being understood).　In Edward II. and III. *rondels d'or,* in "Carlaverok" *gasteaus d'or,* and in Edward III. *pelots d'or.*

The *roundle argent.*　In Henry III.'s reign *torteux d'argent* and *gastelles d'argent;* Edward II. and Edward III.'s reigns *pelotes d'argent;* and in Edward II.'s reign *rondels d'argent.*

The *roundle gules.*　In Henry III.'s reign we have *torteux de gules,* and throughout Edward II. and Edward III. *rondels*

Ronant, (fr.) : of a peacock with its tail spreading.

Rondel, i.q. *roundle.*
Rondeus.　See *Roundles.*

de gules. In one case we meet with *pelletts de gules*, and in Carlaverock "*rouges rondeaux.*"

The roundles of *sable* or *azure* are rare, we find *rondels d'azure* and *pellets d'azure*, and also *peletts* de sable. No other roundles appear named in the early rolls. Several examples of the device will be found given under *hurts*, *pellets*, *plates*, and *torteaux*, and a few others are here added to illustrate the variety.

Sire Amori de SEINT AMAUNT, de or frette de sable; od le chef de sable a iij rondeus de or—Roll, temp. ED. II.

Ele Amauri de SAINT AMANT   O trois gasteaus de or derechief
... De or e de noir fretté; au chief   Roll of Carlaverok, c. 1300.

Monsire de ST. AMOND, port d'or frette de sable; une cheif de sable, trois rondeus d'or—Roll, temp. ED. III.

Sire Robert de ESTAFFORD, de or a un cheveron de goules e iij besanz de or—Roll, temp. ED. II.

Monsire LA ZOUCH, gules une bend d'argent entre vj besants—Roll, temp. ED. III.

Roger de HUNTINGFEILD, d'or a la fesse de goules et trois torteux d'argent e la fesse—Roll, temp. HEN. III.

Sire William de HONTYNGFELD, de or e une fesse de goules a iij rondels e argent—Roll, temp. ED. II. [See *Ibid.* ED. III. under *pellets.*]

Hugh WAKE, d'or a deulx barres de goules ove trois torteux de goules en le cheif—Roll, temp. HEN. III.

Del bon Hue de Courtenay   De or fin o trois rouges rondeaus
La baniere oubliée ne ay   E azurins fu li labeaus.

Roll of Carlaverok, c. 1300.

Sire Hue de COURTENAY, de or a iij rondeux de goules e un label de azure—Roll, temp. ED. II.

Sire Felip FITZ ERNYS, de argent a iij rondes de goules.

Sire Richard de BASCREVILE, de argent a un Cheveron de goules e iij rondels de azure—Roll, temp. ED. II.

COURTENAY.

The modern English rules, however, limit the several names to the several tinctures,—

Or called always *Bezants.*		Vert called always *Pomeis.*	
Argent ,, ,, *Plates.*		Purpure ,, ,, *Golpes.*	
Gules ,, ,, *Torteaux.*		Sable ,, either *Pellets,*	
Azure ,, ,, *Hurts.*		*Ogresses* or *Gunstones.*	

Under most of these terms many examples will be found. There are also roundles of the rarer tinctures, viz. *sanguine* and *tenné*, which have been named by later heralds respectively *guzes* and *oranges*.

The French use as a rule only the term *besants* for the two metals, and *tourteaux* for all else, but the latter is applied sometimes to metals also. The terms *heurtes, gulpes, volets* (for *pomeis*), *ogresses,* and *guzes* seem also to be used.

D'azur a trois tourteaux d'argent au chef de gueules—CARBONEL, Normandie.

D'or a trois chevrons de sable accompagnés de trois tourteaux de sinople—DESCHAMPS.

De gueules, coupé d'azur a trois tourteaux a hermine—CANISY.

The result is that the term *roundle* (written sometimes *rundle* and *ronde*) is retained only for cases where the circle is party-coloured, or *charged* with an ordinary or other charge. It may be *ermine*, or *vair*, or it may be *barry-wavy* (and if argent and azure it is then termed a *fountain*, q.v.). A case may occur also where the field being of more than one tincture and the roundles *counterchanged*, that term is used for convenience to cover the whole series, though one might be a *bezant* and another a *torteau*. The old *rondel* or *rondelet voided* is a term found applied to a figure like an *annulet*, and perhaps its equivalent.

Sable, three roundles quarterly argent and gules [otherwise gyronny of eight argent and gules, otherwise gyronny argent and azure]—DERWARD.

Argent, three pellets, on each a bend of the field—BENEVILLE, Devon.

Argent, three pomeis, on each two bendlets wavy of the field—MILTON.

Argent, three roundles cheveronny of six gules and azure—CARRANT [Sheriff of Dorset. sub Hen. VI.]

Argent, three ogresses, on the first a cross flory of the field—HEATHE.

Per pale gules and azure, three plates, each charged with a cross engrailed vert between four ermine spots sable—HEATHCOTE.

Azure, three plates, each charged with a squirrel gules, cracking a nut or—CRESWELL, co. Northampton. [Confirmed to Robert Cresswell 31 Elizabeth.]

Rook. See *Raven,* also *Chess-rook.*

Rope-hook. See *Hook.*

Roue, (fr.): *Wheel.*

Rouge. See *Gules.*

Rouge Croix and Rouge Dragon, Pursuivants. See *Herald.*

Azure, a roundle chequy or and azure between three boar's heads couped of the second—GORDON, Scotland.

Gules, three roundles vair, on a chief or a lion passant sable—PARTRICK.

Three roundles barry wavy of six argent and vert—THEMILTON.

Per bend or and azure, three roundles in pale counterchanged—BAYNES, London.

Per fesse argent and gules three roundles counterchanged—BEAUFORD.

Sire John de PLESSIS d'argent ove six faux rondeletts de goules—Roll, temp. HEN. III.

Sire Robert BORGYLOUN, quartele de or e de goules, a une bende de sable; en les quarters de goules rondels perces de argent—Roll, temp. ED. II.

The French *besant-tourteau* (or tourteau-besant) is used when the roundle is partly metal and partly colour.

D'azur, à l'étoile à huit rais d'or chargée d'un besant-tourteau, écartelé en sautoir d'argent et de gueules—BONVISY.

There is no limit to the number of roundles in a shield; a single one is frequently found, and every number up to 13. Also 15 and 18 are found.

Barry of six, or and gules, thirteen roundles counterchanged, three, two, three, two, and three—CAUNTER.

Argent, eighteen hurts, nine, four, three, and two—HUNTING.

Rowel *of a spur* (fr. *molette*). As already pointed out under *Mullet*, in the ancient rolls the word *rowel* seems to be identical with it, and that again to be interchangeable with *estoile*. In taking the five rolls of arms which have been chiefly made use of in exhibiting the ancient examples, namely, (*a*) the Roll of Henry III. in the Royal College of Arms, (*b*) that preserved in a copy by Leland and similar to that in the Harleian Collection, (*c*) the Roll of the siege of Carlaverock, and (*d*) the Rolls of Edw. II., and (*e*) of Edw. III., the number of instances of the use of the three terms are as follows:—

	Rowel.	Estoile.	Mullet.
Henry III. (R. C. A.)	—	1	4
Henry III. (Harl. or Leland)	5	—	2
Carlaverock	—	2	5
Edw. II.	9	—	51
Edw. III.	—	1	32
	14	4	94

As the rolls represent the chief families, many names being repeated in two or three of the rolls, the unequal distribution points to the somewhat arbitrary use of the three terms, though, as will be observed, the term *mullet* is not only the most frequently used, but is the only term common to all five rolls. The examples also shew that the terms *mullet* and *rowel* seem to be used indiscriminately in respect of the same families. There does not seem to be sufficient evidence that the difference in the terms used is at all due to the fact of the charge being pierced or not (see under *Mullet pierced*), though the ancient *rowel* probably was always so represented. See *Spur-rowel*.

Gauter BERTANT, pale dor et de goules a une cauntel dazur a une rouel dargent—Roll, temp. HEN. III.

Sire Johan de ASCHEBORNHAM, de goules, a une fesse e 6 rouwels de argent—Roll, temp. ED. II.

John de SEIN JOHN, dargent a chef de goules a deux roueles dor un vers chef—Roll, temp. HEN. III.

Sire Johan de SEIN JOHAN, de argent od le chef de goules a ij moles de or—Roll, temp. ED. II.

Li preus Johans de SAINT JOHAN . .
Ki sur touz ses guarnemens blancs
Et chief rouge ot de or deus molectes.

Roll of Carlaverock.

Argent, on a chief gules, two mullets of eleven points or, pierced vert—John de SAINT JOHN [glass at Dorchester, Oxfordshire].

John de PLESCY, dargent a treis molettes de goules perces—Another Roll, temp. HEN. III.

Sire Hue de PLECY, de argent a vj rouwels de goules—Roll, temp. ED. II.

Sire Huge de CULY, de argent a un cheveron e iij rouwels de goules—*Ibid.*

SAINT JOHN.

Monsire Hugh de CUILLY, port dargent, a une cheveron de sable entre trois mulletts de sable—Roll, temp ED. III.

Sire Johan de CRETINGE, de argent, a un cheveron e iij rouwels de goules—Roll, temp. ED. II.

Rouke: *old* fr. for Chess-rook.

Rounded, (fr. *arrondie*), e.g. of a *Mirror.*

Rousant. See *rising* under *Wings.*

Rouvre, (fr.) : a knotted oak.

Rowan tree. See *Ash.*

Ruby. See *Gules.*

Ruche, (fr.) : Beehive.

Monsire de CRETINGE [port d'argent a une cheveron de gules] a trois mullets gules percées—Roll, temp. ED. III. [*Ibid.* in the Roll of Carlaverock].

The modern term '*spur-rowel*' is occasionally employed.

Argent, two spur-rowels in chief pierced of the field, and a spear's head in base azure—AUCHMUTY.

The term *roelé* in the arms of Rauf de GORGES has been thought to mean a whirlpool (see *Gurges*), but by a roll temp. ED. II. it would appear the family bore *mascles*.

Royal Exchange: this is given as an example of the extent to which a departure from the simplicity of ancient heraldry has been carried.

Azure, on a mount vert the Royal Exchange proper adorned and embellished or, in chief two ships, the dexter under sail, hulk of the last, mast, sail and rigging as the third, the sinister ship riding at anchor sails furled blazoned like the dexter all proper—ROYAL EXCHANGE ASSURANCE COMPANY.

Rudder: this device occurs but in few arms. The usual position seems to be with the hooks to the dexter, but they are sometimes drawn turned the other way, and should be so noticed in the blazon. Guillim suggests that the *rest* (q.v.) was intended for a rudder.

Rudder.

Vert, the rudder of a ship argent on a chief of the last three buckles azure—SCOLLAY, Scotland.

Azure, on a bend argent between two estoiles of six points or three rudders sable—PUTLAND, Ireland.

Azure, three dolphins naiant embowed argent, on a chief or, three rudders sable—BURRIDGE, co. Devon.

Azure, a lion rampant argent supporting a rudder or, on a chief of the second an anchor sable between two 3-foils proper—HENLEY, Waterperry, co. Oxford.

Ruins: this singular device is rare in English arms. In French heraldry the word "*masure*" is used to signify in ruins, and the device is more frequent. *Decouverte* also is used of a building with its roof destroyed.

Ruffled: said of *hands* having ruffs, or ruffled on the wrists.

Rundles. See *Roundles*.

Rushes. See *Reeds*.

Russet, a *colour* used of a *Parrot*.

Rye. See *Wheat*.

Or, a lion rampant couped in all the joints of the first within a bordure embattled gules— MAITLAND, Dundrennan, co. Kircudbright, quartering argent the ruins of an old abbey on a piece of ground proper.

Rustre, or *Mascle round-pierced:* a lozenge with a circular perforation. Certain ancient armour composed of links of this shape sewed upon cloth is thought to have supplied the origin of the charge. It is, however, very rarely found.

Rustre.

Or, a rustre sable—CUSTANCE.
Or, three rustres sable—PERY, Ireland.
Argent, a fesse between three rustres sable—PARRY, Ireland.

Sable, (fr. *sable*): the heraldic term for black, the term being probably derived from certain animals with black feet called *Sabellinæ* (*mustela zibellina* of Linnæus). It is called *Saturn* by those who fancifully blazon by the planets, and *Diamond* by those who use the names of jewels. Engravers represent it by numerous perpendicular and horizontal lines crossing each other.

Sable.

Arms simply sable are found to have been borne by the following families:—GOURNEY (a Norfolk family); DOMBALE; GLEGG; and LORRAINE.

Sabre: there are several kinds of swords with broad curved blades; and first of all the *Sabre* (fr.), which is usually represented as in the margin.

Or, a lion rampant sable holding in his dexter paw a sabre or crooked sword proper, all within a double tressure flory counterflory of the second—MAC CAUSLAND, Strabane, Ireland.

Gules, a fesse cotised or, over all two sabres addorsed saltireways azure hilt and pomel of the second—AGALL.

Sabre.

S stands in *tricking* and heraldic notes and sketches for *sable*.
SSS, Collar of. See *Collar*.
Sackbut. See under *Pipe*.

Sacre, or *Saker :* said to be a kind of falcon with grey head, dark brown back, and light blue legs, but no example given.

So similar are the *Falchion*, called also the *Hanger*, and the *Scimetar* (the latter sometimes represented with the back engrailed) that practically no difference can be made in the drawing, except that the falchion should have a blade somewhat wider in the middle. The *Cutlass* is also found.

Or, a lion rampant double tailed and ducally crowned, brandishing in the dexter paw a falchion all gules— PAUL, Middlesex; granted 1758.

Falchion. Scimetar (engrailed).

Azure, a falchion in pale argent hilt gules—TATNELL, co. Chester.

Gules, three hangers or falchions barwise in pale the points toward the sinister part of the shield argent, hilts and pomels or—HUDGSON, Boston, co. Lincoln.

Azure, three scimetars in pale argent hilts and pomels or, the points to the sinister—HODGSON, Tooting and Buckland, Surrey.

Ermine, on a chief gules three cutlasses erect argent hilts or—HODGSON, Framfield, Sussex; granted 1628.

Or, three bars wavy gules with a scimetar in pale argent, hilt and pomel of the field—DRUMMOND.

Argent, a cutlass in bend sable—ELAM, Kent.

Gules, three cutlasses in pale barry argent [?] neufes or—TROSS, co. Devon.

A French term *Badelaire* is found sometimes used; it seems to be similar to the *sabre*.

De gueules, à trois badelaires d'argent rangés en pal— DU BOIS, Bretagne.

Seax, (Anglo-Saxon *Seax*, Icelandic *Sax*), is also another term used, and signifies a broad curved sword with a semicircular notch at the back of the blade.

Gules, three seaxes barwise proper, hilts and pomels or [handles to the dexter and edges of blades uppermost] —County of MIDDLESEX.

Argent, a lion rampant sable; on a chief gules two seaxes in saltire of the first, tilts and pomels or—GOMME [Middlesex, 1761]

Seax.

Sagittarius. See under *Satyr*.

Sail. See under *Ship;* also under *Windmill.*

Saker = Sacre.

Salamander. See *Phœnix.*

Salix. See *Willow.*

Saddle, (fr. *selle*), is at times found represented separately in heraldry as well as in connection with horses which have saddles (fr. *sellé*), bridles (q.v.), &c. It is represented as in the margin.

Azure, a chevron between three saddles with stirrups [otherwise three manage saddles complete] or—COMPANY of SADDLERS, London.

Argent, three saddles sable—HARVEY, Norfolk.

Saddle complete.

Gules, a horse armed or, bridled and saddled of the first, with a plume on his head, and trappings, and on his shoulder a cinquefoil of the last : on his hip an escutcheon charged with a cross all between three garbs of the second—MALT.

Le roy de Norwey de goules a un cheval dor selle — Roll, temp. HEN. III.

The *Pack-saddle* is a saddle employed for the conveyance of burthens, and may be represented as in the margin, and certainly without stirrups.

Azure, three pack-saddles or—HERVEY, Tiddington, Oxon.

Pack-saddle.

Saints : the figures of Saints and martyrs are scarcely suitable for heraldic bearings : still in the later middle ages, in connection with certain northern Sees and Burghs, Saints are introduced, though perhaps rather as seal-devices than as true coats of arms. A figure of *S. Andrew* appears as in the Insignia of S. ANDREW's : of *S. Boniface* in those of the See of Ross : of *S. Bryce* on the seal of the Burgh of KIRKALDIE : of *S. Edmund* in the Insignia of the Bishopric of the ISLES : *S. Giles* in those of the See of MORAY ; *S. Magnus* in those of the See of ORKNEY : *S. Margaret of Scotland* in those of the Burgh of QUEENSFERRY : *S. Michael* in those of the See of ABERDEEN, as well as of the Burghs of LINLITHGOW and of DUNDEE : and *S. Ninian* in those of the See of GALLOWAY.

In the blazon of the Insignia of the Irish Bishoprick of CASHEL, EMLY, &c., simply a *Saint* is mentioned, but no name ; the same also occurs in those of the Burgh of BRECHIN.

It will be seen that the figures of Saints are variously placed and habited; moreover, the blazon varies considerably, each writer adopting his own method of description, for practically they are without the pale of ordinary heraldry.

The list here given might be, perhaps, somewhat enlarged, but it is sufficient to shew the way in which Saints are introduced. See also the example of *S. Nicholas* under *Bishop*, (generally, but erroneously, blazoned as *S. Michael*), the Blessed *Virgin Mary*, &c. Besides these the emblems are often mentioned, e.g. the *Cross of S. George*, the Cross or Standard of *S. Andrew* (i.e. the *saltire*), the knives of *S. Bartholomew*, the wheel of *S. Katherine*, the scourges of *S. Guthlac*, &c., &c.

Azure, the Apostle S. Andrew proper surrounded with a radiation or, vested of the field, tied to his cross, argent; in base a boar of the last tied to a tree of the second—Burgh of S. ANDREW'S, Scotland.

Argent, S. Boniface on the dexter habited gules his hand across his breast proper; on the sinister a bishop vested in long robe close girt purpure, mitred and in his sinister hand a crosier or—See of Ross, Scotland.

The figure of S. Bryce vested in long garments with a mitre on his head, all proper standing in the porch of a church argent, which is ensigned on the top with a cross pattee of the third; his dexter hand holds a fleur-de-lys or, and the sinister hand is laid upon his breast; the whole between a decrescent and a star in fesse of the last—Seal of the Royal Burgh of KIRKALDIE, Scotland.

Azure, S. Columba in a boat on waves of the sea all proper; in chief a blazing star or [otherwise dexter chief a star gold]—Bishopric of THE ISLES, Scotland.

Azure, a church argent, S. Giles standing in the porch in a pastoral habit proper mitred and in his dexter hand holding a passion cross, the sinister hand holding a book proper—See of MORAY.

Argent, S. Magnus vested in royal robes, on his head an antique crown in his dexter hand a sceptre, all proper—See of ORKNEY, Scotland.

Argent, in the sea azure a galley, her sails furled sable; in the middle thereof S. Margaret, Queen of Scotland, standing richly apparelled, in the dexter hand a sceptre ensigned with a fleur-de-lis or, in the sinister which is plain on her breast a book folded purpure—Burgh of QUEENS-FERRY, Scotland.

Argent, the Archangel Michael proper vested in a long garment azure; in the dexter hand a crosier or, on the head a mitre, and below his feet a serpent nowed, both proper—Burgh of DUNDEE.

Azure, S. Michael with wings expanded, treading on the belly of a serpent in base lying fessways with its tail nowed, all argent, with a spear in his dexter hand piercing the serpent's head proper and holding in the sinister an inescutcheon charged with the royal arms of Scotland —Burgh of LINLITHGOW, Scotland.

Argent, S. Ninian clothed in a pontifical robe purple, on his head a mitre and in the dexter hand a crosier, both or, the sinister hand across the breast—See of GALLOWAY, Scotland.

Per fesse gules and azure, in base a Cross Calvary supported by a Saint on steps proper ; in chief two keys saltirewise or—Bishopric of CASHEL, EMLY, WATERFORD, and LISMORE.

Salient, (fr. *saillant*): usually applied to a wild beast when borne as if leaping at his prey. Sometimes also to a *goat*, (q.v.), instead of *clymant*, and to a *dog, cat,* &c.

Salient appears to have been originally only an accidental variation from *rampant*, but custom has sanctioned this term being used, in contradiction to the other, where both the hind paws are resting on the ground, and both the fore-paws are drawn as if level with each other.

Counter-salient is used to signify leap-ing in contrary directions, that facing the *sinister* usually being uppermost. See *Rampant* under LION.

Argent, a lion salient gules—PETIT, Cornwall.
Vert, three bulls salient argent—Rowland LEE, Bp. of Lichfield and Coventry, 1534–43.
Azure, a cat salient argent—BLAIR.
Argent, a greyhound salient party per long sable and of the first—DE LA FORDE, Iver, co. Bucks.

PETIT.

Argent, a bear salient sable ; a canton gules—John BEERE, Kent, 1586.
Argent, two foxes counter salient in saltire gules, the dexter sur-mounted by the sinister—WILLIAMS, Anglesey.

Salmon, (fr. *saumon*): this fish is frequently blazoned in heraldry, though no very definite drawing has been noted. It is very frequently used for the sake of the play upon the name ; sometimes by towns, perhaps, such as Kingston-on-Thames,

---

Saltant, (fr.): a term sometimes applied to small animals spring-ing forward, instead of *rampant*,

e.g. of a *goat*, or *ram ;* perhaps not to be distinguished from salient.

Peebles on the Tweed, Lanark on the Clyde, in consequence
of salmon being plentiful near them; and by families in consequence of the fish thriving on their estates.　Mr. Moule, in his
work on the heraldry of fish, has collected many stories ac-
counting for the device.　That on the insignia of the town of
Glasgow is supposed to be in allusion to a remark of S. Kentigern the first bishop.

Sable, three salmon hauriant argent — John
SALMON, Bp. of Norwich, 1299—1325.

Gules, three salmon hauriant argent—Family
of GLOUCESTER.

Gules, two salmon in pale argent finned or—
SAMS, co. Essex.

Gules, a salmon in fesse argent—PISAGE.

Argent, a tree growing out of a mound in base,

SALMON.

surmounted by a salmon in fesse all proper, in his mouth an annulet or;
on the dexter side a bell pendent to the tree of the second—Royal Burgh
of GLASGOW.

Three salmon hauriant in pale argent—Town of KINGSTON-UPON-THAMES.

Gules, a salmon's head couped argent with an annulet through its nose
proper, between three cinquefoils of the second—HAMILTON, Scotland.

With the salmon is allied the *Trout* (fr. *truite*), and there
is practically no difference in the drawing.　Mr. Moule thinks
when a fish is shewn in, or near, a river, and not distinctly
named, it is intended for the *trout,* but does not give conclusive
reasons.　The French employ the trout, and frequently apply
to it the term *marqueté,* i.e. in reference to
the spots.

Azure, three trout [interlaced, or] fretted in triangle, 'testes aux queues' argent—TROUTBECK of
Cornwall.

Azure, two trout [? ged] in saltire argent—
GEDNEY, or GEDENEY.

Gules, a trout in bend argent—NEVE.

Argent, on a bend sable three trout or—OS-
BORNE, London.

Sable, a chevron or between three trout hauriant argent—FOREMAN, Scotland.

TROUTBECK.

D'azur, à une truite d'argent en bande, marquetée de sable, accompagnée de 6 étoiles d'or en orle—ORCIVAL, Auvergne.

There are one or two other fish which should be here noted, such as the *smelt* (fr. *eperlan*), known in Scotland as the *sparling*. The '*grayling*' is perhaps intended in the crest of the family of GRAYLEY; while the French name for the same, *ombre*, may have suggested the fish in the arms of the UMBRELL family.

Azure, a chevron between three smelts naiant argent—SMELT, co. York.

Erminois, three sparlings hauriant two and one proper—SPARLING, Petton, co. Salop.

Argent, three umber fish naiant—UMBRELL.

The *salmon spear* occurs on the arms of two branches of the Cornish family of GLYN. The form this spear takes has been given under *Eel-spear*.

Argent, three salmon spears points downwards sable—GLYNN, co. Cornwall.

Salt-cellar, called also a *Sprinkling salt*, is the device of one of the London companies. The ' salt,' however, is also borne by one family.

Per chevron, azure and gules, three salt-cellars [otherwise sprinkling salts] overflowing argent—The SALTERS' COMPANY, London. Arms granted, 1530. [Example on brass at All Hallows, Barking.]

Sprinkling salt.

Sable, a bend argent between three covered salts or—FELLINGHAM.

Saltire, or *saltier*, (fr. *sautoir*): this honourable ordinary is supposed to represent the cross whereon S. Andrew was crucified, and the standard or banner of S. Andrew is one bearing the saltire argent on a field azure.

The plain saltire is nothing but a cross placed in a different position, and whatever was the origin of the one as a device upon a shield, was probably also the origin of the other. Almost all the forms incident to the cross are likewise applicable to the saltire. They may be

FITZ-GERALD.

humetty, and in a French example to which the term *engoulé* is applied, the arms of the cross are terminated by Leopards' heads, their mouths holding the ends.

As will be observed, the '*sautoir*' occurs in the ancient rolls, and it may be added that in one roll temp. ED. II., out of twenty-eight examples of the *saltire* only ten are plain and eighteen are engrailed.

Robert de BRUS, d'or, ung saltoir de goules; et ung cheif de goules—Roll, temp. HEN. III.

Foulke de ESCHARDESTON, de goules ung sautoir d'argent engrele—*Ibid.*

Sire Raudolf de NEVYLE, de goules a un sautour de argent—Roll, temp. ED. II.

Monsire Rauf de NEVILL, port de gules une salter d'argent—Roll, temp. ED. III.

Monsire de TIBETOT, port d'argent une salter engrele de gules—*Ibid.*

Argent, a lion sejant gardant gules armed and langued azure holding in his dexter paw a thistle proper, and in his sinister a shield of the second, on a chief azure a S. Andrew's cross of the first—LYON OFFICE, or OFFICE OF ARMS AT EDINBURGH.

Argent, on a saltire gules an escallop or—See of ROCHESTER. [The Cathedral Church being dedicated to S. Andrew.]

Argent, a saltire counter embattled sable—Richard KIDDER, Bp. of Bath and Wells, 1691—1703.

Argent, a saltire azure botonny or—BASINGHOLD.

Gules, on a saltire argent, another humetty of the field; in chief a mitre coroneted, stringed or—Arms ascribed to GERARD; Bp. of Hereford, 1096; of York, 1100–8.

KIDDER.

Gules, four quatrefoils two and two or; in base a saltire couped argent—PALMER, co. Warwick.

Argent, a cross moline saltirewise—BANESTER.

Or, a lion rampant supporting a saltire engrailed humetty gules — John WOLTON, Bp. of Exeter, 1579–94.

Ecartelé aux 1 et 4 d'azur, au chevron ondé d'argent, accompagné de trois têtes de léopard d'or languées de gueules; aux 2 et 3 de gueules, au sautoir d'or engoulé de quatres têtes de léopard mouvantes des angles chargé en cœur [i.e. in fesse point], d'une autre tête de léopard du champ—DE JACOB DE LA COTTIERE.

WOLTON.

As to the expression a *saltire lozengy*, as has been said respecting the *Cross lozengy* (see § 8), there seems to have been great carelessness in the blazon by the heralds of the seventeenth and eighteenth centuries. It should be described where there is one tincture, a saltire *of so many lozenges*, &c. The first example of the following is clear; the others leave it obscure as to what is meant, and how the lozenges, &c., should be arranged.

Or, a saltire lozengy gules and argent—BELHOUSE.
Or, a saltire lozengy vert—BELHOUSE.
Vert, a saltire lozengy or—FRANKES, also MALCAKE.
Vert, a saltire fusily or—FRANKE.

The Cross of S. Julian is a *saltire crossed*, or as otherwise described, a cross crosslet placed *saltirewise*. It is borne by the Company of INNHOLDERS, in consequence of their claiming S. Julian as their patron.

JULIAN.

Argent, a cross of S. Julian [otherwise cross crosslet in saltire] sable—JULIAN, co. Lincoln.

Argent, five crosses Julian in saltire sable—THOROWGOOD.

Azure, a chevron per paly and per chevron gules and argent counterchanged, between three garbs or; on a chief argent two batons crossed at each end sable in saltire, the dexter surmounted by the sinister, commonly called S. Julian's Cross —INNHOLDERS' Company, [Inc. 1514].

The saltire may be *parted per saltire* (to which the awkward term *saltiery* has been given); more frequently the expression *quarterly per saltire* is used; an example, as it occurs in the see of WELLS before it was united with BATH, has been given under *Quarterly*.

BATH and WELLS.

Azure, a saltire per saltire quartered or and argent; on the dexter side two keys erect, interlaced at the bows, one or the other argent; on the sinister a sword erect—Bishoprick of Bath and Wells united, as borne by Bp. MONTAGUE in 1608 (*Edmondson*).

Sandbox. See *Penner*.   Sand-glass. See *Hour-glass*.

A singular figure, borne on the insignia of the borough of
SOUTHWARK, has been blazoned as a *sal-
tire conjoined in base.* It has all the
appearance of a *merchant's mark.*

Azure, an annulet ensigned with a cross
patteé or, interlaced with a saltire conjoined
in base of the last—Borough of SOUTHWARK.

Saltirewise, and *in saltire,* (fr. *passé en
sautoir*), are words used to describe the
position of charges placed in the form
of that ordinary. The former is properly

Borough of SOUTHWARK.

applied to two long charges, as *swords,* q.v., *fishes,* &c., when
crossing each other bendwise, and the latter to five charges,
placed 2, 1, 2; but, as will be observed, the terms are practically
interchangeable, the latter, however, being more frequently used.

With reference to the former, it is necessary to state that the
sword in bend dexter should be uppermost unless otherwise
directed, because the dexter side, and consequently any thing
placed in bend dexter, is more honourable than the sinister,
though the distinction is but little attended to in practice.
See examples under *Keys, Mace, Scythe,* &c.

Gules, two scythes in saltire argent—PRAYERS.

Gules, a fesse countercompony or and azure between six crosses
crosslet argent placed saltireways—BUCK, Wisbeach, co. Cambridge.

Gules, five crosslets fitchy in saltire between four escallops or—TOWN-
SON, Bp. of Salisbury, 1620–21.

The term *saltorel* is sometimes used when three or more
saltires occur, but it is hardly required.
It is needless to say that they must be
couped; but it should be noted that the
ends are not cut at right angles to the
arms, but horizontally, and when the saltorel is *engrailed* the ends are left plain.

Argent, three saltires vert—GREENLAND.

Or, a saltire gules surmounted by another
ermine, on a chief of the second three saltorels
engrailed of the first—DYON, co. Lincoln.

GREENLAND.

Per saltire, see *Quarterly per saltire.*

Sanguine, or *Murrey :* blood colour, fancifully called by heraldic writers in the arms of princes *Dragon's tail,* and in those of lords *Sardonyx.* It is a tincture of very unfrequent occurrence, and not recognised at all by most writers. In engraving it is denoted by numerous lines in saltire.

Sanguine.

Per bend sanguine and vert, two greyhounds courant bendwise argent—CLAYHILLS, Innergowrie, Scotland.

Satyrs: amongst monsters the human figure came in for its share in combination with the lower animals. The *Satyrs* and *Satyrals* are not found in arms except as supporters (e.g. to the arms of Lord STAWELL), but satyrs' *heads,* q.v., occur in one coat of arms. The *Mantiger* or Lampago, called by writers *Montegre* and Manticora, also occurs, e.g. the body of an heraldic tiger, with the head of an old man with long spiral horns. The supporters, however, to the arms of the Earl of HUNTINGDON are without horns. The *Triton,* or mer-man, occurs as a supporter, e.g. to the arms of Lord LYTTELTON, and in more than one instance as a crest, e.g. of Sir Tatton SYKES and of the family of LANG in Leicestershire and Suffolk. The *Neptune,* q.v., in the arms of Sir Isaac HEARD, Garter King of Arms 1750, is sometimes blazoned as a *Triton.* The supporters to the Insignia of 'The ACADEMY OF THE MUSES,' London, were 'dexter, a *Satyr ;* sinister, a *Mer-man.*'

Argent, on a bend sable three satyr's heads couped at the shoulders of the first horned or—WHEYWELL.

Sable, three man-tigers (or lampagoes) in pale argent—RADFORD, Cheynstone, Chawleigh, co. Devon.

Sanglant: bloody, embrued ; from fr. *ensanglanté.*

Sanglé, (fr.): seems to have been used of a horse, &c., with a ceinture round the body.

Sanglier. See *Boar.*

Sans: used by heralds for *without,* e.g. a dragon *sans* wings.

Sans nombre: without any definite number. See *Semé.*

Sapin, (fr.): *Fir-tree.* See under *Pine.*

Sagittarius, or a *Centaur,* is composed of half man and half horse, the former holding an arrow upon a bended bow. It is one of the twelve zodiacal signs, and King Stephen is said to have assumed it, because the sun was in that sign when he ascended the throne.

Gules, the bodies of three lions passant to the neck, with man's heads or [otherwise sagittarii]—Fictitious arms ascribed to King STEPHEN.

Gules, a sagittarius argent, his bow and shaft sable—BLOYS.

A sagittarius in full speed proper, shooting with a bow or and arrow argent—Crest of ACADEMY OF THE MUSES, London.

Saw: this device is rare; an example of a *framed* saw has already been noted as borne by the company of FANMAKERS. (See *Fan.*) One also occurs in the crest of HAMILTON. A *handsaw* is blazoned on one coat of arms, and a crooked *saw* is sometimes so blazoned on another.

Out of a ducal coronet an oak-tree fructed proper, cut through the main stem by a framesaw proper, the frame or—Crest of HAMILTON, Duke of Hamilton and Brandon.

Argent, a chevron engrailed gules between

HAMILTON.

in chief two escallops of the last, and in base a handsaw palewise azure handle or—SAWERS, Scotland.

Or, within a double tressure flory counterflory with fleur-de-lis sable a lion rampant of the second, holding in his dexter paw a crooked saw proper [otherwise a sabre]—MAC CAUSLAND, Strabane, Ireland.

Sceptre: this ensign of royal authority is but seldom borne singly. It is occasionally found in connection with a sword, the two placed *saltirewise,* or held in the hand of some king or saint. (See example in the insignia of the Town of BERWICK under *King;* and in those of the See of LINCOLN under *Nimbus.*)

Azure, a sceptre in hand between two crowns or; a chief of the last—Fox.

Vert, a sceptre surmounted of another in saltire or—PERSE.

Azure, three sceptres in bend or—PORTREA, Barnstaple.

Azure, three fleurs-de-lis or for Montgomery; quartering in Sceptre.

second and third gules three annulets or gemmed azure for Eglinton; all within a bordure gold charged with a double tressure flory counterflory gules; on a surcoat [i.e. escutcheon over all] of the last a sword and sceptre saltireways proper—MONTGOMERY, Earl of Mount Alexander.

Scissors, as used by tailors, are borne by one of the Companies, and *shears,* (fr. *force*), will be found noted under *Weavers'* implements.

Azure, a pair of scissors expanded in saltire, their points in chief or—Company of TAILORS, Edinburgh.

Scoop: this singular device is a part of the arms of SCOPHAM, of Scopham, Lincolnshire. Being sometimes obscurely drawn they have occasioned an extraordinary blazon, namely, a *Jew's harp.* (See under *Harp.*)

Scoop.

Argent, a scoop sable, with water therein wavy purpure, between four leaves in saltire of the second—SCOPHAM, co. Lincoln.

Scorpion: this is generally borne erect, and represented as in the margin. When it is borne with the head downwards it is described as reversed.

Argent, a fesse between three scorpions erect sable —COLE, Somersetshire.

Argent, a fesse engrailed between three scorpions reversed sable—COLE, Brancepeth, Durham.

Argent, a chevron between three scorpions reversed gules—COLE, co. Devon; and Walden, Essex.

Argent, a bend of five lozenges conjoined azure between two cotises vert, and as many scorpions sable—O'SINAN, Ireland; Harl. MS. 4039, fo. 235.

COLE.

Scourge: scourges with three lashes to each, which occur in the insignia of Croyland Abbey, (see under *Knife*), are referred to as *S. Guthlac's scourges.*

Sapphire. See *Azure.*

Saracen's *head.* See *Head.*

Sarcelled, or *Sarcelly.* See *Cross,* § 6, § 32, and § 24: also *Recercellé.*

Sardonyx. See *Sanguine.*

Saturn. See *Sable.*

Sauterelles, (fr.): *grasshoppers.*

Sautoir, (fr.). See *Saltire.*

Savage. See *Man.*

Saviour. See the Blessed *Virgin Mary;* also *Crucifix.*

Scotland, *Insignia* of: the heraldic insignia of this ancient kingdom are mythically said to have
been assumed by FERGUS I., who is supposed
to have reigned from A.D. 403 to 419, viz.

Or, a lion rampant gules—SCOTLAND.

The lion first appears distinctly upon the seal
of Alexander II., 1214-49, but whence derived,
or whether then first assumed, it is impossible
to say.   Afterwards the Lion was surrounded
by a double tressure.

SCOTLAND.

The parliament of James III. in 1471, "ordanit that in tyme
to cum thar suld be na double trezor about his armys, bot that
he suld ber hale armys of the lyoun, without ony mur."   Notwithstanding this enactment, the double tressure is still a pro-
minent part of the arms of Scotland.

The arms are now blazoned as
follows :—

Or, a lion rampant within a double
tressure, flory counterflory gules.

The *Crest* [Upon an imperial crown
proper].   A lion sejant affronté gules,
imperially crowned or, holding in his
dexter paw a sceptre, and in his sinister
a sword [both proper].

Supporters.   Two unicorns argent,
gorged with a royal coronet and
chained or.

The double tressure is sometimes
referred to as the *Bordure of Scotland.*

Crest of Scotland.

Sea-Gull, (lat. *larus*): to the family of *Gulls* (*laridæ*) belong
the *sea-gulls* and *sea-mews*, as well as the *terns*, all of which are
found in coats of arms.   Probably the general term *sea-fowl*,

Saxon. See *Head.*	to which the antlers of a *deer*
Scales. See *Balances.*	are attached. See *Attires.*
Scallop. See *Escallop.*	Scarpe, or *Escarpe :* a diminu-
Scalp: the portion of the skull	tive of the *bend sinister,* q.v.

and the name *sea-pewit* (perhaps given to the gull from its manner of flight), both of which occur, should be referred to the common *sea-gull*.

Azure, three sea-gulls argent—David LLWCH.

Gules, a fesse wavy argent between three sea-gulls proper; a crescent for difference—MEDLAND, Launceston, co. Cornwall; granted 17 May, 1730.

Gules, three sea-mews argent beaked and legged or—MEWY, co. Devon.

Azure, three mews argent beaked and membered gules—ASHE.

Azure, a fesse ermine between six sea-mew's heads erased argent—SPENCER, Wormleighton, co. Warwick.

Gules, a fesse engrailed between three sea-mews argent—SYER, Isham, co. Northampton; granted 1614.

Gules, a fesse between three tern-fowls argent—YERLE.

Or, a fesse dancetty ermine, in chief a sea-pewit vert beaked and legged gules—QUARLES, co. Northampton.

SPENCER.

Gules, a chevron between three sea-pewits argent—SAYER, Preston, co. Durham.

Sable, a chevron between three sea-fowl close argent—SEAFOWLE.

Sea-horse: this monstrosity is in heraldic drawing repre-sented by the upper part, i.e. head and fore-legs of a horse joined to the tail of a fish, which is twisted back, as shewn in the illustration; at the same time when correctly drawn the legs terminate in slightly webbed feet instead of in hoofs. Further a scalloped fin is substituted for the mane, and is continued down the back. Besides appearing as supporters to the insignia of the towns of Cambridge and of Ipswich, sea-horses appear in the following coats of arms.

Sea-horse.

Scimetar. See *Sabre*.

Scrip, *Palmer's*. See *Pilgrim's*.

Scrogs. See under *Tree*.

Scroll. See *Escroll*.

Scutcheon. See *Escutcheon*.

Scythe. See *Sickle*.

Sea, *The*. See *Ocean*; also exam-ples under *Ships*, &c.

Argent, in a sea vert a sea-horse issuing rampant proper—ECKFORD, Scotland.

Azure, a chevron between three sea-horses or—TUCKER, of Milton, Kent.

Barry wavy argent and azure; on a chevron crenelly or, between three sea-horses silver, finned and unguled of the third, seven gouttes-de-poix—TUCKER, co. Devon.

Azure, four bars argent between three sea-horses or; over all on a chevron crenelly of the last five gouttes-de-poix—TOOKER.

TUCKER.

Per pale or and azure; on the dexter compartment a tower gules, and on the sinister on a mount vert a sea-horse argent, mane, fins, and tail of the first; on a chief gold three mullets of the second—GARRICK, Middlesex.

Argent, on a fesse gules between three sea-horses sable a cross crosslet fitchy between two trefoils slipped of the first—NORDEN, Kent.

Barry of six argent and azure; surtout three sea-horses naiant or—William GLYNN, Bp. of Bangor, 1555-58.

Chequy argent and gules, a lion rampant gardant or; on a chief of augmentation wavy azure a sea-horse naiant proper between two Eastern coronets or, and above the word " Havannah "—POCOCK, co. Durham, Bart.

GLYNN.

Similar to this is the *sea-lion* (or as it is sometimes called from the French *lion poisson*), in which the upper part is that of a lion, the lower that of the body and tail of a fish. The *mane* is sometimes also represented *crested* or escalloped. Besides occurring as the supporters of the arms of Viscount FALMOUTH, it appears in the following coats of arms.

Argent, a sea-lion couchant azure, crowned, armed and langued gules—SILVESTER.

Sea-lion.

Sea-aylet.   See *Cormorant.*
Sea-bear.   See *Bear.*
Sea-calf.   See *Seal.*
Sea-lion, &c.   See *Sea-horse.*

Sea-pewit, Sea-mew, Sea-fowl, &c.   See *Sea-gull.*
Sea-pye.   See *Lapwing.*
Seals : attached to a *book,* q.v.

Azure, a bridge of three arches embattled at top in fesse argent, masoned sable, between three sea-lions passant or—BRIDGEN, Lord Mayor of London, 1764.

Or, on a bend wavy between two sea-lions sable three buck's heads caboshed argent—Sir Robert HARLAND, Bart., Orwell Park, Suffolk. [A sea-lion supporting an anchor, crest of the same.]

The *sea-dragon* is also to be classed amongst monstrosities, though it has been suggested it is intended for the *conger-eel*, and thus the heads in the insignia of KING's LYNN have been blazoned '*dragon's heads.*' Again, when the term occurs in the blazon of the crest of Sir Jacob GERRARD, Bart., 1662, it is said to be a *wyvern.*

Per chevron gules and or; three sea-dragons ducally crowned counterchanged—EASTON, co. Devon.

The *sea-dog* is still more uncertain. It has been suggested that the device is intended for a crocodile, but this results only from bad drawing. With better reason it is suggested to be a fanciful representation of the *otter :* but like all monstrosities the origin must be looked for in the imagination of the draughtsman rather than in the realm of nature. It is drawn like a talbot, with the whole body scaled, and the tail of a beaver. The feet are webbed and the back scalloped like that of a sea-horse.

Argent, three demi sea-dogs passant in pale sable—JESSE.

Per fesse nebuly . . . and . . . three sea-dogs passant counterchanged—HARRIS, Cornwall.

[Baron STOURTON has two such animals, sable, scaled or, for his supporters.]

The *sea-wolf* also belongs to the same category, and this has been supposed only to be the *seal.*

Argent, a chevron engrailed gules between three marine wolves (or sea-dogs) naiant sable finned, ventred, and dented of the first, langued of the second—FENNOR, Sussex; granted 10 November, 1557.

It should be added that the French treat several land animals in this manner by adding the tails of fish to them, and they have a special term to signify the same, viz. *mariné.*

Seax. See *Sabre.*

Sedant, or *Segeant*, i.q. *Sejant.*

Seeded : a word chiefly used with relation to the heraldic *rose*, &c.

Sea-urchin: the figure representing the commonest existing species of the Echinidæ on our own sea-shore seems to have found a place amongst heraldic devices, though when blazoned from bad drawing the figure may often be described as a *Hedgehog*, (q.v.), or even a *Porcupine*.

Azure, three sea-urchins erect argent [Otherwise Gules, three sea-urchins in pale argent]—AL-STANTON.

Azure, three urchins passant in pale or—WOOD.

ALSTANTON.

Seaweed: the *laver* occurs in the insignia of the town of Liverpool, (in allusion to the name). The same arms were borne also as an augmentation by the Earl of Liverpool, created Earl in 1796. In a French example *feuille de varech*, i.e. of wrack, has been observed in one blazon.

Argent, a [lever or] cormorant sable beaked and legged gules, holding in the beak a branch of seaweed called laver inverted vert [originally the eagle of S. John holding a penner and inkhorn]—City of LIVERPOOL.

D'argent, a une feuille de varech de gueules accostée de deux croissants d'azure—BEUARD, Normandie.

Seal: this marine mammal has been adopted in some few coats of arms. It seems to have been fancifully called by some heraldic writers the *sea-calf*, and *sea-wolf;* possibly, too, by the *sea-bear* is meant the *seal* (see under *Bear*). The whole animal, however, does not appear to be represented; only the *paws* and the *head*, and then but rarely.

Seal's paw.

Argent, a chevron between three seal's paws erased and erect sable—Town of YARMOUTH, Norfolk.

Or, a seal's foot erect and erased proper—BERINGBURGH.

Azure, a ducal coronet or between three seal's heads erased argent—BURMAN, Stratford, co. Warwick.

Argent, a chevron between three seal's heads bendwise couped sable—LEY, co. Wilts, Barony, 1625; also LEY, co. Devon.

Lord LEY.

Sejant, (fr. *assis*): this term when applied to beasts signifies that they are in a sitting position; but the position of a *squirrel* sejant differs from most others, from having the fore paws raised.   A lion thus borne would be *sejant rampant*

Argent, three conies sejant—STRODE, co. Somerset, 1716.

Argent, a chevron between three spaniels sejant gules—HOMLING.

Sable, a chevron sable between three lions sejant gardant azure—LYONS.

Or, a bear rampant sejant sable—BERNEK.

Gules, a lion sejant on a chair, and holding in the paws a battle-axe or—Fictitious arms assigned to ALEXANDER the Great.

STRODE.

Sejant affronté is applicable to a lion borne in full aspect. See the crest of *Scotland.*

Semé, (fr.), sometimes written *semy :* means that the field is sown or strewed over with several of the charges named, drawn small and without any reference to the number.   Various synonyms are used by heraldic writers.   In a roll temp. HEN. III., *poudré* is most frequently used, meaning precisely the same; in another roll *plein de* is found.   More modern writers used such terms as *aspersed, replenished with,* and two old French terms *averlye* and *gerattie* are also given in glossaries. Some writers use *sans nombre,* and a very fanciful distinction has been made between this and *semé,* namely, that when all the charges are drawn entire *sans nombre* should be used, but if the outline of the field or any ordinary cuts any of the charges that then *semé* should be used.   In the case of *semé* of *crosslets, billets, bezants,* the special terms *crusily, billetty,* and *bezanty,* already noted in their proper places, are preferable. *Platy, hurty,* and *tortoily,* are not so.   The term is somewhat awkwardly applied to *Chequy* in the blazon of the arms of the Bishop of ELY as given in Wharton's '*Anglia Sacra.*'

Segreant: applied by most writers to the *griffin* instead of *rampant.*   It includes the wings being expanded.   Applied also to the *Leopard* in arms of HETHERFIELD.

Sr JOHN de Bretaigne, porte eschekere d'or et d'azur, ou le cantell d'ermyne ou le bordure de gulez poudre ou lepars d'or—Roll, temp. HEN. III.

Per fesse gules and sable, a lion rampant argent semy of crosses croslet of the first—LODGE, co. York.

Gules, semy of nails argent, three stems of a flower vert—ASHBY.

Azure, semy-de-lis and a lion rampant argent—HOLLAND.

Gules, semy-de-lis or, a lion rampant and a canton ermine—MARKS, Suffolk.

Or, semy of hearts and in chief a lion rampant gardant azure—GOTHES.

Or, on a chevron gules, within a bordure azure semée of mitres [better, charged with eight or more mitres] of the first—Edmund STAFFORD, Bp. of Exeter, 1395 —1419.

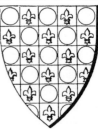

Chequy argent, semée of torteaux, and azure semée of fleur-de-lys or—Louis de LUXEMBOURG, Bp. of Ely, 1438-43, [and Archbishop of Rouen, 1443-56].

Le REY DE FRAUNCE, de asur poudre a flurette de or—Roll, temp. HEN. III.

Rauf le FITZ NICOLE, de goules, ung quintefueil de or; le champ pleyn des escallopes d'argent—*Ibid.*

DE LUXEMBOURG.

Or, the field replenished with estoiles azure, a lion rampant gules—GALLYHALT.

Sengreen is a name for the plant called house-leak (the *saxifraga nivalis* of Linnæus): it occurs only in the very extraordinary arms of one of the founders of a college in Cambridge. The illustration here given is from the college book-plate, with the words of the grant as printed by Gibbon.

" Gold semied with flowers gentil, a sengreen in chief over the heads of two whole serpents in pale, their tails knit together (all in proper colour) resting upon a square marble-stone vert, between these a book sable garnisht gules buckled gold "—Dr. John KAYE [co-founder with GONVILLE of Gonville and Caius College, Cambridge, temp. Queen Mary].

KAYE.

Sellé, (fr.): of a horse with a saddle on.

Senestré par, (fr.): having another charge on the left hand.

Serpent: the serpent or snake, for they are in heraldry absolutely synonymous, (fr. *serpent*), is found in the ancient rolls under the name of *bis;* the word survives in the Italian *biscia*, or cobra of Milan. The reptile occurs rather frequently in coats of arms, and its position should be described. As seen in the case of the arms of CAIUS above, it may be represented *erect*. It may also be drawn *gliding* or *fessways*.

It may be *involved* or *encircled* (both terms meaning the same), as shewn in the margin, in which position it occurs in the arms of WHITBY Abbey. The device was probably suggested by the fossil Ammonites, found in the lias clay there, and which were at first supposed to be petrified snakes. When *involved*, the French heralds seem to use the word *guivre* for snake.

Erect.

Involved.

Le Counte de TRERSTEYN, d'or a un byse de goules—Roll, temp. HEN. III.

Monsire William MALBIS, d'argent a une cheveron de gules a trois testes de bys rases gules—Roll, temp. ED. III.

Argent, a chevron gules between three serpents erect proper—COTTER, Bart. 1763.

Argent, two serpents erect endorsed—LONGSHARE.

Or, three serpents erect wavy sable—CODLEW, or CUDLEW.

Argent, three serpents gliding in pale azure—DUCAT.

Argent, two bars gules; over all as many serpents erect, respecting each other, vert—REFUGE.

Argent, a serpent involved vert—O'DRONE, Ireland. [Another family, three snakes involved vert.]

Argent, three serpents voluted—DIGON, or TROGONE, Ireland.

Azure, three serpents encircled or; two and two—WHITBY Abbey.

D'argent à la guivre d'azur, tortillante en pal, [generally blazoned 'couronnée d'or,'] 'engloutissante un enfant' issante de gueules—Duché de MILAN.

Senestrochère, (fr.): a sinister arm represented starting from the dexter side of the shield.

Sepurture: a term applied to the *wings* of birds, q.v.; synonymous with *endorsed*.

Snakes are also represented *nowed*, (q.v.), or twisted in a knot. In the crest of CAVENDISH the reptile is represented as in the margin, and theoretical heralds contend that if represented as in the lowest of the two figures it would be *nowed* reversed. Also, as will be seen, there are complications of the nowed position.

Nowed.

Nowed reversed.

One or two other varieties are given, but heraldic writers such as Holme devote several pages to imaginary positions of serpents, and fanciful terms to fit them, none of which, however, are found to occur in any coats of arms. They are sometimes represented with tails in their mouths; at others round a pillar, or round necks of children. (See arms of VAUGHAN under *Enveloped*.)

See also *Adder*, from which there is little or nothing to distinguish the charge in heraldic drawing.

Argent, two serpents nowed and linked together in pale between two stars gules—ARWELL, Scotland.

Gules, three snakes nowed in triangle argent—EDNOWAIN AP BRADWEN, Merionethshire.

Gules, three snakes nowed in triangle argent, within a bordure engrailed or—LEWIS, Warwickshire.

Vert, a serpent bowed embowed debruised, the head erect, the tail torqued or—BLOORE.

Azure, three serpents, each encircled, their tails in their mouths argent [in French blazon, 'D'azur, a trois serpents d'argent arrondis se mordant la queue, posées 2 et 1']—DE LAUZON, Poitou.

EDNOWAIN AP BRADWEN.

Azure, a bend or in chief three boy's heads couped at the shoulders argent, each enwrapped about the neck with a snake proper; in base as many griffin's heads erased of the third—MADOCK, co. Gloucester.

Gules, a stellion [?] serpent proper—BUME.

Serrated : having a saw-like edge, e.g. of a *sickle* blade.

Seraph. See *Head*.

Sesant : i.q. *Issant*.

Sex-foil: the term *sex-foil* is found in one or two old rolls of arms, and seems to be used for what are elsewhere blazoned as *roses:* but though the *five-foil or cinque-foil* is very common, it has not been observed in modern coats. See also *Narcissus*.

Uẖ̶ẖ̶ẖ̶ A̶ V̶u̶u̶u̶, d̶u̶ g̶u̶u̶l̶u̶u̶ t̶r̶u̶i̶s̶ s̶i̶x̶f̶u̶e̶i̶l̶l̶u̶s̶ d'ormyn Roll, temp. HEN. III.

Monsire de PIERPOUNT, port d'argent, a une lyon de sable rampant et une urle de seyfoils [often drawn as cinquefoils] gules—Roll, temp. ED. III.

Sire Johan DARCY de argent, a un escuchon de sable, od les rosettes [otherwise blazoned sistefoils] de goules assis en la maniere de bordure —Roll, temp. ED. II.

Argent, ten six-foils [intended for roses] gules, four, three, two, and one—Joan ROSELEE, Roll, temp. ED. I.

Sable, three sixfoils within a bordure engrailed or—Walter de WIG-TONE—[From the coloured roll in possession of Society of Antiquaries].

Angemmes, (fr. from lat. *ingemmæ*), are described as a series of round ornaments drawn like quatrefoils, but with six leaves, and seem to be confined to French heraldry.

De gueules, à un écusson d'argent à la bordure d'angemmes d'or— TANCARVILLE.

Shake-fork: this is a bearing resembling a pall couped and pointed, and is almost entirely confined to Scotch families, and chiefly to those of CUNNINGHAM, who bear it in a variety of ways. It is in one instance blazoned a *Pale furché.*

CUNNINGHAM.

Argent, a shake-fork sable—CUNNINGHAM.

Argent, a pale furché between two cotises sable—CUNNINGHAM.

Argent, a shake-fork sable charged with a cinquefoil of the first—CUNNINGHAM, Glengar-nock.

Argent, a rose vert between three shake-forks sable—SMALLSHAW, Bolton, co. Lancaster.

Azure, on a shake-fork between two mascles in chief, and a boar's head erased in base or, three laurel leaves vert—KINLOCH, Scotland.

Shacklebolt. See *Fetterlock.*
Shadowed, (fr. *ombré* or *tracé*). See *Adumbration.*

Shafferoon. Corruption of *Chap-eronne.*

Shambrogue, or *Shambrough*, is defined by Berry and other heraldic writers as a kind of ship; but it is more probably a kind of boot, (cf. Irish *brogue* under *boot*).

Azure, on a bend or three shambrogues gules—PEDE, Bury, Suffolk.

Or, on a bend sable, three shambroughs argent [otherwise Or, on a bend sable three legs in armour couped at the thigh, and erased at the ankle proper]—BLAGRAVE.

Shark: this fish occurs in one or two coats of arms, and in one or two crests: the *dog-fish* occurs also in the same way.

Azure, a shark or; a chief of the last—VALLIANT.

A shark issuing regardant swallowing a man—Crest of family of YEATES, Ireland.

A shark's head regardant and swallowing a negro—Crest of family of MOLTON.

Argent, three dog-fishes naiant in pale sable—GESSE.

A demi dog-fish—Crest of family of MEER, Dorset.

Sheep: although the *Ram* and the *Lamb* are found frequently blazoned in British Heraldry the sheep is not found so. With the French heralds both *mouton* and *brebis* are found, the former used generally, the latter only when it is feeding (*paissante*).

D'azur, a trois moutons passant d'argent, accornés de sable, accolés de gueules, et clarinés d'or; à la bordure engrêlée et gueules; au chef cousu de France—BOURGES.

D'azur, a une brebis d'argent—BERBISY, Bourgogne.

Shield, (Anglo-Sax. Scȳlð): from the earliest times no doubt the shield borne on the arm to protect the bearer in battle was ornamented with various devices, one object of which was that the bearer should be recognised by his friends in the midst of the fight; and to the devices on these shields there can be no question armorial bearings chiefly owe their origin. The fact that the devices were afterwards pourtrayed on the mantles and on the surcoats, on the trappings of the horses, or on flags and pennons, does not militate against this origin, since

---

Shafted, (fr. *futé*): applied to the shaft of an *arrow;* also to the quill of a feather; but seldom needed.

Shamrock. See *Trefoil.*

Shapourne: a corruption of *Chaperonne.* See also *Point champaine.*

such were later developments. The *crest* on the helmet, however, may perhaps be considered in theory to have as early an
origin as the device on the shield, but throughout the middle ages
it was the device on the shield which marked the man, and
afterwards his family, far more than the crest.

From the much more frequent occurrence on the earlier arms
of the simpler devices, such as the *fesse*, the *bend*, the *chevron*,
&c., it may reasonably be presumed that these had their origin
in the structure of the shield itself, i.e. from the bars of wood,
or more probably of metal, which passed athwart the shield
to strengthen it. The example so frequently referred to as
an early device, namely, the *escarboucle*, (q.v.), is essentially
such as a thirteenth-century armourer would adopt to strengthen
woodwork, and a similar device is not unfrequently found on
doors of churches. It was not *originally* deemed a charge but
merely an ornament, like *diapering* was. Cf. old fr. *bouclier*,
and English synonym *buckler*.

Concurrently with the plain devices (which have in systematic
heraldry received the name of *ordinaries*, see Synoptical Table),
devices derived from the animal, and perhaps in a few cases from
the vegetable, kingdom were adopted, and since these gave far
greater variety they tended to supplant, as well as to supple-
ment the others. The *Lion*, as the emblem of strength and
courage, was of course the favourite device amongst animals,
as the *Eagle* amongst birds, and the *Dolphin* amongst fishes.

The *shield*, in its practical sense, was pourtrayed in sculpture
and in stained glass throughout the middle ages for the purpose
of containing the device; and though the outline was frequently modified—particularly in later years—to harmonize
with the architectural details surrounding it, the shield form,
ending in a point, was nearly always retained. The various

Shave. See *Currier's* shave.

Shavehook. See *Plumber's instruments*.

Shaving-iron occurs in the insignia of the Company of FAN-
MAKERS. See *Fan*.

Shears. See *Weaver's*.

Sheaves of *Arrows*, *Reeds*, &c.
q.v. also of *Corn*. See *Wheat*
and *Garbe*.

Sheldrake. See *Duck*.

Shepherd's Crook. See *Staff*.

modifications of the outline, as found carved on monuments, or engraved on brasses, or painted in glass of windows, or outlined on the seals, &c., at different periods is an interesting study, but beyond the limits of a glossary. In some cases, though rarely in England, a circle is adopted on Seals instead of a shield, but there is no evidence that this was due to anything but the fancy of the artist, since ecclesiastics and laymen, warriors, and religious or municipal communities, have sometimes the shield, sometimes the circle.

Women of all ranks (the sovereign alone excepted) are now supposed to bear their arms on lozenge-shaped figures rather than on shields (see *Achievements*), but formerly all ladies of rank bore shields upon their seals.

The *shield* is, for convenience sake, partitioned out into certain divisions, usually reckoned as nine in number, and called *Points*, q.v.

Shields in some rare instances are themselves borne as armorial bearings, usually blazoned as *Escutcheons*, q.v. In one modern case the mythical *shield of Pallas* is named, and a plain shield is the crest of FORTESCUE.

Azure, on a chevron sable, a gauntlet of the first between two pairs of swords in saltire of the last, hilts and pommels or; on a chief of the second, an oval shield of the field charged with a cross gules encircled with a carved shield of the third, between two peer's helmets proper garnished gold—Company of ARMOURERS, incorporated temp. HEN. VI.

Argent, on a mount in base the trunk of an oak tree sprouting out two branches proper with the Shield of Pallas hanging thereon or, fastened by a belt gules—BOROUGH, co. Derby.

The *target* may be reckoned amongst shields, occurring as it does in the feudal coat of the Lordship of ROTHSCHILD. An archery *Target* seems also to have been adopted.

Gules, a target between three antique crowns or—GRANT, Ballindalloch, co. Elgin.

Ship-lantern.　See *Lantern*.
Shods.　Used for the metal points of arrows.　See under *Palewise*.
Shoe.　See *Boot*.

Shoemaker's Knife.　See *Knife*.
Shovel.　See *Spade*.
Shoveller.　See *Duck*.
Shrine.　See *Church*.

Ship, (fr. *navire* or *vaisseau*): this is a very frequent device, and especially in the insignia of sea-port towns and of merchant companies. The form varies greatly in different examples, being for the most part copied from the existing fashion. When ships are named they should be most scrupulously blazoned, care being especially taken to state the number of *masts* and *top-masts*, whether there are any *sails* (fr. *voiles*), and if any, whether they are furled or not. The *rigging*, too, it will be seen is often of a different tincture. It will be noted that the *hulk* of the vessel is often named, and sometimes the *stern*. *Ships* and *Castles* are so exceedingly varied in form that they present greater difficulties than almost any other bearings.

It will be found that a ship proper is generally represented with three masts; if with one mast it is perhaps better blazoned as a *Lymphad* (q.v.), (which may have oars as well), or a *galley*, though the latter may have three masts.

MEARES.

Argent, a three-masted galley, her sails furled proper [otherwise a ship with three masts, sails furled and shrouded proper]—MEARES.

A ship of three masts in full sail on the waves of the sea; the mainsail charged with a lion rampant, and the sail on the foremast charged with a cross of S. George; on the round top of each mast are four spears with their barbed points upwards—Seal of town of ALDBOROUGH, Suffolk; granted 1561.

Gules, a fesse ermine, in base a ship with three masts, sails furled proper—CRAWFURD, Passell.

Argent, in base a lion passant gules and in chief a three-masted ship sails set . . .—O'LEARIE, Ireland.

Azure, semy-de-lis or, a lion rampant of the last; on a canton argent, a ship in full sail proper—POOLE, co. Chester.

Argent, on waves of the first and azure a three-masted ship in pale sailing to the sinister sable; on a chief of the third a lizard or—MAC SHEELEY.

Quarterly, first and fourth or, a lion rampant gules; second azure a ship at anchor within a royal tressure or; third azure, a ship in full sail or; over all dividing the quarters, a cross engrailed gules—SINCLAIR, Mey, Scotland.

Azure, in base a sea with a dolphin's head appearing in the water all proper; on the sea a ship of three masts in full sail all or, the sail and rigging argent, on each a cross gules; on the dexter chief point the sun in splendour; on the sinister chief point an estoile of the third; on a chief of the fourth a cross of the fifth charged with the lion of England—Company of SPANISH MERCHANTS.

Azure, on a sea in base proper a ship with three masts in full sail or, between two rocks of the second, all the sails, pennants and ensigns argent, each charged with a cross gules; a chief engrailed of the third; in base a sea-horse proper—LEVANT COMPANY [TURKEY MERCHANTS].

Azure, three ships of as many masts rigged and under full sail, the sails, pennants and ensigns argent, each charged with a cross gules, on a chief of the second . . . (see *Pale*)—EAST INDIA COMPANY; arms granted 1600.

Barry wavy of six argent and azure; over all a ship of three masts in full sail proper, sails, pennants, and ensigns of the first each charged with a cross gules all between three bezants; a chief or, on a pale between two roses gules seeded or barbed vert a lion passant gardant of the fifth—RUSSIA MERCHANTS, incorporated 1555.

With the French when the *masts* are of a different tincture the term *equipé* is used, and when the sails are so, *habillé*.

D'azur, au navire d'or, equipé et voilé d'argent, flottant sur des ondes de même—HERAIL, Languedoc.

De gueules, au navire d'or, habillé d'hermine, voguant sur des ondes au naturel; au chef cousu d'hermine—Ville de NANTES.

The *hull* or *hulk* of the vessel is sometimes figured separately on arms, and in a few cases (the insignia of the CINQUE PORTS being the characteristic example), a portion only of the hull is shewn. Often, too, the *hulk* is conjoined to some

Demy Hull.

other charge. The *sails* and the *masts* are also used separately as devices; the former is sometimes drawn with a portion of the mast, or at least of the yard-arm.

Barry of six argent and azure three hulks sable; on a chief gules three lions passant gardant or— City of WATERFORD.

Sail.

Shruttle. See *Basket*.
Shuttle. See *Weaver's Shuttle*.

Silver. See *Argent*. The word is used to avoid repetition.

Per pale gules and azure; on the dexter three demi-lions passant gardant issuing from the centre and conjoined to so many demi-hulks of ships on the sinister argent—CINQUE PORTS.

Per pale gules and azure, three demi-lions passant gardant in pale or; joined to as many demi-hulks of ships argent; over all in pale a crosier or—FEVERSHAM ABBEY.

Gules, a lion rampant gardant or impaled with azure, three demi-hulks of ships joined to the impaled line of the last—Town of IPSWICH, Suffolk; confirmed 1561 [elsewhere Per pale gules and azure a lion rampant or between three sterns of ships argent].

CINQUE PORTS.

Gules, three pieces of masts couped, with the tops argent two and one—CROMER.

Gules [otherwise vert], three sails argent —CAVEL.

Argent, three sails of a ship fastened to their yards gules—LOCAVELL, or CAVELL.

The term *antique* or *ancient ship* sometimes means the *Lymphad*, q.v. When *oars* are named (as in the arms of SIN-CLAIR), though the charge is called a ship, it is meant probably for a *galley*. A *Spanish merchant-ship* occurs in the arms of FAVENC (see under *Mulberry*), and the *Noah's ark*, borne by the Company of SHIPWRIGHTS, has been mentioned in its proper place. The *shambrogue* (q.v.), which writers refer to as a ship, seems not to be a ship at all.

An antique vessel with one mast; two men in the vessel, one blowing a horn, and two men lying on the yard arm—Seal of the Corporation of HYTHE, Kent.

Azure, an ancient ship of three masts, sails furled or—WRANGHAM.

De gueules, au navire antique d'argent, voguant sur des ondes de même; au chef semé de France—Ville de PARIS. [The ship is variously drawn, and the chief has been several times altered.]

Azure, a ship at anchor, her oars in saltire within a double tressure flory counterflory or—SINCLAIR or ST. CLAIR, Baron Sinclair.

Or, a galley, sails furled and oars in action gules, flags azure—NOBLE, Ireland.

Or, on a fesse azure between in chief a bull's head couped, and in base a galley with oars erected saltirewise sable, a Saint Andrew's cross argent—RICHARDSON, Scotland.

Barry wavy of six argent and azure; over all a fishing vessel of one mast sans sail or—ROYAL FISHING COMPANY.

It has been said that several towns bear *ships* on their insignia. The following represents a list of those which have been noticed. Where an asterisk is placed the statement is derived only from the seal.

*ALDBOROUGH, Suffolk; *BEAUMARIS; BERWICK, (North); *BIDEFORD, Devon; BRISTOL; BURNTISLAND; CAMBRIDGE; *CARDIGAN; DARTMOUTH, Devon; *DUNWICH, Suffolk; *EAST LOW, Cornwall, *FOWEY, Cornwall; *HARWICH, Essex (crest); HASTINGS, Sussex; *HYTHE, Kent; IPSWICH, Suffolk; LYDD, Kent; *LYMINGTON, Hants; *MALDON, Essex (rev.); *NEWTOWN, Hants; PLYMOUTH, Devon; QUEENSFERRY, Scotland; RENFREW, Scotland; SANDWICH, Kent; TENTERDEN, Kent; TRURO, Cornwall; WATERFORD, Ireland; WEXFORD, Ireland; WEYMOUTH, Dorset; WINCHELSEA, Sussex; *YARMOUTH, Hants.

Shot: there are one or two names given to the kinds of shot used. The *star stone*, as it is sometimes called from its appearance, is figured in the margin. Possibly the *chain shot* is synonymous — called by Guillim 'a murdering chain shot.' (See also *Fireball*.)

Star Stone.

Gules, on a chevron argent a rose between two lions counterpassant of the first, in base a star stone proper—George HEPBURN.

Azure, three chain shots or [quartered by CLIFFORD, Earl of Cumberland].

Or, two chain shots, one in chief and the other in base sable—SOMBRÉ.

An ancient form of shot is represented in the margin, where the two ends are united by a *bar* instead of by a chain. The *gun stones*, though no doubt called so from their use as projectiles from guns, are considered as one of the *roundles*. (See *Pellets*.)

Bar Shot.

Sinister, (fr. *sinistre*): the left hand side. As shields are always supposed to be upon the arm of the bearer, it is *his* left-hand side which is meant; consequently the sinister is on the spectator's right hand.

Sinistré par, (fr.): signifies having something on the left or sinister side.

Sinople: old French term for *vert*, and now always used by French heralds.

Siren. See under *Mermaid*.

Shrimp: besides the *crab* and the *lobster* we find the *shrimp,* which in one or two cases is blazoned *prawn.* There appear to be, however, only one or two families bearing the device. The position, unless otherwise described, is *displayed tergiant barwise,* the head to the dexter.

Barry wavy of six ermine and gules, a chevron between three shrimps [otherwise prawns] or, charged with a rose of the second barbed vert seeded gold between two lilies in line with the

ATTWATER.

chevron slipped vert—William ATTWATER, Bishop of Lincoln, 1514-21; granted 1509.

Gules, on three bars wavy or, as many shrimps of the field, [otherwise barry wavy of six argent and gules, three shrimps or]—ATSEA.

Or, two bars wavy between three shrimps in pale gules, [otherwise ' Or, on two bars gules as many shrimps naiant argent ']—ATSEA.

Barry wavy of six or and gules, three prawns naiant of the second—SEA or ATSEA, Herne, Kent.

Sickle, (fr. *faucille*), or ordinary *reaping-hook,* is borne but by few families, and is represented as in the margin.

Sable, three sickles interwoven argent—SICKLEMORE, co. Suffolk.

Vert, on a fesse between two garbs in chief or and a sickle in base argent, handled of the second, an arrow barways gules headed and flighted of the third between two estoiles azure—DUBERLY, co. Monmouth; granted 1766.

Sickle.

Gules, three reaping-hooks argent—SASSELL or SAWSEFELE.

Per chevron sable and or ; in base a moorcock of the first combed and wattled gules, in chief two pair of reaping-hooks endorsed and entwined, the blades argent the handles gold—HOCKMORE, Buckyate, co. Devon,

Argent, three reaping-hooks, their bows conjoined in fesse [point] sable—TREMERE, co. Cornwall.

De gueules, à trois faucilles d'argent emmanchées d'or, les pointes au cœur de l'ecu—MAYÈRE, Flandre.

Skean or *Skene.* See *Dagger.*
Skiff. See *Boat.*

Skulls, *human.* See *Bones;* also *Heads.*

Similar to the above is the *pruning-hook*, the only difference, perhaps, being that the handle should be drawn somewhat longer. Pruning-hooks occur notably in the crests of TAY and NANFANT, the former bearing two, the latter three.

Gules, three pruning-hooks, blades argent, handles or—CUTCLIFFE, Ilfracombe, co. Devon.

The *Scythe* (fr. *faux*) is also frequently found.

Argent, a scythe in pale, blade in chief, the sned [or handle] in bend sinister sable; in the fesse point a fleur-de-lis of the last—SNEYD, co. Stafford.

Argent, a scythe sable—SNELSON, co. Chester; also Sir James LEE, co. Stafford.

Argent, a fesse gules between three scythes sable —ALCOCK, co. Chester.

Gules, a scythe argent, handle in pale, blade in chief—BOGHEY, co. Stafford.

Per chevron sable and or, in base a moorcock of

SNEYD.

the first, in chief four scythes conjoined two and two argent, the handles of the second—HUCKMORE, co. Devon.

Or, on a chief gules three scythes erect argent—SETHINGTON.

D'azur, à trois faux d'or—FAUQUIÈRES, Bourgogne.

Scythes are also borne by the families of SNELYTONE, London; MAINWARING; KEMPLEY or KEMSEY, co. Salop; PRAYERS or PRAERS, co. Chester; PARTRIDGE, co. Stafford; RIDLER, co. Gloucester.

It will be observed that the *blades* of the sickle and scythe (fr. *rangier*) are sometimes borne without handles.

Gules, two scythe blades, the edges inward and points upward in saltire, the dexter surmounted of the sinister argent—VAN MILDERT, Bishop of Llandaff, 1819; Durham, 1826-36.

Argent, the upper half of a sickle blade serrated on the inner [dexter] edge erect sable—ZAKESLY.

De gueules, à trois rangiers d'argent—SORNY DES GRESLETS, Champagne.

Slea, or *Slay.* *Weaver's,* q.v.

Sleeve. See *Maunch.*

Slip. See *Tree.*

Slipped, (fr. *tigé*): (1) applied to the stalks of trefoils, and of leaves, sprigs of trees, &c., im-

plying that they are as it were torn off, not couped. See *Trefoil.*

(2) Applied to flowers when they have stalks and leaves to denote the tincture. See *Rose.*

Slippers. See *Weaver's Spindle.*

Side: a portion of the shield, not more than one sixth of its breadth, cut off by a perpendicular line. Theoretically it may be dexter or sinister; but it seems not to be adopted by any English family, though it appears in the arms of a German family resident here. In one MS., too, a quartering bearing a *side* is introduced into the arms of Bp. Edward Fox.

Side.

Argent, on a mount vert, three pine-trees proper, a side dexter or—GROTE, Kent.

Argent, on a bend sable, three dolphins embowed bendwise naiant or —Edward Fox, Bp. of Hereford, 1535-8. Quartering, argent, a plain inescutcheon and a side dexter indented sable—Cotton MS., Tiberius D. 10, fol. 865.

Silk: in the insignia of the SILK-THROWERS' COMPANY, in London, occurs the only reference to this product. Of the three *hanks* or *bundles* of silk, it will be seen that the central one is drawn differently from the others. In the chief is a representation of the silk-throwers' *mill*.

Argent, three bundles or hanks of silk in fesse sable; on a chief azure a silk-thrower's mill or —Company of SILK-THROWERS, London; incorporated 1630.

Company of SILK-THROWERS.

Silkworm-fly: this occurs but in one coat of arms.

Per chevron argent and vert; in chief three silkworm-flies paleways en arriere in fesse; in base a mulberry branch; all counterchanged— BASSANO, Lichfield, co. Stafford.

Silphium: this plant occurs but in one coat of arms, and that a singular one. The flower is similar to that of the chrysanthemum.

Vert, a chevron gules between two couplecloses erminois [*sic*] and three Turk's heads couped proper turbaned or; on a chief argent a silphium plant proper issuant from a mount vert inscribed with the letters ΚΥΡΑ gold—Admiral SMYTH.

Sling: the ancient means for hurling missiles against the enemy (called also a *swepe*) occurs in one or two coats of arms, though not in any ancient ones, so far as has been observed. The *sling*, or *staff-sling*, is represented as in the margin.

CAWARDEN.

The *sweep* (more correctly spelt *swepe*) is used as if synonymous. It is, however, the same as the *balista*, and is so blazoned in one coat; it is a more formidable engine of warfare, similar to the catapult or *mangonel*, whence in one case the play on the name.

Sable, a staff-sling in bend between two pheons argent—CAWARDEN, or CARDEN, co. Cheshire and Hereford.

Gules, a sling or hand-bow between two broad arrows argent—CAWARDEN, co. Stafford.

Argent, a sweep (or sling) azure charged with a stone or—MAGNALL.

Argent, on a mount vert a balista azure charged with a stone proper, a chief per fesse embattled or and gules—MAGNALL, Manchester and London; granted 1765.

MAGNALL.

Snail, or *House-snail*, (fr. *limaçon*): this occurs but rarely.

Sable, a fesse between three house-snails argent— SHELLEY.

Snail.

Gules, three snails argent in their shells or—BARTAN, Scotland.

Argent, a fesse vert between three house-snails azure — STUDMAN, Scotland.

Argent, a fesse vert between two snails in their shells in chief azure, and in base a thistle, leaved proper—STEDMAN.

Quarterly, first and fourth, per fesse or and gules a lion rampant counterchanged; second, or, a lion rampant with two heads azure; third, argent, a chevron gules between three snails sable—MASON, Yorkshire.

Slogan, or *Sloghorn*, [Scottish].
　See *Motto*.
Smelts. See *Salmon*.

Smew. See *Duck*.
Snagged. See under *Tree*.
Snake. See *Serpent*.

Snipe: of birds belonging to the family of the *scolopaidæ* we find single instances of the *snipe*, of the *curlew*, and of the *avocetta*, as follows.

Gules, a snipe argent gorged with a crown or—SNITTERTON.

Azure, a fesse dancetty between three curlews or—SCOGAN.

Azure, the head of an avocetta proper—BINDER.

Sovereign: an old French term found in some Rolls, signifying *chief* or *upper*. In the examples of the arms of BORDET and FLEMING it would refer to the uppermost bar, and in those of CUSANCE it would mean in the upper part of the bend.

Sire Robert BORDET, [de azure a ij barres de or] en la sovereyne barre iij merelos de goules—Roll, temp. ED. II.

Monsire John FLEMINGE, barre d'argent et d'asur a trois oreillers de gules en la sovereign barre.—*Ibid.*

Monsire William CUSANCE, port d'argent a une bend engrele sable a une escalop en le sov'reign peice—Roll, temp. ED. III.

Spade: the spade is generally pointed and shod with iron. The handle is sometimes like that of the figure in the margin, but often merely a short piece of wood at right angles with the upright piece. The *half-spade* is also borne, and in some instances the term *shovel* is used.

Azure, two spades or—DAMPORT.

Azure, three spades argent within a bordure or —AYNESWORTH.

Azure, three spades argent, helved or—KNIPERS-LEY.

Spade. Half-spade.

Sned, (written sometimes *snathe*); handle of a *scythe*. See under *Sickle*.

Snout: of a *mole*, &c., when of a different tincture.

Soaring or *rising*. See *Wings*.

Sol. See *Or*.

Soldering iron. See *Plumbers' Instruments*.

Sole. See *Turbot*.

Soleil. See *Sun* and *Rose en soleil*.

Sommé par, (fr.): when one charge has another *in chief* of it.

Song-book. See *Book*.

Souche, (fr.): a stump of a *Tree* shewing the roots.

Soutenu par, (fr.): when one charge has another below it.

Spalding: a fish. See under *Herring*.

Spancelled. See *Horse*.

Spaniel. See *Dog*.

Argent, on a bend vert three shovels bendwise in bend of the first—SWETTENHAM. [Various branches of the family vary the arms.]

Paly of six argent and gules, on a bend vert three half-spades of the first — SWETENHAM, Somerset.

Azure, three shovels argent—BEECHTON.

Azure, three irons or digging spades or — BECHETON.

Azure, three half-spades or, the side of each spade to the sinister—DAVERPORT.

SWETTENHAM.

Argent, a chevron between three half-spades [otherwise garden-spades] sable—STANDELFE.

The *Spade-iron:* the iron edge of a wooden spade, but it is not impossible that the figure is intended for a *boteroll,* or *crampet.*

Azure, three spade-irons or, [otherwise blades of spades]—BECKTON.

Spade-iron.

Sparrow: the common *sparrow* has been chosen for the sake of the name by one family, and an imperfect blazon may be noted as regards another family, the name *Phillip* being sometimes applied to a tame sparrow.

Argent, six sparrows, three, two and one sable; on a chief indented gules, two swords in saltire between as many wolf's heads erased or—SPAROW, London; granted 1516.

. . . three sparrows . . .—PHILLIP, Brignell, co. York.

Spear: it might have been expected that this charge would have been found in ancient arms, but so far as has been observed it is not the case. It is, however, not unfrequent in later arms. The *tilting-spear* proper should have the *vamplet* shewn, i.e. the funnel-shaped projection near where the hand holds it. The *cronel* also belonging to the tilting-spear has been already mentioned.

With the spear must be included the *lance* (fr. *lance*), *dart*, or *javelin* (fr. *javelot*). (See *Pheon*). It is difficult to distinguish them, but the *lance* is much longer than the dart or javelin, and the head is not barbed. The *dart* may, perhaps, be represented as a long *arrow* (q.v.), and like the *javelin* should have a *barbed* head. A *broken spear* (fr. *eclarté*) signifies the lower half, the upper having been broken off. Spears may be represented in *parcels*. A *half spear* signifies the upper half of the spear.

Or, on a bend sable, a [tilting] spear of the field headed argent—SHAKSPERE, Warwick. [Granted by Dethick to the father of the dramatist, 1546.]

Argent, five barrulets gules between three martlets in chief, and as many tilting spears paleways in base, azure—M'CALZIEN.

Azure, a battle-axe and tilting-spear in saltire argent headed or, in chief an arrow barways of the second headed and feathered of the third—GARBRAND.

Gules, a fesse ermine, over all two spears in saltire argent—CRAWFURD, Scotland.

SHAKSPERE.

Argent, seven half spears sable headed azure, three, one and three——DOCKER.

Sable, three spear-heads argent — PRYCE, Hunts.

Sable, a chevron between three leopard's heads or; on a chief as many spear-heads of the first embrued proper—PRICE, Marden, co. Hereford.

Or, on a bend azure a star between two crescents of the first, in chief a broken lance gules—SCOT, Whitislaid, Scotland.

Vert, a dart between two garbs or; on a chief

PRYCE.

azure a cherub's head proper between two estoiles argent—THACKERY.

Sable, a hand couped at the wrist grasping three darts, one in pale and two in saltire argent—LOWLE, Somerset.

Sable, a chevron between three darts, points upwards, shafts broken argent—AKENSIDE.

Sable, on a cross or between four unicorn's heads erased argent, armed, maned and tufted of the second, a cross engrailed gules charged with a javelin erect gold, headed as the third—WRIGHT, Manchester.

Sable, nine tilting-spears argent in parcels, three in each, viz. one in pale, two in saltire, wreath or—GARTEN, Sussex.

Azure, three fleurs-de-lis or, two and one; in chief spears issuing from the top of the field argent, each having a hook of the second, and beard on the dexter side—UNWYN, Horton, Yabington, co. Hants.

For salmon-*spear* and eel-*spear*, see under *Eel-spear*.

Spectacles: besides appearing in the insignia of the Company, these are borne by one or two families.

Argent, three pairs of spectacles vert, garnished or—Company of SPECTACLE MAKERS, London; Inc. 1629.

Gules, a chevron between three pairs of spectacles argent—STURMYN.

Argent, an oak-tree growing out of a mount in base vert; on one of the branches a pair of spectacles azure; on the top of the tree an eye proper—WAITE.

Sphere, (fr. *sphére*): the Terrestrial Sphere, or *Globe*, is rare in arms but not uncommon as part of a crest, e.g. of families of HOPE, DRAKE, &c. It is often environed with a meridian, and sometimes placed in a frame or stand. A remarkable example of late heraldic invention, and one of the worst, is seen in the arms of Sir John Ross.

A terrestrial sphere.

Similar to the *sphere*, but plain and (as a rule) surmounted by a cross, is the mound or *Orb*, q.v.

Azure, a sphere or—HARME, Surrey.

Azure, a pelican or, vulned proper, standing on a globe argent—John PIERSE, Bishop of Rochester, 1576; Salisbury, 1577; Archbishop of York, 1588-94.

Gules, three estoiles in chevron between as many lions rampant argent; [for augmentation] a chief or, thereon a portion of the terrestrial globe proper, the true meridian described thereon by a line passing from north to south sable, with the arctic circle azure; within which the place of the magnetic pole in latitude 70° 5′ 17″, and longitude 96° 46′ 45″ west, designated by an inescutcheon gules, charged with a lion passant gardant of the first; the magnetic meridian shewn by line of the fourth passing through the inescutcheon with a correspondent circle, also gules, to denote more particularly the said place of the magnetic pole; the words following inscribed on the chief, viz., "Arctæos Numine Fines"—Sir John Ross, C.B., Capt. R.N.

Azure, a globe, whereon are represented the Straits of Magellan and Cape Horn all proper; in the sinister chief point two herrings haurient in saltire argent crowned or; on a canton the united arms of Great Britain of the second—SOUTH SEA COMPANY, established 1712.

Azure, a cross patty fitchy or; on a chief of the last three globes azure—ELDRED, Olavers, Stannaway, Essex.

Both the *Armillary* and *Celestial sphere* are named ; the latter with a foot occurring in the crest of the Company of CLOCKMAKERS.

Gules, an armillary sphere or within an orle argent charged with eight mullets azure —CHAMBERLAIN, Baronetcy, 1828.

Upon a helmet properly mantled gules, doubled argent, and wreath of three colours, a celestial sphere with a foot, or—Crest of the Company of CLOCKMAKERS.

On a wreath argent and gules, a cloud proper, thereon a celestial sphere azure, with the circles or; on the zodiac the signs Aries, Taurus, Gemini, and Cancer—The crest of BULL, Watchmaker to Queen Elizabeth.

Crest of the Company of CLOCKMAKERS.

A *Hemisphere,* or *Demi-globe,* occurs only as part of a crest.

Sphinx, (fr. *sphinx*), is a monstrosity of Egyptian origin, composed of the head and breast of a woman, the body of a lion, and the wings of an eagle. It is more often used as a crest than in coats of arms.

Argent, on a fesse engrailed azure three mullets of the field, in chief a sphinx proper, all within a bordure engrailed gules—MOORE [as borne by Sir John Moore, K.B., the hero of Corunna].

Gules, three bars or, on a bend ermine a sphinx between two wreaths of laurel proper; on a chief embattled, a view of a fortified town with the word ACRE thereunder—CAMERON, co. Argyll.

Ermine, on a fesse engrailed azure three fleurs-de-lis or; in chief two branches of palm in saltire vert; in base a sphinx couchant proper— BERRY, Catton, Norfolk; extinct Baronetcy, created 1806.

Harpy, (fr. *harpie*): an imaginary creature represented as a vulture with the head and breast of a woman.

Vert, a fesse engrailed argent surmounted of another gules between three harpies of the second crined or—MOODY, co. Wilts; Baronetcy, 1621.

Azure, a harpy displayed, crined, crowned and armed or—Given as the Insignia of NUREMBURG. [Guillim, ed. 1632, p. 263.]

De gueules, semé de fleurs-de-lis d'argent à une harpie de même— CALOIS DE MESVILLE.

Allied to the harpy is a badge which is found sometimes carved on stonework during the reign of Richard III., and is usually attributed to this king. It is supposed, however, to represent a falcon, not a vulture, with the head of a woman.

Badge of RICHARD III.

The *Chimera* is said to have the face of a maiden, the mane and legs of a lion, the body of a goat, and the tail of a dragon, but is only used as a crest.

Spiders are found but very rarely on coats of arms. One example only has been noted.

Or, three spiders azure—CHETTLE.

Spire : the term is sometimes found in connection with towers of castles, &c., to describe the conical roofs. In one case only, so far as has been observed, it is used as a charge.

... on a mount vert a castle with five spires argent—Town of QUEENBOROUGH, Kent.

Gules, three spires argent, on each a ball and cross or—DAKECOMBE, or DAKEHAM, Linc. and Salop. [Originally of Stepleton, Dorset.]

Spire.

Spoon : a single example is given of this charge in Glover's Ordinary.

Sable, three spoons erect or—SPONELL.

Spur, (fr. *éperon*) : gilt spurs are proper to knights, and white ones to esquires. When employed as heraldic charges they are generally borne with the straps pendent, and the rowel downwards.

Spurred is also used (see example under *Leg*). The spurs are generally represented with the *leathers* attached.

Spur.

Gules, a dexter hand holding a spear bendways between two spurs with leathers argent—GIB, Cariboer, Scotland.

Spindles, *Weaver's*, q.v.
Spires of *Grass*, q.v.
Splendour, *In his.* See *Sun*.

Spokeshaves. Probably an erroneous blazon. See under *Glaziers' Nippers*.

Argent, three palets gules; on a canton of the second a spur with the rowel downwards leathered or within a bordure engrailed sable—KNIGHT, Ruscombe, co. Berks.

Paly of six argent and azure; on a canton as the last a spur or—KNIGHT.

Gules, a spur-leather and buckle or; on a chief argent three cock's heads erased of the field, combed and wattled gold—COCKES, Somerset.

Argent, a chevron gules, between in chief two spurs, and in base a battle-axe azure, shaft or—CONNELL, Ireland.

The term *Spur-rowel* is sometimes used in modern heraldry to signify a mullet, of six points, pierced. See old fr. *rouwel*, &c., under *Rowel*.

Azure, two talbots in chief and a spur-rowel in base or—VIVIAN, France.

Vert, a horse argent caparisoned or; on a chief of the second three spur-rowels gules—STUDHOLME, co. Cumberland.

Argent, a bend engrailed between in chief two spur-rowels gules and in base a hunting-horn of the second garnished sable—GLASSFORD, Borrostounness, Scotland.

Square : an instrument used by carpenters, also by masons. With the carpenter's square may be noted the single instance of the carpenter's *reel*.

Square.

Argent, a chevron between three carpenter's squares, points dexter sable—ATHOWE, or ATLOWE.

Argent, a chevron between three carpenter's squares, the angles in sinister chief, gules—Elias SYDALL, Bishop of St. David's, 1731; Gloucester, 1731–33.

Per pale argent and sable, a chevron between three mason's squares counterchanged—MASON.

Sable, a carpenter's square or—BEVILL.

Argent, on a chevron between three pairs of compasses extended sable, a joiner's square or, and a golden reel of line as the first—Company of CARPENTERS, London (Cotton MS. Tib. D. 10), [elsewhere, 'and a reel as the last,' stringed azure].

SYDALL.

Spool. See *Spindle*.

Spoonbill. See *Heron*.

Spot: rarely used to denote marks on an animal, e.g. a *Lion* with spots, q.v. See also *ermine* spots. See also spotted *cat*, spotted *dog*, &c.

Sprats. See *Herring*.

The term *square* is found sometimes written for *squire* or *Esquire,* q.v., in the arms of MORTIMER, &c., and *per square* is found fancifully and improperly used for *quarterly.*

Squirrel, (fr. *écureuil*): this animal is always borne sejant, and usually cracking a nut.

Argent, two squirrels addorsed gules—SAMWELL.

Argent, a chevron azure, between three squirrels sejant, cracking nuts sable—LOVELL, Norfolk.

Gules, a squirrel sejant cracking a nut or; on a chief of the last three fleurs-de-lis azure—STOKES.

Azure, a fesse between three squirrels argent cracking nuts or, within a bordure engrailed of the second—STOCKWOOD.

Ermine, on a chevron sable between three squirrels proper, with beads and chains of gold about

SAMWELL.

their necks, three roses argent—Company of TAUYERS [or GREYTAWYERS, i.e. dressers of white leather], London ; [Arms granted, 1531].

Two squirrels proper are the supporters of the arms of BOYD, Merton Hall, co. Wigton.

Staff: the term is usually qualified by some word expressing its special purpose or character, such as *Pilgrim's* or *palmer's staff,* q.v.; *pike-staff,* generally drawn like the first figure of the *pilgrim's staff,* but without the hook; *flag-staff; quarter-staff,* used by foresters, &c.; *Cross-staff,* q.v., and *pastoral-staff,* see under *Crosier.* Sometimes the kind of staff is implied, as a *Banner and staff* (see under Paschal *Lamb*); a *crozier* with the *staff* of such a tincture, &c.

Sable, three pikestaves argent, two and one, on the top of each an annulet or—PIKE, Gottenburgh, Sweden ; granted 1751.

Argent, a chevron erminois between three flag-staves proper—HAWKE.

Azure, a chevron between three quarter-staffs argent—LONGSTAFF.

Gules, a griffin segreant or, holding a flag-staff bendy argent and sable, thereon a banner flowing to the dexter of the third, charged with an

---

Spread, i.q. *Displayed.*

Sprig. See *Tree.*

Springing: a term sometimes applied to beasts of chase instead of *salient;* also to fishes borne bendwise.

Sprouting afresh: a trunk of an oak tree so blazoned.

Square pierced: pierced with a small square orifice. See *Cross quarterly pierced,* § 5.

imperial eagle of the fourth—GABOTT, Acton-Burnell; also GARBETT. [Given by the Emperor Maximilian, Visit. London, 1568.]

Per chief indented azure and or; over all in bend a crosier, the staff gules, the crook of the first—Cistercian Abbey of BUCKLAND, co. Devon.

The *staff raguly*, or *ragged-staff*, occurs very frequently, and the term implies a branch of a tree, with the twigs lopped, and resembling a *club*. It is generally drawn *couped*, and then the term *trunked* is used; when *throughout* the better blazon would be a *fesse* or *bend raguly*. It will be observed that it is sometimes represented *flammant*, but perhaps in that case a *fire-brand raguly* would be the better blazon.

Azure, a fesse quarterly sable and argent between three ragged staves bendways or—WOODHOUSE, Calais.

Argent, a ragged staff embowed to the sinister gules—ALTEN.

Argent, two ragged staves couped at the ends embowed one to the other sable—BOWSTOCK.

Argent, a lion rampant sable supporting a ragged staff azure—WILLISBY.

Sable, an eagle displayed argent, armed and standing upon a ragged staff fesswise or—BARLOW, co. Lancaster.

Sable, on a chevron argent between three staves raguly or, inflamed proper, a fleur-de-lys azure between two Cornish choughs—MERYCK, Bp. of Sodor and Man, 1575–99.

MERYCK.

Argent, three staves raguly sable, flammant at the top proper—LAYLAND.

The *shepherd's staff* or *crook* is a long staff slightly curved at the top, or at least less so than the *staff* represented under *crosier*.

Vert, two shepherd's crooks in saltire or between three lambs passant, two and one argent—James SHEPHERD, New Green, Surrey.

Sable, two shepherd's crooks in saltire or between three garbs of the second—BENNETTE.

Squire, (as in the arms of Mortimer). See *Esquire*.

SS. Collar *of*. See *Collar of SS*.

Stafford's Knot. See *Cords*.

Stag. See *Deer*.

Stag-beetle. See *Beetles*.

Stainand colours, used in theoretical heraldry, are tinctures, which being applied to the figures called *abatements*, are supposed to be disgraceful. They are *sanguine* and *tenné*.

Some peculiar names occur, e.g. a *Jacob's staff* (possibly a shepherd's crook, but probably St. James' *pilgrim's staff*); the *crutch staff*, i.q. *potent*, and the *Jedburgh staff*. The *Patriarchal staff* is a staff surmounted by a double or *Patriarchal cross*. See *Cross*, § 28.

Azure, a Jacob's staff in pale between two estoiles or—John THURLOW, Burnham Overy, Norfolk; [granted 1664].

Gules, on a horse salient argent furnished azure a chevalier armed at all points grasping in the right hand a kind of lance called the Jedburgh staff proper—Burgh of JEDBURGH, Scotland.

The term *staves* is used in the sense of the handles of axes. See battle-*axe*, (*hafted* is a better term). Also of the rays of an *escarboucle*, q.v. *Staved* is also applied to branches; see under *Tree*.

With the staff may be grouped examples of the *club* (fr. *massue*), see *Mace;* also the *truncheon;* the first being usually held by a savage or woodman (see under *Man*), and is not uncommonly held by such when appearing as *supporters*. The *club* also has been drawn so as to be mistaken for the icicle. See *Gouttes*.

Argent, a savage gules, holding a club over the shoulder vert— GILHAM.

Argent, three spiked clubs sable—BARSTON.

Argent, a chevron between three truncheons, each held in a sinister hand couped at the wrist or—STEVENSON.

Azure, three clubs [? icicles] in bend or—HARBOTTLE.

D'argent, a trois massues garnies de pointes de gueules rangées en fasce—BRUSSE, Pays Bas.

De gueules, à trois massues renversées d'argent—MACE, Normandie.

Staff-tree: this shrub is the *Celastrus* of Linnæus, and its leaves are borne in one coat of arms.

Azure, a chevron argent between three staff-tree leaves slipped or, as many bees volant proper—LEAF, Streatham, Surrey.

Stalked; used mostly of ears of *wheat;* but sometimes of *plants, flowers*, &c. Cf. *slipped*.

Stalking: sometimes applied to long - legged birds, instead of '*walking*.'

Staple: this charge is borne in several instances for the sake of the play upon the name. Sometimes the term *door-staple* is used.

Staple.

Argent, on a pile sable, a staple affixed to the centre of the pile interlaced with a horseshoe or — DUNSTAPLE PRIORY, Beds.

Argent, three staples sable—STAPLETON.

Argent, on a lion rampant sable a staple or on the shoulder—STAPLETON, co. Lancaster.

Argent, a chevron ermine between three staples sable—STAPLES.

Argent, a chevron between three door-staples gules—BRETON.

Argent, a saltire gules between four door-staples sable—STOCKTON.

DUNSTAPLE PRIORY.

Star: for the conventional heraldic form of star see *Estoile*. In some late examples of arms, however, the *polar stars* are represented. See also under *Telescope* and *Neptune*. A *comet*, q.v., is sometimes called a blazing star.

Sable, a fesse wavy between the two polar-stars argent—Sir Francis DRAKE (the first English circumnavigator).

Azure, on a rock proper an eagle rising or, between in chief the arctic and in base antarctic polar stars; on a canton of the third a wreath of laurel vert fructed of the second—SOMERSET, London; granted 1771.

Azure, a mast of a vessel issuant from the base, thereon a sail hoisted and pendent flying proper between two estoiles in fesse or, representing the arctic and antarctic polar stars — ENDERBY, London; granted Aug. 12, 1778.

Azure, the sun and full moon in chief, and the seven stars in orbicular form (?) in base, all or—DE FONTIBUS, Bp. of Ely, 1220–25.

Starling: this bird occurs but rarely. Probably the *stern* in the arms of DUKE means the same, and not as sometimes supposed the stern of a vessel.

Sable, an escutcheon between starlings in orle argent—CALVERLEY.

Or, six starlings between three mullets sable, each charged with a bezant—PELTON.

Standard. See *Flag;* also *Arrow.*

Standish. See *Dish.*

Stangue, (fr.): shank of an *anchor.*

Star-fish. See *Mullet.*

Erminois, a fesse wavy azure between three starlings sable, beaked and legged gules—GAMBIER, Baron Gambier.

Azure, a chevron between three sterns argent, beaked and legged gules—DUKE, co. Suffolk.

Statant, (fr. *arrété*): a term signifying standing still with all the feet touching the ground, applied generally to animals, e.g. to a *lion* and *wolf*, q.v.; to some birds, e.g. a *stork*, q.v.; the *heron* being generally drawn so. Frequently it is applied to the *griffin*. To stags when in this position and *gardant* the term '*at gaze*' is applied. The head of an animal statant may be *gardant*, but if so it should be mentioned.

Argent, a griffin statant sable, armed azure—HALTON.

Azure, a griffin statant or—GARDENER, London.

Stilts: this singular charge seems only to be borne by one family. The stilts thus borne are represented as shewn in the illustration given in the margin.

Argent, two stilts in saltire sable, garnished or—NEWBY, Yorkshire.

NEWBY.

Stirrup, (fr. *étrier*): generally borne pendent, attached to a leather strap, with a buckle: in one case the leather is borne separately.

Gules, three stirrups with leathers in pale or—DEVERELL.

Azure, three stirrups with leathers or—GIFFORD, Staff.

Gules, three stirrups leathered and buckled or—SCUDAMORE, co. Hereford.

Azure, three stirrups or—PUREFOY, co. Leicester.

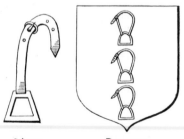

Stirrup.   DEVERELL.

Staved: applied to a *branch*. See under *Tree*.

Steeple. See *Spire*, and *Temple*.

Stem: the stem of *flowers*, &c., is frequently referred to as of a different tincture, when the term *Slipped* is generally used.

Steps or *degrees*. See *Cross*, § 15.

Azure, a stirrup between three mitres argent—Benedictine Abbey, EVESHAM, co. Worcester.

Vert, a chevron engrailed argent between in chief semy of torteaux two stags statant at gaze or, and in base a stirrup-leather gold—ROBINSON, co. Leicester.

Stones. These are very seldom found separately. Two remarkable cases of cranes holding a stone by their feet are given under *Crane*. The stones in walls are represented by *Masoning*. The *flag-stones* are found in the insignia of the PAVIOURS' Company; and a *marble-stone* will be found in the singular coat of arms given under *Sengreen*. *Tombstones* and *Millstones* will be found under their several headings; while the *Star-stone* is only another name for a *Shot* (q.v.) of a particular sort, and *gun-stone* for *Pellet* (q.v.). Also used with a *balista*. See *Sling*. As regards the *flint-stone*, it is supposed by some to mean a *shot*, but most probably it is simply a *flint* which is intended.

Argent, three wall-stones [? bricks] in pale or—BRICKLEY.

Or, a chevron quarterly azure and gules between three flint-stones of the last—STONE, co. Gloucester.

Vert, three flint-stones argent—FLINT.

See also stone *Billets;* stone-bills under *Wedge;* and stone-fountains under *Wells.*

Stork: this bird is found in several coats of arms, as well as the *heron* and *crane,* although in the actual drawing it is difficult to distinguish them. The bird is frequently represented with the right leg raised.

Or, a stork statant—John de EGLESCLIFF, Bp. of Connor, afterwards of Llandaff, 1323–47.

Argent, on a chevron between three storks, as many swans proper—POULTERERS' Company, [Inc. 1504].

Or, a stork proper—SERJEANTS' INN, Chancery Lane.

Argent, a stork sable, beaked and membered gules—STARKEY, co. Derby.

DE EGLESCLIFF.

Stern. See *Ship,* also *Starling.*
Still. See *Distillatory.*

Stock (1) of a *Tree,* q.v., (2) of an *Anchor,* q.v.

Azure, three storks, wings expanded argent—GIBSON, Swindon, co. Wilts.

Azure, three storks rising argent—GIBSON, Bp. of Lincoln, 1716, and of London, 1723–48.

Party per fesse argent and sable, a pale counterchanged, three storks close of the second —Edward STOREY, Bp. of Carlisle, 1468, and of Chichester, 1478—1502.

GIBSON.   STOREY.

Straps: these only incidentally occur in connection with *armour, collars, stirrups,* &c. In one case they are distinctly mentioned, namely, as *wrist straps,* and in another case they are named as part of a badge of office.

Azure, three clubs argent, with wrist straps gules—MAZZINGHI, London.

Azure, an oak-tree growing out of a mount in base or, and on one of the branches two keys of the first fastened by straps gules [for the office of Thane of Fettercairn]—WOOD, Balbegno, Scotland.

Strawberry: the leaf only is the part usually borne, though in one case sprigs *fructed* occur. The more frequent term for the strawberry-leaf is the *frasier,* which is a Scotch term for a *cinquefoil;* hence some contend that this charge should be represented merely as such.

Sable, on a bend between in chief a greyhound courant bendwise and in base a dolphin haurient argent, three torteaux; a chief of the second charged with three sprigs of strawberry fructed proper—HOLLIST, Midhurst, Sussex.

Azure, three garbs or with a strawberry leaf in the centre—CUMING, Moray, temp. James V.

Azure, three frasiers argent—FRASER, Pitcallain.

Azure, a lion rampant argent crowned with an antique crown or armed and langued gules within a bordure of the second charged with six frasiers of the first—MAC DOUGALL, Mackerston, co. Roxburgh.

Stone-bow: probably only an ordinary *cross-bow,* or arbalette, but called thus on account of the name of the bearer, HURLSTONE. See *Bow.*

Stoned: adorned with precious stones, e.g. of a gem-*ring.*

Straps. See examples introduced under *Staff* (club), and under *Tree.*

Sturgeon: this fish occurs in two coats of arms, evidently on account of the play upon the name.

Azure, three sturgeons argent fretty gules—STURGNEY.

Azure, three sturgeons naiant in pale or, over all a fret gules—STURGEON, Whipsted, Suffolk.

Sugar-cane: a modern bearing, no doubt first assumed by persons who had accumulated wealth in the West Indian colonies.

Argent, two sugar-canes in saltire proper surmounted by a fleur-de-lis gules; on a chief azure three plates, each charged with a mullet sable—FOULKS.

Argent, on a fesse wavy azure, between in chief two bucks trippant and in base two sugar-canes in saltire, surmounted by a bill in pale all proper, three estoiles or—TIMPORIN, co. Hertford.

SUGAR-CANE.

Or, on a chevron gules, between three martletts sable, two sugar-canes of the first—FENWICK.

Sugar-loaves were borne by one family in Somerset, and Dr. Sugar added a Doctor's *Cap* in chief.

Sable, three sugar-loaves argent, in chief a Doctor's cap—Dr. SUGAR, New College, Oxford.

Sun, (fr. *soleil*): this luminary is usually borne *in his glory*, or *splendour*, that is to say, with a human countenance (fr. *figuré*), and rays (sixteen or more), alternately straight and waved. When depicted without a face, the French blazon it *ombre de soleil*.

Rays of the sun, or *beams*, are occasionally borne singly, and so in the ancient rolls, but more frequently they are represented issuant from charges, when the term *radiant, rayonné,*

Streamer: a long narrow flag.

Strewed, used by some writers for *Semé*.

Stringed: applied to *bugle-horns, harps, bows, mitres,* &c., when their strings are of a different tincture.

Studded: applied to a collar with studs of a different tincture.

Stump. See *Tree.*

Subinscribed: i.e. with *Letters,* or a name written beneath the charge; found only in very modern arms.

Sufflue: a curious name applied to the *Rest,* q.v.

Super charge: a charge *surmounting* another is by some writers referred to by this term.

or *rayonnant* is used. (See under *Ray*.) It is not improbable that some families have adopted it on account of the play on the name, e.g. THOMPSON, JOHNSON, &c.

Gules, the sun in his glory argent—RICHMOND.

Argent, the sun in splendour or—DELAHAY.

Or, on a pile azure, between two lions rampant combatant in base gules, the sun in splendour proper—PEARSON, co. Lincoln.

Azure, a sun in splendour or—Town of BANBURY.

Gules, two bars ermine in chief three suns in glory or—NICHOLSON, co. Down.

Azure, the sun rising from behind a hill or—HILL, Edinburgh.

RICHMOND.

Gules, an eagle displayed or looking against the sun in its splendour placed toward the dexter chief—The feudal coat of the lordship of CARDROSS.

Or, a sun gules [otherwise radiated gules]—HAYS, co. Dorset.

Per pale or and azure, a sun counterchanged—ST. CLERE, Tidwell, co. Devon.

Azure, seven suns or, three, three and one—ELHAM.

Azure, on a fesse, between three goat's heads couped argent collared gules, the sun radiated or between two mascles sable—GASON, Kent [temp. Hen. VIII.].

D'or, à l'ombre de soleil d'azur—DUPONT, Languedoc.

Sun Eclipsed : the *sun* or *moon* when borne eclipsed is drawn exactly as when in his glory, or her complement, but sable.

Argent, a sun eclipsed issuing out of the dexter chief, the beams or—WELDAY, Wheelhurst.

Azure, the sun half-eclipsed [i.e. per pale, sable and or]—DYSON, co. Worcester.

See also the curious example in the insignia of the DISTILLERS' COMPANY under *Distillatory*.

Super inscribed : i.e. with the name written above the charge ; generally over some *fort* or *castle*, and in two or three cases Indian names.

Supplanting : said to mean bestriding. See the example under *Apollo*.

Supporting : applied to animals holding up some other charge, e.g. of a *Lion* holding a battle-axe. See under *Altar* and *Saltire*. The terms *supporting* and *supported by* are also sometimes used very irregularly for *surmounting*, or *surmounted by*.

Sunflower, (fr. *soleil*): this appears only in one English coat of arms, and in this case the family is of foreign extraction. It is blazoned *heliotrope*, just as the French *tournesol* is sometimes used for the sunflower.

Azure, a heliotrope (or sunflower) or issuing from the stalk sprouting out of two leaves vert; in chief the sun in splendour proper—FLUMIO [originally of Spain; granted 1614].

D'argent, au tournesol d'or tigé feuillé et terrassé de sinople—GUILLOIS, Ile de France.

Supporters, (fr. *supports* and *tenants*, the former applied to animals, the latter to human beings): the figures placed on each side of the shield to support it. There is much difference of opinion concerning their origin. They are found attached to the arms of Edward III. and Richard II., but the only examples (e.g. in glass, &c.) are of later date, and cannot be accepted as authorities. Perhaps the earliest for which there is contemporary evidence are those supporting the arms of Henry VI. Not many supporters are found even for peers much before the reign of Henry VIII.

At present supporters are used in this country by

The *Sovereign* and *Princes of the blood.* (See ARMS, *Royal.*)

Peers and *Peeresses,* the supporters being hereditary.

Knights of the Garter and *Knights Grand Crosses of the Bath* are also dignified with supporters granted to them by Garter King of Arms at their creation.

Some *Baronets* and untitled *Gentlemen* have also the right of bearing supporters, either by patent, or because their ancestors bore them before their ordinary use was restricted to the peerage. In the case of baronets they are usually confined to the holder of the title.

Supporters have been granted to several cities and towns as well as to the principal *Mercantile Companies* of the city of London. They are generally of later date than the insignia which they support, and in some instances in very bad taste.

Suppressed by: used rarely to mean *debruised,* or *surmounted by* some other ordinary or charge.

Surgerant, or *surgeant,* rising: said of birds, and especially of the *falcon,* q.v. See *Wings.*

Surcoat: a coat embroidered with the arms of the wearer, or in the case of heralds, &c., those of his lord. It was at first without sleeves and girt with a belt, but in later times sleeves were added and the belt laid aside. The first English king on whose seal a surcoat appears is King John.

The usual practice was for the arms, whether single or quartered, to appear upon the surcoat both before and behind, and also upon each of the sleeves.

The figure given is that of one of the TURVILLE family, from glass in Wolston Church, Warwickshire, the arms (upon the surcoat and emerasses) being

Sir Richard (?) TURVILLE.

Gules, a chevron vair, between three mullets pierced argent—TURVILLE.

The other figure represents John TALBOT, Earl of Shrewsbury, temp. Hen. VI., and is taken from an ancient painting at Castle Ashby.

The quarters seen upon the body of the surcoat are, Argent, a bend between six martlets—FURNIVALL: and checquy or and azure, a chevron ermine—arms of the ancient Earls of WARWICK. On the sleeve, Gules, a lion rampant with a bordure engrailed or—TALBOT: Azure, a lion rampant with a bordure or—DE BELESME: Gules, a fesse between six crosscrosslets or—BEAUCHAMP: Argent, two lions passant gules—STRANGE of Blackmere: together with FURNIVALL, and WARWICK as before.

Sir John TALBOT.

Ladies formerly wore the arms of their husbands upon their

Surtout, also *sur le tout* (fr.): the English 'over all' is more usually substituted; while the French use the term *brochant sur le tout;* it is especially applied to an *escutcheon* of pretence.

Sur le tout du tout, practically equivalent to the former.

mantles, and their own upon their close-fitting vests. Eleanor,
Countess of Arundel, who died 1372, is thus depicted in the
east window of Arundel church, Sussex. At a later period the
arms were borne impaled on the outer garment; e.g. Elizabeth,
wife of John SHELLEY, Esq., on a brass at Clapham, Sussex, 1513.

Surcoat is sometimes improperly used instead of an *escutcheon
over all*. See an example under *Sceptre*.

Surmounted by: a term used when a bearing is placed
over another of a different tincture. In
cases where more than one ordinary or
charge is surmounted by another, the term
Over all, q.v., must be used. It is needful
to mark the distinction between *surmounted*
and *charged*, which will appear from the
arms of DYXTON. If the pile had been
charged with the chevron, the latter would
not have extended beyond the bounds of
the former. The term may also be rightly

DYXTON.

used of two charges placed in saltire to denote the uppermost
one. (See under *Mace*, *Scythe*, &c.) *Debruised*, q.v., has also
a similar meaning to *surmounted*, and is frequently used, as also
the terms *depressed* and *oppressed*.

Sable, a pile argent, surmounted by a chevron gules—DYXTON.

Gules, a cross patonce or, surmounted of a
bend azure semy of fleurs-de-lys of the second—
HUGH LATIMER, Bp. of Worcester, 1535-39.

Gules, a chevron chequy or and azure surmounted by a bend ermine—HANSTED.

Argent, a fir-tree growing out of a mount vert
in base, surmounted by a sword in bend proper;
on a dexter canton azure a royal crown proper—
GREG, co. Chester.

Gules, a fesse argent surmounted by a chevron
azure [From *Burke's Armory*]. Gules, a fesse ar-

LATIMER.

gent, over all a chevron azure [From *Papworth's Ordinary*]—BROADHURST.

Sustaining, (fr. *soutenant*): a
similar term for *supporting*, e.g.

a *Lion rampant* sustaining a
battle-axe.

The above being the correct signification of the term it must not be overlooked that it is sometimes used irregularly for describing one charge above, i.e. *in chief of*, another, and this is especially the case in modern French heraldry, when *surmonté* or *sommé de* is very frequently, if not always, used with this signification. The terms *brochant* (or *bronchant*) *sur le tout* are more usually employed by French heralds for the true signification of *surmounted by*. (See *Over all*.)

Argent, a heart gules, surmounted by [should be ensigned with] a regal crown, on a chief azure three mullets argent—Douglas. [From *Burke's Illustrations*.]

Per chevron argent and gules three skenes surmounted with as many wolf's heads [better, 'on the point of each a wolf's head'] counterchanged—Skene, Newtile, Scotland. [From *Burke's Armory*.]

Gules, a castle surmounted with a tower argent; in base a lion passant gardant or—City of Norwich. [From *Papworth's Ordinary*.]

De gueules, au chêne d'argent surmonté d'une fleur-de-lis d'or [i.e. with the fleur-de-lis in chief]—De Reals, Languedoc.

De gueules, à une forteresse d'or a trois tours du même, celle du milieu sommée d'une grue, tenant sa vigilance du même [i.e. the crane stands on the top of the central turret]—De Boileau de Castelnau, Languedoc.

Swallow, (fr. *hirondelle*), and from the French word a family of Arundel, as well as the borough of that name in Sussex, are supposed to have taken their arms. The bird, however, is found adopted by several other families. When the *martin* is named it is probably intended for the *martlet*.

Sable, six swallows 3, 2, 1, argent—Family of Arundel of Wardour.

Argent, a swallow volant in bend sinister sable—Town of Arundel, Sussex.

Or, a fesse azure between four barrulets wavy of the last: on a canton of the second two barrulets argent, charged with three swallows volant sable, viz. on the first two, second one—Allott, co. York; granted 1729.

Argent, a fesse between three swallows volant sable—Swallow.

Argent, a cross raguly gules between four swallows [otherwise 'birds'] azure legged of the second—Anstis, Cornwall.

Argent, a chevron between three martins sable—Martinson, Newcastle-on-Tyne.

Swaddled. See *Child*.   Sweep. See *Sling*.

Swan, (lat. *cygnus*, fr. *cygne*): this graceful bird has for various reasons been a favourite charge in armorial bearings. Swans are generally blazoned as *proper*, i.e. white, else they are described as argent, but they are frequently beaked and legged of other tinctures. The bird is generally borne with expanded wings, and it seems desirable that the position should be noticed, though as a fact it is only seldom so. Sometimes they are drawn swimming towards each other, and for this the word '*respectant*' or '*incontrant*' seems to have been used by some heraldic writers.

Azure, two swans close in pale argent between as many flaunches ermine—MELLISH.

Azure, a swan proper—SWAN, Kent.

Azure, a fesse between three swans argent— SWAN, ob. 1487.

MELLISH.

Gules, three swans argent—SWANLAND, Lord Mayor of London, 1329.

Sable, a swan with its wings expanded argent, within a bordure engrailed or—MOORE, Hants.

Azure, a fesse or, between three swans argent beaked and legged gules —GISLINGHAM, Suffolk.

Gules, a bend sable between two cotises or, and as many mullets and as many swans argent—RUSSELL.

Per saltire; in chief argent, a cross gules; in the dexter flank gules, a lion passant gardant or; in the sinister flank or, a red rose; in base azure, a swan eating an eel proper—Town of GOREY, Ireland; granted 1623.

Sable, two swans in pale, wings addorsed argent, between as many flaunches or, on a chief gules a garb between two fleurs-de-lis of the third—FITLER.

Per pale sable and gules, a swan, wings expanded argent, ducally gorged and [sometimes] chained or—Town of BUCKINGHAM.

Azure, a fesse engrailed or, surmounted of another gules charged with three roses argent, all between as many swans sans legs proper—RIVERS, Kent; Lord Mayor of London, 1573.

Sable, two swans [rather geese] incontrant [otherwise in fesse incontrant regardant] argent—TREGOSSE.

Swans are borne by the following families amongst others:—

ATWATER, Kent.—BADBY, Suffolk.—BALDEN, Norfolk.—BOLDEN, Lancaster. — BRACY. — BRODERIP.—BRYSE.— CAZIER, London.—CHARLTON, London.—CLARKE (see under *Pellet*).—COBB (see under *Herring*).—COBLEY.—COPPARD, Sussex.—CRESSINGHAM.—DALE, York and Northumber-

land. —DAWES, Norfolk. —DELANEY. —ELKINGTON. —FATTOR, Norfolk. —
FOLNARBY. — HOBBES, Wilts. — JENYSONN, Norfolk. —LANNOY, Hammer-
smith. —LEIGHAM. —LIGHT, Oxfordshire. —LOVENHAM. —LYTE, Somerset.
—MICHELL, Somerset. —MOLSFORD, Devon. —MORE, Devon. —PELFYN.—
PHILLPOT, Hereford. —PICKERELL, London. —REDDIE. —SCOTER. —SHEL-
DON. — STORMER. — SUTER. — SYNNOT, Wexford. — SWABEY, Bucks. —
VAUGHAN. —WALTON, Lancashire. —WATERS [York Herald, *temp.* Ric. II.].
—WOLRICH, Salop. —WYBERNE, Kent. —YEO, Devon.

The head and neck of a swan are blazoned *a swan's neck;* the
wings are also met with.

Argent, five swan's necks erased argent—LACY,
alias HEDGES, London; also co. Oxford.

Sable, three swan's heads couped at the neck
argent — Samuel SQUIRE, Bp. of S. David's,
1761–66.

Argent, a martlet sable; on a chief azure three
swan's wings endorsed of the first—SWANSTON,
Scotland.

The *Cygnet* sometimes occurs; and a   LACY.
cygnet royal implies a swan gorged with a ducal coronet, having
a chain affixed thereunto and reflexed over its back.   It should
rather be blazoned a swan proper, ducally gorged and chained
or, a cygnet being properly a *young* swan.   It was one of the
badges of Henry V.   The term, however, may properly be used
when there are two or more swans in one coat, like *lioncel.*

Azure, a bend engrailed between two cygnets argent gorged with ducal
crowns, with strings reflexed over their
backs or—PITFIELD, Dorset.

Gules, a cygnet argent—Thomas ASDALE.

A beacon or, inflamed proper.—An antelope gorged with a crown and chained.—

A swan adorned in a like manner.   Three   Badges of HENRY V.
badges of HENRY V., from cornice of his chantry, Westminster Abbey.

Swivel: a charge generally drawn something like a pair
of *Shackbolts* (see under *Fetterlock*).   It appears only to be borne by the IRONMONGERS'
Company.

Swivel.

Argent, on a chevron gules between three steel gads azure as many
swivels, the middle one palewise, the other two in the line of the chevron
or—Company of IRONMONGERS; arms granted, 1455: confirmed, 1530.

Sword, (fr. *epée*), or *arming* sword : the usual form is a long straight blade, with a cross handle, and it is borne in a variety of ways, so that its position should be distinctly stated. The sword in the insignia of the city of London is sometimes called the sword of S. Paul, that apostle being patron of the city. The blade may be waved, omb, and, &c. A sword is often represented piercing an animal or a human heart.

The *hilt* and *pomel* are also frequently named, as they are often of a different tincture from the sword itself. A sword *proper* is *argent* with hilt and pomel *or*.

Or, a sword in bend sable—SMALLBROOK, co. Worcester.

Sable, a sword erect in pale argent, hilt and pomel or—DYMOCK.

Azure, three swords, one in pale, point uppermost, surmounted by the other two in saltire, points downward, argent—NORTON.

Gules, a man's head couped at the shoulders between three swords proper headed or—SWORD.

Gules, a lion rampant argent between two swords, pomels downwards, points to the dexter and sinister chief proper—DEMSEY.

Gules, three pairs of swords in saltire argent, hilts and pomels or, viz. two pairs in chief and one pair in base—CUTLERS' COMPANY, [Incorporated 1417 ; arms granted 1476].

NORTON.

Argent, a sword in pale azure, hilted or; a chief gules—MENZIES, Culdairs.

Gules, on a chief argent two swords in saltire azure—BRADDYLL.

Argent, a two-handed sword in pale azure—SPALDING, Scotland.

Gules, a two-handed sword bendwise between two mullets or—SYMONSTON, Symonston.

Azure, a waved sword erect in pale proper, hilt and pomel or, between two mullets in fesse pierced argent—DICK.

Argent, a sword erect, point upwards; from the blade issuing drops of blood—O'DAVOREN, Ireland.

Gules, a fesse between three pheons argent on a canton or, a dexter gauntlet sable holding a broken sword erect of the second embrued in blood—EGERTON, Dublin.

Azure, two swords in saltire, blades argent, hilts and pomels or, pierced through a human heart proper; in chief a cinquefoil azure—PARSONS.

Or, three sword points proper, two and one—PROCTOR.

There are different kinds of swords mentioned in blazon, e.g. the *arming* sword, the sword of *state*, the *Irish sword*, the Highlander's *Claymore*, &c.

> "The Highlander, whose red *claymore*
> The battle turned on Maida's shore."
> *Scott's Marmion, Introd. to Canto VI.*

Others also will be found already given under *Sabre*, q.v.

Sable, an arming sword, the point in chief argent—MARMION.

A sword of state palewise, point downwards, surmounted of two lions passant; impaling quarterly, first and fourth chequy argent and sable, second and third gules, two barrows [*sic* but *Qy.*] or—Seal and Arms of the Corporation of DROITWICH, co. Worcester.

Argent, issuing from the sinister side of the shield a cubit dexter arm vested gules, cuffed azure, the hand proper grasping an old Irish sword, the blade entwined with a serpent proper—O'DONOVAN, Ireland.

Azure, a cat rampant argent, on a chief the standard of St. Andrew and a claymore, point downwards, in saltire proper—SMITH, London.

The sword may be *sheathed*, i.e. in its *scabbard*, the termination of which is called the *crampet, chape,* or *boteroll*, (fr. *bouterol*); and this termination is sometimes found as a separate charge. [The *habick* of the CLOTH-WORKERS' Company is found wrongly blazoned as a *crampet*.]

Argent, two swords in their scabbards in saltire sable, hilts and chapes or—GELLIBRAND, co. Kent, temp. HEN. VIII. [N.B. Brand is a word for sword.]

Sable, a sword in pale, point downwards, scabbard and belt argent, on the sinister side a Katherine wheel argent—GARAT GROCH.

A crampet or, the inside per pale azure and gules, charged with the letter r of the first—Badge of Earl DE LA WARR.

Azure, three bouterolls or—BECHETON [or Becketon].

Sable, three sword chapes or—ADDERTON, co. York.

Badge of DE LA WARR.

Sword-fish: this fish has been observed named but in one of arms.

Gules, a blade of a sword-fish argent crowned or—LESSIEURE, Middlesex.

Synobolt, *Sinople*, is spelt thus in the Boke of S. Albans.

Sykes. See *Fountain*.

Syren. See *Mermaid*.

Tail, (fr. *queue,* old fr. *couwe, cowe,* and other spellings),
is referred to very frequently in the blazon, and several examples have already been given under *Lion.* It will have
been observed that in the old rolls of arms the lion is very
frequently represented with the *tail forked* (*od la couwe
fourchée*), or, as is sometimes, but erroneously, blazoned *double
queued.* Also that the tail may sometimes be *nowed* (for which
the old French *croisé* and the modern French *passée en sautoir*
seem to be equivalent); *double nowed,* and even *forked* and
nowed (*fourchée* et *renouée*) occur, but such are rare. The tail
may be *erect* (for which the fr. term *estroict* is found) or *extended,* the latter only in the case of the lion passant, meaning
that the tail is stretched out horizontally. Tails, it will be seen,
are blazoned as *inverted, introverted,* and turned over the head;
also *coward,* when the tail hangs down between the hind legs.
The end of the tail is called the *brush* or *tuft.*

Le counte del MONTE, d'argent, a un lion rampant de goules a la
cowe croyse, corone d'or, a une labeu dazur—Roll, temp. HEN. III.

De sable, au lion d'argent, armé, lampassé, et couronné d'or; la
queue fourchue, nouée, et passée en sautoir—BOURNONVILLE, Champagne.

De gueules, a deux lions adossés et passés en sautoir d'or; les queues
en double sautoir—FOSSEZ de COYOLLES, Valois.

Argent, a lion rampant double tailed gules, one of the tails coward—
WALLIS.

The same varieties are found in the tails of other animals
than *Lions,* but not so frequently, e.g.

Sable, a bull statant argent, the tail between his legs [i.e. coward]—
FITZ-GEFFREY, co. Bedford.

Ermine, a griffin segreant coward gules, beaked and legged azure—
GRANTHAM, co. Lincoln.

Argent, two bars sable, on the upper one a wivern volant, tail extended of the field—MANFELD.

Tabard, a *surcoat:* the surcoats of officers of arms are so called; but it was originally the name of the frock worn by the pea-santry. Mentioned in Chaucer and gave the name to the Inn in Southwark.

Tabernacle: i.q. *Tent.*

The tail is also sometimes borne separately from the animal, nd when so, is generally *erased* at the lower extremity.

Sable, three lion's tails erected and erased argent—CORKE, Cornwall.

Argent, a chevron gules between three beaver's tails erect proper—LEWES, co. Kent.

Argent, three lion's tails double queued erect sable—PINCHBECK.

Or, on a mount gules three lion's tails erect of the second, tails turned to the sinister—TAYLARD.

CORKE.

Different names have been fancifully given by some heralds to the tails of different animals, such as the *single*, the *wreath*, the *scut*, &c., but no instances have been observed of their use.

Telescope: this is fancifully used in one coat of arms.

Argent, on a mount vert a representation of the 'forty-feet reflecting telescope' with its apparatus proper, a chief azure, thereon the astronomical symbol of 'Uranus' or 'Georgium Sidus' irradiated or—HERSCHEL, co. Bucks; Baronetcy, 1838.

Temple: examples of this device occur rarely, e.g. in the See of ABERDEEN, where the *church* is blazoned as a *temple* (see under *Bishop*). The *antique temple* occurs, but as *steeples* are named, it is probable the charge is meant for an ancient *church*.

Argent, on a mount in base vert an antique temple of three stories, each embattled; from the second battlement two steeples, and from the top, one, each ending in a cross sable—TEMPLAR, [granted 1765].

Quarterly azure and gules, the perspective of an antique temple argent, on the pinnacle and exterior battlements a cross or; in the first quarter an eagle displayed; in the second a stag trippant regardant of the last —TEMPLER, co. Devon.

Azure, a temple or—TEMPLE, Scotland.

Table d'attente, (fr.): a fanciful term given to shields of a single tincture without any charge.

Tacheté, (fr.): speckled; applied to the salamander.

Tadpole. See *Frog*.

Taillé, (fr.): used when the shield is divided diagonally, from left to right, into two equal parts = *party per bend sinister*.

Talbot. See *Dog*.

Talent: a bezant.

Talons of an *Eagle*, q.v.

Taon, (fr.): the oxfly in the arms of the family of THOU, Ile de France.

Tenné, *Tawney, Orange*, or *Brusk:* Orange colour. In engravings it should be represented by lines in bend sinister crossed by others barways. Heralds who blazon by the names of the heavenly bodies call it *Dragon's head*, and those who employ jewels, *Hyacinth*, or *Jacynth*. It is very rarely found mentioned, but was one of the colours forming the livery of the royal House of Stuart. Further, it is one of the colours which when applied to *abatements* is called in heraldic treatises *stainand*.

Tenné.

Argent, a maunch tenne—TICKELL.

Tent, (fr. *tente*): this is represented as in the margin. It often has a *pennon* attached, which should be named. A *tent royal* should be made more ornamental than the figure, and should have a split pennon flowing towards the sinister. [See example of MERCHANT TAYLORS, given under *Robe*.]

The terms *Pavilion* and *Tabernacle* generally imply a tent like the above, while in the grant of arms to the UPHOLDERS' COMPANY the tents are termed *spervers*.

Tent.

Argent, a chevron between three royal tents sable—TINTEN, St. Fudy, Cornwall.

Azure, a chevron between three tents argent—MAYBANK.

Sable, three pavilions argent, lined ermine—Company of UPHOLDERS' Chester.

Sable, three pavilions [or spervers] ermine, lined azure, garnished or; within the pavilion in base a lamb couchant argent, on a cushion or tasselled of the last; over the head a cross fitchy gules, [Elsewhere blazoned Sable, on a chevron or, between three tents without poles, ermine, lined azure (another, 1730, gules); as many roses gules]—Company of UPHOLDERS, granted 1465.

Tapestry: mentioned in the arms of NEWCASTLE - ON - TYNE. See *Castle*.

Taré, (fr.): a technical term applied to the *Casque* or Helmet for describing its position = *posé*.

In French arms a *Pavilion,* or tent, was sometimes adopted for surrounding the shield—especially the Royal shield—instead of the *Lambrequin* or *Mantle.* For one form also the term *Capeline* seems to be used.

Thistle, (fr. *chardon*): this plant, though occurring in coats of arms, is found more frequently as a badge; it is generally represented *slipped,* as in the margin. The *leaves* are found also separate.

Thistle.

Per pale azure and gules three lions rampant argent; a chief per pale or and argent, charged on the dexter side with a rose gules, and on the sinister with a thistle vert—PEMBROKE COLLEGE, Oxford, founded 1620.

Azure, on a fesse argent between a thistle in chief or and a trefoil in base of the second a cinquefoil gules—STEERS, Ireland.

Gules, a crosier or and sword argent saltirewise; on a chief of the second a thistle vert—KIRK, Scotland.

Argent, a lion passant gardant gules gorged with an open crown and crowned with an imperial one proper, holding in the dexter paw a sword of the last defending the thistle placed in the dexter chief point vert, ensigned with a crown or—OGILVIE, co. Kincardine.

Gules, a bend engrailed argent, in chief a thistle leaved or—GEMMILL, Scotland.

Or, a fesse azure between three thistles slipped vert, flowered gules—Miles SALLEY, Bp. of Llandaff, 1500–16.

A thistle slipped and leaved, ensigned with the imperial crown, all proper — Badge of SCOTLAND; [it occurs also amongst the badges of the STUARTS].

D'azur, a trois chardons d'or—De CARDON, Lorraine et Artois.

Badge of the
STUARTS.

Target. See *Shield.*

Tarjant: i.q. *Torqued.*

Tassel. See *Cushion;* also *Purse.*

Tassy vairy. See *Potent.*

Tau. See *Cross,* § 34.

Taupe, (fr.): *mole.*

Tawney. See *Tenné.*

Teal. See *Duck.*

Teazel. See *Thistle.*

Teeth are very rarely referred to, but are included in the term *armed.* Boars, &c., are, however, often represented *tusked.* In French arms the term *denté* occurs.

Templars. See *Knights* Templars.

Tenants, (fr.). See *Supporters.*

Tench. See *Barbel.*

Tenter-hook. See *Hook.*

Argent, on a fesse gules three oval buckles or ; in base three thistle-leaves conjoined vert—LESLIE, co. Monaghan.

With the thistle may be grouped the *Teazel*, used especially in dressing cloth, and it will be seen to be used both in the insignia of the Exeter WEAVERS' Company (see under *Weavers*), and of the CLOTH-WORKERS (see under *Clothiers*).

Argent, a chevron sable between three teazels stalked and leaved proper—FULHAM.

Argent, three teazels slipped proper—BOWDEN.

Teazel.

Thorns, Crown of: this sacred emblem is very similar to the other *chaplets* (q.v.) already described. It is borne in arms of a private family and in the insignia of a See.

Argent, a cross Tau gules, in chief three crowns of thorns vert—TAUKE, Sussex.

Azure, a crown of thorns or, between three saltires or—See of CAITHNESS, Scotland.

Crown of thorns.

Throughout: means extending to the sides of the escutcheon, and is used when the charge under ordinary circumstances does not do so. An ordinary *Cross* is properly so, but for *Cross pattée throughout*, see § 26. The words *firm, fixed,* and *entire,* have been used by writers with a similar signification. *Passant,* q.v., when used with reference to the plain cross, is supposed to be equivalent to *throughout*.

Azure, a lozenge throughout or, charged with a crescent gules—PRAED.

Baudewin de FRIVILLE de veyr a une croyz passant de goules—Roll, temp. HEN. III.

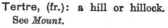

Tergiant : of a *Tortoise*, &c., having the back turned towards the spectator.

Tern. See *Seagull*.

Terrassé, (fr.) : having a *mount* in base, and represented as covered with verdure. Especially applied to *Trees*.

Terrestrial globe. See *Sphere*.

Terrier. See *Dog*.

Tertre, (fr.): a hill or hillock. See *Mount*.

Testes aux queues, (fr.): heads to tails, used of a fish.

Thatch-rake and Thatcher's-hook. See *Rake*.

Thicket. See *Wood*.

Thistle, Order of the. See under *Knights*.

Thorn. See *Hawthorn*.

Thunderbolt: a bearing derived from the classic mythology, in which the emblem is ascribed
to Jupiter. In one instance it is only
outlined or *chased* on the escutcheons.
It is the crest of the families of CAR-
NAGIE and of HAWLEY.

Azure, Jupiter's thunderbolt or, shafted
and winged argent—TOMYRIS.

Azure, a chevron between three escutcheons or, on each a thunderbolt chased—
EDMONDS.

Azure, a sun between three thunderbolts
winged and shafted or—STRICKSON, granted
June 14, 1707.

Jupiter's thunderbolt

Tiara: the pope's triple crown occurs in the arms of one
Company, and has not been observed elsewhere.
It is said that the royal crown in the insignia
of the Church of York was originally a tiara.

Azure, three clouds proper, rays issuing therefrom
downwards or, surmounted by as many tiaras [or
triple crowns], the caps gules, the crowns gold—
DRAPERS' Company, London; granted 1439.

Tiger: this beast, as drawn by ancient
painters, is now often called the *heraldic*
tiger, as distinguished from the natural. Such

Tiara with rays.

distinctions of course are not real, since the old heralds
drew the tiger as they did many animals, conventionally. The
heraldic form of the tiger is shewn in the margin. The
tiger looking into a *mirror* (q.v.) is a very
remarkable bearing. Amongst other extraordinary ideas which our ancestors entertained respecting strange animals was
this—that in order to rob the tigress of
her young, it was only necessary to lay
mirrors in her way, in which she would
stop to look at her own image, and thereby
give the robbers time to escape. Tigers'
heads and *faces* also occur.

LOVE.

Vert, a heraldic tiger [possibly a wolf, i.e. *loup*] passant or. mane and uft of the tail argent—Love, co. Norfolk; granted 1663.

Argent, a tiger rampant collared and chained or—O'Halie.

Or, a tiger passant gules—Lutwyche, Salop.

Gules, a chevron argent, between three tigers, regardant [into mirrors] of the second—Butler of Calais.

Per fesse ermine and sable a heraldic tiger argent, in chief two mascles of the second—Daniels, Lymington, co. Hants.

Vert, within two bars ermine between two heraldic tigers passant, one in chief and one in base or, three garbs of the last—Minton, Stoke-upon-Trent, co. Stafford.

Or, two bars gemel gules between three tiger's heads [otherwise boar's heads] sable, two and one—Jenkinson.

Sable, a lion rampant regardant argent, on a chief embattled or a sword erect proper, hilt and pomel gold, enfiled with an eastern crown gules, between two [natural] tiger's faces also proper—Floyd.

Timbre, (fr.): this French term, for which there is, perhaps, no exact English equivalent, comprises the exterior ornaments of the *escutcheon*, that is (1) the *helmet*, (2) the *mantelling*, (3) the *crest*. By some, however, it is held to include (4) the *escroll*, (5) the *wreath*, (6) the *motto*, (7) the *supporters*, as well as (8) the cap of dignity and *crown*.

Tincture, (fr. *email*, pl. *emaux*): the *metals, colours,* and *furs* used in armoury are called *tinctures*.

As a general rule, a charge of metal should never be placed upon a metal field, nor a coloured charge upon a coloured field, but to this there are some exceptions. First, what the French call *armes pour enquerir*, or *armes à enquerre*, as the insignia of the kingdom of Jerusalem (see *Cross*, § 31), where gold appears on silver; and in other cases where colour appears on colour, e.g.

Gules, a cross vert—Denham, Suffolk.

Three, two, and one; a term often used in *blazon*, q.v., to shew the position of six charges.

Tierce, (fr.): a charge occurring in some French arms, consisting of three triangles arranged generally in fesse. There may be two tierces in the same shield.

Tiercé, (fr.), *tierced*, or *triparted*: in French arms the term is generally of the shield when it is divided into three parts per *fesse*; but the shield also may be blazoned as tiercé per *pale* or per *bend*. See under *Party*.

Secondly, the rule does not extend to *chiefs, cantons,* and *bordures,* which, however, are in such cases by some heralds represented as *cousu,* i.e. giving the idea of the charge being sewed to, and not laid upon, the field. Marks of cadency also, such as labels, bendlets, and batons are exempt from the rule.

The third exception is of a party-coloured field (as *quarterly, gyronny, barry, checquy, vair,* &c.), which may receive a charge either of metal or colour indifferently, and *vice versa.*

Barry of ten argent and azure, a lion rampant gules—STRATFORD, Gloucester.

Barry of ten or and gules, a lion rampant argent — STRATFORD, Coventry.

Per pale azure and gules, an oak-tree proper supported on the sinister side by a lion rampant argent—THOMAS, co. Hereford.

The fourth is, when charges are borne of their *natural colour,* not being one of the recognised tinctures of heraldry. (See *Colours.*) Such charges are nevertheless generally placed upon a field of a contrasted tincture.

The fifth and last exception, and the most frequent case to which this rule does not extend, is when animals are *armed, attired, unguled, crowned,* or *chained* of a tincture different from that of their bodies.

The nine tinctures are as follows, though numbers 8 and 9 are not so clearly recognised as the seven others. See also *Colours* and *Proper.*

1. *Or*	Gold	Sun	☉	Topaz.
2. *Argent*	Silver	Moon	☽	. Pearl.
3. *Gules*	Red	Mars	♂	. Ruby.
4. *Azure*	Blue	Jupiter	♃	. Sapphire.
5. *Sable*	Black	Saturn	♄	. Diamond.
6. *Vert*	Green	Venus	♀	. Emerald.
7. *Purpure*	Purple	Mercury	☿	. Amethyst.
8. *Tenné*	Tenny	Dragon's Head		. Hyacinth.
9. *Sanguine*	Blood colour	Dragon's Tail		. Sardonix.

The *Furs* are in a sense *tinctures,* and to a certain exten- follow the rule of the others; that is to say, *Ermine* is considered as argent, and *Ermines* as sable, so far as the tinctures of the superimposed charges are concerned.

| Ermine. | Ermines. | Pean. | Vair. |
| Erminois. | Erminites. | Meirri. | Verry. |

A brief notice of each of the above will be found beneath their respective headings.

The mode of representation of the tincture by lines was an invention which must be attributed to Silvester Petra Sancta, an Italian Jesuit, whose book, entitled *Tessaræ Gentilitiæ*, printed at Rome in 1638 (or rather his earlier book, *De Symbolis heroicis*, libri ix., 1634), seems to have been the first work in which the system was used. The claim of Marie Vulson de la Colombiere will not hold, as his work did not appear till 1639.

Some whimsical heralds have called the tinctures borne by kings by the names of *Planets* and other heavenly bodies, as given above; and this method so far made way that in some few heraldic MSS. the tinctures are expressed in the tricking by the astronomical marks denoting the planets.

Other heraldic writers again have given to the tinctures of the arms of peers the names of *precious stones*, also shewn above, but this practice is now looked upon as absurd, and calculated to bring the science into ridicule. Sir John FERNE, in his Blazon of Gentry issued in 1586, enumerates fourteen different methods of blazon as follows:—1. By colours; 2. By planets; 3. By precious stones; 4. By virtues; 5. By celestial signs; 6. By the months of the year; 7. By the days of the week; 8. By the ages of man; 9. By flowers; 10. By the elements; 11. By the seasons of the year; 12. By the complexions of man; 13. By numbers; 14. By metals. Such fanciful arrangements, however, tend to degrade the study of heraldry into a mere amusement. Happily they were never much used.

Tierce-feuille: a *trefoil* leaf, but without a stalk.

Tigé, (fr.): used when stalks or stems are of a different tincture.

Tilting-spear. See *Spear*.

Tines: of stags' antlers. See *Deer*.

Tipped: sometimes used of ends of horns and the like when of a different tincture.

Tire, (fr.): a term used for the several rows in *vair*.

Tires. See *Attires* of stags; also under *Deer*.

Tobacco : this plant is found in the insignia of a Company ; also on the arms of a Spaniard naturalised in this country.

Argent, on a mount in base vert three plants of tobacco growing and flowering all proper—Company of TOBACCO-PIPE MAKERS, London ; incorporated 1663.

Sable, five bezants in saltire ; a chief indented argent, thereon three stalks of tobacco, each consisting of three leaves proper—CARDOZO ; granted to Samuel Nunez Cardozo, Hackney, near London.

Tombstone : the seat of *Prester-John* (q.v.) in the insignia of the See of CHICHESTER, and of S. Mary in those of the See of LINCOLN (see *Nimbus*), is so called, though in neither case is it at all probable that the bearing is intended for such.   The Tombstone, sometimes called an Altar, on which the Holy Lamb stands, in the Arms of the College of ASHRIDGE is probably a Tomb, the device signifying the Resurrection.   Other examples occasionally occur, e.g.

Argent, a tombstone gules—ALBON.

Vert, three tombstones argent—TOMBS [represented as coped stones crossed].

Tops : a very few examples of this toy are found.

Sable, three bars nebuly vert, in chief as many playing tops argent [otherwise, Sable, three bars vert ; on a chief indented gules as many tops argent]—TOPP.

Sable, on two bars argent three water-bougets vert, two and one ; a chief gules charged with three playing tops of the second—TOPP.

Argent, three playing tops sable, two and one—ANVINE.

. . . . a chevron . . . . between three pegtops . . . . —TOPCLYFF, [in the church at Topcliffe, co. York, 1391].

Torch, (fr. *flambeau*), or *fire-brand*, is often borne raguled ; and a *Staff raguly flammant* (q.v.) is practically the same.

Argent, three torches proper—COLAN.

Azure, three torches or, fired [or lighted] proper—COLLINS, Ottery S. Mary, co. Devon.

Azure, three fire-brands proper—COLLENS, Barnes Hill, co. Devon.

Argent, a fire-brand (or staff) with one ragule on each side, sable, and inflamed in three places proper—BILLETTES.

Toad. See *Frog*.	Tomahawk. See under Danish *Axe*.
Tobias. See *Ararat*.	Tongs. See *Founders'*.
Tod. See *Fox*.	Tongue (1) of a *buckle*, q.v. ; (2)
Toison. See *Fleece*.	of animals, e.g. *bear*, lion, &c.

Torteau, (fr. *tourteau de gueules*) : the name now always applied to a *roundle gules.* At the same time the French apply the word to roundles of all tinctures, including even *or* and *argent.* (See *Roundle.*) Literally *tourteau* (and it is found in ancient rolls) means a little tart or cake, and the figure is said to have been intended to represent the sacred Host. The term *gastel* is also used (which in the form *gâteau* is still used for a cake), and in the older rolls, though the *torteau* is found more frequently tinctured *gules*, both that and the *gastel* are found tinctured as a metal. The examples of the blazon of the arms of CAMOYS in different rolls will clearly illustrate the variety of terms used.

Walter de BASCREVILE, argent, ung cheveron et trois torteux de goules—Roll, temp. HEN. III.

Hugh WAKE, d'or, a deulx barres de goules, ove trois torteux de goules en le cheif—*Ibid.*

CAMOYS.

Sire Huge WAKE, de or, a ij barres de goules, en le chef iij rondels de goules, el un baston de azure—Roll, temp. ED. II.

Rauf de CAMOIS, d'or; ung cheif de goules a trois torteux d'argent—Roll, temp. HEN. III.

Rafe de CAMOYS, dor; al chef de goules a tres gastelles d'argent en chef—*Ibid.* [Harl MS. 6589].

Sire Rauf de CAMOYS, de or; od le chef de goules a iij rondels de argent—Roll, temp. ED. II.

Le Sire de CAMOYS, port d'or, au cheif de gules, a trois pellets en le chief d'argent—Roll, temp. ED. III.

Argent, on a chief gules three plates—CAMOYS, Broadwater, Surrey.

Argent, a torteau between three escutcheons sable—LOUDON, Scotland.

Or, six torteaux, two, two, and two—WALSHALL.

Argent, three cups sable, a torteau [? for difference]—Richard GRENE-ACRES.

It is said in books that *tortoilly* may be used for *semé* of *torteaux*, but it has not been observed.

Argent semy of torteaux; on a pile azure a lion rampant of the field—HENSLEY.

Sable fretty argent, on each crossing a torteau gules—EAGAR.

Torqued : *bowed-embowed*, especially of a *serpent's* tail ; also *wreathed.*

Tortilly, (fr. *tortillant*): a term applied to Ordinaries which are *wreathed*, as shewn in the margin; the term *wreathy* is also found. The French apply the term *tortil* to the *wreath* or turban with which heads, and especially those of Moors, are adorned in heraldry. See *Wreathed*.

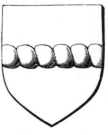

Argent, a fesse tortilly [or wreathed] azure and gules [otherwise, but not so well, a wreath in fesse throughout]—CARMICHAEL.

Argent, a cross wreathed gules and azure [otherwise, a fesse wreathed gules and azure, depressed by a pale wreathed as the fesse]—SERESBY.

Or, a lion rampant gules, a chief tortilly gules and vert charged on the first with a crescent argent between two mullets of the last in the second—MACRITCHIE, Edinburgh.

CARMICHAEL.

Argent, a bend tortilly azure and or—OARE, Sussex.

De gueules, au tortil d'argent—ZBONSKI DI PASSEBON, Provence.

Tortoise : this animal is usually borne *displayed tergiant in fesse*, which position is sometimes described as *passant*. The term *gradient* seems to be used to mean the same, and *tergiant* seems to be implied though not expressed. When upright it should be blazoned *erect*, though *haurient* is found.

Argent, a tortoise displayed, tergiant barwise [otherwise passant] vert—GAWDY, Norfolk.

Argent, on a cross azure between in dexter chief and sinister base a tortoise gradient vert five fleurs-de-lis of the first—LE NEVE, London.

Azure, a tortoise erect or—COOPER.

Vert, three tortoises haurient or—HARPENY.

GAWDY.

Tower, (fr. *tour*): towers and turrets are more frequently named in connection with the *Castle* (q.v.), but they are also found in some cases as distinct charges. Though a castle is sometimes represented as consisting of a single tower,

it generally has at least three. The ordinary *tower* is drawn
as the first example given in the margin.

Azure, a tower or—TOWERS, Northampton.

Gules, in chief a castle surmounted with a
tower argent; in base a lion passant gardant or
—City of NORWICH.

Sable, three high towers argent—DE TOUR,
Shrewsbury.

Sable, a plate between three towers argent—
WINSTON.

Argent, five towers, two, two and one gules—
CORNELL.

TOWERS,
Northampton.

But the *tower* is also frequently represented as bearing three
smaller towers or turrets, and then it is blazoned *triple towered,*
or triple turretted: in that case it is drawn as the annexed
figure in the margin, sometimes with the turrets slightly sloping
outwards, sometimes upright. It is frequently described as
having a *dome* or *cupola,* both terms being
used for the same thing; and sometimes
a *spire* or conical roof. Also as provided
with a *port* or entrance, *port-holes* or windows, *battlements,* &c.

Azure, a tower triple-towered or—TOWERS,
Isle of Ely.

Argent, on a mount vert a tower triple-
towered sable—CHIVERTON, Lord Mayor of London, 1658.

TOWERS,
Isle of Ely.

Azure, a castle triple-towered argent, port-
holes and gate gules—M'LEOD.

Azure, two lions rampant argent chained or,
supporting a tower triple-turretted of the second
—KELLY, Ireland.

A tower triple-turretted of the second—OWEN,
co. Montgomery.

Azure, a tower [otherwise with a cupola] argent, embattled and domed, the port gules—
Gilbert DE LA TOUR, Dorset.

Azure, on a mount vert a castle embattled
with three towers domed, on each a pennon, all
or—Town of CLITHEROW, Lancashire.

DE LA TOUR.

Azure, on a mount proper couped a castle triple-towered argent, the middle tower with dome and pennon—NIELSON, Bothwellshiels.

Gules, a four-square castle in perspective with as many towers and cupolas, one at each angle, argent, standing in water azure—RAWSON, co. York.

Azure, on a bend between two water-bougets or three leopard's faces gules; a chief as the last charged with a castle triple-towered argent, having from the centre tower of a pyramidical shape a banner displayed like the first—HUNT, Limerick.

Sable, a quadrangular tower with four towers in perspective argent, masoned proper; the base of the escutcheon water of the last—Town of PONTEFRACT, Yorkshire.

Gules, a triple circular tower in a pyramidal form or, the first with battlements mounted with cannon of the last, all within a bordure azure charged with eight towers domed or—Town of LAUNCESTON, co. Cornwall.

Azure, a square castle embattled above the gate and at the top, triple-towered, the central tower larger than the dexter and sinister; on each side the central tower a sentinel-house or watch-tower, which are with the three towers pyramidally roofed, all argent, masoned sable, the portcullis and windows gules; the middle tower ensigned with a staff and banner charged with the Royal arms of Scotland—Burgh of FORFAR.

The term *turret* is sometimes used alone, separate from the *tower*, and can only be represented as a smaller tower. The terms *tourelle* and *torele* are also found.

Le Roy de PORTUGAL, de goules poudre a turelles d'or a une labeu lazur —Roll, temp. HEN. III.

Le Counte de POYTERS, party dazur et de goules; per le goules poudre a turelles dor; lazur poudre o flurettes dor—*Ibid.*

Gules, three turrets or—TERRETZ.

Gules, three bars argent, on a quarter of the last a "torele" or a castle sable—John DENE.

Town, (fr. *ville*), *or city:* this device has been introduced occasionally into late coats of arms. An example of the city of NAKSIVAN will be observed under *Ararat*, and of ACRE under *Sphinx.* Examples more frequently occur in French arms.

. . . . the castle, church and town of Tiverton with Lowman's and Exe bridges; beneath them a woolpack . . .—Seal of the Town of TIVERTON.

De sable, au lion d'or, surmonté d'une ville d'argent—MAVAILLES.

D'argent, la ville en perspective du côté du midi, l'hotel de ville girouetté, les églises, le château et les bâtiments ajourés du même, essorés de gueules, les tours ajourées et maçonnées de sable, la porte ouverte et dans l'ouverture un maillet d'or—Ville de JOIGNY, Bourgogne.

Trangles, (fr.): used by French heralds for bars and barrulets when their number is uneven, instead of *burelles;* but the examples shew a want of consistency in this respect.

Palé d'argent et d'azure de six pieces a une trangle de sable brochant sur le tout—DUPORT.

D'or, a cinque trangles de gueules—AUBERY, Poitou.

D'argent, à quatre trangles ondées d'azur—AUTRET, Bretagne.

Tree, (fr. *arbre*): the *tree* is a very common bearing in later heraldry, but is very rare, if used at all, in early arms. In the arms of Sir Rauf de CHEYNDUT the *cheyne* probably means only the *acorn*, as in the arms of MORIENS the leaves only of the mulberry-tree are intended. But in later arms several examples will be found, both of trees generally and special kinds of trees and shrubs (fr. *arbustes*). Amongst these are found the *oak* (fr. *chêne*), (the most frequent); *apple* (fr. *pommier*); *orange* (fr. *oranger*); *fig* (fr. *figuier*); *ash* (fr. *frêne*); *elm* (fr. *orme* and *ormeau*); *hawthorn* (fr. *aubépin*); *holly* (fr. *houx*); *laurel* (fr. *laurier*); *maple; palm* (fr. *palmier*); *pine* (fr. *pin*); *fir* (fr. *sapin*); *cedar; cypress* (fr. *cyprès*); *poplar* (fr. *peuplier*); *willow* (fr. *saule*); and *yew.* Also the leaves and branches of several other trees, e.g. *beech* (fr. *hêtre*); *mulberry* (fr. *murier*); *olive* (fr. *olivier*); *walnut* (fr. *noyer*); *nut* (fr. *noisetier*). (See Synopsis.)

In French arms, besides those noted above, have been observed, *baume* (balsam); *buis* (box); *cormier* (service-tree); *châtagnier* (chestnut); *aubier* (sap-wood); *gui* (mistletoe); *neflier* (medlar); but no English examples of these have been observed.

When the term *tree* only is named without any adjunct, it may be considered to be that of the *oak*, and may be drawn like the example given under that term. But more frequently it is subjected to some special treatment, e.g. it may have the appearance of being torn up by the roots, to which the term *eradicated* (fr. *arraché*) is applied (and this is a better term

---

Trabe, (fr.): the stock of an *anchor*, q.v.

Tracé, (fr.): said to be the same as *ombré*.

Traits, (fr.) *pieces:* e.g. *pily* of six traits, or *chequey* of six traits.

Trammels (?). See under *Tremoiles*.

than *erased*, which should only be applied to parts of animals).
The tree is often *trunked*, i.e. *truncated* (fr. *étété*), *pollard* (fr.
écimé), or *lopped* (fr. *écoté*); or it may be *couped*, so that the
section is seen in perspective, and in that case
the term *snagged* should be applied. Again it may
be *withered* (fr. *sec*); or it may be *broken*, or
blasted, or *without branches* (fr. *ébranché*). A full-
grown tree is said to be *accrued*. A tree may be *fructed* (fr.
fruité), and this applied to the *oak* (q.v.) would signify with
acorns (fr. *englanté*). When the trunk is of a different tincture
from the rest of the tree the French use the term *fûté*.

Snagged.

Argent, a tree growing out of a mount in base vert, in chief three
mullets gules—WATT, Scotland.

Argent, on a mount in base a branched tree
vert—BARETREY.

BOROUGH.

Gules, the stem and trunk of a tree eradicated
as also couped, in pale, sprouting out two branches
argent—BOROUGH, Leicester.

Per pale argent and gules, a lion rampant of the
first on the sinister side, supporting a tree eradicated proper on the dexter—WINSTONE, co. Brecknock.

Gules, an oak-tree eradicated proper; crossing
the stem and near the root a greyhound courant argent—BOLGER, Ark-
low, Ireland.

Argent, an oak-tree erased proper; over all a fesse wavy azure—NEAL.

On a mount a withered tree; in sinister a representation of a cherub's
head with wind issuing therefrom towards the tree; on a chief an eagle
displayed crowned with a celestial crown—PIOZZI.

Argent, a tree in bend couped at the top and slipped at the bottom
sable—TANKE.

Argent, an arm proper, habited gules, issuing out from the side of the

---

Tranché, (fr.): is the equivalent
of *party per bend*.

Transfixed: *pierced through*.

Transfluent: applied to a river
running under a bridge.

Transparency, i.q. *Adumbration*.

Transposed: reversed, or otherwise placed contrary to the usual
position: e.g. of a *Pile*, q.v.,
or of the arrangement of three
charges when one is in chief and
two in base, and so contrary
to the rule. See under *Apple*,
Violin, &c.

escutcheon and holding the lower part of a broken tree eradicated vert, the top leaning to the dexter angle—ARMSTRONG, Scotland.

Coupé d'or et de gueules, à l'arbre sec au naturel brochant sur le tout —BESCOT, Ile de France.

D'argent, à un murier (mulberry) de sinople fûté de sable ; et un chef d'or chargé d'une tête de Maure de sable tortillée d'argent—MOREL, Burgundy.

But besides the trees themselves, parts of trees are frequently borne. We find the *trunk* (fr. *tronc d'arbre*), *stock*, *stem*, *stump* (fr. *souche*), or *body*, the terms appearing to be used indiscriminately by heralds, but meaning the same thing ; these are generally blazoned as *couped*, and if not it is implied ; they are also frequently *eradicated*, and it should be stated when they have *branches* (as in the arms of BOROUGH above) or *slips*, as in the arms of STOCKDEN below.

We find also the term *limb* used, and this is generally represented *raguly* (similar to which, perhaps, is the fr. *noueux*). It should be drawn so as to give the appearance of wood, and not to be mistaken for a *fesse* or *bend raguly ;* and its position should be denoted ; if not it should be drawn *in pale*.

We next find *branches* (fr. *branches*), *boughs* (fr. *rameaux*), *twigs*, *sprigs*, *slips*, and the term *scrogs :* to these terms certain differences are assigned, but the rules laid down are not very rigorously followed. The *branch*, if unfructed, should consist of at least three *slips*, but if with fruit then four leaves are sufficient ; the *sprig* should have at least five leaves, the *slip* should have but three. The branches represented borne in the beaks of doves are no doubt *olive* branches. Many of the terms noted on the previous page as applied to the *tree* are also found applied to the *branches*, &c. As to *staved* branches (if the word is not a misreading of starved = withered), it may mean that they are lopped to represent *staves*.

Trappings. See under *Horse*.

Traverse, (1) = *transverse*, i.e. across the shield horizontally ; (2) a *traverse* with French heralds seems to be a *filet*, though Guillim implies it is the figure called by the French *embrassé*. See under *Emanche*.

Traversed = *contourné*, that is, turned to the sinister.

Trecheur : i.q., *Tressure*.

Tree of Life. See *Paradise*.

Gules, the trunk of a tree eradicated and couped [otherwise snagged] in pale, sprouting two slips argent—STOCKDEN, Leicester.

Vert, three trunks of trees raguly and erased argent—STOCKTON, Ipswich, co. Suffolk.

Argent, three trunks of trees, couped under and above sable—BLACKSTOCK, Scotland.

Argent, the trunk of an oak-tree sprouting afresh—HERE.

De gueules, a deux troncs écotés d'or passés en sautoir soutenant une tour donjonnée de deux tourelles d'argent—LA SALLE DE PUYGERNAND, Auvergne.

STOCKDEN.

Argent, three stocks [or stumps] of trees couped and eradicated sable —RETOWRE.

Argent, three stocks of trees couped and eradicated sable, sprouting anew—GEALE, Ireland.

Per fesse, argent and azure, a stock [or trunk] of a tree couped and eradicated in bend or—AHLEN.

Argent, the stem of a tree couped and eradicated in bend proper— HOLDSWORTH, Warwick.

Gules, the stem of a tree couped at both ends in bend or—BRANDT.

Argent, a fesse embattled gules, in base a stump of a tree proper— RICHARDS.

Argent, three stumps of trees couped and eradicated vert—CORP.

Gules, a chevron between three stumps of trees or—SKEWIS, co. Cornwall.

D'or, a trois souches de sable—WATELET DE LA VINELLE, Flanders.

Argent, on a mount in base vert, the body of a tree sable, branched and leaved proper, between two lions rampant combatant gules—BOYS.

Gules, the limb of a tree, with two leaves in bend argent—BESSE.

Argent, a limb of a tree raguled and trunked, with a leaf stalked and pendent on each side vert—BOODE.

Sable, an eagle displayed argent, armed or, standing on the limb of a tree raguled and trunked of the second—BARLOW.

Ermine, on a chevron sable, three withered branches argent— FRESE.

D'argent, à la branche de frêne de sinople posée en bande—BAUTHER.

De gueules, au saule [= willow] terrassé et étêté d'or, ayant six branches sans feuilles, trois a dextre trois a senestre ; au chef cousu de France—Ville de MONTAUBAN.

Argent, a fesse vairy or and azure between three doves proper, bearing in their beaks a branch vert—BUCKLE, Warwick.

Argent, three staved branches slipped sable, two and one—BLACKSTOCK.

Per fesse, argent and gules, a bird standing upon the top of a tree vert, with a bell hanging from a sinister bough, and over all in base a fish on its back [otherwise blazoned, a salmon in fesse], with a ring in the mouth—City of GLASGOW.

Gules, three trefoils, the stalks embowed at the end, and fixed to a twig, slipped, lying fessewise argent—DRUMMEN.

Argent, three sprigs conjoined in base vert ; on a chief gules a crescent between two mullets of the field—CHAWDER, Scotland.

Argent, a slip of three leaves vert—BROBROUGH.

Or, a chevron azure between two scrogs in chief, and a man's heart in base proper— SCROGIE, Scotland.

Argent, three scrogs blasted sable—BLASTOCK of that Ilk. [Cf. BLACKSTOCK above.]

Trefoil, (fr. *trèfle*): the term 'iij foils,' i.e. 'trefoils' seems to occur in blazon as early as Edward II.'s reign ; but whether the 'three leaves' were conjoined or separate there is no evidence to shew; the term may possibly afterwards have been adopted to represent the *clover leaf.*

The ordinary form is that shewn in the margin, but it is subject to variations. It is, however, always borne with a stalk, generally ending in a point, when the term *slipped* is used.

Trefoil.

If, however, the stalk is not represented as torn off (which the term *slipped* implies) it must be described as *couped.* A trefoil *doubly slipped* would be drawn as the first figure in the margin; but if *raguly* and *couped*, as the second figure. With French heralds the *trèfle* is distinguished

1. Double slipped.   2. Raguly and couped.

from the *tiercefeuille* by the former having a stalk and the latter not.

Sir Edmon de ACRE, de goules, a les iij foilles [probably=semé of trefoils] de or e iij escalops de argent—Roll, temp. ED. II.

Sire Thomas FILOL, de or, a une fesse e ij chevrons de goules ; en la fesse iij treyfoyls de argent.

Argent, three trefoils slipped sable—CHAMPION, Berks.

Or, a trefoil double slipped raguly proper [i.e. vert]—ASKERTON.

Gules, a chevron between three trefoils slipped raguly and couped or—NICOLL.

Argent, ten trefoils in pile [otherwise blazoned 4, 3, 2, and 1] slipped vert—Thomas TURTON, Bp. of Ely, 1845–63.

Per fesse sable and argent, in base two trefoils slipped of the first—RODD, co. Cornwall.

Argent, three trefoils slipped paleways in bend sinister azure—RAUNSTON.

Gules, three trefoils pierced argent—BACON, co. Suffolk.

Per chevron argent and sable, three trefoils slipped counterchanged—KNIGHT.

TURTON.

Sable, a trefoil or, charged with a German text 𝔱—LINNE, London.

D'or, a un trèfle de sinople vêtu de gueules [i.e. Or, on a lozenge throughout gules a trefoil vert]—BENTOUX, Gapençois.

With the trefoil may be classed the *shamrock*, i.e. the three-leaved clover, which is considered the badge of Ireland, being traditionally associated with S. Patrick, who is said to have adopted it as a symbol of the doctrine of the Trinity.

Gules, on a bend or three bald-coots sable beaked and legged of the first; in the dexter chief a key with a sprig of shamrock; in the sinister chief a unicorn's head erased gold holding a sprig of shamrock in the mouth proper—William MARSDEN, Secretary to the Admiralty, temp. George III.

Azure, three hake fishes haurient in fesse argent; on a chief of the second three shamrocks proper—HACKETT, co. Carlow.

The *Cross botonny*, § 14, is by some called *treflée*, and not inappropriately, but the former is the more usual term.

Tremoile or *Tremaille :* this puzzling name occurs in an ancient roll, and the copyist in 1562 supposed the bearing to be 'men's hearts.' It has been thought that they were trefoils, and that both the name and the drawing had been mistaken.

Trellised, (fr. *trelissé*, or *treillé*): sometimes used, perhaps, for *fretty* when with a smaller mesh; and this is usually so with French heralds; but with English heralds it is said to be equivalent to *Lattised*, q.v.

Trench. See *Castle*.

Mr. Wyatt Papworth puts them under 'mill-hoppers' (Qy. the wooden troughs belonging to a corn-mill) in noting these arms, but gives no reason. The family of TREMAYLE seem to bear three *brogues* (see under *Foot*), but in one blazon they are described as bearing *trammels,* the meaning of which is doubtful.

Monsire ELMINDBRIGHT, gules, une cheif d'or; en le cheif trois tremoiles vert—Roll, temp. ED. III.

Tressel: a three-legged frame to support a table, borne chiefly by branches of one family.

Gules, a fesse humetty between two tressels argent—John STRATFORD, Abp. of Canterbury, 1333–48.

Tressel.

Gules, a fesse humetty or [= the board for placing on the tressels] between three tressels argent—Robert STRATFORD, Bp. of Chichester, 1337–62. Also of Nicholas STRATFORD, Bp. of Chester, 1689—1707.

Sable, a hawk argent, belled or, standing on a tressel of the second—HAWKER, Essex.

Tressure, (old fr. *tressour,* fr. *trecheur*): a subordinary, considered by some as a diminutive of the *orle.* It may be single or double (and some say even triple), but is mostly borne double, and fleury-counterfleury, as in the royal arms of *Scotland,* q.v., whence the charge is sometimes called 'the *royal tressure.*' When impaled, it is said to follow the rule of the *bordure,* and not to be continued on the side of the impalement, but several exceptions may be found. When an ordinary is described as within a tressure it should extend only to the inner side of the tressure.

Three owls within a tressure counterfleurée—Dr. John BRIDGES, Bp. of Oxford, 1618. Impaled with the arms of the Episcopal See. [From the brass in Marsh Baldon church.]

BRIDGES.

Sire Johan CHIDEOK, de goulys a un escouchon de argent a un duble tressour de argent—Roll, temp. ED. II.

Azure, three mullets, within a double tressure flory and counterflory—MURRAY, Duke of Atholl.

Azure, a ship at anchor, her oars in saltire, within a double tressure flory counterflory or—St. Clare, Gloucester.

Or, a lion rampant sable, in the dexter forepaw a heart gules, within a bordure of the second charged with a double tressure flory counterflory of the first—Buchanan.

Or, a fesse chequy azure and argent, surmounted by a bend engrailed gules between two lion's heads erased of the last, all within the royal tressure of the fourth—Stuart, Mains, Scotland.

Triangle, (fr. *triangle*) : is simply a charge in the shape of the mathematical figure so called.

Sable, on a triangle voided argent, twelve torteaux— Shone.

Argent, two triangles voided and interlaced sable ; in the centre a heart gules—Villages.

Triangle.

D'azur, a trois triangles d'or posés 2 et 1—Ciprianis, Provence.

De gueules, à deux triangles d'or entrelacés l'un dans l'autre en forme d'étoile—Bonchamps, Poitou.

Charges may be described as *fretted in triangle,* e.g. in the arms of Troutbeck (under *Salmon*), or *nowed in triangle,* as in those of Bradwen under *Serpent.* The insignia of the Isle of Man are sometimes blazoned as *flexed in triangle* (see under *Leg;* also *Arm*). The term has also been awkwardly applied by some writers to cases where charges are borne *transposed* (as is very rarely the case), i.e. *one* (in chief) *and two* (in base).

Trick: *In trick,* or *tricking,* is an expression used when the arms instead of being blazoned in the ordinary way are roughly sketched in, and the tinctures added, and other notes (such e.g. as the repetition of the charge) by abbreviations or signs. The letters usually adopted by the heralds, many of whose note-books we possess, compiled during their visitations, are, **o** for *or;* **a** for *argent;* **b** for *azure* (instead of az. which might be mistaken for ar.); **g** for *gules;* **v** for *vert;* **s** for *sable;* **p** for *purpure;* **er** for *ermine* (rarely ; ⚹ being more often used); **ppr** for

Trian aspect, *In:* neither passant, nor affronty, but the medium between those positions. Rarely used. See *Aspect.*

Incorporated: having three bodies, e.g. of a *Lion,* q.v.

Triparted, or *triple-parted.* See *Cross,* § 8.

proper. The accompanying figures are taken from a copy made by Nicholas Charles in 1606 [Harl. MS. No. 6589, fol. 5 and fol. 6 *verso*] of a Roll of Arms temp. Ed. I. Besides copying the blazon, he has also here and there added the coats of arms *in trick*. It will at once be seen how simple the system is. At the same time in some of the visitations of heralds the arms are very difficult to decipher, and the animals and birds are generally drawn very roughly.

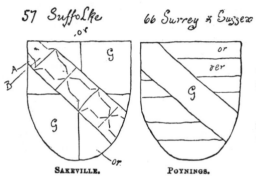

Andreio de SAKE-VILLE, quarterly or and G.,a bend verry.

Michaell de POYN-INGS, barry 6 or and vert, a bend gules.

SAKEVILLE. POYNINGS.

Trident: a fork of three prongs barbed, sometimes associated with *Neptune* (q.v.) in heathen mythology. It is borne in the arms of one or two families.

Argent, a fesse between three tridents sable—RUSSELL.

Gyronny of eight argent and azure, an eagle displayed erminois; on a chief wavy ermine a trident or surmounting in saltire a flagstaff proper, thereon hoisted a pennant gules, both passing through a chaplet of laurel vert—NICOLAS, Cornwall, granted 1816.

Azure, on a lion rampant argent, holding in the dexter paw a trident or, a key in pale of the field—OCHTERLONY, certified 1779.

Per chevron embattled or and gules, in base two battle-axes in saltire argent; on a chief azure, parted from the field by a fillet wavy, a demi-lion rampant naissant of the third holding in both paws a trident of the first—DYCE.

Triple crown. See *Tiara*.
Triple towered. See *Castle* and *Tower*.

Trippant of Stags: equivalent to *passant* of other animals. See *Deer*.

Trinity: the symbol of the Holy Trinity in an azure field was the heraldic ensign of the Priory of Black Canons, near Aldgate, in the city of London, called CHRIST CHURCH.

Shields charged with this device are of frequent occurrence in churches, but they are not to be considered as heraldic in any case except where referring to this monastery, or (perhaps) to that of the Holy Trinity, IPSWICH. A banner of the Holy Trinity having this device in a red field is recorded to have been borne at Agincourt. An ingenious attempt to blazon the device heraldically has been made, but it is naturally unsatisfactory, and is therefore not given here.

CHRIST CHURCH, London.

Azure, a representation of the Trinity argent, inscribed sable—CHRIST CHURCH, London.

Trivet: a frame of iron standing on three feet. It is sometimes drawn circular, at others triangular. Occasionally it is ornamented with cuspings.

Argent, a round trivet sable—TRYVETT, Somerset.

Argent, a triangular trivet sable — BARCLAY, Devon.

Argent, a trivet within a bordure engrailed sable —John TRYVETT.

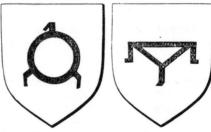

TRYVETT.   BARCLAY.

Argent, a chevron gules between three trivets azure—BASKERVILL.

Argent, three bars sable, in chief as many trivets of the last—REVETT, co. Cambridge.

Tristram knot. See *Cord.*

Triton. See under *Satyr.*

Trois-deux-un, (fr.): *three, two, and one.* See *Blazon.*

Tronçonné, (fr.): i.q. *Dismembered.*

Trotting of a *horse*, q.v.

Trout. See *Salmon.*

True lovers' knot. See *Cord.*

Truncated, applied to a *Tree*, or parts thereof, when *couped.*

Truncheon. See *Staff.*

Trowel: used by plasterers, and borne by the PLASTERERS' Company, in which it appears as in the margin.
The arms will be found blazoned under the word *Hammer*.

Trowel.

Trumpet: this musical instrument is found not unfrequently in the older rolls of arms, and has several shapes, but that annexed is the most common; sometimes it is drawn flexed, taking the shape of the letter S. The trumpet in the insignia of the Benedictine Abbey of ATHELNEY is shaped like a cow's horn.

Sire Giles de TROMPINTONE, de azure crusule de or a ij trompes de or—Roll, temp. ED. II.

Monsire de TRUMPENTON, port d'asure a deux trumpes d'or [et] croisèle or—Roll, temp. ED. III.

Azure, two trumpets in pile between twelve crosses crosslet or—TRUMPINGTON. [From the ancient brass to Roger Trumpington, ob. 1289, in Trumpington Church, Cambridgeshire.]

Sire James de NEYVILE, de goules, crusule de or a ij trompes de or—Roll, temp. ED. II.

Monsire James de NEVILL, port gules a deux trumpes d'or [et] croisele or—Roll, temp. ED. III.

Argent, a chevron engrailed between three trumpets barwise sable—THUNDER, Ireland, 1619.

Or, a cock mounted on a trumpet sable—HODDING.

Trumpet.

Azure, semy of trefoils two trumpets in pale or garnished gules—WADRIEPONT.

With the trumpet may be classed the *Hautboy*, a form of which is represented as in the margin, and appears to be chosen in the first instance for a play on the name (i.e. the fr. *bourdon*).

Azure, three hautboys, wide ends downwards, two and one, between as many crosses crosslet or—BOURDEN.

Gules, two hautboys in saltire between four crosses crosslet or—NEVELL, Sussex.

Hautboy.

Trundles. See *Embroiderer's.*

Trunk. See *Tree;* also *Elephant.*

Trunked: i.q. *truncated* of a *tree,* or branch, &c., which is *couped.*

Tulip: this flower appears in the blazon of only one coat of arms.

Argent, a horse (bay colour) passant, holding in his mouth a tulip slipped proper—ATHERTON.

Tun, (fr. *tonneau*, but if small, *barillet*): a large barrel, represented usually as in the margin, that is lving lengthways. They are sometimes represented with the *hoops* of another tincture. It occurs in the insignia of the BREWERS' and VINTNERS' Companies, as well as in the arms of a few families. Sometimes the term *hogshead*, or *barrel*, or even *tub*, is used, and per-

Tun.

haps in that case the charge should be drawn upright. It was very commonly used in the *Rebus*, q.v., so many names ending in ton. [See example of the lion hopping on a tun for name of Hopton under *Lion*.]

Sable, a chevron between three tuns barwise argent, [sometimes erroneously given as Argent, a chevron between three barrels sable]—The VINTNERS' Company, London; granted 1442.

Gules, on a chevron argent between three pairs of barley garbs in saltire or, as many tuns sable hooped of the third—BREWERS' Company, incorporated 1438; arms granted 1468, confirmed 1560. [On a brass in All Hallows, Barking.] The same arms are borne by the Company of BREWERS, Exeter.

Barry of five argent and azure; on a canton of the second a tun or—KNIGHTON, co. Hertford.

Argent, on a fesse azure between three crosses crosslet fitchy sable, two tuns or—CROXTON, co. Chester.

... three hogsheads, two and one ...—Adam de ORLETON, Bishop of Hereford, 1317–27; Worcester, 1328; and Winchester, 1334–45. [From carving on gatehouse at Esher.]

Gules, three barrels in pale argent—MATON.

Argent, a chevron gules between three barrels [or tuns] standing on their bottoms sable, hooped or—NORTON.

Argent, three tubs gules—BRICKMAN.

Trussed: of a bird; synonymous with *close*.

Trussing is used for *preying*. See under *Falcon*.

Turbot: both the *turbot* and the *sole* are made use of in English heraldry, apparently on account of the name only, as the following examples shew.

Azure, three turbots argent, two and one, joined or—TURBUTT, Ogston Hall, co. Derby; [same borne by TURBUTT, co. York; three turbots naiant proper by TARBUTT of Scotland, and three turbots fretted by TAR-BUTT of Middlesex].

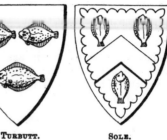

Argent, a chevron gules between three soles haurient [proper] within a bordure engrailed gules—SOLE, Bobbing Place, Kent; also SOLES, Brabanne, co. Cambridge.

TURBUTT.   SOLE.

Gules, three solefish argent—John de SOLES, Kent.

Vert, a chevron between three soles naiant—SOLEY, Shropshire.

Per pale or and gules, a chevron counterchanged between three soles azure and argent—SOLEY, Worcestershire.

A *demi-turbot* erect tail upwards is the crest of the family of LAWRENCE, [and so borne by Sir Thomas Lawrence, the celebrated painter].

Crest of LAWRENCE.

With the above must be grouped the *flounder*, or *flook*, as it is called in Scotland, which is probably not to be distinguished from them. Mr. Moule also finds that at Yarmouth this fish is called a *butt;* in Cornwall he has found the local name to be the *carter* fish, hence he concludes that the fish borne respectively in the arms of BUTTS and CARTER are meant for a fish of this kind. What the *bret* fish is, or the *birt*, he does not seem to have determined. The following examples are taken from his work.

Argent, a saltire gules between four ermine spots; on a chief of the second three butt fish haurient of the first—BUTTS, Dorking.

Tub. See *Tun.*

Tubbe fish. See *Gurnet.*

Tufted: applied to an antelope or goat when the tuft is of a different tincture, and in one or two cases to the extremity of a *tail.*

Tufts of *grass*, q.v.

Gules, three flooks (or flounders) argent—ARBUTT.

Sable, a flook argent—FISHER.

Sable, a chevron ermine between three *carter* fish haurient argent—CARTER, London.

Azure, three *brets* naiant—BRETCOCK.

Azure, a *birt* fish proper—BIRT.

Turkey: this bird occurs in the arms of one or two families, and like the peacock, it may be borne '*in his pride.*'

Argent, a chevron chequy azure and vert between three turkeys proper—WIKES, co. Devon.

Argent, a chevron sable between three turkey-cocks in their pride proper—YEO, co. Devon.

Turnip: only one family seems to bear this. Randal Holmes gives the word *wisalls* (? *wurtzels*), as meaning the green tops of this or some similar roots.

Sable, a turnip leaved proper; a chief or, goutty de poix—DAMMANT.

Turnstile, sometimes called *turnpike:* the charge has been in one case blazoned a *reel*, but this is probably an error. Three forms occur, as shewn by the figures in the margin.

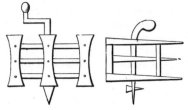

Argent, three turnpikes [elsewhere blazoned turnstiles or reels] sable — WOOLSTON, Withie.

1 and 2. Turnstiles.

A turnpike or, on a wreath argent and gules—Crest of SKIPWORTH, Linc. (Bart. 1622). Fig. 3.

Possibly the *cross-gate* mentioned in the following coat of arms may be of the same character.

Argent, a saltire between a cross-gate in chief and another in base and a crescent in each flank gules—HEGENS, Scotland.

3. Turnpike.

Tunique: the *Surcoat*, or *Tabard* of King of Arms, called so in distinction from that worn by a Herald or Pursuivant.

Turk's head. See *Head.*

Turnpike. See *Turnstile;* also *Gate.*

Turret. See *Tower.*

Undy, or *ondy* (old fr. *undé* and *oundé*, mod.fr. *ondé*), frequently termed *wavy :* one of the lines of division (as its name implies) drawn like the waves of the sea. It is found in the earliest rolls of arms, being more frequently applied to the *fesse* or *bar,* though also to the *bend,* and occasionally even to the *cross, chevron, &c.* ' *Oundé de long* ' pro bably means *paly wavy.* (See *Bar* and *Paly.*)

SANDFORD.

William GERNON, ounde de long d'argent et de goules—Roll, temp. HEN. III.

Etienne BASAN, unde d'argent et de goules a ung quartier noire—*Ibid.*

Sire William le BLOUNT, oundee de or e de sable —Roll, temp. ED. II.

Monsire DAUMARY, port unde argent et gules de vi peeces—Roll, temp. ED. III.

William de SAMFORD, ounde d'argent et de goules—Roll, temp. HEN. III.

Azure, three bars wavy argent—Henry de SANDFORD, Bp. of Rochester, 1227-35.

Argent, a bend wavy sable—WALLOP (anciently WELHOP), Hants.

Barry wavy of six, argent and gules—BASSET, Leicester.

Sable, two bars wavy paly wavy azure and argent—ROGERWAY.

WALLOP.

Argent, a cross wavy gules ; in the dexter chief a crescent sable—TREVILE.

Argent, two chevrons wavy between three fleurs-de-lis sable—PILLAND, co. Devon.

Twig. See *Tree.*

Two and one, (fr. *deux un*): when there are three charges two are placed in chief and one in base, so that this term is not needed ; when the contrary, i.e. one and two, the charges are said to be transposed. See *Blazon.*

Twyfoil. See *Foil.*

Two and two : neither this expression, nor *in quadratum*, are needed for four charges: they would naturally be placed in this position.

Tyrwhitt. See *Lapwing.*

Ulster. See *Kings of Arms* under *Herald ;* also under *Baronet.*

Umber fish. See *Grayling,* under *Salmon.*

Umbration, i.q. *adumbration.*

Unbent, very rarely used of a cross-*bow.*

Uncelles, of a *cock :* same as the gills.

Unicorn, (fr. *licorne*): this fictitious animal, so well known from being the sinister supporter to the royal arms, consists of a *horse,* from the forehead of which proceeds a single horn like that of an ibex. The tail is tufted like that of a lion. It occurs in several coats of arms, and may be represented as *trippant, sejant, salient, couchant, courant, climant, rampant, passant,* &c. The *head* alone also is sometimes found.

Argent, a unicorn passant gules, armed or—STANSAM. [From *Glover's Ordinary.*]

Argent, on a bend sable three unicorns [one family bear calves] passant of the first—VEALE.

Argent, an unicorn rampant, [otherwise blazoned climant, also sejant,] sable, armed and unguled or —HARLING, Suffolk.

Or, an unicorn rampant sable—HOYE.

Gules, a fesse argent, in chief an unicorn courant or—SWANSEY, co. Hereford.

Argent, crucilly or, an unicorn couchant, tail erect argent—DOON or DONNE.

STANSAM.

Argent, an unicorn salient sable, horned or—KERR, Scotland.

Quarterly, first and fourth; azure an unicorn salient argent, unguled, armed, and crined or within a bordure of the last, charged with eight thistles proper; second and third argent, three inescutcheons gules—Robert Hay DRUMMOND, Bp. of S. Asaph, 1748; of Salisbury, 1761; and Abp. of York, 1761–76.

Argent, a bend and in chief an unicorn's head erased sable—DENNISTOUN.

Ermine, a bend between two cotises; and in chief a unicorn's head couped; in base a cross crosslet fitchy gules—Edmund DENISON, Bishop of Salisbury, 1837–54.

Unicorns are also found in the arms of the following families: —COOKE, Middlesex; CRATFORD, Worcester; CROLE; DOANE or DONNE; EDWARDS, Cornwall; EDGEBURY; FARINGDON, Devon; FLOWER, Oxon; HUNNIS, Middlesex; LAYER, Norfolk and Essex; MELDRUM; MISTERTON;

MEAUTYS, Essex; O'NEYLAN, Ireland; STEEDE; STYLEMAN, Wilts; TREVITHICK, Cornwall; WILKINSON.

Unicorns' heads—BEVERLEY, York; CHEVALIER, Scotland; CROSBY; FREELING; GODLEY, Leitrim; GOFTON, Surrey; JAMES, Surrey; OVER-TON, Bp. of Lichfield; PARISH; PRESTON, Scotland; SHELLEY; SMITH, Dinderton, Suosox; SMITH-BARTELOTT, Sussex; SMITH, Stockton on Trent; WOMVILL.

Urn: both *urns* and *vases* are occasionally named, and may be drawn of the usual classical shape. They are, perhaps, sometimes blazoned as *cups*.

Or, three urns sable with flames issuant from each proper—BLANDY, Letcombe-Basset, co. Berks.

Sable, three vases with double handles [otherwise flower-pots] argent —FLANKE.

Azure, a sun in chief and a vase in base or—VASSAL.

Vair, (fr. *vairé*), generally written *vairy* when definite tinc-tures are named: a party-coloured fur, properly argent and azure, which tinctures are always implied when no others are mentioned; but, as will be seen, it occurs even in the early rolls of different tinctures. For instance, at the siege of Car-laverock ' the valiant Robert DE LA WARDE, who wards his ban-ner so well,' bore it ' vairy of white and of black.'

| Apres li vi-je tout premier | Ke ben sa baniere rewarde |
| Le vaillant Robert de la Warde | Vairie est de blanc e de noir. |

The origin of the name is not clear, but the most probable con jecture is that it is derived from a little animal whose fur was much in request, the *ver*, or *vair*, differently spelt, and which appears in Latin as *varus*. The word seems to have been used in-dependently of heraldry for *fur*, and the following curious error may be noted in passing. The familiar fairy tale of Cinderella was brought to us from the French, and the slippers made of this costly fur, written probably *verré* for *vairé*, were erro-

---

Urchin. See *Sea Urchin;* also *Hedgehog.*

Urdé. See *Cross*, § 35.

Urinant: applied to a *Dolphin,* and perhaps to other *fish,* when

with the head downwards, it is supposed to be diving.

Urle, i.q. *Orle.*

V, in *tricking,* stands for *vert.*

Vache, (fr.), *cow.* See *Bull.*

neously translated '*glass* slippers,' which of course was an impossible material, but has been repeated in all nursery tale-books.

Menu-vair is used by French heralds when there are more than four rows, the term being considered as implying a diminutive *vair*. It is borne much by Flemish families, possibly in connection with trade associations. The *menu-vair*, or, as we call it, *minever*, was a term used in the Middle Ages for the fur lining of robes of state.

Beffroi, or *gros vair*, is used when there are less than four rows. The name is evidently derived from the bell-like shape of the *vair*, the word *beffroi* being anciently used in the sense of the alarm-bell of a town. It is said that when French heralds use the term *vair* only, that four rows exactly are intended.

De menu-vair de cinq tires, au chevron de gueules — STESSIN, Flanders.

Plein de menu-vair—BANVILLE DE TRUTEMNE, Normandie.

De beffroi, d'or et d'azur—D'AUBETERRE, Champagne.

In modern heraldry the figures of a shield-shape are gene-rally drawn as in the second figure (arms of BEAUCHAMP), but in the older designs it was similar to that shewn in the arms of the Earl FERRERS, Earl of Derby, 1254-65, the sketch being taken from almost contemporary stained glass in Dorchester Church, Oxon; and sometimes the division lines are drawn after the same manner as *nebuly*.

Le Conte de FERRERS.

Le Conte de FERRERS, verree de or et de goules—Roll, temp. HEN. III.

Hugh de FERRERS, vairre de argent et d'azur—*Ibid.*

Robert de BEAUCHAMP, de vairrie—*Ibid.*

Piers de MAULEE, de veirre a la manche de goules—*Ibid.*

Sire Huge de MEYNI, verre de argent e de sable, e un label de goules—Roll, temp. ED. II.

Monsire John de BEAUCHAMP de Somersetshire, port de verre—Roll, temp. ED. III.

Monsire de NOWERS, port verre d'argent et de gules—*Ibid.*

Monsire La WARD, port verre d'argent et sable—Roll, temp. ED. III.

Vairy argent and azure—BEAUCHAMP.

Vairy argent and gules—GRESLEY, Norfolk.

Vairy argent and sable—MAYNELL.

Vairé, ermine and gules—GRESLEY, Derby-shire.

BEAUCHAMP.

Besides being applied to the *field*, it is often found applied to ordinaries and some few charges; and in some cases even to *animals*.

Or, [another gules], a saltire vair—WILLING-TON of Umberleigh, co. Devon, and Hurley, co. Warwick.

Sire Johan de HOORNE, de goules a une frette de veer—Roll, temp. ED. II.

Quarterly, or and gules, a bend vair—SACKVILLE.

Paly of six or and gules; a chief vair—Francis AT-TERBURY, Bp. of Roches-ter, 1713–23.

Argent, a bend sable and chief vair—Michael de NORTHBURG, Bp. of London, 1461–66.

Barry of six, vaire gules, and ermine, and azure—

SACKVILLE.   ATTERBURY.

Giles de BRAOSE, Bp. of Hereford, 1200–16.

Sire Adam de EVERINGHAM, de goules, a un lion rampaund de veer—Roll, temp. ED. II.

But different forms of *vair* occur, apart from the tincture. The term *counter vair* (fr. *vairé contre vairé*) has been adopted to signify that the shield-like forms instead of alternat-ing singly alternate in pairs, so that each 'piece' represents a pair of shields united at their tops, as shewn in the margin; but this form does not seem to have been adopted in any arms which can be said to be distinctly English, though some of the families may possibly

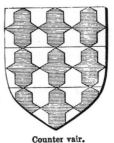

Counter vair.

be represented in England. The form has probably arisen only from incorrect drawing.

Counter-vary or and gules—BROTIER.

De contre-vair; au franc canton d'hermine—SALPERWICK, Artois.

Vairé contrevairé d'or et d'azur—TRAINEL, Ile de France.

Again, *Vair en pointe* is a term applied by Nisbet to an arrangement by which the azure shield, pointing downwards, has beneath it an argent shield, also pointing downwards, and *vice versa,* by which the effect shewn in the margin is produced. There are one or two coats of arms so blazoned, but it is not at all clear that this is the design meant. Also one coat appears with four tinctures.

Vair en pointe.

Vairy en point argent and azure—DURANT.

Vairy en point gules and argent—MONKHOUSE.

Vairy argent, azure, gules, and or en point—Roger HOLTHOUSE.

Heraldic writers also speak of *varry* as meaning one of the pieces of which the vair is composed; they also use the terms *vairy cuppy* and *vairy tassy* for *potent counter potent*, perhaps from the drawings in some instances resembling *cups*, and that is the possible meaning of *tassa*. It may be said that all these variations of the ancient *vair* arise from mere accident (generally bad drawing), supplemented by over refinement on the part of the heraldic writers who have described them.

Vambraced : the term signifies that the arm is entirely covered with armour, but from the etymology of the term (*avant bras*) it seems that it formerly covered the fore part only. The *brassarts* are shewn in the illustration protecting the elbow.

ARMSTRONG.

Gules, three dexter arms vambraced argent, hands proper—ARMSTRONG.

Azure, a fesse embattled ermine between two dexter arms vambraced argent, garnished or—FRANKE, co. Leicester; granted 1689.

Azure, a dexter arm vambraced grasping a sword erect in pale proper, hilted and pomelled or, between three boar's heads couped of the third, langued gules—GORDON, co. Banff.

Vane, (1) a *Weather-cock*, (fr. *girouette*): this device by itself seems to occur only in one coat of arms; but *castles* and *towers* are sometimes blazoned as bearing *vanes*, e.g. in the insignia of EDINBURGH. (See under *Castle*.) As regards the arms ascribed to a Lord Mayor of London in the twelfth century, they are probably of sixteenth-century invention, though not unlike earlier Merchants' marks. In Stow's Survey the weather-cocks are drawn like the figure in the margin.

Weather-cock.

Gules, on a saltire argent, between four weather-cocks (the supporters and vanes of the second, the cross crosslets or) five martlets of the field— Arms ascribed to Henry FITZ-ALWYN, first Mayor of London, and Roger FITZ-ALWYN, his successor.

Per fesse sable and azure, a castle with four towers, the gate displayed argent; on each tower a vane or—RAWSON.

Gules, a castle with two towers or, embattled and masoned sable, adorned with four vanes argent—CHASTELANI, France. [De gueules, au chateau à deux tours d'or maçonné de sable—CASTELLANI, Provence.]

D'azur, à un château sommé, de trois tours, pavillonnées et girouettées d'argent, le tout maçonné de sable—CHASTELAIN DE SERTINES.

2. A Winnowing basket. See *Basket*.

Verge: in one case only this term has been observed to have been made use of to signify the edge or margin of the escutcheon.

Azure, two lions passant gardant; the verge of the escutcheon charged with demi-fleurs-de-lis or—Augmentation granted to Katharine HOWARD, fifth wife of Henry VIII.

Vallary. See *Crown*.

Vamplet: of a *Spear*, q.v.

Vannet, (fr.), a winnowing-basket. See under *Basket*; also under *Escallop*.

Variated, or *Warriated*. See *Champagne*.

Variegated. See under *Flowers*.

Varvals, or *Vervels*: the rings belonging to the *hawk-bells*. See under *Falcon*.

Vase. See *Urn*.

Venus. See *Planet*; *Vert*; also under *Letters*.

Verdoy. See under *Bordure*.

Vergette, (fr.): the diminutive of the *pale* and *vergettée* = *paly*.

Vermeil. See *Gules*.

Verrou, (fr.). See under *Lock*.

Versé, (fr.), i.q. *reversed*: of charges when upside down.

Vessel, (fr. *vaisseau*). See *Ship*.

Vert, (fr. *sinople*) : green; absurdly called *Venus* by those who adopt planets, and *Emerald* by those who adopt the name of precious stones instead of the true name of the tincture. It is expressed in engravings by lines in bend. The French are said to have called it *Sinople*, from a town in the Levant (probably Sinope in Asia Minor) from which were brought the best materials for dyeing green, or silks and stuffs of a brilliant green colour, but the term does not occur

Vert.

before the fifteenth century. In the ancient rolls *vert* seems to be used occasionally (e.g. in the Roll of Carlaverock spelt *verde*). The term *prasin* has also been fancifully used, from the Greek πράσον, a leek.

Vine, (fr. *vigne*) : the *vine* is frequently represented in later arms, sometimes with and sometimes without the fruit, and very frequently also the leaves and the fruit, i.e. a bunch or *cluster* of grapes separately. When blazoned *proper* the leaves should be *vert*, the fruit *purpure*. The bunch of grapes should always be represented hanging, i.e. with the stalk in chief. The French use the term *cep de vigne* when the lower portion is shewn, with leaves and bunches of grapes (*grappes* or *raisins*), and *pampre* when only a *branch* of the vine is shewn with *leaves*, but generally without *fruit*. The term *pampré* of such a tincture refers to the leaves; *fruité*, to the grapes; the *échalas* is the vine-stick, by which the dwarf vines, chiefly cultivated abroad, are supported.

Argent, a vine growing out of the base leaved and fructed between two popinjays endorsed, feeding upon a cluster of grapes all proper—WINCHESTER, Scotland.

Vêtu, (fr.) : (1) *clothed,* e.g. of an arm; (2) a peculiar term signifying that the shield is charged with a large *lozenge,* the four points extending to the edge of the shield. See arms of BENTOUX under *Trefoil;* and of CORRARO and HINXLEY under *Point.*

Argent, a vine with leaves and fruit proper, over all on a bend sable three escallops of the first—LEVINZ, co. Northampton.

Gules, a man's arm couped and embowed, the hand holding a branch of vine fructed, leaved and slipped all proper—CORNEILLES.

Or, three vine leaves vert—ARABIN.

Argent, a chevron between three bunches of grapes proper—BRADWAY, co. Gloucester.

Argent, a bear's head proper holding a bunch of grapes in its mouth between three torteaux; a chief gules—BEARSLEY, Coventry; granted 1730.

D'argent, à un cep de vigne de sinople [entortillé autour d'un echalas du même et] fruité de deux grappes de sable planté sur une terrasse du même mouvante de la pointe de l'écu, et surmonté d'une etoile d'azur—DE LESSEPS, Bayonne.

DE LESSEPS.

D'argent, au cep de vigne, pampré et terrassé de sinople, fruité de gueules, soutenu d'un échalas de sable—GUYON, Normandie.

De sable, au cep de vigne, chargé de ses pampres, et soutenu d'un échalas de sable—LA TREICHE, Normandie.

De gueules, au pampre d'or feuillé de sinople—Ville de DIJON.

D'or, au chevron de gueules accompagné de trois raisins d'azur—OLIER-NOINTEL.

Violet, (fr. *violette*): is found in one English example.

Argent, a chevron sable fretty or between three violets purpure stalked and leaved vert—DIKENS.

D'argent, a trois violettes au naturel, tigées de sable, et un chef d'azur, chargé d'une molette d'éperon d'or a huit pointes—POL, Comtat Venaissin.

Violin: the *violin* or *fiddle* is found named in a few coats of arms. It should be drawn with the handle downwards.

Gules, three treble violins transposed argent, stringed sable—SWEETING, Somerset.

Azure, three violins transposed two and one argent, stringed sable—SUTTIE, Inveresk, Scotland.

Azure, three fiddles argent—SUETING.

Vires, (fr.): a term derived from the Latin *viriæ*, and applied to a series of *annulets* conjoined, generally with the smaller one in the midst. It only occurs in French blazon, and but rarely.

D'azur, à trois vires d'argent—GLATIGNY, Normandie.

Virgin: a figure of a *saint*, when the name is not known, may be thus blazoned, but usually only the head, or the upper portion, is shewn, and the term *demi-virgin* is used, as in the insignia of the MERCERS' Company. (See under Eastern *Crown.*) Similar figures are sometimes blazoned *maidens' heads :* and those in the insignia of the See of OXFORD, being veiled, are blazoned *nuns' heads* (sometimes *ladies' heads*). See under *Head.*

Vert, a demi-virgin couped at the waist proper, mantled gules turned down ermine, her hair dishevelled, on her head an Eastern crown or—Company of PINMAKERS [Inc. 1636].

Virgin Mary: the figure of the *Blessed Virgin Mary* occurs in the insignia of one or two Sees (that of LINCOLN has already been given, see *Nimbus*), and of several religious foundations, and of one or two Scotch Burghs; also on those ascribed to a King of England of the tenth century. It will be seen that the Virgin is variously represented, but always with the infant Saviour.

Azure, our Lady the Virgin Mary with a circle of glory over her head, holding in her dexter arm the infant Jesus, head radiant; in the sinister a sceptre all or—See of SALISBURY.

Argent, upon three ascents the Virgin Mary standing with her arms extended between two pillars; on the dexter pillar a church; in base the ancient arms of Man on an escutcheon ensigned with a mitre—Seal of the Bishopric of SODOR and MAN [but often improperly adopted as the Insignia of the see, which are simply those of the Isle ensigned with a mitre].

Vert, a cross botonné argent; on a canton of the last the Virgin Mary and Child proper [but there are several variations]—GLASTONBURY Abbey.

Azure, three lions passant gardant in pale or; on a chief gules the Virgin and Child of the second—Augustinian Priory of NEWSTEAD, co. Nottingham.

Argent, the Virgin Mary looking at the child Jesus in her arms, a radiated glory round each of their heads, all proper, their vestments azure—Burgh of LAUDER, Scotland.

Vidé, (fr.): *voided.*

Viper. See *Adder.*

Virols: the rings which commonly encircle *Bugle-horns,* (q.v.); and hence *virolled* or virolly, (fr. *virolé*), is used when a circular band of a different tincture is thus encircled.

Gules, the Virgin Mary holding the child Jesus in her arms or—Burgh of BANFF, Scotland.

Vert, a cross potent fitchy argent; in the dexter chief the Virgin and Child in glory—Arms fancifully ascribed to King EDRED, ob. 955, Harl. MS. 4033 [sometimes also King Arthur].

The charge also appears to be borne in the insignia of the See of TUAM, Ireland; in those of TAMANI Hammony, Dorset; and in those of the Deanery of WORCESTER.

Viscount: the fourth order of the peerage of England, being the intermediate rank between earl and baron. The title was originally the official name of the deputy of an earl, whence the name *vice-comes*, then Shire-reeve or Sheriff of a county. It was afterwards granted as a title of honour to John, Lord Beaumont, to whom King Henry VI., 1440, gave by patent the title of Viscount Beaumont in England and France, and hence the distinguishing affix, ' The Lord Viscount '

Visitations: early in the reign of Henry VIII. it was deemed advisable to collect and record genealogical and armorial information, and from this arose those journeys of the heralds termed *visitations*. The earliest, made by virtue of a royal commission, seems to be that of Gloucester, Worcester, Oxford, Wilts, Berks, and Stafford, in 1528-29. From this time the several counties were visited at irregular intervals until the Great Rebellion. Soon after the Restoration the practice was revived, but no commission has been issued since the Revolution. The last is dated May 13, 1686. Most of these ' Visitations' have been printed by Societies or by individuals, but some still remain only in MS., the chief being in the collections in the British Museum.

Viure, or *Wiure*, or *Wyer*. This term, variously spelt, is said by heraldic writers to signify a very narrow fillet or *riband*, generally nebuly (though no case of nebuly is cited, nor has one been found) which may be placed in bend, in fesse, or otherwise. It is probably only the common English word ' wire,' which some heraldic writer has written according to old spelling.

Argent, three bars gemels azure, on a chief gules a viure or—HAYDON, co. Devon

Vivré, a French term (not in any way connected with the previous term) applied to the *fesse, bend,* &c. It is practically equivalent to *dancetty,* except that the indentations are more open, i.e. the lines forming them produce right angles, instead of the acute angles which are usually represented in the drawing of *indented* or *dancetty.* The illustration of the arms of FITZ-JOCELYNE, given under the latter word, has by chance been drawn according to the French form *vivré,* and the difference will at once be seen by a comparison of this with the illustration of the arms of VAVASOUR given on the same page. When applied to the *bend* or *chevron,* the appearance of rectangular steps is produced.

D'or, a la fasce vivrée d'azur, accompagnée de trois alérions de sable 2 et 1—SEIGNEURET, Orléanais.

De gueules, à la fasce d'or, au chef vivré du meme—JAUCHE, Brabant.

D'or, à la bande vivrée d'azur—LA BAUME MONTREVEL, Bresse.

De gueules, au chevron d'argent, chargé d'un chevron vivré de sable accompagné de trois croissants d'or—DE LA GRANGE-TRIANON.

Voided, (fr. *vidé*): this term applied to ordinaries and subordinaries signifies that the middle is removed so that the field is visible through it; thus a plain *chevron* voided has the appearance of two *couple-closes,* and a *bend* voided that of a pair of *cottises.* Heralds, however, make some minute distinctions, and these will be found noticed under *Chevron voided.*

The *voiding* of certain ordinaries is of ancient practice. It will be observed that the *cross 'recercelée'* is sometimes blazoned *'voide'* (see § 32). So also *'faux crois'* signifies a cross voided (see § 6), while *faux lozenge* in one roll is used for a *mascle,* though the mascle itself is sometimes found blazoned *voided.* See *Mascle* and *Masculy.* Again, *faux rondelets* are found meaning *annulets,* (see under *Roundels*); and the *'faux escocheon'* is now blazoned an orle. In some cases the term *percée,* or *pierced,* is used to mean the same as *voided;* and in others *voided* is used of a *mullet* when *pierced* is meant; but as a rule

---

Visor or Vizor: that part of the *Helmet* covering the face.

Voiders: diminutives of *Flanches.*

Vol and demi-vol. See *Wings.*

Volant. See under *Wings.*

Voluted. See *Serpents.*

the *piercing* involves only a small aperture, and generally circular, while *voiding* involves a larger aperture, and one following the outline of the charge.

When the term is used by itself the tincture of the opening is understood to be that of the field, but an ordinary may be *voided* of another tincture.

Argent, a cross voided and double cottised sable, within a bordure or —BROMHOLME PRIORY, Norfolk.

Monsire Gerard SALVAYN, port d'argent; au cheif de sable deux molletts d'or, voydes vert—Roll, temp. ED. III.

Monsire GORNILL, port d'or; cheif sable, deux molletts d'argent, voydes de gules—*Ibid.*

Argent, two bars voided gules; over all a bend sable—BURTON.

Vorant: devouring or swallowing whole; used of one fish swallowing another, or more accurately of a *dolphin*, &c., swallowing a *fish.* (See under *Whale.*) The terms *engoulant,* or *ingullant,* are given by heraldic writers as meaning the same thing. The term *devouring* is also used.

Sable, a dolphin naiant proper vorant a fish of the last—JAMES.

Sable, a dolphin embowed or vorant [otherwise blazoned, holding in the mouth] a fish—SYMONDS, Herefordshire.

Argent, a serpent erect in pale azure, vorant [otherwise devouring] an infant gules—Duchy of MILAN. [See variations of these Insignia under *Serpent.*]

Vulned, (fr. *ensanglanté*): used of an animal wounded and bleeding. *Vulning herself* is frequently applied especially to the *Pelican,* q.v. Sometimes the expression distilling *drops of blood* (or *gouttes de sang*) is used, but this term is more properly applied to a severed head.

Vert, a lion rampant argent, vulned on the shoulder proper—BULBECK.

Argent, a lion rampant vert, vulned proper at the mouth—Tyrwhitt-JONES, co. Salop.

BULBECK.

Or, a lion rampant sable, vulned gules at the breast—SAMMES, co. Essex.

Per pale azure and gules, a wolf salient or, vulned of the second at the shoulder—HAWK.

Argent, a stag's head erased gules [otherwise sable], attired or, distilling drops of blood—CRAWFURD, Scotland.

Embrued, which is used properly of *Spears,* &c., is also sometimes (but wrongly) applied to animals.

Or, two wolves passant sable, mouths embrued gules—Oliver PEARD, Mayor of Barnstaple, co. Devon, 1575.

Vulture, (fr. *vautour*): this bird seems to be named in a solitary instance in English coats of arms, and is not common in French ones.

Ermine, a vulture seizing her prey gules—SIMINGES.

D'or, au vautour essorant de sable—VAULTIER, Normandie.

Wagon: this charge seems to occur only in the coat of arms of one family.

Argent, on a bend engrailed sable a wagon of the first [and a mullet for difference(?)]—BINNING, Scotland.

Wales: the armorial insignia assigned to Wales generally are those of South Wales only. Those of North Wales are distinct.

Quarterly gules and or, four lions passant gardant counterchanged—SOUTH WALES.

Argent, three lions passant gardant in pale gules, their tails passed between their hind legs and reflected over their backs—NORTH WALES [MS. Harl. 4199].

Wall, (sometimes called a *dyke,* fr. *mur*): this is generally found named in connection with *castles* or *towns* which are *walled* (*muraillé*). A wall of this kind should be masoned (fr. *maçonné*) and embattled (fr. *crenellé*), even though this be not specified.

Argent, a tower flanked by a wall and two turrets gules—DAMAN.

Gules, a tower embattled with a round roof between two other turrets standing on a wall extended in fesse, arched inarched ... —BRIDGMORE.

.... On a mount rising out of water a castle with three towers embattled and domed and joined to each other by a circular wall ... — Seal of the town of BOSNEY, Cornwall.

Or, a dyke [or wall] fesswise [masoned proper] broken down in some places gules; on a chief sable three escallops of the first; in base a rose as the second—GRAHAM, Inchbrakie, Scotland [similar arms borne by GRÆME of Stapleton].

Walnut: the leaves of this tree only have been observed.

Sable, three walnut leaves or between two bendlets argent—WALLER, co. Berks.

Argent, on a bend gules three walnut leaves of the first—UVEREY.

Argent, a chevron between three walnut leaves [otherwise oak leaves] vert—TUYSTALE.

Water: this occurs indirectly in many ways. It is conventionally represented by *barry wavy argent* and *azure*, and thus the *roundle* so tinctured is technically called a *fountain*, and is supposed to represent the water lying at the bottom of the well or spring.

The base of the shield is often made to represent the *ocean* (q.v.), and sometimes with *ships* sailing upon it. A *river* (fr. *rivière*) also is often introduced into coats of arms, and this especially in connection with bridges. An example of a *ford* will be found noticed under *Bull, Camel*, &c., and possibly a *pond* is intended in the example given below, as borne by OHENLOYNE, though the tincture being *vert* it is doubtful. The *loch* is mentioned in one or two coats of arms (see those of LITHGOW under *Otter*). The singular device of *Water-bubbles* is also blazoned and figured in one Heraldic work as belonging to the name of BUBBLEWARD, but it is a question whether it occurs in actual Heraldry, or whether it is an invention of some fanciful writer.

Argent, three demi-lions gules issuant out of water proper—MULLIKEN, Scotland.

Azure, in base water vert, thereon a bridge of three arches argent; on the centre a turret of the last flagged gules—VINICOMBE.

Argent, a field and river proper, on the field a buck gules drinking in the river—BARNEVELT.

Argent, a cross moline azure placed in a loch proper [?], and in chief two mullets of the second—MILLER, Gourlebank, Scotland.

D'azur, à la rivière d'argent posée en fasce et chargée d'un bateau de même—BOUDET, Auvergne.

Wake's Knot. See *Cords.*

Wallet. See *Palmer's Scrip* and *Purse.*

Wand. See *Willow.*

Warden. See *Pear.*

Warriated. See *Champagne.*

Wassail. See *Bowl.*

Wastel, or Wastel-cake. See under *Basket.*

Watchman. See *Man.*

Per fesse gules and water proper, a fesse arched with three towers or, all masoned sable [otherwise, Gules, on a fesse arched three towers or, all masoned sable]; in chief a fleur-de-lis between two roses of the second argent seeded gold; in base three ships with one mast and yard, each sable, two and one [otherwise, in base a river proper, thereon three vessels each with one mast and yardarm of the third]—Town of CAMBRIDGE.

Or, in a pond (?) vert [otherwise, however, Or, on ground vert] a boar passant sable—OHENLOYNE [known as Hibernicus SYLVESTRIS].

A tree, from the root whereof runs a spring of water; on the sinister thereof stands a stork picking up a fish, on the dexter is another bird resembling a Cornish chough—City of WELLS, co. Somerset [see also another under *Wells*].

Per fesse, each piece argent; within its base barry wavy argent and azure three ducks swimming, their bills in the water or, waves of the second; over all on a fesse engrailed gules as many roses silver—REVERS. [From *Glover's Ordinary*.]

Azure, three water-bubbles proper—AIRE.

Argent, two bubbles and a third rising out of water in base—BUBBLEWARD. [From *Berry's Encyclopædia*.]

BUBBLEWARD.

Water-bouget: a yoke with two large skins appended to it, formerly used for the conveyance of water to an army. It has been differently drawn at different periods, as the figures, which are arranged in something like chronological order, will shew. Many more slight varieties of form might be given, and as the form has varied so has the name. It is not easy to determine the primary form, but in the earlier rolls it is spelt, as will be seen by the examples, in a variety of ways, i.e. *bouges, bouz, buzes, buz, bouces;*

Early forms of water-bougets.

Later forms of water-bougets.

and in rolls of Edw. III.'s reign we find *bouges, boustes, bustes,* and *busteaux; oge* is also found.

Waterhouses.   See *Well.*

Water-leaves.   See *Leaves.*

Water-pots.   See *Pots,* as well as *Water-bougets.*

William de Roos, de goules, a trois bouges d'argent [in other copies, 'd'azur a trez buz d'or,' and 'trois bousses d'or']—Roll, temp. HEN. III.

Robert de Roos, de goules, a treis buz d'argent [in another copy, a trois buzes d'argent]—*Ibid.*

Sire Johan de Ros, de goules, a iij bouces de sable—Roll, temp. ED. II.

Sire Robert de Ros, de goules a iij bouces de ermyne—*Ibid.*

Guillemes de Ros assemblans   I fu rouge o trois bouz blans,

Roll of Carlaverock.

Monsire TRUSBUTT [elsewhere R. TRUSSEBUZ], d'argent, a une daunsy ... entre trois bouges sable [elsewhere blazoned 'tres boutz,' a play on the name]—Roll, temp. ED. III.

Monsire de BINGHAM, port d'or, sur fes gules trois boustes d'argent—*Ibid.*

Monsire de SAUNSCHEVERELL, port d'argent, une salter d'asur, au busteaux d'or en le salter—*Ibid.*

Gules, a water-bouget argent—DELAMORE.

Or, on two bars gules three water-bougets argent—WILLOUGHBY, co. Derby.

Argent, a bend between two water-bougets sable—LOCKEY, Essex; co. Hereford; HOMES, co. Hertford; and co. York.

The term *dossers* is sometimes found; it is an old English term signifying some receptacle carried on the backs of men or of animals; and in the latter case equivalent to the term 'panniers;' so that the figures in the arms of BANNISTER are sometimes blazoned as *baskets*.

Dossers.

Sable, two dossers suspended by an annulet argent; on a chief gules three fleurs-de-lis or—BANESTER, Darwyn, co. Lancaster.

Argent, two buckets suspended by an annulet saltirewise sable between three fleurs-de-lis gules—BANISTER.

Finally, it will be seen that the same figures in the same coat of arms are blazoned as *buckets* (q.v.), and this is possibly the modern form of the ancient '*bougets.*'

Water-cress. An example occurs of the leaves of this plant.

Quarterly; first and fourth three bendlets ermine; second and third gules, five water-cress leaves in saltire argent — GUEVERA, Lincoln. [Granted or allowed 1617.]

Wattled : of the gills of a *cock* when of a different tincture.

Waves. See *Ocean.*

Wavy. See *Undy.*

Weasel, (fr. *belette*): besides the common *weasel (mustela vulgaris)* the *marten (mustela martes ;* fr. *martre)*, as well as the variety with the white throat, the *foine (mustela foina;* fr. *fouine)* are found in blazon; and more important than all, the *ermine,* q.v. *(mustela erminea;* fr. *hermine)*, which has supplied the most common of the *furs* used in heraldry.

Argent, a fesse gules; in the dexter chief point a weasel passant proper—BELET.

Gules, three weasels courant argent—SCHOPPIN.

Sable, a chevron ermine between three weasels passant argent—BYRT-WYSELL, Amcote Hall, co. Lancaster.

Argent, a foine [? marten] sable, on a chief indented gules three escallops or—MARTEN, Sussex.

Or, on a chief vert an ermine passant proper—WATSON, Newport, Salop.

De gueules, à une hermine au naturel, passante, accolée d'un manteau d'hermine, doublé de toile d'or voletant—Ville de VANNES, Bretagne.

De gueules, à une grille d'or, supportant une hermine passante d'argent—Ville de S. MALO.

Weavers' Implements: these are of various kinds, viz. the *spindle,* the *shuttle,* the *slea,* the *burling-iron,* the *shears,* and the *teazel,* and it will be found that several of these are borne by families apart from the COMPANIES OF WEAVERS.

Azure, on a chevron argent between three leopard's heads or, each having in the mouth a shuttle of the last, as many roses gules seeded of the third barbed vert—WEAVERS' COMPANY OF LONDON; Inc. temp. Hen. I., arms granted 1487.

Per saltire azure and gules, in fesse two shuttles filled paleways or; in chief a teazel; in base a pair of shears lying fessways argent; on a chief ermine a slea between two burling-irons of the third—Company of WEAVERS, Exeter.

The *spindle* is, perhaps, better known in its conventional and heraldic shape as the *fusil* (q.v.), but it is represented in its

---

Weathercock. See *Vane.*
Welk. See *Whelk.*

Wervels, or Varvells. See under *Falcon.*

natural form also, as the reference to the 'threading' or to the 'slippers' implies.

Argent, a chevron between three wharrow spindles sable—TREFUSIS, Cornwall.

Argent, three spindles in fesse threaded or—BADLAND.

Argent, three fusils upon slippers gules—HOBY, Neath Abbey, co. Glamorgan ; HOBBY, co. Berks.

Argent, a chevron between three spindles of silk sable—DARDAS.

Azure, three spindles of silk or ; a canton ermine —BISHOPTON.

TREFUSIS.

The *Weaver's shuttle* (fr. *navette*) is represented as in the margin, and is borne by several families.

Azure, on a fesse argent between two bees volant in chief proper and in base a wolf's head couped or, a wheel-shuttle in fesse, also proper—MILLER, Preston, co. Lancaster; granted 1821.

Weaver's shuttle.

Or, fretty azure ; on a chief of the last a bee volant between two shuttles in pale of the first—HORROCKS, co. Lancaster.

Argent, three weaver's shuttles sable, tipped and furnished with quills of yarn, the threads pendent or—SHUTTLEWORTH, co. Lancashire and Yorkshire; also by SHUTTLEWORTH, Bp. of Chichester, 1840–42.

Argent, three weaver's shuttles in fesse sable—SHAKERLEY.

Azure, three shuttles or, quills argent—PEIRSON

SHUTTLEWORTH.

The *Weaver's slay*, or *slea*, or *reed*, as this instrument appears to be also called, was borne only as the insignia of the Company exercising their craft at Exeter. It was represented as in the margin.

Weaver's slay.

The *burling-irons* (q.v.) represented on either side of the slea have already been figured, and it will be seen they are borne by private families for the sake of the play on the name.

The *Weaver's shears*, used in the process of dressing cloth, were usually represented as in the margin, and the same figure will often be found on brasses and incised slabs in churches, emblematic of the man's trade. They are somewhat different from the *Scissors*, q.v., borne by the TAILORS' Company of Edinburgh.

Weaver's shears.

Azure, a chevron between in chief two swans, and in base a pair of shears argent—DELANEY; also LANNOY, Hammersmith.

The *teazel* has been already noticed under *Thistle*, and it is adopted by the CLOTH-WORKERS' as well as by the Exeter WEAVERS' Company.

Wedge: this is one of the irregular and doubtful terms sometimes made use of. The charges may, after all, in some of the cases be only intended for *nails*, q.v., but being badly drawn have misled the heralds. Another name given in heraldic books to the same figure is the *stone-bill*.

PROCTOR.

Or, three wedges [? nails] sable—PROCTOR, Norfolk.

Vert, three wedges [? nails] argent—ISHAM, Northumberland.

Argent, on a chevron between three wedges sable five mullets of the first—WADGE, Upton, Lewanneck.

Argent, a chevron between three wedges [or piles] sable—PEGGE, Beauchief Abbey.

Argent, a chevron between three stone-bills sable—BILLESBY.

Weel: *Fish-weel* or *Fish-basket* is a contrivance still used in rivers to catch fish. The charges appear to be drawn in various ways, but of those shewn in the margin the first is the more ordinary form of a *weel*, while the second seems to be usually blazoned a *fish-basket*. The terms *eel-pots, weir-baskets*, occur in describing certain crests, and they have been mistaken for *flasks, jars*, &c., e.g. in the arms of WILLARD.

Weel.

Or, a chevron between two fish-baskets [weels or eel-pots]—FOLE-BARNE.

Argent, a chevron ermine between three fish-baskets, hoops outward vert—WYLLEY, 1716.

Per bend gules and azure, a fish-basket weel, or eel-pot in bend or; on a chief azure a wolf's head erased sable between two ogresses—WHEELER, co. Worcester.

Gyronny of eight, gules and or, a fish-weel in fesse sable—FORTON.

Fish-basket.

Argent, on a chevron sable between three flasks or jars [they are weels] proper five ermine spots of the first—WILLARD, Eastbourne, Sussex.

A weir-basket filled with fish—Seal of William WEARE, of Weare Gifford, Devonshire.

An eel-pot per pale argent and vert—The Badge of Lord WILLIAMS of Thame (now borne by the Earl of Abingdon).

Weir, or *Wear :* a dam, or fence against water, formed of stakes interlaced by twigs of osier.

Argent, a weir vert—ZORVIS of that Ilk, Scotland.

A wivern with wings endorsed gules, standing on a fish-weir devouring a child and pierced through the neck with an arrow—Crest of family of VENABLES, Kinderton, Cheshire.

ZORVIS.

Well, (fr. *puits*): the well with masonry round it, is sometimes borne as figured in the margin; though the roundle called a *fountain* (q.v.) is an heraldic representation of the same thing, and is accordingly borne by several families in allusion to the meaning. At the same time it is by no means clear always what is meant, as apparently the same arms are found blazoned as having in one case *fountains*, in another *wells.* A *stone fountain* appears to be undoubtedly a well. The term *cold well* found blazoned in the arms of CALDWELL is but an ordinary well; and *water-houses*, in which the devices are probably intended for stone-built conduits.

Well.

Gules, three wells argent, masoned sable—HADISWELL.

Azure, a fesse between three wells argent—HODSALL.

Azure, a fesse wavy between three stone fountains argent—HODSOLL, London and Kent.

Gules, three square wells argent, water azure—HODISWELL.

Sable, three round wells argent—BOXTON.

Argent, out of a well gules an oak-tree vert—WELLWOOD, co. Fife.

Vert, a heron argent drinking from a well tenne—Arms ascribed to St. Hugh, Bishop of Lincoln, 1186—1200.

Per fesse argent and vert, a tree proper issuing from the fesse line; in base three wells two and one masoned—A variation of the insignia of the City of WELLS, co. Somerset.

Per pale azure and sable, a hart's head couped or, and in chief three cold [?] wells proper—CALDWELL, Glasgow.

Gules, three wells [or water-houses] argent, the doors sable; the water undy of six argent and azure—Old arms of WATERHOUSE, Conisborough, co. York.

Whale, (fr. *baleine*) : this mammal was considered as one of the great fish of the sea, but so far as has been observed, it rarely occurs beyond the arms of the families of WHALLEY, and the insignia of the Abbey of that name.

Whale's head erased.

The head is represented as in the margin, but the French heralds are said to draw it with teeth gules, and to blazon the animal as *fierté*. The head occurs also as a crest.

Gules, three whales haurient or, in the mouth of each a crosier [otherwise vorant as many crosiers] of the last—WHALLEY ABBEY, co. Lancaster [founded 1309].

Ermine, on a bend sable three whale's heads erased or—WHALLEY.

Argent, three whale's heads erased and erect or —WHALLEY.

Or, two bars wavy, and in chief three whale's heads erect and erased sable—COLBECK, co. Bedford.

WHALLEY ABBEY.

Per pale azure and purpure, three whale's heads erased or, each ingulphant of a spear-head argent—Sir Hugh VAUGHAN, Littleton, Middlesex [temp. Hen. VIII.].

Wharrow. See *Weaver's.*

Wheel shuttles. See *Weaver's.*

Whirlpool. See *Gurges.*

White. See *Colour;* also *Argent.*

Wheat, (fr. *blé*) : this was represented in the older arms in *sheaves* only, to which the name *Garb* was given; and under this term wheat continued to be most frequently represented. Some early examples have been given under *Garb*, q.v. In later examples it will be seen they are often *banded* of another tincture. When the term *proper* is used it probably signifies *or*.

In later arms *ears* of *wheat* or *corn* have been adopted as devices (and may be represented as in the margin), and of other grains, such as *barley*, *oats*, and *rye*. When *bearded* they are said to be *aulned*. To the stalk and ear thus borne the French give the name *epis*, and when the stalk is of a different tincture it is *tigé* of such tincture.

Ear of Wheat.

The *wheat* in the arms of the family of GRAUNDORGE (whose name is spelt in a variety of ways) is found blazoned *guinea-wheat*, but no doubt from the name [i.e. *grain d'orge*] barley grain is intended. It may be that from a play on the name (grand) the term *big-wheat* arose, a term adopted in blazoning the arms of BIGLAND and BIGNELL, but White Kennett notes *big* as a kind of barley.

Azure, a wheatsheaf between three thistles or, all within a bordure of the last—BAIN, Berwick.

Gules, two garbs in saltire or, banded azure—SERJEANTS' INN, Fleet-street.

Gules, three garbs in bend or, within two bendlets argent and between two lozenges vair—RICKARDS, Westminster.

Vert, a garb banded, and bowed in the head proper—BOWER.

Sable, five garbs in cross or—MEREFIELD, London.

Gules fretty or, on a canton azure two ears of wheat slipped without blades of the second—WHYSHAW, Lees, co. Chester.

Argent, on a fesse gules between six martlets sable three ears of wheat stalked and leaved or—GILLIOT.

Ermine, on three bars humetty sable fifteen wheat ears or, five and five—STOKES.

Sable, two bars ermine between fifteen wheat ears or, five, five and five, a bordure of the second—STOKES.

Per bend sinister azure and argent; on the dexter side three ears of wheat on one stalk or ; and on the sinister side three fleurs-de-lis one and two of the first—SOLTAU, co. Devon.

Gules, a chevron between nine ears of wheat tied in three parcels or—JOHN WHEATHAMSTEAD, Abbot of S. Albans, ob. 1464.

Azure, a chevron argent between three ears of corn as the second slipped and bladed or—Thomas EYRE, co. Buckingham, granted 1476.

Ermine; on a chief vert three wheat-sheaves [i.e. garbs] argent—PROSSER.

Vert, on a fesse between three bundles of wheat (or barley), each consisting of as many stalks, one erect and two in saltire or, a greyhound courant argent pied proper—MATCHAM.

D'azur, au fer de moulin d'argent, accosté de deux epis de blé d'or, les tiges passées en sautoir vers la pointe de l'ecu—JACOBE DE NAUROIS, Champagne.

Azure, three ears of guinea-wheat couped and bladed or, two and one —GRAUNDORGE, Donington, co. Lincoln.

Azure, two ears of big-wheat in fesse, stalked and bladed or—Ralph BIGLAND [afterwards] Garter, to whom they were granted 1760.

Ermine, a lion rampant gules, on a chief azure an ear of big-wheat couped and bladed or, between two estoiles argent—BIGNELL, Salisbury.

Barley is specified in some cases as in the insignia of the BREWERS of London and Exeter; the *garbs* are sometimes blazoned as *barley garbs*, but they are not distinguishable from others. (See *Tun.*)

Gules, three cups or, in the middle fesspoint as many ears of barley, two in saltire and one in pale of the last—GOODALLE, Scotland.

Quarterly, 1 and 4; azure, a dolphin embowed between three ears of barley or, a bordure engrailed of the second; 2 and 3, argent, three eel spears, tynes upwards sable; on a chief azure a lion passant gardant or —John FISHER, Bp. of Rochester, 1504.

Gules, on a chevron argent between three handsfull of barley ears (each containing five) or three bees proper—SMITH, Yarmouth, Norfolk, granted 1722.

Mention is made of *oats* (fr. *avoine*) at an early date, when the term *aveye* is used (see under *Garb*), and one or two instances occur in later coats of arms. Heraldic writers say the term *rizom* should be applied to the *ears* of *oats*.

Sire .... de BEUMEYS, de azure, a les garbes de aveye de or—Roll, temp. ED. II.

Azure, three oat-sheaves or—BENNIS, Clare, Ireland.

Argent, on a bend azure three oat-sheaves or—OTTLEY, co. Salop.

Quarterly, first and fourth; argent, on a bend azure three oat-sheaves or, second and third argent, an eagle displayed sable—Adam OTLEY, Bp. of St. David's, 1713-23.

The *rye* is distinguished from other grain by representing the
ear drooping, as shewn in the margin. It is
used by one or two families on account of the
play upon the name.

Gules, on a bend argent three rye-stalks sable—
RYE, Suffolk, 1716.

Argent, a chevron gules between three ears of rye
proper, slipped and bladed vert—RIDALE [or RIDELL]
Scotland ; Baronetcy, 1628.

Argent, a fesse between three rye-sheaves azure—
RIDDELL, co. Northumberland.

Rye.

Argent, five stalks of rye growing out of the ground in base vert—
AHRENDS.

Wheel, (fr. *roue*): the more frequent charge is the *Katherine-
wheel*, the instrument of the martyrdom
of S. Katherine, represented as in the arms
of BELVOIR.

Azure, a Katherine-wheel or—BELVOIR, co.
Lincoln ; also WYTHERTON.

Argent, a Katherine - wheel between two
columns or ; in chief a regal crown proper ; in
base an axe argent, handled of the second,
lying fessways, the blades downwards [S. Katherine with her wheel is the crest of the same
Company]— TURNERS' COMPANY, [Inc. 1604].

BELVOIR.

Gules, a Katherine-wheel or — S. KATHERINE'S HALL, Cambridge,
[founded 1475].

Per fesse gules and azure ; in chief a sword barwise argent, hilt and
pomel to the dexter side or ; in base a demi-Katherine-wheel of the last
divided fessways, the circular part towards the chief—S. KATHERINE'S
HOSPITAL, London.

Azure, a Katherine-wheel with a Cross Calvary projecting from it in
chief argent—Augustinian Nunnery, FLIXTON, Suffolk.

Azure, two bars or, in chief a Katherine-wheel between as many
buglehorns argent—MERTINS, Lord Mayor of London.

Gules, three bars argent, on a chief azure three Katherine-wheels or
—LEPTON, co. York.

Argent, on a chief azure two Katherine-wheels of the first—WHEELER,
co. Salop.

Azure, a sword argent, between three Katherine-wheels or—BAYLE.

D'azur, à trois roues de Sainte Catherine d'or—CATHERINE, Bourgoyne.

Other wheels are found named, i.e. the *Cart-wheel,* usually of eight spokes. In one case the *Water-wheel* is named, and for *Mill-wheels* see under *Mill.*

Gules, a wheel of eight spokes or—MARTEJOYS.

Gules, a fesse between three cart-wheels or—CARRINGTON, co. York.

Gules, a chevron between three wheels or; on a chief argent an axe lying fessways proper—WHEELWRIGHTS' Company, [Inc. 1670].

Azure, a horse argent, bridled gules, between three wheels or—MORCRAFT.

Or, a camel statant sable, between three half-wheels azure; on a chief of the third a wheel argent enclosed by two bezants—John WHEELER, Stoke, Surrey, 1543. [From *Glover's Ordinary.*]

MARTEJOYS.

Argent, a wheel or, vert between the spokes—LLES AP COEL.

Azure, a wheel of a watermill or; on a canton of augmentation the royal badge of England and Scotland, viz. the rose and thistle conjoined palewise proper—De MOLINE, Ambassador from the Doge of Venice, temp. King James.

Whelk: this mollusc is borne by several branches of the SHELLEY family, and some others, and may be represented as in the margin.

Argent, a chevron gules between three whelks sable—SHELLEY, co. Lincoln.

Sable, a fesse engrailed between three whelk-shells or—Sir John SHELLEY, co. Sussex.

Sable, on a fesse engrailed or between three whelks argent, as many maiden's heads proper crined of the second—SHELLEY.

Whelk.

Gules, a chevron [otherwise a fesse] vair between three whelk-shells or—WILKINSON, co. Durham; granted 1538.

Gules, on a chevron between three whelks argent as many demi-lions rampant sable—WILKINS, Kent.

Sable, on a fesse argent three whelks lying fessways gules—JOCE.

Whip: this has been observed only in one case.

Gules, three whips of three lashes, each argent—SWIFT, Scotland.

White nun. See *Duck.*   **Whitethorn.** See *Hawthorn.*

Whistle: the *Boatswain's whistle* occurs as a charge on the insignia of the Newcastle Company, and on the arms of Baron HAWKE.

Argent, an anchor pendent azure, the ring and timber [i.e. crosspiece] or ; on a chief of the second a boatswain's whistle and chain of the third, the chain supporting the anchor—MASTERS' and MARINERS' Company, Newcastle-on-Tyne.

Argent, a chevron erminois between three boatswain's whistles azure—HAWKE, co. York ; Barony, 1776.

Lord HAWKE.

Willow-tree: this is found named, as also the *Salix* (for the sake of the name) and *Osiers ;* for the branches of the last the term *wands* is used.

Argent, a willow-tree vert—BENNISON.

Argent, six osier wands (or bastons) interlaced in saltirewise in true love (sometimes in cross) proper, [i.e. sable]—Walter SKIRLAWE, Bishop of Lichfield, 1386 ; Bath, 1386 ; Durham, 1388—1406.

Argent, a chevron gules between three willow-trees proper—WILLIS, Dean of Worcester, ob. 1596.

Or, a salix proper [quarterly with the arms of Fane, &c.]—Count DE SALIS.

Argent, five palets couped at the top, wrapped with osiers in fesse gules, fretty in base with a serpent vert ; in chief three roses—ANGUISH.

Argent, four wands [otherwise bendlets] interlaced in saltire azure between four eagles displayed . . .—Seal of R. D. HAMPDEN, Bishop of Hereford, 1847-68.

Windmills, (fr. *moulin a vent*), and *windmill-sails,* occur in armoury. They vary in the drawing at different periods and even in different examples of the same date.

Or, on a mount vert a windmill sable—SAMPSON.

Per pale sable and azure, a windmill or—Walter LEPULL, co. Dorset.

Azure, a chevron or between three windmill-sails crosswise argent—MILNES, Scotland.

Argent, four windmill-sails conjoined in saltire sable—BAXTER.

Whiting. See *Cod.*

Whittal's-head : a fanciful device used as a crest. See under *Head.*

Wild duck. See *Duck.*

Wild man. See *Man.*

Wimble. See *Augur.*

Windows : mentioned incidentally under *Castle, Church,* &c.

Wine-piercer, or *Wine-broach,* is borne by two families; the same charge appears also to be blazoned both as a *fret* and as a *gimlet.* (See *Awl.*)

Argent, a chevron azure between three frets [or wine-piercers] of the second, screws or—BUTLER, co. Sussex.

Argent, a chevron engrailed [azure] between three frets [otherwise wine-piercers] or, the handles sable, banded gold—BOTELLER [Harl. MS. 1404].

Wine-piercer.

Argent, a chevron between three gimlets azure, the screws or—BUTELLER, Harl. MS. 1386.

Argent, on a chevron gules a fret [wine-broach or piercer] of the first—CLAPHAM.

Wine-press: this has been observed but in one instance.

Argent, a wine-press gules—ANHAULT.

Wings, (fr. *ailes*), occur frequently as heraldic devices. If no description is given or implied the wing must be drawn like an eagle's wing, and with the tip upwards Wings are borne singly, or two are *conjoined.* In the former case it must be stated whether it is a dexter or a sinister wing.

In the latter case, when the term *conjoined* alone is used, it is said to be equivalent to the French *vol,* that is, the wings are placed with the tips upwards, back to back, and joined at the base. When the

A dexter wing.

term *conjoined in lure* is used (and this is more frequently the case), then they should be drawn with the points downwards, and joined at the top.

Gules, three [dexter] wings elevated argent—NEWPORT.

Argent, three sinister wings gules—SEXTON.

Wings conjoined, (fr. *vol*).

Wings conjoined in lure.

Argent, a fesse between three sinister wings sable—DARBY, Walton, co. Leicester.

Winged bull. See under *Pegasus.*   **Winnowing-basket.** See *Basket.*

Azure, three bars argent, on a chief of the last as many pair of wings conjoined gules—FLEMING.

Argent, a stag trippant surmounted by a tree eradicated vert; on a chief azure two wings expanded and conjoined of the field—RENNY.

Gules, a pair of wings conjoined in lure [otherwise inverted and conjoined] or—SAINT-MAUR.

Argent, on a pale azure three pairs of wings conjoined in lure of the first—B. POTTER, Bp. of Carlisle, 1629—1649

Gules five martlion's wings in saltire argent—Sir Arthur PORTER of Newark (Guillim, 1612, p. 225).

D'azur, à la fasce d'or chargée d'un lion leopardé de gueules, accompagnée en pointe de deux vols d'or—PASSERAT DE SILANS, Bugey.

Wings, too, are very often attached to animals, &c., and though *eagle's* wings are generally intended, the *dragon's wing* is sometimes distinctly named; for the mode of drawing see under *Cockatrice, Griffin,* &c. In the Evangelistic symbols the *Lion* and *Bull* are represented with wings, as well as the *Angel* and the *Eagle*.

Argent, a wivern with wings endorsed gules between two flaunches of the last—DRAKE.

Argent, a stag trippant with wings attached to the buttocks and hind legs proper, between the attires a rose or—JONES, co. Brecknock.

Paly of six or and azure, a fesse chequy argent and sable, on a canton gules a dragon's wing erect of the third, in base a sword proper, pomel and hilt gold, surmounting a silver key in saltire—CURTIS [Lord Mayor of London, 1796].

Argent, a fesse counter-compony or and azure between three roses gules; on a chief of the second as many lion's gambs fixed to dragon's sinister wings sable; all within a bordure gobony of the third and purpure—WHITTINGTON.

But the *wings* play an important part in the description of *birds*. For them heralds have devised quite a system of nomenclature, though, as a matter of fact, it is to a very slight degree put in practice, the choice of terms being very arbitrary, and the mode of drawing, perhaps, more so.

Practically where the wings were open, if they had been described as *downwards* or *elevated* it would have met all real requirements, but accidental differences in drawing seem to have given occasion for a pedantic nomenclature, which has naturally become confused because it has had no foundation in fact. It has, however, been thought necessary to give a list of the terms, and attempt some account of what is probably intended by them.

Displayed (fr. *éployé;* old fr. *espanié*) signifies that the wings are somewhat open, with the points upwards. In nine cases out of ten the *eagle* is so represented, and it is generally allowed that even when no description is given to the eagle it should be drawn *displayed*. (See engraving under *Eagle*.)

Expansed.

Similar to *displayed* is *expanded* or *expansed*, and some writers contend that while the first term is applicable only to the eagle or other birds of prey, the latter terms should be employed for birds of a tamer kind, but such distinction appears to be theoretical; and in connection with this it may be noted that *displayed* is generally applied to the *Bat* or reremouse (q.v.), as also to the *Cockatrice*.

Examples of *displayed* will be found under *Eagle, Pelican,* and *Dove,* and of *expanded* under *Eagle, Swan, Stork,* and *Heathcock.*

Azure, six seagulls, three, two, and one argent, the dexter wing displayed, the sinister close—APILBY, co. Salop.

Argent, an eagle, wings expanded gules, standing on the trunk of a tree raguly vert—PORTER.

Gules, a swan, wings expansed argent—DALE, co. Northumberland.

Argent, a chevron between three ravens expansed sable—ROOKEBY.

Argent, a reremouse displayed sable—BAXTER, Scotland.

Sable, a cockatrice displayed argent, crested, membered, and wattled gules—BOGAN, co. Devon.

Disclosed, on the other hand, is used of a bird with the wings open but pointing downwards. At the same time it will be found that such expressions as *displayed downwards* (see example under *Eagle*), *displayed inverted* (see example under *Pelican*), and *expanded inverted* (see under *Dove*), are also used with the same meaning.

Disclosed.

It seems, too, that the expressions *overt* or *overture*, *flottant*, and *hovering* practically mean the same thing, i.e. with the wings open but bent downwards. The expression *overt* is often employed in conjunction with others, e.g. with *rising*. The expression also *overt inverted* will be observed. An example of *hovering* and of *overt* will be found under *Falcon*, and of *overture* under *Eagle*.

Vert, a parrot, wings disclosed, holding up the left foot or—Antick.

Gules, on a canton argent a bird, wings expanded [or overt] and inverted sable—Hutton.

Argent, a chevron gules between three sea-pies rising overt inverted brown—Trevenour.

Where the expression *preying* or *trussing* (fr. *empiétant*) is used, the bird should be represented with the wings *overt inverted*. See illustration of a *hawk trussing* under *Falcon*.

Another term very frequently used is *Rising* (fr. *essorant*), meaning that the bird is opening its wings as if prepared to take flight. *Surgerant*, as also *soaring* and *levant*, mean the same. The word *roussant*, given by some writers, but not observed in any blazon, is said to be restricted to birds attempting to fly whose weight renders them unable to do so: so also some writers use the technical word *collying* for *falcons*, &c., when about to rise.

Rising.

Examples of *Rising* will be found under *Goose*, *Cornish Chough*, *Stork*, *Bustard*, and *Dove*, and combined with other terms under *Eagle* and *Falcon*.

Quarterly ermine and azure, in the second and third quarters an eagle rising [otherwise volant] or—Adams.

Argent, a fesse humetty gules between three ravens rising sable—Peirce, London.

Or, three birds (probably lapwings) surgerant . . . a bordure vert—Sir Rhys Hen, co. Caernarvon.

Gules, on a chief or two swallows rising overt proper—Speed, London.

Quarterly gules and vert, a dove rising, wings overt inverted, between three round buckets or—Bramston.

Quarterly ermine and azure; in the second quarter an eagle rising wings overt inverted; and in the third quarter another rising wings displayed or—Sir Adam de Berry.

Endorsed with its synonym *sepurture* signifies that the wings are only slightly elevated, but thrown back so as almost to touch each other.

Argent, on a raven, wings endorsed proper between four cross crosslets fitchy, one, two and one, another gules—CROSS.

Gules, on a fesse wavy, between three swans with wings endorsed argent, as many crosses patty sable, each charged with five bezants—LANE, London.

Endorsed

Sable, a chevron ermine between three pelicans with wings endorsed or—MEDDOWES.

Erect probably means that the points of the wings are raised higher than in *endorsed.* Examples will be found under *Eagle.*

Gules, four swans erect argent—ROOSE, co. Cornwall.

Argent, on a chevron engrailed gules, between in chief two birds with wings erect and in base an anchor or, five bezants—BOASE, co. Cornwall.

Erect.

Elevated perhaps means something between *endorsed* and *erect.*

Azure, a chevron between three mallards, wings elevated [otherwise swans rising] argent—WOLRICH, co. Suffolk.

Azure, a pelican, wings elevated or, vulning her breast gules, between three fleurs-de-lis of the second—KEMPTON, co. Cambridge.

Volant is a term used to signify that the wings are extended in a horizontal position, and representing the bird *in full flight.* The head should be towards the *dexter,* unless otherwise expressed. (See under *Swallow.*) The position of birds so borne may be distinguished from rising, by their legs being drawn up towards their bodies.

Volant.

Volant en arrière seems to be used of insects rather than of birds, and signifies that they have their back to the spectator. *Volant recursant* means the same, but the head should be slightly turned round; and *Diversely volant,* i.e. flying about in different directions is applied to *bees.* (See under *Beehive.*)

Examples of *volant* will be found under *Eagle, Heathcock, Raven,* Rook, &c.

Argent, a fesse azure between three birds volant gules—TREWINCAN.

Gules, an eagle volant recursant in bend, wings overt or—BEES.

Argent, a heron volant in fesse azure membered or—HERONDON.

Azure, a chevron argent between three martlets volant or—BYERS.

Last of all we have the wings *Close* (fr. *pld*), that is with the wings closed towards the bird. See examples under *Eagle, Falcon, Goose, Barnacle-goose, Swan, Sea-fowl, Stork, Lapwing, Parrot, Kingfisher,* &c., under several of which Illustrations will be found, as well as under *Heathcock, Heron, Moorcock, Owl, Raven,* &c.

All birds are to be represented close when not otherwise described, except *eagles,* which were in ancient arms nearly always represented displayed; as to *swans,* in the old cognizance they were represented open or close very indifferently.

Wire: a *bundle* of occurs in the insignia of one Company.

Azure, on a mount vert a square brazen pillar supported on the dexter by a lion rampant regardant, and on the sinister by a dragon segreant, both or; in chief, on the top of the pillar a bundle of wire tied and bound together of the last between a bezant on the dexter side and a plate on the sinister—SOCIETY OF MINERAL AND BATTERY WORKS, London; incorporated 1568.

Wire-drawers' implements: these occur only in the insignia of the London Company of WIRE-DRAWERS.

Copper.   Drawing-iron.

The *copper* round which the wire was drawn; two of these are borne *in chief.*

The *point;* two of these, crossed in saltire, are borne *in base.*

The *drawing iron,* through which the wire has to pass. With this the chevron is charged.

Point.   Ring.

Also the two *rings.* All of the above are shewn in the margin.

Wisals. See *Turnip.*

Azure, on a chevron or, between in chief two coppers of the second, and in base two points in saltire argent, a drawing-iron between two rings sable—Company of GOLD AND SILVER WIRE-DRAWERS.

To these may be added the *engrossing block*, as it is termed, and which appears as their crest.

Two arms embowed, vested gules, cuffed argent, holding between the hands proper an engrossing block or—Crest of the above Company.

Engrossing
block.

Wolf, (fr. *loup*): this animal is found in a good many arms, and also in a few early instances, being adopted by families into whose names some form of the word 'Lou' enters. The *head* is, perhaps, more frequently borne than the whole animal. It may be *rampant, salient, combatant, statant,* but most frequently simply *passant*, &c. It occurs also very frequently in crests, especially the head.

Gules, a wolf passant argent—LOWE, co. Wilts.

Sire Johan LE Low, de argent a ij barres de goules, en le chef iij testes de lou de goules—Roll, temp. ED. II.

Sire William VIDELOU, de argent a iij testes de lou de goules—*Ibid.*

Gules, three wolf's heads couped or—LOCARD, Ireland.

Argent, three wolves passant sable—LOVATT, co. Stafford.

Argent, a chevron between three wolf's heads erased gules—LOVELL, Norfolk.

LOWE.

On a bend three wolf's heads erased—John LOWE, Bp. of S. Asaph, 1433, afterwards of Rochester, 1444—67.

Sable, a wolf salient, and in chief three estoiles or—Thomas WILSON, Bp. of Sodor and Man, 1697—1755.

Azure, a wolf rampant argent collared and chained or; in chief three crosses patty fitchy of the second—BUSHE, co. Wilts.

Gules, a chevron ermine between three wolves, the two in chief combatant or—GRENFORD.

Azure, a war-wolf passant and three stars in chief argent—DICKISON, Scotland.

Gules, a demi-wolf proper issuing to the sinister, feet erected each side of the head argent—BETWILL.

D'argent, à deux loups de sable, l'un sur l'autre [= in pale]; et une bordure denchée de gueules—DE SALVE, Provence

Wood, (fr. *forêt*): a small group of trees (generally on a mount) is found named in heraldry under various terms, e.g. a *wood*, a *grove* (see grove of *firs* under *Pine*), or a *thicket*, and in one case a *forest*. The term '*hurst*,' too, means the same thing, and perhaps *bowers* in the arms of GILLAM.

Argent, a lion seiant in a wood all proper; on a chief wavy gules a harp between two anchors or—WOOD, Ireland [conf. 1647].

Or, on a mount a stag lodged in a grove of trees proper, on a chief gules a cinquefoil between two mullets of the field—FERNIE, Scotland.

Gules, a stag argent lodged in a thicket of trees vert; between the attires three stars of the second—FAIRNIE, Scotland.

Argent, out of a mount in base a forest of trees vert—BUSCHE, also FORREST.

Argent, in base a mount vert, on the sinister side a hurst of oak-trees, therefrom issuant a wolf passant proper [otherwise, Argent, a wolf issuing from a wood proper]—O'CALLAGHAN, Ireland.

Argent, on a mount in base a hurst proper; on a chief wavy azure three fleurs-de-lis or—FRANCE, Bostock Hall, co. Chester.

Sable, on a chevron or, between three dolphins embowed proper, as many bowers vert—GILLAM, Essex.

D'argent, à une forêt de sinople—Ville de NEMOURS, Ile de France.

Wool-card: an instrument used for combing wool, represented as in the margin, and differing, as will be seen, from the wool-comb.

It is said that the *stock-card* is a similar tool used by wool-combers, and is represented as below. The blazon both of the arms of CARDINGTON and LAYNNE is taken from Glover's Ordinary.

Wool-card.

Ermine, three wool-cards gules—ALVÉRINGE.

Sable, three wool-cards [otherwise working-cards], teeth outwards or—CARDINGTON.

Argent, three wool-cards sable, the back parts outward—LAYNNE.

Stock-card.

Woman, bust of. See *Heads*.
Woodbill. See *Bill*.
Woodbine. See *Honeysuckle*.

Wood-doves. See *Doves*.
Woodman. See *Man*.
Wood-pigeon. See *Dove*.

Wool-comb, *Flax-comb,* or *Jersey-comb,* is also found in one coat of arms.

Sable, three wool-combs argent [in another branch, Sable, two flax-combs in pale argent]—Brom-ley.

Wool-comb.

Wool-pack, or as it is sometimes blazoned, *Wool-sack,* is borne by one or two Companies (e.g. that of the Bonnet Makers, Edinburgh, see under *Bonnet*). It is also borne by individuals, possibly from their having made their fortune in the wool trade. (See *Cushion.*)

Company of Wool-packers.

Azure (some say gules), a wool-pack argent —The Company of Wool-packers, London.

Vert, a wool-pack corded argent—Staple's Inn, London.

Sable, a chevron between three packs or, cushions argent, tied of the first—Company of Dyers, London.

Azure, a wool-pack argent—Johnson.

Argent, a bend sable, on a chief of the second three wool-packs of the first—Johnson, Bp. of Gloucester, 1752; afterwards of Worcester, 1759–74.

Gules, three woolsacks argent [in chief a mullet or]—Ashley, London.

Gules, a chevron between three woolpacks argent—Wooll, Rugby, co. Warwick.

Per saltire argent and gules, a lion rampant gardant or, on a chief wavy azure a wool-pack of the first between two bezants—Back.

Argent, on a chevron between three woolsacks azure as many garbs or—Wolsay, Norfolk.

Gules, on a fesse or voided of the field between three wool-packs argent three crescents gold—Cook, Blackheath, Kent.

Gules, a lion rampant or on a bend azure three wool-packs of the second within a bordure argent charged with eight roses of the field—Dunbar, Scotland.

Woodwallis. See *Parrot.*

Word. See *Letter.*

Working-card. See *Wool-card.*

Wound. See *Golpe.*

Wounded. See *Vulned;* also un der *Lion.*

Wrapped. See *Enveloped.*

Wrist-straps. See *Strap.*

Wreath, (fr. *tortil,* also *bourrelet*): the *wreath,* technically speaking, is the twisted band composed of two strips of gold or silver lace and silk by which the crest is joined to the helmet; though some wreaths of the fifteenth century were of four tinctures. It is sometimes, but improperly, called a *roll,* at others a *torse.* It was, perhaps, copied by the crusaders from the wreathed turbans of the Saracens. The first noticed is that of Sir John de Harsich, 1384.

Wreaths should always shew an equal number of divisions (now restricted to six), which are usually tinctured with the principal metal and colour of the arms alternately. Every *Crest* is understood to be placed upon a *wreath,* unless a chapeau or some coronet be expressly mentioned.

But *wreaths* also sometimes occur as charges; e.g. we find a *circular wreath.* This is meant for the same object as the above, but viewed from a different point. Animals also are sometimes represented with *wreaths* on their heads.

See also *Hatband,* as borne by BURY; and under *Harrow* a *circular wreath* will be found figured in the arms.

Azure, a circular wreath argent and sable, with four hawk's bells joined thereto in quadrature or—JOCELYN, Essex.

Gules, three lions rampant or with wreaths on their heads azure—KELLAM.

JOCELYN.

Although the *wreath* proper is composed of one or more coloured stuffs, the *Chaplets,* q.v. of oak, laurel, and *garlands* of flowers, &c., are frequently blazoned as *wreaths.*

Azure, on a fesse between three garbs or a wreath of oak vert between two estoiles gules—Sandbach, co. Lancaster.

Ermine, a rose gules on a chief embattled or two banners in saltire, the staves enfiled by a wreath of laurel proper, a canton gules charged with a representation of a medal—NIGHTINGALL, co. Norfolk.

Pean, three mountain-cats passant in pale argent, on a canton or a fesse gules surmounted by an anchor of the third encircled by a wreath of laurel vert—KEATS, Dorrant House, Dover; quartering Goodwin.

Wreathed, (fr. *tortillé*): i.e. encircled with a *wreath*, is not an unusual term. A good example is shewn on the head in the crest of MOORE.

Savages are frequently wreathed about the temples and loins with ivy, &c. The term is also sometimes applied to ordinaries instead of the term *tortilly*, q.v., and when so applied, means the same thing, and some examples will be found under that word.

On a wreath argent and sable a moor's head in profile couped proper, wreathed or and of the second—Crest of MOORE or MORE.

Argent, a bend wreathed azure and or—OARE, Sussex.

Or, two bars wreathed bendy of eight azure and gules—JAKYS.

Crest of MOORE.

D'argent, à trois têtes de Maure de sable, tortillées du champ—RIGAUD, Auvergne.

Wren: the *Wren* and the *Robin Redbreast* have been assumed as devices chiefly on account of the name. See also arms of ALDRIDGE, under *Hawthorn*.

Argent, a chevron sable between three wrens close sable (otherwise brown, and in another case back vert and breast gules)—WRENBURY.

Argent, on a chevron azure three wrens of the first, a chief gules charged with as many horse's heads erased purpure—WREN [the chief or, charged with as many heads erased brown—WRENNE, Harl. MS. 1404].

Argent, on a chevron between three wrens gules, as many mullets of the first—MANIGHAM.

Per pale argent and azure, a fesse nebuly counterchanged between three robin redbreasts proper—ROBYNS, Alderman of London.

Nebuly argent and azure, four birds (? robins) counterchanged—ROBYNS, co. Cornwall.

Wyn ɪ a small *flag*.

Wyvern, or Wivern. See *Cockatrice.*

Yarn. See *Quills.*

Yellow. See under *Colour,* also *Or.*

Yeux, (fr.): *eyes.*

Yale: a beast so called was the sinister supporter of Henry Fitzroy, Duke of Richmond, natural son of Henry VIII.

A yale argent bezanty, accorned, hoofed, gorged with a coronal and chained or.

The late Mr. J. G. Nichols, in "Inventories of the Wardrobe, &c., of Henry Fitzroy, Duke of Richmond" (in the Camden Miscellany, vol. iii.), says (at p. lxxxviii.), "I am not aware that this animal is elsewhere known either in natural or heraldic zoology. . . . It differs from the heraldic antelope in having horns like those of a ram, and a tail like a dog's." The term *yale* occurs in the College records.

Yard-measure, or *Measuring-yard*, is only found in one or two examples. It should be drawn sufficiently elongated so as not to be confused with the *billet*, since it does not appear to have always the inches marked upon it. In neither of the examples on the Brasses in Cheam Church, Surrey, to ancestors of the YERDE family, are the measures so marked.

Gules, a chevron between three yard-measures erect or—YARD, Devonshire.

Gules, a chevron between three measuring-yards argent—YARD, Kent.

Yard-measure.

Argent, a chevron between three measuring-yards gules—INRYS.

Yew: this tree is found only in one or two instances.

Ermine, two crosses patty vairy argent and gules ; on a chief azure an annulet between two yew-trees or ; a crescent for difference—BROADWOOD.

Ermine, two palets vairy or and azure ; on a chief of the last a bezant between as many yew-trees of the second—BRANDWOOD, Durham.

Argent, a bugle-horn sable, in chief three yew-trees proper—MORSE, co. Somerset.

Yoke, or *Double ox-yoke*: this device appears variously represented, and two kinds are given in the margin. The first figure is copied from a MS. c. 1580 ; the second is later. The device is borne but rarely ; one instance, that in the arms of PYBERS, where the yoke is

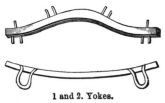

1 and 2. Yokes.

made of bamboo, will be found already noted under *Cinnamon*, and there are one or two others.

Argent, three escutcheons gules, in chief a pair of ox-yokes or—HAY.

Argent, a yoke sable—NEWTHALL, co. Chester.

Argent, a yoke proper and a crescent azure in chief, and in base three escutcheons gules—HAY-DALRYMPLE, co. Wigton.

Zodiac, Signs of the. See *Sphere*.　　　Zule. See *Chess-rook*.

INDEX

Where an asterisk is placed it signifies that an illustration is given.
The mere reference to families as bearing a certain charge are not noted in
the Index.
The various spellings of names follow those given in the course of the
Glossary.